Anonymous

The standard Library Cyclopaedia

Of political, constitutional, statistical, and forensic Knowledge - Vol. II

Anonymous

The standard Library Cyclopaedia
Of political, constitutional, statistical, and forensic Knowledge - Vol. II

ISBN/EAN: 9783337132620

Printed in Europe, USA, Canada, Australia, Japan

Cover: Foto ©ninafisch / pixelio.de

More available books at **www.hansebooks.com**

THE

STANDARD LIBRARY

CYCLOPÆDIA

OF

POLITICAL, CONSTITUTIONAL, STATISTICAL
AND FORENSIC KNOWLEDGE.

FORMING

A WORK OF UNIVERSAL REFERENCE

ON SUBJECTS OF

CIVIL ADMINISTRATION, POLITICAL ECONOMY, FINANCE,
COMMERCE, LAWS AND SOCIAL RELATIONS.

IN FOUR VOLUMES.
VOL. II.

LONDON:
HENRY G. BOHN, YORK STREET, COVENT GARDEN.
1860.

LONDON:
PRINTED BY HARRISON AND SONS,
ST. MARTIN'S LANE, W.C.

CATHEDRAL. Certain churches are called cathedrals or cathedral churches, in consequence of having a seat of dignity (*cathedra*, a Greek term for such a seat) appropriated to a bishop or archbishop. Thus there is the cathedral church of Canterbury, the cathedral church of Norwich, &c. The collegiate churches of Manchester and Ripon were constituted cathedral churches of the new sees of Manchester and Ripon by 6 & 7 Wm. IV .c. 77, the act under which these sees were created.

CATHOLIC CHURCH (Roman). Although in ordinary language this name is often used to designate the ruling authority or power in the Catholic religion, as if distinct from the members of that communion, yet the definition which Catholics give of the church is such as to comprehend the entire body of its members as well as its rulers, the flock as much as the shepherds. Thus we hear of Catholics being under the dominion of their church, or obliged to obey it, as though it were something distinct from themselves, or as if they were not a part of their church. This preliminary remark is made to explain a certain vagueness of expression, which often leads to misapprehension, and serves as the basis of incorrect ideas regarding the peculiar doctrines of that church. The Catholic church therefore is defined to be the community of the faithful united to their lawful pastors, in communion with the see of Rome, or with the pope, the successor of St. Peter and vicar of Christ on earth.

Simply developing the terms of this definition, we will give a brief sketch of the constitution or fundamental system of this church under the heads of its government, its laws, and its vital or constitutive principle.

I. The government of the Catholic church may be considered monarchical, inasmuch as the pope is the ruler over the entire church, and the most distant bishop of the Catholic church holds his appointment from him, and receives from him his authority. No bishop can be considered lawfully consecrated without his approbation. The dignity or office of pope is inherent in the occupant of the see of Rome, because the supremacy over the church is believed to be held in virtue of a commission given to St. Peter, not as his own personal prerogative, but as a part of the constitution of the church, for its advantage, and therefore intended to descend to his successors; as the episcopal power did from the apostles to those who succeeded them in their respective sees.

The election of the pope, therefore, devolves upon the clergy of Rome, as being their bishop; and it is confided to the college of cardinals, who, bearing the titles of the eldest churches in that city, represent its clergy, and form their chapter or electoral body. The meeting or chapter formed for this purpose alone is called a *conclave*. The cardinals are appointed by the pope, and compose the executive council of the church. They preside over the various departments of ecclesiastical government, and are divided into boards or congregations, as they are called, for the transaction of business from all parts of the world; but every decision is subject to the pope's revision, and has no value except from his approbation. On some occasions they are all summoned to meet the pope on affairs of higher importance, as for the nomination of bishops, or the admission of new members into their body; and then the assembly is called a *consistory*. The full number of cardinals is seventy, but there are always some hats left vacant.

The Catholic church, being essentially episcopal, is governed by bishops, who are of two sorts, bishops in ordinary, and vicars apostolic. By the first are meant titular bishops, or such as bear the name of the see over which they rule; as the Archbishop of Paris, or of Dublin; the Bishop of Cambray, or of New Orleans. The manner of appointing such bishops varies considerably. When they are unshackled by the government, the clergy of the diocese meet in chapter, according to old forms, and having selected three names, forward them to the Holy See, where one is chosen for promotion. This is the case in Ireland, Belgium, and perhaps in the free states of America. In most countries however the election of bishops is regulated by *concordat*, that is, a special agreement between the pope and

*2 G

the civil government. The presentation is generally vested in the crown; but the appointment must proceed from the pope.

The powers of bishops, and the manner of exercising their authority, are regulated by the canon law; their jurisdiction on every point is clear and definite, and leaves no room for arbitrary enactments or oppressive measures. Yet it is of such a character as, generally considered, can perfectly control the inferior orders of clergy, and secure them to the discharge of their duty. In most Catholic countries there is a certain degree of civil jurisdiction allowed to the bishops, with judicial powers, in matters of a mixed character; as in cases appertaining to marriages, where a distinction between civil and ecclesiastical marriage has not been drawn by the legislature. Some offences connected with religion, as blasphemy or domestic immorality, are likewise brought under their cognizance.

Where the succession of the Catholic hierarchy has been interrupted, as in England, or never been established, the bishops who superintend the Catholic church and represent the papal authority are known by the name of *vicars apostolic*. A vicar apostolic is not necessarily a bishop—an instance of which we had a few years ago at Calcutta—where the vicar apostolic was a simple priest. Generally, however, he receives episcopal consecration; and, as from local circumstances, it is not thought expedient that he should bear the title of the see which he administers, he is appointed with the title of an ancient bishopric now in the hands of infidels, and thus is called a bishop *in partibus infidelium*, though the last word is often omitted in ordinary language. A vicar apostolic, being generally situated where the provisions of the canon law cannot be fully observed, is guided by particular instructions, by precedents and consuetude, to which all the uniformity of discipline through the Catholic church gives stability and security. Thus the vicars apostolic, who rule over the four episcopal districts of England, have their code in the admirable constitution of Pope Benedict XIV., beginning with the words *Apostolicum ministerium*. The powers of a vicar apostolic are necessarily more extended than those of ordinary bishops, and are ampler in proportion to the difficulty of keeping up a close communication with Rome. Thus many cases of dispensation in marriage which a continental bishop must send to the Holy See may be provided for by an English or American vicar apostolic; and other similar matters, for which these must consult it, could at once be granted by the ecclesiastical superiors of the Mauritius or of China. The nomination of vicars apostolic is solely with the pope.

The inferior clergy, considered in reference to the government of the church, consists mainly of the parochial clergy, or those who supply their place. In all countries possessing a hierarchy, each country is divided into parishes, each provided with a *parochus* or curate,* who corresponds to the rector or vicar of the English established church. The appointment to a parish is vested in the bishop, who has no power to remove again at will, or for any cause except a canonical offence juridically proved. The right of presentation by lay patrons is, however, in particular instances fully respected. In Italy the parish priests are generally chosen by competition: upon a vacancy, a day is appointed on which the testimonials of the different candidates are compared, and they are examined before the bishop in theology, the exposition of scripture, and extemporaneous preaching; and whoever is pronounced, by ballot, superior to the rest, is chosen.

Under an apostolic vicariate, the clergy corresponding to the parochial clergy generally bear the title of *apostolic missionaries*, and have *missions* or local districts with variable limits placed under their care; but are dependent upon the will of their ecclesiastical superiors.

Besides the parochial clergy, there is a considerable body of ecclesiastics, who do not enter directly into the governing

---

* The parish priest in Ireland corresponds to the cure in France, the curato (or in the country, arciprete) of Italy, and the cura of Spain. The curate in Ireland, as in the church of England, is equivalent to the vicaire of France and the sotto-curato of Italy.

part of the church, although they help to discharge some of its most important functions. A great number of *secular* clergy are devoted to the conduct of education, either in universities or seminaries; many occupy themselves exclusively with the pulpit, others with instructing the poor, or attending charitable institutions. A certain number also fill prebends, or attend to the daily service of cathedrals, &c.; for in the Catholic church pluralities, where the cure of souls exists, are strictly prohibited, and consequently a distinct body of clergy from those engaged in parochial duties, or holding rectories, &c., is necessary for those duties. Besides this auxiliary force, the *regular* clergy, or monastic orders, take upon them many of these functions. The clergy of the Catholic church in the west are bound by a vow of celibacy, not formally made, but implied in their ordination as *sub-deacons*. This obligation of celibacy is only reckoned among the disciplinary enactments of the church. The clergy of that portion of the Greek and Armenian church which is united in communion with the see of Rome may be married; that is, may receive orders if married, but are not allowed to marry after having taken orders. A similar discipline, if thought expedient by the church, might be introduced into the West.

The only point concerning the government of the Catholic church which remains to be mentioned is the manner in which it is exercised. The most solemn tribunal is a *general council*, that is, an assembly of all the bishops of the church, who may attend either in person or by deputy, under the presidency of the pope or his legates. When once a decree has passed such an assembly, and received the approbation of the Holy See, there is no further appeal. Distinction must be, however, made between *doctrinal* and *disciplinary* decrees; for example, when in the Council of Trent it was decreed to be the doctrine of the church that marriage is indissoluble, this decree is considered binding in the belief and on the conduct, nor can its acceptance be refused by any one without his being considered rebellious to the church. But when it is ordered that marriages must be celebrated only in presence of the parish priest, this is a matter of discipline not supposed to rest on the revelation of God, but dictated by prudence; and consequently a degree of toleration is allowed regarding the adoption of the resolution in particular dioceses. It is only with regard to such decrees, and more specifically the one we have mentioned, that the Council of Trent is said to have been received, or not, in different countries.

When a general council cannot be summoned, or when it is not deemed necessary, the general government of the church is conducted by the pope, whose decisions in matters of discipline are considered paramount, though particular sees and countries claim certain special privileges and exemptions. In matters of faith it is admitted that if he issue a decree, as it is called, *ex cathedrâ*, or as head of the church, and all the bishops accept it, such a definition or decree is binding and final.*

The discipline or reformation of smaller divisions is performed by provincial or diocesan synods. The first consist of the bishops of a province under their metropolitan; the latter, of the parochial and other clergy under the superintendence of the bishop. The forms to be observed in such assemblies, the subjects which may be discussed, and the extent of jurisdiction which may be assumed, are laid down at full in a beautiful work of the learned Benedict XIV., entitled 'De Synodo Diœcesana.' The acts and decrees of many such partial synods have been published, and are held in high esteem among Catholics; indeed, they may be recommended as beautiful specimens of deliberative wisdom. Such are the decrees of the various synods held at Milan under the virtuous and amiable St. Charles Borromeo.

II. The *laws* of the Catholic church

---

* The great difference between the Transalpine and the Cisalpine divines, as they are termed, is whether such a decree has its force prior to, or independent of, the accession of the body of bishops to it, or receives its sanction and binding power from their acceptance. Practically there is little or no difference between the two opinions; yet this slight variety forms a principal groundwork of what are called the liberties of the Gallican church.

may be divided into two classes; those which bind the interior, and those which regulate outward conduct. This distinction, which corresponds to that above made between doctrinal and disciplinary decrees, may appear unusual, as the term *laws* seems hardly applicable to forms of thought or belief. Still, viewing the Catholic church under the form of an organized religious society, and considering that it professes to be divinely authorized to exact interior assent to all that it teaches, under the penalty of being separated from its communion, we think we can well classify under the word *law* those principles and doctrines which it commands and expects all its members to profess.

Catholics often complain that doctrines are laid to their charge which they do not hold, and in their various publications protest against their belief being assumed upon any except authoritative documents; and as such works are perfectly accessible, the complaint is reasonable and just. There are several works in which an accurate account is given of what Catholics are expected to believe, and which carefully distinguish between those points on which latitude of opinion is allowed, and such as have been fully and decisively decreed by the supreme authority of the church. Such are Veron's ' Regula Fidei,' or Rule of Faith, a work lately translated into English, and Halden's ' Analysis Fidei.' But there are documents of more authority than these; for example, the ' Declaration' set forth by the vicars apostolic or bishops in England, in 1823, often republished; and still more the ' Catechismus ad Parochos,' or ' Catechism of the Council of Trent,' translated into English not many years ago, and published in Dublin. A perusal of such works as these will satisfy those who are desirous of full and accurate information regarding Catholic tenets, of their real nature, and show that the popular expositions of their substance and character are generally incorrect.

The formulary of faith, which persons becoming members of the Catholic church are expected to recite, and which is sworn to upon taking any degree, or being appointed to a chair in a university, is the creed of Pius IV., of which the following is the substance:—

The preamble runs as follows · " I, N. N., with a firm faith believe and profess all and every one of those things which are contained in that creed which the holy Roman church maketh use of." Then follows the Nicene creed.

" I most steadfastly admit and embrace apostolical and ecclesiastical traditions, and all other observances and constitutions of the same church.

" I also admit the holy scriptures, according to that sense which our holy mother the church has held and does hold, to which it belongs to judge of the true sense and interpretation of the scriptures : neither will I ever take and interpret them otherwise than according to the unanimous consent of the fathers.

" I also profess that there are truly and properly seven sacraments of the new law, instituted by Jesus Christ our Lord, and necessary for the salvation of mankind, though not all for every one, to wit: baptism, confirmation, the eucharist, penance,* extreme unction, holy orders,† and matrimony : and that they confer grace; and that of these, baptism, confirmation, and orders cannot be reiterated without sacrilege. I also receive and admit the received and approved ceremonies of the Catholic Church, used in the solemn administration of the aforesaid sacraments.

" I embrace and receive all and every one of the things which have been defined and declared in the holy Council of Trent, concerning original sin and justification.

" I profess likewise that in the mass there is offered to God a true, proper, and propitiatory sacrifice for the living

---

* Under penance is included confession ; as the Catholic sacrament of penance consists of three parts: contrition or sorrow, confession, and satisfaction.

† The clerical orders of the Catholic church are divided into two classes, *sacred* and *minor* orders. The first consists of subdeacons, deacons, and priests, who are bound to celibacy and the daily recitation of the *Breviary*, or collection of psalms and prayers, occupying a considerable time. The minor orders are four in number, and are preceded by the *tonsure*, an ecclesiastical ceremony in which the hair is shorn, initiatory to the ecclesiastical state.

and the dead: and that in the most holy sacrament of the eucharist there is truly, really, and substantially, the body and blood, together with the soul and divinity of our Lord Jesus Christ; and that there is made a change of the whole substance of the bread into the body, and of the whole substance of the wine into the blood, which change the Catholic church calls *transubstantiation*. I also confess that under either kind alone Christ is received whole and entire, and a true sacrament.

"I firmly hold that there is a *purgatory*, and that the souls therein detained are helped by the suffrages of the faithful.

"Likewise, that the saints reigning with Christ are to be honoured and invocated, and that they offer up prayers to God for us; and that their relics are to be had in veneration.

"I most firmly assert that the images of Christ, of the mother of God, and also of other saints, ought to be had and retained, and that due honour and veneration are to be given them.

"I also affirm that the power of indulgences was left by Christ in the church, and that the use of them is most wholesome to Christian people.

"I acknowledge the holy Catholic Apostolic Roman church for the mother and mistress of all churches: and I promise true obedience to the bishop of Rome, successor to St. Peter, prince of the apostles and vicar of Jesus Christ."

Then follow clauses condemnatory of all contrary doctrines, and expressive of adhesion to all the definitions of the Council of Trent.

It is obvious that this form of confession was framed in accordance to the decrees of that council, and consequently has chiefly in view the opinions of those who followed the Reformation.

Such is the doctrinal code of the Catholic church; of its moral doctrines we need not say anything, because no authorised document could be well referred to that embodies them all. There are many decrees of popes condemnatory of immoral opinions or propositions, but no positive decrees. The moral law, as taught in the Catholic church, is mainly the same as other denominations of Christians profess to follow.

Of the disciplanary or governing code we have already spoken, when we observed that it consisted of the Canon Law, which, unlike the doctrinal and moral code, may vary with time, place, and accidental circumstances.

III. The last head was the essential or constitutive principle of the Catholic church. By this we mean that principle which gives it individuality, distinguishes it from other religions, pervades all its institutions, and gives the answer to every query regarding the peculiar constitution, outward and inward, of this church.

Now, the fundamental position, the constitutive principle of the Catholic church, is the doctrine and belief that God has promised, and consequently bestows upon it, a constant and perpetual protection, to the extent of guaranteeing it from destruction, from error, or fatal corruption. This principle once admitted, every thing else follows. 1. The infallibility of the church in its decisions on matters concerning faith. 2. The obligation of submitting to all these decisions, independently of men's own private judgments or opinions. 3. The authority of tradition, or the unalterable character of all the doctrines committed to the church; and hence the persuasion that those of its dogmas, which to others appear strange and unscriptural, have been in reality handed down, uncorrupted, since the time of the apostles, who received them from Christ's teaching. 4. The necessity of religious unity, by perfect uniformity of belief: and thence as a corollary the sinfulness of wilful separation or schism, and culpable errors or heresy. 5. Government by authority, since they who are aided and supported by such a promise must necessarily be considered appointed to direct others, and are held as the representatives and vicegerents of Christ in the church. 6. The papal supremacy, whether considered as a necessary provision for the preservation of this essential unity, or as the principal depository of the divine promises. 7. In fine, the authority of councils, the right to enact canons and ceremonies, the duty of repressing all attempts to broach new opinions; in a word, all that system of rule and authorilative teaching which must strike every one as the leading feature in the constitution of the Catholic church.

The differences, therefore, between this and other religions, however complicated and numerous they may at first sight appear, are thus narrowed to one question; for particular doctrines must share the fate of the dogmas above cited, as forming the constitutive principle of the Catholic religion. This religion claims for itself a complete consistency from its first principle to its last consequence, and to its least institution, and finds fault with others, as though they preserved forms, dignities, and doctrines which must have sprung from a principle by them rejected, but which are useless and mistaken the moment they are disjoined from it. Be this as it may, the constitution of the Catholic church should seem to possess, what is essential to every moral organized body, a principle of vitality which accounts for all its actions, and determines at once the direction and the intensity of all its functions.

We conclude this account of the Catholic church with a sketch of the extent of its dominions, by enumerating the countries which profess its doctrines, or which contain considerable communities under its obedience. In Europe, Italy, Spain, Portugal, France, Belgium, the Austrian empire, including Hungary, Bavaria, Poland, and the Rhenish provinces of Prussia, which formerly belonged to the ecclesiastical electorates, profess the Catholic religion as that of the state, or, according to the expression of the French *charte*, that of the majority of the people. In America, all the countries which once formed part of the Spanish dominions, both in the southern and northern portion of the continent, and which are now independent states, profess exclusively the same religion. The empire of Brazil is also Catholic. Lower Canada and all those islands in the West Indies which belong to Spain or France, including the Republic of Haiti, profess the Catholic faith; and there are also considerable Catholic communities in the United States of North America, especially in Maryland and Louisiana. Many Indian tribes, in the Canadas, in the United States, in California, and in South America, have embraced the same faith. In Asia there is hardly any nation professing Christianity which does not contain large communities of Catholic Christians. Thus in Syria the entire nation or tribe of the Maronites, dispersed over Mount Libanus, are subjects of the Roman see, governed by a patriarch and bishops appointed by it. There are also other Syriac Christians under other bishops, united to the same see, who are dispersed all over Palestine and Syria. At Constantinople there is a Catholic Armenian patriarch who governs the *united* Armenians as they are called, large communities of whom also exist in Armenia proper. The Abbé Dubois, in his examination before a committee of the House of Commons in 1832, stated the number of Catholics in the Indian peninsula at 600,000, including Ceylon, and this number was perhaps rather underrated than otherwise. There are at present an archbishop who is vicar apostolic of Bengal, bishops who are vicars apostolic of Madras, Bombay, and Ceylon respectively, and they are assisted by coadjutor bishops. [BISHOPRIC.] A new one has been added for Ceylon. We have not the means of ascertaining the number of Catholics in China, but in the province of Su-Chuen alone they were returned, 22nd September, 1824, at 47,487 (*Annales de la Propag. de la Foi*, No. XI. p. 257); and an official report published at Rome in the same year gives those in the provinces of Fo-kien and Kiansi at 40,000. There are seven other provinces containing a considerable number of Catholics, of which we have no return. In the united empire of Tonkin and Cochin-China the Catholics of one district were estimated at 200,000 (*Ibid*, No. X. p. 194), and, till the late persecution, there was a college with 200 students, and convents containing 700 religious. Another district gave a return, in 1826, of 2955 infants baptized, which would give an estimate of 88,000 adult Christians. A third gave a return of 170,000. M. Dubois estimates the number of native Catholics in the Philippine Islands at 2,000,000. In Africa, the islands of Mauritius and Bourbon are Catholic, and

CAVALRY. [463] CAVALRY.

all the Portuguese settlements on the coast, as well as the Azores, Madeira, the Cape Verd, and the Canary Islands.

CAUCUS, a word in use in the United States of North America, which is applied to public meetings which are held for the purpose of agreeing upon candidates to be proposed for election to offices, or to concert measures for supporting a party, or any measure of a public or local nature; but its use is more generally confined to meetings of a political character. The word is to be found in nearly every American newspaper, and the 'American Cyclopædia' states that it is one of the very few 'Americanisms' which belong entirely to the United States. It is used in Gordon's 'History of the American Revolution,' published in London in 1788. Gordon says, that more than fifty years prior to the time of his writing, "Samuel Adams' father, and twenty others in Boston, one or two from the north end of the town, where all ship business is carried on, used to meet, make a caucus, &c." It has therefore been supposed that "caucus" was a corruption of "caulkers," the word meeting being understood.

CAVALRY (remotely from the Latin *caballus*, 'a horse') is that class of troops which serve on horseback. In the British army it consists of the two regiments of Life Guards, the royal regiment of Horse Guards, seven regiments of Dragoon Guards, and seventeen regiments of Light Dragoons, of which the 7th, 8th, 10th, 11th, and 15th are Hussars, and the 9th, 12th, 16th, and 17th are Lancers. A complete regiment of cavalry is divided into four squadrons, and each of these into two troops. The full strength of a troop is 80 men; and to each troop there is appointed a captain, a lieutenant, and a cornet.

The charge of the regimental establishments of the Life and Horse Guards in the year 1845, was—Life Guards, each regiment 29,803*l.*; Horse Guards, 26,295*l.* The number of rank and file in each of these regiments is 351; non-commissioned officers, trumpeters, and drummer 53; officers 32: total 436. The pay in the Life and Horse Guards is higher in every grade than for the cavalry of the line. Fourteen regiments of dragoons cost altogether 239,442*l.* One regiment of Dragoon Guards (the 1st) contains 479 of all ranks, and costs 22,264*l.* The cost of six regiments of Light Dragoons, each with 791 officers and men, in service in India, is defrayed by the East India Company, and amounts to 34,638*l.* per annum for each regiment. The cavalry in the pay of this country for 1844-5 was 7970 officers and men, out of a standing army of 99,707, exclusive of cavalry in India; or including the Queen's troops in India, the charge for cavalry for 1844-5 was—

808 Officers £190,322
1059 Non-Commissioned Officers 44,382
9634 Rank and File 235,519
                                    —————
                                    £470,223

Dragoons are a species of light cavalry trained to act either on horseback or on foot as may be required. They appear to have been introduced into the English service before the middle of the seventeenth century; but the oldest regiment of dragoons in the army is that of the Scotch Greys, which was raised in 1681. Dragoons perform the duty of advanced guards and patroles; they escort convoys, and harass the enemy in his retreat; or, in reverses of fortune, they protect the dispersed and defeated infantry. The name Dragoon appears to come from the Latin Draconarius, the appellation given to a standard-bearer, who carried a standard or colour with the figure of a dragon on it. (Ammianus Marcell. xx. 4, and the notes in the edition of J. Gronovius; Vegetius, ii. 7.)

Hussars are also a species of light cavalry, which originally constituted the national militia of Poland and Hungary. They are usually employed to protect reconnoitring and foraging parties, and to serve as patroles.

The Lancers were introduced into the British service in order to correspond to the corps of what were called Polish Lancers in the French army. The long lance carried by this class of troops was supposed to be of use in a charge against infantry; and the fluttering of the flag at the extremity of the lance, by alarming the horse, to give an advantage over a dragoon otherwise armed.

In the late war a portion of the French cavalry was furnished with cuirasses, and, in imitation of them, the English Life Guards and Horse Guards have since borne the same heavy armour. These troops carry a sword, two pistols, and a carabine; the heavy cavalry in general carry carabines, pistols, and swords; and the light cavalry very small carabines, pistols, and sabres.

In the French budget for 1845-6, the estimate for the army was for 81,689 horses and 340,000 men. There are fifty-four regiments of cavalry, of five squadrons each, in the French service, besides four regiments (the African Chasseurs), each composed of six squadrons. The fifty-four regiments consist of—Carabiniers 2; Cuirassiers 10; Dragoons 12; Lancers 8; Chasseurs 13; and Hussars 9 regiments.

In the Austrian service the number of regiments of Cavalry of the line is 37: Cuirassiers 8; Dragoons 6; Light-horse 7; Hussars 12; Uhlans, 4.

The Russian cavalry in 1835 consisted of 86,800 men, besides 4000 Cossacks.

The Prussian cavalry in 1843 amounted to 19,960 men.

CEMETERY. [INTERMENT.]
CENSOR. [CENSUS, ROMAN.]
CENSORSHIP OF THE PRESS. [PRESS.]

CENSUS, THE, at Rome, was a numbering of the Roman people, and a valuation of their property. It was held in the Campus Martius, after the year B.C. 432. (Liv. iv. 22; Varro, *De R. R.* iii. 11.) Every Roman citizen was obliged, upon oath, to give in a statement of his own name and age, of the name and age of his wife, children, slaves, and freedmen, if he had any. The punishment for a false return was, that the individual's property should be confiscated, and he himself scourged and sold for a slave. Taxation depended on the results of the census; many kinds of property were excepted, while, on the other hand, some sorts of property were assessed at several times their value. Constant changes were made by successive censors in the valuation of taxable property. Cato and Flaccus rated the taxable value of high-priced slaves at ten times the purchase-money. (Niebuhr, ii. 402.) It appears from a passage in Livy (vi. 27) that the census also showed the amount of a man's debts and the names of his creditors.

According to the valuation of their property at the census, the citizens were divided into six classes; each class contained a number of centuries or hundreds. That a century did not always consist of a hundred men is clear, from the fact that the richest centuries were the most numerous, and consequently must individually have contained fewer persons than the centuries of the poor. (*Hist. of Rome*, by the Society for the Diffusion of Useful Knowledge, p. 21.) The first class consisted of those whose property amounted to 100,000 ases, about 322*l.* 18*s.* of English money: the second class consisted of persons worth 75,000 ases; the fortune of the third class amounted to 50,000 ases; that of the fourth to 25,000; that of the fifth to 11,000; and the sixth class included all below the fifth, even those who had no estate whatever. This was naturally the fullest of the six, but was accounted only as one century. Now, as the richer classes contained far more centuries than the poorer, so much so that the first class contained more than all the rest together, and as the votes in the Comitia Centuriata were taken within the centuries individually, and then the voice of the majority of centuries was decisive, it is obvious that the influence of wealth was greatly preponderant in this assembly. Cicero (*De Repub.* ii. 22) assigns this as the object aimed at in the institution. The real object of the Comitia Centuriata was (as Niebuhr supposes) to bind the different orders of the state together in one consistent and organised body. In the Comitia Centuriata the people always appeared under arms, and each class had a particular kind of armour assigned to it.

The census was held at first by the kings, afterwards by the consuls, and, from B.C. 442, by two magistrates called Censors (Censores), who were appointed every five years. After the census a sacrifice of purification was generally, but not always, offered. The victims were a sow, a sheep, and a bull, which were led thrice round the army, and then slain: the sacrifice was called Suovetaurilia.

It does not appear that the census was held with strict regularity. It was sometimes altogether omitted. (Cic. *Pro Arch.* 5. 11.) The usual interval was five years; and in allusion to the sacrifice of purification, the interval was commonly called a lustre (lustrum).

When a person was duly entered on the books of the censors, this was taken as a proof of his citizenship, even if he were a slave, provided he had been registered with his master's consent. (Cicero, *De Or.* i. 40; Ulpian, *Frag.* tit. i. 8; Gaius, i. 17.) As the census was held at Rome, citizens who were in the provinces, and wished to be registered, were obliged to repair there on that occasion (Cicero, *Ad Att.* i. 18, &c.); but this was sometimes evaded, and was made a matter of complaint by the censors. The census, accompanied with the ceremony of the lustrum, seems to have fallen into disuse after the time of Vespasian; but the numbering of the population, and the registration of property, continued under the empire.

The term *census* is also used in Latin authors to signify the amount of a person's estate, and hence we read of census equestris, the estate of an eques, and census senatorius, the estate of a senator.

The nature of the Roman census may be collected from various particulars. One object was to ascertain the number of men capable of bearing arms; and another, to ascertain the amount of each person's property, and the various heads of which it consisted. Cicero's treatise on Laws, though it contains a picture of an ideal republic, appears in one passage (iii. 3, 4) to describe what the Roman census was as it existed in his time. He says—"Let the censors take a census of the ages of the people, the children, the slaves, the property; let them look after the temples of the city, the roads, waters, treasury, the taxes; let them distribute into tribes the parts of which the people consist; then let them distribute the population according to property, classes; let them register the children of the cavalry and the infantry; let them forbid celibacy; let them regulate the morals of the people; let them leave no infamous man in the senate; let there be two censors; let them hold their office for five years, and let the censorial authority be always continued. Let the censors faithfully guard the law; and let private persons bring to them their *acta*" (probably their vouchers or evidences). Thus the Romans must have had an immense mass of statistical documents, collected every five years, from which the population and the wealth of the community at each quinquennial period could be accurately known. Florus (i. 6) observes, "that by the great wisdom of King Servius the state was so ordered that all the differences of property, rank, age, occupations, and professions were registered, and thus a large state was administered with the same exactness as the smallest family." The Roman law fixed the age of legal capacity, and the ages at which a man could enjoy the various offices of the state. There must consequently have been a register of births under the republic; and a constitution of the emperor Marcus Antoninus, as to the registration of births for a special purpose, is recorded. (Jul. Capitolinus, *M. Antonin.* c. 9.)

In addition to this we have from the Codes of Theodosius and Justinian various particulars as to the census under the empire, and particularly from a valuable fragment of Ulpian, entitled 'De Censibus.' (*Dig.* 50, tit. 15, s. 2, 3, 4.) These authorities have preserved even the form of the registration under the Roman census. These registers showed the number, class, age, and property of all free persons, and also indicated the heads of families, mothers, sons, and daughters; they also comprised the slaves, male and female, with their occupations and the produce of their labour. They also contained all the lands, and indicated the mode in which they were cultivated; whether as vineyards, olive-yards, cornland, pastures, forest, and so forth. They showed the number of acres (jugera), of vines, olives, and other trees. In fact, the Roman census under the empire was a complete register of the population and wealth of all the countries included within the limits of the Cæsar's dominions. These remarks are from Dureau de la Malle, 'Economic Politique des Romains,' who has given at the end of

2 H

one of his volumes the form of the registration tables.

CENSUS. Before the first enumeration of the people of this country, in 1801, the number of the population was a fruitful topic with party writers. By some it was contended that England was far less populous than it had been formerly. Arthur Young, writing in 1769, states (vol. iv. p. 556, 'Northern Tour') that these writers asserted we had lost a million and a half of people since the Revolution. Even so intelligent a writer as Dr. Price was of opinion that in 1780 England and Wales contained no more than 4,763,000 souls. The increase of manufactures, and the greater abundance of employment, which had of course the effect of raising wages, might also be regarded from another, though a one-sided point of view, as the result of the decline of population. It was in vain to tell such persons that all the circumstances of the country were favourable to the increase of population; and that while agriculture was improving, manufactures and commerce rapidly extending, wages higher, and provisions continued at a reasonable price, it was not in the nature of things that population should even continue stationary, but that it would be most likely to increase with great rapidity. It is now known that the population of England increased upwards of two millions and a quarter between 1750 and the end of the century; but it was not until a census was actually taken that an end was put to the disputes as to the amount of the population.

Having once obtained an enumeration of the people, it has been possible to apply the facts to antecedent periods, in order to form an approximative estimate of the amount of population. This task was undertaken by the late Mr. Rickman, who, in 1836, addressed a circular letter to the clergy throughout England and Wales, asking for their assistance in preparing returns from the parish registers of the births, marriages, and deaths at different periods. Out of about ten thousand parishes in England, one-half possess registers which were commenced prior to 1600, and of these, three-fourths commence as early as the year 1570. From these registers Mr. Rickman was supplied with the number of births, marriages, and deaths for six periods, each embracing three consecutive years, from which he calculated the average population of each period. It was then assumed that the births, marriages, and deaths were in the same proportion to the population of each period as in 1801. The result of Mr. Rickman's estimate, according to his mode of calculation, showed that the population of England and Wales in each of the following years was as under:—

	England.	Wales.
1570	3,737,841	301,038
1600	4,460,454	351,264
1630	5,225,263	375,254
1670	5,395,185	378,461
1700	5,653,061	391,947
1750	6,066,041	450,994

1. *Census of* 1801.—The first census of Great Britain was limited to the following objects: 1, The number of individual inhabitants in each parish, distinguishing males from females; 2, The number of inhabited houses, and the number of families inhabiting the same in each parish; 3, The number of uninhabited houses; 4, A classification of the employment of individuals into the great divisions of agriculture, trade, manufactures and handicraft, and a specification of the numbers not included in either of those divisions; 5, The number of persons serving in the regular army, the militia, and the embodied local militia. The inquiry under the fourth head entirely failed, through "the impossibility," as Mr. Rickman states, "of deciding whether the females of the family, children, and servants, were to be classed as of no occupation, or of the occupation of the adult males of the family. (*Statement of Progress under Pop. Act of* 1830.) The results of the census were, however, very valuable in putting an end to doubts and controversy on the subject of the numbers of the people.

2. *Census of* 1811.—The second census embraced all the points which were the subject of inquiry in 1801; but the question respecting the number of houses was subdivided, so as to distinguish the number of houses building, which, in the

first census, were classed under the head of uninhabited houses. With a view also of obtaining a more accurate return of the occupations of the people, the form of inquiry under this head was modified so as to ascertain, 1st, What number of *families* (not persons, as in 1801) were chiefly employed in or maintained by agriculture; 2nd, How many by trade, manufactures, and handicraft; and, 3rd, The number of families not comprised in either class.

3. *Census of* 1821.—The heads of inquiry were the same as in 1811, with an additional head respecting the ages of the population. For the first time it was attempted to ascertain the age of every person, distinguishing males from females. The first head included persons under the age of five; and the quinquennial period was adopted for all persons not exceeding 20, after which the ages were classified in decennial periods; and there was a head which comprised all persons aged 100 and upwards. The ages of 92 out of every 100 persons were thus ascertained.

4. *Census of* 1831.—The new features in this census were an alteration in the form of inquiry respecting occupations. In 1801 the attempt to ascertain the occupation of every individual was, as already stated, a failure; and the inquiry in 1811 and 1821 had reference only to the heads of families; but this form was altered, in consequence, as Mr. Rickman states, of "the often recurring and unanswerable doubt as to what is to be deemed a family." The returns to the questions, as modified under the census of 1831, showed, as in 1811 and 1821, the number of families employed in, 1, Agriculture; 2, In trade, manufacture, and handicrafts; and 3, The number of families not comprised in either class; but they also showed, in addition to the information procured at any former period, the number of *persons* (males aged twenty years and upwards) employed in, 1, Manufacture or in making manufacturing machinery; 2, Retail trade or handicraft, as masters or workmen; 3, The number of capitalists, bankers, and other educated men; 4, Labourers employed in non-agricultural labour; 5, Other males aged twenty years and upwards (not including servants); 6, Male servants aged twenty and upwards; and also male servants under twenty. The number of female servants was also returned under a separate head. The returns also showed, in reference to the occupation and cultivation of the land, the number of—1, Occupiers employing labourers; 2, Occupiers not employing labourers; 3, Labourers. The inquiry respecting age, which had on the whole been so successful in 1821, was abandoned, except in so far as it went to ascertain the number of males aged twenty years and upwards, on the ground that it imposed "too much labour in combination with the other inquiries," and that, for so short an interval as ten years, the information was "unnecessary and inconclusive." With regard to males aged twenty and upwards employed in trade, manufactures, and handicrafts, an attempt was made to show the number employed in different branches of these employments. The following was the plan adopted for this purpose:—A form, containing a list of one hundred different trades and handicrafts, comprising those most commonly carried on, was furnished to the overseers in each parish or place required to make a separate return, to be filled up with the number of males aged twenty and upwards; and the overseers were authorized to add to the list such additional trades as were not included in the printed form. The absence of uniformity in describing occupations not inserted in the official formula, and the difficulty of testing the accuracy of that part of the classification which was left to the discretion of the overseers, were the principal defects of this plan. The number of distinct occupations returned in the census was 598.

The censuses of 1801, 1811, 1821, and 1831 were each superintended by the late Mr. Rickman, clerk assistant of the House of Commons, and the business of enumeration was conducted by the overseers of the poor in England and Wales, and by the parochial schoolmasters in Scotland.

Census of 1841.—This is far more complete and comprehensive than any preceding census. The heads of inquiry were more numerous and more minute, while the results obtained are more accurate. In consequence of the death of Mr. Rickman, two census commissioners (Edward Phipps and Thomas Vardon, Esqrs.) were appointed, and the officers of the registrar-general of births, marriages, and deaths were employed as enumerators, instead of the less intelligent parochial overseers. England and Wales were divided into about 35,000 enumeration districts, each containing not less than twenty-five nor more than two hundred houses, so that each district might be completed in a single day. Public institutions, barracks, gaols, workhouses, &c. were required under the Census Acts, 3 & 4 Vict. c. 99, and 4 Vict. c. 7, to be enumerated by the several officers residing therein. Two very important improvements were made as to the inquiry respecting ages and occupations. Instead of quinquennial and decennial periods being taken, as in 1821, or only the age of males aged twenty and upwards, as in 1831, the exact age of every person was ascertained. In reference to occupations, the enumerators were directed to ascertain the employment of *every* person, distinguishing sex, and whether above or under twenty years of age. A new head of inquiry was also introduced for the purpose of showing the number of persons born in the county in which they resided; the number born in other counties of the same country; and the number born in Scotland (for Scotland the number born in England), Ireland, the colonies, and in foreign parts.

The number of parishes which made a return of all the above particulars was 9942 for England, and 838 for Wales. In the volumes of Abstracts of the Population Returns the population is given separately for 17,476 parishes and other divisions in England, and 1984 in Wales; and for Great Britain the population is separately stated for 22,303 parishes, towns, hamlets, &c., which is 5601 more than under the census of 1831. The analysis of this immense body of facts was very admirably arranged under the superindendence of the census commissioners.

An examination into the results of the census of 1841 is treated of under a separate head. [CENSUS of 1841.] The following is a comparative summary of each census from 1801 to 1841 inclusive:—

	1801.	1811.	1821.	1831.	1841.
England	8,331,434	9,538,827	11,261,437	13,091,005	14,995,508
Wales	541,546	611,788	717,438	806,182	911,321
Persons travelling at night, June 6	..	..	..	..	4,696
England and Wales	8,872,980	10,150,615	11,978,875	13,897,187	15,911,725
Scotland	1,599,068	1,805,688	2,093,456	2,365,114	2,628,957
Islands in the British Seas	..	..	89,508	103,710	124,079
Total Great Britain	..	..	14,161,839	16,366,011	18,664,761
Ireland	..	..	6,801,827	7,767,401	8,175,124
Total United Kingdom	..	..	20,963,666	24,133,412	26,839,885

The first census of Ireland was taken in 1813, but in a very imperfect and incomplete manner. Six counties and the cities of Limerick and Kilkenny were omitted altogether. In 1821, and again in 1831, a census was taken in a manner which afforded no ground of complaint. The inquiry respecting age in 1821 was more successful than in Great Britain, where it was defective in respect of 8000 in every 100,000, while in Ireland the defect was only 126 in each 100,000. The preface to the Abstracts of the Census Returns of 1841 is a very elaborate disquisition on the results which the returns present, and it embraces a comprehensive view of the social condition of the country. [CENSUS OF 1841.]

Amongst the defects of the census of Great Britain and Ireland may be mentioned the absence of information concerning the number of persons belonging to each religious denomination.

In 1834 a specific census was taken in Ireland with a view of ascertaining for purposes of legislation the religious persuasion of the people. This inquiry was not repeated at the last census, and it has never found a place in the census of either England or Scotland.

In the Colonial possessions of Great Britain a census is taken at intervals, under acts of the local legislature or under the direction of the governor. In some cases the ages of the population are ascertained; in others the religious persuasion; and in many the value and amount of stock and produce are returned.

In France there have been six enumerations of the people during the present century: in 1801, 1806, 1821, 1826, 1831, 1836, and 1841. The census is now taken every five years. In the census of 1801 the sexes were distinguished, and those in each sex who were or had been married, and those who were single. In 1806, widowers and widows were also distinguished. The census of 1826 was simply an enumeration without distinction of age or sex; but in 1836, and at each subsequent census, the inquiry was pursued in the same form as in 1821.

In Belgium the census distinguishes the town and country population, sexes and ages, the number of single and married persons, and widowers and widows. The occupations of the people are also shown, divided into two classes, liberal and industrial. The first includes seven subdivisions, and the second twelve subdivisions. The number of persons belonging to each religious profession is also given.

In Holland the census is taken on the 1st of January in each year.

In Saxony the census embraces inquiries as to sexes, age, number of families, number unmarried and married, widowers and widows, religious profession, and the number of the blind, deaf and dumb.

In Prussia the census is taken every three years. The ages of males and females are given in five classes, and in this respect the census is less minute than might have been expected. The numbers belonging to each religious denomination are also given.

Sweden has long been remarkable for the minute and even ultra-inquisitorial character of its census. A board called the "Table Commission" was organised in 1749 for collecting and digesting accurate statistics of the population, which are supplied by the clergy. The Swedish census exhibits the circumstances of all the households, arranged in three classes: 1st, the number who have more than they require for subsistence, or are in good circumstances; 2nd, the number who can support themselves; and 3rd, those who are in bad circumstances, or have less than they want for subsistence. The number of the poor and by whom they are supported is accurately ascertained. Censuses are also taken by the civil officers for the purposes of taxation, but they are not so exact as the enumeration by the clergy. It is said, indeed, that during the progress of the civil census the poor labourers, especially in the towns, contrive to go away or conceal themselves.

In Norway the census is taken by the magistrates in towns, and in the country by the rectors of parishes. The inquiries extend to the number of cattle and the production of grain. Temporary absentees are returned in the family to which they belong, and as casual strangers and visitors are not returned, the census comprises those only who have house and home in the country. The number of idiotic and of deaf and dumb persons is distinguished. Under the head of occupations, persons having more businesses than one are returned under each. A general census has been five times taken in Norway: in 1769, 1801, 1815, 1825, and in 1835; and as the census is taken decennially, there will be one in 1845.

In Denmark the census is both varied and minute, and in the information which it gives it does not differ much from the Swedish census.

The census of Sardinia, made in 1838, is said to be as complete in its objects and method as any in Europe. It was executed under the superintendence of a

Central Statistical Commission, assisted by local committees for the several provinces, consisting each of five members, besides the "Intendente" of the province, who acted as its president. The system of enumeration by *names* was adopted, and the returns showed, for each person in a population of 4,650,370 souls, the name and surname; age; civil condition, whether single, married, or widowed; place of birth, whether in the province in which they resided, or subjects born in some other province; residents who were foreign subjects; occupation; and religious profession.

In Austria the census is taken every year, but neither sex nor occupations are distinguished; but this defect is partially remedied by the very accurate registry which is kept of the births, marriages, and deaths.

In the vast empire of Russia a census of the population is taken, but we are unable to state at what intervals; and there is a registration of births, marriages, and deaths.

In Portugal a census was taken in 1841. In Spain a census has been taken at irregular periods; but at present the number of the population is only conjectured.

There is not at the present time a single European state (Turkey excepted) in which a census of the population is not taken with more or less minuteness; and this is accompanied, with few exceptions (amongst which are Scotland and Ireland), by a more or less perfect system of registering every birth, marriage, and death. [REGISTRATION OF BIRTHS, DEATHS, AND MARRIAGES.] In addition to these means of information respecting the population, there are in most states returns respecting property, which further illustrate the condition of the people. [STATISTICS.]

In the United States of North America the representative system is based on numbers, and whenever direct taxation is resorted to, it is apportioned on the same principle. A census is therefore indispensable; and provision was made respecting it by the constitution of the United States. There are other reasons which render a census of peculiar importance. Professor Tucker, of the university of Virginia, remarks:—"Our changes are both greater and more rapid than those of any other country. A region covered with its primeval forests is, in the course of one generation, covered with productive farms and comfortable dwellings, and in the same brief space villages are seen to shoot up into wealthy and populous cities. The elements of our population are, moreover, composed of different races and conditions of civil freedom, whose relative increase is watched with interest by every reflecting man, however he may view that diversity of condition, or whatever he may think of the comparative merit of the two races." The first census was taken in 1790, and referred to the 1st of August of that year; the second in 1800, and subsequently in every tenth year. In 1830 the period of enumeration was changed to the 1st of June, so that the preceding decennium was two months short of ten years. The last census was taken on the 1st of June, 1840.

In the first census of the United States the heads of inquiry were five, and the numbers were ascertained of—1, Free white males, aged sixteen and upwards. 2, The same under sixteen. 3, Free white females of all ages. 4, Slaves. 5, Free persons of colour, for the phrase "all other persons" could comprise only them. In the second census the ages of the white population were ascertained and distributed under five heads, showing the number under 10; between 10 and 16; 16 and 26; 26 and 45; and 45 and upwards. The census of 1810 was taken in the same manner as that of 1800. In the succeeding census, in 1820, free coloured persons and slaves were for the first time classified as to age and sex, and they were distributed in four divisions of ages. A column was added for white males aged between 16 and 18. The population was also classified as to occupations in the three great divisions of agriculture, commerce, and manufactures. In 1830 the population was distinguished with greater minuteness as to age. The white population under 20 was classed into quinquennial periods, and from 20 and upwards into decennial periods. The free coloured persons and slaves were classed, in respect to age, in six divisions. The number of persons blind, and deaf and dumb, were ascertained in each class of the population, and their ages distinguished. No notice was taken in the census of 1830 of the occupations of the people. The census of 1840, on the contrary, is remarkable for its attempt to supply minute details of every branch of industry in the United States, but in other respects the heads of inquiry were the same as in 1830. Not only were the people classified according to their occupations, but estimates were obtained relative to the annual products of industry, under the six heads of—Mines, with nine subdivisions; Agriculture, with twenty-nine; Commerce, with five; Fisheries, with five; the Forest, with five; Manufactures, with forty-six subdivisions. It appears, however, from the 'American Almanac' (Boston, 1845) that the statistical details of productive industry are not so correct as could be wished. Professor Tucker, however, is of opinion that the errors so balance and compensate each other, as to afford on the whole "an approximation to the truth, which is all that the subject admits of." (*Progress of the United States in Population and Wealth in Fifty Years, as exhibited by the Decennial Census*. By George Tucker, Prof. of Moral Philosophy and Political Economy in the University of Virginia, Boston, 1843. This is a valuable and useful work, and it is to be regretted that no writer of this country has undertaken a similar task for the five censuses of Great Britain, the results of which are only to be found in the cumbrous volumes of Parliamentary Returns which give the details of each census.)

CENSUS OF 1841. In June, 1841, was taken the decennial census of Great Britain and Ireland, the results of which, when compared with other statistical returns, afford the means of examining the condition and prospects of the country. It is not proposed, in this article, to enter with any minuteness either upon the manner in which the census was taken, or upon the detailed results appearing in the reports of the commissioners; but it is intended to present a comparison of the increase and distribution of the population, with their means of employment, their command of the necessaries and conveniences of life, the growth of capital, the extension of trade and manufactures, and with other indications of the progress of society. If it shall appear that in all these respects the means of enjoyment have increased more rapidly than the population, this review of the national resources will be most encouraging; and may be more generally acceptable than a tedious examination of the specific results of the census itself. As the selection of the various subjects of comparison will be made without reference to any preconceived theory, the accuracy of the facts may be relied on: and it is hoped that no conclusions will be drawn from them which they do not fairly justify.

In several particulars, it will be necessary to advert to Great Britain and to Ireland separately; but it will be convenient, in the first place, to present a summary of the population of the United Kingdom in 1831 and in 1841, with calculations of the rate of increase per cent.

	1831.	1841.	Increase per cent.
England	13,091,005	14,995,138	14·5
Wales	806,182	911,603	13
Scotland	2,365,114	2,620,184	10·7
Army, navy, and registered seamen afloat	277,017	198,453	
Persons travelling on the night of June 6	..	5,016	
Islands in the British Seas	103,107	124,040	19·6
GREAT BRITAIN	16,643,028	18,844,434	13·2
IRELAND	7,767,401	8,175,124	5·25
United Kingdom	24,410,429	27,019,558	10·6

The Irish census commissioners (Report, p. xi.) enter into certain calculations, by which they raise the per centage of increase in the population of Ireland from 5·25, as actually shown in the returns, to nearly 12 per cent. If the same principles of calculation were applied to the population of Great Britain, the increase would also be greater; but it will be sufficient, for the purposes of this inquiry, if the entire population of the United Kingdom, during the ten years from 1831 to 1841, be assumed to have increased 12 per cent.

In judging of the condition of the people, the first point which may be investigated is their consumption of those articles which are used more or less in proportion to their means. Unhappily there are no means of estimating the quantities of bread and meat or other staples of food produced in this country; but the quantities of auxiliary articles of food and luxury imported from abroad for home consumption, or manufactured in this country, are fair indications of the means possessed by the people of enjoying the comforts of life. If the increase in the consumption of such articles be in a greater proportion than the increase of population, it may reasonably be inferred that their means of enjoyment have generally increased; or, in other words, that the people enjoyed more comforts in 1841 than in 1831, relatively to their numbers.

The quantities of several articles which paid duty for home consumption in the United Kingdom, in 1831 and 1841 respectively, and the rate of increase, will appear from the following table :—

		1831.	1841.	Rate per cent. of increase.
Butter	cwts.	121,193	251,255	106·4
Cheese	,,	130,039	248,335	90·9
Cocoa	,,	502,806	1,930,764	283·9
Coffee	lbs.	22,715,807	28,420,980	25·1
Tea	,,	29,937,055	36,396,078	21·3
Rice	cwts.	140,100	245,887	75·5
Eggs	No.	58,464,690	91,830,187	57·1
Tallow	cwts.	918,733	1,243,112	35·3
Soap (hard)	lbs.	103,956,030	156,008,290	43·1
Tobacco	,,	19,333,840	22,308,385	14·2
Crown-glass	cwt	103,803	116,893	12·6
Plate glass	,,	14,019	27,639	97·1
Green or bottle glass	cwts.	288,760	499,581	73·0
Paper	lbs.	62,738,000	97,103,548	54·7

This list might be extended much further; but it will suffice to show that the consumption of these articles (restrained in some cases by too heavy a taxation) was enjoyed in a larger ratio than the increase of population, and that the comforts of the people must have been proportionately greater in 1841 than in 1831.

Concurrently with this increased consumption of articles of comfort and luxury, it is worthy of special notice that the use of intoxicating drinks had apparently decreased. We are not aware of any causes which encouraged the smuggling or adulteration of spirits in 1841 which did not exist in 1831; and yet it appears, from the returns, that the consumption of duty-paid spirits of all kinds, whether British or foreign, had decreased in that interval to the extent of 7·8 per cent. In the same period the consumption of all wines had increased only 3·9 per cent. The consumption of beer cannot be ascertained, but the quantity of hops that paid duty had fallen from 36,500,028 lbs. in 1831, to 30,504,108, or 19·6 per cent.; and of malt, from 40,334,987 bushels to 35,656,713, or 13·1 per cent. From these facts, however, no certain inference can be drawn, on account of the great varieties in the natural produce of these articles in different years, and of the free use of other ingredients by brewers.

Our view of the evidences of increased consumption may be closed by the notice of the three articles of timber, cotton-wool, and wool, all of which are used solely in giving employment to productive industry. Taking all the different kinds of imported timber, there appears to have been an increase of 37·5 per cent. In cotton-wool there was an increase of 61·1 per cent.; and in sheep and lambs' wool imported, of 78·7 per cent.

The next subject of comparison may be the exports of British and Irish produce and manufactures from the United Kingdom, in 1831 and in 1841, from which the manufacturing and commercial condition of the country, and the employment of its people, at those periods, may be collected.

The quantities and declared value of some of the principal articles of export are exhibited in the table in the following page :—

On referring to the two last columns of this table, it appears that the value of the exports did not always increase in the same ratio as the quantities; but the total declared value of all British and Irish produce and manufactures exported in 1831 was 37,64,372*l.*; in 1841,

	1831.		1841.		Increase per cent.	
	Quantities.	Declared value.	Quantities.	Declared value.	In the quantity	In the declared value.
		£.		£.		
Apparel................	—	790,293	—	1,217,975	—	54·1
Brass and Copper ma- } cwts. nnfactures .... }	181,951	803,124	327,247	1,523,744	79·8	89·7
Cordage............. ,,	36,276	81,986	63,822	130,414	75·9	71·2
Cotton manufactures ... yds.	421,385,304	12,163,513	751,125,624	14,985,810	78·2	23·2
Cotton twist and yarn .. lbs.	63,821,440	3,975,019	123,226,519	7,266,986	93·0	82·9
Earthenware .... pieces	37,028,897	461,090	53,150,903	600,759	43·5	30·3
Glass (entered by weight)....	177,915	420,044	338,890	405,168	90·4	—
—— (entered at value)	—	9,580	—	21,708	—	127·2
Hardwares and cutlery cwts.	336,194	1,622,429	·353,348	1,623,961	5·1	0·09
Iron and steel (wrought } tons. or unwrought) ..... }	124,312	1,123,372	360,875	2,877,278	174·2	156·1
Leather .... lbs.	1,314,931	246,410	2,623,075	332,573	99·4	34·9
Linen manufactures .... yds.	69,253,802	2,400,043	90,321.761	3,200,467	30·4	33·3
—— thread, tapes, &c. ,,		61,661		147,098		138·5
—— yarn .... lbs.	110,188	8,705	25,220,290	972,466	22788·4	11071·3
Machinery and mill-work ...	—	105,491	—	551,361	—	422·6
Silk manufactures	—	578,874	—	789,894	—	36·2
Tin and pewter wares	—	230,143	—	390,621	—	69·7
Wool, British........... lbs.	3,494,275	173,105	8,471,235	555,620	142·4	220·9
Woollen and worsted yarn ,,	1,592,455	158,111	4,903,291	552,148	207·9	249·2
——— manufactures, pieces	1,997,348	4,580,902	2,291,273	4,821,820	14·7	5·2
——————— yards.	5,797,546	500,956	9,831,975	695,462	69·5	39·4
——— hosiery, &c........	—	150,555	—	228,391	—	51·7

51,634,623*l.*; thus showing an aggregate increase of 38·9 per cent.

Another evidence of the increased commerce of the country is afforded by the returns of shipping. In 1831, 20,573 ships (British and foreign) engaged in the foreign and colonial trades, entered inwards; of which the total tonnage amounted to 3,241,927. In 1841 the number of ships had increased to 28,052, and the tonnage to 4,652,376; thus showing an increase of tonnage in the proportion of 43·5 per cent. In 1832, 119,283 ships were employed (including their repeated voyages) in the coasting trade, of which the tonnage amounted to 9,419,681. In 1841 the number of ships had increased to 146,127, and the tonnage to 11,417,991, showing an increase of 21·2 per cent. in the tonnage employed.

Thus far an increased prosperity can admit of no doubt. It is evident that consumption, production, and commerce all increased in a greater ratio than the population. But it may here be asserted that profits were low, and that, notwithstanding the outward signs of prosperity, the capital, available for further enterprises, was not increasing with corresponding rapidity. The evidences of accumulation cannot be of so distinct a character as those of consumption and production; but it may be asked, in the outset, how could so vast an increase in the productive industry of the country, in the value of its exports, in its shipping and commerce, have been supported without prodigious additions to its capital? The best evidence of the quantity of capital in a country is its results. Without a sufficient quantity, production and consumption could not continue to increase: and as capital is likely to be applied to production and consumption as much at one period as at another, all that seems necessary for ascertaining the increase of capital, is to know the increase of its immediate results. If, in addition to the vast increase of production and consumption which could only have been supported by a proportionate amount of capital, we see the price of all public securities high, the interest of money low, and capital seeking investment in every speculative enterprise, and devoted to religious and charitable objects over the whole world, it is absurd to doubt the abundance of capital. But in addition to this indirect evidence of the increase of capital, there are other indications of its accumulation, of a more direct nature, a few of which may suffice :—

Notwithstanding the discouragement of insurance, caused by a duty of 200 per cent., the sums insured against fire, in the United Kingdom, amounted in 1831 to 526,655,332*l*., and in 1841 to 681,539,839*l*.; being an increase of 29·4 per cent. The accumulations annually made through the instrumentality of life assurance are known to be enormous, but no reasonable estimate can be made of their amount, nor any comparison of the rate of increase in the period of which we are treating. The most interesting evidence of accumulation is presented by the returns of savings' banks. In 1831 there were 429,503 depositors, whose deposits amounted to 13,719,495*l*.: in 1841 there were 841,204 depositors, and the amount of their deposits had increased to 24,474,689*l*.; so that, both in number and amount, the deposits may be said to have been doubled in this short period of ten years. The capital invested in railways in the same period may safely be estimated at upwards of 60,000,000*l*. (see 'First Report on Railways,' 1839, Appendix); and the sums authorised by Parliament to be raised for various public purposes—for roads, bridges, docks, canals, navigations, markets, lighting and improving towns, afford evidence of the abundance of capital which was constantly seeking investment, in addition to its customary employment in commerce and manufactures.

The returns of the assessment of property for the income tax will not present any comparison of the wealth of the country in 1831 and in 1841; but very important results may be deduced from them, which must not be overlooked. The annual value of real property, as assessed to the property tax in 1815, was returned at 51,898,423*l*.; in 1842 it was returned at 82,233,844*l*.; and the tithes at 1,668,113*l*. In Scotland the real property was assessed in 1811 at 5,972,523*l*.; in 1842 at 9,284,382*l*. In the absence of any intermediate assessment a rough estimate only can be made of the increase in the value of real property between 1831 and 1841; but we are inclined to think it was not less than from 20 to 25 per cent. In 1815 the annual profits of trade in England and Wales were assessed at 35,028,051*l*. No similar account for 1842-3 has yet been published ; but as the actual receipts by government amounted to 1,466,985*l*. at 2*l*. 18s. 4*d*. per cent., after exempting all profits under 150*l*. a year, the annual amount of all profits above 150*l*. a year may be fairly estimated at 50,153,333*l*.; and after adding a fifth, or 10,000,000*l*., for profits under 150*l*., the proportion of increase which accrued between 1831 and 1841 will not be overrated at 20 per cent.

The amount of capital upon which legacy-duty had been paid in Great Britain, from 1797 to 1831 inclusive, was 741,648,197*l*.; in 1841 it amounted to 1,163,284,207*l*. Thus, in this period of ten years, legacy-duty had been paid upon a capital of 422,636,009*l*. 19s. 5*d*., or considerably more than one-half of the aggregate amount upon which the duty had been paid in the thirty-four preceding years. In 1831 the produce of the stamp-duties upon probates of wills and letters of administration in the United Kingdom amounted to 918,667*l*.; in 1841 to 1,012,481*l*., showing an increase of 10·2 per cent.

These various statements all confirm, more or less distinctly, the conclusion which had been suggested by less direct, but not less conclusive evidence, viz., that the capital of the country appears to have increased in the period of ten years from 1831 to 1841, in a greater ratio than the population; and, consequently, that the funds necessary for the employment of labour and for maintaining the growing population in increased comfort, had multiplied more rapidly than the people for whose use they were available.

Having now compared the increase of national wealth with the increase of population, so far as the statistics of consumption, production, and accumulation afford such comparison; a confirmation of the results presented by our analysis is to be found in the Reports of the Census Commissioners, together with many singular facts illustrative of the state and destinies of our country. In following these, however, it will be necessary to consider Great Britain and Ireland separately.

The first point illustrative of the condition of the people is, that the increase in the number of inhabited houses in England and Wales since 1831 was two per cent. greater than that of the population. Too much reliance, however, must not be placed upon this bare statistical result, as the quality of the houses may be a more important matter than their positive number; but so far as it goes it is satisfactory. The misery and destitution which prevail in many parts of Great Britain are undeniable; squalid poverty and glittering wealth meet the eye in every street; but the apparent fact of an increased house accommodation should make men hesitate before they declare that poverty is spreading at one extremity of society while wealth is agglomerating at the other. Apart from this direct evidence that one of the most painful results of poverty, the overcrowding of many families into the same houses, though painfully prevalent in Liverpool and some other places, has not generally increased—it may be asked what better proof, amongst many, can be given of the general prosperity of the masses of the people than the application of so vast a capital to productive industry as must have been required for the building of 500,000 new houses in a space of ten years?

It is well known that the rate of increase of the population from 1831 to 1841 in England and Wales was apparently less than in the preceding ten years, by 1½ per cent.; and if the bare fact of numerical increase were taken as a test of national strength and prosperity, this fact might be deemed a symptom of decay. To this discouraging view, however, a complete answer is given by the commissioners, who ascribe the apparently diminished rate of increase wholly to emigration. " The additional population which would be required in order to make the ratio of increase equal to that of the former decennial period would be 208,998, being 1½ per cent. on the population of 1831; and from returns which have been furnished from the Emigration Board, it appears that the total excess of emigration in the ten years ending 1841, compared with the ten years ending 1831, may be estimated at 282,322." (See Preface, p. 11.) Thus, instead of attributing this apparent decrease to the pressure of poverty by which the natural growth of population was checked, we must ascribe it to a cause which is calculated to raise the wages of labour in this country, while it affords to the emigrants a wider field and,-we trust, a larger reward for their industry.

Another fact of the highest importance is clearly proved, viz.—that the commerce and manufactures of Great Britain alone afford employment for the increasing population. While the increase upon the whole kingdom amounted, as already stated, to 13·2 per cent., the increase in the manufacturing and commercial counties was greatly above that proportion, and in the agricultural counties considerably below it. In Chester the increase was 18·3 per cent.; in Durham, 27·7; in Lancaster, 24·7; in Middlesex, 16; in Monmouth, 36·9; in Stafford, 24·3; in Warwick, 19·3; and in the West Riding of York, 18·2. In Buckingham the increase was only 6·4 per cent.; in Cumberland, 4·9; in Devon, 7·8; in Dorset, 9·9; in Essex, 8·6; in Hereford, 2·4; in Norfolk, 5·7; in Oxford, 6·2; in Suffolk, 6·3; in Westmoreland, 2·5; and in the North Riding of York 7 per cent. It is useless, therefore, to discuss the relative importance of agriculture and manufactures in the abstract; for agricultural counties cannot support their own population; while the manufacturing and commercial counties find employment for their own natural increase and for the surplus of other counties which the land cannot maintain.

The relative increase of the agricultural and commercial population is shown by the following proportions per cent. :—

	Agricultural	Commercial.	Miscellaneous.
1831	28	42	30
1841	22	46	32

But in 1831 the returns referred to families, and in 1841 to individuals; and as a greater number of children are employed in manufactures than in agriculture, the difference may have been slightly augmented by this form of enumeration. A still more important point of comparison is the relative increase of different classes of occupations in the same period of 10 years from 1831 to 1841. A comparative return of the Commissioners (Preface, p. 21) includes males only aged 20 years and upwards, and exhibits the following results:—The number of occupiers and labourers in agriculture had decreased in that period from 1,251,751 to 1,215,264; but the Commissioners explain this result by supposing that numerous farm-servants had been returned in 1841 as domestic servants instead of as agricultural labourers. Persons engaged in commerce, trade, and manufacture had increased from 1,572,292 to 2,039,409 (or 29·7 per cent.): capitalists, bankers, professional and other educated men, from 216,263 to 286,175 (or 32·3 per cent.): labourers employed in labour not agricultural had *decreased* from 611,744 to 610,157: other males 20 years of age, except servants, had increased from 237,337 \o 392,211: male servants 20 years of age and upwards had increased from 79,737 to 164,384, including, however, as already noticed, many farm-servants. For the purpose of instituting a just comparison of the relative increase of particular employments, it must be understood that the total number of male persons 20 years of age and upwards (exclusive of army, navy, and merchant seamen) had increased, in this period of ten years, from 3,969,124 to 4,707,600 (or 18·6 per cent.). Making due allowance for the probable error in the return of agricultural labourers, we are forced to conclude that that class had either not increased at all or had increased in a very small degree: and that the class of labourers not agricultural had positively diminished: while capitalists, bankers, professional and other educated men, had increased 32·3 per cent.; persons engaged in trade and in manufactures 29·7 per cent.; and domestic servants 106 per cent., or allowing for farm-servants, say 90 per cent. Thus the two classes who earn the lowest wages were alone stationary or retrograde: the highest class in wealth and intelligence had increased 32·3 per cent.; and the domestic servants, whose numbers are a certain indication of the means of their employers, had increased 90 per cent. Nor must another important fact be omitted in connexion with the decrease in the class of labourers, viz. the immense numbers of Irish who notoriously perform the most laborious parts of industry. In Lancashire the persons born in Ireland formed, in 1841, 6·3 per cent. upon the whole population; in Cheshire, 3 per cent.; in Middlesex, 3·6 per cent.; in Ayrshire, 7·3; in Dumbartonshire, 11; and in Lanarkshire and Renfrewshire, upwards of 13 per cent. It would seem, therefore, that the class of British labourers are gradually raising themselves into a higher condition and more lucrative employments; and that the demand for the lowest description of labour, caused by their withdrawal from it, is supplied by their Irish brethren.

The number of female domestic servants increased in Great Britain from 670,491 in 1831, to 908,825 in 1841, or 35 per cent.

In concluding this statement of the industrial occupations of the people of Great Britain, it is gratifying to learn that the whole of the "almspeople, pensioners, paupers, lunatics, and prisoners" amounted in 1841 to 1·1 per cent. only upon the population.

We may now pass to some of the most material facts disclosed by the census of Ireland. The constant migration of labourers from the agricultural counties of England to the manufacturing districts, and the extensive emigration of the last ten years, have been already noticed ; and precisely the same circumstances are observable in Ireland. In the period from 1831 to 1841 no less a number than 403,459 persons left Ireland, either to settle in the populous towns of Great Britain or to emigrate to the British Colonies or the United States; while an extensive migration was taking place, within Ireland itself, to Dublin and to other commercial and manufacturing places.

The returns of house accommodation in Ireland present a very lamentable picture. The Commissioners have adopted a judicious classification by which the houses are distinguished under four classes, the last being that of the cabin or mud hut with one room, and the third class but one degree better. The following statement shows the proportion per cent. which the number of families in each class of accommodation bear to the total number of families:—

	1 Class.	2 Class.	3 Class.	4 Class.
Rural districts	1·2	15·3	40·	43·5
Civic districts	7·	22·4	33·9	36·7

The value of this classification is obvious, and if hereafter adopted in England it will render the statistics of house accommodation of considerably greater weight, in estimating the social condition and habits of the people. A mud hut upon a common ought not to rank even, in the array of figures, with the mansions of wealthy cities.

Even in Ireland it appears that manufactures are attracting the agricultural population; for the number of families engaged in trade and manufactures have increased five per cent. since 1831; and the number employed in agriculture have diminished in a corresponding proportion.

The population have been divided by the commissioners into three great classes, nearly equivalent to the three ordinary grades of society: and the proportions of families appear as follow:

	Rural.	Civic.
Vested means, Professions, &c.	1·8	6·6
The direction of labour	28·3	50·
Their own manual labour	68·	36·4
Means not specified	1·9	7·

The occupations of all individuals above 15 years of age are classified: 1st, as ministering to food; 2nd, as ministering to clothing; 3rd, as ministering to lodging, &c.; 4th, as ministering to health, education, &c.; and 5th, as unclassified or miscellaneous; each class bearing respectively the following proportions to the entire population, viz. 23·3; 11··2·; 17·; and 6·. But as no similar classification had ever been adopted before, no comparison is practicable with any preceding period.

The report of the Irish Census Commissioners abounds in highly interesting inquiries into the condition of the Irish people; but as they do not afford any comparison with the year 1831, the object which we had proposed cannot be carried any further with respect to that country.

This succinct view of the material progress of society, as far as it admits of elucidation by statistics, is certainly incomplete without a consideration of its advances or retrogression in religion, in morals, and in education; but these questions, far more important in themselves than any we have here discussed, are not so immediately connected with the results of the Census.

CENTRAL CRIMINAL COURT. [CIRCUITS.]

CERTIFICATE. [BANKRUPT, p. 292.]

CERTIORA'RI, in law, is a writ issuing from one of the superior courts, directing the judges or officers of an inferior court to transmit or cause to be certified (*certiorari facias*) records or other proceedings. The object of the removal is either that the judgment of the inferior jurisdiction may be reviewed by the superior court, or that the decision and the proceedings leading to it may take place before the higher tribunal. An instance of the former is where the convictions of magistrates or the judgments or orders of courts of quarter-sessions are removed by certiorari into the court of King's Bench by way of appeal against their validity, in which case the decision which has previously been given is re-considered, and is confirmed or set aside. An instance of the latter is where an indictment found against a peer by an inferior jurisdiction is certified or transmitted into the Court of Parliament or the Court of the Lord High Steward, in order that the further proceedings and the adjudication may take place before the proper tribunal. By this writ, indictments, with the proceedings thereon, may, at any time before actual trial, be removed from the assizes or quarter-sessions into the Court of

King's Bench, as the supreme court of ordinary criminal jurisdiction. The 5 & 6 Wm. IV. c. 33, enacts that no certiorari shall issue to remove indictments or presentments from inferior courts to the Court of King's Bench, at the instance of a prosecutor, without leave obtained from the court, as by a defendant. In order to avoid the occurrence of frivolous appeals, it is usual in statutes which give summary jurisdiction to inferior tribunals to restrict, or altogether take away, the right to a certiorari.

CE'SSIO BONO'RUM, in the law of Scotland, is the name given to a process by which, as by the insolvency system in England, the estate of an insolvent person who does not come within the operation of mercantile bankruptcy is attached and distributed among his creditors. The term is derived from the deed of cession, or the assignment by which, as the counterpart of the relief afforded to him from the immediate operations of his creditors, the insolvent conveys his whole property for their behoof. Both the nomenclature and the early practice of the system are taken from the Roman law. (Dig. 42, tit. 3, "de cessione bonorum.") According to the more ancien' law, the person released from prison on a cessio bonorum was bound to wear a motley garment called the dyvour's habit. In later times this stigma became the penalty of fraud, and it was subsequently disused. Before the passing of the late act, the jurisdiction in the awarding of Cessio was entirely confined to the Court of Session, and the insolvent was required to have been a month in prison before he could sue out the process. By 6 & 7 Will. IV. c. 56, the system was remodelled. The process may now be sued out either in the Court of Session or in the sheriff's local court. It may be taken advantage of by any person who is in prison for civil debt, or against whom such a writ of imprisonment has issued. It proceeds on notice to the creditors, and an examination and surrender of the insolvent. Proceedings instituted in the Sheriff Court are liable to review in the Court of Session. Cessio bonorum exhibits, like the insolvency system in England, this important difference from mercantile bankruptcy, that the person who obtains the privilege is not discharged from his debts, but only from proceedings against his person for payment of past debts, his estate continuing to be liable to the operations of his creditors. In Scotland, however, the common law means of attaching a debtor's property are simple and effectual, and there does not appear to have been there the same inducement as in England to make the process for the distribution of the debtor's effects an instrument of their discovery. The Scottish system, moreover, cannot be used by the creditors as a means of compelling their debtor to distribute his estate. It is a privilege of the debtor, and being seldom resorted to except by persons in a state of destitution who are harassed by vindictive creditors, the improvement of the system has not been a matter of much interest either among lawyers or legislators.

CESSION. [BENEFICE, p. 349.]
CESTUI QUE TRUST. [TRUSTEE.]
CHALLENGE. [JURY.]
CHAMBERLAIN (custos cubiculi, or cubicularius, keeper of the chamber). Cubicularius was the Roman name for a slave whose special business was to look after the rooms or chambers in the house, introduce visitors, and the like. The cubicularius was thus a confidential slave or freedman, as the case might be, and a kind of guardian of his master's person. Under the emperors the cubicularii were officers in the imperial household; and were called the "cubicularii sacri cubiculi," the chamberlains of the imperial chamber. (Cod. xii. tit. 5.) The emperor's wife, the Augusta, also had her chamberlains. This office, like many others in royal households, is derived from the usages of the later Roman Empire. In the Anglo-Saxon times, in England, the chamberlain appears to have had the name of Camerarius, and had the keeping of the king's treasure (Ealred, in Vit. S. Edw. Confess., c. ii. p. 9), by which name this officer also occurs in the Domesday Survey. The word chamber (French, chambre) is from the Latin camera.

The office of lord great chamberlain of England was once of the highest dignity, and was held in grand serjeanty from the second year of King Henry I. by the family of De Vere, from whom it passed, by a female heir, to the family of Bertie. By the statute of precedency, 31 Hen. VIII., the great chamberlain's place was next to that of the lord privy seal. In 1714 the Marquess of Lindsay, then hereditary great chamberlain of England, having been raised to the dukedom of Ancaster, surrendered this precedency for himself and his heirs, except only when he or they should be in the actual execution of the duties of the said office, in attending the person of the king or queen, or introducing a peer into the House of Lords. This surrender was confirmed by 1 Geo. I. c. 3. The duties which now devolve upon the great chamberlain are, the dressing and attending on the king at his coronation; the care of the ancient Palace of Westminster; the provision of furniture for the Houses of Parliament, and for Westminster Hall, when used on great occasions; and attendance upon peers at their creation, and upon bishops when they perform their homage. On the death of Robert, the last duke of Ancaster but one, in 1779, the office of hereditary great chamberlain descended to his two sisters, Priscilla, Lady Willoughby de Eresby, and Georgiana Charlotte, Marchioness Cholmondeley. The office is now jointly held by the families of Cholmondeley and Willoughby de Eresby, and the honours are enjoyed in each alternate reign by each family successively.

The office of lord chamberlain of the king's household is changed with the administration. He has the control of all parts of the household (except the ladies of the queen's bed-chamber) which are not under the direction of the lord steward, the groom of the stole, or the master of the horse; the king's chaplains, physicians, surgeons, &c., as well as the royal tradesmen, are by his appointment; the companies of actors at the royal theatres, as part of the household, are under his regulation, and he is also the licenser of plays. [THEATRE.] One of the officers in his department is styled Examiner of Plays.

The chamberlain of the corporation of the city of London is an officer elected by the freemen who are liverymen. By an act of common council of 5 Henry IV. the office is an annual one, but it is very rarely that the existing officer is opposed. There has been no such opposition since 1778. The duties of the chamberlain are judicial and administrative. He admits on oath all persons entitled to freedom of the city, and hears and determines all matters of complaint between masters and apprentices, and may commit either. He may discharge the apprentice from his indentures, and a part of the premium may be recovered by a peculiar process in the Lord Mayor's Court. An appeal is said to lie from the decision of the chamberlain to the lord mayor. The chamberlain has the conservation of lands, monies, or goods of citizens who die intestate, leaving orphans, on the application of such orphans or others on their behalf, for which purpose the chamberlain is deemed in law a corporation sole; but such applications are now rarely made. As treasurer of the corporation he has to receive all rents, profits, and revenues of markets and other items of receipt forming the income of the corporation, and to pay all money on account of the corporation upon competent warrants or orders. The fixed annual income of the chamberlain is 1160*l*. 9*s*. 4*d*.: his "ancient bill of fees" is 94*l*. 4*s*. a-year. He obtains an annual profit of from 1000*l*. to 2000*l*. from balances of the corporation money retained in his hands. This principle of remunerating a public officer is strongly objected to by the Commissioners of Corporation Inquiry (*Second Report*, p. 102). \

In the Exchequer Court of the County Palatine of Chester there is a chamberlain, an office generally held by some nobleman; and there is also a vice-chamberlain.

There was an officer called the chamberlain in two hundred and three of the municipal corporations investigated in 1834 by the Commissioners of Corporation Inquiry.

CHANCEL. This is rather a term of ordinary discourse than one which would be used in a technical description of the several parts of a Christian church. As far as we have observed, 't is now used to denote that part of a church in which the communion table or altar is placed, with the area before it, in which the congregation assemble when the Eucharist is administered. An outcry was raised at the Reformation against the rubric prefixed to the Common Prayer, which ordained that the chancels should remain as in times past. The more ardent reformers asserted that this ordinance tended only to magnify the priesthood; and hence the modern practice of performing divine service in the body of the church, though the chancel still remains as a separate part of the edifice. In many churches the Epistles and Gospels and the Commandments are read at the communion-table, the proper place for which is the chancel. The chancel was often separated from the nave or body of the church by lattice-work, *cancelli*, and it was from this circumstance that the term chancel seems to have originated. The word cancelli is used by Cicero and other Latin writers to express a partition made by upright and cross pieces of wood or metal for the purpose of making any barrier or separation in courts of justice, in a theatre, and so forth.

In some churches we may hear of the chancel of a particular family. This is in cases in which some particular family has had a private oratory within the church, which has usually been also the burial-place of the family. These private chapels or chantries are sometimes called chancels, for the same reason that the great choir is sometimes so called; that is, in consequence of being divided from the rest of the church by *cancelli*.

CHANCELLOR (in Latin, *Cancellarius*). The primary meaning of cancellarius is "qui ad cancellos assistit," one who is stationed at the lattice-work of a window or a door way, to introduce visitors, &c. A cancellarius in this sense was no more than a door-keeper. The emperor Carinus made one of his cancellarii praefect of the city, a promotion which caused great dissatisfaction. (Vopiscus, *Carinus*, c. 16.) In another sense, cancellarius was a kind of legal scribe, so called also from his position at the cancelli of the courts of law. The cancellarius, under the later emperors, and in the Constantinopolitan court, was a chief scribe or secretary (ὁ μέγας λογοθέτης), who was ultimately invested with judicial powers, and a general superintendence over the rest of the officers of the emperor. He was called cancellarius because he sat *intra cancellos* (within the lattice), a screen which divided off a portion of a larger room for the sake of greater privacy; from which circumstance the chancel of a church also acquires its name.

The prelates of the Roman church had likewise an officer so called; in the Church of England, each bishop has a chancellor, who exercises judicial functions. All the modern nations of Europe have or have had chancellors, though the powers and duties seem to have varied in each.

In England the chancellor was originally the king's chief secretary, to whom petitions were referred, by whom patents and grants from the crown were approved and completed, and by whom reports upon such matters were, if necessary, made to the king; hence he was sometimes styled Referendarius. This term occurs in a charter of Ethelbert, A.D. 605; and Selden (*Treatise on the Office of Chancellor*) considers it synonymous with chancellor, a name which, he says, first occurs, in the history of England, in the time of Edward the Elder, about A.D. 920.

In the capacity of secretary he was the adviser of his master; prepared and made out his mandates, grants, and charters, and finally (when seals came into use) affixed his seal. Hence, or perhaps because in early times he was usually an ecclesiastic, he became keeper of the king's conscience, examiner of his patents, the officer by whom prerogative writs were prepared, and keeper of the great seal. The last ecclesiastic who exercised the office was John Williams, archbishop of York, who was lord keeper from July 10, 1621, to November 1, 1625; his friend and secretary, John Hacket, who became bishop of Lichfield and Coventry wrote his life in a volume of singular interest, which he entitled 'Scrinia Reserata.'

The interference of the king, as the source of justice, was frequently sought against the decisions of the courts of law, where they worked injustice; and also in matters which were not cognizable in the ordinary courts, or in which, from the maintenance or protection afforded to his adversary, the petitioner was unable to obtain redress. The jurisdiction with which the English chancellor is invested had its origin in this portion of discretionary power, which was retained by the king on the establishment of courts of justice (*Legal Judicature in Chancery stated*, p. 27, *et seq.*). Though the exercise of these powers in modern times is scarcely, if at all, less circumscribed by rule and precedent than the strict jurisdiction of the courts of law [EQUITY], controversies have at times arisen as to the powers of the chancellor; the particulars of one dispute have been preserved to us entire. (*The Jurisdiction of the Court of Chancery vindicated*. Printed at the end of 1 *Ch. Rep.* and in the 1st vol. of *Collect. Jurid.*)

The style of the Chancellor in England is Lord High Chancellor of Great Britain. He takes rank above all dukes not of the blood royal, and next to the archbishop of Canterbury. He is appointed by the delivery of the great seal into his custody, though there are instances of his having been appointed by patent. The resumption of the great seal by the king determines his office. By virtue of his office he is the king's principal adviser in matters of law, and a privy counsellor; speaker and prolocutor of the House of Lords, chief judge in the Court of Chancery, and the head of the profession of the law; visitor in the king's right of all hospitals and colleges of royal foundation; and patron of all crown livings under the value of 20*l.* a year, according to the valuation made in the reign of Henry VIII., and confirmed in that of Elizabeth. [BENEFICE, p. 352.] He appoints and removes all justices of the peace, though usually only at the recommendation of lords-lieutenants of counties. He issues writs for summoning parliaments, and transacts all business connected with the custody and use of the great seal. To him was intrusted the care of infants and their property upon the dissolution of the court of wards and liveries: and he has

the jurisdiction over idiots and lunatics by special delegation from the crown. He also exercises a special jurisdiction, conferred upon him by various statutes, as original and appellate judge, as to charitable uses, friendly societies, infant lunatic and idiot trustees, in certain appeals from the court of review, in bankruptcy, and in many other cases. He is a conservator of the peace, and may award precepts and take recognizances to keep the peace; and has concurrent jurisdiction with the other judges of the superior courts, with respect to writs of habeas corpus. Except in the case of service of process, given to him by some recent statutes, the lord chancellor has no jurisdiction in Scotland.

The authority of lord chancellor and lord keeper are made the same by the stat. 5 Eliz. c. 18: it is not now customary to appoint a lord keeper, and of course there cannot now be a lord chancellor and lord keeper at the same time. The last lord keeper was Lord Henley, in 1757. The great seal is however sometimes put into commission during the temporary vacancy of the office, or the sickness of the chancellor, the seal being intrusted to the chief commissioner. (1 Will. and M. c. 21.)

The chancellor has also important political functions: he has a seat in the cabinet, and usually takes an active part in public measures. He resigns office with the party to which he is attached.

By 3 & 4 Wm. IV. c. 111, § 3, in consideration that the Chancellor had lost the patronage of certain offices then abolished, the king is empowered to grant an annuity of 5000*l.* a year to the Lord Chancellor or Lord Keeper on his resignation of office. The salary of the Lord Chancellor is 10,000*l.* a year, and is paid out of the Suitors' Fee Fund. He has besides a salary as Speaker of the House of Lords. There is also a Lord High Chancellor of Ireland, whose authority within his own jurisdiction is in most respects the same as that of the Lord High Chancellor of Great Britain. The salary of the Irish Chancellor, which is paid out of the Consolidated Fund, is 8000*l.* a year. His retiring pension is 3692*l.* a year. (Selden, *Off. Ch.*; Black-

CHANCELLOR. [482] CHANCELLOR.

stone, *Com.*; Story *On Equity;* and the *Books of Chancery Practice.*) [CHANCERY.]

The *Chancellor of a Diocese* or *of a Bishop* is Vicar-general to the bishop, holds his courts, and directs and assists him in matters of ecclesiastical law. He has a freehold in his office, and he is not necessarily an ecclesiastic; but if he is a layman, or married, he must be a Doctor of the Civil Law. (Blackstone, *Com.*; 37 H. VIII. c. 17.)

The *Chancellor of a Cathedral* is an officer who superintends the regularity of the religious services.

The *Chancellor of the Duchy of Lancaster* presides either in person or by deputy in the court of the Duchy of Lancaster concerning all matters of equity relating to lands holden of the king, in right of the Duchy of Lancaster. His salary is 2000*l*. a year, and that of the Vice-Chancellor is 600*l*.: the fees, which amount to 30*l*. or 40*l*. annually, are deducted from the salary. The Vice-Chancellor holds courts both in Westminster and in Lancashire.

The *Chancellors of the Universities of Oxford and Cambridge* are elected by the respective corporate bodies of which they are the heads; they exercise exclusive jurisdiction in all civil actions and suits where a member of the University or privileged person is one of the parties, except in cases where the right to freehold is concerned. In both the English Universities the duties of the Chancellor are in nearly all cases discharged by a Vice-Chancellor.

The *Chancellor of the Exchequer* is under-treasurer, and holds the seal of the Exchequer. The office of Lord High Treasurer is now executed by the Lords Commissioners of the Treasury. The Chancellor of the Exchequer is the principal finance minister of the crown: the office is sometimes held by the Prime Minister when he is a member of the House of Commons. The legal functions of the Chancellor of the Exchequer are now merely formal. [EXCHEQUER.] Bills in the Exchequer were addressed to him, and to the barons of that court, so long as the equity jurisdiction of the Exchequer existed, and on some occasions (as on his appointment) he sits in court; but all the legal business is transacted by the barons. If the chief baron and barons are equally divided in opinion, the Chancellor of the Exchequer may be required to re-hear the cause with the barons, and give his decision. The last instance occurred in 1735, when Sir Robert Walpole gave his decision upon a question of considerable doubt and difficulty, which is said to have given great satisfaction. (Blackstone, *Com.*; Fowler's *Exchequer Practice.*)

The *Chancellor of the Order of the Garter* and other orders of knighthood seals and authenticates the formal instruments of the chapter, and keeps the register of the order. He exercises various functions at the installation of the knights, and during their meetings and processions.

CHANCELLOR OF SCOTLAND, As in England, the chancellor of Scotland was always a high officer of the crown, and had great influence with the king and authority in his councils. As in England too, that authority at length extended itself beyond its former limits, and affected the whole judicial power of the kingdom. Its operation and effect in the two countries, however, was different: for while in England the chancellor only carved out for himself a jurisdiction in equity, in Scotland he reached the head of the administration of justice, and sat in a court which dispensed both equity and common law, and the course of proceeding in which all the other judicatures of the realm were bound to follow.

In 1425, which was shortly after the return of King James I. from his long captivity in England, the "chancellor and with him certaine discreete persones of the thre estates chosen and depute by the king" were erected into the court of the session, for the final determination of all matters competent to the king and his council. The court of the session, however, expired with Bishop Wardlaw, from whom in all likelihood it originated; the chancellor's office being taken, on his death, from his protégé, Bishop Cameron, and given to Sir William Crichton, a layman, when the former policy of determining suits by the old common law was restored. This continued (with the exception of an attempt to the contrary in 1457, probably under the influence of Bishop Shorsewood, the favourite and confessor of King James II.) till the time of Bishop Elphinstone, to whom undoubtedly may be ascribed the crafty acts passed in 1487 for the recovery of the large jurisdiction of the chancellor and court of the session, as well as the act 1494, c. 5, to enforce in the courts the study and practice of the canon and civil laws. Nor perhaps shall we greatly err in conceiving his zeal to have been employed in establishing in 1503 the court of daily council, which was essentially a restoration of the old court of the session. But all these proved only preparatory steps to the erection of the court of council and session, or college of justice, which was instituted in 1532, and has continued to our own time. Of this college the chancellor, or, as he then began to be styled, lord chancellor of Scotland, was to be principal; and as on the one hand it was the supreme court of the kingdom, and on the other all inferior courts were required to copy its proceedings, it wielded the whole judicative power of the country. It early claimed also, and exercised, a large legislative power under the statutes permitting it to pass acts of sederunt; and the officers who executed its warrants and decrees were either its own macers or else messengers, over whom it obtained complete control. These powers the court wielded so as to effect nearly an entire change of the law. The ecclesiastical estate for some time predominated both on the bench and at the bar. The consequence was, the canon and civil laws became, what indeed they used to be styled, the common law of the land, and the old common law became obsolete and antiquated. Much of this has been corrected since the Reformation; and still more since the union with England, where the old common law has ever continued the antagonist of Roman jurisprudence. At the Reformation the authority of the canon law ceased, and not long afterward ministers of the gospel were disabled by statute from being either of the bench or bar. The authority of the canon law was in like manner essentially broken by the Union, when both portions of the island became one great mercantile community, to which the civil law was in many respects unsuitable; and since that event various provisions have been made to improve and assimilate the laws and practice of the two kingdoms.

The similarity of procedure in the court of session in Scotland and the high court of chancery in England is striking. Both courts indeed, and the ecclesiastical courts of both countries, borrowed their forms from the court of Rome, and with these last the forms of the court of session in many respects still agree. The bill or written supplication to the court for letters, whether of summons or of diligence, is of the same nature with the supplication for letters in the court of Rome, and it is observable that when the desire of the bill is granted, it is in the same terms in both courts. The condescendence and answers are plainly derived from the articuli and responsiones of the papal tribunal. The initialia testimonii, or purging of a witness, are identical with the interrogatoria generalia of that court. Letters of advocation, suspension, and reduction are well known there. The " malè appellatum et benè processum" is but verbally translated in the phrase of the Scots court, "finds the letters orderly proceeded;" and letters of horning, caption, and relaxation bear their papal origin impressed upon them. It appears also that from an early period the court issued commissions to its macers to perform judicial duties, as the ecclesiastics appoint the inferior church officers their legates and commissaries for the like purposes; and at an early time also the judges began the yet subsisting custom of changing their name on their elevation to the bench, in imitation, as it seems, of the like custom on elevation in the papal hierarchy.

From what is above stated, we may see why there is no court of chancery in Scotland, separate from the courts of common law, as in England; the whole judicatures of Scotland having become subject to the court of session, where the chancellor presided, dispensing both equity and common law. But from the earliest times there was an office of chancery in

CHANCERY. [484] CHANCERY

Scotland, and we shall find that many of the early chancellors had been 'clerici cancellarii.'

In the list of chancellors for Scotland in the 'Penny Cyclopædia,' art. "Chancellor," various errors are corrected which occur in Crawford's 'Officers of State' in the series of chancellors of Scotland. In Beatson's 'Political Index' there is a chancellor as early as the reign of Malcolm III., but the more authentic series begins with Constantine, earl of Fife, who was chancellor in the time of Alexander I.

By art. 24 of the treaty of Union, it was provided that there should in future be but one great seal for the United Kingdom, and that a seal should be kept and used in Scotland for such private rights or grants as had usually passed the great seal of Scotland. The office of chancellor of Scotland then properly expired, and none have been appointed to it since the earl of Seafield, who was chancellor at the time of the Union.

CHANCERY (*Cancellaria*); the term is derived from Chancellor, *Cancellarius*, and signifies the court where that judge exercises his functions. There are several chanceries, as there are several chancellors; but the place where the Lord High Chancellor's judicial functions are exercised is called the High Court of Chancery.

The principal part of the business of the Court of Chancery consists in the administration of Equity, a name which in this country comprehends those rules of law, which are applicable to such matters as belong to the jurisdiction of the court. The Court of Exchequer had a similar jurisdiction, which was abolished by 5 Vict. c. 5. [EQUITY.]

The Lord Chancellor, the three Vice-Chancellors, and the Master of the Rolls, are the judges by whom equity is administered in Chancery. Each of them has a separate court. In term-time they sit in Westminster Hall; in vacation, the Chancellor and Vice-Chancellors sit in Lincoln's Inn, and the Master of the Rolls at the Rolls, in Chancery-lane.

The Master of the Rolls is appointed by the crown by letters patent, and holds his office on the same terms as the common law judges, that is, during good behaviour. He has the power of hearing and determining originally the same matters as the Lord Chancellor, excepting cases in lunacy and bankruptcy; orders and decrees pronounced by the Master of the Rolls are good and valid, but they must be signed by the Lord Chancellor before they are enrolled, and they are subject to be reversed by the Chancellor. The Master of the Rolls has precedence next to the Lord Chief Justice of the King's Bench. This office is one of high antiquity. The salary is 7000*l*. a year under 1 Vict. c. 46. The Master of the Rolls in Ireland has 3969*l*. a year under 4 Geo. IV. c. 61.

The office of Vice-Chancellor was created by 53 Geo. III. c. 24. This officer (who, in Chancery, takes precedence next to the Master of the Rolls) is appointed by the crown by letters patent, and holds his office during good behaviour. Rank and precedence are given him by 5 Vict. c. 5 next after the Lord Chief Baron of the Exchequer. If a member of the Privy Council, he is also to be a member of the Judicial Committee. He has power to hear and determine all matters depending in the Court of Chancery, either as a court of law or as a court of equity, or as incident to any ministerial office of the said court, or which are subjected to the jurisdiction of such court or of the Lord Chancellor by any special act of parliament, as the Lord Chancellor shall from time to time direct. All orders and decrees of the Vice-Chancellor are valid, but subject to be altered or reversed by the Chancellor; and they must be signed by the Lord Chancellor before they can be enrolled. It is expressly provided by the act that the Vice-Chancellor has no power to alter or discharge any decree or order made by the Lord Chancellor, unless authorised by the Lord Chancellor, nor any power to alter or discharge any order or decree of the Master of the Rolls. The salary is 6000*l*. a year, granted by 2 & 3 Will. IV. c. 116. On the next appointment of a Vice-Chancellor, under 53 Geo. III. c. 24, the salary will be 5000*l*., with a retiring pension of 3500*l*. Since the appointment of two additional Vice-Chancellors by 5 Vic. c. 5, he is styled the Vice-Chancellor of England.

The act appointing two additional judges (Vice-Chancellors) to assist in the discharge of the functions of the Lord Chancellor is the 5 Vict. c. 5. They are respectively styled the first Vice-Chancellor and the second Vice-Chancellor, and hold office during good behaviour. The act prohibits the appointment of a successor to that one of the two new Vice-Chancellors who was appointed second. The salaries of the new Vice-Chancellors are 5000*l.* a year each, paid out of the interest arising from the Suitor's Fund. The salaries of the secretary, usher, and train-bearer, of each Vice-Chancellor are fixed by the act at 300*l.* a year for the secretary, 200*l.* for the usher, and 100*l.* for the train-bearer. After fifteen years' service, or when incapacitated for the duties of office by infirmity, a pension not exceeding 3500*l.* a year may be granted to each Vice-Chancellor. If he holds any other office of profit under the crown the annuity will be reduced, so that on the whole his public income may not exceed 3500*l.* a year.

An appeal (which, strictly speaking, is nothing more than a re-hearing of the cause) may be made from any decision of the Master of the Rolls or the Vice-Chancellors to the Lord Chancellor, and the court of the Lord Chancellor has been of late years much occupied with such appeals: original causes are generally confined to the courts of the Master of the Rolls and the Vice-Chancellors. The appeal from the decree of the Lord Chancellor is to the House of Lords.

There are officers of the Court of Chancery by whom certain parts of the equitable jurisdiction are exercised. These officers have however no original power for this purpose, but derive all their authority from special delegation by one of the judges in Chancery. The principal of these officers are the Masters in Ordinary, and the Accountant-General. The Masters in Ordinary are eleven in number, besides the Master of the Rolls, who is the chief of them, and the Accountant-General. The number of Masters was increased from ten to eleven when the equity jurisdiction of the Court of Exchequer was abolished by 5 Vict. c. 5. They were formerly appointed by the Lord Chancellor, but are now appointed by the crown, and hold office during good behaviour. (3 & 4 Wm. IV. c. 94.) The salary is 2500*l.* a year. It is the duty of the Masters to execute the orders of the court upon references made to them, whether in exercise of its original jurisdiction, or under the authority of an act of parliament, and to make reports in writing upon the matters that are referred to them. The Masters' reports must be confirmed by the court in order to make them effectual. The heads of reference to the Masters are almost as numerous as the subjects of the court's jurisdiction. The principal subjects of reference are, to examine into any alleged impertinence contained in pleadings, and into the sufficiency of a defendant's answer; to examine into the regularity of proceedings taken in any cause, or into alleged contempts of court; to take the accounts of executors, administrators, and trustees, or between any parties whatsoever; to inquire into, and decide upon, the claims of creditors, legatees, and next of kin; to sell estates, and to approve of the investment of trust-money in the purchase of estates, and, for this purpose (or for any other, as the case may be), to investigate titles, and settle conveyances; to appoint guardians for infants, and to allow proper sums for their maintenance and education; to tax the costs of the proceedings in any suit, or under the orders of the court: and generally to inquire into and inform the equity judge upon all matters of fact, which are either disputed between the parties, or not so far ascertained by evidence as to preclude all doubt on the subject.

The *Accountant-General* is an officer created by the stat. 12 G. I. c. 32, which also regulates his duties. [ACCOUNTANT-GENERAL.]

The proceedings in the Court of Chancery are conducted by Bill and Answer. But besides the jurisdiction, of which a sketch has been given above, a summary jurisdiction, upon Petition only, has been given to Courts of Equity in certain cases by acts of parliament. The principal cases in which this summary jurisdiction has been granted are those where trustees or mortgagees die without heirs or leaving infant heirs, or where trustees are out of the jurisdiction, or refuse to convey property to the persons beneficially entitled to it. In these, and many similar cases, the court is empowered, upon petition of the parties beneficially interested, to direct a conveyance or assignment of the property held in trust or on mortgage by the infant, or in case of a trustee having died without heirs, or being out of the jurisdiction of the court, or refusing to convey, to appoint some other person to convey in his place. The principal statutes relating to this branch of the jurisdiction of the court are, 1 Wm. IV. c. 47, 1 Wm. IV. c. 60, 1 Wm. IV. c. 65, 4 & 5 Wm. IV. c. 23, 5 & 6 Wm. IV. c. 17.

The stat. 52 G. III. c. 101 gives the court a summary jurisdiction in cases of abuse of charitable trusts. The court also appoints guardians for infants upon petition merely.

The jurisdiction exercised in Chancery over *infants* and *charities* is partly derived from the general equity jurisdiction, and partly from acts of parliament. (As to the origin of the jurisdiction over infants, see Coke upon Litt., by Hargrave, 88 b. n. 16; 2 Fonbl. *on Eq.*, p. 226, 232.)

The jurisdiction over infants is exercised principally in directing *maintenance* to be given them out of the property which they will enjoy on attaining their full age; in appointing and controlling *guardians* of them; and in providing suitable *marriages* for them.

A distinct part of the business in Chancery, though but a small part, arises from what is called *the common law jurisdiction of the Court of Chancery*.

It has chiefly respect to actions by or against any officer or minister of the Chancery, and to judicial proceedings respecting the acts of the king, when complained of by a subject. 3 Blackstone, *Com.* 48.

In actions depending in the Court of Chancery by virtue of its common law jurisdiction, the court has no power to try issues of fact. For this purpose the record of the pleadings must be delivered to the Court of King's Bench, and that court will have the issues tried by jury, and give judgment in the actions: and, from a judgment on demurrer in this court, it is said that a writ of error lies to the Court of King's Bench.

To the common law jurisdiction of the Court of Chancery belongs the power of issuing certain *writs*; particularly the writ of *habeas corpus*, and the writs of *certiorari* and *prohibition*, for restraining inferior courts of justice from assuming unlawful authority. (1 Madd. *Chanc.* 17, &c.)

The place where the common law jurisdiction of the Court of Chancery is exercised is the *petty bag office*; which is kept solely for this purpose. No part of the equity business of the Court of Chancery is carried on there.

The Court of Chancery, in respect of its common law jurisdiction, is said to be a court *of record*, which, as a court of equity, it is not. (Spelm. *Gloss.* 3 Bl. *Com.* 24.)

"In this ordinary or legal court," says Blackstone (vol. iii. 49), "is kept the *officina justitiæ*, out of which all original writs that pass the great seal, all letters patent, and all commissions of charitable uses, bankruptcy, sewers, idiotcy, lunacy, and the like do issue." The issuing of original writs, however, is now unfrequent. These writs, which were formerly the foundation of all actions in the courts of law at Westminster, have, with few exceptions, been abolished by recent statutes. Commissions of bankruptcy also are now never issued, owing to the late alterations in the bankrupt law. [BANKRUPT.]

The principle of the High Court of Chancery in England has led to the establishment of courts of equity in the British dominions and dependencies. Some of these are called Courts of Chancery. In each of the counties palatine of Lancaster and Durham, and also in Ireland, there is a court so named, which dispenses the same equity within the limits of its jurisdiction, as the High Court of Chancery. By 6 & 7 Wm. IV. c. 19, the palatine jurisdiction of Durham was separated from the bishopric and vested in the king, but the courts were expressly reserved. In the Irish Court of Chancery the Lord Chancellor for Ireland presides. From these courts the appeal is immediately to the House of Lords.

In most of our colonies there are Courts of Chancery (Howard's *Laws of the Colonies*). From the colonial courts an appeal now lies to "the judicial committee of the Privy Council." (Stat. 2 & 3 Wm. IV. c. 92.)

There are Chancery Courts in some of the states which compose the North American Union.

CHANCERY, INNS OF. [INN.]

CHANTRY (Cantária, in the middle age Latin), a private religious foundation, of which there were many in England before the Reformation, established for the purpose of keeping up a perpetual succession of prayers for the prosperity of some particular family while living, and the repose of the souls of those members of it who were deceased, but especially of the founder and other persons named by him in the instrument of foundation. The French word Oratoire appears to correspond to chantry.

Chantries owed their origin to the opinion once generally prevalent in the Christian church of the efficacy of prayer in respect of the dead as well as the living. Among the English, it prevailed in all ranks of society. The inscriptions upon the grave-stones of persons of ordinary condition in the times before the Reformation almost always began with "Orate pro animâ," "Pray for the soul," which was an appeal to those who resorted to the churches to pray for the soul of the person who slept below. Princes and persons of great wealth, when they founded monasteries, included amongst the duties of the religious for whose use they gave them, that they should receive in them their bodies, and for ever make mention of them in their daily services. When a taste for founding monasteries declined, which may be referred to about the close of the twelfth century, the disposition to secure the same object, by the foundation of chantries, began to prevail extensively in the better classes of society, and it continued to the Reformation, when all such foundations were swept away as superstitious.

A chantry did not necessarily require that any edifice should be erected for it. Chantries were usually founded in churches already existing: sometimes the churches of the monasteries, sometimes the great cathedral or conventual churches, but very frequently the common parish church. All that was wanted was an altar with a little area before it and a few appendages; and places were easily found in churches of even small dimensions in which such an altar could be raised without interfering with the general purposes for which the churches were erected. An attentive observation of the fabric of the parish churches of England will often show where these chantries have been; in some churches there are perhaps small remains of the altar, which was removed at the Reformation, but the traces of them are seen more frequently in one of those ornamented niches called piscinas, which were always placed near the altars. Sometimes there are remains of painted glass which was once the ornament of these private foundations, and more frequently we see one of those arched recesses in the wall which are called Founders' Tombs, and which in many instances no doubt were the tombs of persons to whose memory chantries had been instituted.

In churches which consisted of only nave and chancel with side aisles, the eastern extremities of the north and south aisles were often seized upon for the purpose of these foundations; in the larger churches, in which the ground-plan resembles the cross on which the Saviour suffered, the transverse beams (transepts) were generally devoted to the purpose of these private foundations. In the great conventual churches and the churches of monasteries, it would appear as if provision was often made for these private chantries in the original construction, each window that looks eastward being often made to light a small apartment just sufficient to contain an altar and a little space for the officiating priest.

It was by no means unusual to have four, five, or six different chantries in a common parish church: in the great churches, such as old St. Paul's in London, the Minster at York, and other ecclesiastical edifices of that class, there were at the time of the Reformation thirty, forty, or fifty such foundations. When the church allowed no more space for the introduction of chantries, it was usual for the founders to attach little chapels to the edifice. It is these chantry chapels, the use and occasion of which are now so generally forgotten, which occasion so much of the irregularity of design which is apparent in the parish churches of England. They were generally erected in the style of architecture which prevailed at the time, and not in accommodation to the style of the original fabric.

When chapels were erected for the especial purpose of the chantries, they were usually also the places of interment of the founder and his family, whence we sometimes find such chapels belonging, even to this day, to particular families, and adorned with monuments of many generations. One of the most beautiful chapels of this kind is in the little village of Sandal, a few miles from Doncaster, the foundation of Rokeby, archbishop of Dublin, who died in 1521. The church of Sandal being small, afforded no scope for the design of this magnificent prelate. Having determined that this should be the place of his interment, he erected a chapel on the north side of the choir, open, however, to the church on one side, being separated from it only by open wainscot. On entering it by the door the whole economy of one of these chapels is manifest. Under the window looking eastward an altar has stood; the piscina on the right remains. On each side of the east window is a niche where once, no doubt, stood an effigies of a saint whom the archbishop held in peculiar honour. In the centre is a brass indicating the spot in which the body of the prelate lies; and in the north wall is a memorial of him, having his arms and effigies, with an inscription setting forth his name and rank and the day of his decease, with divers holy ejaculations. The stone and wood work have been wrought with exquisite care, and the windows appear to have been all of painted glass. The Beauchamp chapel at Warwick contains the very fine monument and effigy of Richard de Beauchamp, Earl of Warwick, who died in 1439.

Sometimes chantries were established in edifices remote from any church, a chapel being erected for the express purpose.

In chantries of royal foundation, or in chantries founded by the more eminent prelates or barons, the service was conducted sometimes by more than one person. But usually there was only one officiating priest. The foundation deeds generally contain a specification of his duties, which consisted for the most part in the repetition of certain masses: but sometimes the instruction of youth in grammar or singing, and the delivering pious discourses to the people, made part of the duty of the chantry priests. They also contain an account of the land settled by the founder for the support of the priest. The names of the persons whom he was especially to name in his services are set forth, as well as the mode of his appointment and the circumstances in which he might be removed. Generally the king was named together with the founder and members of his family. This, it was supposed, gave an additional chance of the foundation being perpetuated. The king's licence was generally obtained for the foundation.

In many towns and country places there are ancient houses called chantry houses, or sometimes chantries, or colleges, which were formerly the residence of the chantry priests, and when called colleges they were the places where they lived a kind of collegiate life. These, as well as all other property given for the support of the chantry priests, were seized by the crown and sold to private persons, when by an act passed in the first year of King Edward VI. cap. 14, all foundations of this kind were absolutely suppressed and their revenues given to the king. An account had been taken a few years before of all the property which was settled to these uses, by the commissioners under the act 26 Hen. VIII. cap. 2, whose returns form that most important ecclesiastical document the 'Valor Ecclesiasticus' of King Henry VIII. The 'Valor' has been published by the commissioners on the 'Public Records' in five volumes folio.

The act of Edward VI. gave the king

all the colleges, free chapels, chantries, hospitals, fraternities or guilds, which were not in the actual possession of King Henry VIII. to whom the Parliament in the thirty-seventh year of his reign had made a grant of all such colleges, &c., nor in the possession of King Edward. The preamble of the act of Edward states that the object of the act was the suppression of the superstitions which such foundations encouraged, and the amendment of such institutions, and the converting them to good and godly uses, as for the erection of grammar-schools, and for augmenting of the universities, and better provision for the poor and needy. But this act was much abused, as the act for dissolving religious houses in King Henry VIII.'s reign had been, and private persons got most of the benefit of it. The money was not only not appropriated as it ought to have been, but both many grammar-schools and much charitable provision for the poor were taken away under the act. As already observed, the teaching of youth was sometimes one of the duties of the chantry priests, and it is probable that wherever there was a school and a chantry provided by the same foundation, the existence of the chantry was made a pretext for suppressing the whole endowment. Thus at Sandwich, in Kent, the chantry of St. Thomas was suppressed. One of the priests of this chantry was bound to teach the children of Sandwich to read. The citizens, feeling the loss of their school, raised money by subscription for making a new school, and Roger Manwood, afterwards chief baron of the Exchequer, was at the head of the subscription. This is the origin of the present free grammar-school of Sandwich. (*Journal of Education,* vol. x. p. 63.) King Edward founded a considerable number of grammar-schools, and the endowments were for the most part out of tithes formerly belonging to religious houses, or out of chantry lands given to the king in the first year of his reign. These schools are now generally called King Edward VI.'s Free Grammar-Schools; and many of them, such as Birmingham for instance, are now well endowed in consequence of the improved value of their lands. (Strype, *Ecclesias-* *tical Memoirs,* ii. 101—103, ii. 423, iii. 222, vi. 495.)

CHAPEL (in French, *chapelle;* in Latin, *capella*), a word common to many of the languages of modern Europe, and used to designate an edifice of the lower rank appropriated to religious worship.

In England it has been used to designate minor religious edifices founded under very different circumstances and for different objects.

1. We have a great number of rural ecclesiastical edifices, especially in the north of England, where the parishes are large, which are not, properly speaking, churches, *ecclesiæ,* though they are sometimes so called, but are chapels, and not unfrequently called parochial chapels. Most of them are of ancient foundation, but still not so ancient as the time when the parochial distribution of England was regarded as complete, and the right to tithe and offerings was determined to belong to the rector of some particular church. In the large parishes a family of rank which resided at an inconvenient distance from the parish church would often desire to have an edifice near to them, for the convenience of themselves and their tenants. On reasonable cause being shown, the bishop would often yield to applications of this kind; but in such cases he would not suffer the rights of the parish church to be infringed; no tithe was to be subtracted from it and given to the newly erected foundation, nor was that foundation to be accounted in rank equal to the older church, or its incumbent otherwise than subordinate minister to the incumbent of the parish church. But the bishop generally, perhaps always, stipulated that there should be an endowment by the founder of such an edifice. Frequently in edifices of this class there was the double purpose of obtaining a place of easier resort for religious worship and ordinances, and a place in which perpetual prayers might be offered for the family of the founder. [CHANTRY.] Others of these rural chapels were founded by the parishioners. The population of a village, which lay remote from the church of the parish within whose limits it was included, would increase, and

thus the public inconvenience of having to resort to the parish church on occasion of christenings, churchings, marriages, and funerals, besides the services on the festivals, become great; they would therefore apply to the bishop in petitions, many of which are in the registers of the sees, setting forth the distance at which they lived, the impediments, constant or occasional, in the way of their ready resort to their parish church, as want of good roads, snow, the rising of waters, and the like, on which the ordinary would grant them the leave which they desired, reserving, however, as seems almost always to have been the case, whatever rights and emoluments had beforetime belonged to the parish church. In the parish of Halifax there are twelve of these chapels, all founded before the Reformation. In the parish of Manchester, and in most of the parishes of Lancashire, such subsidiary foundations are numerous. Those foundations of this class which could be brought within the description of superstitious foundations were dissolved by the act of 1 Edward VI. for the suppression of chantries; but while the endowment was seized, it not unfrequently happened that the building itself, out of the piety of the person into whose hands it passed in the sale of the chantry lands, or the devotion of the persons living near it, and long accustomed to resort to it, continued to be used for religious worship in its reformed state, and remains to this day a place of Christian worship, the incumbent being supported by the casual endowments of the period since the Reformation, and especially by what is called Queen Anne's Bounty, in which most of the incumbents of chapels of this class have participated.

2. The term chapel is used to designate those more private places for the celebration of religious ordinances in the castles or dwelling-houses of persons of rank. These chapels, says Burn, were anciently all consecrated by the bishop. We find in some of the oldest specimens of the castles of England some small apartment which has evidently been used for the purposes of devotion, and this sometimes in the keep, the place of last resort in the time of a siege. An instance of this is at Conisbrough, near Doncaster. But more frequently chapels of this kind were erected near to the apartments appropriated to the residence of the family. Most of the baronial residences, it is probable, had chapels of this kind. How splendid they sometimes were we may see in St. George's Chapel at Windsor and St. Stephen's Chapel at Westminster, both chapels of this class attached to the residences of our kings.

3. The chapels of colleges, as in the two universities; of hospitals, or other similar foundations.

4. Chapels for private services, chiefly services for the dead, in the greater churches, as the chapel of Saint Erasmus, and others, in the church of Westminster. Additions made to the parish churches for the support of chantries are sometimes called chantry chapels.

5. Places of worship of modern foundation, especially those in towns, are called chapels of ease, being erected for the ease and convenience of the inhabitants when they have become too numerous for the limits of their parish church. Most of these are founded under special Acts of Parliament, in which the rights and duties of the incumbent and the founders are defined. Under the Church Building Acts the commissioners may assign districts to chapels under care of curates. By 3 Geo. IV. c. 72, they may convert district chapelries into separate parishes. [BENEFICE, p. 343.]

6. The word chapel is pretty generally used to denote the places of worship erected by various sects of Dissenters under the Act of Toleration, though the Quakers and some of the more rigid Dissenters of other denominations, out of dislike to the nomenclature of an ecclesiastical system which they do not approve, prefer to call such edifices by the name of meeting-houses. The name chapel is now also generally given, by Protestants at least, to the Roman Catholic places of worship.

CHAPLAIN (*capellanus*, a word formed from the middle Latin, *capella*, chapel). A chaplain is properly a clergyman officiating in a chapel, in contradistinction to one who is the incumbent of a parish church. But it now generally de-

CHAPLAIN. [491] CHAPLAIN.

signates clergymen who are either (1) residing in families of distinction and actually performing religious services in the family; or (2) who are supposed to be so, though not actually so engaged. This fiction proceeds on the assumption that every bishop and nobleman, with some of the great officers of state, have each their private chapel, to which they nominate a priest, or more than one. Certain privileges respecting the holding of benefices belonged to these chaplains, by reservation out of the Act against Pluralities, 21 Henry VIII. c. 13, which were restricted by 57 Geo. III. c. 59; and by 1 & 2 Vict. c. 106, both these acts were repealed so far as they related to the subject of pluralities. By 21 Henry VIII. the number of chaplains which noblemen and other persons may nominate was limited: an archbishop may nominate eight; a duke or a bishop, six; a marquis or earl, five; a viscount, four; a baron, a knight of the garter, or the lord chancellor, three; the treasurer of the king's house, the comptroller of the king's house, the clerk of the closet, the king's secretary, the dean of the chapel, the almoner, and the master of the rolls, may nominate each two; the chief justice of the King's Bench and the warden of the Cinque Ports, each one; a duchess, marchioness, countess, and baroness, being widows, are allowed to nominate each two.

The Speaker of the House of Commons appoints his chaplain, who reads prayers daily at the House before business commences. In the House of Lords prayers are read by the bishop last raised to the episcopal bench.

A chaplain is appointed to each of her Majesty's ships when in active service. He must have been regularly ordained, and a graduate of Oxford, Cambridge, Dublin, or Durham, and not above the age of thirty-five. He undergoes an examination by some competent person appointed by the Admiralty, and must produce testimonials of good moral and religious conduct from two beneficed clergymen. The pay of a chaplain is 12*l.* 5*s.* per month for ships of all rates, and the half-pay is 5*s.* or 10*s.* a day, according to length of service. In the army it is not necessary to appoint a chaplain to each regiment, but there are a few clergymen appointed for the army under the name of Chaplains to the Forces.

The magistrates in quarter-sessions are required by 4 Geo. IV. c. 64, to appoint a chaplain to every prison within their jurisdiction. His salary is regulated by the number of persons which the prison is capable of containing, and must not exceed 150*l.* when the number of prisoners does not exceed fifty, nor 200*l.* if the number of persons which the prison can contain does not exceed one hundred; and the salary may be fixed at the discretion of the justices when the number of prisoners exceeds two hundred. A chaplain to a prison must be a clergyman of the Church of England, and be licensed by the bishop before he can officiate. The magistrates have the power of removing him from his office in case of misconduct and neglect, and of granting him an annuity when incapable from infirmity of performing his duties: his duties are pointed out by the above act, and amongst other things he is required to keep a journal. The duties of chaplains in jails are further regulated by 2 & 3 Vict. c. 56. They must not reside more than a mile from the prison. A chaplain in any jail in which the number of prisoners confined at one time during the three years preceding his appointment was not less than one hundred, cannot hold a benefice with cure of souls, or any curacy with the office of chaplain. An assistant chaplain or chaplains may be appointed in jails where the number of prisoners exceeds 250. The reports of chaplains are sometimes of great interest and throw light upon the causes of crime. Appended to the act 2 & 3 Vict. c. 56, are a number of questions, the answers to which are annually returned to the Secretary of State; and the 28th question relates to the duties of the chaplain.

Chaplains are required to be appointed to every County Lunatic Asylum.

The Poor Law Amendment Act (4 & 5 Will. IV. c. 76) empowers the Poor Law Commissioners to appoint paid officers of parishes and unions, and this includes chaplains. The act contemplates that the inmates of union workhouses, of whatever religious persuasion, should have instruction in that persuasion. It is not peremptory to appoint a clergyman of the Church of England as chaplain, and the guardians may appoint a dissenting minister.

Both in jails and union workhouses licensed dissenting ministers are allowed to visit the inmates of their respective persuasions at reasonable times and under certain restrictions. By the Irish Poor Law Act (1 & 2 Vict. c. 56) three chaplains may be appointed for the union workhouses, one of the Established Church, one Roman Catholic priest, and one Protestant dissenter.

CHAPTER. The canons in the cathedral or conventual churches, when assembled, form what is called the chapter, *capitulum*; anciently the council of the bishop. Other religious communities, when assembled for business, sat in *chapter*. Attached to many cathedral and conventual churches are buildings for the meeting of the chapter, called chapterhouses. The buildings of this kind connected with the churches of Westminster and York are octagonal and of singular beauty.

The members of the College of Arms, that is, the king's heralds and pursuivants, are said to hold a *chapter* when they confer on the business of their office; and in like manner chapters of the order of the Garter are held.

CHARGE' D' AFFAIRES. [AMBASSADOR, p. 126.]

CHARITABLE USES. [USES, CHARITABLE.]

CHARTA MAGNA. [MAGNA CHARTA.]

CHARTE, from charta, "paper," was the name given to the letters of franchise granted by the kings of France during the middle ages to several towns and communities, by which they were put in possession of certain municipal privileges, such as the free election of their local magistrates and others. The word Charte has been used in France to signify the solemn acknowledgment of the rights of the nation made by Louis XVIII. on his restoration in 1814. The Charte was the fundamental law of the French constitutional monarchy. One article of this charte, having given occasion to a false interpretation, of which the ministers of Charles X. availed themselves to issue the ordonnances which gave rise to the revolution of July, 1830, was altered on the accession of Louis-Philippe, and it was clearly explained that "the king issues the necessary ordonnances and regulations for the execution of the laws, without having the power in any case to suspend the course of the law or to delay its execution." The "Charte de 1830," with this and one or two more modifications of minor importance, was sworn to by Louis-Philippe on the 9th of August, 1830. After that date, a change was made by the legislature in the constitution of the Chamber of Peers. The Peers were only for life, and the peerage was consequently not hereditary.

As France is so closely connected with England in the progress of constitutional history, we give an abstract of the "Charte de 1830." The general outline of the late government of France bore a resemblance to our own, being an hereditary constitutional or limited monarchy. Its general constitution is defined in the charter granted by Louis XVIII. upon his restoration in A.D. 1814; modified in 1830, after the revolution which drove out the elder branch of the Bourbons; and further modified since that time. The Charte, as modified after the revolution of 1830, and as it stood in February 1848, consisted of sixty-seven articles, arranged under seven heads.

1st head, containing eleven articles.— *Droit public des Français (Public or national Rights of the French).*—This head provides for the equality of all Frenchmen in the eye of the law, their equal admissibility to civil and military employments, and their equal freedom from arrest otherwise than by legal process. It guarantees the full enjoyment of religious liberty; and while it recognises Catholicism as the religion of the majority of Frenchmen, it provides for the payment not only of the Catholic priesthood, but of the ministers of other Christian denominations, out of the public purse.* It ensures the liberty to all

---

* A law of Feb. 8, 1831, includes payment to the ministers of the Jewish religion.

Frenchmen of printing and publishing their opinions, and prohibits for ever the re-establishment of the censorship.* It abolishes the conscription; provides for the oblivion of all political offences previous to the restoration of the Bourbons; and guarantees the security of property (including the so-called "national domains" sold during the first Revolution), except when the public good, as made out in a legal manner, requires the sacrifice of individual property, in which case the owner must be indemnified.

2nd head, containing eight articles.— *Formes du Gouvernement du Roi* (*Limits of the Kingly Power*).—This head secures to the king the supreme executive power, the command of the army and navy, the right of making war and treaties of peace, alliance, and commerce; of nominating to all the offices of public administration; and of making all regulations needful for the execution of the laws, without the power of suspending them or dispensing with them. It provides that the legislative functions shall be exercised by the king, the Chamber of Peers, and the Chamber of Deputies; that every law must be agreed to by a majority of each chamber (the discussions and votes of which are to be free), and sanctioned by the king; that bills may originate with any of the three branches of the legislature, except money bills, which must originate in the Chamber of Deputies; and that a bill rejected by any branch of the legislature cannot be brought in again the same session. The civil list is fixed at the commencement of every reign, and cannot be altered during that reign.

3rd head, containing ten articles.— *De la Chambre des Pairs* (*Of the Chamber of Peers*).—This head provides for the assembling of this chamber simultaneously with the deputies, and renders every sitting illegal (except when the chamber is exercising its judicial power) unless it is held during the session of the deputies. The nomination of the peers is vested in the king (the princes of the blood are peers by right of birth); their number is

* The law of Sept. 9, 1835, restrains the freedom of the press by several severe enactments.

unlimited, and their dignity is for life only; art. 23 of the "Charte," which related to the peerage, having been replaced by the law of 9th December, 1831, which abolished an hereditary peerage. This law is incorporated in the "Charte." It points out the class of persons from whom peers must be selected; and prohibits pensions being attached to the dignity of a peer. The ordonnance of nomination must mention the services for which the honour is conferred. The peers have no right of entry into the chamber under twenty-five years of age or of voting under thirty. The chancellor of France is president, or, in his absence, a peer nominated by the king. The sittings of the peers are public. The chamber takes cognizance of offences against the state. A peer can only be arrested by the authority of the chamber, and is not amenable to any other tribunal than the chamber in criminal matters.

4th head, containing sixteen articles.— *De la Chambre des Députés* (*Of the Chamber of Deputies*).—This head provides for the election of the deputies and the sittings of the chamber. The electors must be not less than twenty-five years of age and the deputies not less than thirty, and each must possess whatever other qualifications the law requires.* (The law of 19th April, 1831, for regulating the electoral franchise was passed in pursuance of a promise given in the Charte.) The deputies are elected for five years, and one-half of the deputies for each department must have their political domicile in it. The remaining heads refer to ministers and the administration of justice; but as the entire Charte has become a nullity by the extraordinary revolution of February 1848, it is unnecessary to dwell further upon it. By the

* The deputies are all chosen by the departments; or, to borrow the language of our own institutions, they are all "county members;" and the electoral qualification consists in the payment of 200 francs direct taxes. The qualification of a deputy is the payment of 500 francs. The votes are given by ballot, both by electors and by the deputies in the chambers. The whole number of deputies is now 459, having been increased within the last few years from 430.

CHARTER. [494] CHARTER.

new constitution promulgated November 4, 1848, the constitutional monarchy of Louis Philippe has been converted into a democratic republic, one and indivisible. Article 1 of the constitution declares, that " in adopting this definitive form of government, the ends proposed are—a freer advance in the path of civilization, and more equitable distribution of the burdens and advantages of society. Next follow declarations abolishing the punishment of death for political offences; slavery cannot exist upon "any French territory;" and confiscation of property is abrogated.

By chap. 4, the legislative power is delegated to a single assembly of 950 members, including the representatives of Algeria and the French colonies. All Frenchmen of the age of 21, enjoying their civil rights, are made electors, and all electors of the age of 25 are eligible to be representatives. The National Assembly is elected for three years, and one half the members and one more is necessary to the validity of any vote upon the laws. No project of a law, except in urgent cases, to be definitively decided upon till after three debates, at intervals of not less than five days.

By chap. 5, the *executive power* is delegated to a citizen, with the title of President of the Republic. He must be thirty years of age, be elected for four years, and not be eligible to be re-elected until after an interval of four years; neither during the same period can the vice-president be chosen, nor any relative of the president to the sixth degree of affinity. The president is chosen by ballot by the election of the Assembly. He is empowered to dispose of the armed force, but not to command it in person. He cannot prorogue or dissolve the Assembly, or suspend in any way the constitution or the laws. He may negotiate public treaties, but no treaty is definitive until approved by the Assembly. He cannot cede territory, nor begin any war without the assent of the Assembly. The president's salary is 600,000 francs, with residence.

CHARTER. This word is from the Latin *charta*, a word of uncertain origin: the Greek form of the word is *chartes*

($\chi\acute{a}\rho\tau\eta\varsigma$). Charta appears to have signified writing material made of papyrus. The term was afterwards applied not only to the materials for writing, but to the writing itself, as to a letter or the leaf of a book. In English law it was used to denote any public instrument, deed, or writing, being written evidence of things done between man and man, and standing as a perpetual record. (Bracton, lib. 2, c. 26.) Among the Saxons such instruments were known as *gewrite*, or writings.

Charters are divided into—I. charters of the crown, and II. Charters of private persons.

I. Royal charters were used at a very early period, for grants of privileges, exemptions, lands, honours, pardon, and other benefits that the crown had to confer; and thus the term became restricted to such instruments as conferred some right or franchise. These instruments did not differ in form from letters patent, being usually addressed by the king to all his subjects, and exposed to open view, with the great seal pendent at the bottom; but such as contained grants of particular kinds were distinguished by the name of charters. Thus as giving was the object of a charter, the term became very popular, and was used in a more extended sense, to denote laws of a popular character.

Whatever may have been the prerogatives and legislative authority of the kings of England, it is certain that from the earliest times there were many rights and liberties which by the law of the land belonged to the people. As these were often restrained and violated, nothing was more acceptable to the nation than a formal recognition of them by the crown: and the popular name of charter was applied to those written laws by which the kings from time to time confirmed or enlarged the liberties of the people. Such laws were regarded not only as concessions from the king, but as contracts between man and man—between the king and his subjects; while, at the same time, they were promulgated as the legislative acts of the sovereign authority in the state.

The charter of William the Conqueror,

for observing the laws throughout England, was in the nature of a public law. It settled the religion of the state and provided for its peace and government, for the administration of justice, the punishment of criminals, and the regulation of markets; it confirmed the titles to lands, and the exemption of the tenants in chief of the crown from all unjust exaction and from tallage. The words are those of a lawgiver appointing and commanding; "*statuimus*," "*volumus et firmiter precipimus*," "*interdicimus*," "*decretum est*," are the forms of expression by which matters are ordered or prohibited. (*Fœdera Rec. Comm. Ed.*, vol. i. p. 1.)

The charters of liberties granted by Henry I., Stephen, Henry II., John, Henry III., and Edward I., are all, more or less, in the nature of public laws, either making new provisions, or confirming, enlarging, and explaining existing laws, and relate to the freedom and good government of the people, and all the most important interests of the country. Some of them are still regarded as authoritative declarations of the rights and privileges which the people of England have enjoyed for centuries.* So valid and binding were the royal charters esteemed as laws, that in the 37 Henry III. (A.D. 1253), in the presence of the king, several of the first nobles, "and other estates of the realm of England," the archbishop and bishops excommunicated and accursed all who should violate change "the church's liberties or the ancient approved customs of the realm, and chiefly the liberties contained in the charters of the common liberties and of the forest, granted by our lord the king." In those times no sanction more solemn could have been given to the authority of any law. It was intended chiefly as a check upon the king himself, whose power had been restrained by the popular concessions made in the charters of liberties, but it was also directed against all

* They are printed at length in the first volume of the 'Statutes of the Realm,' published by the Record Commissioners. With the exception of one charter in the 25th Edw. I., they are all in the Latin language.

his subjects who should violate the liberties of the people. [MAGNA CHARTA.]

These charter-laws, though often expressed to have been made by the advice of the king's council, implied an absolute legislative power vested in the crown; and as royal prerogative became restrained and the public liberties enlarged, legislation by charter was gradually superseded by the statutes and ordinances made in Parliament. During the reigns of Henry III. and Edw. I. laws were promulgated in both forms; but since that time statutes and ordinances have been the only records of legislation—not differing materially, at first, either in form or in the nature of the authority from which they emanated, from the charters of earlier reigns, but gradually assuming their present character as acts agreed to by the entire legislature.

But notwithstanding the discontinuance of the practice of promulgating general laws by royal charter to bind the whole kingdom, the exercise of prerogative, by means of charters, has partaken of a legislative character throughout the entire history of the British government. Some of the most ancient and important of these were charters to boroughs and municipal bodies, conferring immunities and franchises, of which the greatest was that of sending representatives to parliament. There are still extant municipal charters of the Saxon kings, and of the Norman kings after the Conquest, conferring various rights upon the inhabitants of boroughs, of which an exclusive jurisdiction was always one; but the first charter of incorporation to any municipal body appears to have been granted in 1439, in the reign of Henry VI., to Kingston-upon-Hull; although, in the absence of prior charters, it has been usual to presume that charters confirming existing usages had been lost.

But though the king's charters have conferred upon boroughs the right of sending members to parliament, it was held in several cases, by the House of Commons, that the right of voting by the common law, could not be varied by charters from the crown. (Glanville's *Reports*, p. 47, 63, 70.) Between the reigns of Henry VIII. and Charles II.

no less than 180 members were added to the House of Commons by royal charter, the last borough upon which that right was conferred, in this manner, having been Newark, in 1673. Several of these were ancient boroughs which had ceased to send members, and whose rights were thus restored by charter; while some towns, expressly created boroughs by charter, did not send members to parliament for centuries afterwards, as Queenborough, for example, to which a charter was granted in 1368, but which did not return members until 1578. Hence it has been argued that, notwithstanding the practice of later reigns, the charter of the crown alone was not sufficient in law to entitle a *town* to send members to parliament, although expressly created a borough, to which, by the common law, the right of sending members was incident. (Merewether and Stephen's *History of Boroughs and Municipal Corporations*, Introduction, and pp. 664, 1256, 1774, &c.) This view derives confirmation from the acknowledged law that the crown was unable, by charter, to exempt a borough from returning members, since that right was always held to be exercised for the benefit of the whole realm, and not for the advantage of the particular place. (Coke, 4th Inst. 49.) Upon these grounds a charter of exemption to the citizens of York was declared void by act of parliament, 29 Henry VI. c. 3. But as parliamentary representation has, at length, been comprehensively arranged for the whole kingdom by the Reform Acts, the legal effect of royal charters upon the elective franchise has become a question merely of historical interest. The peculiar rights of corporations have also been determined by the Municipal Corporations Act; but a power has been reserved to the crown, with the advice of the Privy Council, to grant charters of incorporation to other towns, upon the petition of the inhabitants, and to extend to them the provisions of the Municipal Corporations Acts (5 & 6 Will. IV. c. 76, § 141). [MUNICIPAL CORPORATIONS.]

Charters were formerly granted by the crown, establishing monopolies in the buying, selling, making, working, or using certain things; an injurious practice, contrary to the ancient and fundamental laws of the realm, which was abolished by the act 21 James I. c. 3. [MONOPOLY.]

The crown has ever exercised, and still retains, the prerogative of incorporating universities, colleges, companies, and other public bodies, and of granting them, by charter, powers and privileges not inconsistent with the law of the land. But as the most considerable bodies ordinarily require powers which no authority but that of parliament is able to confer, such corporations as the East India Company and the Bank of England, which were originally established by royal charter, have long since derived their extraordinary privileges from acts of parliament, as well as other public companies which have been incorporated in the first instance by statute.

But the largest powers now conferred by royal charter are those connected with the colonies and foreign possessions of the crown. Whenever a new country is obtained by conquest or treaty, the crown possesses an exclusive prerogative power over it, and by royal charters may establish its laws and the form of its government; may erect courts of justice, of civil and criminal jurisdiction, and otherwise provide for its municipal order, for the raising its revenue, and the regulation of its commerce. (Chitty, *On Prerogatives*, c. iii.) This sovereign power, however, is always subject to the ultimate control of parliament; and even if deputed to a legislative assembly, or other local government, possessing rights and liberties defined by charter, the crown cannot recall the charter, and govern by any laws inconsistent with its provisions, or at variance with the common law.

II. Charters of private persons are the title-deeds of lands, many of which are the ancient grants of feudal lords to their tenants. These pass with the land as incident thereto, and belong to him who has the inheritance; or, if the land be conveyed to another and his heirs, the charters belong to the feoffee. A charter of the crown, granted at the suit of the grantee, is construed most beneficially for the crown, and against the party; but a private charter is construed most strongly against the grantor. (Fleta, lib. iii. c. 14; Comyn's *Digest*, tit. Charters; Coke, 1st *Inst.* 6 a, 7 a, 2nd *Inst.* 77; Cowel, *Law Dictionary*; Blackstone and Stephen's *Commentaries*; Preface to *Statutes of the Realm*, &c.)

CHARTER PARTY. [SHIPS.]

CHARTISTS, the name given to a political party in this country, who propose extensive alterations in the representative system, as the most direct means of attaining social improvement, and whose views are developed in a document called the "People's Charter." The principal points of this proposed charter are, universal suffrage, vote by ballot, annual parliaments, the division of the country into equal electoral districts, the abolition of property qualification in members and paying them for their services. The principles of the charter and the means of carrying them into effect have also been embodied in the form of a bill. It was prepared in 1838 by six members of the House of Commons, and six members of the London Working Men's Association; and the following are the most important of its enactments:—I. The preparers of the Bill allege the low state of public feeling as an apology for not admitting women to the franchise, and it is therefore only provided that every male inhabitant be entitled to vote for the election of a member of the Commons' House of Parliament, subject however to the following conditions:—1. That he be a native of these realms, or a foreigner who has lived in this country upwards of two years, and been naturalized. 2. That he be twenty-one years of age. 3. That he be not proved insane when the lists of voters are revised. 4. That he be not convicted of felony within six months from and after the passing of this act. 5. That his electoral rights be not suspended for bribery at elections, or for personation, or for forgery of election certificates, according to the penalties of this act. II. That the United Kingdom be divided into 300 electoral districts, so as to give uniform constituencies of about 20,000 voters each. III. That the votes be taken by ballot. IV. That a new Parliament be elected annually; that the elections take place on the same day in all the districts; and that electors vote only for the representative of the district in which they are registered. V. That no other qualification be required for members than the choice of the electors. VI. That every member be paid 500*l*. a year out of the public treasury for his legislative services; and that a register be kept of the daily attendance of each member.

There is nothing new in the principles or details of the People's Charter. They have, either separately, or some one or other of them in conjunction, been a prominent subject of discussion at various intervals within the last seventy years. In 1780 the Duke of Richmond introduced a bill into the House of Lords for annual parliaments and universal suffrage. In the same year the electors of Westminster appointed a committee to take into consideration the election of members of the House of Commons, and in their report they recommended the identical points which now constitute the main features of what is called the People's Charter. The Society of the Friends of the People, established in 1792, three years afterwards published a declaration which recommended a very large extension of the suffrage. In seasons of national distress, the amendment of the representative system has always been warmly taken up by the people of this country.

In 1831 the wishes of a large mass of the middle classes were realized and satisfied by the passing of the Reform Act. A season of political repose, and, as it happened also, of commercial prosperity, followed the excitement which preceded the passing of that measure. A victory had been gained, and the people waited for the benefits which they were to derive from it. In the next period of distress which arose, the amended state of the representative system and the advantages which it had brought were narrowly scanned; and the consequence was, the gradual formation of a party who were dissatisfied with its arrangements, and sought to attain the ends of political and social good by a more extensive change. This is briefly the origin of Chartism and of the Peo-

2 K

ple's Charter. The middle classes were, however, well satisfied on the whole with the overthrow of the rotten boroughs and the enfranchisement of the large towns, and therefore the Chartists stood alone, and began to regard them with a feeling of hostility. Chartists were sometimes found, as in all other parties, ready to assist the party which differed most widely from them, with the object of thwarting the political objects which the middle classes had at heart. In 1838 they had become a large party and embraced a great number of the working classes employed otherwise than in agriculture. The number of signatures attached to the petition presented at the commencement of the session of 1839 in favour of the People's Charter was upwards of one million and a quarter. Unfortunately the idea began to be entertained amongst a certain class of the Chartists, that physical force might be justifiably resorted to if necessary for obtaining political changes; and the party became divided into the Physical Force Chartists and the Moral Force Chartists. The former became implicated in disturbances which took place at various times in several parts of the country; and many persons of this class never having had correct views respecting the wages of labour, it appeared as if they had adopted the cry of "a fair day's wages for a fair day's work" as an additional point of the People's Charter. The disturbances in 1842 in the midland and northern counties were to some extent encouraged by the less intelligent of the Physical Force Chartists. At the close of 1841, however, an attempt was made to combine the middle classes with the Chartists in their attempt to obtain an extension of the suffrage. Early in 1842 a Complete Suffrage Union was formed at Birmingham, and in April of the same year a Conference, consisting of eighty-seven Delegates, was assembled at Birmingham, which sat for four days; three of which were spent in agreeing upon a basis of union between the middle and working classes, and the last day in adopting plans of practical organization. The six points of the People's Charter were adopted by the Conference, and the details were left for settlement to a future Conference. It was resolved also at this conference to establish a National Complete Suffrage Union. The proposed National Conference commenced its meetings in December, 1842, and was attended by 374 delegates. Here a rupture took place between the Chartists and the Complete Suffrage party, and the latter were outvoted on the question of adopting the People's Charter instead of the Complete Suffrage Bill. The minority, however, proceeded to act upon their views as developed in the Complete Suffrage Bill. This Bill does not contain any disqualifying clauses. In other respects it differs from the People's Charter only in matters of detail. These are the only two plans connected with the extension of the franchise which are at present supported by any large class in this country. The Chartists and the Complete Suffragists are only nominally distinct parties; but the former may be characterized as possessing a greater hold on the working classes than the Complete Suffragists, whose ranks are chiefly recruited from the middle classes: their objects, however, are so similar, that they may at any time unite without any sacrifice of principle.

CHASE. [FOREST.]

CHATTELS (in Law Latin, Catalla). This term comprehends all moveable property, and also all estates in land which are limited to a certain number of years or other determinate time. All moveable goods, as horses, plate, money, and the like, are called Chattels Personal. Estates or interests in land, which are comprehended in the term chattels, are called Chattels Real. "Goods and Chattels" is a common phrase to express all that a man has, except such estates in land as are freehold estates; but the word chattels alone expresses the same thing as "goods and chattels." The word goods is merely a translation of the Latin word Bona, which was used by the Romans to express all property, and generally all that a man was in any way entitled to. (*Dig.* 50, tit. 16, s. 49.) The nature of personal property in England is further considered under PROPERTY. Chattels of each description pass to the personal representatives of the deceased proprietor, and are comprehended under the general term "Personal Property." The law as to chattels is now, owing to the great increase of wealth, and particularly of moveables, of equal importance with the law relating to land; but under the strict feudal system, and the laws to which it more immediately gave rise, chattels (including even terms for years) were considered of small importance in a legal point of view, and, indeed, prior to the reign of Henry VI., were rarely mentioned in the law treatises and reports of the day. (Reeve, *Hist. Eng. Law*, 369.) Many articles which are properly chattels, owing to their intimate connexion with other property of a freehold nature, and being necessary to its enjoyment, descend therewith to the heir, and are not treated as chattels. Thus, for instance, the muniments of title to an estate of inheritance, growing trees and grass, deer in a park, and such fixtures as cannot be removed from the freehold without injury to it, are not chattels, because they pass to the heir. In the hands of a person however who has a limited interest in such things they become his chattels, and pass to his executor. Chattels, except so far as they may be heir-looms, cannot be entailed, though they may be limited so as to vest within twenty-one years after the death of a person or persons in being. They are not within the Statute of Uses, inasmuch as the proprietor of a chattel is said to be *possessed* of it, not *seised*, which is the word used in that statute. The same forms were not required in passing a chattel by devise, as in the case of real property, and a will of chattels might also be made at an earlier age than one which disposed of real estate; at fourteen years of age by a male, and twelve by a female. But this is now altered by 1 Vict. c. 26, and no person under twenty-one years of age can now dispose of anything by will. Chattels do not go in succession to a corporation sole, except only in the cases of the king and the chamberlain of the city of London. (Co. Litt.; Blackstone, *Comm.*)

CHEQUE, an order on a banker by a person who has money in the bank, directing him to pay a certain sum of money to the bearer or to a person named in the cheque, which is signed by the drawer. Cheques are immediately payable on presentment. They are not liable to stamp-duty, and are therefore limited in their functions in order to prevent their circulating as bills of exchange. They must, for example, be payable on demand, without any days of grace, and must be drawn on a banker within fifteen miles of the place where they are issued. The place of issue must therefore be named, and they must bear date on the day of issue. A cheque should be presented on the day which it is received, or within a reasonable time. One of the first rules to be observed in writing a cheque is to draw it in a business-like manner, so as to prevent a fraudulent alteration in the amount, for if otherwise the drawer may be liable. A "crossed" cheque is an ordinary cheque with the name of a particular banker written across the face of it for security, or it may be crossed simply "& Co."; and in this case it will only be paid through that banker. If presented by any other person, it is not paid without further inquiry. The 'Bankers' Magazine' for Oct. and Nov. 1844, and Jan. and Feb. 1845, contains some valuable information on the Law of Cheques.

One of the great advantages of a banking account is the convenience of drawing cheques. A person is thus relieved of the necessity of keeping ready money in his hands, and a cheque is some evidence of payment in the absence of a proper receipt. The Bank of England allows cheques to be drawn for sums of 5*l.*, but a few years ago it allowed no cheques under 10*l.*

CHICORY. [ADULTERATION.]
CHIEF JUSTICE. [COURTS.]
CHILD-KILLING. [INFANTICIDE.]
CHILD-STEALING. [ABDUCTION.]
CHILTERN HUNDREDS. A portion of the high land of Buckinghamshire is known by the name of the Chiltern Hills. "Formerly these hills abounded in timber, especially beech, and afforded shelter to numerous banditti. To put these down, and to protect the inhabitants of the neighbouring parts from their depredations, an officer was appointed under the crown, called the steward of the Chiltern Hundreds." (*Geog. of Great Britain*,

2 K 2

by the Society for the Diffusion of Useful Knowledge.) The duties have long since ceased, but the nominal office is retained to serve a particular purpose. A member of the House of Commons, who is not in any respect disqualified, cannot resign his seat. A member therefore who wishes to resign, accomplishes his object by applying for the stewardship of the Chiltern Hundreds of Stoke, Desborough, and Bodenham, which, being held to be a place of honour and profit under the crown, vacates the seat, and a new writ is in consequence ordered. This nominal place is in the gift of the chancellor of the exchequer. As soon as the office is obtained it is resigned, that it may serve the same purpose again. Another office which is applied for under similar circumstances, is the stewardship of the manors of East Hendred, Northstead, and Hempholme. The offices which have been held to vacate seats may be collected from the several General Journal Indexes, tit. "Elections."

In the session of 1842 a committee of the House of Commons was appointed "to inquire whether certain corrupt compromises had been entered into in specified boroughs, for the purpose of avoiding investigation into gross bribery, alleged to have been practised in them;" and a member for one of these boroughs (Reading) having applied to the chancellor of the exchequer, requesting that the stewardship of the Chiltern Hundreds might be conferred on him, the chancellor of the exchequer, who anticipated similar applications from members of some of the other boroughs implicated, decided upon refusing the appointment. The reasons he alleged for this refusal, in a letter addressed to the member for Reading, were as follows:—" Under ordinary circumstances I should not feel justified in availing myself of the discretion vested in me in order to refuse or delay the appointment for which you have applied, when sought for with a view to the resignation of a seat in parliament. But after the disclosures which have taken place with respect to certain boroughs, of which Reading is one, and after the admission of the facts by the parties interested, I consider that by lending my assistance to the fulfilment of any engagement which may have been entered into as arising out of any such compromise, I should, in some sort, make myself a party to transactions which I do not approve, and of which the House of Commons has implied its condemnation. I feel, moreover, that by a refusal on my part of the means by which alone such engagements can be fulfilled, I afford the most effectual discouragement to the entering into similar compromises in future, and thus promote, so far as is in my power, the intentions of the House of Commons."

CHIMNEY-SWEEPER, a person whose trade it is to cleanse foul chimneys from soot. The actual sweepers were formerly boys, of very tender age, who were taught to climb the flues, and who, from the cruelties often practised upon them by their masters, had for the last half-century become objects of particular care with the legislature. The first and chief act by which regulations concerning them were enforced was the 28 Geo. III. c. 48. In 1834 the act 4 & 5 Will. IV. c. 35, was passed for the better regulation of Chimney-sweepers and their Apprentices, and for the safer Construction of Chimneys and Flues. From that date no child who was under ten years of age could be apprenticed to a chimneysweeper. A particular form of indenture of apprenticeship is required in the case of chimney-sweeps. In 1840 another act (3 & 4 Vict. c. 85) was passed, 7th August, for the regulation of chimney-sweepers and of chimneys. This act annulled existing indentures of chimney-sweepers' apprenticeship, where the apprentice was under sixteen, and prohibited in future the binding of any child under that age. Any person who compels, or knowingly allows, any young person under the age of twenty-one, to ascend or descend a chimney, or enter a flue, for the purpose of sweeping or extinguishing fire, is liable, under this act, to a penalty not exceeding 10l. and not less than 5l. That part of the act 3 & 4 Vict. c. 85, which related to chimneys is repealed by 7 & 8 Vict. c. 84 (the Metropolitan Buildings Act), which substitutes new regulations as to the dimensions and construction of chimneys.

CHURCH-RATES. [501] CHURCH-RATES.

The number of persons returned as chimney-sweepers in 1841 was 4620 in England, 56 in Wales, and 331 in Scotland. Two-fifths (1974) were under twenty years of age.

About the beginning of the present century, a number of individuals joined in offering considerable premiums to any one who would invent a method of cleansing chimneys by mechanical means, so as to supersede the necessity for climbing-boys. Various inventions were in consequence produced, of which the most successful was that by Mr. George Smart. The principal parts of the machine are a brush, some hollow tubes which fasten into each other by means of brass sockets, and a cord for connecting the whole.

CHIVALRY, COURT OF. [COURTS.]
CHURCH BRIEF. [BRIEF.]
CHURCH-RATES are rates raised, by resolutions of a majority of the parishioners in vestry assembled, from the parishioners and occupiers of land within a parish, for the purpose of repairing, maintaining, and restoring the body of the church and the belfry, the churchyard fence, the bells, seats, and ornaments, and of defraying the expenses attending the service of the church. The spire or tower is considered part of the church. The duty of repairing and rebuilding the chancel lies on the rector or vicar, or both together, in proportion to their benefices, where there are both in the same church. But by custom it may be left to the parishioners to repair the chancel, and in London there is a general custom to that effect.

The burden of repairing the church was anciently charged upon tithes, which were divided into three portions, one for the repair of the church, one for the poor, and one for the ministers of the church. Pope Gregory had enjoined on St. Augustine such a distribution of the voluntary offerings made to his missionary church in England; and when Christianity came to be established through the land, and parish churches generally erected, and when the payment of tithes was exacted, the tithes were ordered to be distributed on Pope Gregory's plan. Thus, one of Archbishop Ælfric's canons, made in the year 970, is as follows:—

" The holy fathers have also appointed that men should give their tithes to the church of God, and the priests should come and divide them into three parts, one for the repair of the church, and the second for the poor, but the third for the ministers of God, who bear the care of that church." (Wilkins, *Concilia*, i. 253.) The same division of tithes was enacted by King Æthelred and his councillors in Witenagemot assembled, in the year 1014. A portion of the fines paid to churches in the Anglo-Saxon times for offences committed within their jurisdictions was also devoted to church repairs. The bishops were likewise required to contribute from their own possessions to the repair of their own churches. A decree of King Edmund and his councillors, in 940, headed " Of the repairing of churches," says that " Each bishop shall repair God's house out of what belongs to him, and shall also admonish the king to see that all God's churches be well provided, as is necessary for us all." (Schmid, *Gesetze der Angel-Sachsen*, i. 94.) One of King Canute's laws says, " All people shall rightly assist in repairing the church;" but in what way it is not said. There is no pretence however for interpreting this law of Canute's as referring to anything like church-rate. A payment tô the Anglo-Saxon church, called cyric-sceat (church scot), has beer erroneously identified with church-rate by some writers. This was a payment of the first-fruits of corn-seed every St. Martin's day (November 11). so much for every hide of land, to the church; and the laws of King Edgar and King Canute direct all cyric-sceat to be paid to the old minster. (Schmid, i. 99, 165.) Cyric-sceat was otherwise called cyric-amber, amber being the measure of payment.

Churches continued to be repaired with a third of the tithes after the Norman conquest, and to as late as the middle of the thirteenth century. How the burden came to be shifted from the tithes to the parishioners is involved in much obscurity. The following conjectural sketch of the rise of church-rates is from a pamphlet by Lord Campbell:—" Probably the burden was very gradually shifted to the parishioners, and their contributions to the expense were purely voluntary. The custom growing, it was treated as an obligation, and enforced by ecclesiastical censures. The courts of common law seem to have interposed for the protection of refractory parishioners till the statute of Circumspecte Agatis, 13 Ed. I., which is in the form of a letter from the king to his common law judges, desiring them to use themselves circumspectly in all matters concerning the bishop of Norwich and his clergy, not punishing them if they held plea in court Christian of such things as are merely spiritual, as "si prælatus puniat pro cimeterio non clauso, ecclesia discooperta vel non decenter ornata." Lord Coke observes, "that some have said that this was not a statute, but made by the prelates themselves, yet that it is an act of parliament." In the printed rolls of parliament, 25 Ed. III. No. 62, it is called an ordinance; but in the statute 2 & 3 Ed. VI. c. 13, § 51, it is expressly styled a statute, and it must now clearly be taken to be the act of the whole legislature. From the year 1285 therefore the bishops were authorized to compel the parishioners by ecclesiastical censures to repair and to provide ornaments for the church." (*Sir John, now Lord, Campbell's Letter to Lord Stanley on the Law of Church-Rates*, 1837.) But for long after the existence of the custom of making the parishioners contribute to the repairs of the church, and after the statute *Circumspecte Agatis*, the original obligation on the clergyman to repair out of the tithes was remembered. Lord Campbell quotes in the same pamphlet a passage from a MS. treatise in the Harleian Collection, written in the reign of Henry VII., by Edward Dudley, a privy councillor of that king, which thus lays down the law for appropriation of the incomes of the clergy:—" One part thereof for their own living in good household hospitality; the second in deeds of charity and alms to the poor folk, and specially within their diocese and cures, where they have their living; and the third part thereof for the repairing and building of their churches and mansions." Lyndwode, who wrote in the fifteenth century, says that by the common law the burden of repairing the church is on the rector, and not on the laity. "But certainly," he adds, "by custom even the lay parishioners are compelled to this sort of repair; so that the lay people is compelled to observe this laudable custom." (*Const. Legatin.* 113.)

Church-rates are imposed by the parishioners themselves, at a meeting summoned by the churchwardens for that purpose. Upon the churchwardens, conjointly with the minister, devolves the care of the fabric of the church and the due administration of its offices. With a view to provide a fund for such expenses, it is the duty of the churchwardens to summon parish-meetings for the purpose of levying rates; and if they neglect to do so, they may be proceeded against criminally in the ecclesiastical courts. They may also be punished by the ecclesiastical courts for neglecting to make repairs for which money has been provided by the parish; but if they have no funds in hand, and if they have not failed to call the parishioners together, they cannot be punished. A mandamus also is grantable to compel the churchwardens to call a meeting. If the parish fail to meet, the churchwardens then constitute the meeting, and may alone impose a rate; but if the parish should assemble, it rests with the parishioners themselves to determine the amount of the rate, or to negative the imposition of a rate altogether.

The repair of the parish church and the provision of the necessaries for divine service are thus entirely at the option of the majority of the parishioners assembled. Before the Reformation the parishioners could be punished in the ecclesiastical courts for failing to repair the parish church; and the punishment was, to place the parish under an interdict, by sentence of excommunication, by which the church was shut up, the administration of the sacraments suspended, and any parishioner who died was buried without bell, book, or candle. But there is now no means of compelling the parishioners to provide church-rates. There is no remedy by mandamus: the Court of King's Bench will grant a mandamus, as has been already said, directing churchwardens to call a parish meeting, but not to compel parishioners to make a rate. The ecclesiastical courts cannot make a rate, nor appoint commissioners to make one. An *obiter dictum* of Chief Justice Tindal in delivering the judgment of the Court of Exchequer Chamber in error in the Braintree case, has lately suggested the possibility of proceeding criminally against parishioners for voting against a a rate, or absenting themselves from a meeting called to consider of a rate, where repairs are needed. In Braintree parish, after the parishioners on meeting had refused to make any rate, the churchwardens had levied a rate of their own authority, and proceeded against a parishioner for refusing to pay his portion. The Court of Exchequer Chamber, to which the churchwardens appealed against a prohibition issued by the Court of Queen's Bench, confirmed the prohibition, and declared the churchwardens' rate to be illegal. But in delivering the judgment of the court, Chief Justice Tindal made the following remark:—" It is obvious that the effect of our judgment in this case is no more than to declare the opinion of the court, that the churchwardens have in this instance pursued a course not authorized by law, and consequently all the power with which the spiritual court is invested by law to compel the reparation of the church is left untouched. If that court is empowered (as is stated by Lyndwode, page 53, *voce sub pœna*, and other ecclesiastical writers) to compel the churchwardens to repair the church by spiritual censures; to call upon them to assemble the parishioners together, by due notice, to make a sufficient rate; to punish such of the parishioners as refuse to perform their duty in joining in the rate by excommunication, that is, since the statute of 53 Geo. III. c. 127, by imprisonment, and under the same penalty to compel each parishioner to pay his proportion of the church-rate; the same power will still remain with them, notwithstanding the decision of this case." In December, 1842, some parishioners of St. George's, Colegate, Norwich, were articled in the Court of Arches for having wilfully and contumaciously obstructed, or at least refused to make, or join and concur in making, a sufficient rate for the repair of the church of the parish. The articles were admitted by Sir Herbert Jenner Fust, the judge of the Court of Arches; but on application to the Court of Queen's Bench the proceedings were stayed by prohibition. Church-rates depend, therefore, entirely on the will of a majority of the parishioners assembled: and this is obviously a state of things which, where dissenters from the established religion abound, may lead to parish churches being left to go to ruin.

The existing poor-rate of the parish is generally taken as the criterion for the imposition of the church-rate; but decisions as to poor-rates are not binding in cases of church-rates, and the proper test for church-rates is a valuation by competent judges, grounded on the rent the tenant would be willing to pay for the premises. All property in the parish is liable except the glebe-land of that parish, and the possessions of the crown when in the actual occupation of the crown, and places of public worship. Stock in trade is not generally rated for church repairs, but a custom may exist rendering it rateable in a particular parish. The ecclesiastical courts have the exclusive authority of deciding on the validity of a rate, and the liability of a party to pay it; but a ratepayer cannot by an original proceeding in those courts raise objections to a rate for the purpose of quashing it altogether. If he wishes to dispute it, he ought to attend at the vestry, and there state his objections; if they are not removed, he may enter a caveat against the confirmation of the rate, or refuse to pay his assessment. In the latter case, if proceeded against in the ecclesiastical court, he may in his defence show either that the rate is generally invalid, or that he is unfairly assessed. The consequence of entering a caveat is an appeal to the ecclesiastical judge, who will see that right is done.

A retrospective church-rate, or rate for expenses previously incurred, is bad. This has been often decided in the courts of common law and equity, and in the ecclesiastical courts. The reason is stated by Lord Ellenborough in the judgment of the court in Rex *v.* Haworth (12 East,

556) :—" The regular way is for the churchwardens to raise the money beforehand by a rate made in the regular form for the repairs of the church, in order that the money may be paid by the existing inhabitants at the time, on whom the burden ought to fall." It has lately been decided by the Judicial Committee, in the case Chesterton v. Hutchins, reversing the decision of the Court of Arches, and confirming the previous decision of the Consistory Court, that a rate not retrospective on the face of it, but admitted to be partly retrospective, was bad.

Previously to 53 Geo. III. c. 127, the only mode of recovering church-rates from parties refusing to pay was by suit in the ecclesiastical court for subtraction of rate. By that statute, where the sum to be recovered is under 10*l.* and there is no question as to the validity of the rate, or the liability of the party assessed, any justice of the county where the church is situated may, on complaint of the churchwarden, inquire into the merits of the case, and order the payment. Against his decision there is an appeal to the quarter-sessions. By several statutes, principally the 58 Geo. III. c. 45, and 59 Geo. III. c. 134, acts passed for the promotion of building churches, the common-law powers of churchwardens have been varied, and extended so as to enable them to raise money on the security of church-rates, and to apply them for the enlargement, improvement, &c. of churches, and for the building of new ones, &c.

The levying of church-rates on dissenters, who are so numerous in this country, has caused so much irritation, and the frequently successful opposition of dissenters at vestry-meetings called to impose rates has rendered church-rates so precarious a resource, that various attempts have been made of late years to abolish them, and to substitute some more certain and less obnoxious provision for the repair of churches and the due celebration of divine worship. Lord Althorp, as chancellor of the exchequer in Lord Grey's government, brought in a bill for the abolition of church-rates in 1834, which proposed to charge the Consolidated Fund with 250,000*l.* a year, to be devoted to the repair of parish churches and chapels (including the chancel), and to be disbursed by commissioners after certificate from the quarter-sessions of the county in which the parish might lie, founded on a report by the county surveyor,—to place on the rector or lay impropriator, relieved of the duty of repairing the chancel, the burden of providing necessaries for the performance of divine service,—to leave the preservation of pews to the owners or occupiers, and to leave the provision and repair of bells, organs, and ornaments to voluntary contributions. This bill fell to the ground, principally owing to the opposition of dissenters, who viewed the substitution for church-rates of a charge on the public taxes as a mere shifting of the burden upon themselves, and objected altogether to being called upon to contribute to a church to which they did not belong. In 1837 Lord Melbourne's government made a second attempt to settle the question; and a bill was brought in by Mr. Spring Rice, chancellor of the exchequer, to abolish church-rates, and provide for the objects of them by a surplus created by a better management of the church lands held by the archbishops, bishops, and deans and chapters; these lands to be managed by commissioners, and 250,000*l.* a year to be the first charge on the surplus. The opposition of the church and of church lessees frustrated this measure, and no measure has since been brought forward by any government.

Lord Althorp stated, in introducing his measure, that the amount of church-rates annually levied was from 500,000*l.* to 600,000*l.*; and about 249,000*l.* was annually expended on the fabrics of churches. Mr. Spring Rice calculated that in 5000 parishes in England no church-rates are levied. There are endowments in many parishes for the repair of the church, which render church-rates unnecessary; and in many parishes arrangements have been made for voluntary subscriptions, to avoid squabblings between churchmen and dissenters, and the scandal of such disputes.

The Parliamentary Returns respecting local taxation issued in 1839 (No. 562) give the following particulars respecting church-rates in England and Wales for the year ending Easter, 1839 :—Total amount of rates and monies received by churchwardens, 506,812l., of which 363,103l. was derived from the church-rates, and 143,709l. from other sources. The total sum expended was 480,662l., and of this sum 215,301l. was expended in the repairs of churches. The debt secured on church-rates amounted to 535,236l. There is a more complete return for the year ending Easter, 1832, which shows some of the principal of the "other sources" alluded to in the return of 1839. In 1831-2 the total amount which the churchwardens received was 663,814l., derived from the following sources :—Church-rates, 446,247l.; estates, &c., 51,919l.; mortuary or burial fees, 18,216l.; poor-rates, 41,489l.; pews and sittings, 39,382l.; other sources not stated, 66,559l. The payments by the churchwardens in the same year amounted to 645,883l., and included 46,337l. for books, wine, &c.; salaries to clerks, sextons, &c., 126,185l.; organs, bells, &c., 41,710l.; and repairs of churches, 248,125l.

CHURCHWARDENS are parish officers, who by law have a limited charge of the fabric of the parish church, of the direction and supervision of its repairs, and of the arrangement of the pews and seats. Certain other duties are imposed upon them on particular occasions. There are usually two churchwardens in each parish, but by custom there may be only one. It is said by some authorities, that by the common law the right of choosing churchwardens is in the parson and the parishioners. This is however by no means universally the case, as a custom prevails in many parishes for the parishioners to choose both, and in some both are elected by a select vestry. The eighty-ninth canon of 1603 directs that "churchwardens shall be chosen yearly in Easter week by the joint consent of the minister and parishioners, if it may be; but if they cannot agree, the minister shall choose one and the parishioners another." It has however been questioned how far these canons are binding upon the laity, even in matters ecclesiastical.

The usual duties of churchwardens are, to take care that the churches are sufficiently repaired; to distribute seats among the parishioners, under the control of the ordinary; to maintain order and decorum in the church during the time of divine service; and to provide the furniture for the church, the bread and wine for the sacrament, and the books directed by law to be used by the minister in conducting public worship. In addition to these ordinary duties, the churchwardens are by virtue of their office overseers of the poor, under the statutes for the relief of the poor; they summon vestries; they are also required to present to the bishop all things presentable by the ecclesiastical laws, which relate to the church, minister, or parishioners. They act as sequestrators of a living. They are also required to perambulate the bounds of the parish. In large parishes there are sometimes officers called sidesmen (*synodsmen*) or questmen, whose business it is to assist the churchwardens in inquiring into offences and making presentments. Churchwardens and sidesmen were formerly required to take an oath of office before entering upon their respective duties; but by a recent statute, 5 & 6 Will. IV. c. 62, § 9, it is enacted that, in lieu of such oath, they shall make and subscribe a declaration before the ordinary (the bishop of the diocese, or the archdeacon, official, or surrogate) that they will faithfully and diligently perform the duties of their offices. This is done at the archdeacon's visitation. It is said by various old writers that the churchwarden might act before he was sworn; but 5 & 6 Will. IV. c. 62, requires that the declaration should be taken first. The old churchwardens usually act until the archdeacon's visitation, about the month of June, though their successors are appointed at Easter.

If churchwardens are guilty of any wilful malversation, or if they refuse to account to the parishioners at the termination of their period of service, they may be proceeded against summarily before the bishop by any parishioner who is interested, or the new churchwardens may maintain an action of account against them at common law; in which action the parishioners, other than such as receive alms, are admissible as witnesses. (3 Will. III. c. 11, § 12.) On the other hand, in all actions brought against them for any thing done by virtue of their office, if a verdict be given for them, or if the plaintiff be nonsuited or discontinue, they are entitled to double costs by 7 Jas. I. c. 5, and 21 Jas. I. c. 12.

Under the 59th Geo. III. c. 12, § 17, churchwardens and overseers are empowered to take and hold lands in trust for the parish as a corporate body; and by a decision under this act, they can also take and hold any other lands and hereditaments belonging to the parish, the profits of which are applied in aid of the church-rate. (Burn's *Justice* and Burn's *Ecclesiastical Law*, tit. "Churchwardens.")

CINCINNATI, ORDER OF, an association established at the termination of the revolutionary war by the officers of the American army, which, in reference to the transition made by most of them from the occupation of husbandry to that of arms, took its name from the Roman Cincinnatus. The society was called an "order," and an external badge was provided of a character similar to those worn by the knights and other privileged orders of Europe. It was moreover provided that the eldest son of every deceased member should also be a member, and that the privilege should be transmitted by descent for ever. This principle of perpetuating a distinction soon became the object of attack. Judge Burke, of South Carolina, endeavoured, in a pamphlet, to show that it contained the germ of a future privileged aristocracy, and that it should not be allowed to develop itself. The society was publicly censured by the governor of South Carolina in his address to the Assembly, and by the legislatures of three states, Massachusetts, Rhode Island, and Pennsylvania. A correspondence ensued between General Washington and Mr. Jefferson concerning the institution in 1784, and Mr. Jefferson expressed himself altogether opposed to the principle of hereditary descent. The public disapprobation did not run less strongly in the same direction. At a meeting of the society soon afterwards, in Philadelphia, the hereditary principle and the power of adopting honorary members were abolished; but the society, in all other respects, was preserved. According to Mr. Jefferson, General Washington used his influence at the meeting in Philadelphia for its suppression, and the society would probably have been dissolved but for the return of the envoy whom they had despatched to France for the purpose of providing badges for the order, and of inviting the French officers to become members. As they could not well retract, it was determined that the society should retain its existence, its meetings, and its charitable funds. The order was to be no longer hereditary; it was to be communicated to no new members; the general meeting, instead of being annual, was to be triennial only. The badges were never publicly worn in America, but it was wished that the Frenchmen who were enrolled in the order should wear them in their own country. In some of the States the society perhaps still exists, and the members hold, or until lately held, triennial meetings. In others it has been allowed silently to expire. That of Virginia met in 1822, and transferred its funds (15,000 dollars) to Washington College. (Tucker's *Life of Jefferson*, vol. i. pp. 184-188.)

CINQUE PORTS. It is stated by Jeake ('Charters of the Cinque Ports'), that in one of the records of the town of Rye is a memorandum that "the five ports were enfranchised in the time of King Edward the Confessor;" the five ports here intended, the original *Cinque Ports* of the Normans, being the towns of Sandwich, Dover, Hythe, and Romney, on the coast of Kent, and Hastings on that of Sussex. Only three of these five ports being mentioned in the Domesday Survey, viz. Sandwich, Dover, and Romney, Lord Coke thence infers that at first the privileged ports were these three only.

Though some part of the municipal constitution of the individual ports may be anterior to the Norman invasion, yet the organization of the general body, as it has existed in later times, is plainly traceable to the policy of the Conqueror in securing, by every means, his communications with the Continent. These ports and their members occupy exactly the tract of sea-coast of which, after the victory of Hastings, he showed most eagerness to possess himself, by sweeping along it with his army before he directed his march towards London; and the surrender into his hands of the castle of Dover, which is the centre of the Cinque Ports' jurisdiction, was one of the stipulations introduced into the famous oath which, in Edward's lifetime, the duke had extorted from Harold. To enable his government to wield the resources of this maritime district with the greater vigour and promptitude, he severed it wholly from the civil and military administrations of the counties of Kent and Sussex, erecting it into a kind of palatine jurisdiction, under a *gardien*, or *warden*, who had the seat of his administration at the castle of Dover, and exercised over the whole district the combined civil, military, and naval authority; uniting in his own hands all the various functions which, to use the terms most intelligible to modern readers, we may describe as those of a sheriff of a county at large, a custos rotulorum, a lord lieutenant, and an admiral of the coast.

To the five ports of the Conqueror's time were added, before the reign of Henry III., with equal privileges, what were called the *ancient towns* of Winchelsea and Rye, lying on the Sussex coast, between Hastings and Romney. To each of these seven municipal towns, except Winchelsea, were attached one or more subordinate ports or towns, denominated *members* of the principal port.

The internal constitution of each port, as well as the Norman denominations of *jurats* and *barons*, which, in lieu of *aldermen* and *freemen*, have constantly prevailed in them all since William's time, concur to show the solidity of his plan for rendering this maritime line one of the grand outworks of the Conquest. The earliest members of the municipal bodies established under these foreign denominations, at a time when the English municipalities in general were subjected to the most rigorous enslavement, were doubtless trading settlers from William's continental dominions; and the term *barons*, as applied to the Cinque Ports' representatives, which in the later periods of English parliamentary history has usually been considered as simply synonymous with *burgesses*, did, before the several elements of the Commons' House coalesced into one homogeneous body, imply a political as well as a municipal superiority.

Until the time of Henry VII. the crown appears to have had no permanent navy: the Cinque Ports constantly furnished nearly all the shipping required for the purposes of the state, and their assistance to the king's ships continued long after that time. When ships were wanted, the king issued his summons to the ports to provide their quota. In the time of Edward I. the number they were bound to provide was fifty-seven, fully equipped, at their own cost: the period of gratuitous service was limited to fifteen days.

Each of the five original ports returned two *barons* to parliament, as early as the 18th of Edward I. The peculiar nature of the relation between the Cinque Ports and the crown must have given the latter, from the commencement, a very powerful influence in their internal transactions; and, in later times, when the parliamentary relations of the municipal towns came to be the grand object of solicitude to the royal prerogative, these municipalities imbibed an ample share of the prevalent municipal as well as political corruption. In the 20th of Charles II. the first open blow was struck by the crown at the liberties of the Ports in general, in the provision of Charles's charter of that year, by which the elections of all their recorders and common clerks were made subject to the royal approbation. Subsequently, in 1685, all the general charters of the Ports, and most of the particular charters of each individual town, were, by the king's special command, delivered up to Colonel Strode, then constable of Dover Castle, and were never afterwards recovered.

Before the Revolution in 1688 the lord-wardens assumed the power and the right of nominating one, and sometimes both, of the members for each of the port-towns having parliamentary representation; but this practice was terminated by an act passed in the first year after the Revolution, entitled 'An Act to declare the Right and Freedom of Election of Members to serve in Parliament for the Cinque Ports.'

The jurisdiction of the Cinque Ports collectively extends along the coast, continuously, from Birchington, which is west of Margate, to Seaford in Sussex. But several of the corporate members are quite inland. Tenterden, in the centre of a rich agricultural district, has not even a river near it. Many of the unincorporate members are not only inland, but situated at great distances from their respective ports, some as far as forty to fifty miles. All the unincorporated members being exclusively under the jurisdiction of their own ports, each of those members was obliged to have recourse to the justices and coroner of its own port. This inconvenience was partially removed by 51 Geo. III. c. 36, entitled 'An Act to facilitate the Execution of Justice within the Cinque Ports.'

The Parliamentary Reform Act of 1832 worked a considerable revolution in the political relations of the Cinque Ports, and the Municipal Reform Act has operated yet more decidedly to break up the ancient organization of the ports, and assimilate their internal arrangements to those of the improved English municipalities at large.

Anciently there were several courts, exercising a general jurisdiction over all the ports and members. The Court of Shepway was the supreme court of the Cinque Ports. The lord warden presided in it, assisted by the mayors and bailiffs and a certain number of jurats summoned from each corporate town. Two other ancient courts are still occasionally held, the Court of Brotherhood and the Court of Guestling. The Court of Brotherhood is composed of the mayors of the five ports and two ancients towns and a certain number of jurats from each of them. The Court of Guestling consists of the same persons, with the addition of the mayors and bailiffs of all the corporate members, and a certain number of jurats from each of them. It is thought that the bodies forming this addition may originally have been merely *invited* by the Court of Brotherhood to give their assistance, and that hence the assembly may have received the name of Guestling. In the Court of Brotherhood the arrangements and regulations were made as to the apportioning of the service of ships to the crown. The necessity for proceedings of this kind no longer exists; and although these courts have been occasionally held of late years, such holding seems to have been mere matter of form, excepting only the Courts of Brotherhood and Guestling, held before each coronation, at which the arrangements have been made respecting the privilege of the *barons* of the ports to hold the canopy over the king's head on that occasion; another mark of the pre-eminence among the municipalities of England given to these towns by the princes of the Norman line.

It remains to notice more particularly the nature of the lord warden's jurisdiction as now exercised. All writs out of the superior courts are directed to the constable of Dover Castle, who is always the lord warden; upon which his warrant is made out, directed to and executed by an officer called the *bodar*. This officer, by a curious anomaly, has also the execution of writs out of the distant civil court at Hastings; and the necessity of having recourse to him has been a source of inconvenience and dissatisfaction to the latter town. The clerk of Dover Castle acts as under-sheriff. The constable's gaol for debtors is within Dover Castle; and by act 54 Geo III. c. 97, their maintenance was provided for by an annual contribution of 300*l*., to be levied on the ports and members in proportions fixed by the act.

The Admiralty jurisdiction of the Cinque Ports, attached to the office of lord warden, is expressly reserved in the Municipal Reform Act. A branch of this jurisdiction appears in the court of Lodemanage, so call from the old English word *lodeman*, a *lead*-man or steerer, which is held for the licensing and regulating of pilots, by the lord warden and a number of commissioners, of whom the mayors of Dover and Sandwich are officially two. The lord warden seems anciently to have held a court of chancery in one of the churches at Dover, but it has long been obsolete. (Jeake's *Charters of the Cinque Ports*, &c.)

CIRCUITS (from the French *circuit*, which is from the Latin *circuitus*, "a going about"), in English law, denote the periodical progresses of the judges of the superior courts of common law through the several counties of England and Wales, for the purpose of administering justice in civil and criminal matters. The ordinary circuits take place in the spring and summer of each year. In 1843 and 1844 a winter assize was held, and it is probable that a third assize will now take place every year. These winter commissions of oyer and terminer and general gaol delivery have not hitherto included the counties of cities. All the circuits take place under the authority of several commissions under the great seal, issued to the judges and others associated with them on each occasion. [ASSIZE.] Most barristers practising in the common law courts in London are attached to one or other of the circuits; and each circuit is constantly attended by a numerous bar. The transaction of judicial business in the presence of a professional audience of this kind, has been justly considered one of the best securities for the due administration of justice; and in consequence of the system of circuits, this advantage is not confined to the metropolis, but is communicated to the most remote parts of England and Wales.

Since the statute 11 Geo. IV. & 1 Will. IV. c. 70, by which the ancient Welsh judicature was abolished, the circuits of the judges are eight in number, and the counties of England and Wales are distributed among them in the following manner:—

The Northern Circuit comprehends the counties of York, Durham, Northumberland, Cumberland, Westmoreland, and Lancaster.

The Western Circuit comprehends the counties of Southampton, Wilts, Dorset, Devon, Cornwall, and Somerset,—and Bristol.

The Oxford Circuit comprehends the counties of Berks, Oxford, Worcester, Stafford, Salop, Hereford, Monmouth, and Gloucester.

The Midland Circuit comprehends the counties of Northampton, Rutland, Lincoln, Nottingham, Derby, Leicester, and Warwick.

The Home Circuit comprehends the counties of Hertford, Essex, Kent, Sussex, and Surrey.

[For several years preceding 1834 one of the judges made a circuit through the counties of Hertford, Essex, Kent, Sussex, and Surrey, in the month of December, for the trial of criminals. But in that year an act was passed (4 Wm. IV. c. 36) for establishing a central criminal court for London and Middlesex, and parts of Essex, Kent, and Surrey, the sessions for which are held at the Old Bailey, at least twelve times a year. The judges are the Lord Mayor, the Lord Chancellor, the Judges, the Aldermen, Recorder, and Common Serjeant of London, and such others as her Majesty may appoint. The jurisdiction of this court extends to all treasons, murders, felonies, and misdemeanours within ten miles of St. Paul's Cathedral. Offences committed on the high seas, within the jurisdiction of the Admiralty of England, are tried in this court.]

The Norfolk Circuit comprehends the counties of Buckingham, Bedford, Huntingdon, Cambridge with the Isle of Ely, Norfolk, and Suffolk.

The South Wales Circuit comprehends the counties of Glamorgan, Carmarthen, Pembroke, Cardigan, Brecon, and Radnor.

The North Wales Circuit comprehends the counties of Montgomery, Merioneth, Carnarvon, Anglesey, Denbigh, Flint, and Chester.

Ireland is divided into the North-East Circuit, the North-West Circuit, the Home Circuit, and the Leinster, Connaught, and Munster Circuits.

Scotland is not divided into Circuits. Assizes are held twice a year in Aberdeen, Inverness, Perth, Ayr, Dumfries, Jedburgh, Glasgow, Inverary, and Stirling: at Glasgow they are held three times a year.

The total number of towns in which assizes are held is, in England, 66; Ireland, 34; and Scotland, 9. In many counties, especially in England, the assizes are held alternately at two different towns of the county. In Surrey they are held in three different towns,—the Spring assizes at Kingston, and the Summer assizes at Croydon and Guildford alternately.

The Commissioners of Insolvent Debtors make circuits thrice a year throughout England and Wales, for the purpose of discharging insolvent debtors. There are four circuits, corresponding with the number of commissioners. The Home Circuit comprises five towns, the Midland twenty-six, the Northern twenty-two, and the Southern twenty-six,—in all seventy-six towns.

The Romans used to divide their Provinces into districts, and to appoint certain places, at which the people within the several districts used to assemble at stated times for the purpose of having their disputes settled by legal process. These places were called Conventus, "meetings," a word which properly signified " the act of meeting," and the assembly or people who met; and the term "Conventus" was also used to express the jurisdiction exercised by the governor at such district courts, and also the districts themselves. The practice was for the governor to make a circuit through the province and hold his courts at each Conventus at stated times, as we see from various passages in Cicero's works and Caesar's 'Gallic War.' (Cicero *Against Verres*, vii. c. 11; Caesar, *Gallic War*, i. 6, v. 2.) During his Gallic War Caesar used to go his Circuits in the winter after the campaign for the year was over. Some towns in the Roman Provinces obtained the privileges of having magistrates of their own (Jus Italicum), but as the governor (proconsul, or praetor) had the supreme authority, there was probably an appeal to him from the decision of such magistrates. Pliny (iii. 1. 3; iv. 22) states that in his time Hispania Citerior, which lay between the Ebro and the Pyrenees, was divided into seven Conventus, or judicial districts, and Hispania Baetica, which was comprised between the Ebro and the Guadiana, was divided into four judicial districts. The Province of Lusitania, which corresponded pretty nearly with modern Portugal, was divided into four judicial circuits. Strabo (xiii. p. 629) has some remarks on the judicial districts in the west part of Asia Minor. The business done at the Conventus was not confined to the settlement of legal disputes; but other matters were also transacted there which required certain forms in order to have a legal effect, such as the manumission of slaves by those who were under thirty years of age (Gaius i. 20).

CITATION, a process in the commencement of a suit by which the parties are commanded to appear before the Consistorial Courts. In the Prerogative Court it is called a Decree.

CITIZEN, from the French word *Citoyen*, which remotely comes from the Latin *Civis*. Aristotle commences the Third Book of his 'Politik' with an investigation of the question, What is a citizen (πολίτης)? He defines him to be one who participates in the judicial and legislative power in a State; but he observes, that his definition strictly applies only to a democratical form of government. The Roman word Civis, in its full sense, also meant one who had some share in the sovereign power in the State. The word citizen then, if we take it in its historical sense, cannot apply to those who are the subjects of a monarch, or, in other words, of one who has the complete sovereign power. It is consistent with ancient usage and modern usage, and it is also convenient to apply the word citizen only to the members of republican governments, which term, as here understood, comprehends [REPUBLIC] constitutitional monarchies. The term constitutional monarchy is not exact, but its meaning is understood : it is a form of republican government at the head of which is a king, or person with some equivalent title, whose power and dignity are hereditary. Constitutional monarchies approach near to absolute monarchies when the constitution gives very little power to the people, and this little power is rendered ineffectual by the contrivance of the prince and his advisers. Constitutional monarchies are of an aristocratical character when much political power is vested in the hands of a minority which is small when compared with the majority; or they may approach to a democracy, and differ from it only in having an elective instead of an hereditary head. Citizenship therefore is here understood as only applying to those States in which the constitution, whether written or unwritten, gives to those who are members of such States, or to some considerable number of them, some share of the sovereign power. The usual form in which citizenship is acquired is by birth; by being born of citizens. In the old Greek states, and generally in those states of antiquity where citizenship existed, this was the only mode in which as a general rule it could be acquired. A person obtained no rights of citizenship by the mere circumstance of being born in a country or living there. Citizenship could only be conferred by a public act either on an individual or on all the members of other communities. Difference of religion was one of the causes of these communities excluding strangers from their political body. The Roman system was at first a close community, but the practice of admitting aliens (peregrini) to the citizenship was early introduced. They were even admitted by the old burgers (the Patricians) in considerable numbers, but only by a vote of the collective body of Patricians. The admission of aliens to the citizenship, either partial or complete, became a regular part of the Roman polity to which Rome owed the extension of her name, her language, and her power. It is true that the process of admission went on slowly, and for a long time the Romans, unwisely, and with danger to their state, resisted the claims of their Italian allies, or subject people, who demanded the Roman citizenship; but this claim was finally settled in favour of the Italians by the Social or Marsic War (B.C. 90), and by the concessions that followed that war. Sometimes the States of Italy declined admission into the Roman political body; they preferred their own constitution to the rights and duties of Roman citizens.

The Roman system did not allow a man to claim the citizenship by birth, unless he was born of such a marriage as the state recognised to be a legal marriage. If a Roman married a woman who belonged to a people with whom the Roman state recognised no intermarriage (connubium), the child was not a Roman citizen; for he was not the child of his father, and it was only as the child of a Roman father that he could claim Roman citizenship.

The English law gives the citizenship to all persons who are born anywhere of a British citizen or of one whose father or father's father was a citizen of Great Britain. The English law also gives the citizenship to every person born in the British dominions; which rule originated in the king claiming such persons as his subjects who were born within his dominions. [ALLEGIANCE.] In the earliest periods of English history, those were properly called subjects who may now properly be designated citizens; though citizenship in England must be divided into two kinds, as it was in Rome. Some native citizens do not enjoy the suffrage, nor are they eligible to certain offices, such for instance as a membership of the House of Commons. But these are not permanent and personal disabilities: they are temporary incapacities arising from not having a certain amount of property, and therefore the complete citizenship may be acquired by every man who can acquire the requisite property qualification. It follows from what has been said that those who happen to be under this disability are not full citizens, but have a capacity to become such. Those who have not the suffrage are in the situation of subjects to that sovereign body, of which those who possess the suffrage form a part. The terms on which foreigners are admitted to the citizenship are different in different countries. A recent act of parliament (7 & 8 Vict. c. 76) has rendered the acquisition of partial citizenship in England much easier and less expensive than it was under the former process of a special act of parliament. [NATURALIZATION.]

The United States of North America have had various rules as to the admission of aliens to citizenship; but at present they require a period of five years' residence as a preliminary to obtaining the citizenship. [ALIEN.] Some persons in that country would extend the period of probation to twenty-one years. This however would be a very impolitic measure, for if foreigners will throng to a country such as the United States, with the view of settling there, the best thing is to make them citizens as soon as they wish to become such; and there would be manifest danger to the United States if the large number of foreigners who settle there should be considered as aliens for a period which would extend to the whole term of the natural life of many of the new settlers. Indeed there seems to be no objection to giving to aliens in republican governments, as soon as they choose to ask for them, all the rights and consequent duties of citizens, if they are ever to have them. It may be prudent to exclude aliens by birth from some of the high offices in a state, which is done in England and in the United States of North America. [ALIEN.]

In ancient Rome, aliens were not always admitted to the full rights of Roman citizens; and indeed in the early history of the state, even the Plebeians formed an order who were without many of the privileges which the Patricians enjoyed. A person might receive the Roman citizenship so far as to enjoy every advantage except a vote at the public elections and access to the honours of the state. This however was not citizenship as understood by Aristotle, nor is it citizenship as understood by the free states of modern times. The acquisition of complete citizenship implies the acquisition of a share of the sovereign power: the acquisition of all the rights of a citizen, except the suffrage and access to the honours of the state, is a limited citizenship; and it is no more than may be acquired in those states where there is no representative body, and in which a man by such acquisition gets not citizenship, but the state gets a subject.

The great facilities for a man changing his residence which now exist, and the increased motives to such change in a desire to better his condition by permanently settling in another country, lead to emigration from one country to another, and more particularly from Europe to America. The advantage which any country receives from the emigration of those who possess capital or peculiar arts is so great, that, under the present circumstances of the world, it is not easy to discover any good reason for Republican governments refusing to give the citizenship to any person who comes to another country with the view of settling there. A difficulty will arise in case of war, when a man owes a divided allegiance, for it is a principle of English law that a man cannot divest himself of his allegiance to the king of England; and probably an American citizen cannot divest himself of his allegiance to the United States. [ALIEN.] And yet the two countries which maintain this legal principle, allow the citizens of any other country to become citizens of their several communities. The Roman principle under the Republic was, that as soon as a Roman was admitted a citizen o another State, he ceased to be a Roman citizen, because a man could not belong to two States at once; wherein we have one among many examples of the precision of Roman political principles. The same principle must certainly be adopted some time into the international law of modern States.

The nations of Europe and the States of the two Americas have all a common religion, which however contains a great number of sects. A person of any religion in the United States of North America may become a citizen, and his opinions are no obstacle to his enjoying any of the honours of the country. But this is not so in England. No man for instance, though an English citizen, can be a member of the House of Commons unless he is, or is willing to profess that he is, a Christian.

CITY (in French *Cité*, ultimately from the Latin *Civitas*). Certain large and ancient towns both in England and in other countries are called cities, and they are supposed to rank before other towns. On what the distinction is founded is not well ascertained. The word seems to be one of common use, or at most to be used in the letters and charters of kings as a complimentary or honorary name, rather than as betokening the possession of any social privileges which may not and in fact do not belong to other ancient and incorporated places which are still known only by the name of towns or boroughs. Richelet (*Dictionnaire*) says that the French word *cité* is only used in general when we speak of places where there are two towns, an old town and another which has been built since; and he adds that " la cité de Paris" means old Paris.

Sir William Blackstone, following Coke (1 *Inst.* 109 b), says, "A city is a town incorporated, which is or hath been the see of a bishop." (*Comm. Introd.*, sec. iv.) But Westminster is a city, though it is not incorporated. Thetford is a town, though incorporated, and once the seat of a bishop. Whether Westminster owes its designation to the circumstance that it had a bishop for a few years of the reign of Henry VIII., and in the reign of Edward VI., may be doubted. But there are, besides Thetford, many places which were once the seats of bishops, as Sherburn, and Dorchester in Oxfordshire, which are never called cities. On the whole, we can rather say that certain of our ancient towns are called cities, and their inhabitants citizens, than show why this distinction prevails and what are the criteria by which they are distinguished from other towns. These ancient towns are those in which the cathedral of a bishop is found; to which are to be added Bath and Coventry, which, respectively with Wells and Lichfield, occur in the designation of the bishop in whose diocese they are situated; and Westminster, which in this respect stands alone.

In the United States of North America the name City is usually given to large towns, as New York, Philadelphia, and others.

CIVIL LAW. [ROMAN LAW.]

CIVIL LIST. The expenses of the English government, including military expenses, were formerly comprehended in one general list, and defrayed out of what was called the royal revenue. For a considerable period after the Conquest this revenue, derived from the rents of the crown lands, and from other sources, was at the command and under the uncontrolled management of the crown through the exercise of the prerogative. Even when at a later period the greater portion of the expenses of the government came to be granted by parliament in the form of supplies, the entire expenditure was still left with the crown, and the supplies were either voted for no specific purpose, or when they were voted for a special purpose, parliament had no control over their application.

This state of things continued to the Restoration in 1660. A distinction was then made between the military expenses of the government, or those occasioned by war, which were considered of the nature of extraordinary expenses, and those incurred in the maintenance of the ordinary establishments of the country. The revenues appropriated to the latter were called the hereditary or civil-list revenues, and were provided for partly from the crown lands that remained unalienated, and partly from certain taxes imposed by parliament expressly for that purpose during the life of the reigning king. In the reign of King William III. the sum applicable to the civil list, on an average of years, amounted to the annual sum of about 680,000*l.* This sum was applied in defraying the expenses of the royal household and of the privy purse, the maintenance and repairs of the royal palaces, the salaries of the lord chancellor, the judges, the great officers of state, and the ambassadors at foreign courts; and out of it were also paid the incomes of the members of the royal family, the secret service money, pensions, and a long list of other claims. The interest of the national debt, however, was never defrayed from the sum allotted for the civil list.

In the reign of Queen Anne the civil list remained of nearly the same amount as in the reign of King William. The principal taxes appropriated to it were an excise of 2*s.* 6*d.* per barrel on beer, which produced about 286,000*l.* per annum, a tonnage and poundage duty, which produced about 257,000*l.*, and the profits of the post-office, from which about 100,000*l.* was derived.

At the commencement of the reign of George I., 700,000*l.* a year was voted by parliament for the civil list, and certain taxes, as usual, were appropriated to that branch of the public expenditure.

2 L

On the accession of George II. it was provided, that if the taxes which had been appropriated to the civil list in the previous reign did not produce 800,000*l*. per annum, the deficiency should be made up by parliament, and that any surplus beyond that sum should be retained by the crown.

At the accession of George III. he surrendered the larger branches of the hereditary revenue of England, and the sum of 800,000*l*. was again voted by parliament for the civil list, but no particular taxes were set apart to provide that revenue. In the course of a few years, however, a large amount of debt had accumulated in this department, and to pay it off, two sums amounting together to considerably above 1,000,000*l*. were voted by parliament in 1769 and 1777. In the latter year also the civil-list revenue was permanently raised to 900,000*l*. This, however, did not prevent further deficiencies, which were again made good by parliament in 1784 and 1786, to the extent of about 270,000*l*.

In 1780 Mr. Burke brought in his bill for the better regulation of the civil list, which, although it was greatly mutilated before it passed into a law (in 1782), abolished several useless offices, and effected some reduction of expenditure.

According to the report of a committee of the House of Commons which sat upon the subject of the civil list in 1802, the total average annual expenditure in that branch since 1786 had been 1,000,167*l*., under the following heads:—royal family in all its branches, 209,988*l*.; great officers of state, 33,279*l*.; foreign ministers, 80,526*l*.; tradesmen's bills, 174,697*l*.; menial servants of the household, 92,424*l*.; pensions, 114,817*l*.; salaries to various officers, 76,013*l*.; commissioners of the treasury, 14,455*l*.; occasional payments, 203,964*l*. At this time another sum of above 990,000*l*. was voted by parliament to pay the debts on the civil list; and in 1804 the civil-list revenue was raised to 960,000*l*. In 1812 it was further augmented to 1,080,000*l*.; besides which, annuities to the amount of 260,000*l*. were then paid to the different branches of the royal family out of the consolidated fund.

Another committee inquired into the subject of the civil list in 1815, and it was upon the report made by this committee that the amount of the civil list was settled, on the accession of George IV., at 850,000*l*. per annum, 255,000*l*. of annual charge being at the same time transferred from this branch to other funds. It was calculated that the distribution of this sum would be under the following heads:— 1. His Majesty's privy purse, 60,000*l*. 2. Allowances to the lord chancellor, judges, and Speaker of the House of Commons, 32,956*l*. 3. Salaries, &c. of his Majesty's ambassadors and other ministers, salaries to consuls, and pensions to retired ambassadors and ministers, 226,950*l*. 4. Expenses, except salaries, of his Majesty's household in the departments of the lord steward, lord chamberlain, master of the horse, master of the robes, and surveyor-general of works, 209,000*l*. 5. Salaries in the last-mentioned departments, 140,700*l*. 6. Pensions limited by Act 22 Geo. III. c. 82, 95,000*l*. 7. Salaries to certain officers of state, and various other allowances, 41,306*l*. 8. Salaries to the commissioners of the treasury and chancellor of the exchequer, 13,822*l*. 9. Occasional payments not comprised in any of the aforesaid classes, 26,000*l*. The crown was left besides in the enjoyment of the hereditary revenues in Scotland, amounting to about 110,000*l*. per annum; and also of a civil list for Ireland, of 207,000*l*.

On the 15th of November, 1830, immediately after the accession of King William IV., the late Lord Congleton, then Sir Henry Parnell, carried in the House of Commons a motion for appointing a select committee to inquire into the civil list. The chief object proposed was the separation of the proper expenses of the crown from all those other charges which still continued to be mixed up with them under that title. The consequence of the success of this motion (besides the overthrow of the Wellington administration and the introduction of the Reform Bill) was another report, upon which was founded the Act 1 Will. IV. c. 25, for the regulation of the civil list. The committee which was appointed on the motion of Sir H. Parnell, recommended that the civil-list charges should be confined to expenses proper for the maintenance of their Majesties' household, and the sum of 510,000*l.* was granted to his Majesty by the above act under the following classes:—1. For their Majesties' privy purse, 110,000*l.* 2. Salaries of his Majesty's household, 130,300*l.* 3. Expenses of his Majesty's household, 171,500*l.* 4. Special and secret service, 23,200*l.* 5. Pensions, 75,000*l.* A separate civil list for Ireland was discontinued; and the Scotch hereditary revenues, as well as the droits of admiralty, and the 4½ per cent. duties, were to be paid into the Exchequer for the use of the public.

Speaking of the civil list as settled by 1 Will. IV. c. 25, and comparing it with the civil list of King Geo. IV., Lord Congleton remarked ('Financial Reform,' p. 205) "that there was no real reduction in that arrangement, for whatever appears to be a reduction, has been produced by a transfer of charge from one head to another of the old civil list. The chief difference in this arrangement from the former consists in the transfer of about 460,000*l.* a year from the civil list to the consolidated fund, and in providing for the gradual reduction of the pensions to 75,000*l.* a year."

William IV. retained the revenues of the duchies of Lancaster and Cornwall, which are considered to be the hereditary revenues, not of the crown, but of the duchies of Lancaster and of Cornwall. The duchy of Lancaster is permanently annexed to the crown, and the duchy of Cornwall belongs to the crown when there is no Prince of Wales. No account of the amount of these revenues had ever been laid before parliament until very recently. In his speech on Economical Reform in 1780, Mr. Burke said, "Every one of those principalities has the appearance of a kingdom, for the jurisdiction over a few private estates; and the formality and charge of the Exchequer of Great Britain, for collecting the rents of a country squire. Cornwall is the best of them; but when you compare the charge with the receipt, you will find that it furnishes no exception to the general rule. The duchy and county palatine of Lancaster do not yield, as I have reason to believe, on an average of twenty years, 4000*l.* a year clear to the crown. As to Wales and the county palatine of Chester, I have my doubts whether their productive exchequer yields any returns at all."*

The Civil List of Queen Victoria was settled by 1 Vict. c. 2. This act contains a very important and salutary provision, which will shortly be noticed, respecting pensions. The preamble of the act states that her majesty had placed unreservedly at the disposal of the commons in parliament those hereditary revenues which were transferred to the public by her immediate predecessors, and that her majesty felt confident that her faithful commons would gladly make adequate provision for the support of the honour and dignity of the crown. It is then enacted, that the hereditary revenue shall be carried to the Consolidated Fund during the life of her majesty, but that after her demise it shall be payable to her successors. The latter part of the enactment is a mere form. By § 3 the clear yearly sum of 385,000*l.* is to be paid out of the Consolidated Fund for the support of her majesty's household and of the honour and dignity of the crown, to be applied according to a schedule as under:—

1. For her Majesty's privy purse £60,000
2. Salaries of her Majesty's household and retired allowances . . . 131,260
3. Expenses of her Majesty's household . . . 172,500
4. Royal bounty, alms, and special services . . 13,200
5. Pensions to the extent of 1200*l.* per annum.
6. Unappropriated monies . 8,040

£385,000

The restriction to which allusion has been made relates to class 5 in the schedule.

---

* The gross revenues of the duchy of Cornwall in 1843 amounted to 40,100*l.* The two largest items were, rents and arrears 14,069*l.*; compensation in lieu of the tin coinage duties 15,741*l.* The sum required to defray salaries, allowances, and annuities was 8,425*l.*. the payments made to the use of the Prince of Wales, and which in the previous reign were enjoyed by the king, were 18,5.9*l.*, and a sum of 2000*l.* was expended in purchasing the surrender of beneficial leases. The sum set down as balances and arrears was 8486*l.* The gross

This check upon the wanton and extravagant disposal of the public money is thoroughly in accordance with just and constitutional principles. The amount which can be granted in pensions by the crown in any one year is not to exceed 1200*l.*; and the Civil List Act restricts, though in a comprehensive spirit, the persons to whom they are to be granted, who must be such persons only as have just claims on the royal benevolence, or who by their personal services to the crown, by the performance of duties to the public, or by their useful discoveries in science and attainments in literature and the arts, have merited the gracious consideration of their sovereign and the gratitude of their country. A list of all such pensions must be laid before parliament yearly. [PENSIONS; WOODS AND FORESTS.]

CIVILIZATION. The words civilization, education, and religion, with many others, are often used without any precise ideas being attached to them; yet there are no words that require to be more thoroughly analysed.

The meaning of a word is often formed by degrees. As soon as a particular fact presents itself to our notice which appears to have a specific relation to a known term, it becomes immediately incorporated with it; and hence the meaning of many terms gradually extends, and finally embraces all the various facts and ideas which are considered to belong to it. On this account, there is more depth as well as accuracy in the usual and ordinary meaning of complex terms than in any definitions which can be given of them, notwithstanding the definition may appear to be more strict and precise. In the majority of instances scientific definitions are too narrow, and owing to this circumstance they are frequently less exact than the popular meaning of terms; it is therefore in its popular and ordinary signification that we must seek for the various ideas that are included in the term civilization.

---

income of the duchy of Lancaster, which, as already explained, is enjoyed by the crown independent of arrangements under the Civil List Act, was 33,037*l.* in 1843. The sum paid out of this revenue to the keeper of her majesty's privy purse was 13,000*l.*

Now, the fundamental notion of civilization is that of a progressive movement, of a gradual development, and a tendency to amelioration. It always suggests the idea of a community, of a political body, of a nation, which is advancing methodically, and with distinct and clear views of the objects which it seeks to attain: progress, continual improvement, is therefore the fundamental idea contained in our notion of the term Civilization.

As to this progress and improvement involved in the term Civilization, to what do they apply? The etymology of the word answers the question. From this we learn that it does not contemplate the actual number, power, or wealth of a people, but their *civil* condition, their social relations, and intercourse with each other. Such then is the first impression which arises in our mind when we pronounce the word *Civilization*. It seems to represent to us at once the greatest activity and the best possible organization of society; so as to be productive of a continual increase, and a distribution of wealth and power among its members, whereby their absolute and relative condition is kept in a state of constant improvement.

But great as is the influence which a well organised civil society must have upon the happiness of the human race, the term Civilization seems to convey something still more extensive, more full and complete, and of a more elevated and dignified character, than the mere perfection of the social relations, as a matter of order and arrangement. In this other aspect of the word it embraces the development of the intellectual and moral faculties of man, of his feelings, his propensities, his natural capacities, and his tastes.

Education, which is the result of a well ordered social arrangement, and also its perfector and conservator, an education which shall give to every member of the community the best opportunities for developing the whole of his faculties, is the end which civilization, or a society in a state of continued progress, must always have in view.

The fundamental ideas then, contained

in the word Civilization are—the continual advancement of the whole society in wealth and prosperity, and the improvement of man in his individual capacity. When the one proceeds without the other, it is immediately felt that there is something incomplete and wanting. The mere increase of national wealth, unaccompanied by a corresponding knowledge and intelligence on the part of the people, seems to be a state of things premature in existence, uncertain in duration, and insecure as to its stability. We are unacquainted with the causes of its origin, the principles to which it can be traced, and what hopes we may form of its continuance. We wish to persuade ourselves that this prosperity will not be limited to a few generations, or to a particular people or country, but that it will gradually spread, and finally become the inheritance of all the people of the earth. And yet what rational expectation can we entertain of such a state of things becoming universal? It is only by means of education, conducted upon right principles, that we can ever hope to see true national prosperity attained, and rendered permanent. The development of the moral and intellectual faculties must go hand in hand with the cultivation of the industrious arts; united, they form the great engine for giving true civilization to the world.

In fact, without the union of these two elements, civilization would stop half way; mere external advantages are liable to be lost or abused without the aid of those more refined and exalted studies which tend to improve the mind, and call forth the feelings and affections of the heart. It must be repeated, civilization consists in the progressive improvement of the society considered as a whole, and of all the individual members of which it is composed.

The means by which this improvement of the whole of a society and of all the members of it may be best effected, will vary somewhat in different countries. European nations consider and call their social state civilized, and they view the social states of other countries, which do not rest on the same foundation, either as barbarous or as less civilized than their own. An impartial observer may allow that if we measure civilization by the rule here laid down, the nations of Europe, and other nations whose social systems have a like basis, are the most civilized. The civilization of Europe and of the nations of European origin is founded mainly on two elements, the Christian religion and the social state which grew up from the diffusion of the power of the Romans. The establishment of feudality in many countries greatly affected the social basis; and the consequences are still seen, but more distinctly in some parts of Europe than in others. The elements of such a social system are essentially different from those on which is founded the system of China, of the nations which profess Mohammedanism, and of the natious of the Indian peninsula. European civilization is active and restless, but still subordinate to constituted authority. It gives to man the desire and the means to acquire wealth at home, and it stimulates him to adventure and discovery abroad. It seeks to assimilate the civilization of other nations to its own by conquest and colonization, and it is intolerant of all civilization that is opposed to itself. Asiatic civilization is at present inert, it is not in a state of progress, and is exposed to the inroads of European civilization. European civilization has been and is most active in increasing the power of states as states, and in increasing their wealth; it also gives facilities for men of talent and enterprise to acquire wealth and power by means recognised as legal and just; and it is now beginning to extend the means of individual improvement among all the members of its communities more widely than any other civilization; but the amount of poverty and ignorance which still co-exist by the side of wealth and intelligence, wherever European civilization has been established, show that much remains to be done before the individual happiness of these States can be as complete and their internal condition as sound as their collective wealth is unbounded and their external aspect is fair and flourishing.

The nations of Europe consider their

social system as the standard by which the civilization of other countries must be measured, and they assume as a fundamental principle, that in countries where there is no individual property in land, and where the land is not cultivated, there is no civilization, and that they may therefore seize it. This assumption is true, if we measure civilization by the rule here laid down, for on individual ownership of land, and the cultivation of land, the whole European system rests. Whether land might be advantageously cultivated in common, and the institution of private property in land might be abolished, is another question, which however has not yet been satisfactorily resolved, and cannot be resolved without destroying the present social systems of Europe.

A recent committee of the House of Commons, appointed to inquire into the state of New Zealand, have put forth the following doctrine :—" The uncivilized inhabitants of any country have but a qualified dominion over it, or a right of occupancy only, and until they establish amongst themselves a settled form of government, and subjugate the ground to their own uses by the cultivation of it, they cannot grant to individuals, not of their own tribe, any portion of it, for the simple reason that they have not themselves any individual property in it." This is not very precise language, but one may collect what it means. Lord Stanley, in a despatch to the governor of New Zealand, dated 13th August, 1844, says, " With respect to this doctrine, I am not sure that, were the question one of mere theory, I should be prepared to subscribe, unhesitatingly and without reserve, to the fundamental assumption of the committee; and I am sure that it would require considerable qualification as applicable to the aborigines of New Zealand. There are many gradations of 'uncivilized inhabitants,' and practically according to their state of civilization must be the extent of the rights which they can be allowed to claim, whenever the territory on which they reside is occupied by civilized communities." After describing the "aborigines of New Holland" as far below " the New Zealanders in civilization, and being wholly ignorant of or averse to the cultivation of the soil, with no principles of civil government or recognition of private property, and little if any knowledge of the simplest form of religion, or even of the existence of a Supreme being ;" he adds, that "it is impossible to admit, on the part of a population thus situated, any rights in the soil which should be permitted to interfere with the subjugation by Europeans of the vast wilderness over which they are scattered ; and all that can be required by justice, sanctioned by policy, or recommended by humanity, is to endeavour, as civilization and cultivation extend, to embrace the aborigines within their pale, to diffuse religious knowledge among them, to induce them, if possible, to adopt more settled means of providing for their subsistence, and to afford them the means of doing so, if so disposed, by an adequate reservation of lands within the limits of cultivation." The principles laid down by Lord Stanley are those which the civilized nations of Europe have long acted on, sometimes tempering their conquests of uncivilized nations with mercy and humanity, and sometimes treating them as if they were merely wild beasts that infested the country. The foundations on which even Lord Stanley places the justification of European occupation are not stated with much precision. The real foundations are, the enterprising spirit of Europeans ; the pressure of difficulties at home, which drive men abroad ; the necessity of possessing land in their new country, as the basis of that edifice of civilization which they propose to erect after the model of the mother country ; and the power to take from those who are too feeble to resist. Europeans admit, and the admission is contained by implication in Lord Stanley's remarks, that the nearer a nation's social system approaches to their own, the safer should it be against unprovoked aggression ; but they contend, as Lord Stanley does, that the same self-restraint will not and ought not to be practised in those cases where the social system, or the mode of life, is altogether opposed to those fundamental principles on which European society is constituted.

CLARENDON, THE CONSTITUTIONS OF, were certain declaratory ordinances agreed to at a general council of the nobility and prelates assembled by Henry II. at his palace or manor of Clarendon, in Wiltshire, in the year 1164. These ordinances were sixteen in number, and were intended to define the limits between civil and ecclesiastical jurisdictions, to prevent the further encroachments of the clergy, and to abolish the abuses which had arisen from the gradual and increasing usurpations of the pope. (Howell's *State Trials*, vol. ii. p. 546.)

− CLEARING-HOUSE. [BANK, p. 273.]

CLERGY, a collective term, under which that portion of the population of a country is comprehended who are in holy orders. It is used in contradistinction to *laity*, which comprehends all other persons. Like most ecclesiastical terms, it is of Greek origin, the word κληρικός (clericus) having been used in the sense of "appertaining to spiritual persons" by the Greek ecclesiastical writers. From *clericus* comes the word *clerk*, which is still a law-term used to designate clergymen, but which appears antiently not to have been confined to persons actually in holy orders, but to have been applied to persons possessed of a certain amount of learning.

The distinction of clergy and laity in the Christian church may be considered as coeval with the existence of the church itself; for in the apostolic period there were officers in the church specially appointed to discharge the duties of pastors or deacons, and even, as many suppose, bishops or overseers, who had the superintendence of various inferior officers. These persons, though they might not perhaps be entirely relieved from the ordinary duties of life, so that they might devote themselves exclusively to their sacred office, yet must necessarily have been nearly so, and it is certain that they were nominated to their offices by some peculiar forms. Very early however the distinction became complete. The bishops, priests, and deacons of the Christian church, each ordained to the office in a manner which it was believed the founders of Christianity appointed, and each supposed to have received a peculiar spiritual grace by devolution from the apostles and from the founder of Christianity himself, soon formed a distinct body of men whom it was convenient to distinguish by some particular appellation.

In Christian nations the distinction has been usually recognised by the state, who have allowed certain privileges or exemptions to the clergy. No inconsiderable share of temporal power, extending not only over the members of their own body, but over the laity, has in most states been conceded to them. In the old German confederation the sovereign power in some of the states was vested in ecclesiastics; while at Rome there has been for many ages an elective head, in whom all temporal and spiritual authority over the states of the church has been vested.

It is easy to account for the ascendency of the clergy in the middle ages, and their acquisition of power. They were the best instructed part of the population. The learning of the age was almost exclusively theirs; and knowledge is a means of obtaining power. Beside this they had the means of working upon the ruder minds of the laity, in the power vested in them alone of administering the sacraments of the church, and of regulating under what circumstances those sacraments ought to be administered. This enabled them to win acquiescence in any favourite design, sometimes by gentle influences and sometimes by terror.

The history of almost every country of modern Europe presents instances of struggles between the laity and the clergy for power or privilege. All power in the clergy of England to erect an authority dangerous to the laity, or to secure to themselves political immunities or privileges inconsistent with the general good, was broken at the Reformation. The clergy of England then became a fragment of a once great and well disciplined body dispersed through the whole of Christendom, which, when acting with common effort, and putting forth all its strength, it had been difficult for any single temporal prince to resist with effect.

CLERGY.

The clergy were before the Reformation in England divided into regular and secular. The regular clergy were the religious orders who lived under some religious rule (regula), such as abbots and monks. The secular clergy were those who did not live under a religious rule, but had the care of souls, as bishops and priests. The phrase *the clergy* now means in the English and Irish established church all persons who are in holy orders. The privileges which the law of England allows to the clergy are but a faint shadow of the privileges which they enjoyed before the Reformation. A clergyman cannot be compelled to serve on a jury, or to appear at a court leet or view of frankpledge. He cannot be compelled to serve the office of bailiff reeve, constable, or the like. He is privileged from arrest in civil suits while engaged in divine service, and while going to or returning from it; and it is a misdemeanour to arrest him while he is so engaged. (5 Geo. IV. c. 31, s. 23.) He is exempted from paying toll at turnpike-gates, when going to or returning from his parochial duty. He could claim benefit of clergy more than once. [BENEFIT OF CLERGY.] The clergy cannot now sit in the House of Commons. This was formerly a doubtful point, but it was settled by 41 Geo. III. c. 63, which enacted that "no person having been ordained to the office of priest or deacon, or being a minister of the Church of Scotland, is capable of being elected;" and that if he should sit or vote, he is liable to forfeit 500l. for each day, to any one who may sue for it. The Roman Catholic clergy are excluded, by 10 Geo. IV. c. 7, § 9. (May's *Parliament*, p. 27.)

The old ecclesiastical constitutions prohibited clergymen acting as judges in causes of life and death; but there was usually a clause saving the privilege of the king to employ whom he thought proper in any way, and the prohibition was therefore of little practical effect. The bishops, however, do not at the present day vote in the House of Lords in any case of life or death. [BISHOP, p. 376.] Ecclesiastical persons have sat as chief justices of the King's Bench in former times. (Blacks. *Comm.* c. 17.) The last ecclesiastic who filled the office of lord high chancellor was Bishop Williams, from 1621 to 1625 [CHANCELLOR, p. 480]; and the last who acted publicly in a diplomatic capacity was the Bishop of Bristol, at Utrecht, when the treaty of 1713 was negotiated. In 1831 a parliamentary paper was issued (No. 39), which showed the number of clergymen in the commission of the peace in England. In many counties the proportion of clergymen was one-third of the whole number of justices; in several counties above one-half; in Derbyshire and Sussex there was not one clergyman in the commission, and in Kent only two. Lord-lieutenants have in some cases made it a rule not to recommend clergymen to the lord chancellor. This is in strict accordance with some of the old constitutions, which were founded on the principle that clergymen should not be entangled with temporal affairs.

By 21 Henry VIII. c. 13. the clergy were forbidden to farm lands, or to buy any cattle or merchandise to sell for profit; but if their glebe-lands were insufficient, they might farm more, in order to maintain their families, and might buy cattle to obtain manure. By 57 Geo. III. c. 99, they were permitted, with consent of the bishop of the diocese, to farm lands to the extent of eighty acres for a term not exceeding seven years.

The act which now applies to farming and trafficking by the clergy is the 1 & 2 Vict. c. 106, which consolidated former acts on this subject: its provisions do not extend to Ireland. The term "spiritual persons" includes persons "licensed or otherwise allowed to perform the duties of any ecclesiastical office whatever." The clause (§ 28) which relates to farming is substantially the same as in 57 Geo. III. c. 99.

The clause (§ 29) respecting spiritual persons engaging in trade, or buying to sell again for profit, enacts that it shall not be lawful for such persons "to engage in or carry on any trade or dealing for gain or profit, or to deal in any goods, wares, or merchandise, unless in any case in which such trading or dealing shall have been or shall be carried on by or on behalf of any number of partners exceeding the number of six, or in any case in which any trade or dealing, or any share in any trade or dealing, shall have devolved or shall devolve upon any spiritual person or upon any other person for him or to his use, under or by virtue of any devise, bequest, inheritance, intestacy, settlement, marriage, bankruptcy, or insolvency; but in none of the foregoing excepted cases shall it be lawful for such spiritual person to act as a director or managing partner, or to carry on such trade or dealing as aforesaid in person."

Spiritual persons holding benefices could not legally become members of a joint-stock banking company before the passing of a short act, 1 Vict. c. 10, which enacted that no association or co-partnership or contract should be void by reason only of spiritual persons being members thereof; and the principle of the act is now adopted in 1 & 2 Vict. c. 106.

It is enacted in § 30 of 1 & 2 Vict. c. 106, " That nothing hereinbefore contained shall subject to any penalty or forfeiture any spiritual person for keeping a school or seminary, or acting as a schoolmaster or tutor or instructor, or being in any manner concerned or engaged in giving instruction or education for profit or reward, or for buying or selling or doing any other thing in relation to the management of any such school, seminary, or employment, or to any spiritual person whatever, for the buying of any goods, wares, or merchandise, or articles of any description, which shall without fraud be bought with intent at the buying thereof to be used by the spiritual person buying the same for his family or in his household; and after the buying of any such goods, wares, or merchandises, or articles, selling the same again or any parts thereof, which such person may not want or choose to keep, although the same shall be sold at an advanced price beyond that which may have been given for the same; or for disposing of any books or other works to or by means of any bookseller or publisher; or for being a manager, director, partner, or shareholder, in any benefit society, or fire or life assurance society, by whatever name or designation such society may have been constituted; or for any buying or selling again for gain or profit, of any cattle or corn or other articles necessary or convenient to be bought, sold, kept, or maintained by any spiritual person, or any other person for him or to his use, for the occupation, manuring, improving, pasturage, or profit of any glebe, demesne lands, or other lands or hereditaments which may be lawfully held and occupied, possessed, or enjoyed by such spiritual person, or any other for him or to his use; or for selling any minerals, the produce of mines situated on his own lands; so nevertheless that no such spiritual person shall buy or sell any cattle or corn, or other articles as aforesaid, in person in any market, fair, or place of public sale."

Under § 31 of the act the bishop of the diocese might suspend a spiritual person for illegally trading, and for the third offence such person might be deprived; but proceedings for this offence would now be regulated by 3 & 4 Vict. c. 86.

This act (3 & 4 Vict. c. 86, commonly called the Church Discipline Act) was passed in 1840, " for better enforcing Church Discipline," and it repeals the old statute (1 Henry VII. c. 4) under which bishops were enabled to proceed against their clergy and sentence them to imprisonment. Before this act was passed, the mode of procedure against spiritual persons for ecclesiastical offences was " by articles in the diocesan or peculiar court, or by letters of request to the court of the metropolitan." (Phillimore's Burn, iii. 365.) Dr. Phillimore states, that " any person, it has been held, may prosecute a clergyman for neglect of his clerical duty." The 3 & 4 Vict. c. 86, enacts, "that no criminal suit or proceeding against a clerk in holy orders of the United Church of England and Ireland, for any offence against the laws ecclesiastical, shall be instituted in any ecclesiastical court otherwise than is hereinbefore enacted or provided," nor in any other mode than that pointed out by the act (§ 3). The act provides, " that in every case of any clerk in holy orders in the United Church of England and Ireland, who may be charged with any offence against the laws ecclesiastical, or concerning whom there may exist scandal or evil report, as having offended against the said laws, it shall be lawful for the bishop of the diocese within which the offence is alleged or reported to have been committed, on the application of any party complaining thereof, or if he shall think fit, of his own mere motion, to issue a commission under his hand or seal to five persons, of whom one shall be his vicar-general, or an archdeacon or rural dean within the diocese, for the purpose of making inquiry as to the grounds of such charge or report: provided always, that notice of the intention to issue such commission under the hand of the bishop, containing an intimation of the nature of the offence, together with the names, addition, and residence of the party on whose application or motion such commission shall be about to issue, shall be sent by the bishop to the party accused fourteen days at least before such commission shall issue." The bishop may pronounce sentence without further proceedings, by consent of the clerk; and such sentence is good and effectual in law. If he refuse or neglect to appear and make answer to the articles alleged, other than an unqualified admission of the truth thereof, "the bishop shall proceed to hear the cause, with the assistance of three assessors, to be nominated by the bishop, one of whom shall be an advocate who shall have practised not less than five years in the court of the archbishop of the province, or a serjeant-at-law, or a barrister of not less than seven years' standing; and another shall be dean of his cathedral church, or of one of his cathedral churches, or one of his archdeacons, or his chancellor; and upon the hearing of such cause the bishop shall determine the same, and pronounce sentence thereupon, according to the ecclesiastical law."

When the charge is under investigation the bishop may inhibit the party accused from performing any services of the church within his diocese until sentence has been passed; but if the person accused be the incumbent of a benefice, he may nominate any person or persons to perform such services during his inhibition, and such persons are to be licensed by the bishop, if they are approved of by him. Appeals under the act are to the archbishop, and are to be heard before the judge of the court of appeal of his province; but if the cause has been heard and determined in the first instance in the court of the archbishop, the appeal is then to the queen in council, and is to be heard before the judicial committee of Privy Council; and at least one archbishop or bishop, who is a member of the Privy Council, must be present.

In the Constitutions and Canons Ecclesiastical of 1603, canons 31 to 76 inclusive relate to " Ministers; their Ordination, Function, and Charge." By the 76th canon " no man, being admitted a deacon or minister, shall from thenceforth voluntarily relinquish the same, nor afterwards use himself in the course of his life as a layman, upon pain of excommunication."

The clergy meet by delegates in convocation at the beginning of every new parliament, but this is now merely a form; the king, as supreme head of the Church of England, invariably dissolves the convocation before they can proceed to any business. They have however still courts in which jurisdiction is exercised touching ecclesiastical affairs, and causes matrimonial, and testamentary so far as concerns the granting of probates and letters of administration, and where the church's censures are directed against particular classes of offenders. To them also belongs the whole ecclesiastical revenue in the Established Church of England, with divers fees or customary payments, and to them also the whole regulation of the terms of admission to their order.

The three great classes of the English clergy are the bishops, priests, and deacons. To be admitted into each of those classes requires a peculiar ordination. This distinction is of an entirely different kind from that which arises out of office or appointment. Of this kind of distinction there is in the English clergy the archbishop, the bishop, the dean and canons of a conventual or collegiate church (some of the canons being in many instances invested with particular characters, as precentors, succentors, and the like), the archdeacon, the rural dean, the dean of some church whose constitution is peculiar, the rector, the vicar, the curate in some chapels called parochial, the minister in some newly-founded chapel, whether a chapel of ease or what is called a proprietary chapel, assistant ministers to aid the vicar or the rector in some churches of antient foundation, and, finally, a body of persons called curates, who are engaged by the incumbents of benefices to assist them in the performance of their duties, but who are not dismissable at the caprice of the incumbent, nor left by law without a claim upon a certain portion of the profits of the benefice.

England is divided into 10,780 districts, varying in extent, called parishes. Each of these parishes must be regarded as having its church, and one person (or in some instances more than one) who ministers divine ordinances in that church. This person, whose proper designation is *persona ecclesiæ*, enjoys of common right the tithe of the parish, and has usually a house and glebe belonging to his benefice. When this, the original arrangement, is undisturbed, we have a parish and its rector; and in other cases the vicar and perpetual curate. [BENEFICE, pp. 341-343.]

CLERGY, BENEFIT OF. [BENEFIT OF CLERGY.]

CLERK IN ORDERS. [CLERGY.]

CLERK OF ASSIZE is an officer attached to each circuit, who accompanies the judges at the assizes, and performs all the ministerial acts of the court. He issues subpœnas, orders, writs, and other processes, draws indictments; takes, discharges, and respites recognizances; files informations, affidavits, and other instruments, enters every *nolle prosequi*, records all the proceedings of the court, and enters its judgments. He is associated with the judges in the commissions to take assizes; and he is restrained by statute 33 Hen. VIII. c. 24, from being counsel for any person on his circuit. He is paid by fees which are charged upon the several official acts performed by him, some, by virtue of established usage, and others, under various statutes, 55 Geo. III. c. 56; 7 Geo. IV. c. 64; 7 & 8 Geo. IV. c. 28; 11 Geo. IV.; & 1 Wm. IV. c. 58. The fees payable on each circuit will be found in *Parl. Paper*, No. 631 of 1843. (*Parl. Paper*, 1843, No. 631; Wood's *Institutes*.)

CLERK OF THE CROWN IN CHANCERY, is an officer of the crown in attendance upon both Houses of Parliament, and upon the great seal. In the House of Lords he makes out and issues all writs of summons to peers, writs for the attendance of the judges, commissions to summon and prorogue Parliament, and to pass bills; and he attends at the table of the House to read the titles of bills whenever the royal assent is given to them, either by the queen in person or by commission. He receives and has the custody of the returns of the representative peers of Scotland, and certifies them to the House; and makes out and issues writs for the election of representative peers of Ireland and their writs of summons. He is the registrar of the Lord High Steward's Court for state trials and for the trial of peers; and he is also registrar of the Coronation Court of Claims.

In connexion with the House of Commons, he makes out and issues all writs for the election of members in Great Britain (those for Ireland being issued by the clerk of the crown in Ireland); gives notice thereof to the secretary-at-war, under act 8 Geo. II. c. 30, for the removal of troops from the place of election; receives and retains the custody of all returns to Parliament for the United Kingdom; notifies each return in the 'London Gazette,' registers it in the books of his office, and certifies it to the House. By act 6 & 7 Vict. c. 18, he has the custody of all poll-books taken at elections, and is required to register them, to give office copies or an inspection of them to all parties applying, and to prove them before election committees. He attends all election committees with the returns of members; and when a return is to be amended in consequence of the determination of an election committee, he attends at the table of the House to amend it.

He is an officer of the lord high chancellor, not in his judicial capacity, but as holding the great seal; and in this department he makes out all patents, commissions, warrants, appointments or other instruments that pass the great seal, except patents for inventions and other patents and charters which are passed in the Patent Office. He also administers the oaths of office to the lord chancellor, the judges, the serjeants-at-law, and all other law officers, and records the same in the books of his office. For these several duties he receives a salary of 1000l. a year, under 7 & 8 Vict. c. 77. (*Parl. Report*, No. 455, *of Session* 1844.)

The office of the Clerk of the Crown is commonly called the Crown Office; but there is also an office in the Court of Queen's Bench called the Crown side of the Court, of which there is a master and other officers.

CLERK OF THE HOUSE OF COMMONS. The chief officer of that House is appointed by the crown for life, by letters patent. Upon entering office he is sworn before the lord chancellor " to make true entries, remembrances, and journals of the things done and passed in the House of Commons; in which duties he is aided by the clerk-assistant and second clerk-assistant. These three officers are more commonly known as " clerks at the table." The chief clerk signs all orders of the House, endorses the bills, and reads whatever is required to be read in the proceedings of the House. He is also responsible for the execution of all the official business of the House, which is under his superintendence. In the patent he is styled " Under Clerk of the Parliaments to attend upon the Commons;" whence it is inferred that on the separation of the two Houses, the under-clerk of the Parliaments went with the Commons, leaving the clerk of the Parliaments in the Upper House. His salary is 3500l. a year, that of the clerk-assistant 2500l., and that of the second clerk-assistant 1000l.; but under act 4 & 5 Will. IV. c. 70, the salaries of the two first offices will be reduced to 2000l. and 1500l. respectively, on the first vacancy. (Hatsell's *Precedents*, vol. ii. p. 251; May's *Proceedings and Usage of Parliament*, p. 157 and Index.)

CLERK OF THE MARKET. [WEIGHTS AND MEASURES.]

CLERK OF THE PARISH. [PARISH CLERK.]

CLERK OF THE PARLIAMENTS is the chief ministerial officer of the House of Lords. His duties (which are executed by the clerk-assistant and additional clerk-assistant) are to take minutes of all the proceedings, orders, and judgments of the House; to sign all orders, to endorse bills, to swear witnesses at the bar, to wait upon the queen when she comes to give the royal assent to bills, and to take her command upon them; and to signify the royal assent in all cases, whether given by the queen in person or by commission. He is also sent occasionally with a master in chancery as a messenger from the Lords to the Commons in the absence of another master. Besides these and other special duties, he is charged with the general superintendence of the official establishment of the House of Lords. He is paid out of the Lords' Fee Fund, of which no account is ever given. It is understood that on the death of Sir G. Rose (aged 73) the office will not be filled up. (May's *Proceedings and Usage of Parliament*.)

CLERK OF THE PEACE is an officer attached to every county or division of a county, city, borough, or other place in which quarter-sessions are held; being the ministerial officer of the court of quarter-sessions. He is appointed by the *Custos Rotulorum* of the county, and holds his appointment so long as he shall well demean himself. In case of misbehaviour the justices in sessions, on receiving a complaint in writing, may suspend or discharge him, after an examination and proof thereof openly in the sessions; in which case the *Custos Rotulorum* is required to appoint another person residing within the county or division. In case of his refusal or neglect to make this appointment, before the next general quarter-sessions, the justices in sessions may appoint a clerk of the peace. (1 Will. III. c. 21, § 6.) The *Custos Rotulorum* may not sell the office or take any bond or assurance to receive any reward, directly or indirectly, for the appointment, on pain of both himself and the Clerk of the Peace being disabled from holding their respective offices, and forfeiting double the value of the consi

CLERK.   [525]   CLIENT.

deration, to any one who shall sue them. (Id. § 8.) To give effect to this provision, before the Clerk of the Peace enters upon the execution of his duties he takes an oath that he has not paid anything for his nomination.

The Clerk of the Peace may execute the duties of his office either personally, or by a sufficient deputy approved by the Custos Rotulorum. He or his deputy must be constantly in attendance upon the court of quarter-sessions. He gives notice of its being holden or adjourned; issues its various processes; records its proceedings; and performs all the ministerial acts required to give effect to its decisions. During the sitting of the court, he reads all acts directed to be read in sessions; calls the jurors, and parties under recognizance; presents the bills to the grand jury and receives them again; arraigns prisoners, administers oaths, and receives and records verdicts. Whenever prosecutors decline any other professional assistance, he is required to draw bills of indictment, for which, in cases of felony, he can charge 2s. only, but in cases of misdemeanor he may charge any reasonable amount for his service.

In addition to these general duties he has other special duties imposed upon him by different statutes, in regard to the summoning of juries, the appointment of sheriffs and under-sheriffs, the enrolment of rules of savings' banks and friendly societies, the custody of documents required to be deposited with him under standing orders of the Houses of Parliament, and other matters.

By act 22 Geo. II. c. 46, § 14, he is restrained, as being an officer of the Court, from acting as a solicitor, attorney or agent, or suing out any process, at any general or quarter sessions, to be held in the county, &c. in which he shall execute his office.

The Clerk of the Peace is paid by fees. Those chargeable upon prisoners acquitted were abolished by the 55 Geo. III. c. 50, for which he is indemnified by the county. By the 57 Geo. III. c. 91, the justices of the peace for the county are authorised to settle a table of fees, to be approved by the Judges of Assize, which may not be exceeded by the Clerk of the Peace, under a penalty of 5l. If he take more than is authorised by such table of fees, he will also be liable to be proceeded against at common law for extortion, and to be removed from his office by the court of quarter-sessions. The sessions cannot, however, compel the payment of these fees by summary process, nor detain the parties until they be paid, but the Clerk of the Peace is left to his remedy by action. A bill, however, is now before parliament, by which Clerks of the Peace are in future to be remunerated by salaries, payable out of the fees collected. (Dickinson's *Quarter-Sessions;* Burn's *Justice of the Peace*)

CLERKS IN ORDINARY OF THE PRIVY COUNCIL. [PRIVY COUNCIL.]

CLERKS AND SERVANTS. [SERVANTS.]

CLIENT (Cliens), supposed by some writers to be derived from the verb *clueo*; but the derivation is somewhat doubtful. From the origin of ancient Rome, there appears to have existed the relation of patronage (patronatus) and clientship (clientela). Romulus, the founder of Rome, was, according to tradition, the founder of this system; but it was probably an old Italian institution and existed before the foundation of the city. The cliens may perhaps be compared with the vassal of the middle ages. Being a man generally without possessions of his own, the client in such case received from some patrician a part of his domains as a precarious and revocable possession. The client was under the protection of the patrician of whom he held his lands, who in respect of such a relation was named patron (patronus), *i. e.* father of the family, as matrona was the mother, "in relation to their children and domestics, and to their dependents, their clients." (Niebuhr.) It was formerly the opinion that every plebeian was also a client to some patrician; but Niebuhr, in speaking with reference to the proposition that "the patrons and clients made up the whole Roman people," affirms that the proposition is only true "if applied to the period before the commonalty (plebs) was formed, when all the Romans were comprised in the original tribes by means of the houses they belonged to." It is most consistent with all the testimony that we have, to view the Roman state as originally consisting of a number of free citizens who shared the sovereign power, and of a class of dependents, or persons in a state of partial freedom (clientes), who were attached to the several heads of houses and had no share in the sovereign power. The commonalty, or Plebs, as the writers call that class who from an early period stood in political opposition to the citizens who had the sovereign power (Patres), was of later growth, and was distinct from the Clients. The Plebeians, whatever may have been their origin, were Roman citizens, from the time that they were recognised as an order by the legislation of Servius Tullus; but they had not all the rights of the Patricians: they only attained them after a long struggle. The legislation of Servius appears also to have placed the Clients on something like the same footing as the Plebs with respect to civic rights.

There existed mutual rights and obligations between the patron and his client, of which Dionysius (*Roman Antiq.* ii. 10) has given a summary. The patron was bound to take his client under his paternal protection; to help him in case of want and difficulty, and even to assist him with his property; to plead for him and defend him in suits. The client on his part was bound in obedience to his patron, as a child to his parent; to promote his honour, assist him in all affairs; to give his vote for him when he sought any office, for it appears that the Clients had votes in the Comitia Centuriata; to ransom him when he or any of his sons was made prisoner; and to contribute to the marriage portion of the patron's daughters, if the patron was too poor to do it himself. The obligation to contribute to a daughter's portion and to ransom the patron or his sons bears some resemblance to the aids due under the feudal system. [AIDS.] The patron succeeded to his property when the client died without heirs; which was also the law of the twelve tables in the case of a freedman (*De*

Bonis Libertorum, Dig. 38, tit. 2) who died intestate and left no heir (*suus heres*). Patron and client were not permitted to sue at law, or give evidence against one another; of which an instance is mentioned by Plutarch in his Life of Marius (c. 5), though the relation of patron and client was not at that time exactly what it once had been.

The relation between patron and client was hereditary; and the client had the gentile name of his patron, by which he was united to his patron's family and to the Gens to which his patron belonged.

Originally patricians only could be patrons; but when, in the later times of the republic, the plebeians had access to all the honours of the state, clients also were attached to them.

The terms patronus and libertus, or even patronus and cliens, as used in the later years of the republic, and under the emperors, cannot be considered as expressing the same relation as the terms patronus and cliens in the early ages of Rome, though this later relation was probably derived from the earlier one. When a foreigner who came to reside at Rome selected a patron, which, if not the universal, was the common practice, he did no more than what every foreigner who settled in a strange country often found it his interest to do. The relationship existing at Rome between patron and client facilitated the formation of similar relations between foreigners and Roman citizens; the foreigner thus obtained a protector and perhaps a friend, and the Roman increased his influence by becoming the patron of men of letters and of genius. (See Cicero *Pro Archia*, c. 3, and *De Oratore*, i. 39, on the 'Jus Applicationis,' the precise meaning of which, however, is doubtful. See also Niebuhr, vol. i. p. 316, &c., and the references in the notes; and Becker, *Handbuch des Röm. Alterthums*, vol. ii.)

As a Roman client was defended in law-suits by his patron, the word client is used in modern times for a party who is represented by a hired counsellor or solicitor. The term Patron is also now in use: the present meaning of the word requires no explanation.

COAL TRADE. The quantity of

coals shipped coastwise from ports of Great Britain to other ports of Great Britain and to Ireland amounted, in the year 1843, to 7,447,084 tons; and the quantity exported to the British colonies and to foreign countries in the same year was 1,866,211 tons; making an aggregate of 9,313,295 tons of coals sea-borne from the maritime districts. The market of London alone required a supply of 2,663,204 tons, for the conveyance of which 9593 ships (which make repeated voyages) were employed. The great towns of Lancashire, of the three Ridings of Yorkshire, of Nottinghamshire, Derbyshire, Leicestershire, Warwickshire, and Staffordshire, are supplied by canals or by land-carriage from collieries in the respective counties here enumerated. In 1816 it was ascertained that the quantity of coals then sent by inland navigation and by land-carriage to different parts of the kingdom was 10,808,046 tons; and the quantity must now be very much greater, not only from the increase of population, but the growth of manufactures. The quantity used in the immediate neighbourhood of the collieries is also very great. The town of Sheffield, for example, alone requires for manufacturing and domestic purposes more than half a million of tons annually drawn from collieries on the spot; and it has been estimated that the iron-works of Great Britain, most of which are situated in spots where coal is found, require every year, for smelting the ore and converting the raw material into bars, plates, &c., nearly seven million of tons. There is good reason for believing that the annual consumption of coals within the United Kingdom is not far short of 35,000,000 tons. In 1841 the number of persons in Great Britain employed in coal-mines was 118,233. In Durham there were more persons employed under ground in coal-mines than in cultivating the surface. On the 10th of August, 1842, an act was passed " to prohibit the employment of women and girls in mines and collieries, to regulate the employment of boys, and to make other provisions relating to persons working therein." No boys can be employed under ground in any colliery who are under the age of ten. This in-

terference of the legislature was founded on an extensive inquiry by the Children's Employment Commission, which prepared three Reports that were presented parliament in 1842.

It was long considered politic to check the exportation of coals to other countries, both through fear of exhausting the mines, and because it was imagined that our superiority as manufacturers might be endangered. A heavy export duty was accordingly levied, amounting to 17s. the chaldron, Newcastle measure, or 6s. 5d. per ton upon large, and 4s. 6d. the chaldron, or 1s. 8d. per ton, upon small coals. In 1831 these duties were modified to 3s. 4d. per ton upon large, and 2s. per ton upon small coals; and in 1835 they were repealed, with the exception of an ad valorem duty of 10s. per cent.; but if exported in foreign ships not entitled to the privileges conferred by treaties of reciprocity, the duty was 4s. per ton, whether the coal was exported to foreign countries or to British possessions. In 1842 Sir R. Peel altered the duties to 2s. per ton on all large coal exported to foreign countries, and 1s. per ton on small coals and culm; but if exported in foreign ships not entitled to the privileges conferred by treaties of reciprocity, the duty was 4s. per ton on large coal, and the same on small coals, culm, and cinders. In the session of 1845 Sir R. Peel, in bringing forward the budget, announced his intention of abandoning the coal-duty; and on the 12th of March it was abolished. This duty had the effect of checking the foreign coal-trade, which had been rapidly increasing for several years, and had, in fact, trebled in amount since 1835. The duty was comparatively insignificant as a source of revenue; it led to greater activity in foreign mines, and reduced the profits of the shipper of English coal, who had to meet foreign competitors.

A considerable revenue was for many years raised from all coal carried coastwise by sea from one part of the kingdom to another. When first imposed, in the reign of William III., this tax was 5s. per chaldron, but was raised during the war of the French revolution to 9s. 4d., at which rate it was continued until 1824·

it was then reduced to 6s., and in 1831 was wholly repealed.

Although the government has remedied the evil so far as the public revenue is concerned, the consumer is still burthened in some places with local or municipal duties, &c. Thus in the city of London the corporation was empowered, by the acts 10 Geo. IV. c. 136, and 11 Geo. IV. c. 64, to levy eight pence per ton "for providing for the payment of the interest and ultimate liquidation of monies borrowed for making the approaches to London Bridge." The produce of this tax, which in 1842 was 89,642l., is mortgaged for the cost of rebuilding London Bridge and approaches. One penny per ton is levied under the act 47 Geo. III. for establishing a market for the sale of coals. This tax realized 11,521l. in 1842. It has been said that the means of establishing the Coal Market might have been provided without difficulty by a more economical management of some of the City departments; but it was an easier task to apply for an act of parliament to levy an additional tax. Under the act 1 & 2 Will. IV. c. 76, four pence per ton is levied "for metage by prescription and charters," making together 1s. 1d. per ton upon all coals brought coastwise to the port of London.

By letters patent granted by Charles II., the Duke of Richmond was entitled to receive 1s. per chaldron, Newcastle measure, on all coals shipped in the river Tyne to be consumed in England; and on the average of ten years ending 1799, the amount of that duty had been 21,000l. a year. On the 19th of August, 1799, the Treasury agreed with the duke for the purchase of this duty by an annuity of 19,000l., which sum was charged upon the consolidated fund, to be paid quarterly. The sum issued by the Exchequer at three several periods for the purchase of a perpetual annuity of 19,000l. for the duke was 490,833l.; but the sums received by the Custom House, as the representative of the Duke of Richmond, from August, 1799, up to March, 1831 when all coasting duties ceased, exceeded the payments made from the Exchequer by 315,000l. The total revenue derived from the coasting duties on coals in 1830, the year preceding its repeal, was 1,021,862l.

A very peculiar regulation has been established by the coal-owners of the northern coal-field, called the "limitation of the vend." It is important that the consumers of coal should understand the nature and effects of this restriction; and the following account of it, by G. R. Porter, Esq., is therefore given at some length. Mr. Porter says:—"The limitation of the vend has existed, with some partial interruptions, since the year 1771. This arrangement is no less than a systematic combination among the owners of collieries having their outlets by the Tyne, the Wear, and the Tees, to raise the price to consumers by a self-imposed restriction as to the quantity supplied. A committee appointed from among the owners holds its meetings regularly in the town of Newcastle, where a very costly establishment of clerks and agents is maintained. By this committee not only is the price fixed at which coals of various qualities may be sold, when sea-borne, for consumption within the kingdom, but the quantity is assigned which, during the space of the fortnight following each order or "issue," the individual collieries may ship. Upon the opening of a new colliery, the first thing to be determined is the rank or "basis" to be assigned to it. For this purpose, one referee is appointed by the owners of the colliery, and another by the coal-trade committee, who, taking into view the extent of royalty or coal-field secured, the size of the pits, the number and power of steam-engines erected, the number of cottages built for workmen, and the general scale of the establishment, fix therefrom the proportionate quantity the colliery shall be permitted to furnish towards the general supply, which the directing committee shall from time to time authorise to be issued. The point to be attained by the owners of the colliery is to secure for their establishment the largest basis possible; and with this view it is common to secure a royalty extending over from five to ten times the surface which it is intended to work, thus burthening themselves with the payment of possibly 500l. per annum, or more, of "dead rent," to the owner of the soil, who, of course, exacts such payment in return for his concession, although his tenants may have no intention of using it. Instead of sinking one or two pits, which would afford ample facility for working the quantity which the mine is destined to yield, a third and possibly a fourth pit are sunk, at an enormous expense, and without the smallest intention of their being used. A like wasteful expenditure is made for the erection of useless steam-power; and to complete and give an appearance of consistency to the arrangements, instead of building 200 cottages for the workmen, double that number are provided. In this manner a capital of 160,000*l.* to 200,000*l.* may be invested for setting in motion a colliery, which will be allowed to raise and sell only such a quantity of coals as might be produced by means of an outlay of one-fourth or one-fifth of that amount. By this wasteful course the end of the colliery owners is attained: they get their basis fixed, if it is a large concern, as is here supposed. say at 50,000, and this basis will probably secure for them a sale of 25,000 chaldrons during the year, instead of 100,000 chaldrons, which their extended arrangements would allow them to raise. The Newcastle committee meet once a fortnight, twenty-six times in the year, and, according to the price in the London market, determine the quantity that may be issued during the following fortnight. If the London price is what is considered high, the issue is increased; and if low, it is diminished. If the "issue" is twenty on the 1000, the colliery here described would be allowed to sell (20 × 50) 1000 chaldrons during the ensuing fortnight. The pit and the establishment may be equal to the supply of 3000 or 4000 chaldrons; orders may be on the books to that extent, or more; ships may be waiting to receive the largest quantity; but, under the regulation of the "vend," not one bushel beyond the 1000 chaldrons may be shipped until a new issue shall be made. By this system the price is kept up; and, as regards the colliery owners, they think it more for their advantage to sell 25,000 chaldrons at 30*s.* per chaldron than to sell 100,000 chaldrons at the price which a free competition would bring about. They may be right in this calculation; but if, under the system of restriction, any undue profit is obtained, nothing can be more certain than that competition for a portion of this undue profit will cause the opening of new collieries until the advantage shall be neutralized, and this result of the system is already fast approaching. Every new colliery admitted into the "vend" takes its share in the "issues," and, to some extent, limits the sales of all the rest. The disadvantage during all this time to the public at large is incontestable. . . . The owners of collieries, being restricted in their fortnightly issues to quantities which their establishment enables them to raise in three or four days, are naturally desirous of finding for their men during the remainder of the time some employment which shall lessen the expense of maintaining them in idleness, and spread over a larger quantity of product the fixed expenses of their establishments and their *dead rents*. To this end coals are raised which must find a sale in foreign countries; and it practically results that the same quality of coals which, if shipped to London, are charged at 30*s.* 6*d.* per Newcastle chaldron, are sold to foreigners at 18*s.* for that quantity, giving a preference to the foreign buyer of 40 per cent. in the cost of English coal. By this means the finest kinds of coal, which in London cost the consumer about 30*s.* per ton, may be had in the distant markets of St. Petersburg and New York for 15*s.* to 16*s.*, or little more than half the London price. Nor is this the worst effect of the system. In working a colliery a great proportion of small coal is raised. The cost to the home consumer being exaggerated, and the freight and charges being equally great upon this article as upon round coal, very little small coal finds a market within the kingdom, except on the spot where it is raised; and as the expense of raising it must be incurred, the coal-owners must of course seek elsewhere for a market at any price that will exceed the mere cost of putting it on board ship. By this means "nut-coal," which consists of small pieces, free from dust, which have passed through a screen, the bars of which are five-eighths of an inch apart, are sold for shipment to foreign countries at the low price of 3s. per ton. The intrinsic quality of this coal is quite as good as that of the round coal from the same pits; it is equally suitable for generating steam, and for general manufacturing purposes; and thus the manufacturers of Denmark, Germany, Russia, &c. obtain the fuel they require, and without which they cannot carry on their operations, at a price not only below that paid by English manufacturers, but for much less than the cost at which it can be raised. The coal-owner might, it is true, sell this small coal at home at a better price than he obtains from his foreign customer, but every ton so sold would take the place of an equal quantity of large coal, upon which his profit is made, and by such home sale he would by no means lessen his sacrifice, but the reverse." (*Progress of the Nation*, vol. iii. p. 98.)

Another regulation affecting the coal trade from the Tyne and the Wear has been established by act of parliament (6 Geo. IV. c. 32), under the provisions of which every ship must be loaded in her turn; and if any colliery refuse to sell, a penalty is imposed of 100l.; but this regulation may be and has been evaded by the coal-owners towards ships the owners of which refuse to be bound by their regulations in the port of discharge; and the mode of evading it is to fix an exorbitant price upon their coal, which may be done although a price below the regulation is not allowed, and by this means the vessels are either brought into conformity with the regulations in the port of discharge, or forced out of the trade. The regulations here alluded to were made in June, 1834, at a meeting of the coal-factors in London, and are to this effect:—" That whenever a greater number than eighty ships reach market on any one day, the factors shall offer them for sale according to the rotation of entry; and that not more than forty of such ships shall be offered for sale on one market-day, unless the prices of best coals be 20s. or upwards, and in that case to be at liberty to sell such further number of ships as each factor may think proper,

giving to every vessel with the same coals her fair and regular turn of sale, by which arrangements the ships will experience little or no detention, and the evil be avoided of pressing for sale at a reduced price a larger quantity of coals than the average demand of the market requires." This rule was altered as follows in January, 1835, as far as regards the number of ships the cargoes of which may be offered for sale in one market-day:—

"When the price of the best Sunderland coals has been on the previous market-day 21s. or less, the number of cargoes to be offered for sale shall be . 40
When 21s. 3d. or 21s. 6d. . . 50
21s. 9d. or 22s. . . . 60
22s. 3d. . . . . . 70."

Some alteration has since been made in this scale, but the principle is fully acted upon. Vessels loaded with coal for gas companies begin to work upon arrival, and also all vessels whose cargoes are for the use of the government.

In May, 1844, the harbour-master of the port of London presented a return to the lord mayor, which shows the operation of the regulations established by the coal-owners in the port of London for keeping up the price of coal. On the 1st of May there were 260 vessels laden with coal, detained in sections waiting their "turn" of sale. On one day in the same month, ten colliers had been detained, with their captains and crews, for forty-six days, and two had been detained above fifty days. On the 27th of May, 109 coal-laden ships were detained in sections, and the price of the best coal had advanced to 24s. and 25s. per ton, or about 34s. per ton to the consumer. "A saving of every shilling per ton on the average consumption of the metropolis is equivalent to an annual saving to its inhabitants of 150,000l." (Railway Report of Board of Trade, 28th Feb., 1845.) During the winter of 1844-5, the price of coal in London has been as high as 40s. a ton. If the " limitation of the vend" and other restrictions on the coal trade were abolished, and there was no detention and waste of time either at the port of shipment or in London, it is believed that the best coal could be brought from Sunderland into the port of London at 15s. per ton, and that 7s. per ton at the pit would be as remunerating to concerns working to their full power as 11s. with their powers limited by the vend regulations; and that a freight of six shillings per ton would be as profitable as the higher freight now paid, part of which is to cover the expense of detention.

The railways now in progress will no doubt in time have an important and most beneficial effect in reducing the price of coal in those parts of the country where it is at present so high as almost to place it beyond the reach of the poorest classes of the population. Soon after the Great North of England Railway, from Darlington to York, was opened, the price of coal at York fell to the extent of from 5s. to 10s. per ton. There will also most probably soon be a large increase in the supply of inland coal in London, as more than one of the great railway companies whose lines extend from London to the midland coal-fields have agreed to convey coal "at rates not exceeding 1d. per ton per mile, including toll and locomotive power." Thus the cost of conveying coal from the south of Staffordshire and Derbyshire will not exceed 10s. and 12s. a ton; and such coal may then be sold with a profit in London at 20s. per ton. Whether in time the opening of additional sources for the supply of coal will have an effect on the restrictions of the coal-owners of the north, cannot of course be as yet safely predicted.

The statistics of the coal-trade are given for the sake of distinctness under the following heads:—1. Coasting Trade. 2. Coal Trade of the Port of London. 3. Foreign Trade.

1. Of 7,447,084 tons of coal shipped at the several ports of the United Kingdom, to other parts of the United Kingdom, in 1843, the shipments from fifteen ports exceeded 70,000 each, viz. :—

	Tons.
Newcastle	2,289,591
Stockton	1,446,069
Sunderland	877,451
Newport	495,419
Swansea	401,893
Whitehaven	300,498
Cardiff	267,303

	Tons.
Goole	175,735
Llanelly	170,608
Irvine, N. B.	169,542
Maryport	124,700
Borrowstoness	91,174
Alloa	86,606
Gloucester	84,773
Ayr	71,015

2. The quantity of coal and the number of ships, including their repeated voyages, in which the same was brought into the port of London in each year, from 1832 to 1844, were as follows:—

Years.	Ships.	Tons.
1832	7,528	2,139,078
1833	7,077	2,020,409
1834	7,404	2,078,685
1835	7,958	2,298,812
1836	8,162	2,398,352
1837	8,720	2,626,997
1838	9,003	2,581,085
1839	9,340	2,625,323
1840	9,132	2,566,892
1841	10,311	2,909,144
1842	9,691	2,723,200
1843	9,593	2,628,520
1844	9,466	2,490,919

The monthly arrivals in the port of London in 1844 were as under; but from April to August there was a strike for wages amongst the colliers, and this circumstance affected the regularity of the supply:—

Ships.		Tons.
799	Jan.	224,633
741	Feb.	205,746
977	March	270,771
751	April	198,674
405	May	84,993
551	June	132,238
517	July	144,130
795	Aug.	192,231
1220	Sept.	319,295
1283	Oct.	337,518
1066	Nov.	296,381
291	Dec.	88,330
9466		2,490,919

The quantity which arrived by inland navigation, in 1843, was 34,684 tons.

COAL TRADE. [532] COAL TRADE.

The quantity of each particular sort of coal which arrived in the port of London is certified by the Fitters; and, in 1844, was as follows:—

	Ships.	Tons.
Newcastle Wallsend	1,428	424,548
Other Newcastle Coal	1,757	577,073
Sunderland Wallsend	2,149	611,662
Other Sunderland Coal	109	28,064
Stockton Wallsend	1,877	482,807
Other Stockton Coal	109	22,016
Scotch Coal	354	66,347
Blyth Coal	313	76,361
Yorkshire Coal	945	94,199
Welsh Coal	318	83,039
Culm	7	1,568
Cinders	54	13,150
From Sundry Places	5	424

3. In 1842 the declared value of 1,999,504 tons of coal exported to foreign countries and British possessions was 734,000*l.*; in 1843 the declared value of coal thus exported was 690,424*l.*, and in 1844 665,584*l.* In 1843 the exports of coal to foreign countries and the colonies were, 815,434 tons from Newcastle, 305,991 tons from Sunderland, and 224,593 from Stockton; or 1,346,018 out of 1,866,211 tons exported in that year.

The exports of coal to foreign countries only have been as follows in the undermentioned years:—

Years.	Tons.	Duty.
1828	228,681	£34,540
1829	244,330	37,170
1830	359,886	56,432
1831	359,039	51,082
1832	415,247	56,507
1833	449,655	64,795
1834	432,406	34,815
1835	548,574	5,340
1836	716,961	8,705
1837	865,774	10,153
1838	1,052,272	7,342
1839	1,192,896	8,587
1840	1,307,722	6,664
1841	1,500,701	10,697
1842	1,647,450	57,884
1843	1,547,297	132,609

The following table shows the principal foreign countries to which coal from the United Kingdom was exported in 1838 and 1843:—

	1838. Tons.	1843. Tons.
France	334,563	462,941
Holland	149,137	153,632
Germany	89,701	153,099
Prussia	60,401	148,197
Denmark	105,109	137,268
Russia	68,051	116,041
Spain	9,049	64,009
Italy	26,709	48,854
Turkey and Greece	33,224	41,504
United States of N. America	57,175	33,948
Foreign West Indies	7,097	30,008
Portugal	34,550	29,057
Sweden	23,690	25,961

In addition to the above, the quantity of coal exported to British possessions in the four years from 1840 to 1843 was—

	Tons.
1840	298,591
1841	347,593
1842	352,054
1843	318,914

In the last of these years the Channel Islands took 80,413 tons; the British West Indies, 74,889 tons; British North America, 67,939 tons; Malta, 37,935 tons; East Indies and China, 30,087 tons.

The quantity of coal raised in France increased 2,744,590 tons from 1814 to 1841, or 412 per cent., and between 1836 and 1841 the increase was 34 per cent. The number of mines in 1841 was 256, and the quantity raised was 13,321 tons each; in 1836 the average of each mine in France was 9863 tons. Each person employed in coal-mines (29,320) raises, on an average, 116 tons a year. The quantity raised in each of the undermentioned years was as follows:—

	Tons.
1814	665,610
1826	1,301,045
1836	2,544,835
1841	3,410,200

The export of coal from France has never reached 50,000 tons in one year. The importation has been constantly increasing, notwithstanding the great addition to the domestic supply. In 1814 the quantity of coal imported into France was 165,345 tons; 505,180 tons in 1826;

999,452 tons in 1836; and 1,619,160 tons in 1841; and of the quantity last mentioned 992,226 tons were received from Belgium, 196,502 from the Rhenish provinces of Prussia and Bavaria, and 429,950 from the United Kingdom. The import duty on sea-borne coal was reduced in 1834 from a uniform rate of fifteen francs per ton, to three, six, and ten francs per ton, according to the district into which it was imported; and on coal brought by land-carriage the duty was reduced from three francs to one-half that amount. In 1841 the increase of imports was 130 per cent., and the productiveness of the French mines had in the same time increased 65 per cent.

(*Mining Industry in France*, by G. R. Porter, Esq., F.R.S.; *Journ. of Lond. Stat. Soc.*, No. 6, 1838, and part iv. vol. vii., Dec. 1844.)

In Belgium there are 352 coal-mines. The Belgian coal is conveyed inland into France as far as Rouen, where it comes into competition with English coal. In 1834 the quantity of coal raised in Prussia was 1,810,000 tons; and in 1839 the quantity had increased to 2,442,632 tons. The coal from the Rhenish provinces comes down the Rhine into Holland, and it also enters into competition with English coal. In 1837 the produce of the coal-mines in the German Customs' Union (including Prussia) was 10,393,470 tons.

In the United States of North America there are extensive collieries in Pennsylvania. Out of 863,489 tons (of 28 bushels) of anthracite coal raised in 1840 in the North American Union, 859,686 tons were raised in Pennsylvania; and out of a total of 27,603,191 bushels of bituminous coal, 11,620,654 bushels were raised in Pennsylvania, 10,622,345 bushels in Virginia, and 3,513,409 bushels in Ohio. Nearly 7000 persons were employed in coal-mines in the United States in 1840.

CODE, CODEX. The original meaning of the Latin word Caudex or Codex was the trunk or stem of a tree. Before the use of more convenient materials, wooden tablets were employed by the ancients for writing on. Such a written tablet was called Codex, of which Codicillus is a diminutive. First they wrote by making notches or indents in these tablets, but afterwards they covered them with wax, and used a style to write with. The notion of the word was then extended, and it had several new significations. 1. Codex denoted any hand-writing on parchment, or paper, or ivory, or other material (*Dig.* 32, s. 52). 2. The diminutive Codicilli (codicil) was used in the plural number in various senses, and finally in that of a testamentary writing. 3. A collection of laws was also called Codex, and is now called a Code in modern languages, as in English and French. In this sense the word is now most commonly used. There are several kinds of codes. A code may be made by merely collecting and arranging in a chronological or systematic order the existing laws of a state, which have been made at various times by the sovereign power. Such a collection is either made by public authority, as was the case with the Codex Theodosianus and Codex Justinianeus, or by private individuals, as was the case with the Codex Gregorianus and Hermogenianus. The Germans call collections of old German laws, made in the middle ages, "Rechtsbücher" (books of law). A code (in German *Gesetzbuch*, book of laws), by which the legislative power makes a new system of laws, is very different from a compilation of existing laws. A mere arrangement and classification of existing laws is more properly called a Digest (Digesta), which is the Roman name for one of Justinian's legal compilations. If to this classification and arrangement selection be superadded, it would still be properly only a Digest. A code, though it may adopt many existing laws and customs, is now generally used to express a new system, founded on new fundamental principles; such principles, for instance, as are set forth in Bentham's 'Leading Principles of a Constitutional Code for any State.' In England, for example, if it were proposed to make a code in the modern sense, it might be found useful or necessary to modify the law of tenures, or to abolish certain kinds of tenures, such as customary tenures; and also to provide positive rules for numerous cases that are still either unprovided for or left doubtful by conflicting decisions, or decisions regarded as of little authority.

CODES, LES CINQ, is the name given to several compilations of laws, civil and criminal, made in France after the revolution, and under Bonaparte's administration. They consist of the Code Civil, Code de Procédure Civile, Code de Commerce, Code d'Instruction Criminelle, and Code Pénal. To these has been added the Code Forestier, or regulations concerning the woods and forests, promulgated under Charles X. in 1827. Hence the whole collection is sometimes called 'Les Six Codes.' But even this name is not correct, as, in addition to the six already mentioned, there are the following codes: Code Administratif; Code de l'Armée; Code des Avocats; Code de la Chasse; Code de la Contrainte par Corps; Code des Contribuables; Code des Cultes; Code Electoral; Code de l'Enregistrement (which includes the Stamp laws); Code de l'Expropriation par Cause d'Utilité Publique; Code des Frais, for regulating the official charges of courts of law; Code de la Garde Nationale; Code de l'Instruction Publique; Code Municipal et Départemental; Code des Officiers Ministériels (advocates, notaries, &c.); Code des Patentes; Code de la Pêche Fluviale; Code des Poids et Mesures; Code de la Police Médicale; Code de la Presse; Code de la Propriété Industrielle et Littéraire; Code Rural; Code des Tribunaux; Code de la Voirie (rivers, canals, highways, streets, and public vehicles). The Charte of 1830 is sometimes called the Code Politique.

Civil Code.—The old laws of the French kingdom were founded partly on the Roman law, partly on the customs of the various provinces, and partly on the ordinances of the kings. Having been abrogated at the Revolution, several attempts were made, by Cambacérès among others, to form a code adapted to the altered state of society; but the fury of the internal factions, the cares of foreign war, and the frequent changes of rulers, prevented any calm deliberation on the subject during the first years of the Revolution. After Bonaparte became First Consul, he appointed, in 1800, a commission, consisting of Tronchet, president of the Court of Cassation, Bigot de Préameneu, Portalis, and Malleville, to draw up a project of a civil code. The project was printed early in 1801, and copies were sent to the different courts of France for their observations and suggestions. The observations and suggestions were likewise printed, and the whole was then laid before the section of legislation of the council of state, which consisted of Boulay, Berlier, Emmery, Portalis, Roederer, Réal, and Thibaudeau. Bonaparte himself, and Cambacérès, his colleague in the consulship, took an active part in the debates. The various heads of the code were successively discussed, after which they were laid before the tribunate, where some of the provisions met with considerable opposition. The code, however, passed at length both the tribunate and the legislative body, and was promulgated in 1804 as the civil law of France—'Code Civil des Français.' Under the empire its name was changed into that of Code Napoléon, by which it is still often designated, though it has now officially resumed the original title of Code Civil. This code defines the civil rights of Frenchmen, and their legal relations to each other and to society at large. In its general arrangement and distribution it resembles the Institutions of Justinian. It consists of three books, divided into titles or heads, each of which is subdivided into chapters and sections. Book I., in eleven heads, treats of persons; specifies their civil rights; regulates the means by which their rights are certified; prescribes the mode of registering births, marriages, and deaths; defines the conditions which constitute the legal domicile of each individual; and provides for cases of absence. It treats of marriage as a civil contract, the forms required, the obligations resulting from it, and, lastly, of separation and divorce. The articles concerning divorce, which gave rise to much debate and opposition at the time, have been repealed since the Restoration, and separation alone is now allowed. The code proceeds to treat of the relations of father and son, of legitimate and natural children, of adoption and guardianship, and of paternal power. Under this last head, the

French code, without adopting the rigid principle of the old Roman law in its full extent, gives to a father the right of imprisoning his son during his minority for a term not exceeding six months, by a petition to that effect, addressed to the president of the local court, who, after consulting with the king's attorney, may give the order of arrest without any other judicial forms being required. The remaining heads treat of minority and emancipation; majority, which is fixed, for both sexes, at 21 years complete; of interdiction, and of trustees who are appointed in certain cases to administer the property of a man who is incapable of doing it himself. Book II. treats of property. The 1st head draws the distinction between *meubles* and *immeubles*, or personal and real property; though these two words do not exactly express, to an English lawyer, the distinction between *meubles* and *immeubles*. The 2nd defines the different rights of ownership. The 3rd treats of usufruct, use, and habitation. The 4th concerns rural servitudes, the *prædiorum servitutes* of the Roman law: all former personal servitudes were abolished at the Revolution. Book III. treats of the various modes by which property is legally acquired, such as inheritance, donation inter vivos, and wills or testaments. A father can dispose by testament of one-half of his property if he has only one legitimate child, of one-third only if he has two, and of one-fourth if he has three or more. The law then proceeds to treat of contracts, and specifies the modes of proving them by written documents, official or private, or by witnesses, or lastly by presumption. The 5th head treats of marriage, and the respective rights of husband and wife according to the terms of the marriage contract. Next come the heads of sales, exchanges, leases, partnerships, loans, deposits, and sequestration. The 12th head concerns the contracts called *aléatoires*, which depend in a great measure upon chance, such as insurance, annuities, &c. The law treats next of power of attorney, of bail and security, and of amicable compromise. The 18th head concerns privileged creditors and mortgages. This subject is very elaborately treated, and has been much extolled as a very valuable part of the Civil Code, on account of the security which it gives to property by means of the public offices for registering mortgages, of which there is one in every district. The registration of mortgages has been adopted in most of the Italian states, and other countries besides France; but even this system is not considered perfect, because there is no obligation to register every sale or transmission of property, nor the servitudes affecting property; and because the French code admits of sales by private contract, and of mortgages in favour of minors or wives, even without registration. In this particular the Austrian code is considered superior, because it enforces the registration of every transmission of property, and of every burthen or servitude, in the book of census, or cadasto, for each district. (Grenier, *Traité des Hypothèques*, 1824: *Introduction*.) The nineteenth head of the French civil code treats of expropriation or seizing, or selling off by execution; and the twentieth, or last, of prescription.

Much has been written on the merits and defects of this celebrated code. In order to judge of its value, we ought to read the reports of the discussions in the council of state by the most distinguished jurists of France. (Locré, *Esprit du Code Napoléon tiré de la Discussion*, 6 vols. 8vo., 1805; and Malleville, *Analyse raisonnée de la Discussion du Code Civil au Conseil d'Etat*, 4 vols., 8vo., 1807.) On the other side, several distinguished German jurists have pointed out its imperfections. (Savigny, *On the Aptitude of our Age for Legislation*, translated from the German by a barrister of Lincoln's Inn; Rehberg, *Ueber den Code Napoleon*, Hanover, 1814; Thibaut, Schmidt, &c.) With regard to the part which Bonaparte took in its discussion, not as a professional man, but as a quick-sighted observer and critic, a lively account is given in Thibaudeau's *Mémoires sur le Consulat*, in which his own original expressions are preserved.

Code de Procédure Civile.—The Code de Procédure is divided into two parts. The first part treats of the various courts: 1st. Of the justices of peace and their jurisdiction. There are about 2840 of these magistrates in France, whose powers are very similar to those of magistrates in England in matters of police; but they also decide petty cases not exceeding 200 francs, and in certain cases not exceeding 100 francs their decision is without appeal. They also act as conciliators between parties at variance, who are not allowed to take proceedings in a court without having first appeared before the juge de paix. 2nd. Of the process before the tribunaux de première instance, which try civil cases without jury. There is one of these courts in every arrondissement. 3rd. Of appeals to the Cours Royales, of which there are 27 established in the larger towns, each having several departments under its jurisdiction: these courts try cases by jury. 4th. Of various modes of judgment. 5th. Of the execution of judgments. The second part treats of the various processes for the recovery of property, separation between husband and wife, interdiction and cession of property by an insolvent debtor. Foreigners are excluded from the benefit of the *cessio bonorum*. The code then passes to the subject of inheritance, the affixing of seals, taking inventories, &c. The last book treats of arbitration.

The Code de Procédure was in great measure founded on the ordonnance promulgated in 1667 by Louis XIV., but with considerable ameliorations. It was framed by a commission appointed in 1800, then discussed in the council of state and the tribunate, and lastly passed by the legislative body. It was put in force in January, 1807. The expenses, duties, fees, &c. attending civil process are now regulated by the Code des Frais. The principal reproach made against the Code de Procédure is the multiplicity of formalities, written acts, registrations, stamps, &c. Another objection is, that in actions in which the state is concerned, it has advantages over private parties. But the publicity of the discussions, the security to all civil proceedings by means of registration, the well-defined authority of the various courts, the independence of the judges, and the establishment of local courts all over the country, and above all the institution of the supreme Court of Cassation—these are essential and lasting advantages.

The *Code de Commerce* was promulgated in January, 1808. It was founded in some measure upon the ordonnances of 1673-81 of Louis XIV. On account of the many modifications which the Code of 1805 had undergone, a new text of the Code was promulgated in January, 1841. The Code de Commerce is considered the best part of French legislation. The institution of the commercial tribunals has been of great advantage to France, and has been adopted in other countries. These courts, of which there are 213, consist of a president and two or more judges, all chosen by the merchants among themselves, and for a limited time; they are not paid, but the greffier or registrar receives a salary. The Code de Commerce consists of four books: the first treats of commerce in general, of the various descriptions of commercial men, of the keeping of books, of companies and partnerships, of brokers, commissioners, carriers, &c.; the second treats of maritime commerce, shipping, insurances, bankruptcy, &c.; the third concerns bankruptcies; and the fourth treats of the commercial tribunals, their jurisdiction and proceedings. By a law of April, 1838, appeals in matters above 1500 francs (formerly 1000 francs) lie to the Cour Royale of the district.

Code d'Instruction Criminelle.—The criminal laws of France under the monarchy were defective, confused, and arbitrary. There was no penal code, but there were various ordonnances for the punishment of particular offences. The ordonnance of Louis XIV. for regulating proceedings in criminal cases introduced something like uniformity, but it maintained torture and secret trial. Torture was abolished by Louis XVI. The first National Assembly in 1791 recast the criminal legislation, introduced the trial by jury, and remodelled the criminal courts after those of England. Bonaparte, when First Consul, appointed a commission, consisting of Viellard, Target, Oudard, Treilhard, and Blondel, to frame a criminal code. The fundamental laws were drawn up in 1801, and were then discussed in the council of state. Bonaparte took a lively part in these first discussions, especially on the institution of the jury, which he strongly opposed on the ground of the probable incapacity or party spirit of jurors: he looked upon the question in a political rather than a judicial light. Portalis, Simeon, Bigot de Préameneu, and Ségur sided with Bonaparte. Treilhard, Berlier, Defermon, Crétet, Bérenger, Merlin, and Louis Bonaparte defended the jury. There is an interesting account of this discussion in Thibaudeau (vol. vii. pp. 88, &c.). The question being put to the vote, the majority was in favour of the jury. The matter, however, was finally settled by suppressing the jury d'accusation, or grand jury, and retaining the jury de jugement. The jurors are taken from the electors who are qualified to vote for a member of the legislature, graduates in law, medicine, and other sciences, notaries, members of the Institute, and of other learned bodies recognised by the State, officers on half-pay who have been domiciled for five years in the department, and whose pay amounts to 1200 francs a-year, &c. A list of persons so qualified is made out by the prefect of the department, from which the President of the Cour Royale, or of the Cour d'Assise, selects the number required to serve. The proceedings in criminal trials are partly written and partly oral. The accused is first brought before the procureur du roi (king's attorney), who examines him, and simply reports the case to the juge d'instruction, without giving any opinion upon it. At the same time, if the accused is charged with a crime punishable with personal and degrading penalties, he orders his detention. For mere délits or misdemeanors, bail is allowed. The juge d'instruction summons and examines the witnesses, and then sends back the report to the procureur du roi, who makes his remarks on the case, which is then laid before the chambre de conseil, consisting of three judges of the tribunal de première instance. These judges investigate the case minutely, and decide if there is ground for further proceedings. In such case the report is laid before the chambre d'accusation, composed of five judges of the Cour Royale, who ultimately decide for commitment or acquittal. If committed for a crime punishable by peines afflictives or infamantes, the prisoner takes his trial before the next cour d'assise of the department. If for mere délit or misdemeanor, he is sent before the correctional tribunal. The courts of assize consist of two of the judges of the Court of First Instance of the town, and the president is a member of the Cour Royale of the department. Their sessions are held every three months in the chef lieu of each department. The jury vote by ballot, and decide by a majority on the fact of the charge; eight constitute a majority. The mode of voting was regulated by a new law, May, 1836. The court then awards the sentence, having a discretion between a maximum and a minimum penalty. By a law passed in 1831 the court was prohibited from setting aside the verdict of the jury and referring the case to a new trial; but by the law of September, 1835, the judges can order the case to be tried at the next assizes by a new jury, when they must pronounce sentence according to the verdict, although it may not differ from that of the first jury. The prisoner may challenge twelve jurors. One or two juges d'instruction are attached to each court of assize for criminal cases; they are generally taken from among the juges de première instance, and for a definite time only. The Code d'Instruction Criminelle consists of the following books: 1. Of the judiciary police and the various officers whose duty it is to inquire after offences, collect the evidence, and deliver the prisoners to the proper courts. These officers are very numerous, including the maires and their assistants, the commissaries of police, the rural guards and forest-keepers, the justices of the peace, the king's attorneys and their substitutes, the juges d'instruction, &c. It also treats of the manner of proceeding by the king's attorney, as already stated; and of the juge d'instruction and his functions. Book 2 treats of the various courts; tribunaux de simple police, which take cognizance of petty offences, and can inflict imprisonment of not more than five days, and a fine not exceeding fifteen francs; tribunaux en matière correctionelle, which are composed of at least three judges of the tribunaux de première instance, and take cognizance of délits or misdemeanors, the penalties for which are defined in the Code Pénal; and cours d'assise, already mentioned, from which there is an appeal for informality or want of jurisdiction to the Court of Cassation. The cours spéciales, or exceptional courts, which Napoleon insisted upon having at his disposal, and which were often resorted to after the Restoration, are abolished by Art. 54 of the Charte of 1830. These special courts were assembled in cases of armed rebellion against the authorities, and they also took cognizance of the offence of coining, and of crimes committed by vagabonds and convicts who have escaped; they were composed of a president taken from among the judges of the Cour Royale, four judges, and three military officers of the rank of captain or above. They tried without jury, judged by majority and without appeal, and the sentence was executed within twenty-four hours. The Chamber of Peers, by virtue of Art. 28 of the Charte, sits as a court of justice in matters of high treason and attempts against the safety of the State. On the subject of the Code d'Instruction, Thibaudeau observes that it retained many of the ameliorations introduced by the National Assembly, especially the publicity of trial and the institution of the jury. Its chief faults are, the great number of officers, whose business it is to follow up offenders, by which circumstance the citizens are often exposed to vexatious interference; the too great extent given to the jurisdiction of the correctional courts, by which, in many cases, the citizens are deprived of the security of the jury; the restrictions on the choice of jurors, which is too much in the power of prefects and other local authorities; and, lastly, the frequent abuse of the power of the police, by which its agents could issue warrants of arrest. This last abuse is now corrected, or at least greatly mitigated. Other provisions of the Code d'Instruction, as well as of the Penal Code, have been also altered for the better by the law of April 28, 1832, entitled 'Modifications aux Codes d'Instruction Criminelle et Pénal,' which is found at the end of the later collections of the French codes.

The *Code Pénal*, or the laws that define crimes and punishments, was completed in January, 1810. Its discussion occupied forty-one sittings of the Council of State. Of these sittings Napoleon attended only one (21st January, 1809). Cambacérès presided at all the rest. "Napoleon was therefore a stranger to its discussions; he only expressed an opinion that the laws ought to be concise, and leave much latitude to the judges and the government in the application of the penalty, 'because,' said he, 'men had feelings of compassion unknown to the law.' He insisted upon the penalty of confiscation being retained in certain cases, because most nations had sanctioned it in cases of conspiracy, rebellion, and false coining. But the definition of crimes and offences, the nature of the penalties, and the mode of their application, were the work of criminal jurists, who were generally inclined to severity, and were well acquainted with the ideas of Napoleon, who was persuaded that criminal legislation ought to be very rigorous in order to maintain order and support the authority of the government." (Thibaudeau, vol. viii. p. 3.) Hence the penalty of death was fixed in numerous cases, and those of perpetual imprisonment, hard work, or transportation for life, in a still greater number. The pillory is also one of the punishments.

If we look at book iii. ch. 1, which treats of the crimes and offences against the safety of the State (a term susceptible of indefinite and arbitrary application), we find that the penalties of death and confiscation are fixed very generally. Confiscation, however, has been abolished by a law passed under Louis XVIII. By the head "Des critiques, censures, ou provocations contre l'autorité publique dans un discours pastoral," any clergyman found guilty of having, in a pastoral charge, sermon, or other public address, spoken or printed, criticised or censured any act of the government authorities, is subject to banishment, transportation, and even death, according to the consequences which have resulted from his act. The following head, "Résistance, désobéissance, et autres manquemens envers l'autorité publique," is equally severe. The article "Délits commis par la voie d'écrits, images ou gravures, distribués sans nom de l'auteur," &c., concerns the press, which was under a strict censorship in Napoleon's time. Since the Restoration the censorship has been abolished, and several laws have been enacted to repress abuses of the press, especially in April and October, 1831. The last law on this subject was promulgated in September, 1835, and consists of five heads: 1. Crimes, délits, et contraventions. 2. Du gérant (editor) des journaux ou écrits périodiques. 3. Des desseins, gravures, lithographies, et emblêmes. 4. Des théâtres, et pièces de théâtre. 5. De la poursuite et du jugement. By the section of the Penal Code entitled "Des Associations ou Réunions illicites," which continues in force to this day, every association of more than twenty persons for the purpose of meeting on fixed days to discuss either political, religious, literary, or other subjects, is declared illegal, unless the approbation of the government is obtained, which can prescribe conditions and fix regulations at its pleasure. The chiefs or directors of any such illegal association are punished by fine. If at the meetings of such assemblies there has been any provocation to crimes or délits, as defined in the other articles of the Penal Code, the chiefs or directors and administrators are liable to imprisonment from three months to two years, besides fine, although they themselves may not have been guilty of the offence. No individual can lend his house or apartments for the meeting even of an authorized association, unless with the permission of the municipal authorities. By a law which passed the Chambers in April, 1834, the above regulations have been made even more strict. Every member of an illegal association is liable to a fine of 1000 francs, and to imprisonment from two months to one year. Under the heads "Vagabondage" and "Mendicité," vagrants are defined to be all those who have no fixed domicile nor means of subsistence, and who do not follow habitually any trade or profession. On the legal evidence of being such, they are condemned to an imprisonment of from three to six months, after which they are under the surveillance of the police for periods varying from six months to ten years. With regard to mendicants or beggars, any person found begging in a place where there is a workhouse or depôt for the poor is subject to from three to six months' imprisonment. In places and cantons where there is no depôt for the poor (which is the case in most rural districts of France), able-bodied beggars may be imprisoned for a period of from one to three months; and if arrested out of the canton where they reside, they are imprisoned for a term of from six months to two years. By Art. 402, fraudulent bankrupts may be punished by imprisonment with hard labour, and bankrupts not fraudulent are liable to imprisonment from one month to two years. Fraudulent brokers are condemned to hard work for a time. The law of France makes a wide distinction between native and foreign insolvents. Foreigners not domiciled in France, having no commercial establishment or real property there, are liable to double the period of imprisonment that a Frenchman is, but it must not exceed two years for a debt less than 500 francs; four years for a higher sum under 1000 francs; six under 3000; eight for less than 5000; and ten years for 5000 and upwards. (Okey, *Concise Digest of the Law, Usage, and Custom affecting the Commercial and Civil Intercourse of the Subjects of Great Britain and France.* There is also a useful epitome of the French law as it affects British subjects in Galignani's *Paris Guide.*) By the head "Violations des réglemens rélatifs aux manufactures, au commerce, et aux arts," any coalition between masters to lower wages is punished by a fine of from 200 to 3000 francs, besides imprisonment not exceeding a month. Coalition among workmen, followed by an attempt to stop the works of a manufactory, is punished by imprisonment of from one to three months; the leaders or originators of the coalition or attempt are subject to imprisonment from two to five years. By Art. 417, any one who, with the view of injuring French industry, has removed to a foreign country the workmen or clerks of a manufactory, may be imprisoned from six months to two years, besides paying a fine of from 50 to 300 francs. Art. 418: Any director, clerk, agent, or workman, of a manufactory, who communicates to foreigners or to Frenchmen residing abroad any secret of the fabric in which he is employed, is punished by a fine of from 500 to 20,000 francs, besides imprisonment at the discretion of the court. Art. 421: All wagers or bets upon the rise or fall of the public funds are punishable by imprisonment from one month to one year, besides a fine of from 500 to 10,000 francs. The offenders may after the expiration of their imprisonment be placed by sentence of the court under the surveillance of the police from two to five years. This sentence, "placed under the surveillance of the high or government police," which is added at the end of numerous penalties, means that the person so placed is to give security for his good conduct; in default of which he is "at the disposal of government," who may fix a particular place for his residence. All individuals who have undergone the punishment of imprisonment and hard labour for a time, or that of banishment or transportation, or those who have suffered a penalty for political crimes, are placed under the surveillance of the high police for the rest of their lives.

The above extracts are sufficient to show the spirit in which the French criminal code has been framed. It is, in fact, as harsh and illiberal in many of its enactments as that of any absolute government in Europe. In speaking therefore of Napoleon's legislation, it is necessary to discriminate between the civil and the criminal law; and again between the laws themselves and the practice and rules of proceeding in the courts. The adoption of the French criminal code met with great opposition in Italy. At Milan the legislative body attempted to modify and adapt it to the habits and wants of the Italians. Two commissions were appointed by the minister of justice, one for the code of instruction, and the other for the code pénal. Their reports were sent to Paris, but were rejected by Napoleon, and an answer came with peremptory orders to translate literally and enforce the two French codes without any alteration. At Naples similar objections were also made, but with no better effect. (Colletta, *Storia del Reame di Napoli*, book vi.)

The French code is retained in Rhe-

nish Prussia; in the kingdom of Naples with some few modifications; in the Canton of Geneva in Switzerland; and in Belgium. The commercial code and the registry of mortgages have been adopted all over Italy.

For comments and strictures by French jurists on the criminal laws of France, see Bérenger, *De la Justice Criminelle en France*, 1818; Dupin, *Observations sur plusieurs points importans de notre Législation Criminelle*; and Bavoux, *Leçons préliminaires sur le Code Pénal*, 1821.

There are in France more than 3000 judges, including those of the commercial courts, besides 2846 juges de paix. The judges of the Tribunaux de Première Instance have salaries varying from 2000 to 6000 francs; those of the Cours Royales, from 3000 to 8000. The presidents and vice-presidents receive more in proportion. The juges de paix receive about 800 francs, besides certain fees. The various courts, magistrates, greffiers, &c. cost the state about fifteen millions of francs annually. (Goldsmith, *Statistics of France*, 1832.)

For a general view of the judiciary system of France, see Meyer, *Esprit des Institutions Judiciaires*, last vol.; 'and Rey, *Des Institutions Judiciaires de l'Angleterre comparées avec celles de France et de quelques autres Etats*, 1826.

CODICIL. [CODE; WILL.]
CODIFICATION. [LAW AND LEGISLATION.]

COFFEE TRADE (French, *Café*; German, *Koffe*, *Koffebohnen*; Dutch, *Koffy*, *Koffebomen*; Italian, *Caffè*; Spanish, *Café*; Turkish, *Chaube*; Swedish, *Koffe*; Russian, *Kofé*). This great branch of commerce has been wholly created since the beginning of the eighteenth century. Nearly all the coffee which now comes to Europe is the produce of trees propagated from a single plant, which, having been raised from seed procured from Mocha in Arabia by Van Hoorn, governor of Batavia, was sent by him to the botanical garden at Amsterdam, and the progeny of which was, in the year 1718, twenty years after its reception from Java, sent to Surinam.

There is a table by Mr. M'Queen in

the appendix to the Parliamentary Report on the Produce of India, which purports to show the quantity of coffee produced in the various countries of its growth; but there scarcely exist accurate data for such information, and the table in question is confessedly only an approximative estimate. The total quantity of coffee produced in all countries is stated to be 359,000,000 lbs. (3,205,351 cwts., or 160,267 tons); but Ceylon, from which in 1844 we received 138,846 cwts., is not given in the table; and the total production of British India, from which in 1841 we imported 15,896,624 lbs., is set down at 6,245,000 lbs. The declining production of coffee in the British West Indies, though favoured by a differential duty, rendered it necessary to admit the coffee of some other region on equally favourable terms, and in 1835 East India coffee was admitted on the same terms as West India. The imports from the East Indies increased from 5,182,856 lbs. in 1835 to 15,896,624 lbs. in 1841; and the coffee of Ceylon increased from 1,870,143 lbs. in 1835 to 15,550,752 lbs. in 1844. From 1831 to 1834 the annual imports of British West India coffee averaged above 21,000,000 lbs.; and in 1841, 1842, and 1843, they did not reach 10,000,000 lbs. In 1843 they were only 8,530,110 lbs.

In 1824 the consumption of coffee in the United Kingdom was 8,262,943 lbs., and the duties were—

On foreign coffee . . 2s. 6d. per lb.
East India . . . 1 6
British West India 1 0

In 1824 there was consumed

Of foreign coffee . . 1,540 lbs.
East India . . . 313,513
West India . . . 7,947,890

In 1825 Mr. Huskisson reduced the duties on

Foreign coffee to . . 1s. 3d. per lb.
East India . . . 0 9
West India . . . 0 6

The consequence was a rapid increase in the consumption, which in 1830 was 22,691,522 lbs. In 1835 there was consumed

Of foreign coffee . . 2,126 lbs.
East India . . 5,596,791
West India . . 17,696,129

The consumption having overtaken the supply of those kinds of coffee which were admissable at the lowest rate of duty, had remained almost stationary for several years. At the end of 1835, therefore, the duty on East India coffee was reduced to 6d. per lb.; and subsequently coffee, of whatever growth, if imported from a British possession eastward of the Cape of Good Hope, or from that place, was admitted at a duty of 9d. Practically speaking, the duty on foreign coffee, instead of being 1s. 3d. per lb., became only 9d., to which 1d. must be added for the cost of additional freight from the Cape of Good Hope, whither it was sent for the purpose of being transhipped for England at a duty of 9d. instead of 1s. 3d., to which it would have been subject if imported direct. The quantity of coffee shipped for the Cape to be re-shipped for this country at the 9d. duty was estimated in 1840 at 7080 tons from Europe, 5060 tons from the foreign West Indies, 5680 tons from Brazil, and 2030 tons from Java; and the additional cost upon this quantity, in one way or other, amounted, according to Mr. Porter's calculation, to 177,000*l*. a year. He showed also that "the price of all the coffee used in this country was increased to the consumer by 28s. per cwt., the difference of duty, in addition to 13s. 7d. per cwt., the expense of sending coffee from Europe to the Cape and back." This increased price amounted to 533,227*l*., but the duty of 9d. per lb. was received only on about half the quantity imported, and the additional sum accruing to the Exchequer was only 192,416*l*.

In 1840 the consumption was as follows:—

	lbs.	Duty.
Of East and West India . .	14,443,398	0s. 6d.
Foreign . .	14,143,438	0 9
Foreign direct	77,504	1 3

By the tariff of 1842 the duties were reduced to 8d. per lb. on foreign coffee, and 4d. on coffee from British possessions.

On the 6th of June, 1844, the duty on foreign coffee was further reduced to 6d. per lb. There are now, therefore, only two rates of duty, 4d. and 6d. per lb.

The influence of high and low duties is shown with great clearness in the following table, taken from Mr. Porter's 'Progress of the Nation:'—

Years.	Number of Pounds consumed. lbs.	Rate of Duty per Pound on British Plantation Coffee. s. d.	Population of Great Britain.	Average Consumption per head. lb. ozs.	Sum contributed per Head to the Revenue. d.
1801	750,861	1 6	10,942,646	0 1·09	1¼
1811	6,390,122	0 7	12,596,803	0 8·12	4
1821	7,327,283	1 0	14,391,631	0 8·01	6
1831	21,842,264	0 6	16,262,301	1 5·49	8
1841	27,298,322	0 6	18,532,335	1 7·55	10½

The stock of coffee on hand in the following places, on the 1st of February, 1845, was as under:—

	Stock. cwts.	Importations, 1844. cwts.
Holland	847,000	1,300,000
Antwerp	140,000	500,000
Hamburg	175,000	620,000
Trieste	57,000	232,000
Havre	31,000	230,000
England	502,000	440,000
	1,752,000	3,222,000

The shipments from these ports to one another are estimated at 350,000 cwts., which reduces the total importation to 2,972,000 cwts. This does not include the whole of the supply received in Europe. Sweden, for instance, in 1840 imported 2,519,986 lbs. from Brazil. In 1835, or within a year or two of that date, the imports into Bremen were 4500 cwts.; St. Petersburg, 2000 cwts.; Denmark, 1400 cwts.; Spain (from Cuba only), 1000 cwts.; Naples and Sicily, 640 cwts.; Venice, 320 cwts.; Fiume, 170 cwts.; but in these last-mentioned places the imports were not wholly direct from the countries of production.

In the nine months ending June 30, 1843, there were imported into the United States of North America 92,295,660 lbs. of coffee, valued at 6,346,787 dollars: the importation from Brazil was 49,515,666 lbs.; from Cuba, 16,611,987; and from Hayti, 10,811,288 lbs. The quantity of coffee re-exported during the above period was 6,378,994 lbs. There is no import duty on coffee in the United States.

For the year ending 5th Jan., 1845, the consumption of coffee in the United Kingdom was 31,394,225 lbs. (19,564,082 British, and 11,830,143 foreign); the importations were—

From British possessions 24,110,283 lbs.
Foreign „ 22,410,960 „

46,521,243 „

Since 1835 we have been gradually enlarging the sources of supply, and the consequence has been increased importation and diminution of price.

The quantity of coffee re-exported from the United Kingdom in 1844 was 6,306,000 lbs., all of which, with the exception of 155,703 lbs., was foreign. Of 9,505,634 lbs. exported in 1842, Belgium took 3,709,400 lbs.; Germany, 1,005,206 lbs.; Holland, 986,122 lbs.; Italy, 926,279 lbs.; Turkey, 850,829 lbs.; and the remainder was sent in smaller quantities to thirty-one other countries.

The price of coffee in London has been gradually declining for several years, and has fallen as follows per cwt.:—

	1839. s.	1845. s.	s.	s.
Jamaica, low middling and middling	111	to 116	72	to 90
Ceylon, good ordinary		102		52
Mocha, ordinary to fine	110	135	40	90
Java		71	80	30 51
Brazil, ordinary to fine		46	53	27 66

From the above statements it will be seen that coffee is an article of the first commercial importance, and in most countries it is made to yield a considerable revenue. In Holland the duty is 3s. 4d. per 100 lbs., and there is no differential duty in favour of the Dutch colonies. In Belgium the duty is 16s. 8d. per 100 lbs.; in Austria, 42s. per 123½ lbs.; in France, 2l. 8s. to 4l. per 100 kilogrammes.

In 1835 the duty on coffee consumed in the United Kingdom was 652,123l.; 564,176l. in 1838; 373,573l. in 1840; and in the years ending 5th July, 1843 and 1844, 375,974l. and 351,101l.

Chicory and other substitutes for coffee are prohibited in several countries; but in England it is becoming an important article in commerce. In 1840 the quantity of raw chicory retained for home consumption was 3932 cwts.; and in the years ending 5th July, 1843 and 1844, 20,775 and 31,720 cwts. The duty of 20s. per cwt. was not altered by the tariff of 1842. The present value of the article is 9s. 6d. per cwt. exclusive of duty.

The effect of rendering such a beverage as coffee cheap has been attended with beneficial moral effects. In 1685 Charles II. issued a proclamation for suppressing coffee-houses, in which he speaks of "the multitude of coffee-houses lately set up in this kingdom" as being the resort of disaffected persons. The proclamation was soon withdrawn. In 1844 the number of coffee-houses in London was above 600. Thirty years ago there was scarcely one where coffee was supplied at less than 6d. a cup; and there were none to which the humbler classes could resort. There are now many houses (coffee-shops) where from 700 to 800 persons a day are served at the charge of 1d. per cup; some where 1500 or 1600 persons are served at 1½d.; and all these houses are supplied with newspapers and periodical publications for the use of the persons who frequent them. A few years ago the working classes had no other place but the public-house to which they could resort for refreshment.

COGNO'VIT is a plea, in an action at law, whereby the defendant acknowledges or confesses the justice of the plaintiff's demand against him (*cognovit actionem*). By this plea a trial is avoided and judgment is entered up for the plaintiff. But where the action is for damages, this judgment is not final, as the amount of damages remains to be assessed by a jury, under a writ of inquiry, which is executed by the sheriff, by the agency of his under-sheriff. When the jury have assessed the damages, the sheriff returns the inquisition, which is entered upon the roll in the form of a *postea*, and the judgment is then complete, the defendant's plea having already confessed the cause of action, and the damages having been assessed by a jury. If the action be for the recovery of a specific amount, as in an action of debt, the judgment entered upon a plea of *cognovit actionem* is conclusive against the defendant, as it confesses the entire declaration. On this account it is a common practice for a debtor to strengthen the security of his creditor by executing a warrant of attorney to an attorney named by the creditor, authorising him to confess a judgment by a plea of cognovit in an action of debt to be brought by the creditor against the debtor for the specific sum due to him. But in order to prevent fraud, it is provided by 1 & 2 Vict. c. 110, § 9, 10, that such warrant of attorney or cognovit is of no force unless there be present an attorney of one of the superior courts, on behalf of the party who gives it, expressly named by him, and attending at his request, to inform him of the effect of the instrument before he executes it, and who must subscribe as a witness to the execution, and declare himself to be the attorney for the party. In order to make this process effectual as against the assignees of the debtor, if he should become bankrupt or insolvent, warrants of attorney and cognovits must be filed in the Court of Queen's Bench within twenty-one days after execution, or judgment must be signed or execution issued thereon within the same period. (3 Geo. IV. c. 39; 6 Geo. IV. c. 16, § 108; 1 & 2 Vict. c. 110, § 60, 61; 6 & 7 Vict. c. 66. Harrison's *Digest of Reported Cases*, titles "Bail," "Warrant of Attorney;" Stephen's *Comm.* vol. iii. p. 634.)

COHABITATION. [CONCUBINAGE.]

COINING. The numerous and complicated laws upon this subject, passed from time to time during several centuries, to protect the coin of the realm, were repealed by the 2 Will. IV. c. 34. The operation of this statute is confined to Great Britain and Ireland; and the former are not repealed, so far as they may be in force in any part of the king's dominions out of the United Kingdom. The making or coining of money being one of the prerogatives of the crown, the counterfeiting of the king's coin was in early periods of the history of English law considered to be a usurpation upon the royal authority, and upon that principle constituted the offence of high treason both by the common law and by various statutes. By 2 Will. IV. c. 34, § 3, it is enacted, with respect to gold and silver coin, That any person falsely making or counterfeiting any coin resembling, or apparently intended to resemble or pass for, the king's current gold or silver coin, shall be liable to transportation for life, or any term not less than seven years, or to imprisonment for any term not exceeding four years. The 4th section of the act imposes the same punishment upon the offences of colouring, washing, or casing over any metal or counterfeit coin so as to pass for the genuine gold and silver coin of the realm ; and of filing, washing, or otherwise altering silver coin so as to pass for gold, or copper coin so as to pass for silver or gold. By § 5, persons impairing, diminishing, or lightening the king's current gold or silver coin, with intent to make it pass for the king's current gold or silver coin, are made liable to transportation for fourteen years, or imprisonment for three years.

By § 6 of the statute it is enacted, That if any person shall buy, sell, receive, pay or put off, any false or counterfeit coin resembling, or apparently intended to resemble or pass for, any of the king's current gold or silver coin, or offer so to do, at or for a lower rate or value than the same by its denomination imports; or if any person shall import into the United Kingdom, from beyond the seas, any false or counterfeit coin resembling, or apparently intended to resemble or pass for, any of the king's current gold or silver coin, knowing the same to be false or counterfeit, he shall be liable to be transported for life, or for any term not less than seven years, or to be imprisoned for any term not exceeding four years.

By § 7 it is enacted, That if any person shall tender, utter, or put off any false or counterfeit coin, resembling, or apparently intended to resemble or pass for, any of the king's current gold or silver coin, knowing the same to be false or counterfeit, he shall be liable to imprisonment for any term not exceeding one year ; and if any person shall tender, utter, or put off any false or counterfeit coin resembling, or apparently intended to resemble or pass for, any of the king's current gold or silver coin. knowing the same to be false or counterfeit, and such person shall, at the time of such tendering, uttering, or putting off, have in his possession, besides the false or counterfeit coin so tendered, uttered, or put off, one or more piece or pieces of false or counterfeit coin resembling, or apparently intended to resemble or pass for, any of the king's current gold or silver coin, or shall, either on the day of such tendering, uttering, or putting off, or within the space of ten days then next ensuing, tender, utter, or put off any more or other false or counterfeit coin resembling, or apparently intended to resemble or pass for, any of the king's current gold or silver coin, knowing the same to be false or counterfeit, he shall be liable to imprisonment for any term not exceeding two years. And it is further declared by the same section, that if any person who shall have been convicted of any of the offences therein before mentioned, shall afterwards commit any of such offences, he shall be liable to be transported for life, or for any term not less than seven years, or to be imprisoned for any term not exceeding four years.

By § 8 it is enacted, That if any person shall have in his custody or possession three or more pieces of false or counterfeit coin resembling, or apparently intended to resemble or pass for, any of the king's current gold or silver coin, knowing the same to be false or counterfeit, and with intent to utter or put off the same, he shall be liable to be imprisoned for any term not exceeding three years ; and if any person so convicted shall afterwards commit the like misdemeanor, or crime and offence, he shall be liable to be transported for life, or for any term not less than seven years, or to be imprisoned for any term not exceeding four years.

The above provisions relate to the protection of the gold and silver coin: by § 12 of the same statute similar provisions were made with respect to copper coin; but the penalties are transportation for seven years, or imprisonment for any term not exceeding two years.

Section 10 of the act contains a provision against making, mending, or having in possession any coining tools. The penalties are transportation beyond the seas for life, or for any term not less than seven years, or imprisonment for any term not exceeding four years.

The form of this act of parliament is a good example of the adherence to established principles. The object of the act is to protect the public interest, and to prevent people from being defrauded by the makers and issuers of base coin; and it is for the public interest that such fraud as coining should be punished with any amount of severity that is necessary to attain the object. But the offence is treated, even in the last act, as if it consisted in counterfeiting the king's coin, and not in injuring the public; and thus the legal offence is made to consist in the imitating of that coin which the king alone, by his prerogative, can make and issue; for it is an offence against the king's prerogative, whether the coin is of base metal or as good as the king's coin. The form of the act, however, accomplishes the object, just as well as if it were based on the principle of the mischief of coining; and the preservation of forms is certainly of some importance in governments of all kinds. The punishment for making coin to imitate the king's coin, even if the metal be as good as the king's, is necessary; for there would be no security for good money if anybody might make it. But some changes have been made by the act of William IV., which have brought the law nearer to its true object. Those offences against the coin which were formerly high treason are now felony; and the punishment of transportation has been substituted for the former punishment of death, a circumstance which tends to render the execution of the law more steady and efficient. [MINT.]

COLLATION. [ADVOWSON; BENEFICE, p. 340.]

COLLE'GIUM, or CONLE'GIUM (from the word Colligo, "to collect or bring together"), literally signifies any association or body of men. The word Corpus was also used in the same sense, and those who were members of a collegium or corpus were hence called corporati; from which come our terms corporation and corporators. The word Corporatio (Corporation) was also used under the Empire. The word Universitas was sometimes used as equivalent to Collegium or Corpus, but it had also the more general signification of "community," or "collective body of citizens." In the Roman polity collegium signified any association of persons such as the law allowed, and which was confirmed by special enactment or by a senatus consultum, or an imperial constitution, in which case it was called Collegium Legitimum. A collegium necessarily consisted of three persons at least. (*Dig.* 50, tit. 16, s. 85.)

In general, any association for the purpose of forming a collegium, unless it had the sanction of a senatus consultum, or of the emperor, was illegal (illicitum); but when dissolved, the members were allowed to divide the property of the association according to their respective shares. The members of a collegium were called Sodales: the terms and object of their union or association might be any that were not illegal. They could make regulations for the administration of affairs, or by-laws as we call them, provided such regulations were not contrary to law. (*Dig.* 47, tit. 22.)

A great variety of collegia (many of them like our companies or guilds) existed at Rome both before and under the empire, as we see by ancient writings and inscriptions, such as the Collegia Fabrorum, Pistorum, Pontificum, Fratrum Arvalium, Virorum Epulonum, Augurum, &c. Some of these, such as the colleges of Pontifices and Augurs, were of a religious character. These collegia possessed property as a corporate body; and in the time of the emperor M. Antoninus, if they were collegia legitima, they could take a legacy or bequest (*Dig.* 34, tit. 5, s. 20) in their corporate capacity. Collegia were allowed, as a matter of course, to have a

2 N

common chest, and an actor, syndicus or attorney, to look after their rights and interests, and appear on their behalf. (*Dig.* 3, tit. 4, s. 1.) The maxims that what was due to a university was not due to the individual members, and that the debts of universities were not the debts of the individual members, and that even though all the members were changed, the university still existed, comprehend the essential notion of a corporation as now understood. In most cases the members probably filled up vacancies in their own body.

The word Collegium was also applied to various magistrates: the Tribunes of the Plebs were called Collegium Tribunorum; and the Prætors, Collegium Prætorum. The word is also applied to the consuls, though they were only two (Liv. x. 22); and the two consuls were called Collegae with respect to one another. Varro (*Ling. Lat.* vi. 66) says that those Roman magistrates were called Collegae with respect to one another, who were elected at the same time (una lecti); and consistently with this explanation, it is stated by M. Messala (quoted by Gellius, xiii. 15), that the Censors were not colleagues of the consuls, but the Prætors were.

Besides the senses above mentioned, Collega was used to express any associate; and Collegium to express any association of individuals. Accordingly Collegia are sometimes called Societates; but the proper sense of Collegium must not be confounded with the proper sense of Societas, which is merely a partnership. The nature of Roman corporate bodies is further considered under UNIVERSITY.

In England a COLLEGE is an Eleemosynary Lay Corporation, of the same kind as an hospital, and it exists as a corporate body either by prescription or by the grant of the king. A college is not necessarily a place of learning. An hospital also is not necessarily a mere charitable endowment, but is sometimes also a place of learning, as Christ's Hospital, London.

A college is called Eleemosynary, because its object is the perpetual distribution of alms (eleemosynae) or bounty of the founder, among such persons as he has mentioned in the terms of the endowment. It is called a Lay corporation, because it is not subject to the jurisdiction of the ecclesiastical courts, or to the visitation of the ordinary or diocesan in his spiritual capacity. (Blackstone, *Comm.* i. p. 471.) These eleemosynary corporations however are generally composed of spiritual persons, and have a spiritual character; but they are considered as Lay corporations for the reason just mentioned.

The particular form and constitution of a college depend on the terms of the foundation. A college generally consists of a head, called by the various names of provost (præpositus), master, rector, principal or warden, and of a body of fellows (socii), and generally of scholars also, besides various officers or servants, according to the peculiar nature of the foundation. A college is wholly subject to the laws, statutes, and ordinances which the founder makes, and to the visitor whom he appoints, and to no others. All elections, and the general management of a college, must be in conformity with such statutes or rules. If a college does not exceed its jurisdiction, the king's courts have no cognizance, and expulsion of a member is entirely within its jurisdiction. If there is no special visitor appointed by the founder, the right of visitation, in default of the heirs of the founder, devolves upon the king, who exercises it by the great seal. When the king is founder, his successors are the visitors.

The general power of a visitor is to judge according to the statutes of a college, to expel and deprive for just reason, and to hear appeals. His precise powers are determined by the founder's statutes, and if there are any exceptions to his power, the jurisdiction in such excepted cases devolves on the king. Certain times are generally named in the statutes for visitation, but the visitor may visit whenever he is called on, for it is incident to his office to hear complaints. So long as a visitor keeps within his jurisdiction his acts cannot be controlled, and there is no appeal from him, as was decided in the well-known case of Philips *v.* Bury, or the case of Exeter College, Oxford.

(Show. P. C. 35.) A visitor is not bound to any particular forms of proceeding, and, in general, want of jurisdiction is the only ground on which he is liable to prohibition. If a visitor's power is not limited or defined, he must use his best discretion. If a power to interpret the statutes is given to any person, as to the bishop of the diocese, this will constitute him and his successors visitors. The heirs of a founder cannot alter the statutes, unless such a power is expressly reserved; and it appears, that where the king is founder, his successors cannot alter statutes without the consent of the college, unless such a power is reserved. But as to the power to alter statutes, it must be observed, that in the case of the crown at least, it has not unfrequently been done, though such a power might possibly be disputed, unless expressly reserved to the founder and his successors by the original statutes.

Whenever a visitor is appointed, the Court of Chancery never interferes with the internal management of a college; but this court exercises jurisdiction on all matters pertaining to the management of the funds, for as to the funds of a college, those who possess the legal estate are in the situation of trustees. If governors, or persons called visitors, have the legal estate, and are intrusted with the rents and profits, the Court of Chancery will make them account. In colleges, when a new foundation is engrafted on the old one, it becomes part of the old one, and subject to the same visitorial authority, unless new statutes are given with the new foundation.

The validity of all elections in colleges must be determined by the words of the founder's statutes or rules. In the disputes that have arisen on elections, the point has generally been, whether the master's concurrence is necessary, or whether a bare majority of the electors, of which electors the master is one, is sufficient. In Catherine Hall, Cambridge, fellows must be elected "communi omnium consensu, aut saltem ex consensu magistri, et majoris partis communitatis;" and it was held by Lord Eldon, upon these words and another clause which follows, that no election was valid in which the master did not concur.

The statutes of Clare Hall, Cambridge, require "that the election of a fellow shall be by the master and the major part of the fellows present;" and here it was held (A.D. 1788) that a valid election might be made without the concurrence of the master. But this interpretation is obviously wrong, and is referred to with disapprobation in the subsequent case of Queen's College, Cambridge (5 Russell).

Colleges (13 Eliz. c. 10) cannot grant leases of their land beyond twenty-one years, or three lives; and in such leases the accustomed yearly rent, or more, must be reserved, payable yearly during the term. By 18 Eliz. c. 6, in all leases made by colleges in the universities, and by the colleges of Winchester and Eton, one-third of the whole rent must be reserved in corn. The Mortmain Act of 9 Geo. II. c. 36, which has put considerable obstacles in the way of gifts of land or money to be laid out in land in England for charitable purposes, does not extend to the two universities of Oxford and Cambridge, or to colleges in the two universities, nor to gifts in favour of the scholars of Eton, Winchester, and Westminster. This statute contained a restriction as to the number of advowsons which a college in either of the universities of Oxford and Cambridge was allowed to hold; but this restriction was removed by 45 Geo. III. c. 101, having been found, as the preamble to this statute sets forth, injurious to learning. These colleges can therefore now purchase and hold as many advowsons as they please.

Of late years various places of learning have been incorporated under the name of Colleges by royal charter, such as University College and King's College, London. Both these colleges consist of a large number of shareholders or proprietors, in whom the property of the college is vested. Both these colleges are governed by a council; and King's College has also a principal, and in other respects is assimilated to the colleges at Oxford and Cambridge. University College has no principal or other corresponding officer: but it has a senate composed of the professors of the college, a president and two vice-presidents; and faculties of arts and laws, and a faculty of medicine. The constitution of King's College assimilates it to the nature of a college at Cambridge or Oxford: that of University College assimilates it more to the character of the universities of Oxford and Cambridge, which are mere civil corporations. Neither University College nor King's College confers degrees; but the students of both colleges may take degrees in the University of London, subject to certain regulations. The College of Physicians in London, and the College of Surgeons, are also instances of civil corporations established under the name of colleges; and the Herald's College is another.

A Collegiate Church is a church that has a college or chapter of canons, but no bishop, and yet it is said to be under the authority of a bishop. But in the case of Manchester College, a mandamus from the Court of King's Bench was directed to the Bishop of Chester, as warden of Manchester College, to admit a chaplain. The bishop happened also to be visitor of the college. It was held by the King's Bench, that in the case of a spiritual corporation the jurisdiction was in that court, unless there was an express visitor appointed, and the court interposed in the present case, because there was no separate visitorial power then existing, owing to the union of the wardenship and visitorship in the same person. This case was afterwards provided for by an express act, 2 Geo. II. c. 29. The canonists require three canons at least to constitute a collegiate church, because three, according to the Roman law, were required to make a college. These collegiate churches are sometimes simply called colleges, and were formerly more numerous. Westminster, Windsor, Eton, Winchester, Southwell, and Manchester are collegiate churches. Probably schools were always a part of such foundations: those of Eton, Westminster, and Winchester have flourishing schools.

As to the relation between the English universities and the colleges within their limits, see UNIVERSITY.

The statutes of all the old colleges in England are in Latin; and, indeed, with the exception of some comparatively modern endowments, probably all college statutes are in Latin. Those of Eton College, of Trinity College, Cambridge, and of St. John's College, Cambridge, which may serve as specimens of the statutes of such foundations, are printed in the Education Reports of the House of Commons, 1818.

Meiners (*Geschichte der Enstehung und Entwickelung der Hohen Schulen*, &c., Göttingen, 1802, vol. i.) has given an interesting chapter on the origin of colleges in universities. The colleges in the University of Paris were the first institutions of the kind in Europe, though it is a mistake to suppose them older than the university itself.

The terms College and University have been often confounded in modern times, and indeed are now sometimes used indiscriminately. Some of the incorporated places of learning in the United States, which confer degrees, are called universities, and some are called colleges, though there is in fact no distinction between the two. Some of these institutions called colleges contain the schools or departments of arts, law, medicine, and theology; and some that are called universities contain only those of arts, law, and medicine. Some of these colleges are more limited as to the objects of instruction, but still they confer degrees. If we look to the origin of colleges and their connexion with universities, it will be evident that the indiscriminate use of these terms is incorrect, and tends to lead to confusion. When an incorporated college, such as the College of Surgeons in London, is empowered to confer a degree or title after examination of candidates, some other name would be more appropriate. According to modern usage, the term university is properly applied to corporate bodies which confer degrees; and this is the title by which the University of London, which is empowered to confer degrees in arts, law, and medicine, is incorporated. It is convenient at present to distinguish colleges as places of learning which do not confer degrees, from universities which do. The word Academia, though an old Greek word,

COLONEL. [549] COLONEL.

is the most modern of all the terms now applied to places of higher instruction: it has been most usually applied to endowed corporate bodies which have for their object the improvement of some particular science or some particular branch of knowledge, in some cases with the power to confer degrees in such particular science, &c., and sometimes without this power. Yet the terms academia and university have often been used, and now are used indiscriminately. (Meiners, vol. iv., *On the Different Names of High Schools*.)

The history of the Scotch universities shows that the terms college and university were, both at the time of the foundation of these institutions and subsequently also, used with little discrimination; and this carelessness in the application of the terms has led to anomalies in their constitution, and no little difficulty in comprehending the history and actual constitution of these bodies. (See the *Report of the Royal Commission of Inquiry into the State of the Scotch Universities*, printed 1831; and Malden's *Origin of Universities*, London, 1835.)

In France, the term college signifies a school, though the constitution of a French college is very different from that of our grammar-schools. It comes nearest, perhaps, to a German gymnasium. Of these colleges there are about 320, every large town having one of them. They are maintained by the towns, and the heads and professors are paid out of the revenues of the communes. They are all under the superintendence of the University of France. There are also about forty royal colleges, in which the directors (*administrateurs*) and professors are paid by the state. The College Royal of France, founded by Francis I., has above twenty professors, who lecture on the various sciences and the Oriental languages. (See *Journal of Education*, No. III. 'On the State of Education in France.')

COLLEGE. [COLLEGIUM.]

COLONEL, the commander of a regiment or battalion of troops; he is the highest in rank of those called field-officers, and is immediately subordinate to a general of division.

The derivation of the word is uncertain. It is supposed to have been given originally to the leader of a body of men appointed to found a colony; or to have come from the word *coronarius*, indicating the ceremony of investing an officer with the command of a corps; or, finally, from the word *columna*, denoting the strength or support of an army.

The title of colonel-general was, for the first time, conferred by Francis I., about the year 1545, on officers commanding considerable divisions of French troops, though, according to Brantome, it had been given to the chief of an Albanian corps in the service of France at an earlier period. When the troops of that country were formed into regiments (the infantry about 1565, and the cavalry seventy years afterwards), the chiefs of those corps were designated *Mestres de Camp*; and it was not till 1661, when Louis XIV. suppressed the office of colonel-general of infantry, that the commanders of regiments had the title of colonel.

In England, the constitution of the army was formed chiefly on the model of the French military force; and the terms regiment and colonel-general were introduced into this country during the reign of Elizabeth. It must, morever, be observed, that in the regulations made by the citizens of London for forming the militia in 1585, it is proposed to appoint *colonels* having authority over ten captains; and that both colonels and lieutenant-colonels are distinctly mentioned in the account of the army which was raised in order to oppose the threatened invasion of the country in 1588. Before the time of that queen, it appears that the commanders of bodies of troops equivalent to regiments had only the general title of captain.

The duties of colonels are described in Ward's 'Animadversions of Warre,' which was published in 1639; and from the account there given, it appears that those duties were then nearly the same as they are at present. To the colonel of a regiment, besides the general superintendence of the military duties performed by the troops composing it, is intrusted the care of providing the clothing of the men and of appointing the agent through whom their pay is transmitted. Colonels take precedence of one another according to the dates of their commissions, and not according to the seniority of their regiments.

The lieutenant-colonel is immediately under the full colonel. He assists the latter in directing the evolutions of the battalion or regiment, which he also commands during the absence of his superior officers.

If appointed after 31st March, 1834, the annual pay of a colonel is, in the Life and Horse Guards, 1800*l*. without other emolument; but in all other regiments the colonel derives emoluments from clothing. The annual pay, exclusive of these emoluments, is—in the Grenadier Guards, 1200*l*.; in the Coldstream and Scots Fusilier Guards, 1000*l*.; in the cavalry regiments generally, 900*l*.; and in the regular infantry, 500*l*. The sum voted for the full pay of 135 colonels, in 1845, was 88,450*l*. The daily pay of a lieutenant-colonel is—in the Life Guards, 1*l*. 9*s*. 2*d*.; in the Foot Guards, 1*l*. 6*s*. 9*d*.; in the Royal Artillery, 1*l*. 7*s*. 1*d*. in the Horse Brigade, and 18*s*. 1*d*. in the Foot; in the Royal Engineers, 18*s*. 1*d*. and 16*s*. 1*d*.; and in the Royal Marines and in the Infantry, 17*s*. The full pay of 176 lieutenant-colonels was 59,180*l*. in 1845. The half-pay of a colonel of cavalry is 15*s*. 6*d*., and of infantry 14*s*. 6*d*. per diem. A lieutenant-colonel of cavalry receives 12*s*. 6*d*., and of infantry, 11*s*.; and in the Artillery and Engineers, 11*s*. 8*d*. For prices of commissions see COMMISSION.

In February, 1845, there were in the British army 374 colonels and 697 lieutenant-colonels.

COLONIAL AGENTS. Most of the British colonies have agents in England, whose duties do not appear to be very accurately defined. The act of 1843, appointing an agent for Jamaica, recites, "that it is necessary the inhabitants of this island should have a person in Great Britain fitly qualified and fully empowered to solicit the passing of laws and to transact other public matters committed to his care for the good of the island." In this case the salary of the agent is 1000*l*. per annum. A person called "the agent-general" acts for the crown colonies; but where there is a local legislature the appointment is generally made by it. Previously to the separation of the North American colonies most of them had a special agent in England for the management of their affairs, to whom a salary was given. They were appointed by the Assemblies, and sometimes confirmed by the governor. Sometimes, as in Massachusetts, the legislative council and the Assembly had each its own agent. The persons generally selected were distinguished lawyers or merchants, usually the former, and often members of parliament. William Knox, under-secretary of state, was agent for Georgia in 1764; John Sharpe, M.P., was agent for Massachusetts in 1755; Charles Garth, M.P., acted for South Carolina from 1765 to 1775, and his correspondence during this period contains a full account of the proceedings of the Imperial Parliament. Richard Jackson, M.P., acted for Connecticut, Massachusetts, and Pennsylvania, about the year 1774. Edmund Burke was appointed agent, by the House of Assembly alone, for New York, December 21, 1770, with a salary of 500*l*. a year, and continued to act until 1775, when all intercourse with the colony was suspended. The House of Assembly of Lower Canada several times appointed special agents, the last of whom was Mr. Roebuck, M.P., who in that capacity, but not at the time an M.P., was heard at the bar of both Houses of Parliament in opposition to the Bill to suspend the constitution of Lower Canada. (Pamphlet *On the Nomination of Agents formerly appointed to act in England for the Colonies of North America*, 1844.)

CO'LONY (in Latin Colonia, a word derived from the Latin verb 'colo,' 'colere,' to till or cultivate the ground) originally signified a number of people transferred from one country or place to another, where lands were allotted to them. The people themselves were called Coloni, a word corresponding to our term colonists. The meaning of the word was extended to signify the country or place where colonists settled, and is now generally applied to any settlement or land possessed by a sovereign state upon foreign soil. Thus Ceylon and the Mauritius are called British colonies, though they are not solely colonized by Englishmen, the former being chiefly inhabited by natives, and the second by French or descendants of French colonists and Africans. The present notion of the word "colony" (as determined by the general use of the term) seems to be a foreign country, either wholly or partly colonized, that is to say, possessed and cultivated by natives, or the descendants of natives, of another country, and standing in some sort of political connection with and subordination to the mother country. The notion of a British colony implies that the waste lands belong to the British crown. The continental possessions called British India are not a colony: the island of Ceylon is a colony.

The formation of colonies is among the oldest events recorded in history or handed down by tradition. Maritime states, such as those of Phœnicia and of Greece, which possessed only a scanty territory, would have recourse to emigration as their population increased. In both these countries the sea afforded a facility for transferring a part of their superabundant citizens, with their families and movables, and their arms, to some foreign coast, either uninhabited or thinly peopled by less civilized natives, who, by good will or by force, gave up to them a portion of their land. The emigration might be voluntary or forced; it was sometimes the result of civil contentions or foreign conquest, by which the losing party were either driven away, or preferred seeking a new country to remaining at home. The report of some remote fertile coast abounding in valuable productions would lead others to emigrate. Lastly, the state itself having discovered, by means of its merchants and mariners, some country to which they could trade with advantage, might determine upon sending out a party of settlers, and might establish a factory there for the purpose of sale or exchange. In fact, commercial enterprise seems to have led both to maritime discovery and to colonization as much as any one single cause. Such seem to have been the cause of the numerous Phœnician colonies which, at a very early date, were planted along the coasts of the Mediterrannean. Tyre itself was a colony of Sidon, according to the 'Old Testament,' which calls it the "daughter of Sidon." Leptis Magna, near the great Syrtis, was also a colony of Sidon, according to Sallust (*Jugurth.* c. 78). Hippo, Hadrumetum, Utica, and Tunes, were Phœnician colonies, and all of greater antiquity than Carthage, which was subsequently settled by Phœnicians in the neighbourhood of Tunes. The Phœnician colonies extended along the north coast of Africa as far as the Pillars of Hercules (the Straits), and along the opposite coast of Spain, as well as to the Balearic Islands, and Sardinia and Sicily. Those on the Spanish coast seem to have been at first small settlements or factories for the purpose of trade between the metropolis or mother country and the natives. Several of them, however, such as Gades (the site of the modern Cadiz), became independent of the mother country. The foundation of Carthage was an instance of another kind. It resulted, according to tradition, from an emigration occasioned by the tyranny of a king of Tyre.

Of the early settlements in the islands of the Ægean Sea we have only traditions referring to times previous to the war of Troy. Thucydides (i. 4) says that the Carians inhabited the Cyclades islands, and carried on piracy, until Minos, king of Crete, drove them away and planted new colonies. Thucydides does not mention the Phœnicians as occupying the Cyclades, but he speaks of the islands of the Ægean generally as possessed by Carians and Phœnicians, who carried on piracy; and he adds that they settled on most of the islands (i. 8). Herodotus (ii. 44; vi. 47) also states that the Phœnicians had once a settlement in the island of Thasus, where they worked the gold-mines. They also had a settlement on the island of Cythera (Cerigo), which lay conveniently for their trade with the Peloponnesus. (Herodotus, i. 105.) Thucydides (vi. 2) mentions that the Phœnicians formed establishments on the promontories and small islands on the coast of

Sicily, from which they traded with the native Siculi; but that when the Greeks came to settle in great numbers in that island, the Phœnicians abandoned several of their posts, and concentrated themselves at Motya, Soloeis, and Panormus, now Palermo (which must have then had another name, for Panormus, or Allport, is Greek), near the district occupied by the Elymi or Phrygian colonists (who had emigrated from Asia after the fall of Troy, and had built Entella and Egesta), trusting to the friendship of the Elymi, and also to the proximity of these ports to Carthage. These three Phœnician settlements merged afterwards into Carthaginian dependencies. The Phœnicians appear also to have occupied Melita or Malta, and the Lipari Islands, one of which retained the name of Phœnicusa. Of the Carthaginian settlements in Sardinia we have the report of Diodorus (v. 13) and a fragment of Cicero *Pro Scauro*, published by Mai. (Compare Pausanias, x. 17; Strabo, p. 225, ed. Casaub.) Caralis (Cagliari) and Sulchi were Carthaginian settlements. A Phœnician inscription was found in a vineyard at Cape Pula, belonging to the monks of the order of Mercy, and was explained by De Rossi, ' Effemeridi Letterarie di Roma,' 1774. But the chief field of Phœnician colonization was the north coast of Africa. There the Phœnician settlements seem to have been independent, both of the mother country and of each other. We have the instance of Utica and Tunes, which continued separate communities even after Carthage had attained great power, Carthage only exercising the hegemony, or supremacy. This seems to have been the case among the original Phœnician towns; Sidon, Tyre, Aradus, and others, each a distinct commonwealth, formed a sort of federation, at the head of which was the principal city, at first Sidon, and afterwards Tyre. A feeling of mutual regard seems to have prevailed to the last among the various Phœnician towns and colonies, including Carthage, as members of one common family.

The colonies established afterwards by the Carthaginians in the interior as well as on the coast of Africa, Sicily, and Spain, were upon a different plan from those of the Phœnicians: they were made through conquest, and for the purpose of keeping the country in subjection, like those of the Romans, with the remarkable exception of the colonies planted by Hanno on the west coast of Africa.

The earlier Greek colonies appear to have owed their origin to the same causes as those of the Phœnicians. Thucydides (i. 12) says, that after the Trojan war, and the subsequent conquest of Peloponnesus by the Dorians, Greece, being restored to tranquillity, began to send out colonies. The Athenians, whose country was overflowing with people from other parts of Greece, who had flocked thither for security, began to send out Ionians, as Thucydides terms the settlers in the country in Asia called after them Ionia, and to many of the islands: the Peloponnesians sent theirs to Italy, Sicily, and some parts of Greece. The Dorians from Megaris, Argos, Corinth, and other places, colonized some of the larger islands, part of Creta, Rhodes, Corcyra, as well as Ægina, Cos, and other islands. They founded the Hexapolis on the south-west coast of Caria, in Asia Minor, which district took from them the name of Doris. A colony of Lacedæmonians founded Cyrene. The Megarians founded Chalcedon, Byzantium, Selymbria, Heraclea, and other places on the coasts of the Euxine. Sicily also was chiefly colonized by Dorians. Syracuse was a Corinthian colony, which afterwards founded Acræ and Camarina; Gela was a colony of Rhodians and Cretans, and Agrigentum was a colony from Gela. The Megarians founded Selinus. The Chalcidians built Naxus, which was the first Greek settlement in Sicily, and afterwards took Leontini and Catana from the Siculi. For a more detailed account of the numerous Dorian colonies, see K. O. Müller's ' History of the Doric Race.'

The Ionians from Attica, who emigrated to the west coast of Asia Minor, which took from them its name Ionia, established there twelve cities or communities, which quickly rose to a high degree of prosperity, and formed a kind of federal union. These Ionians who settled in Asia were a mingled people, of whom the Ionians who emigrated from Athens considered themselves the best part. They gave the name Ionia to their new settlements in Asia from the country in the Peloponnesus, once called Ionia, and subsequently Achæa, from which they had been driven by Achæans who settled there. As the Ionians consisted of twelve states in their old country, so they made twelve states in their new settlements. (Herodotus, i. 143, &c.) Four generations before the Ionian emigration, according to Strabo (p. 582, ed. Cas.), the Æolians and some Achæans, two nearly allied races, being driven away from part of the Peloponnesus by the Dorians, had emigrated to the coast of Asia Minor, where they formed colonies from Cyzicus on the Propontis as far southwards as the Hermus. Phocæa was the most northern of the Ionian towns, and it was on the borders of Æolis. The Æolians also colonized the islands of Lesbos, Tenedos, and others in that part of the Ægean. These emigrations were posterior to the time of Homer, who mentions other people as occupying that coast. The Athenians at a later date colonized Eubœa, where they founded Chalcis and Eretria; and they also sent colonies to Naxos, to the islands of Ceos, Siphnos, Seriphos, and other islands of the Ægean. Many of these colonies, having thriven and increased, became colonizers in their turn. The enterprising mariners of Phocæa formed various colonies, the most celebrated of which is Massilia (Marseille), on the south coast of Gaul. Miletus, also one of the Ionian cities, was the parent of numerous colonies, many of which were on the south coast of the Black Sea. The Chalcidians of Eubœa founded Cumæ, on the west coast of Italy, in the country of the Opici. Pirates from Cumæ founded Zancle in Sicily, on the Straits of Messina; but a fresh colony of Samians and some Milesians escaping from the Persian invasion, in the time of the first Darius, B.C. 494, took Zancle, and were afterwards in their turn dispossessed by Anaxilas, tyrant of Rhegium, who called the town Messene (now Messina), from the name of his original country in the Peloponnesus. The Æolians founded Dicæarchia, afterwards Puteoli, in Italy, and they, with the Cumæans, are supposed to have founded Parthenope (Naples).

The Greek colonies on the east coast of Italy, setting aside the confused traditions of Arcadian and other immigrations, consisted chiefly of Dorians and Achæans from the Peloponnesus. Croton, Sybaris, and Pandosia were Achæan colonies. Tarentum was a colony of Lacedæmonians, and Locri Epizephyrii of the Locrians. Greek colonies were settled both on the north and east sides of the Pontus (Black Sea), and also on the north coast and in the modern Crimea. Many of them, as already observed, were Milesian colonies.

The relation which subsisted between the Greek colonists and the prior inhabitants of the countries which they occupied, was undoubtedly in most cases that of conquerors and subjects. Either the natives withdrew into the interior and left the ground to the new occupants, as the Siculi did in several instances, or they resisted, in which case, when overpowered, the men were exterminated or reduced to slavery, and the conquerors kept the women for themselves. In some instances the older inhabitants were reduced to the condition of serfs or bondmen to the new settlers. The records of authentic history do not present us with an instance of any colony being settled in a country where there were not previous inhabitants. The consequence of the immigration of a new race, who seek to possess themselves of the land, must be the extermination or gradual decay of the prior race, unless the old inhabitants are made slaves. So far as we trace the history of Greek colonies in the scattered fragments of antiquity, such were the consequences of their colonial settlements. On the coast of Italy it would appear that the Greeks pursued a more humane or more politic course. They are said to have allied themselves to and intermarried with the natives, and by their superior civilization to have acquired great influence. It may here be remarked that the Greeks, so far from being averse to foreign intermixture, as some have said, mingled their blood freely with that of all the nations with whom they came into contact, and thus the civilization of the

Hellenic stock was gradually introduced among nations less advanced in the useful arts.

The relations between these Greek colonies and the mother country, and between those colonies that were of a kindred race, may be gathered pretty clearly from Thucydides (i. 24, &c.). Epidamnus was a colony of Corcyra: but the leader of the colony (οἰκιστής), the founder of the colony, or the person under whose conduct it was settled, was a Corinthian, who was called or invited, says Thucydides, from the mother city (called by the Greeks the metropolis, μητρόπολις, or parent state), according to an ancient usage. Thus it appears that if a colony wished to send out a new colony, this was properly done with the sanction of the mother country. Some Corinthians and other Dorians joined in the settlement of Epidamnus, which became a thriving community, and independent both of Corcyra and Corinth. In the course of time, however, civil dissensions and attacks from the neighbouring barbarians induced the Epidamnians to apply to Corcyra, as to their metropolis, for assistance, but their prayers were not attended to. Being hard pressed by the enemy, they turned themselves to the Corinthians, and gave up their town to them, as being the real founders of the colony, in order to save themselves from destruction. The Corinthians accepted the surrender, and sent a fresh colony to Epidamnus, giving notice that all the new settlers should be on an equal footing with the old settlers: those who did not choose to leave home were allowed to have an equal interest in the colony with those who went out, by paying down a sum of money, which appears to have been the price of allotments of land. Those who went out gave their services; those who stayed at home gave their money. "Those who went out," says Thucydides, "were many, and those who paid down their money were also many." For the moneyed people it was in fact an affair of pure speculation. The Corcyræans, themselves originally a colony from Corinth, having become very powerful by sea, slighted their metropolis, and "did not pay to the Corinthians the customary honours and deference in the public solemnities and sacrifices, as the other colonies were wont to pay to the mother country." They accordingly took offence at the Corinthians accepting the surrender of Epidamnus, and the result was a war between Corcyra and Corinth.

Again, the Corcyræan deputies, who were sent to seek the alliance of the Athenians against Corinth, stated in answer to the objection that they were a colony of Corinth, that "a colony ought to respect the mother country as long as the latter deals justly and kindly by it, but if the colony be injured and wrongly used by the mother country, then the tie is broken, and they become alienated from each other, because, said the Corcyræans, colonists are not sent out as subjects, but as free men to have equal rights with those who remain at home." (i. 34.) This shows the kind of relation as understood by the Greeks between the metropolis and its colonies. The colonies were in fact sovereign states, attached to the mother country by ties of sympathy and common descent, so long as those feelings were fostered by mutual good-will, but no further. The Athenians, it is true, in the height of their power, exacted money from their own colonies as well as from the colonies of other people, and punished severely those who swerved from their alliance, such as Naxos; but this was not in consequence of any original dominion as supposed to belong to the mother country over the colony. Many of the colonies, especially the earlier ones, which were the consequence of civil war or foreign invasion, were formed by large parties of men under some bold leader, without any formal consent being asked from the rest of the community: they took their families, their arms, and their moveables with them, to conquer a new country for themselves; they left their native soil for ever, and carried with them no political obligations. Those that went off in more peaceful times, by a common understanding of the whole commonwealth, went also away for ever, freely and voluntarily, though under a leader appointed by the parent state, to seek a country where they could find an easier subsistence than at home. In either case it was a complete separation of a member from the body. Such were the proper colonists (ἀποικίαι) of the Greeks; but they were not colonies in the modern sense of the word, nor colonies in the Roman sense. We have derived from the Romans the name of colony, and our colonies resemble theirs in a great degree, and bear no resemblance to the so-called Greek colonies. Indeed, the Greek colonies should be called by another name; and the word "foreign settlements," or the German term "auswanderung," comes nearer to the sense of Apoikia (ἀποικία) than the term colony. When the Athenians, in later times, took possession of parts of Euboea (Thucyd. i. 114), and of Aegina (ii. 27), of Melos (v. 116), and shared the lands among their own citizens who went there, the relationship thus formed was of a different kind, and came nearer to the nature of a Roman and a modern colony. Yet Thucydides calls the settlers in Melos, Apoikoi (ἄποικοι); but the name Cleruchi was usually given to such settlers: and their allotments were called Cleruchiae (κληρουχίαι). In the case of Aegina the whole population, which was of Hellenic stock, was turned out, and a body of Athenians occupied their place, with the express object of being as a body or community subordinate to the state of Attica, in order to prevent the annoyance to which Attica had long been subject by the proximity of an independent island so well situated both for the purpose of annoying Attica and for self-defence. The relation between the settlers called Cleruchi and the parent state of Athens appears not to have been always the same; that, in some cases at least, they retained all the privileges of Athenian citizens is sufficiently clear. Of these Athenian settlements the earliest is the instance mentioned by Herodotus (v. 77), which belongs to the last part of the sixth century B.C., of the settlement of four thousand Athenians in Chalcis on the conquered lands. The system subsequently was extended to other places, as appears from the passages above referred to; and, among other places, the island of Lesbos received Athenian settlers. (Thucydides, iii. 50.) The battle of Aegospotami (B.C. 401) deprived the Athenians of their foreign dependencies, though they were partially recovered. But Athens never succeeded in establishing a system of colonies on a sure and lasting basis, as the Romans did.

That the Greek settlements of a kindred race should feel a common interest in opposition to those of a rival branch is natural, and is proved, among other instances, by the case of the deputies from Egesta in Sicily, who, while requesting the assistance of the Athenians against the Syracusans and Selinuntians, urged as an additional plea that the Leontines, who were originally Chalcidians, and therefore akin to the Athenians, had been expelled from their town by the Syracusans, and showed that it was the interest of the Athenians to assist a kindred people against the prevailing power of the Dorian colonies in Sicily. (Thucyd. vi.)

Before we pass to the Roman colonies, we must say something of the system of colonization among the other inhabitants of the Italian peninsula in the ante-Roman times. The Etruscans extended their conquests north of the Apennines in the great plain of the Po, and founded there twelve colonies, the principal of which was Felsina (Bologna). Afterwards, having defeated the Umbrians, many years before the assumed foundation of Rome, they extended themselves into East and South Italy, penetrated into Latium, and took Campania from the Oscans, where they founded likewise twelve colonies, the principal of which was Capua. The Etruscans, being skilled in architecture, surrounded their towns with solid walls built of massive stones without any cement; they were also well versed in agriculture and hydraulics, and several of the earliest drains and canals in the Delta of the Po are attributed to them. They subjected, but at the same time civilized, the people among whom they settled. Their colonies seem to have formed independent communities, though allied by a kind of federation. The Etruscans also founded colonies in the Picenum, such as Hatria, Cupra Montana, and Cupra Maritima. They took from the Ligures the country around the gulf now called Della Spezia, and founded the city of Luna. They likewise sent colonies to the islands of Elba and Corsica, for the Etruscans were a commercial as well as agricultural people; they navigated the sea, and in the sixth century B.C. they defeated the Phocæans, and drove them out of Corsica. The Etruscans contributed to civilize Italy by means of their settlements; but, unlike Rome, they did not keep them united under a central power.

The Sabini, an agricultural and pastoral people, lived in the Apennines of Central Italy, and occupied part of the modern Abruzzi: they sent out colonies in very early times to other parts of Italy. It was a custom common among many of the old Italians, after the lapse of a certain number of years, to celebrate solemn sacrifices in the spring season, and to consecrate to the gods a number of young men, who were to quit their native land, and proceed under the auspices of Heaven to seek a new country. (Dionysius, *Roman Antiquities*, i. 16.) In this manner the Piceni and the Samnites are said to have been colonies of the Sabini. The Samnites in their turn sent out other colonies, and the Lucanians were one of these. The Samnites, as well as the Sabini, were entirely given to agricultural pursuits.

Rome, in the earliest ages, adopted the system of sending out colonies to those parts of Italy which she conquered. Colonies were established during the kingly period (Livy, i. 11, 27, 56); and the practice was continued after the expulsion of Tarquinius Superbus, the last king (Livy, ii. 21, 39). But the Roman colonies were different from those of most other people, inasmuch as they remained strictly subject to the mother country, whose authority they were the means of enforcing upon the conquered nations. They were, in fact, like so many garrisons or outposts of Rome. Servius (Æn. i. 16) gives the following definitions of a colony, taken from much older authorities:—"A colony is a society of men led in one body to a fixed place, furnished with dwellings given to them under certain conditions and regulations." Again, "Colonia is so called a colendo; it consists of a portion of citizens or confederates sent out to form a community elsewhere by a decree of their state, or with the general consent of the people from whom they have departed. Those who leave without such a consent, but in consequence of civil dissensions, are not colonies." The notion of an early Roman colony was this: the colonists occupied a city already existing; and this, with perhaps one exception or two, was the general character of the early Roman colonies in Italy. These colonists were a part of the Roman state; they secured her conquests and maintained the subject people in obedience. When the Romans afterwards extended their conquests into countries where there were no regular towns, or where the population was fierce and hostile, and the Roman settlers must be ever on their guard against them, they built new towns in some favourable position. Such was the case in several parts of Gaul, Germany, and Spain. The first Roman colony beyond the limits of Italy was that founded on the site of Carthage, in the tribunate of Caius Gracchus, B.C. 122. This colony, which was originally called Junonia, did not succeed, or was neglected, owing to the dissensions at Rome: it was restored, or finally established, by C. Julius Cæsar. (Plutarch, *Caius Gracchus*, c. 11.) Narbo Martius, Narbonne in the south of France, was one of the early colonies beyond the limits of Italy. The early Roman colonies then in Italy consisted of Roman citizens, who were sent as settlers to fortified towns taken in war, with land assigned to them at the rate generally of two jugera of arable land or plantation for each man, besides the right of pasture on the public or common land. The old inhabitants were not ejected, or dispossessed of all their property; the general rule was, that one-third of the territory of the town was confiscated and distributed among the colonists, and the rest was left to the former owners, probably subject to some charges in the shape of taxes or services. The colonists constituted the *populus* of the captured place; they alone enjoyed political rights and managed all public affairs. The ownership of the publicum or public property, including the pasture land, was probably also vested in the new settlers. It is natural to suppose, that for some generations at least, no great sympathy existed between the old and the new inhabitants, and hence we frequently hear of revolts of the colonies, which means, not of the colonists against the mother city, but of the old inhabitants, who rose upon and expelled the colonists. (Livy, ii. 39; vi. 21.) But these events generally ended by a second conquest of the place by Roman troops, when the old inhabitants were either put to the sword or sold as slaves, or, under more favourable circumstances, lost at least another third of their property. In later times, during the Civil Wars of Rome, which commenced with the disputes between Marius and Sulla, new colonies were sent by the prevailing party to occupy the place of the former ones; and the older colonists were then dispossessed of their property either wholly or in part, just as they had dispossessed the original inhabitants. Sometimes colonies, especially at a great distance from Rome, having dwindled away, or being in danger from the neighbouring people, asked for a reinforcement, when a fresh colony was sent, which also received grants of land. (Livy, ii. 21; vi. 30; xxxi. 49.) Each of the older colonies, it is observed by Gellius (xvi. 13), was a Rome in miniature; it had its senators called Decuriones, its Duumviri, Ædiles, Censores, Sacerdotes, Augurs, and other officers.

A distinction must be made between Roman colonies and Latin colonies. The citizens who went out to form a Roman colony retained all their civic rights, although Sigonius and some others pretend that they lost the franchise (jus suffragii); and yet, in various passages of Livy and elsewhere, colonists are styled cives and Romæ censi. The members of Roman colonies which were called Latin (Coloniæ Latinæ), had not the Roman citizenship, and those Roman citizens who went out in such a colony thereby lost their suffrage; they voluntarily renounced part of their civic rights in consideration of a grant of lands. The practice was for those persons who were willing to join a colony, to give in their names at Rome, and as the consequence of joining a Latin colony was a loss of civic rights, Cicero (*Pro Cæcina*, c. 33) argues that the joining such colony must be a voluntary act. There is also no reason for supposing that the joining of a Roman colony was compulsory; and if it was, it follows from what has been said, that a Roman colonist retained his civic rights. These Latin colonies were Roman colonies, inasmuch as they were subject to the Roman state; and hence they are sometimes called Roman colonies, which in one sense they were. But as opposed to Roman colonies which consisted of Roman citizens (Coloniæ civium), they were called Latin colonies, by which term was denoted their political condition. Before the Social War (B.C. 90), the following was the classification of people in the Roman dominions:—

1. Cives Romani, Roman citizens, that is, the inhabitants of Rome, the citizens of the Coloniæ Civium or proper Roman colonies, and the citizens of the Municipia without reference to the stock to which they belonged.

2. Latini, or the citizens of the old towns of the Latin nation, with the exception of those towns which were raised to the rank of Municipia; and also the numerous and important Coloniæ Latinæ.

3. Socii (Allies), the free inhabitants of Italy who did not belong to the two classes first enumerated, and belonged to very various national stocks.

4. Provincials: the free subjects of the Romans beyond the limits of Italy.

This is the division of Savigny (*Zeitschrift für Geschichtliche Rechtswissenschaft*, xi. 6); and it appears to be consistent with all the best ancient authorities. He adds that as to the political condition of the people included under these four heads, those included under the first head, Cives Romani, were alone Cives; those included under the three other heads were Peregrini (aliens). According to this view, the members of Latin colonies before the Social War were simply subjects of the Roman state: they had none of those political capacities which were the characteristics of Roman citizenship. As the term Peregrinus, however, was very comprehensive, and included all who were not Cives, it follows that, according to this view, the Latinæ Coloniæ and foreigners not under Roman dominion were precisely on the same footing as to the privileges of Roman citizens; but their condition differed in this, that foreigners (aliens, properly so called) were not Roman subjects, but the members of Latin colonies were. This view is perhaps on the whole right, yet the inhabitants of Latin colonies were in a sense Cives, as contrasted with foreigners not subject to Rome, though they were not Roman citizens, in the sense of those who had all the capacities of Roman citizenship.

The result of the Social War was, that the Roman citizenship (civitas) was given to all the inhabitants of Italy south of the Po: all became Romani Cives; and the Latini—the inhabitants of Coloniæ Latinæ—and the Socii were all merged in the class of Cives. The distinction of Romani Cives and Peregrini still subsisted; but the class of Roman citizens had become enlarged. A new class of persons was now established, and distinguished by the name of Latini. This term now did not denote a particular people, but a political status—an imperfect citizenship, by virtue of which this new class had the right of acquiring property (commercium) just like Roman citizens; but they had not the connubium, or civic right of contracting such a marriage as would be a Roman marriage; in other words, a Roman citizen who married a woman in the condition of a Latina, was not according to Roman law the father of his children, and the children consequently were not Roman citizens. But in certain cases, a Latinus might acquire the Roman citizenship, for instance, by holding the high offices in his city. This rule was first established for the people north of the Po, and then given to many towns, and to large tracts out of Italy. The privilege of thus acquiring the Roman citizenship was the Jus Latii (Appian, *Civil Wars*, ii. 26), or Latinitas (Cicero, *Ad Atticum*, xiv. 12); and it was given to some towns founded after the Social War, as Novum-Comum, which was founded in Italy north of the Po, by C. Julius Cæsar, B.C. 59. The privilege which the Romans sometimes conferred on a town or district, under the name of Jus Italicum, was a different thing from the Jus Latii. "It had no reference to the status of individuals, but to the condition of many communities. When a Provincial town received as a special favour by a Privilegium those rights which were the peculiar privileges of the Italian towns, this favour was called Jus Italicum. It consisted of three things: a free constitution, with the choice of their own magistrates, such as are mentioned in the Italian Municipia and Colonies (Duumviri, Quatuorviri); exemption from land-tax and poll-tax; the capacity of the land within the limits of the community to be held in Roman ownership (ex jure Quiritium), and the consequent application to such land of the Roman rules of law, as to Mancipation and Usucapion." (Savigny, *Zeitschrift*, &c., xi.)

The correctness of this view of the nature of the Coloniæ Latinæ, the Latinitas, and the Jus Italicum, will hardly be disputed now.

The Roman Agrarian Laws, or the laws for the distribution of public land, were often passed with the view of founding a colony: and this became a usual mode of providing for veteran soldiers. Perhaps one of the earliest instances is mentioned by Livy (xxxi. 4). The senate passed a decree for the measurement and distribution of public land in Samnium and Apulia among those veteran soldiers who had served in Africa under P. Scipio. But after Sulla had defeated his opponents, the grants of lands to soldiers became more common, and they were made to gratify the demands of the army, at the cost of former settlers, who were ejected to make way for the soldiers. Julius Cæsar and Octavianus Augustus added to the number of these military colonies, and the practice of establishing them in parts beyond Italy existed under the Empire.

These colonies are distinguished by having military ensigns on their coins, while the Coloniæ Togatæ, or citizen colonies, have a plough on theirs. The coins of some colonies have both marks, which means that the original colony consisted of citizens, after which a second was sent, composed of soldiers. In Tacitus (*Annal.* i. 17), the veterans complain that, after their long service, they were rewarded only with lands situated in swampy tracts or on barren mountains.

The early system of colonies adopted by Rome had a double political object; to secure the conquered parts of Italy, and to satisfy the claims of its own poorer citizens by a division of lands among them. The importance of the Roman colonies is well expressed by Cicero, who calls them "propugnacula imperii et speculæ populi Romani." Such they doubtless were, and at the same time, by their extension beyond Italy, they were the germ of the civilization of Northern and Western Europe. A nation of civilized conquerors, whatever evils it may inflict, confers on the conquered people greater benefits. By their colonies in Spain, Gaul, on the banks of the Rhine, and in Britain, the Romans established their language and their system of administration. The imprint of their Empire is indelibly fixed on all the most civilized nations of Europe.

The difference between a Roman Colonia and an Italian Municipium is, that the latter was a town of which the inhabitants, being friendly to Rome, were left in undisturbed possession of their property and their local laws and political rights, and obtained moreover the Roman citizenship, either with or without the right of suffrage; for there were several descriptions of Municipia. The Roman colonies, on the contrary, were governed according to the Roman law. The Municipia were foreign limbs engrafted on the Roman stock, while the colonies were branches of that stock transported to a foreign soil. There is, however, some difficulty as to the precise character of an Italian Municipium in the republican period of Rome; and the opinions of modern writers are not quite agreed.

The Roman Provincial system must not be confounded with their Colonial system. A Roman province, in the later sense of that term, meant a country which was subjected to the dominion of Rome, and governed by a praetor, propraetor, or proconsul sent from Rome, who generally held office for a year, but sometimes for a longer period. Thus Spain, after the Roman conquest, was a Roman province, and was divided into several administrative divisions. The earliest foreign possession that the Romans formed into a province was Sicily (B.C. 241). Sardinia (B.C. 235) became a Roman province, and the system was extended with the extension of the Roman power to all those parts of Europe, Asia, and Africa which were subjected to Roman dominion. A province was originally a foreign dependency on Rome; after all Italy became Roman, at the close of the Republican period, we may view all the provinces of Rome as foreign dependencies on Italy, of which Rome was the capital. The condition of the provinces, viewed as a whole, with respect to Rome was uniform: they were subject countries, subject to the ruling country, Italy. But the condition of the towns in the provinces varied very greatly: some had the Jus Italicum, or privilege of Italian towns, in the sense already explained, and these were probably in most cases settlements of Roman citizens; some towns retained most or perhaps all of their old privileges; and others were more directly under the Roman governor. Thus while the whole country was a dependency on Rome, particular cities might have all the privileges of Italian cities; and others would be in a less favoured condition. Both under the Republic and the Empire, but still more under the Empire, the Romans established colonies both of Roman citizens and Latin colonies, in their provinces; and in this way they introduced their language and their laws. Tracts of land were doubtless seized as public land and distributed from time to time, but there does not appear to have been any claim on all the lands in any province, as lands that the Roman state might distribute, though undoubtedly the theory under the Empire was that all land in the provinces belonged to the Cæsar or the Roman state (Gaius, ii. 7). And this theory would have a practical effect in all cases where an owner of land died and left no next of kin, or anybody who could claim his land. The maxim also implied the duty of obedience to the Roman state, and that rebellion or resistance to the Romans would at once be a forfeiture of that land which was held by provincials, according to this theory, as a precarious possession. But the Romans never gave the name of Colony to any of their Provinces. There were Roman colonies in Britain, but Britain itself was not a Colony; it was a Province. In modern usage, whenever the word colony is applied to a country, it includes all the territory of such country.

The Northern tribes who overthrew the Western Empire did not found colonies; they overran or conquered whole provinces, and established new states and kingdoms. The same may be said of the Saracen conquests in Asia and Africa. But, after a lapse of several centuries, when Europe had resumed a more settled form, the system of colonization was revived by three maritime Italian republics, Pisa, Genoa, and Venice. Their first settlements on the coasts of the Levant and Egypt were mercantile factories; which the insecurity of the country soon induced them to convert into forts with garrisons, in short into real colonies. The Genoese established colonies at Famagosta in Cyprus, at Pera and Galata. opposite to Constantinople, and at Caffa in the Crimea, in 1266; they also acquired possession of a considerable extent of coast in that peninsula, which was formed into a district subject to Genoa under the name of Gazaria. Another tract, on the coast of Little Tartary, called Gozia, was also subject to the Genoese, who had there the colony of Cembalo. In the Palus Mœotis they had the colony of La Tana, now Azof. On the south coast of the Euxine they possessed Amastri; they had also a factory with franchises and their own magistrates at Trebizond, as well as at Sebastopolis. These colonies were governed by consuls sent from Genoa, and the order and justice of their administration have been much extolled. In the archives of St. George, at Genoa, there is a valuable unpublished MS. containing the whole colonial legislation of the Genoese in the middle ages.

The Pisans, having taken Sardinia from the Moors, sent colonies to Cagliari and other places. Their settlements in the Levant were mere commercial factories.

The Venetians established colonies in what are now called the Ionian Islands, and in Candia and Cyprus. Their system resembled that of Rome; by means of their colonies and garrisons they governed the people of those islands, whom they left in possession of their municipal laws and franchises. These were not like the settlements of the Genoese, merely commercial establishments — they were for conquest and dominion; in fact, Candia and Cyprus were styled kingdoms subject to the Republic. The Venetians had also at one time factories and garrisons on various points of the coasts of the Levant, but they lost them in the Morea, Eubœa, Syria, and the Euxine, either through the Genoese, or afterwards by the arms of the Ottomans. We can hardly number among their colonies the few strongholds which they had until lately on the coast of Albania, such as Butrinto, Prevesa, and Parga, any more than those once possessed by the Spaniards and Portuguese on the coast of Barbary, Oran, Melilla, Ceuta, and others. They were merely forts with small garrisons, with no land attached to them. The name used in the Mediterranean for such places is presidii; and they are often used as prisons for criminals.

An essential qualification of a Colony in the Roman sense, and in the present sense of the word is, that it should have land, and contain a body of settlers who are cultivators. The question agitated in France, with regard to Algiers, turned upon this,—whether the French were merely to occupy the towns on the coast as military and in some degree commercial colonies, or to establish an agricultural colony in the interior, by taking possession of and cultivating the land. This question touches several points both of justice and policy. When a colony is sent to a country occupied by a few hunting tribes, as was the case in North America when the English settled there, and as is now the case in New Holland, taking possession of part of the land for the purpose of cultivation is attended with the least possible injury to the aborigines, while, at the same, it has in its favour the extension of civilization. [CIVILIZATION.] The savages generally recede before civilized man; a few of them adopt his habits, or at least the worst part of his habits, and the rest become gradually extinct. When the limits are confined, the progress towards extinction is exceedingly rapid. The aborigines of Van Diemen's Land having been reduced to a very small number, were wholly removed to a small island in Bass's Straits; and there is every probability that their race will soon be extinct. This has been, from the earliest times, the great law of the progress of the human race. But the case is much altered when the natives are partly civilized, have settled habitations, and either cultivate the land or feed their flocks upon it. The colonists in such case do what the Romans did in their colonies; they take part of the arable land, or the whole of the common or pasture land, and leave to the natives just what they please, and if the natives resist they kill them. Such was the system pursued by the Spaniards in various parts of America, by the Dutch at the Cape of Good Hope and the Molucca Islands, and by all maritime nations in some part or other of Asia, Africa, or America; and this is now done by the French against the Arabs and Kabyles of the state of Algiers. The French have sent numerous colonists to Algiers, and among the colonists are many old soldiers who have received a grant of lands after the Roman fashion. The case may be one of greater or less oppression: according as the land is either enclosed and cultivated, or merely used for pasture or the chace; and according as the natives are more or less numerous in proportion to the land, colonization may proceed on a milder or harsher system. The system of purchase from the natives has been practised both by the English and Anglo-Americans in North America; but though it has the specious name of bargain, it has often been nothing more than a fraud, or sale under compulsion. The man of Europe has been long accustomed to regard the possession of the soil as that which binds him to a place, and gives him the most secure and least doubtful kind of property. His habits of accumulation, and of transmitting to his children a permanent possession, make him covet the acquisition of land. In whatever country he has set his foot, and once got a dominion in the soil, neither contracts, nor mercy, nor feelings of humanity, nor the religion which he carries with him, have prevented him from seizing on the lands of the natives, and punishing their resistance with death. British colonization is at present conducted on principles more consistent with justice and humanity, as we see in the case of New Zealand. [CIVILIZATION.]

European colonies in Asia and America have been formed partly on the Roman or Venetian and partly on the Genoese or old Phœnician principle. When the Portuguese first began their voyages of discovery in the fifteenth century, they took possession of some islands or points on the coasts of Africa and of India, and left there a few soldiers or sailors under a military commander, who built a fort to protect the trade with the natives, and afterwards also to keep those natives under a sort of subjection. No great emigrating colonies were sent out by them, except in after times to Goa and the Brazils, which latter is really a colony of Portuguese settlers. The Spaniards, on the contrary, when they discovered America, took possession of the soil, and formed real colonies kept up by successive emigrations from the mother country. In the West India Islands the natives were made slaves, and by degrees became extinct under an intolerable servitude. On the mainland they were exterminated in some places, and in others reduced to the condition of serfs or tributaries. The Spaniards colonized a great part of the countries which they invaded. The Spanish American colonies had for their objects both agriculture and mining. The English North American colonies were the consequence of emigration, either voluntary or produced by religious persecution and civil war at home. The Puritans went to New England, the Quakers to Pennsylvania, and the Cavaliers to Virginia. They formed communities under charters from the crown, and local legislatures, but were still subject to the sovereignty of the mother country. The mother country sent its governors, and named, either directly or indirectly, the civil functionaries. The precise amount of obedience that the colonies then owed to the mother country cannot be exactly defined. The American revolution only showed that it did not extend to a certain point, without showing how far it did extend.

A new feature has appeared in modern European colonization, that of penal colonies, which was an extension of the principle of the presidii on the coast of Barbary, already mentioned. Convicts were sent by England first to North America, and afterwards to New Holland, by France to Guiana, by Portugal to the coast of Angola, and by the Dutch to Batavia. They were either employed at the public works, or hired to settlers as servants, or were established in various places to cultivate a piece of land, for which they paid rent to the government. The policy of penal colonies has been much discussed. They may afford a temporary relief, but at a great cost to the mother country, by clearing it of a number of troublesome and dangerous persons, especially so long as criminal legislation and the system of prison discipline continue as imperfect as they are at present in most countries of Europe; but with regard to the convicts themselves, and the prospect of their reformation, everything must depend upon the regulations enforced in the colony by the local authorities. If we look, however, at the horrid places of confinement to which convicts are sent by most continental governments, and which are sinks of every kind of corruption and wretchedness, we cannot help feeling disposed to think more favourably of such colonies, under proper management, and to prefer the penal colonies of Great Britain to such ill-regulated places of punishment, which do not even affect to be places of reformation. [TRANSPORTATION.]

The advantages which may result from colonies to the mother country appear to be, the extension of the manufactures and the trade of the mother country by the demand for home products which arises in the colonies, the consequent impulse given to industry in the mother country, and the opportunities which industrious labourers and small capitalists have of mending their condition by emigrating to a country where labour is wanted, and where land can be had at a moderate price. The establishment of a colony draws capital from the mother country, which is a disadvantage to the parent state, unless the colony also draws off superabundant labourers; and without a due supply of labour the exportation of capital to a colony is unproductive to the colony, while it diminishes the wealth and the productive power of the parent state. If a colony is to be a matter of expense to the state, if the administration of it is to be maintained entirely or in part at the expense of the mother country, that is a direct loss to the parent state. And if, in order to support such colony, or the interests of any body of persons that are connected with it, the trade of the mother country is encumbered by regulations which diminish the free interchange of commodities with other countries, and render foreign products dearer to the citizen of the parent state, that is another manifest loss to the parent state. The history of modern colonization, on the whole, shows that the parent states have sustained great loss by the system of colonization that has been adopted; but it cannot therefore be inferred that colonization may not be placed on such a footing as will make it both advantageous to the parent state, and to those who live in the colony under its protection.

Much has been written upon this subject by political and economical writers, and the advantages of colonies have been exaggerated by some, and too much underrated by others. In a general point of view, as connected with the progress of mankind, a busy prosperous colony on a land formerly desert is undoubtedly a cheering sight. Commercial colonies or factories are likewise useful for protecting traders in remote and half-barbarous countries.

The Colonies of England are mentioned subsequently.

France has the French West India Islands, and French Guiana in America; Senegal, on the coast of Africa; the island of Bourbon; Pondicherry, in the East Indies; and Algeria, on the north coast of Africa.

Spain has lost her vast dominions in Mexico and South America, but has retained the fine islands of Cuba and

Puerto Rico; she has also the Philippine Islands.

Portugal has lost the Brazils, but has still numerous settlements on the coast of South and East Africa, at Angola, Benguela, Loango, and on the Mozambique; but these settlements are the most degenerated of all European colonies. In India, the Portuguese retain Goa, and they have a factory at Macao, and a settlement on the northern part of the island of Timor.

The Dutch have the islands of Curaçao and St. Eustaz, and Surinam in Guiana. In Asia they have the great colony of Batavia with its dependencies, various settlements on the coasts of Borneo, Sumatra, Celebes, and the Molucca islands.

The Danes are possessed of the islands of St. Cruz and St. Thomas in the West Indies; Christianburg, near Accra, on the Guinea coast; and Tranquebar in the East Indies.

The Swedes have the island of St. Bartholomew in the West Indies.

A society of North American philanthropists has founded, since 1821, on the Guinea coast, a colony of emancipated negroes, who have been transferred thither from the United States. The colony is called Liberia.

On the subject of modern colonies, Raynal, *Histoire des Etablissemens des Européens dans les deux Indes,* may be useful, though it is often exaggerated and turgid; but the best authorities are the original accounts of the various discoverers and founders of the colonies, such as have been published by Navarrete for the Spanish, and Barros for the Portuguese.

England was not the first among European nations that planted settlements in parts beyond Europe. But by her own colonization, and by the conquest of the settlements of other nations, she has now acquired a more extensive dominion of colonies and dependencies than any other nation.

The *English Colonies* have, as a general rule, local legislatures, elected by the people, and a governor and executive council named by the crown. In New South Wales, which obtained a legislative council in 1842 (5 & 6 Vict. c. 76), twelve of the thirty-six members are appointed by the crown and the remainder are elected by the people. The colonies which are governed by the secretary of state for the colonies without the interference of a local legislature are termed Crown Colonies. In such colonies there is an executive council, which consists partly of *ex-officio* members who hold offices at the pleasure of the crown, and partly of persons selected from among the principal inhabitants, who are likewise removable at pleasure. The foreign commerce of these colonies is regulated by the sovereign parliament of the mother country, and put on such a footing as generally to allow the products of the colonies admission into British ports on more favourable terms than the like products of other countries. To the amount of this protecting duty, the colonies then have the advantage of a monopoly in the markets of the mother country. The old strict colonial system of excluding foreign countries from direct commercial intercourse with the colonies, had the double object in view of securing all the supposed advantages of the exchange of British for colonial products, and giving employment to the British merchant navy. The rigour of this system, however, has gradually relaxed, and given way to clearer views of self-interest. Still the colonial system, as maintained by Great Britain, presents in many instances examples of foreign possessions which are expensive to the country without any equivalent advantages; and also of foreign possessions the trade with which is so regulated as to be designedly put on a footing which shall be favourable to the colony and unfavourable to the parent state. This is effected by discriminating or differential duties, as they are termed, the effect of which is to make the consumer of sugar (to take that as an example) in Great Britain pay to the favoured colonists a sum equal to the difference between the duty on colonial sugar and the higher duty on other sugar. The mother country which imposes this additional duty to protect her colonial subjects, not only gets no revenue by such ill-timed partiality in favour of her foreign dependencies, but she loses the increased revenue that she might have,

2 o 2

if she would allow her own people to buy foreign sugar on the same terms as the sugar of the colonies.

The direct expenditure in some of the colonies for the purposes of administration is beyond the means of the colonial revenues to meet, and the deficiency must of course be supplied by the parent state. Colonial possessions put some amount of patronage at the disposal of the home government, and colonies are therefore looked upon as profitable things by those who participate in the advantages of posts and places in them. On the other hand, those who only contribute to these expenses may reasonably ask for some proof of solid advantage to the parent state in return for the deficiency which she supplies. Setting aside the interests of those concerned in the administration of the colonies, it is asked, in many cases, what advantage does the rest of the nation receive? So far as some colonies may be desirable posts for protecting British commerce and shipping, the advantage of maintaining them may be fully equivalent to the expense. But in every particular instance the question as to the value of a modern colony to the mother country (omitting, as before mentioned, the value of the patronage to those who confer places in the colonies, and the value of the places to those who receive them) is simply this;—what advantage is this said colony to the productive classes of the country? a question not always easy to answer; but this is the question, the solution of which must decide whether a colony ought to be maintained or not, if we look only to the interests of the mother country. If we look to the interests of the colony, it may be in many, and certainly is in some cases, the interest of the colony to remain as it now is, under the protection and sovereign authority of the mother country; for it is protected at little or no cost to itself, and it often gets commercial advantages which, if the relationship to the mother country were to cease, would cease with it. But again the question recurs, what is the advantage to the mother country? If some advantage cannot be shown, the maintenance of a useless colony is a pure act of national benevolence towards the colony and to those few of the mother country who have places or property in it. If our present relation with a colony such as Jamaica or Canada entails any expense on the mother country, we may ask whether all the commercial advantages that result from this relation, whatever they may be, would not be equally secured, if only a free commercial relation existed, and that of administration were to cease. In support of this view, it is shown that the commerce of Great Britain with the United States, now free and independent, has increased most wonderfully since the separation, and probably more rapidly than it would have increased under the colonial system. This being the case, a similar increase might be anticipated in the trade with all those foreign possessions whose trade is really of any importance. This argument, to which it is difficult to reply, is met by saying that if we give up those colonies that cause expenditure on the part of the mother country, some of them at least would be a prize for other nations, who would exclude us from the commerce of those former colonies, or allow it only on unfavourable terms; or that these colonies would throw themselves into the arms of foreign nations, and the same result would follow. To this it is replied, that no other nation is in a condition to take on itself the management of expensive colonies; that nations, like individuals, will, if let alone, buy where they can buy cheapest, and sell where they can sell dearest; and that if we should be shut out from the commerce of any of our present colonies, there are equally good or better markets from which we are now in part or altogether excluded owing to those very regulations, which only exist because we have colonies to maintain.

The colonial administration of the British colonies is an important department of the general administration. At the head of it is the principal colonial secretary.

Historical and Statistical View of British Colonies, &c.

The word Colony is not applicable to all the foreign possessions of Great Britain. Gibraltar, Malta, and Heligoland may be more correctly termed Possessions, Port Essington, on the northern coast of Australia, is a Settlement; British India is a Dependency, and so likewise are the Channel Islands and the Isle of Man; Van Diemen's Land, New Zealand, &c. are Colonies. The seven Ionian Islands are under the protection of Great Britain. Tenasserim, Singapore, Penang, Malacca, Aden, and some other places, are Dependencies of the East India Company. The Chatham Islands are Dependencies of New Zealand, and Norfolk Island of Van Diemen's Land. In the British Colonies the waste lands belong to the British Crown, and they are now disposed of by sale only, under one tolerably uniform system. The mode in which these lands are sold, and leased, or depastured under licences, and the mode in which emigration to them is now conducted, are considered under the head of EMIGRATION.

I. Date of Capture, Cession, or Settlement.

Canada, capitulation, 18th Sept. 1759, and 8 Sept. 1760, and cession by treaty, 1763.

New Brunswick, Nova Scotia, Cape Breton, Prince Edward's Island, and Newfoundland—fisheries or settlements, established soon after their discovery in 1497.

Antigua, settlement, 1632.
Barbados, settlement, 1605.
Dominica and Grenada, ceded by France, 1763.
Jamaica, capitulation, 1655.
Montserrat, settlement, 1632.
Nevis, settlement, 1628.
St. Kitt's, settlement, 1623.
St. Lucia, capitulation, 22 June, 1803.
St. Vincent and Tobago, ceded by France, 1763.
Tortola and Anguilla, settlement, 1666.
Trinidad, capitulation, 18 Feb. 1797.
Bahamas, settlement, 1629.
Bermudas, settlement, 1609.
British Guiana, including Demerara, Essequibo, and Berbice, capitulation, September, 1803.
Honduras, treaty, 1670.
Gibraltar, capitulation, 4 Aug. 1704.
Malta and Gozo, capitulation, 5 Sept. 1800.
Cape of Good Hope, capitulation, 0 Jan. 1806.

Sierra Leone, settlement, 1787.
Gambia, settlement, 1618.
Gold Coast, African Forts, 1618.
Ascension Island, taken possession of by permission of Spain, 1827.
Fernando Po, taken possession of, 1815.
Ceylon, capitulation, 17 Sept. 1795.
Mauritius, capitulation, 3 Dec. 1810.
New South Wales, settlement, 1787.
Van Diemen's Land, settlement, 1803.
Western Australia, settlement, 1829.
South Australia, settlement, 1834.
New Zealand, settlement, 1839.
Falkland Islands, taken possession of, 1833.
St. Helena, ceded by Holland, 1673.
Hong-Kong, treaty, 1842.

The immense territory in North America which lies north of the British Colonies, and extends to the Pacific, where it is bordered on the north-west by the Russian possessions, and on the south by the Territory of the United States, is administered by the Hudson's Bay Company under a charter. Another vast territory in North America, which lies between the Rocky Mountains and the Pacific, and is called the Oregon Territory, is claimed by Great Britain as far south as the Columbia river; but it is partly occupied by citizens of the United States, and partly by British subjects; and there are conflicting claims between the two governments as to the right of sovereignty.

II. Population of the principal British Colonies in 1842, or according to the latest census.

Eastern (Lower) Canada	678,590
Western (Upper) Canada	486,055
New Brunswick . .	156,142
N. Scotia and C. Breton	178,237
Prince Edward's Island	47,034
Newfoundland . .	75,094
Antigua . .	36,405
Barbados . .	122,198
Dominica . .	18,291
Grenada . .	29,650
Jamaica . .	377,433
Montserrat . .	7,119
Nevis . .	7,470
St. Kitt's . .	21,578
St. Lucia . .	21,001
St. Vincent . .	27,248

COLONY. [566] COLONY.

Tobago	..	18,208
Tortola	..	8,500
Anguilla	..	2,934
Trinidad	...	60,319
Bahamas	..	25,244
Bermudas	..	9,930
Demerara and Essequibo, and Berbice	..	102,354
Honduras	..	10,000
Gibraltar	.	11,318
Malta and Gozo	.	118,759
Cape of Good Hope	.	159,451
Sierra Leone	..	39,839
Gambia	..	4,495
Ceylon	..	1,421,631
Mauritius	..	174,699
New South Wales	.	130,856
Van Diemen's Land	.	50,216
Western Australia	.	3,476
South do.	.	15,527
New Zealand	..	17,000
St. Helena	..	4,834

III. Form of Government.

By a Governor, Legislative Council, and Assembly.

Canada	Jamaica
New Brunswick	Montserrat
N. Scotia and C. Breton	Nevis
	St. Kitt's
Prince Edward's Island	St. Vincent
	Tobago
Antigua	Tortola
Barbados	Anguilla
Dominica	Bahamas
Grenada	Bermudas

By a Governor and Legislative Council.

New South Wales	Van Diemen's Land

By a Governor and Executive Council, and Orders of Queen in Council.

St Lucia	Gibraltar
Trinidad	Malta and Gozo
British Guiana, consisting of Demerara, Essequibo, and Berbice	Cape of Good Hope
	Ceylon
	Mauritius
	Hong-Kong

By a Governor and Executive Council, and British Acts of Parliament.

Sierra Leone	South Australia
Gambia	New Zealand
Gold Coast	Falkland Islands
Western Australia	St. Helena

By a Superintendent and Magistrates.

Honduras, &c.

IV. Imports into the United Kingdom from British Colonies, and Declared Value of British and Irish Produce exported from the United Kingdom to the same:

	Imports.	Exports.
	£.	£.
Canada	922,731	1,589,169
New Brunswick .	171,155	146,513
Nova Scotia . .	50,801	268,149
P. Edward's Island & Newfoundland .	246,568	276,650
Antigua. . . .	272,397	87,338
Barbados . . .	520,097	266,942
Dominica . . .	109,293	32,258
Grenada . .	133,857	48,882
Jamaica . . .	1,818,227	1,161,146
Montserrat. . .	22,574	3,884
Nevis	38,790	4,884
St. Kitt's . . .	164,426	55,533
St. Lucia . . .	132,795	23,750
St. Vincent . .	234,233	72,625
Tobago	82,564	21,845
Tortola . . .	9,316	97
Trinidad . . .	572,879	223,647
Bahamas . . .	59,626	45,448
Bermuda . . .	16,958	55,103
Demerara and Essequibo . . .	788,884	332,613
Berbice. . . .	174,347	43,625
Honduras . . .	864,502	111,804
Gibraltar . . .	39,891	937,719
Malta	232,414	289,304
Cape of Good Hope	280,324	369,076
Sierra Leone, &c..	89,823	132,112
Ceylon	1,012,266	248,841
Mauritius . . .	960,396	244,922
New South Wales	298,507	598,645
Van Diemen's Land	134,150	260,730
Western Australia	1,297	22,579
South Australia .	23,127	34,212
New Zealand . .	10,998	42,758
Falkland Islands .	1,077	384
St. Helena . . .	3,729	17,530

V. Tonnage Entered Inwards and Cleared Outwards, in the trade between British colonies and the United Kingdom:

	Entered.	Cleared.
	Tons.	Tons.
Canada	322,145	267,492
New Brunswick. .	173,544	107,965
Nova Scotia . . .	25,309	44,753
P. Edward's Island & Newfoundland .	19,450	25,360
Antigua	10,298	13,383
Barbados . . .	26,085	51,758
Dominica . . .	3,051	2,678

COLONY. [567] COLONY.

	Entered. Tons.	Cleared. Tons.		Entered. Tons.	Cleared. Tons.
Grenada	4,358	11,045	Bermudas	968	18,488
Jamaica	47,776	61,923	Berbice	6,158	5,985
Montserrat	804	481	Honduras	13,028	5,257
Nevis	1,995	1,147	Gibraltar	20,602	43,508
St. Kitt's	6,072	5,271	Malta and Gozo	21,583	40,141
St. Lucia	3,321	2,238	Cape of Good Hope	4,980	16,408
St. Vincent	7,911	7,952	Sierra Leone, &c.	18,464	13,519
Tobago	3,323	3,752	Ceylon	9,666	10,959
Tortola	146	283	Mauritius	28,650	16,397
Trinidad	19,219	21,866	Australian Settlements	22,865	51,234
Bahamas	3,864	2,312	New Zealand	1,341	9,651
Demerara and Essequibo	33,316	45,525	Falkland Islands	92	216
			St. Helena	350	2,086

VI. Summary of Population and Trade.

	N. American Colonies.	W. Indies.	Other Colonies.	Totals.
Population, 1842, or last census	1,621,152	901,082	2,152,101	4,674,355
Imports from into the United Kingdom	1,391,255	6,015,765	3,087,999	10,495,019
Declared Value of British and Irish produce and manufactures exported	2,280,481	2,591,424	3,198,812	8,070,717
Vessels entered inwards from the United Kingdom;				
Ships	1,552	714	522	2,788
Tons	540,448	191,688	128,593	860,729
Cleared outwards from the United Kingdom:				
Ships	1,329	896	852	3,077
Tons	4,455,570	261,344	204,119	911,033

VII. Revenue and Expenditure of British Colonies in 1842.

	Revenue.	Expend.		Revenue.	Expend.
Gibraltar	£31,454	£31,445	Montserrat	£1,871	£2,244
Malta	120,852	110,759	St. Kitt's	6,892	6,933
Canada	476,304	465,141	Nevis	8,834	8,678
Nova Scotia	95,899	84,869	Virgin Islands	2,332	2,440
New Brunswick	81,920	55,792	Dominica	8,504	7,880
Prince Edward's Island	19,626	13,411	British Guiana	243,985	237,759
Newfoundland	56,686	40,787	Trinidad	109,545	71,674
Bermuda	19,342	17,435	Bahama	21,943	23,570
Honduras	13.459	12,515	Mauritius	259,075	206,355
Jamaica	321,945	303,195	St. Helena	17,756	17,643
Barbados	17,707	15,957	Ceylon	311,248	301,791
Tobago	8,532	8,514	Cape of Good Hope	226,261	226,025
Grenada	15,933	12,643	Sierra Leone	26,206	24,165
St. Lucia	11,694	11,409	Gambia	9,592	7,472
St. Vincent	13,892	12,236	New South Wales	844,265	804,982
Antigua	17,110	15,880	Van Diemen's Land	182,622	160,003
			Western Australia	18,334	17,031
			South Australia	84,531	81,813
			New Zealand		

VIII. Principal items of Revenue and Expenditure in British Colonies in the year 1842.

Gibraltar. Revenue: — Wine duty, 2717*l.*; spirit duty, 8101*l.*; auction fees, 3207*l.*; ground and house rents, 3836*l.*; post rates and duties, 5806*l.*; licences on taverns and wine-houses, 3153*l.* Expenditure:—Government, 5013*l.*; post department, 5031*l.*; police, 3889*l.*; revenue department, 3527*l.*; judicial, 2975*l.*; civil secretary's department, 1862*l.*

Malta. Revenue: — Import duties, 81,649*l.*; tonnage dues, 4618*l.*; quarantine dues, 3855*l.*; post-office, 2431*l.* Expenditure: — Governor's establishment, 5177*l.*; chief secretary's office, 3142*l.*; courts of justice, 6575*l.*; interior police, 7374*l.*; marine police and quarantine, 6240*l.*; University and Lyceum, 2679*l.*; primary schools, 679*l.*; charitable institutions, 4173*l.*; pensions, 9920*l.*; alms to the poor, 3086*l.*; hospitals and asylums, 9061*l.*

Canada. Revenue:–Customs, 238,784*l.*; excise, 27,617*l.*; territorial, 31,648*l.*; public works, 11,160*l.*; American Land Company, 10,000*l.* Expenditure:— Governor-general, 6937*l.*; judicial establishment, 15,666*l.*; pensions and salaries of crown officers and contingencies, 22,716*l.*; chief secretary, provincial secretaries (east and west) and their offices, and registrar, 12,981*l.*, &c. &c., making a total for civil establishments of 74,566*l.* which is provided for in the Union Act. The chief expenses provided by provincial enactments are,—Legislature, 14,423*l.*; interest on loans, 68,554*l.*; education, 20,478*l.*; rural police, 10,999*l.*; improving navigation, 11,029*l.*; hospitals and charities, 11,064*l.*; printing laws, &c., 9587*l.*; roads and bridges, 4917*l.*; public works, 179,291*l.*; emigration, 12,388*l.*

Nova Scotia. Revenue :—-Customs, 30,937*l.*; excise, 35,022*l.*; rents, &c. of coal-mines, 4389*l.* Expenditure :—Governor and civil establishment, exclusive of customs, 11,374*l.*; judicial, 5614*l.*; ecclesiastical, 7640*l.*; custom-house, 10,069*l.*; legislature, 4707*l.*; roads and bridges, 27,319*l.*; grammar schools, 1095*l.*; common schools, 1095*l.*; colleges, 1225*l.*

New Brunswick. Revenue : — Provincial revenue, 20,935*l.*; customs' duties under imperial acts, 15,001*l.* Expenditure:—Civil list, 13,050*l.*; pay and expense of legislature, 6991*l.*; collection and protection of revenue, 3202*l.*; parish and Madras schools, 12,480*l.*; college and grammar schools, 2025*l.*; roads, 6373*l.*; bye roads and bridges, 14,853*l.*

Prince Edward's Island. Revenue:— Customs, 5931*l.*; land assessment, 1896*l.*; parliamentary grant, 3070*l.*; governor, judicial and civil establishments, 5116*l.*; roads, bridges, &c., 5387*l.*

Newfoundland. Revenue :—Customs, 41,119*l.* Expenditure :— Civil departments, 24,611*l.*, including customs' establishment, 6038*l.*; courts of law, 5837*l.*; police, 3785*l.*; legislature, 3255*l.*

Bermudas. Revenue:—Customs, 7582*l.*; parliamentary-grant salaries, 4049*l.* Expenditure:—Civil establishments, 10,718*l.*, including 2988*l.* for the governor and his establishment.

Honduras. The principal item of revenue is 4721*l.* duty on wines, spirits, and cordials.

St. Helena. Customs' revenue, 6441*l.*; harbour dues, 2555*l.*; and the total expense of the civil establishments is 14,064*l.*

Ceylon. Revenue : — Sea customs, 90,476*l.*; land customs, 10,305*l.*, principally bridge and ferry tolls; land rents, 43,318*l.*; licences for arrack and toddy farms, 44,768*l.*, and for salt farms, 31,322*l.*; stamps, 17,560*l.*; postage, 5163*l.* Expenditure :—Governor, 7100*l.*; archdeacon of Colombo, 7207*l.* ; schools, 3318*l.*; with other items in the civil department, 95,127*l.*; judicial establishment, 47,603*l.* ; revenue department, 49,784 ; military expenditure, part of which is defrayed by the imperial government, 97,000*l.*

Cape of Good Hope. There are assessed taxes on servants, horses, carriages, a capitation and an income tax, which produce 7632*l.*; stamps, 19,288*l.*; customs, 56,485*l.* ; auctions, 11,627*l.* ; post-office, 6454*l.* The expense of the civil establishments was 17,817*l.*; judicial, 10,799*l.*; revenue and magistracy, 22,584*l.*; church establishments, 8049*l.*; post-office, 5769*l.*; police, 5861*l.*

Sierra Leone. The customs' duties

were 7584*l.*, and the greater part of the disbursements are paid out of parliamentary grants. The expenses of the liberated African department were upwards of 9000*l.*

New South Wales. Revenue :—Sydney, Spirits imported, 107,924*l.*, and 5155*l.* on spirits distilled; tobacco duty, 41,222*l.*; duties ad valorem on foreign goods, 24,944*l.*; post-office, 17,266*l.*; auctions, 10,094*l.*; spirit licences, 15,275*l.*; assessments on stock beyond the limits of location, 15,357*l.* Port Philip revenue :— Spirits, 41,510*l.*; tobacco, 10,394*l.* : ad valorem duties, 7229*l.*; spirit licences, 2923*l.*, assessments on stock, 6107*l.* In the Sydney district the proceeds of land sales were 11,387*l.*; quit-rents, 14,855*l.*; licences to depasture-stock on crown lands, 8782*l.* In the district of Port Philip the sale of land produced 17,728*l.*; pasture licences, 7775*l.* The cost of the civil establishments was 93,505*l.*, which included 20,053*l.* for the surveyor-general's department; 12,000*l.*, colonial engineer; 18,484*l.*, post-office. The judicial department cost 23,812*l.*; police, 77,882*l.*; gaols, 10,242*l.*; clergy, 18,144*l.*, which included payments to the Established Church, Presbyterians, Wesleyans, and Roman Catholics; and 7568*l.* was paid on account of the schools belonging to those religious denominations; and the sum of 12,867*l.* was contributed towards erecting their churches and chapels, and dwellings for their ministers. Bounties on immigration at Sydney, 143,413*l.*; at Port Philip, 99,492*l.* There were other disbursements on account of Port Philip amounting to 59,007*l.*

Van Diemen's Land.—Revenue from Customs, 80,969*l.*; Post-office, 7321*l.*; retail wine and sp'rit licences, 6550*l.*; quit rents, 3423*l.*; land sales, 30,518*l.* Expenditure : — Governor and judges, 5351*l.*; Customs establishment, 5024*l.*; Post-office, 6081*l.*; police, 36,395*l.*; courts of law and their officers, 9775*l.*; public works, roads, bridges, and public buildings, 20,571*l.*; Church of England, 10,864*l.*; Church of Scotland, 2697*l.*; Church of Rome, 1873*l.*; Queen's Orphan Schools, 5683*l.*; day-schools, 3775*l.*; Wesleyan and Methodist missions, 525*l.*

Western Australia.—The sum of 4493*l.* was received on imported spirits, and there are other import duties and various licences. The total expense of the civil establishment was 9778*l.*, and the largest items were 1729*l.* maintenance of a colonial vessel, and 1606*l.* for the survey department.

South Australia.—The sum of 36,607*l.* was received on account of drafts drawn on the home government; and the principal items of local revenue were, Customs' duties on spirits, 8502*l.* ; on tobacco, 3504*l.*; licences, 2271*l.*; land sales, 17,830*l.* The total expenses of the civil establishment amounted to 34,410*l.*, which includes 1725*l.*, governor and judge; survey department, 3434*l.*; Customs, 2279*l.*; harbour department, 2019*l.*; police, 8551*l.*

Jamaica.—The principal items of receipt are given under the following heads :—Additional Duty Act, 18,252*l.*; Customs' Tonnage Act, 14,200*l.*; Import and Export Act, 127,821*l.*; Land-tax Act, 19,980*l.*; Rum Duty Act, 43,239*l.*; Stamp Duty Act, 4800*l.*; Sugar Duty Act for island consumption, 8596*l.*; and a similar duty on coffee, 750*l.*; Tea Duty Act, 1290*l.*; tax on stock, wheels, hereditaments, rent, trade, dogs, &c. &c., 66,587*l.* Expenditure :—Revenue establishments, 35,495*l.*; clergy stipends, 11,500*l.*; curates' stipends, 15,963*l.*; police, 41,399*l.*; immigration, 33,323*l.*; public hospital, 11,371*l.*; roads and bridges, 10,106*l.*; military, 15,166*l.*; judicature, 55,333*l.*; Assembly, 3969*l.*; governor, his secretary and island agent, 12,078*l.*, but in this sum the salaries of five quarters are included. The debt of the island was 613,297*l.*

British Guiana. — Tax on income, 12,558*l.*; on produce, 47,908*l.*; wine and spirit duties, 14,229*l.*; import duty, 66,160*l.*; rum duty, 25,189*l.*; spirit retail licences, 15,039*l.*; shop-tax, 1551*l.*; huckster licences, 3241*l.*; colony craft-tax, 1086*l.* Expenditure :—Civil List, 36,621*l.*; police, 29,457*l.*; gaols, 8906*l.*; colonial hospital, 9010*l.*; immigration, 39,624*l.*; penal settlement expenses, 7515*l.*; grants to the Established, Dutch, and Roman Catholic churches.

Trinidad.—There are several kinds of import duties, and under the head "foreign duties on imports" the receipts were

17,507l.; import duties, 8834l.; wines and spirit duty, 1495l.; tonnage duty, 3930l.; export duties, 13,745l.; fees of public offices, 4182l.; spirit licences, 3200l. The civil, judicial, ecclesiastical, and police establishments cost 33,894l.

Other West India Islands.—It is not necessary to give details of the revenue and expenditure of each island. The revenue is principally derived from customs' duties, licences, export duties on island produce, direct taxes, licences, and some other sources; and it is expended in defraying the cost of civil establishments, improvement of roads, and for churches, schools, &c. &c.

Mauritius.—Revenue of Customs: Imports, 53,968l.; exports, 37,902l.; port collections, 14,312l.; direct taxes, 5269l.; licences, 35,136l.; registration fees, 33,162l.; stamps, 5240l.; canteens, 9070l. Expenditure:—Civil List, 26,000l.; judicial, 32,050l.; ecclesiastical, 3273l.

The mother-country does not levy taxes or duties in any colony except for their use; but the colonies do not usually defray all the cost of their own establishments, and the entire charge of them to England, inclusive of naval and military outlay, is above 3,100,000l. annually. The colonial revenues are expended in maintaining establishments which are often not only expensive, but sometimes nearly useless. The charges of collecting colonial revenues are frequently greater than the produce of the revenue. The sum of 166,067l. of the public money was voted by Parliament in 1838 for religious establishments in the colonies: of this sum 134,450l. was for the established church; church of Scotland 9967l.; Roman Catholic church 14,763l.; Dutch church 6886l.; besides 2175l. to Jews, Baptists, and Wesleyans for religious purposes. But it is the drain upon the military resources of the mother-country which render the British colonies so heavy a burden. From 1839 to 1843 inclusive, the charges incurred on account of Canada in respect of the army, navy, ordnance, and commissariat, was 5,532,957l. (Parl. Paper, 304 Sess. 1844.)

COMBINATION LAWS. The laws known by this name were repealed in 1824. Till then any combination of any two or more masters, or of any two or more workmen, to lower or raise wages, or to increase or diminish the number of hours of work, or quantity of work to be done, was punishable at common law as a misdemeanor: and there were also thirty-five statutes in existence, most of them applying to particular trades, prohibiting combinations of workmen against masters. The act passed in 1824 (5 Geo. IV. c. 95) repealed all the statute and common law against combinations of masters and of workmen, provided a summary mode of conviction, and a punishment not exceeding two months' imprisonment for violent interference with workmen or masters, and for combinations for violent interference; and contained a proviso with regard to combinations for violent interference, that no law in force with regard to them should be altered or affected by the act. But all the common law against combinations being repealed by the act, this proviso was considered as of no force; and the act also went beyond the intentions of the framers in legalizing combinations unattended with violence for the purpose of controlling masters in the mode of carrying on their trades and manufactures, as well as peaceable combinations to procure advance of wages or reduction of hours of work. The act was passed after an inquiry into the subject by a committee presided over by Mr. Hume, which reported to the house the following among other resolutions:—

"That the masters have often united and combined to lower the rates of their workmen's wages, as well as to resist a demand for an increase, and to regulate their hours of working, and sometimes to discharge their workmen who would not consent to the conditions offered to them; which have been followed by suspension of work, riotous proceedings, and acts of violence.

"That prosecutions have frequently been carried on under the statute and the common law against the workmen, and many of them have suffered different periods of imprisonment for combining and conspiring to raise their wages, or to resist their reduction, and to regulate their hours of working.

"That several instances have been

stated to the committee of prosecutions against masters for combining to lower wages, and to regulate the hours of working; but no instance has been adduced of any master having been punished for that offence.

"That it is the opinion of this committee that masters and workmen should be freed from such restrictions as regard the rate of wages and the hours of working, and be left at perfect liberty to make such agreements as they may mutually think proper.

"That therefore the statute laws which interfere in these particulars between masters and workmen should be repealed; and also that the common law, under which a peaceable meeting of masters or workmen may be prosecuted as a conspiracy, should be altered."

Immediately after the passing of this act a number of widely organized and formidable combinations arose in various trades and manufactures for the purpose of controlling the masters as to the way in which they should conduct their business; and the extent to which the act had repealed the common law being doubtful, and the act having clearly gone beyond the resolutions on which it was grounded in legalizing combinations, Mr. Huskisson, then President of the Board of Trade, moved early in the session of 1825 for a committee to consider the effects of the act 5 Geo. IV. c. 95; and a committee was appointed with Mr. (afterwards Lord) Wallace, then Vice-President of the Board of Trade, for its chairman. This committee recommended the repeal of the act of the previous session, and the enactment of another; and in consequence of their recommendation the 6 Geo. IV. c. 129, was passed, which is the act now in force relative to combinations.

This act repealed the 5 Geo. IV. c. 95, and all the statutes which that act had repealed. It relieved from all prosecution and punishment persons meeting solely to consult upon rate of wages or hours of work, or entering into any agreement, verbal or written, on these points. And it provided a punishment of not more than three months' imprisonment, with or without hard labour, for any one using violence or threats to make a workman leave his hiring, or return work unfinished, or refuse to accept work, or belong to any club, or contribute to any common fund, or pay any fine for not belonging to a club, or contributing to a common fund, or refusing to conform to any rules made for advance of wages or lessening of the hours of work, or regulations of the mode of carrying on any business, and for any one using violence to make any master alter his mode of carrying on his business.

By the act 6 Geo. IV. c. 129, therefore, combinations of masters and workmen to settle as to rate of wages and hours of labour are made legal and freed from all punishment; but the common law remains as it was as to combinations for otherwise controlling masters.

By 9 Geo. IV. c. 31, assaults in pursuance of a combination to raise the rate of wages are made punishable by imprisonment and hard labour.

A committee of the House of Commons sat in 1838, presided over by Sir Henry Parnell, to consider the effect of combinations of workmen; but nothing followed from this committee.

COMMANDER. [CAPTAIN.]

COMMANDERY, a species of benefice attached to certain foreign military Orders, usually conferred on knights who had done them some especial service. According to Furetière, these Commanderies were of different kinds and degrees, as the statutes of the different orders directed. The name of Commandery in the Order of St. Louis was given to the pension which the King of France formerly assigned to twenty-four commanders of that order, of whom eight received 4000, and sixteen 3000 livres each. The Order of Malta had commanderies of justice, which a knight obtained from long standing; and others of favour, of which the grand master had the power of disposal.

In England, commanderies were the same amongst the Knights Hospitallers as preceptories had been among the Knights Templars: they were societies of those knights placed upon some of their estates in the country under the government of a commander, who were allowed proper maintenance out of the revenues under their care, and accounted for the remainder to the grand prior at London. At the dissolution of religious houses, in the time of Henry VIII., there were more than fifty of these commanderies in England, subordinate to the great priory of St. John of Jerusalem. A few of these held productive estates, and had even the appearance of being separate corporations, so much so as to have a common seal; but the greater part were little more than farms or granges. The Templars' term of preceptory was as frequently used to designate these establishments as the term commandery. (Furetière, *Dictionnaire Universel*; Tanner, *Notitia Monastica*, edit. 1787, pref. p. xvii.; Dugdale's *Monasticon Anglicanum*, last edit. vol. vi. pp. 786, 800.)

COMMENDAM. [BENEFICE, p. 350.]

COMMISSARY, an officer who is delegated by a bishop to act in a particular part of the diocese, to exercise jurisdiction similar in kind to that exercised by the chancellor of the diocese in the consistory court of the diocese. A commissary has, generally speaking, the authority of official principal and vicar-general within his limits. An appeal lies from his decisions to the metropolitan. In some dioceses there is a commissary court for each archdeaconry. The commissarial courts were established for the convenience of the people in parts of the diocese remote from the consistory court. A commissary must be learned in the civil and ecclesiastical law, a master of arts or bachelor of law, not under the age of twenty-six, and he must subscribe the Thirty-nine articles (Canon 127).

In Scotland the same classes of questions which in other parts of Europe were arrogated to the ecclesiastical judicatories came under the authority of the bishop's courts while the episcopal polity continued, and subsequently devolved on special judges, who were called commissaries. The four commissaries of Edinburgh constituted the Supreme Commissary Court, which had jurisdiction in questions of divorce, and of declarations of the existence or non-existence of marriage. The district commissaries had the administrative authority of confirming executors to persons deceased, a function resembling the granting of letters of administration in England. By 4 Geo. IV. c. 97, the functions of the provincial commissaries were vested in the sheriffs of the respective counties, who, before the passing of that act, were usually appointed the commissaries of their districts. By 11 Geo. IV. 1 Wm. IV. c. 69, the jurisdiction of the commissaries of Edinburgh, as above, was vested in the Court of Session.

COMMISSION. This word appears to be used generally to express the instrument by which authority is delegated by one person to another; and it is particularly used to express the instrument by which the crown gives authority to a person or persons to do any act. A commission, then, is a warrant or letter patent by which a person is empowered, or persons are empowered, to do any act, either ordinary or extraordinary. Some commissions in England issue from the king under the Great Seal, and others are only signed by the king. There was formerly a High Commission Court, but it was abolished by 16 Charles I. c. 11, and 13 Charles II. c. 2.

An enumeration of some of the principal kinds of commissions will show the nature of the power thereby given, and the objects of it:—

Commissions of Oyer and Terminer, and Gaol Delivery. [ASSIZE.]
Commission of Lunacy. [LUNACY.]
Commission of the Peace. [JUSTICES OF THE PEACE.]
Commissions, Naval and Military, and others. [COMMISSIONS, MILITARY.]
COMMISSION. [AGENT; BROKER; FACTOR.]
COMMISSION ECCLESIASTICAL. [ECCLESIASTICAL COMMISSION.]

COMMISSION, in military affairs, is the document by which an officer is authorized to perform duty for the service of the state.

In England in former times the regular mode of assembling an army, either to resist an invading enemy, or to accompany the king on a foreign expedition, was by sending a royal command to the chief barons and the spiritual lords, that they should meet at a given time and place with their due proportion of men, horses, &c. properly equipped, according to the tenure by which they held their estates; and these *tenants in capite* appear to have appointed by their own authority all their subordinate officers. But commissions were granted by the kings to individuals, authorizing them to raise men for particular services; thus, in 1442, Henry VI. gave one to the governor of Mantes, by which he was appointed to maintain 50 horsemen, 20 men-at-arms on foot, and 210 archers, for the defence of that city. According to Père Daniel, the commission was written on parchment, and, that it might not be counterfeited, the piece was divided, by cutting it irregularly, into two portions, of which doubtless each party retained one.

Commissions of array, as they were called, were also issued by the king in England, probably from the time of Alfred, for the purpose of mustering and training the inhabitants of the counties in military discipline; and in the reign of Edward III. the parliament enacted that no person trained under these commissions should be compelled to serve out of his own county except the kingdom were invaded. Of the same nature as these commissions of array was that which, in 1572, when the county was threatened with the Spanish invasion, Queen Elizabeth issued to the justices of the peace in the different counties, authorizing them to muster and train persons to serve during the war. Those magistrates were directed to make choice of officers to command bodies of 100 men and upwards; and such officers, with the consent of the magistrates, were to appoint their own lieutenants. This privilege of granting commissions to the officers of the national militia continued to be exercised by the lord-lieutenants of counties, the king having the power of confirming or annulling the appointments; and it was made law in the reign of Charles II. The militia has been disembodied for several years; but commissions in the yeomanry cavalry, a force which is still kept up in England, are granted by the lord-lieutenants. It appears, however, that before the Revolution, the lieutenants and ensigns were recommended for commissions by the captains of the companies.

In the French service, between the reigns of Francis I. and Louis XIV., we find that the kings reserved to themselves the nomination of the principal commanders only of the legions or regiments, and that the commanders were permitted to grant commissions under their own signature and seal to the subordinate officers, who were charged with the duty of raising the troops and instructing them in the use of arms.

In the British regular army all the commissions of officers are signed by the king. The several commissions in the navy are a sort of warrant, and are signed by the Lords Commissioners of the Admiralty; but the documents are called commissions, and they are signed in the name of the king. In the navy, in the regiment of artillery, and in the corps of engineers and marines, the commissions are conferred without purchase; and to a certain extent this is the case with the commissions granted to officers of the line. Those cadets who have completed a course of military education in the Royal College at Sandhurst are so appointed. In other cases, gentlemen obtain leave to enter the army by the purchase of an ensigncy, the prices of which, in the different classes of troops, are regulated by authority; and they proceed to the higher grades on paying the difference between the price of the grade which they quit and of that which they enter.

The commissioned officers of a battalion of infantry are as follow: Field-officers—colonel, lieutenant-colonel, and major. Regimental officers — captains, lieutenants, and ensigns. Staff-officers— chaplain, adjutant, quartermaster, and surgeon.

The prices of commissions in the British army are as follows:—Life Guards— lieutenant-colonel, 7250*l.*; major, 5350*l.*; captain, 3500*l.*; lieutenant, 1785*l.*; cornet, 1260*l.* Royal Regiment of Horse Guards—lieutenant-colonel, 7250*l.*; major, 5350*l.*; captain, 3500*l.*; lieutenant, 1600*l.*; cornet, 1200*l.* Dragoon Guards and Dragoons — lieutenant - colonel, 6175*l.*; major, 4575*l.*; captain, 3225*l.*; lieutenant, 1190*l.*; cornet, 840*l.* Foot

Guards—lieutenant-colonel, 900*l.*; major, with rank of colonel, 830*l.*; captain, with rank of lieutenant-colonel, 480*l.*; lieutenant, with rank of captain, 205*l.*; ensign, with rank of lieutenant, 120*l.* Regiments of the Line—lieutenant-colonel, 450*l.*; major, 320*l.*; captain, 180*l.*; lieutenant, 70*l.*; ensign, 45*l.* Fusilier and Rifle regiments—1st lieutenant, 70*l.*; 2nd lieutenant, 50*l.*

Commissions in the military service of the East India Company are given by the Court of Directors.

In the British colonies where a militia is kept on foot commissions are given in it by the governor as captain-general.

In the National Guards of France the officers are selected by their comrades.

COMMISSIONERS, LORDS. [ADMIRAL; ASSENT, ROYAL; PARLIAMENT.]
COMMISSIONERS OF BANKRUPTS. [BANKRUPT.]
COMMISSIONERS OF LUNACY. [LUNACY.]
COMMISSIONERS OF SEWERS. [SEWERS.]

COMMITTEE OF PUBLIC SAFETY, Comité de Salut Publique, the name given to a committee of members of the National Convention, who exercised a dictatorial power in France for about fifteen months, which is known by the name of the Reign of Terror. The National Convention having abolished the royal authority at the end of 1792, and proclaimed the republic, found themselves invested with the whole sovereign power. They delegated the executive part of it to several committees or departments of government, and placed a Committee of Public Safety over all. This committee consisted of ten members of the Convention, appointed for three months, but re-eligible indefinitely: they were commonly called the decemvirs. Their business was to watch over the conduct of the public authorities, and to promote the cause of the revolution. By degrees their powers attained a most extensive range; all the constituted authorities and public functionaries, civil and military, were placed under their immediate inspection. This was after the successful insurrection on the 31st of May, 1793, when the Mountain or terrorist party in the Convention gained the victory, by means of the armed multitudes of Paris, over their fellow-deputies of the Gironde party, who wished to govern the republic according to legal forms, and when the leaders of the Girondins were sent to prison and to the scaffold. From that time Robespierre and his friends monopolized all the power of the Committee of Public Safety. By a decree of the Convention, 4th of December, 1793, the committee had the power of appointing and removing all the administrative authorities, all the agents and commissioners sent to the departments and to the various armies, and the agents sent to foreign countries. They were to watch and direct public opinion, and denounce all suspected persons. By another decree, of 28th July, 1793, the committee was invested with the power of issuing warrants of arrest. There was another committee, called de Sureté Générale, which has been sometimes confounded with the Committee of Public Safety, but was subordinate to it, and concerned itself with the internal police and judicial affairs. " The Committee of Public Safety," says a witness and a member of the Convention, " did not manifest its ambition at the outset; it was useful at first. But that prudent conduct ceased after the revolt of the 31st of May, when the Convention, its several committees, and especially that of General Security, fell under the yoke of the Committee of Public Safety, which acted the part of the Council of Ten and of the three inquisitors of the Venetian government. Its power was monstrous, because it was in a manner concealed—because it veiled its acts amidst the multitude of other committees—because, by renewing itself perpetually from among men of the same stamp, it took away the responsibility from its members, although its measures were ever the same. The committee concentrated itself at last in three of its members: Robespierre, who was the real chief, though half-concealed from view, and Conthon and St. Just. There was perfect unanimity among these three down to the moment of their fall; in proportion as the Mountain itself became divided, and its chiefs perished on the scaffold, the alliance between the three became more firmly cemented. There is reason to believe that they had resolved to perpetuate their power by establishing a supreme council of three consuls, in which Robespierre would have had the perpetual presidency, with the departments of justice, exterior, and finance; Couthon that of the interior, and St. Just the war department." (*Histoire pittoresque de la Convention Nationale*, par un Ex-Conventional, 4 vols. 8vo. Paris, 1833.) The means by which these men contrived to maintain their usurped power are shown by Mignet in his 'History of the French Revolution.' Acting in the name of the National Convention, the Committee was in fact master of that assembly, which it compelled to adopt its reports and resolutions; it decreed the proscription of any member who resisted its will; it had at its command the armed multitudes of Paris and the suburbs, whose passions and fears it kept constantly excited by suspicions of royalists and traitors; it was supported by the numerous clubs and revolutionary committees distributed all over the country, the poorer members of which received by a decree of the Convention, extorted from that assembly on the 31st of May by the armed mob, an allowance of forty sols a day; and it sent commissioners to the armies, who impeached every general suspected of disaffection, and easily prevailed on the deluded soldiers to give him up. "It had at its command the law against the suspected passed by the Convention, by which it could arrest any citizen; the revolutionary tribunals which summarily sent the accused to the scaffold; and the decrees of confiscation, forced loans and requisitions, and the maximum upon provisions, by which it disposed of the property of all." This law of the maximum fixed the highest legal price of provisions and other necessaries, both for wholesale and retail dealers, and forbade them to ask more. (*Tableau du Maximum de la République Française décreté par la Convention Nationale le 6 Ventose, An II.*) The net was so widely spread that it took in all France; and a few obscure men exercised in the name of liberty a tyranny infinitely greater than that of the most arbitrary king of the old dynasty. In the Convention, from which nominally they derived their power, they were supported by a few bold men, who frightened the rest with the pikes of the mob and with threats of the scaffold. But when these men, Tallien, Barras, and others, discovered that they themselves stood in the way of Robespierre's ambition, and were destined to the common lot of the guillotine, they turned upon him and his friends of the Committee, and the majority of the Convention, which had through fear acquiesced in all their measures, immediately sided with them; the National Guards, weary of useless proscriptions, stood by their representatives, and Robespierre and his few friends found themselves alone, without any military man to support them. Even in the Committee of Public Safety, Collot d'Herbois and Billaud Varennes turned against Robespierre. On the 9th Thermidor, July 28, 1794, Robespierre, Couthon, and St. Just were executed. From that time the moderate party gradually, though slowly, acquired the ascendency in the Convention.

COMMITTEES. [PARLIAMENT.]

COMMODORE (*Comendador*), in the royal navy, is the officer commanding a small number of ships of war, when detached for any particular service from the fleet. His rank is immediately below that of a rear-admiral, and he is classed with a brigadier-general in the army His ship is distinguished by a red pendant at the mast-head. The title is sometimes given to the senior captain in a fleet of merchant ships.

In the French service the commander of a detachment of ships is called *Chef d'Escadre;* and in the time of Louis XIII. the commander-general of the fleet was so called when he had not the rank of admiral.

The highest rank in the navy of the United States of North America is that of commodore, which is given to the commanders of squadrons at the six stations at which a naval force is maintained by the United States government.

COMMON LAW. In its most general signification the expression Common Law denotes the ordinary law of any country:

when used in this sense it is called *common*, as prevailing generally over a whole country, in contradistinction to *particular* laws, the operation of which is confined to a limited district or to a peculiar class of inhabitants. In England the Common Law is that body of customs, rules, and maxims which have acquired their binding power and the force of laws in consequence of long usage, recognised by judicial decision, and not by reason of statutes now extant. The common law is therefore called, in early periods of our legal history, the "lex et consuetudo Angliæ," and at the present day the appellation is used to denote "lex non scripta," in opposition to "leges scriptæ," or statutes. Sir Matthew Hale, in his 'History of the Common Law of England,' divides all the laws of England into two kinds, lex scripta, the written law, and lex non scripta, the unwritten law; and he adds, "although all the laws of this kingdom have some monuments or memorials thereof in writing, yet all of them have not their original in writing; for some of these laws have obtained their force by immemorial usage or custom, and such laws are properly called *leges non scriptæ*, or unwritten laws or customs" (chap. 1). He confines the term leges scriptæ, or written laws, in which he is followed by Blackstone, to statutes or acts of parliament; but this is not quite correct, for there are other rules, such as rules of court, made by the judges of the common-law courts, and orders in chancery, made by the judges in chancery pursuant to power given to them, which are laws, and "written laws," according to Hale's definition, for the "original" of them is in writing. The term unwritten law also is applicable to a great part of that kind of law called equity, for the original of it does not exist in writing. A large part of the law of equity is founded on judicial decisions made in conformity with some established principles, and therefore it resembles that part of the common law which is recognised as such by the decisions of common-law judges. In addition to customs and usages, whose particular origin is unknown, many portions of the common law consist of statutes passed before the time of legal memory, that is, the beginning of the reign of Richard I., which, though known historically to have been acts of parliament, have no authority as laws in that character, but derive their obligation from immemorial usage, recognised by judicial decision. The provisions of the common law are, however, quite as binding as acts of the legislature, for they have received the character of law by force of judicial decisions. In very early times it is probable that the system of rules which composed the common law was wholly traditional. In course of time the decisions of the king's ordinary courts of justice were recorded, and became the most authoritative evidence of such customs and maxims as formed part of the common law, according to the rule of the civil law, that what the emperor had once judicially determined was to serve as a guide in all like cases for the future. (Cod. 1, tit. 14-12.) In addition to the recorded judgments of courts, technically called precedents, the treatises of Bracton, Fleta, Britton, Staundforde's 'Pleas of the Crown,' and Coke's 'Commentary upon Littleton,' are acknowledged as evidence of what is Common Law. Of the whole system the judges of the superior courts are the expositors; they declare the law by applying certain established rules and principles to cases which come before them for judgment, but they have no power to add to or vary the law in any other way than by their decisions upon particular cases that are brought before them. Law made by judicial decision is called by Bentham *judge-made* law; a term which, as already intimated, belongs to a part of the law called equity, which is administered in the courts of chancery.

Learned writers have indulged in much speculation respecting the origin of the common law of England, though Sir Matthew Hale says it is "as undiscoverable as the head of the Nile." It seems, however, to be well ascertained that the customs which in ancient times were incorporated with it were of compound origin, and introduced at various times in consequence of the political vicissitudes of the country; some being Saxon, others Danish, and others Norman. It is also evident, from the adoption of the

Roman terms of art and many Roman provisions, that many of the rules and maxims of the common law were derived from the civil law. Bracton's work contains many passages which are taken directly from the 'Digest' and the 'Institutions' of Justinian. Again, many parts of the common law have gradually arisen from the necessary modification of its ancient doctrines and principles, in order to render them applicable to new states of society, produced by enlarged commerce and advancing civilization. From this cause some branches of our system of jurisprudence have wholly sprung into existence in modern times. Thus almost the whole of the law of evidence, now perhaps the most important part of our practical jurisprudence, has appeared as part of the common law since the time of the Commonwealth. But perhaps the most remarkable instance of the total change in common-law institutions with the progressive improvement of society is the trial by jury, which may be traced through all its gradations, from a rude kind of trial, in which the jury were merely witnesses called from the neighbourhood, in order that they might declare the truth to the judge, to the present system, where the jury themselves decide upon the truth of facts by the testimony of witnesses examined before them. On the other hand, many rules and provisions of the common law have wholly disappeared, having either become obsolete from disuse, or been gradually declared inoperative by decisions of the judges as they became inapplicable to the altered state of society. So great has been the alteration of the common law which these accessions and abstractions have occasioned, that it can scarcely be termed with propriety the same body of law that it was six hundred years ago, unless it be upon the principle upon which Sir M. Hale maintains its identity: that the changes have been only partial and successive, whilst the general system has been always the same, "as the Argonauts' ship was the same when it returned home as it was when it went out, though in that long voyage it had successive amendments, and scarce came back with any of its former materials."

(Hale, *History of the Common Law*; Blackstone, *Commentaries*, vol. i. p. 63; Reeve, *History of English Law*, vol. i.; and Hallam, *Middle Ages*, vol. ii., 'On the Origin of the Common Law.')

COMMON PLEAS, COURT OF, a superior court of record, which has jurisdiction over England and Wales in all common pleas or civil actions commenced by man against man. It is at present composed of five judges, one of whom is chief justice and the other four are *puisne* justices. All are created by the king's letters patent.

This court has been stationary at Westminster Hall for several centuries. During the existence of the Aula or Curia Regis, established by the Conqueror in the hall of his usual residence, the palace at Westminster, that single tribunal had supreme jurisdiction in all temporal causes, which were adjudicated by the principal officers of the royal household, often assisted by persons learned in the law, called the king's justiciars. In this state of things, the poorer class of suitors in the common civil pleas, or actions between man and man in which neither the king's revenue nor his character of prosecutor of offences on behalf of the public were concerned, laboured under the inconvenience of either attending the frequent and distant progresses of the court, or of losing their remedies altogether. This evil, as well as the jealousy entertained by the crown of the ascendancy of the chief justiciar, who presided over the whole Aula Regis, occasioned the article in Magna Charta, that common pleas should not follow the king's court, but be held in some certain place. This court thereupon became gradually detached from the Aula Regis, and assumed its present separate form. It has ever since continued its sittings daily during the four terms of each year, without removal from the palace of Westminster or its immediate vicinity, except on a few occasions, in time of plague or contagious disease.

Before the passing of the statute of 3 & 4 Will. IV. c. 27, this court had an exclusive jurisdiction in all those actions which, as they concerned freeholds or realty, were called real. including as well those on which the common assurances of

2 P

fines and recoveries passed, as the others which were commenced by the king's original writ out of chancery. On this account it was styled by Coke the "lock and key of the common law." Since the abolition of real actions by the above-mentioned act (with three exceptions), dower and quare impedit are the only forms of action in which this court has exclusive jurisdiction; for in mixed and personal actions the King's Bench and Exchequer of Pleas have long exercised concurrent power. The Court of Common Pleas is a court of appeal from the decision of the revising barristers in the matter of disputed claims to vote for members of parliament. (6 Vict. c. 18, § 42.)

In the original constitution of this court, and down to the beginning of the reign of William IV., its proceedings in actions between persons not its officers were founded on original writs issued out of the Court of Chancery, though in process of time they did not actually issue except in cases where it became necessary to perfect the record. But now by a statute (2 Will. IV. c. 39) introduced by the late Lord Tenterden, to secure the uniformity of process in personal actions in the three superior courts of law, certain forms of process, called writs of summons and capias, are provided as the only means for commencing personal actions in any of those courts, and they may be issued from any of them.

Before 1830 the appeal from the judgments of this court was by writ of error to the justices of the King's Bench, a vestige of superiority in the Bench as the remnant of that Aula Regis from which this court as well as those of Chancery and Exchequer have been gradually detached. But now by 11 Geo. IV. & 1 Will. IV. c. 70, the judgments of this court can only be reviewed by the judges of the King's Bench and the barons of the Exchequer, who form a court of error in the Exchequer Chamber; the further appeal is by writ of error returnable in the Lords' House of Parliament.

[For an account of the privileges of sergeants-at-law in the Court of Common Pleas. see SERGEANT.]

COMMON, RIGHTS OF, in law, is the right of taking a *profit* in the land of another in *common* with others. It may either be such a right as is enjoyed in common with others to the exclusion of the owner of the land, or it may not exclude the owner of the land. The commoner has no interest in the soil of the land on which he has a right of common.

The profits which may be the subjects of common are the natural produce of land (or water, which is included in the legal signification of land); such as grass and herbage, turf, wood, and fish. The commons relating to these subjects are accordingly called common of pasture, turbary, estovers, and piscary. Other things which cannot be called products of land, but rather part of the land itself, as stones and minerals, may also be the subjects of common right. Rights of way and other accommodations in the land of another, though enjoyed in common by several persons, do not bear that name, but are called Easements.

Of all commons, that of pasture is the most frequent. It is the right of taking grass and herbage by the mouths of grazing animals. It differs from that property which may exist in the *vesture* or vegetable produce of the land, without any property in the land itself, and which is a corporeal hereditament; whereas all rights of common are incorporeal rights. The same remark applies to other rights of common, the subjects of which—as for instance woods and mines—may belong as corporeal hereditaments to one, while the land generally belongs to another.

Common of turbary is the right of taking *turf* for fuel, and common of estovers is the right of taking *wood* for fuel, and for the repairs of houses, fences, and implements of husbandry. These supplies of wood are called fire bote, house bote (which includes the former), plough bote, and hedge or hay bote. These estovers or botes may also be taken by every tenant for life or years from the land which he himself occupies, but in that case they are not subjects of *common* rights.

Common of piscary is the right of *fishery* in rivers not navigable; the right of fishing in the sea and in navigable rivers is common to all persons in the realm.

The extent of rights of common depends very much upon the *title* to them. There are four titles on which such rights may be founded; common right (which seems to be nearly the same thing as the common law), prescription, custom, and grant (deed).

The title by common right arose with the creation of manors, when land was granted out in fee to be *held* of the grantor as lord. As such grants were forbidden by the statute "*quia emptores*" (18 Edw. I. c. 1), it follows that all commons appendant now existing must have been created before the date of that statute. The law allowed to every such grantee, as common right, common of pasture, turbary, estovers, and piscary in the *waste* of the lord, or that part of his lands which was neither taken by him into his *demesnes* or actual occupation, nor granted out by him to others. These implied rights of common, however, were allowed no farther than necessity seemed to require, and rights of common thus originating are still confined nearly within their ancient limits. As they originated in grants of land, they were considered as inseparably *appendant* to the land, so that they could not be separated from the land without becoming extinct. Accordingly what is called Common Appendant is a right of common which a man enjoys in respect of his title to a piece of land. The right is appendant or attached to the land. The common of pasture was confined to the purpose of maintaining from seed-time to harvest the cattle of the commoner which were used by him in cultivating his land, and which that land would maintain through the winter, or which were, as the law styled it, *levant* and *couchant* upon it. Horses, oxen, kine, and sheep, used either for tilling or manuring land, were the *commonable* cattle. The land to which the common was appendant must have been originally arable, though the subsequent change of arable into meadow, &c. does not extinguish the right. Common of turbary appendant was confined to the purpose of supplying fuel for the domestic use of the tenant; and so strictly must this right be still confined within its ancient limits, that it must be appendant to an ancient messuage or house, and no more turves can be taken under it than will be spent in the house. Common of estovers appendant gives, as it gave originally, only the right of taking wood for the repair of ancient fences and houses. Common of piscary appendant was only for supplying the tenant's own table with fish, and it must be still limited to this purpose.

Common claimed by prescription (which supposes a grant) may be as various as grants may be. A right of common thus founded may be either annexed to land (when it is said to be appurtenant), or altogether independent of any property in land, when it is said to be *in gross*. Common in gross must be claimed either by prescription or by deed; and is not appendant or appurtenant to any certain land. If common of pasture, it may be for any kind of animals, whether commonable or not, as swine and geese. The number of animals may be fixed, or absolutely unlimited, and they need not be the commoner's own.

Common appurtenant may be severed from the land to which it was originally annexed, and then it becomes common in gross.

The title to common by custom is peculiar to copyholders and may also give the commoner various modifications of right.

Right of common of pasture may also be claimed because of *vicinage*, or neighbourhood. This is where two wastes belonging to different lords of manors adjoin each other without being separated by a fence. The cattle lawfully put upon the one common may then stray, or rather are excused for straying, into the other.

The rights of the owner of the soil over which a right of common exists, are all such rights as flow from ownership, and are not inconsistent with the commoner's rights.

Rights of common are conveyed, like all other incorporeal hereditaments, by deed of grant. When they are annexed to land, they will pass with the land by any conveyance which is adapted to transfer the land.

Rights of common are liable to be extinguished in several ways, and often contrary to the intentions of parties. It is a rule, that if the owner of common appurtenant purchase any part of the land over which the right extends, the right of common is *altogether* extinguished; it is the same if he release his right over any part of the land. This unreasonable rule, however, does not extend to common *appendant*, though that will be extinguished if the commoner becomes the owner of *all* the land in which he has common, and partial extinguishment of the common will follow from acquisition of part of the land. The enfranchisement of a copyhold to which a right of common is annexed extinguishes the right.

The most common mode of extinguishing rights of common in modern times is by inclosure under act of parliament. (INCLOSURE; also generally on this subject Woolrych, on 'Rights of Common;' Coke on Littleton, 122 a; Comyn's *Digest*, tit. 'Common;' and Blackstone's *Commentaries*, book ii. chap. 3.)

COMMONS. [INCLOSURE.]

COMMONS, HOUSE OF. The object of this article is to present a compendious view of the history and actual state of the House of Commons as a part of the Imperial Parliament of Great Britain and Ireland.

Long after the first signing of the great charter, the levying of *tallage* upon the burgesses, as upon the *villains*, was still claimed as an inherent right of the Anglo-Norman crown, and was of itself an abundant source of vexatious oppression. To show the galling nature of this exaction, we may instance the levy made by Henry II., on pretext of a crusade, in 1087, one of the last years of his reign:—He had a list made out of the richest citizens and burgesses of all the municipal towns, and had them individually summoned to appear before him at an appointed time and place. The honour of being admitted into the presence of the Conqueror's great grandson was in this manner granted to two hundred citizens of London, one hundred of York, and to a proportionate number in the other cities and boroughs. The letters of convocation admitted neither of excuse nor of delay. The burgesses thus summoned were received a certain number at a time, at several different days and places; and as each band presented themselves, it was notified to them, from the Norman king, through an interpreter, what sum he required from them. "And thus," says a contemporary historian (Roger de Hoveden, *Annales*), "did the king take from them a tenth of their properties, according to the estimate of good men and true, that knew what income they had, as likewise what goods and chattels. Such as he found refractory he sent forthwith to prison, and kept them there until they had payed the uttermost farthing. In like manner did he to the Jews within his realm, which brought him incalculable sums." This assimilation of the great mass of Anglo-Saxon burgesses to the Jews gives us the exact measure of their political condition at the commencement of the second century of the régime of the Conquest.

To the sagacity of Simon de Montfort, the great Earl or rather Count of Leicester, who led the national resistance to the tyranny of the weak and treacherous Henry III., the first general summoning of representative citizens and burgesses to parliament seems to be attributable, for it was in the year 1265, while Henry was a captive in De Montfort's power, after the battle of Lewes, that, in calling a parliament, he issued the earliest writs requiring each sheriff of a county to return, together with two knights for the shire under his jurisdiction, two citizens for each city, and two burgesses for each borough within its limits. Although the defeat and destruction of De Montfort, shortly after, by the exertions of Prince Edward, appear to have prevented this plan of representation to the commons from taking immediate effect, yet it was permanently adopted by Edward himself, at least from the twenty-third year of his reign, as an amelioration which, under the existing internal circumstances of the country, sound policy dictated.

It is plain, however, that in this measure little was contemplated by Edward beyond the facilitating of the extraordinary supplies of money, indispensable for the prosecution of those schemes of national aggrandizement which so actively and steadily occupied his vigorous reign. The advantage immediately derived to the burgess population from the substitution for the arbitrary and vexatious mode already described of summoning their deputies to the king's court for the purposes of taxation, of the uniform practice of calling them together at the same times and places at which the established estates of the Anglo-Norman parliament were convened, was, not so much the lightening of their pecuniary burdens on the whole, as the effecting and maintaining a more equal and regular distribution of them. The Anglo-Norman king and his great council, into which, among the laity, none but his immediate feudal tenants and a few summoned by his personal letters were yet admitted, still claimed and exercised the power of taxing the burgesses almost at discretion. Although the *knights of the shires*, at that period, that is, the representatives of the county freeholders at large, were first regularly summoned to attend on parliament at the same time as the representative burgesses, and, like them, for the purpose of taxation only, yet they and the burgesses were for some time longer regarded as forming two distinct representative bodies. Thus the writs for the parliament of the 23rd of Edward I. expressly direct that the elected citizens and burgesses shall have full power to act on behalf of the citizens and burgesses at large separately (*divisim*) from the county representatives, for transacting what shall be ordained by the great council (whose composition is above described) " in the premises," that is, in providing remedies for the dangers of the kingdom, as set forth in the preamble of the writ, sufficiently intimating that a " grant of supply," as it is now termed, was a primary object of this parliamentary convocation. And we find that while the county freeholders at large, as regards the rate of impost on their personal property, were placed on the same level as the tenants-in-chief, the citizens and burgesses were constantly called upon to give a full third more.

This very circumstance, however, the large proportion which they were made to bear of the burden which each great pecuniary exigency of the state imposed, inevitably accelerated their advance towards the attainment of a permanent control over all the great operations of government, by rendering their peaceable assent to the several impositions the more indispensable. The lasting establishment just described, of the practice of convoking them collectively, at the same places and times as the legislative estates of parliament, indicates the first great step in this progression. Arbitrary intimidation was no longer felt to be the best means of exacting through the town delegates the desired contributions. It was found expedient that they should at least hear the objects stated and discussed, to which the proceeds were to be applied. Their second step naturally was, to exercise a judgment on the wisdom and fitness, first, of the objects themselves, and next of the means by which they were to be prosecuted. So rapid was the march of the delegated body of citizens and burgesses in this career, that in the year 1297, the 25th of Edward I., we arrive at the first solemn recognition of their political existence in the *statutum de tallagio*, which has been commonly called *statutum de tallagio non concedendo*, by which the right of taxing them arbitrarily was finally relinquished. The statute declares—" No tallage or aid shall be taken or levied by us or our heirs in our realm without the good will and assent of the archbishops, bishops, earls, barons knights, burgesses, and other freemen of the land." At this date then we may fix that important step in the constitutional progression, the union of the representative freeholders or knights of the shire with the representative citizens and burgesses in one assembly.

In the great national measure of the year 1327, which closed the calamitous reign of the second Edward, we find them confounded together under the general name of *commons*, by whose " counsel and assent," as well as by that of " the prelates, earls, barons, and other great men" of the kingdom, it is stated in the writs issued to the sheriffs on that occasion by the young Edward to proclaim himself king, that his father had " removed himself" (that is, had been deposed), and he (the younger Edward) had taken upon him the government.

And according to the preamble of the statutes made at the first parliament of Edward III., the acts were passed "at the petition of the commons presented to the king in his council of parliament, by the assent of the prelates, earls, barons, and other great men." This form of *petitioning* the king in parliament, that is, in the baronial assembly or house of lords, was long the only mode possessed by the commons of introducing a measure sanctioned by themselves into that higher assembly, and remained a memorial of their first seemingly timid advances towards the complete legislative character, until, on their attainment of the latter station, they abandoned the term *petition* for the more business-like and less submissive one of *bill*. [BILL IN PARLIAMENT.]

In this very reign of Edward III., they proceeded so far as to claim an absolute veto upon all enactments affecting those great bodies of the people which they represented, by declaring to the king in parliament that they would not be compelled by any of his statutes or ordinances, *made without their assent*. Edward III. had too much general sagacity, and was too mindful of the popular concurrence in the revolution which had deposed his father, to seek to evade or oppose this legislative assent of the Commons.

It should be borne in mind that the original basis of the representation, in the time of Edward I., was very different from what we must suppose it would have been made, had the crown and its advisers at that period contemplated in this arrangement any such thing as the composition of a legislative assembly. The very large proportion of the whole number of its members that were sent from the towns, at a period when the population and general importance of the towns, as compared with those of the counties at large, were vastly less than they are now, was manifestly a circumstance repugnant to all the political notions and tendencies of the government of that day. Under Edward I. the town representatives bore so large a proportion to those of the shires as 246 to 74; and under Edward III. as 282 to 74. The reason why, on the first settling of the representative system into regularity and permanency, each constituency was uniformly summoned to elect *two*, members, without regard to its known or presumed proportion of wealth or populousness, seems to have been very simple and very natural. So long as the parliamentary voice of the commons was confined to matters of taxation merely, the only thing that appears to have been seriously regarded in fixing the number of delegates was the securing such a delegation from each constituency as at the smallest inconvenience and expense to it should have full power to treat of the pecuniary business in question, and *two*, being the smallest number compatible with the important conditions of mutual consultation and joint testimony, was fixed upon as the number that imposed the smallest burden on the constituents, and was also most convenient for avoiding a too crowded assemblage of representatives. And thus it seems to have been that the periodical and frequent shire and borough courts presenting the most natural and convenient modes and occasions of appointing the parliamentary deputies of the several communities, two representatives, and two only, were summoned, indifferently from the shire as from the borough, and from the largest shire or borough as from the smallest.

When the power and authority of the commons in parliament had become so firmly consolidated under the first three Edwards as to exercise an effective control over all the great measures of government, the composition of the representative body was an object of constant attention and solicitude to the crown. As the number and names of the counties entitled to send members admitted neither of doubt nor of dispute, the right of the *boroughs* became the first object of attack from that quarter. The attempts of this nature, made through the arbitrary exercise of the presumed power of the sheriff to select or omit boroughs, were defeated by parliamentary enactment of the 5th of Richard II.; and, in like manner, statutes were passed in the three following reigns to restrain the corrupt and irregular proceedings of the sheriffs both in county and in borough elections.

Hitherto, however, the parliamentary determinations of the commons, as regarded the constitution of their own house, had constantly tended to maintain the political rights of their constituents against invasion on the part of the crown. But that firm and lasting establishment of their own power as a distinct legislative body, which may be dated from the great revolution that first brought the house of Lancaster to the throne, seems, by that very additional security which it gave them against royal encroachment, to have tended to embolden the house, not, as formerly, to maintain the elective franchise to the utmost with the same zeal with which they upheld their own interest and independence as a legislative chamber, but to commence a sort of reaction against the constituent bodies by narrowing the basis of the suffrage itself. The earliest of these disfranchising enactments, and one of the most remarkable, is that of the 8th Henry VI., which restricts the county franchise, formerly possessed by all freeholders, to such only whose freeholds were worth clear forty shillings a year, a sum at least equal to twenty pounds of the present day. The next remarkable instance, though very different in its nature, of legislative enactment respecting the constitution of the Commons' House, appears in the parliamentary incorporation of Wales and Cheshire in the reign of Henry VIII., which brought an accession of sixteen county and fifteen borough members.

The *borough* representation in general was still the great object of attention to the crown in undermining the independence of the House of Commons. This part of its policy was diligently pursued under the later reigns of the Tudors, and carried to the utmost limit by the Stuarts: 1st, by creating or reviving parliamentary boroughs, and at the same time remoulding their municipal constitutions according to the views of the crown; 2nd, by proceeding to assimilate the municipal constitutions of the old parliamentary boroughs to those of this newly created class. Of the 46 parliamentary boroughs first created in the reigns of Edward VI., Mary, and Elizabeth, no fewer than 27 appear in schedule A of the Reform Act of 1832, besides five of the same number which are in schedule B; a very clear indication as to the description of places which were chiefly selected at that period to exercise for the first time the parliamentary franchise. The last addition to the English representation, previous to the recent changes, was, under Charles II., the enfranchisement by statute of the county and city of Durham, and the creation by charter of the parliamentary borough of Newark. James I., by virtue of his royal prerogative, had already conferred the right of electing two members upon each of the two universities of Oxford and Cambridge, quite independently of the city and borough representation of those places already existing: thus introducing an anomaly, as well as novelty, into the representative system.

Those who conducted the revolution of 1688 made much more effectual provision against the return of Roman Catholic ascendency than they did for the purification of the representative system. The Bill of Rights does, indeed, express, "that the election of members of parliament ought to be free;" but this vague declaration seems to have amounted to nothing more than an indication of the prevailing public opinion on the subject. We find another strong proof that the public attention had now begun to be directed not merely, as in former times, to upholding the authority of the Commons' House as constituted in parliament, but to the nature of the relations, on the one hand, between the house and the constituent body of the nation, on the other between the several members and their individual constituencies, in the enacting of the statute commonly called "the Triennial Act," which deprived the crown of the power of continuing the same House of Commons for a longer period than three years. The Triennial Act of 6 & 7 William and Mary, c. 2, was an enactment wholly on the side of electoral freedom. The discretionary power previously exercised by the crown, not only of dissolving, but of continuing at pleasure, was highly favourable to any such view, on the part of the crown, as that of forming a tacit compact with a corrupt or servile majority of the Commons' House, and was therefore, as had been lately seen under Charles II., exceedingly convenient both to king and commons, when the latter happened to be sufficiently pliant. So strongly, however, was the popular opinion on this point expressed at the period in question, that it compelled the commons to persist in the measure in spite of King William's refusal of assent to the bill after its first passing the two houses, so that on the second occasion his assent was reluctantly yielded. The same activity of the public opinion of that day respecting the composition of the commons, produced the several acts of that reign which disqualify various classes of placemen for seats in the house.

The legislative union with Scotland, effected in 1707 by statute 6 Anne, c. 8, brought an accession to the English (which thereby became the British) House of Commons, of thirty members for counties, and exactly half that number for cities and boroughs; exhibiting between the numerical amount of the county and that of the borough representation a proportion quite the reverse not only of that which existed in England, but of that which had previously appeared in the Scottish parliamentary representation.

The same reign presents us with an enactment of the British House of Commons respecting its own future constitution, totally different in character from those of William III.'s time just referred to. This is the very important act (9 Anne, c. 5) which established the qualification of landed property for English members, whether for counties or boroughs. In the reign of Henry VI., which gave birth to the enactment disfranchising the smaller county freeholders, was passed an act, in the same spirit, restricting the choice of those freeholders who still retained the franchise. The very terms of this statute imply, that in the case of the counties, as in that of the boroughs, there was originally no legal distinction between the qualification of the electors and that of the elected, but that the former were simply called upon to return two of their own number according to their own best discretion. The circumstance, too, of the daily expenses uniformly paid under legal obligation by the constituents to each representative while absent on parliamentary duty, may in this place be properly mentioned as a striking evidence of the fact, that the qualification of considerable property, how much soever it might be regarded in the judgment of the constituents, was originally not at all contemplated by the law. The statute in question (23 Henry VI. c. 14) declares, that thenceforward the county representatives shall be "notable knights of the same counties, or shall be able to be knights," that is, shall have freehold to the amount of 40*l.* per annum, and that no man shall be eligible " that stands in the degree of a yeoman or under." On this legal footing the county representation remained until the ninth year of Queen Anne, when not only was the landed property qualification re-enacted for the counties on a scale nearly proportioned to the decrease in the nominal value of money, but an unprecedented step was taken, by including in the very same clause of the same act a provision, that while every knight of the shire should possess a freehold or copyhold estate of clear 600*l.* per annum, so also every citizen, burgess, and baron of the Cinque Ports should have the like landed qualification to the amount of 300*l.* per annum. The statute of the 1st of George I., commonly called the Septennial Act, which extended the legal duration of parliaments from three years to seven, how cogent soever might be the political motives of the chief promoters of the measure, is another memorable instance of the lengths to which the House of Commons could now venture in dealing with the elective rights of its constituents.

After all that royal prerogative and parliamentary enactment had now done to undermine the originally free and independent basis of the national representation in general, little more seemed necessary in order to render the subversion of this part of the legislative constitution complete; and the door was permanently shut against the prosecution of any scheme for reforming or improving the constitution of the Commons' House, originating within the assembly. It would require volumes to describe the operation and effects of this great political machine during the period that followed—the period of its most absolute perversion to ministerial and to party purposes, and at the same time to trace the fearful and fluctuating conflict thus excited and protracted between the vitiated constitution of the house and the growing strength and intelligence of public opinion. It is no matter of conjecture; it is a momentous and significant fact in the history of this great political institution, that it was "the pressure from without," and that alone, forcibly stimulated, indeed, by the recent success of a popular revolution in France (July, 1830), that drove the House of Commons to compel, first, the formation of a ministry pledged to amend the constitution of the representative body in general, and secondly, by adopting and perseveringly supporting the measure of amelioration consequently brought forward, to force the acquiescence of the hereditary chamber of the legislature in this degree of purification of the representative.

One of the most important operations of the British House of Commons during the period above mentioned, was the enacting of the statute, passed in 1800 and taking effect from January 1st, 1801, by which it incorporated the parliamentary representation of Ireland with that of Great Britain. For the previous history of the Anglo-Irish representation, and the degree of alteration made in it by the Act of Union, we refer to PARLIAMENT OF IRELAND. Sixty-four members for counties, thirty-five for cities and boroughs, and one for Dublin university, were thus added to the number of the British House of Commons. In this instance, as in that of the Scottish union, the ancient proportion between the city and borough representation was reversed, and an additional weight consequently thrown into the scale of the county representation of the United Kingdom at large.

The following is a view of the present state of the representative system, with the alterations made by the Reform Acts of 1832 : 2 Will. IV. c. 45, England; 2 & 3 Will. IV. c. 65, Scotland; 2 & 3 Will. IV. c. 88, Ireland:—

1. *As regards the number and local limits of constituencies, and the number of representatives.*

COUNTIES.

ENGLAND AND WALES.—The number of county constituencies before the Reform Act was 52, returning collectively 94 members: viz. two for each county of England, except Yorkshire; four for the latter county, and one for each county of Wales. The several cities and boroughs which are counties-corporate were excluded from the limits of the several shires within which they were locally situated: viz., from Carmarthenshire, the town of Carmarthen; from Kent, the city of Canterbury; from Cheshire, that of Chester; from Warwickshire, that of Coventry; from Gloucestershire, that of Gloucester; from Yorkshire, the town of Kingston-upon-Hull and the city of York; from Lincolnshire, the city of Lincoln; from Middlesex, London; from Northumberland, the town of Newcastle-upon-Tyne; from Dorsetshire, Poole; from Worcestershire, the city of Worcester· and from Hampshire, the town of Southampton.

The Reform Act increased the number of constituencies to 82, by dividing into two electoral districts each of the 25 counties in schedule F of the act: constituting each of the three ridings of Yorkshire a distinct district for the same purpose; and in like manner severing the Lindsey division of Lincolnshire from the other portion of that county, and the Isle of Wight from Hampshire. The number of county members was raised from 94 to 159, as follows:—Two are assigned to each division of each of the counties in schedule F and of Lincolnshire; two to each riding of Yorkshire : one member is added to each of the seven undivided counties included in schedule F 2 of the act; one to each of the three Welsh counties of Carmarthen, Denbigh, and Glamorgan; and one is assigned to the Isle of Wight, separately from Hampshire.

SCOTLAND.—The number (30) of county constituencies and of county members, as existing before the Reform Act, remains unaltered. But for two of the 27 counties which returned one member each, viz., Elgin and Ross, are substituted Bute and Caithness, which before sent only in alternate parliaments; and the remaining six counties, instead of electing alternately as before, now return jointly as follows :— Elgin and Nairn, one member; Ross and Cromarty, one; Clackmannan and Kinross, one. To the last-mentioned electoral district are also annexed three whole parishes, and part of two others, detached by the act from the shire of Perth, and one entire parish from that of Stirling. And, to obviate the inconvenience arising from the great irregularities in the boundaries of some of the Scottish counties, it is enacted that all detached portions of counties shall, for election purposes, be held to be in the several shires within which they are locally included.

IRELAND.—The Irish Reform Act of 1832 made no change in the county representation as to local limits or number of representatives; two members were still returned for each of the 32 counties.

CITIES AND BOROUGHS.

ENGLAND AND WALES.—The whole number of the cities and boroughs, or districts of boroughs, previously to the act, was 208, returning collectively 415 members. For total extinction as parliamentary boroughs, those were selected the population of each of which, according to the parliamentary returns of 1831, was below 2000. Within this description came the 56 English boroughs which returned collectively 111 members. For reduction from the sending of two representatives to that of one only, those were selected the population of which, according to the same census, was under 4000. These were the 30 English boroughs from whose proportion of the representation 30 members were deducted; to these must be added two members deducted from the four formerly sent by the united boroughs of Weymouth and Melcombe Regis; making altogether a total of 143 borough members struck out of the old frame of the representation.

Of the distribution of this number among the new constituencies of the United Kingdom (as the total number of members remains unaltered), we have here to speak only of the portion assigned to the populous parliamentary boroughs now created in England and Wales. To these was transferred the election of 63 members out of the 143 thus taken from the old constituencies. Of the 43 new boroughs, 22, containing each a population of 25,000 and upwards, and including the great metropolitan districts, were empowered to return two members each; and the remaining 21, containing each 12,000 inhabitants or upwards, to send one member.

New Boroughs created by the Reform Act, passed June 7, 1832.

Ashton-under-Lyne	(Lancash.)	1
Birmingham	(Warwickshire)	2
Blackburn	(Lancashire)	2
Bolton	(Do.)	2
Bradford	(Yorkshire)	2
Brighthelmstone	(Sussex)	2
Bury	(Lancashire)	1
Chatham	(Kent)	1
Cheltenham	(Gloucestershire)	1
Devonport	(Devon)	2
Dudley	(Worcestershire)	1
Finsbury	(Middlesex)	2
Frome	(Somerset)	1
Gateshead	(Durham)	1
Greenwich	(Kent)	2
Halifax	(Yorkshire)	2
Huddersfield	(Do.)	1
Kendal	(Westmorland)	1
Kidderminster	(Worcestershire)	1
Lambeth	(Surrey)	2
Leeds	(Yorkshire)	2
Macclesfield	(Cheshire)	2
Manchester	(Lancashire)	2
Marylebone	(Middlesex)	2
Merthyr Tydvil	(Glamorganshire)	1
Oldham	(Lancashire)	2
Rochdale	(Do.)	1
Salford	(Do.)	1
Sheffield	(Yorkshire)	2
South Shields	(Durham)	1
Stockport	(Cheshire)	2
Stoke-upon-Trent	(Staffordshire)	2
Stroud	(Gloucestershire)	2

Sunderland (Durham)	2
Swansea, sharing with Aberavon, Kenfig, Loughor, and Neath: formerly contributory to Cardiff, now detached (Glamorganshire)	1
Tower Hamlets (Middlesex)	2
Tynemouth (Northumberland)	1
Wakefield (Yorkshire)	1
Walsall (Staffordshire)	1
Warrington (Lancashire)	1
Whitehaven (Cumberland)	1
Whitby (Yorkshire)	1
Wolverhampton (Staffordshire)	2

Contributory Boroughs added by the Reform Act in Wales.

To Beaumaris—
 Amlwch ⎫
 Holyhead ⎬ Anglesey
 Llangefrii ⎭
To Carmarthen—
 Llanelly . Carmarthenshire
To Carnarvon—
 Bangor . Carnarvonshire
To Denbigh—
 Wrexham . Denbighshire
To Flint—
 Holywell ⎫
 Mold ⎬ Flintshire
 St. Asaph ⎭
To Haverfordwest—
 Fishguard ⎫
 Narberth ⎬ Pembrokeshire
To Montgomery—
 Llanfyllin ⎫
 Llanidloes ⎪
 Machynlleth ⎬ Montgomeryshire
 Newtown ⎪
 Welsh Pool ⎭
To Pembroke—
 Milford . Pembrokeshire
To Radnor—
 Presteigne . Radnorshire

In the important matter of *boundaries*, two great objects were to be attained; the fixing of appropriate limits to the boroughs of large population newly created, and the extending the limits of the old boroughs in the many instances in which a considerable population had, in the lapse of ages, accumulated without the ancient boundary. A large agricultural district was also annexed, for the purposes of parliamentary election, to each of the four boroughs of Aylesbury, Cricklade, East Retford, and New Shoreham. And as regards the Welsh districts of boroughs, it may be observed that the principle laid down in the act of Henry VIII., that *all* the boroughs in each county should share the representation—a principle which the arbitrary interference of the Crown, and the decisions of election committees, had since rendered in many instances inoperative—was now restored in its full vigour.

SCOTLAND.—The number of town representatives was raised from 15 to 23; two instead of one being assigned to the city of Edinburgh; two to that of Glasgow; one to that of Aberdeen; one each to the towns of Dundee and Perth; and one each to the large modern towns of Greenock and Paisley. As regards the districts of burghs, their number, their general locality, and their proportion of members (one to each district), remain nearly as before; but as regards the particular places joined in the respective districts, various alterations were made by the Reform Act. Some towns were disfranchised, and others which had formerly been unrepresented were included. The great increase in the population of the maritime vicinity of Edinburgh has occasioned the creating of one district entirely new, comprising the three towns of Leith, Portobello, and Musselburgh, without, however, increasing the previous number of districts, the towns in the old arrangement being all distributed in the new. New and suitable parliamentary limits are assigned in the schedules of the act, as well to the several ancient boroughs as to those newly created.

IRELAND.—In the list of cities and boroughs which sent representatives, no alteration was made by the Irish Reform Act; but two members each, instead of one, were assigned to Belfast, Galway, Limerick, and Waterford, thus raising the whole town representation from 35 members to 39. The limits of the parliamentary boroughs are defined, and to greater number of them new limits are assigned by the Boundary Act.

UNIVERSITIES.

One member was added by the Irish Reform Act to the one previously returned by the University of Dublin.

2. *Elective Franchise.*

COUNTIES.

ENGLAND AND WALES.—Until the Reform Act, the parliamentary franchise in counties had remained without extension or alteration, as limited full three centuries before by the statutes of the 8th & 10th of Henry VI., the former of which confined the right to such "as had freehold land or tenement to the value of 40s. by the year at least, above all charges;" the latter to "people *dwelling and resident* within the county, &c., whereof every man shall have freehold to the value of 40s. by the year." In order to render a man a freeholder, and complete his qualification for voting, it was necessary not only that he should have a freehold interest in his lands and tenements, but that he should hold them by freehold tenure: consequently copyholders, holding by what is technically termed *base* tenure, as well as *termors*, having only a chattel interest in their estates, were excluded from voting. Doubts having been raised as to the right of copyholders, it was expressly enacted by the 31 Geo. II. c. 14, that no person holding by copy of court-roll should be thereby entitled to vote. The Reform Act extends the franchise by admitting not only copyholders, but leaseholders, and even occupiers, under certain limitations; and abridges in some cases of freeholds not of inheritance, as also in all cases of land situate in a city or borough, and which, being occupied by the proprietor, would give him a parliamentary vote for that city or borough. In establishing the right to the county franchise, questions of tenure and interest have become of comparatively little importance, except as they are connected with value; for now what is commonly, though improperly, called a tenant at will (that is, from year to year) occupying land of the annual rent of 50l. has a right to vote for a county, without reference to the tenure by which the lessor holds the land, or the interest that

he may have in it. By 18 Geo. II. c. 18. § 5, it was enacted that no person should vote for a county until he had been for *twelve* calendar months in actual possession of the rents and profits to his own use, except in particular cases. But by the statute of 1832, by § 26 it is enacted that no person shall be registered as a freeholder or copyholder, unless he was in actual possession of the rents and profits for *six* months previous to the last day of July of the year wherein he claims to be registered. Leaseholders and their assignees, and yearly tenants, must have occupied for *twelve* months before the same period, except in the cases excepted by the above-mentioned statute of Geo. II. Value, therefore, has now become the criterion upon which, in many cases, the right of voting wholly depends; and in all cases it is a most material subject of inquiry, in order to determine in what character, whether as freeholder, copyholder, leaseholder, or occupier, an elector should make his claim to be registered.

1. If lands or tenements are held at a yearly rent of 50l., bare occupation as tenant from year to year is sufficient to qualify; no further interest in the lands, &c. being necessary, and it being immaterial by what tenure they are held. 2. So also is the occupation of lands, &c. of 50l. yearly value, as sub-lessee or assignee of any under-lease, which lease was created originally for a term of not less than 20 years, how small a portion soever of the original term may remain unexpired. 3. The original lessee of a term created originally for 20 years, of lands of 50l. yearly value, or the assignee of such term, is entitled to vote in like manner, whether or not he is the occupier of such lands. 4. The occupier of lands of 10l. yearly value, as sub-lessee or assignee of any under-lease of a term of not less than 60 years. 5. So likewise the original lessee or the assignee of such a term of the lands of 10l. yearly value is entitled, whether occupying or not; nor is the nature of the tenure material in any of the above cases; but twelve months' possession previous to the last day of July of the year in which he claims to be re-

gistered is required in all. 6. The being seised of an estate—whether of inheritance or for a life of lives—whether freehold, copyhold, or of any other tenure, to the like yearly value of 10*l*., entitles.

Freehold lands or tenements of 40*s*. yearly value, § 18, are still sufficient to give a vote in the four following cases:—
1. If it be an estate of inheritance. 2. If not an estate of inheritance, but only an estate for life or lives, if the elector was seised previously to the 7th of June, 1832 (the day on which the act received the royal assent), and continues so seised at the time of registration and of voting. 3. If acquired subsequently to that day, if the elector be in actual and *bonâ fide* occupation at the time of registration and of voting. 4. Or if acquired subsequently to that day, if it came to the elector by marriage, marriage settlement, devise, or promotion to any benefice or any office.

Of freehold or copyhold estates six months' possession, and of leasehold estates twelve months', is required, previously to the last day of July in the year of registration, except they come by descent, succession, marriage, marriage settlement, devise, or promotion to any benefice or office.

Now, also, it has become material to consider how the lands or tenements are locally situated, §§ 24, 25: for if they are freehold within a city or borough, and in the freeholder's own occupation, so as to confer a right to vote for such city or borough—or if copyhold or leasehold, and occupied by him or any one else so as to give the right of voting for such city or borough to him or to any other person—they cease to qualify for a county vote.

However, by the 18th section of the act, an express reservation is made of all *existing* rights of suffrage possessed by county freeholders, provided they are duly registered according to the provisions of the act itself.

SCOTLAND.—Under George II. enactments were made which rendered the proving of the old forty-shilling votes yet more difficult, so that many more of them disappeared, and at the close of the last century very few remained. Although the Scottish act of 1681 enacted that the right of voting should be in persons publicly infeoffed in property *or* superiority of lands of 40*s*. old extent, or of 400*l*. Scots valued rent, thus making a distinction, it should seem, between property and superiority, yet it was constantly interpreted to mean that superiors, that is, tenants-in-chief, or persons holding immediately of the crown, were *alone* entitled to vote. Thus proprietors of estates of whatever value, holding from a subject, were excluded from the franchise. It is computed that in several counties nearly one-half the lands were held in this manner, and in the whole kingdom one-fifth of the lands were so held. The class of landholders thus excluded comprised not only the middling and smaller gentry, and the industrious yeomen and farmers who had inherited or acquired some portion of landed property, but also some men of estates worth from 500*l*. to 2000*l*. per annum; while many persons, who had not the smallest actual interest in the land, possessed and exercised the elective franchise. When a person of great landed property wished to multiply the votes at his command, his course was to surrender his charter to the crown, to appoint a number of his confidential friends, to whom the crown parcelled out his estates in lots of 400*l*. Scots valued rent, and then to take charters from those friends for the real property, thus leaving them apparently the immediate tenants of the crown, and consequently all entitled to vote. This operation being open as well to peers as to great commoners, they availed themselves of it accordingly, thus depreciating or extinguishing the franchises of the smaller proprietors. This legal fraud began in the last century, and was chiefly practised subsequently to the accession of George III. Among the various modes by which it was performed, the most common were by life-rent charters, by charters on *wadset* or mortgage, and by charters in fee. The parliamentary representation of the Scottish counties therefore had, according to the expression of a learned lord, "complety slid from its basis." The total number of county voters, as compared with the number of persons directly interested in the property of the soil, was extremely small, and of these the number of real votes scarcely exceeded that of the fictitious ones.

The new basis of county suffrage appears, by the Reform Act for Scotland, to be assimilated, as closely as the difference between the modes of possessing and occupying lands, &c. in the two countries will permit, to the system established for England and Wales. While the old class of rights to the suffrage are preserved to the individuals in actual possession of them before March 1, 1831, provision is made against their perpetuation; while the body of electors newly admitted consists of owners to the value of 10*l.* a year, —of leaseholders for 57 years or for life, whose clear yearly interest is not less than 10*l.*—of leaseholders for 19 years, where such yearly interest is worth not less than 50*l.*,—of yearly tenants whose rent is not less than 50*l.* per annum,—and of all tenants whatsoever who have paid for their interest in their holding an amount not less than 300*l.* The same difference is made as in the English act, between the freeholder and the mere occupier, as to the *six* months' proprietorship required in the former case and the *twelve* months' occupancy in the latter; and the like exceptions from this condition as to the length of possession in favour of cases wherein either ownership or lease comes to a person by inheritance, marriage, marriage settlement. " *mortis causâ* disposition," or appointment to any place or office.

IRELAND.—The Act of Union made no alteration in the parliamentary suffrage of the Irish counties. The qualification of a freeholder remained the same as before, a clear annual forty-shilling interest for a life; and as it was customary in Ireland to grant leases on lives, freeholders were thus created whose votes, from their extreme poverty, and consequent inability to discharge their legal obligations to their landlord, were disposable by him as a matter of course. This practice of multiplying freeholds for election purposes merely was carried to an excessive and most mischievous extent, reducing the franchise almost to universal suffrage, among individuals who, by the very instrument by which they were professedly made free, were reduced to the most abject state of political bondage. Thus many of the counties, in choosing their representatives, lay under the absolute dictation of some great territorial proprietor ; and there were few in which a coalition of two or three of the principal landowners would not determine the election according to their own wishes. Under these circumstances, the provision of the Catholic Emancipation Act of 1829, which raised the freehold qualification in the counties of Ireland from 40s. to 10*l.*, can hardly be regarded as a virtual disfranchisement.

The whole civil organization of Ireland having been introduced directly from England, and the system of tenures in particular being the same in both countries, the provisions of the Irish Reform Act which have reference to the territorial franchise are more strictly analogous to those of the act for England than those of the Scottish act could well be made, at least in appearance. The existing freehold rights being preserved here, as in the other two divisions of the empire, to their individual possessors, and the 10*l.* freehold franchise being already established by the above-mentioned provision of the act of 1829, the classes of electors newly created are—1, the 10*l.* copyholders ; 2, lessees or assignees having a clear yearly interest of 10*l.* in a leasehold created originally for 60 years or upwards, or of 20*l.* in a leasehold of not less than 14 years, whether in their actual occupancy or not; 3, sub-lessees or assignees of any under-lease in either of the two cases just mentioned, actually occupying ; 4, the immediate lessees or assignees, and they only, having a 10*l.* yearly interest in a 20*l.* lease, and actually occupying. The like provision is made as in the English act, against any title to the county franchise being derived from any holding whatever that would entitle to vote for a city or borough.

CITIES AND BOROUGHS.

ENGLAND AND WALES.—The want of any uniform basis of suffrage in the parliamentary boroughs, the endless diversity of the claims to its exercise derived from the various political as well as local influences that had operated upon them in the course of ages,—a diversity which the numerous, various, and often conflicting decisions of election committees of the House of Commons had additionally complicated and confused—was one of the most grievous defects of the old representative system. The generally prevailing custom, too, that the non-residence of borough voters entailed no disqualification, was one of the most serious evils comprised under this head. The Reform Act prepared the way for sweeping off all the claims to the franchise founded on the old and long-abused titles to borough freedom, by establishing a uniform qualification, resting chiefly on the basis of inhabitancy.

It provides, § 27, that in every city or borough which shall return members, every male person of full age and not subject to any legal incapacity, who shall occupy, within such city or borough, or within any place sharing in elections with it, as owner or tenant, any house, warehouse, counting-house, shop, or other building, either separately or jointly with any land, of the clear yearly value of not less than 10*l.*, shall, if duly registered, as directed in another part of the act, be entitled to vote in the election of members for such city or borough; provided always, that no such person shall be so registered in any year, unless he shall have occupied such premises for twelve calendar months previous to the last day of July in that year; nor unless such person, where there shall be a rate for the relief of the poor, shall have been rated to all the rates for the relief of the poor made during such his occupation; nor unless such person shall have paid, on or before the 20th of July in the same year, all the poors' rates and assessed taxes due from him previously to the 6th of April preceding; provided also, that no such person shall be so registered unless he shall have resided for six calendar months previous to the last day of July in such year within the city or borough, or within the place sharing in the election, or within seven miles thereof. The premises in respect of the occupation of which any person shall be entitled to be registered as a voter, need not be always *the same* premises, § 28, but may be different premises occupied in *immediate* succession by such person during the twelve calendar months next previous to the last day of July in such year: such person having paid, on or before the 20th of July in such year, all the poors' rates and assessed taxes due before the 6th of April preceding, in respect of *all* such premises so occupied by him in succession.—Furthermore, § 29, when any premises in any such city or borough, or place sharing in the election, shall be *jointly* occupied by more persons than one, each of such joint occupiers shall be entitled to vote, in case the clear yearly value of such premises shall be of an amount which, when divided by the number of such occupiers, shall give a sum of not less than 10*l.* for each occupier. And, § 30, in every city, borough, or place sharing in election, it shall be lawful for any person occupying as above specified in any parish or township in which there shall be a rate for the relief of the poor, to claim to be rated; and upon such occupier so claiming, and actually paying or tendering the full amount of the rates, the overseers are to put the name of such occupier upon the rates; and in case such overseers shall neglect or refuse so to do, such occupier shall nevertheless be deemed to have been rated.

The formerly anomalous position of cities and towns which are counties of themselves, as regards the possession of the elective franchise, is rectified by the act, § 18. Such counties of cities and towns are now included, for the purposes of county elections, in the several counties at large, or divisions of counties, in which they are locally situated—with this restriction only as regards freeholds *for life*;—that no person shall be entitled to vote in the election of knights of the shire, or of members for any city or town a county of itself, in respect of any freehold whereof such person may be seised for his own life, or for the life of another, or for any lives, except such person shall be in the actual occupation, or except the same shall have come by marriage, marriage settlement, devise, or promotion to any benefice or to any office, or except the same shall be of the clear yearly value of not less than 10*l*. It is further provided, § 31, that in every city or town being a county of itself, in the election for which freeholders or burgage tenants, either with or without any superadded qualification, now have a right to vote, every such freeholder or burgage tenant shall be entitled to vote, if duly registered; but no such person shall be so registered in respect of any freehold or burgage tenement, unless he shall have been in actual possession thereof, or in receipt of the rents and profits for his own use, for twelve calendar months previous to the last day of July (except where the same shall have come to him, within such twelve months, by descent, succession, marriage, marriage settlement, devise, or promotion to any benefice or office), nor unless he shall have resided for six calendar months previous to the last day of July within such city or town, or within seven miles of it; — the limits of such city or town a county of itself, being, for the purpose of this enactment, those settled by the general parliamentary Boundary Act for England and Wales. Similar provision as to length of occupancy, &c. was made in the case of persons having a previous freehold qualification to vote for any of the boroughs of Aylesbury, Cricklade, East Retford, or New Shoreham.

Such are the provisions which constitute what is popularly called, by reference to their most prominent feature, "the ten-pound householder qualification."

But as in the settling of the places which were thenceforward to elect, and in apportioning the members, the new act made a large compromise with the old system, so also it made no inconsiderable one, for a season at least, in sparing to a certain extent the rights to the parliamentary franchise grounded on the old titles to borough freedom. In all such cases, however, it imposes the very important condition of *residence*. It provides that every person who would have been entitled to vote in the election of members for any city or borough as a burgess or freeman, or in the city of London as a freeman and liveryman, shall be entitled to vote if duly registered; and that every other person having, previous to the act, a right to vote in the election for any city or borough by virtue of any other qualification than those already mentioned, shall retain such right so long as he shall be qualified as an elector according to the usages and customs of such city or borough, or any law in force at the passing of the act, and shall be entitled to vote if duly registered; but in both of the above cases it is enacted that no such person shall be so registered unless he shall, on the last day of July, be qualified in such manner as would entitle him then to vote if such day were the day of election; nor unless for six calendar months previous to that day he shall have resided within such city or borough, or within seven miles from the place where the poll shall heretofore have been taken, or, in the case of a contributory borough, within seven miles of such borough. As regards the second class of voters last mentioned, it is further enacted that every such person shall for ever cease to enjoy such right of voting if his name shall have been omitted for two successive years from the register of parliamentary voters for such city or borough, unless he shall have been so omitted in consequence of his having received parochial relief within the twelve calendar months previous to the last day of July in any year, or of his absence on naval or military service.

The expedient to which, to serve party purposes during the agitation of the Reform measure, many of the governing bodies of corporations had resorted, of admitting unusually large numbers of freemen, occasioned the following limitations of the above reservation of the elective franchise of freemen to be introduced into the act, viz:—That no person who shall have been elected, made, or admitted a burgess or freeman since March 1, 1831, otherwise than in respect of birth or servitude, or who shall hereafter be so, shall be entitled to vote, § 32; that no person shall be entitled as a burgess or freeman in respect of birth, unless his right be originally derived from or through some person who was a burgess or freeman, or was entitled to be admitted as such, before the said 1st of March, 1831, or from some person who since that time shall have become, or shall hereafter become, a burgess or freeman in respect of servitude, § 32; and that no person shall be entitled to vote for any city or borough (except it be a county of itself) in respect of any estate or interest in any burgage tenement or freehold which shall have been acquired by such person since the same 1st of March, 1831, unless it shall have come to such person previously to the passing of this act, by descent, succession, marriage, marriage-settlement, devise, or promotion to any benefice or office, § 35.

It is also provided in general that no person shall be entitled to be registered in any year as a voter for any city or borough who shall, within twelve calendar months previous to the last day of July in that year, have received parochial relief or other alms which, according to the previously existing law of parliament, disqualified from voting.

SCOTLAND.—Owing to the previous absence of all pretence or shadow of popular suffrage in the Scottish boroughs, the revolution made in their parliamentary constituencies by the Reform Act of 1832 was effected simply, completely, and at once. The franchise is taken from the members of the town councils and their delegates, in whom as such it was before exclusively vested, and a 10l. qualification, by ownership or occupancy, substituted in its place, with the like conditions, as in the English act, of twelve months' previous occupancy, payment of assessed taxes, registration, and non-receipt of parochial relief.

IRELAND.—In the Irish cities and boroughs the change immediately worked by the Parliamentary Reform Act was relatively greater than in England, owing chiefly to the fact that the municipal corporations of the former country existed in a state yet more thoroughly anomalous and corrupt than those of England. Here again, the actually existing and the inchoate titles to the parliamentary suffrage being reserved, as in the English act, on condition of residence within seven miles, and honorary freemen created since March 30, 1831, being excluded, the 10l. ownership or occupancy qualification is established as the new basis of suffrage, on condition of registration with *six* months' previous occupancy and payment of all rates due for more than one half-year. Reservation was also made, as in the English boroughs, of rights by freehold under 10l., when accruing before the passing of the act, by descent, marriage, &c. The clause of the Catholic Emancipation Act, which raised the freehold qualification in counties at large to 10l., left it at the old amount of 40s in the several counties of cities and towns; but the Reform Act raised it there to the same scale as in the counties at large (only reserving for life the existing 40s. rights), and at the same time gave the parliamentary franchise for such corporate counties to the same classes of leaseholders, and on the same conditions, whom it admitted in the counties at large.

UNIVERSITIES.

In the two English universities the parliamentary suffrage is independent of residence, property, or occupancy, being vested in the doctors and masters of arts of Cambridge and Oxford respectively, so long as they keep their names on the boards of their respective colleges. In that of Dublin, in like manner, it is possessed by the fellows, scholars, and graduates of Trinity College, on the like condition.

The establishment of a general and uniform system of registration of voters, calculated to obviate much of the inconvenience of contested returns, is another very important feature of the Reform Acts; for the various and rather complicated details of which we must refer the reader to the acts themselves.

Having thus given a view of the qualifications for exercising the parliamentary franchise as now established throughout the British Islands, it remains to notice the principal of those legal disqualifications which are of a personal nature, and operate independently of all proprietorship or occupancy.

Every woman, of whatever age, and however independently situated as to property and social relations, is as much excluded from voting as from being elected. As to age in male persons, the only exception is that which excludes all minors, that is, all who have not com-

2 Q

pleted their twenty-first year. As to the exception which regards *aliens*, this is not the place in which to examine the various difficulties that in many cases have arisen and still arise in strictly defining who are aliens and who are not. By the ancient "law of parliament," which forms an integral portion of the common law, lunatics are very reasonably incapacitated, as also are paupers in city or borough elections. It was resolved by the House of Commons in 1699 (14th December), that "no peer of parliament" has a right to vote for members of that house. After the Union with Ireland, this resolution, which was usually repeated at the beginning of every session, was altered into the following form : " That no peer of this realm, except such peer of that part of the United Kingdom called Ireland as shall for the time being be actually elected, and shall not have declined to serve, for any county, city, or borough of Great Britain, hath any right to give his vote in the election of any member to serve in parliament." The vast increase, since the commencement of the last century, owing to the establishment of so many new branches of revenue, in the number of persons employed immediately by the crown as revenue-collectors, occasioned the enactment of several statutes of exclusion from the parliamentary franchise. Thus the 22 George III. c. 41, excludes every class of officers concerned in the collection or management of the excise, customs, stamp duties, salt duties, window and house duties, or in any department of the business of the post-office. By 3 George IV. c. 56, § 14, it was first enacted that no justice, receiver, surveyor, or constable, appointed by that act at any one of the eight police-offices of the English metropolis, shall be capable of voting for Middlesex, Surrey, Westminster, or Southwark ; and by 10 George IV. c. 44, which established the new system of police in certain districts of the metropolis (the operation of which has since been extended to meet the local extension of the police-system), it was enacted that no justice, receiver, or person belonging to the police-force appointed by virtue of that act, shall be capable of voting for Middlesex, Surrey, Hertfordshire, Essex, or Kent, or for any city or borough within the metropolitan district. By 2 Geo. II., c. 24, § 6, persons legally convicted of perjury or subornation of perjury, or of taking or asking any bribe, are thereby for ever incapacitated from voting.

As regards religious grounds of disqualification in general, it should be observed, that as no oaths are now required to be taken, nor declarations to be made, as preliminary either to registration or to voting, all such disabilities as might have arisen from refusal to take or make them are of course removed.

3. *Qualifications of Candidates.*

Of the close relation so long subsisting between the grounds of the elective franchise and of eligibility, and which had sprung from their original identity, we find distinct traces in the similarity between the heads of disqualification in either case. Women, minors, aliens, and lunatics are of course excluded in the latter case as well as in the former. It would be needless to remark, that peers of *parliament*, that is, actual members of the House of Lords, are ineligible to the House of Commons, except in order to point out this distinction—that any Irish peer, not being among the twenty-eight sitting in the House of Lords for the time being as representatives of the Irish peerage, and being, therefore, though a peer of the realm, not a peer of parliament, is eligible to represent any constituency in the United Kingdom, although such is not the case with Scotch peers who are not representative peers. No person concerned in the management of any duties or taxes created since 1692 (except commissioners of the treasury), nor any officer of the excise, customs, stamps, &c., nor any person holding any office under the crown created since 1705, is eligible. In like manner, pensioners under the crown during pleasure, or for a term of years, are wholly excluded. Any member, however, who accepts an office of profit under the crown existing prior to 1705, though he thereby vacates his seat, is capable of being re-elected. Contractors with government are ineligible ; and it is enacted, that if any person so disqualified shall sit in the House, he shall forfeit 500l. per day for so doing; and that if any person having a contract of this nature admits a member of the house to share in it, he shall forfeit 500l. to the prosecutor. Again, by 3 Geo. IV. c. 55, no police justice of the metropolis can sit in parliament.

The judges of the superior courts of common law are disqualified. The three vice-chancellors also are excluded, though the master of the rolls is not. The clergy are also excluded. [CLERGY.] Sheriffs of counties, and mayors and bailiffs of boroughs, as being themselves returning-officers in parliamentary elections, are ineligible for the several districts respectively for which it is their duty to make returns.

The repeal of the Corporation and Test Acts in 1828, and the passing of the Catholic Emancipation Act in 1829, have worked one very important alteration in the constitution of the Commons' House, by removing nearly altogether the widely operating religious disqualifications which previously existed. The engagement "on the true faith of a Christian," to abstain from all designs hostile to the church as by law established, which the latter act has substituted for the oath and declaration formerly required, excludes no man professing Christianity in however general terms, and seems indeed to have no effective operation but against individuals of the Jewish race and creed, to whose admission this bar is still opposed.

Such are the chief personal disqualifications, at common law and by statute, from sitting in the Commons' House of Parliament; presenting, as already remarked, a general analogy to those existing against the voter.

We now come to the other branch of the subject, the qualifications by property and residence; and here, in the case of the English and Irish representation at least, the analogy no longer holds good. The qualification for an English, Welsh, or Irish member, was not altered by the Reform Acts, and was—for a county member a clear estate of freehold or copyhold of 600l. a year, and for a city or borough member, 300l. To represent a university no property qualification is requisite. In 1838 an act was passed (2 Vict. c. 48), which amends the laws relating to the qualifications of members to serve in parliament : a knight of the shire must be entitled, for his own use and benefit, to real or personal property, or both together, to the amount of 600l. ; and to be a citizen or burgess, only one-half the qualification is required. The only *personal* exceptions from this condition are in favour of the eldest sons of peers, of bishops having seats in the House of Lords, and of persons legally qualified to be county members. The qualifying property may be situated in any part of England, Wales, Ireland, or Berwick-upon-Tweed. As regards the Scottish part of the representation, it is worthy of especial remark, that the property qualifications enacted for England within a very few years after the union with Scotland, have never been extended to the latter portion of the kingdom ; and that consequently the conditions of suffrage and of eligibility have remained there, according to the original constitution of the representative system in both countries, one and the same, excepting only the antiently essential condition of *residence*, which has long been done away throughout the United Kingdom without any reservation or limitation whatever; and excepting also that the Scottish Reform Act of 1832 has rendered unnecessary for county members the qualification of an *elector* formerly required.

Issuing of Writs for a General Election; Election Proceedings and Returns.

An essential and very important part of the representative machinery is that which regards the due transmission from the central to the local authority of the summons to elect, the superintendence of the election proceedings, and the due return from the local to the central authority of the names of the individuals chosen. When the lord chancellor, the highest officer of state, has received the written command of the king in council for the summoning of a new parliament, he thereupon sends his warrant in order to the highest ministerial officer acting under him, the clerk of the crown in chancery, to prepare and issue the *writs*, or written authorities for that purpose, to the several sheriffs, whether of counties at large or of counties corporate.

In the early periods of our history, when the shire-motes, or county courts, were held regularly once a month, and the borough courts once a week or once a fortnight, there was no need to incur the trouble and inconvenience of a special meeting of the members of those courts, that is, of the freeholders in the former case and the burgesses in the latter, to elect the parliamentary representatives; and accordingly the sheriff was simply required to cause the election of the county members at the next county court, held in the regular course, or at an adjourned meeting of that court, in case such adjournment were necessary in order to allow time for giving due notice of the election. It was not until the importance of the county courts declined, that a different arrangement became necessary; nor was it until the 25 George III. that it was enacted that the sheriff, on receipt of the writ, should call a *special* county court for the purpose of the election.

The writ, thus addressed under the great seal to the sheriff of a county at large, requires him not only to cause the election of the county representatives, but also of those of each city and borough within his jurisdiction. And accordingly, on receiving this command, he issues a *precept* under his own seal to the head of each municipality enjoying the elective franchise, which precept is to be returned to him within a limited time, together with the name of the person or persons chosen;* in like manner as he himself is bound to return, before a certain day previous to that on which the parliament is summoned to assemble, to the clerk of the crown, from whom he received it, the writ, with the names of the persons chosen, whether as county or as borough members. Such, in brief, as regards the returning-officers and responsible conductors of elections, has been the system from the commencement of the general representation.

* In the universities, the vice-chancellor, as returning-officer, receives and returns the sheriff's precept of election.

In fourteen of the forty-three new and populous parliamentary boroughs created by the Reform Act for England and Wales, which had already a municipal or other chief civil officer or officers in whom this function could be appropriately vested, it is so intrusted by the Act. As regards the others, it is provided, that the sheriff of the respective counties shall, in the month of March in each year, by writing under his hand, to be delivered to the clerk of the peace for that county within a week from its date, and be by him filed with the records of his office, appoint for each of such boroughs a fit person resident therein to be the returning-officer until the nomination to be made in the March following. In case of such person's death or incapacity from sickness or any other sufficient impediment, the sheriff, on notice thereof, is forthwith to appoint in his stead a fit person, resident as aforesaid, to be the returning-officer for the remainder of the year. No person so nominated as returning-officer shall, after the expiration of his office, be compellable thereafter to serve again in the same office. Neither shall any person in holy orders, nor any churchwarden or overseer of the poor, be so appointed; nor shall any person so nominated be appointed a churchwarden or overseer during the time he shall be such returning-officer. Any person qualified to serve in parliament is exempted from such nomination as a returning-officer, if within one week after receiving notice of such appointment he make oath of his qualification before any justice, and forthwith notify the same to the sheriff. In accordance, however, with all previous usage, it is provided that "in case his Majesty shall be pleased to grant his royal charter of incorporation to any of the said boroughs named in the said schedules (C) and (D), which are not now incorporated, and shall by such charter give power to elect a mayor or other chief municipal officer for any such borough, then and in every such case such mayor or other chief municipal officer for the time being shall be the only returning-officer for such borough; and the provisions hereinbefore contained with regard to the nomination and appointment of a returning-officer for such borough shall thenceforth cease and determine."

The division of both counties and boroughs into convenient polling-districts, —the shortening of the time of polling in contested elections, from the old period of fifteen days to two days in England, Wales, and Scotland, and to five in Ireland,—the restriction of inquiry at the poll into the elector's right to the ascertaining the identity of name and qualification with those contained in the register of voters (thus abolishing the old tediously litigious practice of election scrutinies),—and the limitation of the necessary expense of election proceedings, borne by the candidates or their proposers—are among the more important of the recent improvements. For details, as we have already done in the case of the new system of registration, we must refer to the several Reform Acts of 1832.

Having thus given, we believe, a tolerably just though succinct view of the history and present state of the representative system of the British empire, so far as it can be distinctly shown without continual reference to the other branches of the legislature, we refer for an account of the organization and operations of the Commons, " in parliament assembled," to the article PARLIAMENT, IMPERIAL.

We have seen how the popular representation arose, first as a convenient, then as a necessary appendage to the feudal parliament of the Anglo-Normans. We have seen how, as early at least as the parliamentary settlement of the crown upon the house of Lancaster, that popular representation, under the title of the House of Commons, had become an effective, integral, independent, and solemnly recognised branch of the legislature. We have traced, from that period downwards, the twofold operation of the crown in undermining this equal and sometimes preponderating independence of the Commons' House, and of that House itself in contracting the limits and abridging the rights of the constituent bodies, until the original constitution of the representative body itself was absolutely subverted. And last of all we have seen that which, in the present day, it is most interesting to consider,—the reaction of an enlarged and enlightened public opinion on the legal constitution of the House. In an historical view it is far less important to examine the merits of the late measures of representative amelioration in detail, than to mark the maturity of a new political element which they indicate, and the new line of constitutional progression which they have begun. No matter that the Reform Acts, as they are called, have made but a compromise with the exceeding corruptions and anomalies of the old system, and have left some of its most important usurpations untouched ; no matter that the Commons' House, which in the days of its pristine vigour was democratic in the fullest sense of the term, is still, though somewhat popularized by the recent changes, a highly aristocratic body; we do not the less find in these changes a successful effort of the national intelligence and will, not so much to replace the legislative representation on the basis on which it stood at the close of the fourteenth century, and which, from the causes we have previously stated, was fixed without any scientific or symmetrical proportioning even of the number of representatives to that of constituents, but to mould it into some shape more accordant with the present advanced state of general information in the great body of the people ; to render it, in short, a popular representation in fact as well as in name. Towards this point, how much soever they have fallen short of it, the late alterations by parliamentary enactment distinctly tend. The spirit that predominates in them plainly shows from what quarter the impulse came to which they owe their being; and it is a reasonable, at least, if not a necessary inference, that nothing short of a retrogression of the public intelligence can prevent the impulse from being repeated until the great object we have stated shall be completely attained.

COMMONS, IRISH HOUSE OF. [PARLIAMENT OF IRELAND.]

COMPANIES, or GUILDS. [COLLEGIUM; GUILDS.]

COMPANIES, JOINT-STOCK. [JOINT-STOCK COMPANY.]

COMPANY. [CORPORATION; PARTNERSHIP.]

COMPURGA'TOR. A practice once prevailed, derived from the common law, of permitting persons accused of certain crimes to clear themselves by purgation. In these cases the accused party formally swore to his innocence, and, in corroboration of his oath, twelve other persons, who knew him, swore that they believed in their consciences that he stated the truth. These twelve persons were called compurgators. (Ducange, *ad vocem* "Juramentum.") This proceeding appears to have existed among the Saxons, and, in process of time, it came into use in England in civil cases of simple contract debts. The ceremony of canonical purgation of clerks-convict, which was nothing more than the formal oath of the party accused, and the oaths of his twelve compurgators, continued in England until it was abolished by the stat. 18 Eliz. c. 7. [BENEFIT OF CLERGY, p. 360.]

CONCEALMENT OF BIRTH. [INFANTICIDE.]

CONCLAVE. [CARDINAL; CATHOLIC CHURCH.]

CONCORDAT is the name given to a formal agreement between the see of Rome and any foreign government, by which the ecclesiastical discipline of the Roman Catholic clergy and the management of the churches and benefices within the territory of that government are regulated. It is, in fact, a diplomatic negotiation and treaty concerning ecclesiastical affairs, which includes also temporalities belonging to the church. The frequent disputes between the popes and the various states of Europe touching the right of appointing to vacant sees and benefices, and also about the claims of the see of Rome to part, or in some cases the whole, of the revenues of vacant sees and livings, and of the first-fruits and tenths of those which it had filled, as well as the immunities claimed in various times and countries by the clergy and supported by Rome, such as exemption from taxation, and from the jurisdiction of the secular courts, the right of asylum for criminals in the churches, and other similar claims; —all these have given occasion to concordats between the popes and particular states, in order to draw a line between the secular and ecclesiastical jurisdictions, and thus put an end to controversy and scandal.

By the concordat of 1516 between Leo X. and Francis I. the king abolished the right exercised by the chapters of electing the respective bishops, a right assured to them by St. Louis and by the states of the kingdom under Charles VII. in 1438. The parliament refused for two years to register this concordat, as contrary to the spirit of the general councils and the liberties of the Gallican church; it registered it at last March 19th, 1518, 'by express and repeated commands of the king.' (Gregoire, *Essai Historique sur les Libertés de l'Eglise Gallicane.*)

Concordats have become most frequent since the middle of the eighteenth century, an epoch from which the European governments have made themselves more independent of the ecclesiastical power, and the popes have been for the most part men of an enlightened and conciliatory spirit. Benedict XIV., by a concordat with the King of Sardinia, in 1741, gave up to the king the right of nomination to benefices in various provinces of the Sardinian kingdom, which the see of Rome had claimed till then, as well as the temporalities of the same during a vacancy. A concordat was made between the pope and Charles, King of Naples, about the same time, by which the property of the clergy became subject to taxation, and the episcopal jurisdiction in temporal matters was greatly limited. By another concordat between Clement XIV. and the King of Sardinia, the right of asylum to criminals in the churches was much restricted, and full power was given to the respective bishops to expel and give up to the secular power those who were guilty of heinous offences. But the most celebrated concordat is that agreed upon between Cardinal Consalvi, in the name of Pius VII., and the first consul Bonaparte, in July, 1801. By it the head of the state had the nomination to the vacant sees, but the pope was to confer canonical institution, and the bishops had the appointment to the parishes in their respective dioceses, subject however to the approbation of the government. The clergy became subject in temporal matters to the civil power, just like laymen. All immunities, ecclesiastical courts, and jurisdictions, were abolished in France, and even the regulations of the public worship and religious ceremonies, and the pastoral addresses of the clergy, were placed under the control of the secular authorities. Most of these provisions remain in force in France to the present day. Regulations nearly similar exist in Austria and other German states. Other concordats have been made with some of the Italian states. By that of 1818 with Naples the king proposes the bishops, subject to the pope's scrutiny, and the pope consecrates them; the bishops have the right of censorship over the press, and the ecclesiastical courts are re-established for matters of discipline and for ecclesiastical causes as defined by the council of Trent. Appeals to Rome are allowed. It appears from the above facts, that the ecclesiastical authority and influence in Roman Catholic countries vary considerably according to the concordats, if there be any, entered into with Rome, or according to the civil regulations adopted and enforced by the respective governments towards the clergy as towards laymen.

CONCUBINAGE is the cohabitation of a man with a woman, to whom he is not united by marriage. Augustus, with the view of preventing celibacy and encouraging marriage, A.D. 9, caused the law called Lex Julia and Papia Poppæa to be passed, which may be considered as much an ordinance of moral police as a measure in favour of population. This law contained several conditions advantageous for those who had the greatest number of children. It also gave to concubinage (concubinatus) a legal character. The union of concubinage seems to have been commonly formed between a man and his liberated female slave. It appears that a man might have either another person's freedwoman or his own freedwoman as a concubine, or even a woman who was born free (ingenua); but they were chiefly taken from the class of persons of mean birth, or those who had been prostitutes. A man could not have a woman of honest life and conversation, a free-born woman, as a concubine, without some formal declaration of his intention. To cohabit with a free woman otherwise than in a matrimonial connection or that of concubinage, was a legal offence (stuprum). It appears that free-born women must have been sometimes had as concubines; for the Emperor Aurelian forbade such unions. By a constitution of Constantine a man could not keep a concubine while he was married. In Roman inscriptions we find instances of a woman raising a monument to her deceased companion, and calling herself his concubina. No female could be had as a concubine if she was under twelve years of age. Several instances are recorded of Roman emperors who, after the death of their wives, took a concubine instead of contracting a legal marriage; Vespasian, Antoninus Pius, and the philosopher Marcus Aurelius. The object of this union was, that the father might not beget children who would have the same rights as his children by his wife; for as concubinatus was not marriage, the children of such a union were not lawful children.

In Germany, among the reigning families, a left-handed marriage (Trauung an die linke hand or morganatische ehe) still sometimes occurs. This kind of marriage resembles the Roman concubinage, as well in its conditions as its consequences. (*Dig.* 25, tit. 5.)

CONFEDERATION OF THE RHINE. The Confederation of the Rhine was established by an act, signed at Paris on the 12th of July, 1806, by the Kings of Bavaria and Wirtemberg, the Elector of Mainz, the Elector of Baden, the Duke of Cleves and Berg (Murat), the Landgrave of Hesse-Darmstadt, the Princes of Nassau-Usingen, Nassau-Weilburg, Hohenzollern-Hechingen, Hohenzollern-Siegmaringen, Salm-Salm, Salm-Kyrburg; the Duke of Aremberg; the Princes of Isenburg, Birstein, Lichtenstein, and the Count of Leyen. By this act the Elector of Mainz received the title of the Prince Primate; the Elector of Baden, the Landgrave of Hesse-Darmstadt, and the Duke of Berg, received the titles of grand dukes, with royal rights and privileges; the Prince of Nassau-Usingen received the ducal, and the Count of Leyen the princely dignity. The French

CONFEDERATION. [600] CONGE D'ESLIRE.

Emperor declared himself Protector of the Confederation. By the establishment of this Confederation many towns and principalities lost their political existence: such were the imperial city of Nürnberg, which was given to Bavaria; and Frankfort, which was given to the prince primate. Several petty sovereign princes were by the same act mediatised, or deprived of their sovereign rights, such as making laws, concluding alliances, declaring war, coining money, &c.: they retained their hereditary estates, but became subjects to the sovereigns who were members of the Confederation. The object of the Confederation was declared to be, the maintenance of external and internal peace by the mutual assistance of all the members of the Confederation as well as of France, in case any one of them should be attacked by an enemy. The affairs of the Confederation were to be conducted by a congress sitting at Frankfort-on-the-Maine, and divided into two colleges—the royal one, in which the grand dukes had also their seats, and the princely one. The president of the congress in general, and of the royal college in particular, was the prince primate, but the president of the princely college was the Duke of Nassau. The Elector of Würzburg joined the Confederation in the same year, and the King of Prussia meditated the establishment, under his own protection, of a similar Confederation, composed of the princes of Northern Germany, in order to counterbalance the power of the Confederation of the Rhine. This project was destroyed by the war of 1806, which was not over when the Elector of Saxony, who had received the title of king, by his treaty with France, on the 11th of December, 1806, joined the Confederation, and his example was followed by all the Saxon princes. By the treaty of Warsaw, on the 13th of April, 1807, the two princes of Schwarzburg, the three ducal lines of Anhalt, the princes of Lippe-Dettmold and of Lippe-Schaumburg, and the princes of Reuss, were received members of the Confederation, which was increased by the accession of the newly erected kingdom of Westphalia, as well as that of both the Dukes of Mecklenburg, and of the Duke of Oldenburg. Thus in 1808 the Confederation comprehended 5916 geographical square (German) miles, with a population of 14,608,877 souls; the army of the Confederation, which was fixed in the beginning at 63,000, was increased to the number of 119,180. The act of the Confederation was violated by its protector himself, who united with France, by a decree of the 10th December, 1810, all the country situated between the mouths of the Scheldt and the Elbe, and deprived many sovereign princes of their dominions, taking away from the Confederation of the Rhine an extent of 532 geographical square (German) miles, with a population of 1,133,057. Napoleon did not observe any better the promise which he gave at the establishment of the Confederation not to meddle with its internal affairs, but treated it in every respect as one of his provinces. The events of 1813 put an end to the Confederation of the Rhine; and the Congress of Vienna established, in 1815, the Germanic Confederation, composed of all the States of Germany. [GERMANIC CONFEDERATION.]

CONFERENCE at Hampton Court, was held on the 14th, 16th, and 18th of January, 1604, in the presence of King James I., who took a leading part in the discussion, between nineteen bishops and inferior clergymen of the Church of England, and four Presbyterian or Puritan divines, to argue certain objections to the doctrine and discipline of the Church, respecting which the Puritans had petitioned his Majesty. It was followed by no result.

CONFERENCE. [BILL IN PARLIAMENT, p. 367; PARLIAMENT.]

CONFISCATION. [FORFEITURE.]

CONFLICT OF LAWS. [INTERNATIONAL LAW.]

CONGE' D'ESLIRE, a term in Norman French, literally signifying 'leave to elect,' which is appropriated to the king's writ or licence to a dean and chapter to elect a bishop, at the time of the vacancy of the see. The right of nominating to bishoprics was in most countries of Europe enjoyed by the temporal princes, with little opposition from the ecclesiastical authorities, until the eleventh century, when a contest began

CONGE D'ESLIRE. [601] CONGRESS.

between the popes and the princes of Europe, which, in the next century, ended in the princes surrendering this power to the clergy. Father Paul (*Treatise of Benefices*, c. 24) says that between A.D. 1122 and A.D. 1145 it became a rule almost everywhere established, that bishops should be chosen by the chapter. In England, by the constitutions of Clarendon, A.D. 1164, the election was vested in the chapters, subject to the king's approbation of their choice. The right of election was afterwards surrendered to the chapters by a charter of King John, by which however he reserved to himself, among other things, the right of granting a congé d'eslire, and of confirming the choice of the chapter. This grant of freedom of election was expressly recognised in Magna Charta, and also by a subsequent statute, 25 Ed. III., stat. 6 (one of the statutes of præmunire), which was passed for the purpose of preventing the popes from interfering with the elections to dignities and benefices in England. This was the law until the passing of 25 Henry VIII. c. 20, which was repealed in Edward the Sixth's reign. It is stated (Blackstone, *Comm.* i. 380, Note by Coleridge) "that the statute (of Hen. VIII.) is held to have been constructively revived and to be still in force, though it does not apply to the five bishoprics created by Henry VIII. subsequently to its passing; these are Bristol, Gloucester, Chester, Peterborough, and Oxford, which have always been pure donatives in form as well as substance." The authorities for this opinion are not given by Coleridge. This act of Henry VIII. provides that upon every avoidance of an archbishopric or bishopric the king may send to the dean and chapter a licence under the great seal to proceed to the election of a successor, and with the licence a letter missive containing the name of the person whom they are to elect. If the dean and chapter delay their election above twelve days after receiving the licence, the king may, by letters patent, nominate any person to the vacant see; if they delay the election beyond twenty days, or elect any other person than the candidate recommended by the king, or do anything else in contravention of the act, they incur the penalty of a præmunire. The ceremony of election is followed by confirmation, investiture, and consecration; after which the bishop sues to the king for his temporalities. Bishoprics in Ireland are donative by letters patent, without a congé d'eslire. (*Irish Stat.* 2 Eliz. c. 4.)

CONGRESS, an assembly of envoys delegated by different courts with powers to concert measures for their common good or to adjust their mutual concerns. The term is given also to a meeting of sovereign princes which is held for the like purpose. The delegates from the Assemblies of the British colonies who met at New York 7th October, 1765, to consider their grievances, called their assemblage a Congress. A second congress, which assembled in June, 1774, and sat for eight weeks, published a Declaration of Rights. Another congress met in May 1775, which proceeded to organize the military and financial resources of the colonies; and thus these assemblies of delegates exercised the functions of a supreme government, and under their authority the war of independence was brought to a successful termination. In 1789 the constitution was re-organized, and a congress of two houses was formed [UNITED STATES, CONSTITUTION OF.] The meeting of envoys or plenipotentiaries which precedes a treaty of peace is sometimes called a Congress; but the term is more generally applied to such meetings when they have to settle, either before or after the peace, an extensive plan of political arrangements and re-organization. This was the business of the Congress of Vienna in 1815. Sometimes a meeting of sovereign princes or plenipotentiaries takes place to concert a certain line of political action, and this is also commonly termed a Congress. At the Congress of Carlsbad, held in August, 1819, measures were adopted by the ministers of Austria, Prussia, Bavaria, Hanover, Saxony, Würtemberg, Baden, Saxe-Weimar, Mecklenburg, and Nassau, touching the affairs of Germany and the question of granting constitutions to some of the German states. The Congress of Troppau, which met in December, 1820, and was afterwards adjourned to Laybach, was held to deliberate on the political condition of Naples, Spain, and Portugal. At the Congress of Verona, which sat from October to December in 1822, it was determined that French troops should march into Spain to restore to Ferdinand VII. his freedom of action, or, in other words, to put down constitutional principles. The Duke of Wellington was present at this congress, and through him the protest of the British Government against interfering with the internal politics of Spain was conveyed to the Congress.

CONSANGUINITY, or KIN, is the relation subsisting between persons who are of the same blood, or, in other terms, who are descended from the same stock or common ancestor. There can be no legal consanguinity without a legal marriage. [BASTARD.] Consanguinity is either *lineal* or *collateral*. Lineal consanguinity subsists between persons who are related to each other in the direct ascending line, as from son to father, grandfather, great-grandfather, &c.; or in the descending line from great-grandfather to grandfather, father, and son. Collateral kindred are those who, though they have the same blood, derived from a common ancestor, and are therefore *consanguinei*, do not descend one from the other. Thus brothers have the same blood and are descended from a common ancestor, but they are related to each other collaterally, and the children and descendants of each of them are all collateral kinsmen to each other. The Canon Law and the Roman Law have different methods of computing the degrees of collateral consanguinity. According to the Canon Law, which has been followed by the law of England, we begin at the common ancestor and reckon downwards to the persons whose degree of consanguinity we desire to ascertain, counting each generation as a degree: and the degree of consanguinity in which they stand to each other is the degree in which they stand to their common ancestor, if they are removed from the common ancestor by the same number of degrees; if they are not, their degree is that in which the more remote of them stands to the common ancestor. Thus (to use the example given by Sir William Blackstone), Titius and his brother are related in the first degree; for from the father to each of them is counted only one; but Titius and his nephew are related in the second degree, for the nephew is two degrees removed from the common ancestor, namely, his own grandfather, the father of Titius. On the other hand, in this supposed case, the Romans place Titius and his nephew in the third degree of consanguinity, for they count all the degrees from one given person upwards to the common ancestor, and downwards from that common ancestor to the person whose degree of relationship to the first person it is the object to establish. Thus they would count from Titius's nephew to his grandfather two degrees, and one more from the grandfather to Titius. By the law of England, all persons related to each other by consanguinity or affinity, nearer than the fourth degree of the Roman law, are prohibited from marrying, excepting in the ascending or descending line (in which the case is hardly possible by the course of nature); and by statute 5 & 6 Will. IV. c. 54, sec. 2, it is enacted, "that all marriages celebrated after the date of that act between persons within the prohibited degrees of affinity or consanguinity, shall be absolutely null and void to all intents and purposes whatsoever." [AFFINITY.] Under the statute of distributions, 22 & 23 Car. II. c. 10, in making the distribution of an intestate's personal estate among the next of kin, the computation of degrees of kindred is according to the Roman law, which has probably been adopted in this case, because the other provisions of the statute are mainly taken from the Roman law. In England real estate descends to the next heir, and the descent is regulated by the general doctrine of consanguinity of the Common Law and the statute of 3 & 4 Will. IV. c. 106. (*Novell.*, 118; Blackstone's *Essay on Collateral Consanguinity*, and Blackstone's *Commentaries*, vol. ii. p. 202.)

The question of consanguinity is the question of relationship between two given persons, as explained above. If one of these persons is called [A] all his lineal ancestors will be found in (*a*) in the ascending line above him, and all his lineal descendants in the descending line below him. His collateral relations will be found in the parallel lines (*b*), (*c*), (*d*), &c. The Roman numerals denote the respective degrees of consanguinity in the Canon, and the Arabic those in the Roman Law. Thus, III. in the ascending line is A's great grandfather, and III. in the descending line his great grandson. In the ascending and descending lines the computation of the Roman and canon laws, as already explained, is the same: in both laws the great grandfather and great grandson are respectively in the third degree from A. No. III. in line (*b*) is A's great uncle, who, according to the mode of reckoning already explained, is in the third degree of consanguinity to A by the canon law; and in the fourth, as denoted by the Arabic numeral 4, placed under III., by the civil or Roman law.

The following are the names for consanguinity in the Roman law. In line (*a*) ascending from A: 1, pater, mater; 2, avus, avia; 3, proavus, proavia; 4, abavus, abavia; 5, atavus, atavia; 6, tritavus, tritavia: all above 6 are included in the general name "majores." In line (*a*) descending from A: —1, filius, filia; 2, nepos, neptis; 3, pronepos, proneptis; 4, abnepos, abneptis; 5, atnepos, atneptis; 6, trinepos, trineptis: all below 6 are included in the general name of "posteri" or "posteriores."

In line (*b*), beginning with 2 and ascending:—2, frater, soror; 3, patruus, amita (uncle and aunt on the father's side); avunculus, matertera (do. on the mother's; 4, patruus magnus, amita magna, avunculus magnus, matertera magna; 5, propatruus, proamita, proavunculus, promatertera; 6, abpatruus, abamita, abavunculus, abmatertera.

In line (*b*), beginning with 3 and descending, the names are, 3, fratris, sororis, filius et filia, and so on.

In (*c*), beginning with 4 and ascending: —4, consobrinus, consobrina, which are the general terms, but properly signify those born of two sisters (quasi consororini); sons born of two brothers are properly called fratres patrueles; daughters, sorores patrueles. 5, proprior, or prior sobrino, proprior sobrina, the sons and daughters of the patruus magnus, amita magna, &c. (Tacit., *Annal*. xii. 64.) Some of the Latin writers used "nepos" to express a brother's or sister's son.

The term consanguinity is derived from the Romans; but among the Romans, Consanguinei were properly only those who had a common father. Cognatio was a larger term, and it was divided into naturalis and civilis. Naturalis cognatio was that which existed without civilis cognatio, that is, without reference to marriage. Accordingly naturalis cognatio existed among all persons who were merely of kin through the mother, whether they were the offspring of a marriage or not. Naturalis cognatio, or the natural propagation of the species, was the element upon which the civilis or legal cognatio was formed. But civilis cognatio might exist without the naturalis, as in the case of adoption. When cognatio resulted from a legal marriage, there was both the naturalis and civilis cognatio combined. The naturalis cognatio was simply called cognatio; the civilis cognatio might be called civilis cognatio, but its proper name was agnatio. All those between whom cognatio existed were Cognati: all those between whom agnatio existed were Agnati. Cognati then were all those who were connected either by father or mother, or both, whether they were agnati also, or were merely connected by the naturalis cognatio. Those only were agnati who were in the power of a father of a family; and among them was the wife, who was in the hand (manus) of her husband; and they were still agnati after his death. They ceased to be agnati if they were adopted into another family. Also those who were adopted into a family became agnati to all who belonged to such families. Accordingly the definition of agnati, which defines it to be those cognati who are related through males, that is, by being begotten by a man in lawful marriage, is not quite exact; for the definition does not comprise those who are adopted into a familia, though by such adoption they became agnati; and it does comprise those who are adopted out of the family, and who thereby cease to be agnati to the members of the family which they have left. In the old Roman law it was only agnatio, that is, civilis cognatio, which was a matter of legal consideration; but under the empire the strict nature of agnatio lost its meaning, and cognatio also was regarded, as we see in the case of succession to intestates. Thus those agnati who had lost their rights to the succession under the old law in consequence of a capitis diminutio were admitted by the praetorium jus to the succession of intestates, for they were cognati, though they had ceased to be agnati. The same equity of mutual succession was extended to a mother and her children when the mother had not been in the hand of her husband, and consequently the legal consanguinity between her and her children was wanting. (Gaius, iii. 24, &c.)

(*Institut.*, iii. tit. 6, *De Grad. Cognationum*; *Dig.*, 38, tit. 10: Ulpian, *Frag.*, tit. 26; Böcking, *Institutionen*, i. 253.)

```
(a)
VI.
 6
 V. .
 5   .  .
        .  .   (b)
 IV. .    .
  4   .     .  V.
       .     .  6
 III. .    .
  3    .    .  IV.
        .    .  5   .
 II. .     .        .   (c)
  2   .     . III.    .
       .    .  4   .    . IV.
 I. .     .        .      6
  1  .    . II.    .
      .   .  3    .    . III.
 ___  .        .    .     5   .
|A |    . I.       .      .    (d)
|__|     2        . II.    .
                 .  4     .   . III.
 I.     II.                    6
  1      3        III.
                   5
 II.    III.
  2      4        IV.
                   6
 III.   IV.
  3      5
 IV.    V.
  4      6
 V.
  5
 VI.
  6
```

CONSCIENCE, COURTS OF. [REQUESTS, COURTS OF.]

CONSCRIPTION is the name given to the mode of recruiting the French army under the Republic and the Empire. Under the old French kingdom the army was recruited chiefly by voluntary enlistment, and the soldiers were taken mostly from the peasantry, by whom the change from the condition of a daily labourer to that of a soldier was considered as an improvement. The officers were appointed from among the higher or educated classes. When the revolution commenced, the old army was broken up, the whole nation was called to arms, and volunteers were found in abundance. But as the soldiers were bound by no permanent obligation, a system of requisition was enforced, by which every district was bound to furnish a certain number of men for the regular army. But even this proved insufficient, and the Executive Directory found itself in want of soldiers to supply the numerous armies on the frontiers. In 1798 General Jourdan presented to the Council of Five Hundred a project of a law for a new mode of recruiting, under the name of Conscription. This project was approved by the legislature, and passed into a law 5th of September, 1798. After setting down as a principle that every Frenchman is bound to defend his country when in danger, the law went on to say, that independently of danger to the country, every Frenchman from the age of twenty to twenty-five is liable to be called out to serve in the regular army. Every year lists were made in every department of the young men of the age above stated, divided into five classes, the first being those between twenty and twenty-one years; the second from twenty-one to twenty-two; and so forth. The number of men required for that year being made known by the government, and voted by the legislature, a distribution was made among the departments and districts of the quota which each was to furnish. The number required was then taken by lot from the first or junior class, and when that was exhausted, from the second, and so on. This operation was repeated every year. The first levy by conscription in 1799 was 200,000 men. Bonaparte, when first consul, found the system already established, and he applied himself strenuously to render it more effective and to carry it to the utmost extent. At the beginning of 1802 a levy was made of 120,000 conscripts, 60,000 of whom were to fill up vacancies in the army on the peace establishment, and the other 60,000 to form a reserve in case of war. In April, 1803, 120,000 more conscripts were levied out of the conscription lists for the years XI. and XII. In October of the same year 60,000 more were levied out of the lists of the year XIII. By an arrêté 19 Vendemiaire, year XII. (12 October, 1803), severe penalties were enacted against refractory conscripts, that is, those who had not joined their regiments. Eleven dépôts in various citadels were marked out for them, where they were to be kept under arrest, and work at the fortifications. They were also condemned to a fine, payable by their relations. In January, 1804, 60,000 men of the list of the year XIV. were levied. On this occasion Bonaparte said to the Council of State that the law of the conscription was the dread and desolation of families, but that it formed the security of the state. (Thibaudeau, tome v. p. 319.) In 1805, just before the war of Austerlitz, a Senatus Consultum ordered a levy of 80,000 men. Till then the levies had been voted by the legislative body, but henceforth a Senatus Consultum was deemed sufficient.

In December, 1806, a levy was ordered of 80,000 men; in 1808, 80,000, besides 80,000 more of the conscription lists of 1810, to be called out in 1809. This was on account of the Spanish war, which the senate said was "politic, just, and necessary." Instead of men of twenty years complete, according to the original law, the young men now taken were not nineteen. In 1809 a new Senatus Consultum, 18th April, ordered a levy of 40,000; and on the 5th October, another of 36.000. In 1810 there was a levy of 120,000 of the lists of 1811, besides 40,000 conscripts of the maritime departments for the service of the navy. In 1811 the levy was 120,000 conscripts, besides those levied in Tuscany, the Roman states, Holland,

and the Hanseatic towns recently annexed to the empire. As the levies increased, the repugnance of young men to the service became greater, and the severity of the government against refractory conscripts increased in proportion. A reward of twenty-five francs was given for seizing one. When there was a considerable number of refractory conscripts in a department, a moveable column was formed to hunt after them, and the soldiers were quartered in the houses of the relations of the fugitives, who were obliged to board them.

The disasters of the Russian campaign occasioned new expedients for raising men besides the regular conscription. Half a million of men was voted by the senate towards the end of 1812, consisting of 150,000 conscripts of 1813, 150,000 of 1814, 100,000 out of the lists of 1809, 1810, 1811, and 1812, who had not been included in the former levies, and 100,000 men of the first ban of the National Guard, who were formed into regiments of the line.

In November, 1813, another Senatus Consultum placed at the disposal of the emperor 350,000 more conscripts of the lists of 1813-14, who had not been included in the previous levies; and by a decree, 17th December of the same year, 180,000 men, taken chiefly from the National Guards, were ordered for the defence of the towns, as the allies threatened the French territory; and yet, notwithstanding these enormous calls, Napoleon, in 1814, had hardly 150,000 regular troops to oppose to the allies.

Besides the above conscriptions of the French empire, the kingdom of Italy furnished the following numbers:—in 1805, 6000; January, 1807, 9000; October, 1807, 10,000; 1808, 12,000; 1810, 11,000; January, 1811, 15,000; November, 1811, 15,000; 1812, 15,000; February, 1813, 15,000; October, 1813, 15,000.

Few soldiers, unless disabled by infirmities or wounds, ever got their discharge under Napoleon. The time of service was unlimited. By art. 11 of the Charte of 1830, the conscription was abolished, and a new law was promised respecting the recruitment of the army and navy.

This law was promulgated 21st March, 1832, and it declares that the army is to be recruited only by voluntary engagements and by the 'appel,' which term signifies a choice by the drawing of lots amongst the young men of each canton who have completed their twentieth year during the year preceding. The following persons are exempt from the 'appel:' any orphan with younger brothers or sisters—an only son or grandson, and the oldest son or grandson of a widow or blind father, or of a father above sixty—but if the eldest son or grandson in either of the last-mentioned cases is blind or infirm, the youngest is exempted. There are also some other exemptions, as persons engaged in public instruction, or who are preparing for the church or the ministry in any religious denomination which is paid by the State, also students who have obtained certain prizes. There is an appeal to a council of revision for those who conceive that they ought to have been exempted. The period of service is seven years. Persons who have drawn lots which render them liable to serve may obtain a substitute, who must be above twenty and not above thirty years of age, or thirty-five if he has already served in the army, or between eighteen and thirty if the brother of a person liable. Substitutes must not be married, or widowers with children. A person under the age of thirty cannot be admitted to any civil or military office unless he has fulfilled the obligations of the law of 21st March, 1832. Napoleon admitted in principle the procuring of substitutes, and even defended it in the Council of State, as necessary " in the present state of society, which was very different from that of Sparta or Rome;" but he afterwards surrounded it with so many difficulties, that substitutes became extremely scarce and expensive.

In Prussia all men able to bear arms from twenty to twenty-five belong to the standing army: they serve three years, and are then discharged for two years, during which they are liable to be called out as the reserve. All those who have served in the standing army belong to the landwehr of the first ban, from the age of twenty-six to thirty-two inclusive. This ban, in time of war, is liable to serve abroad as well as at home. It is called out every year to exercise. The second ban is called out only in time of war, and includes all men capable of bearing arms till the age of thirty-nine. All older men fit for service belong to the landsturm. For an account of the Prussian military system see Laing's 'Notes of a Traveller.' [MILITIA.]

CONSERVATORS OF THE PEACE, before the comparatively modern institution of justices of the peace, were officers who by the common law of England were appointed for the preservation of the public peace. These conservators, whose powers were far inferior to those of modern justices of the peace, consisting almost entirely of the authority to take sureties for the peace and for good behaviour, were of several kinds. In the first place, certain high functionaries were general conservators by virtue of their offices. Thus the king, the lord chancellor or lord keeper, the judges of the Court of King's Bench, and the master of the rolls, were intrusted by the common law with the general conservancy of the peace throughout the realm, as incidental to their several offices. Other officers again were conservators only in special places; thus the judges of the common pleas and barons of the exchequer were conservators of the peace only within the precincts of their several courts. In like manner, judges of assize and jail delivery within the places limited by their commissions; coroners and sheriffs within their several counties; the steward of the Marshalsea within the verge of the king's household; and constables and tithingmen within their hundreds or tithings, were all conservators of the peace at common law; and all the officers above enumerated retain their authority at the present day. But besides these official conservators there were others who were expressly intrusted with the charge of the peace, either by prescription, election, or tenure. Thus it is said that the owner of a manor might have prescribed that he and his ancestors, whose estate he had, were entitled to be conservators of the peace within such manor. So also as sheriffs were formerly elected, and as coroners still are elected, by the freeholders of the county, certain persons were, before the reign of Edward III., elected conservators of the peace in different counties. There were also instances in which lands were granted by the king to hold of him by knight's service, and also by discharging the duties of conservation of the peace within the county where the lands lie. Besides these, there were conservators of the peace appointed by letters-patent from the Crown, in cases of emergency, to defend particular districts, where breaches of the peace were apprehended in consequence of foreign invasion or intestine tumult. All the different kinds of conservators of the peace above noticed, excepting those who have the duty cast upon them as incidental to other offices, were entirely superseded upon the establishment of the system of justices of the peace, in the early part of the reign of Edward III. [JUSTICES OF THE PEACE.] (See also full details upon this subject in Lambard's *Eirenarcha*, book i., c. 3.)

CONSERVATOR OF THE STAPLE, in the law of Scotland, an officer in the nature of a foreign consul, resident at Campvere, in the Netherlands. By the act 1503, c. 81, passed, as the preamble states, for the welfare of merchandise, and to provide remedy for the exorbitant expense of pleas in foreign courts, the conservator of Scotland was vested with a jurisdiction to do justice between merchant and merchant in the parts beyond sea, such merchants being the king's lieges, and the conservator exercising his jurisdiction by advice of at the least four merchants, his assessors; and it was further provided by the act, that no Scotch merchant sue another before any other judge beyond sea, nor do in the contrary of the statute, under the penalty set down therein. By subsequent acts he was empowered to put the usury laws and other like laws in execution among the same merchants; so that the conservator might be regarded as a commercial judge, with a civil and criminal jurisdiction over native Scotsmen beyond the realm.

From the chapter immediately following that first above cited, wherein the conservator is required to come yearly home, or send a procurator for him, to answer

CONSIDERATION. [608] CONSIDERATION.

all matters laid to his charge, we might suppose that appeal lay from him only to the king and council. But since the erection of the Court of Session, in 1532, he has been regarded as an inferior judge, and his court as an inferior court, which it is accordingly considered by Erskine in his 'Institutes,' b. i. tit. 4, sec. 32. In the case of Hoy v. Tenant, June 27, 1760, the Court of Session went still further, and held itself as the *forum originis* of all Scotsmen, to have a cumulative jurisdiction with the conservator.

CONSIDERATION. This is a Latin word, "consideratio," which, as well as the verb "considero," was used by Cicero and others to express "careful observation," or "reflection," or "deliberation before action." It has nothing to do with looking at the stars, as the Latin grammarian Festus states; but it implies something which is nearer to the business of common life than star-gazing: it implies the sitting down of a man in a place alone or with others. The word "consideration" means 'deliberation' in the English language of common life.

But consideration has also a legal and technical meaning, which seems to flow naturally from its primary and vulgar meaning. A consideration is something which enters into all contracts, and is a part of all transfers of property, except they are made by will or testament. The following are examples of *expressed* considerations, from which examples the technical meaning of consideration may be collected:—If a man agrees to sell his land to another for 100*l.*, the 100*l.* is the consideration for which he agrees to part with his land; or if a man promises to give 1000*l.* to another man if he will marry his daughter, the man is entitled to the 1000*l.* if he does marry the daughter. There is an *implied* consideration in many cases where none is expressed. A man may undertake to do a piece of work for another without any express bargain that he shall be paid; but if he does the work according to his agreement, the other man may be compelled to pay him. The implied consideration here is the implied promise to pay if the work is done.

The word consideration applies either to agreements about something which is to be done, which in England are generally called contracts, or to something that is done, some transfer of property, which is generally done by the act which is called a deed.

Contracts cannot be enforced if there is no consideration. A man may promise to give another 1000*l.*, but the promise cannot be enforced unless there is a consideration, which has been defined to be a reason which moves the contracting party to enter into the contract. This is not a very good definition, but it will do: the meaning is, there must be a motive which the law considers a sufficient motive. A consideration must of course be a thing lawful.

Considerations are sometimes divided into valuable considerations and good considerations. Marriage, as in the instance just given, that is a marriage intended, and afterwards carried into effect, is a valuable consideration; money, and any other thing which is of the nature of property, and has a money value, are valuable considerations. Therefore, if a man parts with his estate for a valuable consideration, the transaction is valid, and he who gets the estate has, so far as the consideration is concerned, a good title. A good consideration is the consideration of natural affection between blood relations, and a man may give his estate to another for such a consideration. But this kind of consideration is not sufficient to maintain the validity of a conveyance of property against the claim of a subsequent purchaser for valuable consideration. Thus if a man after his marriage settles an estate upon his wife and children in consideration of his natural affection, and then sells the estate for money, the purchaser will have the estate, and not the wife and children. (Hill v. Bishop of Exeter, 2 Taunt. 69.) Such a settlement after marriage is called voluntary or gratuitous. A settlement of property made in consideration of a future marriage, which afterwards takes place, is a settlement for valuable consideration. The actual settlement may be made after marriage, if it is made pursuant to a written agreement entered into before marriage.

In the statute 13 Eliz. c. 5, the object of which is to prevent persons from cheating their creditors by disposing of their real or personal property, it is declared that the provisions of the act do not extend to estates or interests made or conveyed "upon good consideration and *bonâ fide*," and the good consideration here means money, or money's worth, or a marriage which is then intended and afterwards takes effect. Good consideration here is therefore equivalent to what has been above defined to be a valuable consideration.

The acts 27 Eliz. c. 4, and 30 Eliz. c. 18, § 3, make void, as against subsequent purchasers, all conveyances, &c. of real property which are made for the purposes of defrauding such purchasers, unless "upon or for good consideration and *bonâ fide*." This statute has received a singular interpretation, for it has been decided that it makes void a previous conveyance, though not made with the intent to defraud any one, if the consideration is not such as the statute intends; and accordingly, as in the case just stated, if a man settles his land after marriage on his wife and children, and then sells it, the prior settlement is void as a fraudulent conveyance.

A voluntary conveyance then by a man who is at the time insolvent, is not valid against his creditors; but if a man is not insolvent at the time, a voluntary conveyance, that is, one where there is no valuable consideration, is valid against future creditors (13 Eliz. c. 5). A conveyance for valuable consideration, such as marriage, is a valid conveyance, even if a man be insolvent at the time. An insolvent man may therefore cheat his creditors by settling his property on a woman with a view to marriage, and then marrying her; but in certain cases, such settlements are not valid against creditors when made by a person who is subject to the bankrupt laws. A voluntary conveyance is not valid against a future purchaser for good consideration: it is a fraudulent transaction according to the construction of the 27th of Eliz., and as such is declared void against the purchaser. If the purchaser knew that there was such a voluntary prior conveyance, that makes no difference; his purchase is valid against such conveyance.

It appears from these instances that the legal notion of consideration is this:— the fact of there being a good consideration is evidence that there is no fraud, and the absence of it is a presumption of fraud. The doctrine of consideration is intended to protect either the giver or grantor, or other persons whom he may wish to defraud by disposing of his property.

Every deed therefore or instrument by which property is conveyed ought to show some consideration for which the person conveys the property to another; for though a deed is valid between the parties to it, when no consideration is expressed, it may be invalid with respect to other persons who are not parties to it. There is no absolute amount of consideration which can be legally required, but a very small amount of consideration might in some cases raise a presumption of fraud; and, indeed, even if the amount of consideration should be the full value of the thing conveyed, it may be necessary in some cases to inquire whether the consideration expressed was actually paid.

In the case of a contract or agreement to give or settle property, the necessity for a consideration is obvious, both for the protection of the giver, and of others to whom he is indebted, or whom it is his moral duty to provide for. No contract to give can be enforced unless there is a sufficient legal consideration. An agreement to settle property on a lawful child is such consideration: an agreement to settle property on an illegitimate child is not such a consideration.

Many curious legal questions have arisen on the doctrine of consideration, such for instance as the case of one man promising to pay the debt of another man. The general principle is, as already stated, that there must be some advantage to the person promising, either certain or prospective, which shall be a reasonable and sufficient inducement for him to promise. If a man were to give his physician a bond which should bind his executors to pay the physician a certain sum after his death, a case which has happened, the validity of the bond might be disputed if the circumstances under which it was given were such as to raise a suspicion of fraud; for instance, if no person was privy to the transaction except the man and his physician, and if the sum should be very large, and the services of the physician altogether disproportionate to the amount.

CONSISTORIUM. [CARDINAL, p. 455.]

CONSISTORY is the court Christian, or spiritual court, formerly held in the nave of the cathedral church, or in some chapel, aisle, or portico belonging to it, in which the bishop presided, and had some of his clergy for assessors and assistants. But this court is now held by the bishop's chancellor or commissary, and by archdeacons or their officials, either in the cathedral church or other convenient place in the diocese, for the hearing and determining of matters of ecclesiastical cognizance happening within that diocese. (Burn's *Ecclesiastical Law*, tit. "Consistory.") The consistory courts grant probates of wills for the goods and chattels of a deceased person which are within their jurisdiction: but if the deceased has *bona notabilia* in two dioceses, the probate must be granted by the prerogative court of the province. The officers of a consistory court usually consist of a judge, deputy-judge, registrar, deputy-registrar, and apparitor.

By stat. 24 Hen. VIII. c. 12, an appeal lies from this court to the court of the archbishop of the province.

CONSOLS. [NATIONAL DEBT.]

CONSPIRACY. Every conspiracy to do an unlawful act which is injurious to individuals or to the public, is a misdemeanor by the common law of England. Many frauds affecting individuals, which cannot be made the subject of prosecution as such, become indictable when they are effected by the co-operation of several confederates. Thus if several persons agree by indirect means to impoverish a third person, as by circulating calumnies injurious to his character or credit, the offence is punishable as a conspiracy, though the concerted acts alone, when committed by individuals, could only have formed the subject of a civil action by the injured party. Another instance of this is the case of a conspiracy among journeymen or servants to raise the price of wages by refusing to work under a certain price. [COMBINATION LAWS.] In former times persons convicted of conspiracy at the suit of the king (the nature of which offence is very doubtful) were liable to receive what was called *villanous* judgment, by which they were rendered incapable of acting as jurors or witnesses, their lands and goods were forfeited for life, and their bodies committed to prison. This judgment was never, however, inflicted upon persons convicted of conspiracies of a less aggravated kind at the suit of the party; and in modern times, the villanous judgment having become obsolete by long disuse, the punishment of conspiracy has been by fine, imprisonment, and sureties for good behaviour, at the discretion of the court.

(Russell, *On Crimes and Misdemeanors*, vol. ii.)

CONSTABLE. This word is supposed by Ducange, Spelman, Cowell, and other legal writers, to be corrupted from *comes stabuli*, which was another name for the *tribunus stabuli*, or *praepositus equorum*, a kind of master of the horse, frequently mentioned as an officer of state in the middle ages. (Ducange, *Glossary*, ad vocem *Comes Stabuli*.) Sir Edward Coke, Selden, and several other writers, insist upon another etymology—from two Saxon words, *koning*, a king, and *stapel* or *stabel*, a stay or support—*quasi columen regis*. Both these derivations are equally remote from the description of the office of our modern constable; but the former appears to be far the more probable; and, in accordance with it, the Constable of France was an important officer of the highest rank in that country, who had the chief command of the army, and had cognizance of military offences: it was also his duty to regulate all matters of chivalry, such as tilts, tournaments, and feats of arms. This office was suppressed in France by an edict in the year 1607: it was revived by Napoleon, and constituted one of the six grand dignities under the French empire; and was finally abolished upon the restoration of the Bourbon dynasty, in 1814.

Immediately after the Norman conquest we find in England an officer of the crown called the lord high constable, whose duties, powers, and jurisdiction were in most respects like those of the Constable of France. The office was one of great dignity and power, both in war and peace, the constable having the command of the army and the regulation of all military affairs. He was the supreme judge of the court of chivalry, in which character his encroachments upon other courts were so heavy a grievance, that the stat. 13 Rich. II. c. 2, was passed to restrict his jurisdiction to "contracts and deeds of arms and things which touch war, and which cannot be discussed or determined by the common law." The office, for several centuries after the Conquest, passed by inheritance in the line of the Bohuns, earls of Hereford and Essex, and afterwards in the line of their heirs-general, the Staffords, dukes of Buckingham, in right of certain manors held by them by the feudal service of being constables of England. The fees of the office were extremely burdensome to the crown; and the possession by a subject of the hereditary right to command the militia of the realm, independently of any royal appointment, was an unusual and frequently a dangerous power; and on this account Henry VIII., in the early part of his reign (1514), consulted the judges respecting the means of abolishing the tenure. He was advised by them, that as the individuals holding the manors were only compellable to exercise the office *ad voluntatem regis*, he had the power of discharging the feudal service altogether; and acting upon this opinion, the king abolished the office, by disclaiming to have the services any longer executed. (Dyer, *Reports*, p. 285 b.) The effect of this was, that Edward Stanley, the last duke of Buckingham in that line, the hereditary high constable of England at the time of this resolution, held the manors after this period discharged of the service of being constable. All doubt which might have been suggested respecting the legal extinction of the office by this means was removed eight years afterwards by the attainder of the duke of Buckingham for high treason, upon which even the manors in question were for-

feited to the crown. Since that time the office of high constable has never been granted to any subject, excepting for some special occasion, such as the king's coronation or trials of peers.

"Out of this high office," says Lambard, in his 'Duties of Constables,' "the lower constableship was first drawn and fetched, and is (as it were) a verie finger of that hand; for the statute of Winchester, which was made in the time of Edward I., and by which the lower constables of hundreds and franchises were first ordained, doth, amongst other things, appoint that, for the better keeping of the peace, two constables in every hundred and franchise should make the view of armour." He then concludes, in justification of his etymology of the term, that "the name of a constable in a hundred or franchise doth mean that he is an officer that supporteth the king's majesty in the maintenance of his peace." This derivation of the office of a common constable seems very improbable, especially as it is the better opinion that these officers were known to the common law before the statute of Winchester. (Hawkins, *Pleas of the Crown*, book ii. cap. 10.) Chief Justice Fineux, in the reign of Henry VII., gives a more reasonable account of the matter. He says that when the superintendence of the peace of a county was found too great a task for the sheriff, hundreds were formed, and a conservator of the peace, under the sheriff, appointed in each, who was called a constable. This was the high constable, or constable of the hundred. As population increased and towns sprung up, it was found expedient to make a further subdivision for the preservation of the peace, and accordingly conservators were appointed for manors, vills, and tithings, who were then called petty constables. (*Year-Book*, 12 Henry VII. pl. 18.)

Constables, in the usual acceptation of the term at the present day, are of two kinds: constables of hundreds, who are still called high constables; and constables of vills or tithings, who are called either petty constables or tithingmen. Both high and petty constables were formerly chosen by the jury at a court leet, and were sworn in and admitted there by

2 R 2

CONSTABLE. [612] CONSTABLE.

the lord or his steward; but until recently the high constables were usually chosen by the magistrates at quarter-sessions. The petty constables are still often chosen by the homage at the court-leet; but by the stat. 13 & 14 Car. II. c. 12, § 15, it is enacted, that if any constable shall die or go out of the parish, any two justices shall make and swear a new constable, until the lord of the manor shall hold a court, or until the next quarter-sessions, who shall approve of them or appoint others. By virtue of this statute, and by reason of the frequent disuse of courts-leet in modern times, the duty of nominating and swearing the constables is now generally discharged by the justices of the peace.

By the Metropolitan Police Acts, 10 Geo. IV. c. 44, and 2 & 3 Vict. c. 47, the police force are appointed by direction of the Secretary of State, and sworn in as constables by the commissioners; and in boroughs affected by the provisions of the Municipal Reform Act (5 & 6 Wm. IV. c. 76), constables are now appointed by the Watch Committee, under the authority of the 76th section of that statute. County and district constables (rural police) may be appointed by the justices at quarter-sessions, under 2 & 3 Vict. c. 93, and 3 & 4 Vict. c. 88; constables (a police) for the protection of property on canals and rivers, by justices in counties, and by the Watch Committee in boroughs, under 3 & 4 Vict. c. 50. By these acts the duties of the office of constable are altered, as well as the mode of appointment. By 5 & 6 Vict. c. 109, parish constables may be appointed by the justices from the lists to be returned by the vestries, and vestries may unite to appoint a permanent and salaried constable for a union of parishes. These recent modifications of the ancient office of constable are noticed under POLICE. The office of constable at common law is a yearly appointment, and if any officer has served longer than a year, the justices at quarter-sessions will, upon his application, discharge him, and appoint another officer in his stead.

Besides these general constables, two or more justices of the peace, upon information that disturbances exist or are apprehended, are authorized by the stat. 1 & 2 Wm. IV. c. 41, to appoint special constables; and by the 83rd section of the Municipal Reform Act magistrates in boroughs are authorized to swear in as many inhabitants as they think fit to act as special constables when called upon. The act 5 & 6 Wm. IV. c. 43, and 1 & 2 Vict. c. 80, enlarged the provisions of 1 & 2 Wm. IV. c. 41, by enabling justices to appoint persons to act as special constables in other places than where they resided, and to pay constables engaged to suppress outrages by labourers and others engaged on railways and other public works.

By 7 & 8 Vict. c. 33, an act was passed for "relieving high constables from attendance at quarter-sessions, in certain cases, and from certain other duties." It was formerly the duty of the high constable to collect and pay the county rates to the county treasurer, but the duty is transferred to the Boards of Guardians; and in parishes which are not in any union, it devolves upon the overseers. High constables for each division are to be appointed at the special sessions held for hearing appeals against the rates, and not at the quarter-sessions, as heretofore.

In general all the permanent inhabitants within a district, borough, parish, or place, are liable to serve as constables; but they must be persons of good character and of competent ability; and the lord or steward of the manor at the leet, or the justices, may exercise a discretion as to the appointment of proper persons. It is obligatory upon a constable who has been legally appointed to serve the office, unless he can show some lawful exemption; and if he refuses to serve, he may be fined or punished by indictment. The following persons are exempt from serving the office; namely, members of the colleges of physicians and surgeons, and the Apothecaries' Company in London, practising barristers, attorneys, dissenting ministers following no trade or other employment except that of a schoolmaster, schoolmasters, parish-clerks, clerks of guardians in poor-law unions, masters of workhouses, churchwardens, overseers and relieving-officers, registrars and superintendent-registrars; and gamekeepers, victuallers, licensed retail beer-sellers, and dealers in exciseable liquors, are disqualified.

The Metropolitan Police Act and the Municipal Reform Act contain provisions that the constables to be appointed under those statutes respectively shall have all such powers and privileges, and be liable to all such duties and responsibilities as any constable has within his constablewick by virtue of the common law of this realm. In consequence of these provisions, it becomes of great practical importance to ascertain with precision the common-law incidents of the office of constable.

1. By the common law, constables are said to have been conservators of the peace; and in consequence of this character, probably, every constable has undoubted authority to arrest all persons who commit an affray, assault, or breach of the peace *in his presence*, and keep them in safe custody until they can be brought before a magistrate. But as his duty is to preserve the peace, and not to punish for the breach of it, it is doubtful whether he can arrest by his own authority and without a warrant, upon the information or charge of a third person, for an affray committed in his absence. (See the case of Timothy v. Simpson, 1 Crompton, Meeson, and Roscoe's *Reports*, p. 760.) By the Metropolis Police Act, and the Municipal Corporation Reform Act, constables appointed under those acts are expressly authorised, in charges of petty misdemeanor in the night time, to take bail by recognizance for the appearance of the offender before a magistrate within a limited time.

2. A constable having reasonable cause to suspect that a felony has been committed, may arrest and detain the supposed offender until he can be brought before a magistrate to have his conduct investigated; and he will be justified in so doing even though it should afterwards appear that in fact no felony was committed. In this case there is a distinction between the authority of a constable and that of a private person; the former may arrest if he can show a reasonable ground of suspicion that a felony has been committed; but a private person, in order to justify himself for causing the imprisonment of another, must prove, in addition to the reasonable suspicion of the individual, that a felony has actually been committed. A constable is bound to arrest any person whom he sees committing a felony, or any person whom another positively charges with having committed a felony; but generally speaking, he has no authority to arrest for a misdemeanor, either upon his own reasonable suspicion or the charge of another person, without a magistrate's warrant. With respect to the authority of a constable to arrest for felony or breach of the peace, Mr. Justice Buller is reported to have said, that "if a peace-officer, of his own head, takes a person into custody on suspicion, he must prove that such a crime was committed; but if he receives a person into custody on a charge preferred by another of felony or breach of the peace, then he is to be considered as a mere conduit; and if no felony or breach of the peace was committed, the person who preferred the charge alone is answerable." Lord Ellenborough, in the case of Hobbs v. Branscomb (3 Campbell's *Reports*, 420), said that "this rule appeared to be reasonable."

3. Constables were authorised by the common law to arrest such "strange persons as do walk abroad in the night-season." (Lambard's *Constable*, p. 12.) This authority, which was perhaps sufficiently definite in times when the curfew was in practice and when watch and ward were kept, is at the present day of so vague a nature, that a peace-officer could scarcely act under it without danger of an action in every particular instance. It is, however, obviously essential to the efficiency of any system of police, that constables should be armed with some general authority of this nature, especially in towns. By the Metropolitan Police Acts (10 Geo. IV. c. 44, and 2 & 3 Vict. c. 47), it is provided that any man belonging to the police force appointed under these acts may apprehend all loose, idle, and disorderly persons whom he shall find disturbing the public peace, and any person charged by another with having recently committed an aggravated assault, or any person whom he shall

have just cause to suspect of any evil designs, and all persons whom he shall find between sunset and the hour of eight in the morning lying in any highway, yard, or other place, or loitering therein, and not giving a satisfactory account of themselves, and deliver them to the constable in attendance at the nearest watch-house, to be secured until they can be brought before a magistrate. The constable may detain persons, and vessels, and carriages conveying property suspected to be stolen, &c. Offenders are to be taken to the nearest station-house, and the horses and carriages of offenders are to be detained. The Municipal Reform Act contains a similar but less comprehensive provision, authorising any constable appointed under that act, while on duty, to apprehend all idle and disorderly persons whom he shall find disturbing the public peace, or whom he shall have just cause to suspect of intention to commit a felony. The constable of a municipal borough under the act has power within any part of the county to which the borough belongs, and also within every other county within seven miles of such borough. Besides the specific authorities which apply to the metropolitan police district and the boroughs affected by the Municipal Reform Act, there is no doubt that in general a constable, by virtue of his common-law authority, may stop any person carrying by night a bundle or goods under circumstances of reasonable suspicion; and if upon examining him his suspicions are not removed, he may detain him in his custody. A constable has also a general authority to apprehend for offences against the Vagrant Act, 4 & 5 George IV. c. 83, or against the Larceny Act, or the Malicious Injuries Act, 7 & 8 George IV. c. 29 and 30.

4. In the execution of a warrant a constable acts only as a ministerial officer to the magistrate who signs it. He is the proper officer to a justice of the peace, and is bound by law to execute his warrants, and may be indicted for disobeying them. It is his duty to execute the warrant of a magistrate as soon as it comes to his hands; and where he arrests or distrains or does any other act, though it is not absolutely necessary that he should show his warrant, he ought always to give notice of it, and he will be wise to produce it in all cases where it is demanded; but as the warrant constitutes his justification, he is not required to part with it out of his possession. If the constable has a legal warrant to arrest for felony, or even breach of the peace, he may break open doors after having demanded admittance and given notice of his warrant; and if, after such notice, he is resisted and killed, it will be murder. If a warrant be directed to a constable by his name of office merely, he is *authorised* by the stat. 5 Geo. IV. c. 18, to execute it out of his own constablewick, provided it be within the jurisdiction of the magistrate who signs it; but he is not *bound* to do so, and may in all cases choose whether he will go beyond his own precincts or not.

5. There are several provisions for the indemnity and protection of constables in the proper discharge of their duty. Thus by the stat. 7 Jac. I. c. 5, if an action be brought against a constable for anything done by virtue of his office, he may plead the general issue and give the special matter in evidence; and if he recovers, he is entitled to double costs. Formerly if a magistrate granted a warrant in a matter over which he had no jurisdiction, the officer who executed it was liable to an action of trespass for so doing; but by the stat. 24 George II. c. 44, § 6, it is enacted, that "no action shall be brought against any constable for anything done in obedience to the warrant of a justice of the peace, until he has neglected or refused to show his warrant on being demanded so to do. And if after he has shown his warrant, any action is brought against the constable alone, without joining the justice who signed the warrant, the defendant, on producing the warrant at the trial, shall be entitled to a verdict, notwithstanding the defect of the justice's jurisdiction; and if the action be brought against the constable jointly with the justice, the constable is to be entitled to a verdict on proof of the warrant." By section 8 of the same statute, all actions against constables for anything done in the execution of their office must be

brought within six months. For the further protection of constables, the stat. 9 George IV. c. 31, § 25, enacts that persons convicted of assaults upon peace-officers in the due execution of their duty may be imprisoned with hard labour for two years, and be fined or required to find sureties for keeping the peace. (For fuller information upon the whole of this subject, see Viner's *Abridgement*; Bacon's *Abridgement*; and Burn's *Justice*, title "Constable.")

For an account of the rural police established in several counties of England, and of the constabulary in Ireland, see POLICE.

CONSTABLE, LORD HIGH, OF SCOTLAND. In the twelfth century we have a list of eleven lord high constables in Scotland. Sir Gilbert de Hay got the office in fee and heritage in the year 1314; since which time the constable's staff, then put into his hands by Bruce, has remained in the Errol family.

The office and jurisdiction of the lord high constable of Scotland differ from those of the like officer in England. No formal distribution of the powers of the lord justiciar of Scotland, such as took place at the breaking up of the aula regis of England, was ever made in the former kingdom; nor when in the course of years this happened, did the once large powers of the justiciar pass to the like officers in the one country as in the other. On the new modelling of the judicial polity of England by King Edward I., the constable and mareschal were set over a court of chivalry, with jurisdiction in matters of honour and arms. But in these the constable of Scotland never had jurisdiction. His jurisdiction was of the nature of that in England, vested by 33 Henry VIII. c. 12, in the lord steward of the king's household, or (in his absence) of the treasurer, comptroller, and steward of the Marshalsea; for according to the Leges Malc. II., he judged jointly with the mareschal in all transgressions committed within certain limits of the king's court. But even this jurisdiction seems to have been exercised in fact by the lord justiciar; the constable only protesting against the interference with his powers. In the reign of King Charles I., a commission was issued to inquire into the nature and extent of the constable's jurisdiction; and they reported that it extended to all slaughters and riots committed within four miles of the king's person, or of the parliament or privy council. No alteration was made at the Union; and by the act 20 Geo. II. c. 43—which swept away so many other heritable jurisdictions—the office and jurisdiction of the lord high constable of Scotland were expressly reserved.

CONSTITUTION, a term often used by persons at the present day without any precise notion of what it means. Such a definition of a Constitution, if it were offered as one, might be defended as equally good with many other definitions or descriptions which are involved in the terms used whenever a constitution is spoken of.

The constitutions which are most frequently mentioned are the English Constitution, the constitutions of the several States composing the North American union, the Federal constitution, by which these same States are bound together, and various constitutions of the European continent.

The *vague* notion of a constitution is that of certain fundamental rules or laws by which the general form of administration in a given country is regulated, and in opposition to which no other fundamental rules or laws, or any rules or laws, can or ought to be made.

The *exact* notion of a constitution cannot be obtained without first obtaining a notion of sovereign power. The sovereign power in any state is that power from which all laws properly so called proceed; it is that power which commands and can enforce obedience. Such a power, being sovereign or supreme, is subject to no other power, and cannot therefore be bound by any rules laid down, either by those who have at any previous time enjoyed the sovereign power in the same community, or by any maxims or rules of conduct practised or recommended by its predecessors in power, whether those rules or maxims be merely a matter of long usage or solemnly recorded in any written instrument. The sovereign power for the time is supreme, and can make what laws it pleases without doing any illegal act, and, strictly speaking, also without doing any unconstitutional act. For this word Constitution, taken in its strongest sense, can never mean more than a law made or a usage sanctioned by some one or more possessed of sovereign power, which law or usage has for many generations been observed by all those who have successively held the sovereign power in the same country. To modify or destroy such a rule or law might be unwise, as being an act in opposition to that which many successive generations had found to be a wise and useful rule; it might be dangerous as being opposed to that to which the experience or prejudices of many generations had given their sanction; and it might lead to resistance on the part of the governed, if either their own interest or their passions were strong enough to lead them to risk a contest with the sovereign power. If (as would generally be admitted) the assembled parliament of Great Britain and Ireland possess the sovereign power, there is no act which they could do which would be illegal, as everybody must admit; and further, there is no possible act which they could do which would be unconstitutional, for such act would be no more than repealing some law or usage having the force of law which the mass of the nation regarded with more than usual veneration, or enacting something at variance with such law or usage. For example, if the next assembled parliament should abolish the trial by jury in all cases, such an act might be called by some persons illegal, unconstitutional, and unwise. But it would not be called illegal by any person who had fully examined into the meaning of the word Law; it would not be called unconstitutional by any man who, having called it illegal, wished to be consistent with himself: it could only be properly called wise or unwise by those who had reflected sufficiently on the nature of the institution and its operations to know whether such a modification would do more good or harm.

The words constitution and unconstitutional appear to be only strictly applicable to those cases where the sovereign power, whether held by one, or two, or five hundred, or all the males of an independent political community who are above a certain age, or by any other number in such a community, lays down certain rules to regulate the conduct of those to whom the sovereign power intrusts the legislative functions. Such are the Constitutions of the several states composing the North American Union, and such is the Constitution of the Federation of these several states. In these several states the people, in the mass, and as a general rule, are the sovereign. The people assembled by their delegates, named for that especial purpose, have framed the existing Constitutions; and they change the same Constitutions in the same way whenever the majority of the people, that is, when the sovereign, chooses to make such change.

These constitutions lay down certain rules, according to which the legislative, executive, and judicial functionaries must be chosen; they fix limits to their several powers, both with respect to one another, and with respect to the individuals who compose the sovereign. "They do ordain and declare the future form of government." For example, the Constitution of Virginia of 1776 declares "that all ministers of the Gospel of every denomination shall be incapable of being elected members of either House of Assembly, or of the Privy Council." The same rule, we believe, forms a part of the amended Constitution of the same state. If the Virginian legislature were to pass an act to enable clergymen to become members of the House of Assembly or of the Privy Council, such an act would be unconstitutional, and no one would be bound to obey it. The judiciary, if such a matter came before it, would, in the discharge of its duty, declare it unconstitutional, and such so-called law could have no further effect than if any unauthorized body of men had made it.

A constitution, then, is nothing more than an act of the sovereign power, by which it delegates a part of its authority to certain persons, or to a body, to be chosen in a way prescribed by the Act of Constitution, which at the same time fixes in a general way the powers of the body to which a part of the sovereign power is thus delegated. And the sovereign power changes this Constitution whenever it pleases, and in doing so acts neither constitutionally nor unconstitutionally, but simply exercises its sovereign power. No body can act unconstitutionally except a body which has received authority from a higher power, and acts contrary to the terms which fix that authority. Wherever, then, there is a sovereign power, consisting either of one, as the Autocrat of Russia, of three members, king, lords, and commons, as in England (provided these three members do possess the complete sovereign power), or of all the males born of American citizens and of a given age, and of all naturalized foreigners, as in most of the United States of North America—such sovereign power cannot act unconstitutionally. For to act unconstitutionally would be to act against a rule imposed by some superior authority, which would be a contradiction.

A constitutional government may be either purely democratical, as those of the United States of North America, or it may be republican, that is, a government in which the sovereign power is simply defined as not being held by one person, as in France and England. It may be of such a kind that it shall approach very near to a monarchy, if the king or other head of the state is by the constitution invested with very great powers, or such powers as may enable him to overpower, overawe, or render incapable of action, the other limbs of the Constitution. A constitutional government may be of the aristocratical kind, as England, where the power of the crown is now very limited in practice, and is in effect wielded by the small number who for the time obtain the direction of affairs by means of being able to get a majority of the House of Commons ; for this body, though elected by the people, cannot yet be considered as a really popular body. The French king, under the Charter, has greater powers than the English king has in fact, though in theory it may seem otherwise. The present King of the French presides in his own Cabinet; the English Cabinet deliberates without the presence of the king, whose wishes, in opposition to those of the Cabinet, can never be carried into effect. The Cabinet consists of the responsible ministers ; they are the king's servants, but so long as they are in office they act as they please. But whatever variety of form there may be in constitutional governments, the essential element to a constitutional government, as here understood, is an assembly of representatives chosen by all the people, or by a considerable proportion of them. This is the body on which a constitutional government depends for its strength, its improvement, and its existence. This is the element out of which ought to come all the ameliorations of the condition of the people which can be effected by legislative measures. The limb or member of a constitutional government, which is composed either of hereditary peers, or of peers named for life by a king, is from its nature an inert body. It may resist unwise and hasty change, but it is not adapted for any active measures.

The policy of having a constitution in a state where the sovereign power is in the hands of all the citizens may be defended on general grounds of convenience. When the community have settled that certain fundamental maxims are right, it is a saving of time and trouble to exclude the discussion of all such matters from the functions of those to whom they have by the constitution intrusted legislative power. Such fundamental rules also present a barrier to any sudden and violent assumption of undue authority either by the legislative or executive, and oblige them, as we see in the actual workings of constitutions, to obtain their object by other means, which, if not less dangerous in the end, are more slow in their operation, and thus can be detected and are exposed to be defeated by similar means put in action by the opposing party. There are disadvantages also in such an arrangement. Constitutional rules when once fixed are not easily changed; and the legislative body when once established, though theoretically, and in fact too, under the sovereign control, often finds means to elude the vigilance and defeat the wishes of the body to which it owes its existence, and from which it derives its power. One of the great means by which these ends are effected is the interpretation of the written instrument or constitution, which is the warrant for their powers. The practice of torturing the words of all written law, till in effect the law or rule is made to express the contrary of what seemed to be at first intended, appears to be deeply implanted in the English race, and in those of their descendants who have established constitutional forms on the other side of the Atlantic. The value of all written instruments, whether called constitutions or not, seems considerably impaired by this peculiar aptitude of men to construe words which once seemed to have one plain meaning only, so that they shall mean anything which the actual circumstances may require, or may seem to require.

It is beside our purpose to discuss the advantage of a Constitution in a community where the sovereign is one. Being supreme, the sovereign may change the Constitution when he pleases. It may be said that if the Constitution is good, and has been allowed to stand by several successive possessors of the sovereign power, it obtains an apparent prescriptive authority, which is the more binding on the sovereign, as the mass of the nation habitually regard this same Constitution as something which even the sovereign cannot touch with impunity. It would shock common prejudice if the actual sovereign were to violate that which has been sanctioned by his predecessors, and is recommended by an apparently higher antiquity than the power which, in the actual sovereign's hands, appears to be of more recent birth. The precise meaning of what is called the English Constitution must be got from the various writers who have made its origin and progress their study. In reading them it may not be amiss to bear in mind that the word Constitution, as used by them, has not the exact, but the vague meaning as explained above.

States where there is a king, or other person with corresponding name and power, are now most usually distributed into the two classes of monarchies and constitutional monarchies. The term Monarchy is a proper term to express a form of government in which one man has the sovereign power, as in Russia. The term Constitutional Monarchies is not an appropriate term, because the word monarchy is not capable of a limitation of meaning without the implication of a contradiction in terms. Still the expression is used, and it is understood to express those states in which the kingly power is limited or defined by a written instrument, which also lays down certain general rules affecting the form of government and the condition of the people, which are not to be varied by any legislative act. Such an instrument is the French Charte [CHARTE], under which France, instead of being a monarchy, as it was once, is now a constitutional state, or, as it is called, a constitutional monarchy. This act, which proceeded from the king (Louis XVIII.), cannot be revoked by any future king consistently with good faith; and, besides this, such revocation would be followed by resistance to the government, if the actual government were not too strong to be resisted. The violation of such a solemn act would, in the opinion of all mankind, justify revolution, and the inflicting the punishment of death on all who advised or participated in so flagrant a violation of good faith.

At present there is a struggle in some countries, as in Prussia for instance, between the sovereign (the king) and his subjects, who call for a constitution. The late King of Prussia, Frederick William III., solemnly promised his people a constitution in the hour of difficulty, on the 22nd of May, 1815, when Napoleon was again threatening Prussia and all Europe. The promise was a reward due to the Prussian nation, for their services in the years 1813, 1814: it was a compensation due for the blood shed at Leipzig, and the overthrow of the enemy of all freedom and constitutions. He promised not only a representative system for the eight provinces of Prussia, but a representative system for all Prussia; the only sure foundation on which that kingdom can now stand. Frederick William III. died on the 7th of June, 1840, without having fulfilled his promise of giving Prussia a general representative system,—without having made good the solemn promise of a king to a people who had again built up his throne that had crumbled to the dust before the armies of France. The son of Frederick William III., King Frederick William IV. of Prussia, has declared to the states of Posen, on the 9th of September, 1840, that his father's promise does not bind him, because his father thought a constitution incompatible with the good of his people, and accordingly gave them, in place of it, the law of the 5th of June, 1823. To this it is replied, that the law of the 22nd of May, 1815, promised provincial estates and representatives for the whole nation. The law of the 5th of June, 1823, established the provincial estates, and gave a prospect of the representatives of the nation being called together; consequently, in making this renewal of his promise, Frederick William III. could not have intended that the second law should stand in the place of the first. (*Das Königliche Wort,* Friederich Wilhelms III., von Dr. Johann Jacoby, dated Königsberg, 16th December, 1844, but printed in London.)

In some monarchical governments, as in Prussia, a constitutional government is of urgent necessity. When a nation has reached a certain point in its social progress, a participation in the sovereign power becomes a universal desire. It does not follow that a nation will be better administered because the people participate in the sovereign power, but they will not be satisfied till they do participate in it; and that is the important matter for an absolute power to consider. The representatives may often, and will certainly sometimes, enact laws which are mischievous to themselves; but that is an incident to, or an accident in, a constitutional system, not its essential. The essential of a constitutional system is to call all men into political activity as members of a state, to secure the highest degree of individual freedom that is consistent with the general interest, to establish a real national character by making each man a potentia land living member of the body corporate, and, above all, to keep a tight and steady hand upon the public purse; to see that no more taxes are raised than are necessary for the due support of the administration, and to see that they are raised in such a way as to bring the largest sum into the treasury with the least detriment to the individual. Freedom of publication, or, as it is usually called, the liberty of the press, is in modern times indispensable as a means of maintaining constitutional freedom where it exists, and of attaining it where it does not. In an absolute government, like Prussia, it is restrained by a censorship: in France, which is a young constitution, it is checked by severe enactments; in England the freedom of the press is amply secured both by law and usage. In the actual state of Germany, in which political life hardly exists, the establishment of a true constitutional government in Prussia would be the commencement of a new æra for the Germanic nation. The Russian subjects of the Czar of Muscovy, or of the greater part of his dominions at least, may be at present as contented and as well governed as they would be under a constitution; for a constitution, in order to be beneficial, must be founded upon a representation of a whole nation which has political knowledge, or of a majority so large that the minority shall be insignificant when compared with it.

In the articles CHARTE and UNITED STATES, CONSTITUTION OF, an account is given of the constitutions of France and the United States of North America, which countries, and England, enjoy a higher degree of constitutional freedom than any other states. Spain has made extraordinary efforts to obtain the advantages of a constitution. [CORTES.] Some of the smaller states of Germany have constitutions, as Würtemberg, Hanover, Baden, Hesse Darmstadt, Hesse Cassel, Nassau, &c. The European states which have no constitution are Russia, Austria, Prussia, Ottoman Empire, Naples and Sicily, Papal States, Grand Dukedom of Tuscany, Dukedom of Parma, Dukedom of Modena, Dukedom of Lucca, Sardinia, the Principality of Monaco, &c. The constitutions of Mexico and of the Republics of South America resemble that of the United States. Brazil has a constitution and a representation.

For the nature of a Federal Government, which necessarily implies the notion of a Constitution, see FEDERATION.

CONSTITUTIONS AND CANONS ECCLESIASTICAL. King James I., in the first year of his reign in England, by his writ directed to the Archbishop of Canterbury, summoned and called the "bishops, deans of cathedral churches, archdeacons, chapters and colleges, and the other clergy of every diocese within the province of Canterbury," to meet in the Cathedral Church of St. Paul in London, to "treat, consent, and conclude upon certain difficult and urgent affairs mentioned in the said writ." The persons so summoned met in Convocation, and "agreed upon certain canons, orders, ordinances, and constitutions, to the end and purpose" by the king "limited and prescribed unto them;" to which the king, out of his " princely inclination and royal care for the maintenance of the present estate and government of the Church of England by the laws of this realm now settled and established," gave his royal assent by letters-patent, according to the form of the statute of the twenty-fifth year of King Henry VIII. The king, by his prerogative royal and supreme authority in causes ecclesiastical, commanded these said canons, orders, and constitutions to be diligently observed, executed, and kept by his loving subjects of the kingdom, both within the provinces of Canterbury and York, in all points wherein they do or may concern every or any of them; and the king also commanded that every minister, by whatever name or title soever he be called, shall in the parish church or chapel where he hath charge read all the said canons, orders, ordinances, and constitutions once every year, upon some Sundays or holydays, in the afternoon before divine service.

The canons and constitutions may be divided into fourteen heads, which treat as follow:—1. Of the Church of England. 2. Of divine service, and administration of the sacraments. 3. Ministers, their ordination, function, and charge. 4. Schoolmasters. 5. Things appertaining to churches. 6. Churchwardens, or questmen, and side-men, or assistants. 7. Parish clerks. 8. Ecclesiastical Courts belonging to the archbishop's jurisdiction. 9. Ecclesiastical Courts belonging to the jurisdiction of bishops and archdeacons, and the proceedings in them. 10. Judges ecclesiastical and their surrogates. 11. Proctors. 12. Registrars. 13. Apparitors. 14. Authority of synods. The number of constitutions is one hundred and forty-one. The authority of these canons is binding on the clergy, but not on the laity, except so far as is stated under the head CANON, p. 446. The authority of Canon 77 may be doubted; it is this : " No man shall teach, either in public school or private house, but such as shall be allowed by the bishop of, the diocese, or ordinary of the place, under his hand and seal; being found meet as well for his learning and dexterity in teaching, as for sober and honest conversation, and also for right understanding of God's true religion; and also except he shall first subscribe to the first and third articles afore mentioned simply, and to the first ten clauses of the second article." The 78th Canon provides that "curates desirous to teach shall be licensed before others ;" and 79 declares "the duty of schoolmasters." The Constitutions and Canons Ecclesiastical have been printed by the Society for Promoting Christian Knowledge, London, 1841. together with the Thirty-Nine Articles of the Church of England.

CONSTITUTIONS, ROMAN. The word Constitutio (from *constituere*, to set up, to establish) signifies any disposition or appointment; for example, an edict of the prætor is called constitutio (*Dig.* 4, tit. 2, s. 1. 9). The decrees and decisions of Roman emperors are also called constitutiones; and, according to Gaius (i. 5), an imperial constitution is what the emperor declares by a decree, or an edict, or a letter (epistola). That modern signification of the term, which denotes the fundamental law of a state, was not in use among the Romans; yet Cicero (*De Republica*, i. 45) employs the word to express a similar notion. An imperial constitution, then, was a rule of law established by the Roman emperor, either as a judge or as a legislator. A Decree (decretum) was a judgment in some matter brought before the emperor either upon appeal or originally. Some of these decreta were final, and, at least after the legislation of Justinian, had the force of law; but interlocutory judgments had not. An Edict (edictum, edictales leges) was an ordinance promulgated by the emperor, and as a general rule applicable to all his subjects. The word Epistola is a general name for any constitution which was promulgated in the form of a letter; and this term also comprises Subscriptiones and Annotationes, which were short answers to questions propounded to the emperor, and written, as these terms import, at the foot or on the margin of the paper which was laid before him. Rescripts (rescripta) were properly answers to an individual who presented a petition to the emperor, or to magistrates who prayed for his advice in any matter. Rescripta, according to their nature, were only applicable to a particular case, though they might contain general principles which would be applicable to other cases, and so in time they would obtain the force of law. Mandata were instructions to the provincial governors for their direction in matters of administration. All these forms of expressing the imperial pleasure, though originally not equally binding as general laws, became in various ways rules of law, and formed a part of what appear in the codes of Theodosius and Justinian as imperial constitutions.

The origin of this system of legislation is properly referred to the time of Octavianus Augustus, who united in his person the various kinds of authority which, under the Republic, were distributed among several magistrates. From the time of Augustus, legislation by the popular assemblies fell gradually into disuse, and the ordinances of the senate (senatus consulta) were the shape in which laws were formally promulgated. The legislation of the senate was superseded by the Orationes Principum, or messages of the emperor to the senate, which contained his proposed laws, to which the senate gave a formal assent. Still later, about the time of Hadrian and the Antonines the edicta and rescripta of the emperor became the usual form of legislation; and finally imperial constitutions, as above explained, became the only source of written law.

In course of time the number of these constitutions became so great, that to prevent confusion collections were made, and called Codes. The first collections made by private persons were the codices Gregoriani and Hermogeniani, of which we know very little; it is even uncertain if they were two separate codes or only one, but the general opinion is that there were two codes. Opinions vary as to the time when these compilers lived. The Gregorianus Codex was divided into books and titles. Of the Hermogenianus only twenty-five constitutions are preserved. These collections, which contained the constitutions from the time of Septimius Severus to Diocletian, are lost, and we have only some fragments, which were first edited by Jac. Sichardus (Basil. 1528, fol.), together with the Codex Theodosianus. The fragments are in Schulting's 'Jurisprud. Vet. Antejust,' Lugd.-Bat. 1712, and in the 'Jus Civile Antejust.,' Berol. 1815.

Another and more important collection was made under the reign of Theodosius II., by public authority. The emperor nominated, in the year 435, a commission of sixteen persons, under the direction of Antiochus, for the purpose of collecting the constitutions from the time of Constantine the Great; and three years afterwards (A. D. 438), the new code, called Codex Theodosianus, was confirmed by the emperor, and published in the Eastern empire. In the same year (438) the code was sent to Rome to Valentinian III., and confirmed as law for the Western empire. This compilation was formed on the model of those of Gregorianus and Hermogenianus. It contains sixteen books, divided into titles, in which the separate constitutions are arranged, according to their subject-matter, in such a way that many of them are subdivided. Some additions, called Novellæ, were afterwards made to the collection of Theodosius. The first five books were lost, but some parts of them have been discovered at Milan, by Clossius (Clossii, 'Theodos. Codic. Genuin. Fragmenta,' Tüb. 1824); and at Turin, by Peyron ('Codic. Theodos. Fragmenta Ined.,' Tur. 1823-24). Carlo Baudià Besme has recently discovered at Turin palimpsests which contain valuable additions to, and means of improving the text of the Theodosian Code. The edition of the Theodosian Code by Jac. Gothofredus. tom. vi. Lugd., 1665, is valuable for the commentary which was also published, together with the text, by Ritter, Leipzig, 1736-54. The last edition is the valuable critical edition of G. Haenel, Bonn, 1837.

In the year 506, Alaric II. caused an abridgment to be made of the Theodosian Code, to which were added excerpts from the codices Gregoriani and Hermogeniani, and of the works of the Roman lawyers Gaius and Paulus, for the use of the Romans then living in the empire of the Visigoths: the collection is called 'Breviarium Alaricianum.'

The last and most important collection of Roman constitutions was made by the order of Justinian, and is entitled Codex Justinianeus. [JUSTINIAN'S LEGISLATION.]

CONSUL. The two chief magistrates who were annually elected by the Romans were called Consuls. Their powers and functions were the same or nearly the same as those of the kings; but they were elected and only held office for a year. The original name was Praetor and not consul. The consuls were chosen solely from the Patricians, or order of old nobles, till B.C. 369, when a law was passed which allowed one of the consuls to be chosen from the commons (Plebs). After this time, sometimes both consuls were plebeians. After the establishment of the imperial power in the person of Augustus, the office of consul was little more than honorary; and the election was transferred from the people to the senate; and it also became the practice for the consuls to hold office only for a few months, in order that the emperor might gratify others with the honorary title. The Romans reckoned their epochs of time by reference to the foundation of the city, B.C. 753, according to the æra of Varro; and they marked the particular years by the names of the consuls. The first consuls were appointed B.C. 509, or in the year of the city (A.U.C.) 245: they were L. Junius Brutus and L. Tarquinius Collatinus. From B.C. 509 there are extant the names of consuls down to A.D. 541. These names were registered in the Roman Fasti, which is the Roman name for the registered list of their magistrates; and though there are some discrepancies in the various authorities from which our complete lists of consuls are compiled, the series is on the whole established by good evidence. The consuls under the Empire were consuls only in name.

The word consul, like many other Roman terms, has passed into the languages of Europe, and modern times have witnessed the establishment of a consulate in France; but in nothing else.

The word consul has been used in various senses in modern times. The Genoese had consuls in the factories or ports which they established. [COLONY, p. 560.] Richelet (*Dictionnaire*) speaks of a consul as a judge at Paris who settled disputes among merchants: his office lasted only a year. He adds that many of the old counts in France were called consuls. The name was also used in the courts of Provence and Languedoc in the sense of Echevin. [ECHEVIN.]

A modern consul is an officer appointed by a government to reside in some foreign country, in order to give protection to such subjects of the government or citizens of the state by which he is appointed as may have commercial dealings in the country where the consul resides, and also to keep his government informed concerning any matters relating to trade which may be of advantage for it to know. To these duties are sometimes added others with objects more directly political, but into this part of a consul's duty it is not necessary to enter at present, as such functions are assigned to consuls not as such, but in the absence of an ambassador or other political agent. The duties of an English consul, as such, cannot perhaps be better described than by giving the substance of the general instructions with which he is furnished by the government on his appointment.

His first duty is to exhibit his commission, either directly, or through the English ambassador, to the authorities of the country to which he is accredited, and to obtain their sanction to his appointment: the document whereby this sanction is communicated is called an exequatur; its issue must precede the commencement of his consular duties, and its possession secures to the consul "the enjoyment of such privileges, immunities, and exemptions as have been enjoyed by his predecessors, and as are usually granted to consuls in the country in which he is to reside." It must be the particular study of the consul "to become conversant with the laws and general principles which relate to the trade of Great Britain with foreign parts; to make himself acquainted with the language and with the municipal laws of the country wherein he resides, and especially with such laws as have any connexion with the trade between the two countries." It is the consul's principal duty "to protect and promote the lawful trade and trading interests of Great Britain by every fair and proper means;" but he is at the same time "to caution all British subjects against carrying on an illicit commerce to the detriment of the revenue and in violation of the laws and regulations of England, or of the country in which he resides;" and he is to give to his own government notice of any attempt at such illicit trading. The consul is "to give his best advice and assistance, whenever called upon, to his majesty's trading subjects, quieting their differences, promoting peace, harmony, and good-will amongst them, and conciliating as much as possible the subjects of the two countries upon all points of difference which may fall under his cognizance." Should any attempts be made to injure British subjects in person or in property, he is to uphold their rightful interests and the privileges secured to them by treaty. If, in such cases, redress cannot be obtained from the local administration, he must apply to the British minister at the court of the country in which he resides, and place the matter in his hands. The consul must transmit to the secretary of state for foreign affairs at the end of every year a return of the trade carried on at the different ports within his consulate, according to a form prescribed. He is also required to send quarterly an account of the market prices of agricultural produce in each week of the preceding three months, with the course of exchange, and any other remarks which he may consider necessary for properly explaining the state of the market for corn and grain. It is further his duty to keep his own government informed as to the appearance of any infectious disease at the place of his residence. The consul is required to afford relief to any distressed British seamen, or other British subjects thrown upon the coast, or reaching by chance any place within his district, and he is to endeavour to procure for such persons the means of returning to England. He is to furnish intelligence to the commanders of king's ships touching upon the coast where he is, and to obtain for them, when required, supplies of water and provisions, and he is to exert himself to recover all wrecks and stores belonging to king's ships when found at sea, and brought into the port where he resides.

In most cases consuls are subjects or citizens of the state by which they are appointed, but this is by no means an invariable rule, and they are sometimes the subjects or citizens of the country in which they reside, or of some other country foreign to both. Persons are usually selected for filling the office from among the mercantile class, and it very commonly happens that they are engaged in commercial pursuits at the port where their official residence is fixed. In this respect the English government is chargeable with some inconsistency, for while, in many instances, British consuls are permitted to trade, in others they are expressly interdicted from so doing. It would be difficult to discover the application of any fixed principle in determining the places where either of these opposite rules has been adopted. We believe the interdiction to be of modern application, and that the desire of diminishing the public expense has since led, in many cases, to the relaxation of what was once intended to be made a general rule, for it is necessary to give a higher salary whenever trading is not allowed. Many traders are willing to undertake the office at a low rate of direct remuneration for the sake of the commercial influence which it brings, and which is frequently of far greater value to them than any salary which the government would give. The policy of this kind of economy has been much questioned. Stations of British consuls, &c. in 1844:—

Russia. — St. Petersburg, Archangel, Riga, Liebau, Wiburg, Warsaw, Odessa, Taganrog, Kertch.
Sweden.—Stockholm and Gottenburg.
Norway.—Christiania and Bergen.
Denmark.—Elsinore and Copenhagen.
Prussia.—Memel, Pillau, Stettin, Königsberg.
Hans Towns.—Hamburg, Bremen, Lubeck, Cuxhaven.
Holland. — Amsterdam, Rotterdam, Flushing.
Belgium.—Antwerp and Ostend.
France. — Paris, Calais, Boulogne, Hâvre, Caen, Granville, Brest, Nantes, Charente, Bordeaux, Bayonne, Marseille, Toulon, Corsica.
Spain. — Madrid, Bilbao, Corunna, Cadiz, San Lucar, Malaga, Carthagena, Alicante, Barcelona, Mahon, Teneriffe, Santiago de Cuba, Puerto Rico.
Portugal.—Lisbon, Oporto, Madeira, St. Michael's, Fayal, Terceira, Cape Verd Islands.
Sardinia.—Genoa, Nice, Cagliari.
Tuscany.—Leghorn.
Roman States.—Ancona.
Two Sicilies. — Naples, Gallipoli, Otranto, Palermo, Messina.
Austrian States. — Venice, Trieste, Fiume, Milan.
Greece.—Patras, Syra, The Piræus, Missolonghi.
Persia.—Tabreez, Tehran.
Servia.—Belgrade.
Wallachia.—Bucharest, Ibraila.
Moldavia.—Jassy, Galatz.
Albania.—Joannina, Prevesa, Scutari.
Turkey.—Dardanelles, Salonica, Adrianople, Enos, Brussa, Smyrna, Mytelene, Scio, Erzeroom, Trebisonde, Kaisseriah, Batoom, Samsoom, Moussul.
Syria. — Damascus, Aleppo, Adalia, Alexandretta, Tarsous, Beyrout, Candia, Cyprus.
Palestine.—Jerusalem.
Egypt.—Alexandria, Cairo, Damietta.
Tripoli.—Bengazi.
Tunis.—Tunis, Sfax.
Algiers.—Algiers, Oran, Bona.

Marocco.—Tangier, Mogador, Tetuan.
United States.—Portland, Boston, New York, Philadelphia, Baltimore, Norfolk, Charleston, Savannah, Mobile, New Orleans.
Texas.—Houston, Galveston.
Mexico.—Mexico, San Blas, Vera Cruz, Tampico, Matamoros.
Central America.—St. Salvador, Mosquito.
Hayti.—Port-au-Prince, Cape Haytien.
New Granada.—Bogota, Carthagena, Panama, Santa Martha.
Venezuela. — Caracas, La Guayra, Puerto Cabello, Maracaibo.
Ecuador.—Guayaquil.
Brazil.—Rio de Janeiro, Maranham, Para, Pernambuco, Bahia, Paraiba.
Monte Video.—Monte Video.
Buenos Ayres.—Buenos Ayres.
Chili.—Santiago, Valparaiso, Concepcion, Coquimbo.
Peru.—Lima, Callao, Arica, Isla.
Bolivia.—Chuquisaca.
China.—Under the treaty of August 29, 1842, consular officers are appointed at the five ports of Canton, Amoy, Foochoo-foo, Ning-po, Shang-hae, to regulate the trade between the Chinese and the subjects of Great Britain. Their duties are of course very important in the present state of our relations with China. The consul at each port is security for the payment of duties, and is bound to prosecute for all infractions of the revenue laws.
Sandwich Islands.—Woahoo.
Society and Friendly Islands.—Tahiti.
The stations of consuls-general, and agents and consuls-general, in 1845, are as follows:—
Consuls-General.—At Odessa, Christiania, Danzig, Hamburg, the Havana, Austrian States, Belgrade, Constantinople, Syria, Houston for Texas, St. Salvador for Central America, Port-au-Prince for Hayti, Bogota for New Grenada, Caracas for Venezuela, Monte Video, Santiago for Chili, Lima for Peru, Woahoo for the Sandwich Islands. The highest salary is 2000*l*. a-year.
Agents and Consuls-General. — For Egypt, Tunis, Algiers, Tangier for Marocco, and at Mosquito in Central America. The total amount paid in salaries to

English consuls, &c. and vice-consuls in 1844 was 107,300*l*.; in 1835, 61,950*l*.; in 1825, 71,716*l*.

Under 6 Geo. IV. c. 87, the contingent expenses of the consular establishment in 1844 were 17,000*l*. They consisted of relief to distressed British subjects, expenses for chaplains, churches, burial-grounds, interpreters in the Levant, &c. The consuls of the United States of North America do not receive salaries, except those for London, Tangier, Tunis, Tripoli, 2000 dollars each, and the consul for Beirout 500 dollars.

CONSUMPTION. [CAPITAL.]

CONTEMPT. A contempt in a court of law is a disobedience of the rules, orders, or process of the court, or a disturbance or interruption of its proceedings. Contempts by resistance to the process of a court, such as the refusal of a sheriff to return a writ, are punishable by attachment; but contempts done in the presence of the court, which cause an obstruction to its proceedings in administering the law, may be punished or repressed in a summary manner by the commitment of the offender to prison or by fining him. The power of enforcing their process, and of vindicating their authority against open obstruction or defiance, is incident to all superior courts; and the means which the law intrusts to them for that purpose are attachment for contempts committed out of court, and commitment and fine for contempts done before the court. (Viner's *Abridgment*, tit. "Contempts.")

If a defendant in Chancery, after being served with a subpœna, does not appear within the time fixed by the rules of the court, and plead, answer, or demur to the bill, he is in contempt, and he is liable to various processes in succession according to the continuance of his disobedience. The first process is attachment, which is a warrant directed to the sheriff ordering him to bring the defendant into court, who is thereupon committed to the Queen's Prison till he complies with the orders of the court.

There are also contempts against the King's prerogative, contempts against his person and government, contempts of the King's title, which fall short of treason or præmunire; and contempts against the king's palaces and courts of justice; all which contempts and their several punishments are discussed by Blackstone (*Comm.* book iv. c. 9).

CONTRABAND, from the Italian *Contrabando*, against the proclamation, a term commonly used in commercial language to denote articles the importation or exportation of which is prohibited by law. Since the adoption of the warehousing system in Great Britain, the list of goods the importation of which is prohibited has been made exceedingly short: it comprises at this time (1845) only the following articles:—

Arms, ammunition, and utensils of war, by way of merchandise, except by license from his Majesty for the public stores only.

Books first printed in the United Kingdom, and reprinted in any other country and imported for sale. Notice must be given by authors or others to the Commissioners of Customs, that copyright is subsisting.

Clocks or watches, with any mark or stamp representing any legal British assay mark or stamp, or purporting to be of British make, or not having the name and abode of some foreign maker visible on the frame and the face, or not being complete.

Foreign goods bearing the names or marks of manufacturers in the United Kingdom are forfeited on importation.

Coin, counterfeit, or not of the established standard in weight and fineness.

Malt.

Snuff-work, tobacco-stalks, and tobacco-stalk flour.

The list of articles contraband as regards exportation from the United Kingdom is still more limited, and comprises only the following articles:—

Clocks and watches: the outward or inward case or dial-plate of any clock or watch without the movement complete, and with the clock or watchmaker's name engraved thereon.

Lace made of inferior metal, in whole or in part, to imitate gold or silver lace.

The schedule of prohibitions to importations was formerly much more extensive. Under the Customs' Act of

CONTRABAND.   [626]   CONVENT.

3 & 4 Wm. IV. c. 56, cattle, sheep, fresh beef and pork, or slightly salted, and fish were contraband; but under the tariff established by 5 & 6 Vict. c. 47, they have ceased to be contraband. Tools, utensils, and machinery were also contraband, but the restriction with respect to machinery was very much relaxed under the power given by act of parliament to the Board of Trade to license upon application the exportation of such tools and machines as in the opinion of the Board might without inconvenience be allowed to go out of the country; and the restriction was at length limited almost entirely to machinery required for the prosecution of the processes of spinning various kinds of yarn. The act 6 & 7 Vict. c. 84, repeals, with some exceptions, the prohibition against machinery.

There are some other prohibitions by which trade in certain articles is restricted, but these refer to the manner in which the trade may be conducted, as the size of the ship, or the package, or the country from or to which the trading may take place, and these being only of the nature of regulations, the articles in question cannot be considered contraband. Of this nature are the prohibitions which extend to our colonies, and which have for their object the encouragement of the trade of the mother country. The list of articles prohibited by many foreign countries is much larger than that enforced in this country.

Another sense in which the term Contraband is applied refers to certain branches of trade carried on by neutrals during the continuance of war between other countries. It has always been held under these circumstances that belligerents have a right to treat as contraband, and to capture and confiscate, all goods which can be considered munitions of war, under which description are comprehended everything that can be made directly and obviously available to a hostile purpose, such as arms, ammunition, and all kinds of naval stores, and all such other articles as are capable of being used with a like purpose, such as horses, and timber for building ships. Under some circumstances, provisions which it is attempted to convey to an enemy's port are contraband, as when a hostile armament is in preparation in that port. These restrictions rest upon principles which are reasonable in themselves, and have been generally recognised by neutrals; others which have at various times been enforced or attempted to be enforced have been contested, but a description of this branch of the subject belongs rather to the matter of International Law than to a description of contraband trading.

CONTRACT, ORIGINAL. [ORIGINAL CONTRACT.]

CONVENT, from the Latin *conventus*, an assembly or meeting together. This word is used in a double sense, first, for any corporation or community of religious, whether monks or nuns; and secondly, for the house, abbey, monastery, or nunnery in which such monks or nuns dwell. Shakspere uses it in the first sense, when he says of Wolsey:—

" At last, with easy roads, he came to Leicester,
Lodged in the abbey; where the reverend abbot
With all his convent honourably received him."
Hen. VIII., act iv. sc. 2.

Addison uses it for the building:— " One seldom finds in Italy a spot of ground more agreeable than ordinary that is not covered with a convent."

Furetiere, who wrote his dictionary in the time of Louis XIV., says there were no fewer than 14,000 convents formerly in France.

Convent, as related to the foreign military orders, meant the principal seat or head of the order. Furetiere says, " La Commanderie de Boisy, près d'Orléans, est le Couvent général de l'Ordre de St. Lazare."

The earliest inhabitants of convents were termed Coenobites, from the Greek words κοινός and βίος, as living in community. They dwelt chiefly in Egypt. Fleury (*Hist. Eccles.* 4to. Paris, 1720, tom. v. p. 14) dates their institution as early as the days of the Apostles; others, probably with more correctness, give them a later origin. St. Pachomius, abbot of Tabenna, on the banks of the Nile, who was born at the close of the third century, is believed to have been the first person who drew up a rule for the Coenobites. (Moreri, *Dic. Histor.*, tom. viii.) [MONASTERY.]

CONVENTION, MILITARY, a treaty made between the commanders of two opposing armies concerning the terms on which a temporary cessation of hostilities shall take place between them. It is usually solicited by that general who has suffered a defeat, when his retreat is not secure and small chance is left of maintaining his position; and it is seldom refused by the victor, since, without incurring the unavoidable loss attending an action, his force becomes immediately disposable for other operations.

In 1757 the Duke of Cumberland, when in danger of being surrounded, entered into a convention with the Duke de Richelieu, through the medium of Denmark, by which, on consenting to disband all his auxiliaries, he was allowed to retire with the English troops across the Elbe. And in 1799, when the Anglo-Russian army failed in the attempt to deliver Holland from the French power, the Duke of York made a treaty with General Brune, by which the invading force was allowed to re-embark, on condition that 8000 French and Dutch prisoners of war in England should be restored.

After the battle of Vimeira in 1808, the Duke of Abrantes, having been defeated, and fearing a general rising in Lisbon against him, sent General Kellerman to the quarters of the British commander-in-chief, to request a cessation of arms, and propose a convention by which the French troops might be allowed to retire from Portugal. This being granted, it was finally arranged in the convention that they should not be considered as prisoners of war; and that, with their property, public and private, their guns, and cavalry horses, they should be transported to France: On the other hand, all the fortresses which had not capitulated were to be given up to the British, and a Russian fleet, then in the Tagus, was to be detained in English ports till after the conclusion of a peace. This is the celebrated convention which was made at Lisbon, and is generally but improperly called "the Convention of Cintra." It excited much dissatisfaction both in Portugal and England, as the cupidity of the French induced them to appropriate to themselves property to which they had no claim. (Napier, vol. i.). By the appointment of a committee consisting of one individual of each of the three nations, all causes of complaint were, however, finally removed.

CONVENTION . PARLIAMENT. Two days after the abdication [ABDICATION] of James II., the lords spiritual and temporal, to the number of about ninety, who had taken their places in the House of Lords, requested the Prince of Orange to issue writs for a "Convention," to meet on the 22nd of January 1689; and on the 26th of December, 1688, an assembly of such persons as had sat in parliament in the reign of Charles II., to the number of about a hundred and fifty, together with the aldermen of London, and fifty of the common council, agreed upon an address similar to that of the Lords. The prince accordingly dispatched circular letters to the several counties, universities, cities, and boroughs, for the election of members. The convention, or parliament, as it was afterwards declared to be, passed the Act of Settlement, which declared the throne vacant, and conferred the crown, with constitutional limitations to its power, on the Prince and Princess of Orange jointly. The Convention Parliament was dissolved 29th January, 1691.

CONVENTION TREATIES. These are treaties entered into between different states, under which they each bind themselves to observe certain stipulations contained in the treaty. In 1843 two acts were passed (6 & 7 Vict. c. 75 and c. 76) for giving effect to conventions between her majesty and the King of the French and the United States of America for the apprehension of certain offenders.

The act relating to France (c. 75) legalizes the convention entered into with the government of that country for the giving up of offenders who may escape from France into England. On requisition duly made by the French ambassador, a warrant will be issued for the apprehension of fugitives accused of having committed the crimes of murder (as defined by the French code), attempt at murder, forgery, or fraudulent bankruptcy; and any justice before whom they may be brought is authorized to commit them to gaol until delivered up pursuant to the ambassador's requisition. Copies of the depositions on which the original warrant was issued, duly certified as true copies, are to be received as evidence. But no justice is to issue a warrant for the apprehension of any French fugitive unless the party applying is the bearer of a warrant or document, issued by a judge or competent authority in France, authenticated in such a manner as would justify the arrest of the supposed offender in France upon the same charge. The secretary of state will order the person committed to be delivered up to the person or persons authorized to receive him. If the prisoner committed shall not be conveyed out of her majesty's dominions within two months from the time of his committal, any of her majesty's judges, on application made to them, and after notice of such application has been sent to the secretary of state (or to the acting governor in a colony), may order such person to be discharged, unless good cause shall be shown to the contrary. The act is to extend to all her majesty's present or future possessions, and to continue in force during the continuance of the convention.

The act relating to America (c. 76) is similar in its nature and purposes to the one relating to France; but the crimes specified include, in addition, piracy, arson, and robbery, and do not include fraudulent bankruptcy.

In 1844 a case occurred of a fraudulent French bankrupt who had escaped to England, and the French government demanded that he should be given up under the Convention Treaty. He was arrested and taken to prison; but before the surrender could take place he applied for a writ of habeas corpus, on the ground that fraudulent bankruptcy was an offence unknown to the law of England, and that therefore it was contrary to law to arrest him or keep him in custody on such a charge. The warrant of commitment did not specify that the prisoner should be given up on requisition duly made according to the act, but the words were, "until he shall be delivered by due course of law." In consequence of the defective application of the Convention Treaty in this particular case the prisoner was discharged.

At the close of 1843, seven persons accused of murder, robbery, and piracy fled for security from Florida, in the United States, to Nassau, one of the Bahama Islands. They were followed by a marshal of the United States, who was authorized by his government to demand that the fugitives should be given up under the Convention Act. The governor, Sir Francis Cockburn, issued his warrant accordingly to the chief justice of the colony, authorizing and directing him to take measures for the fulfilment of the act. In anticipation of the application of the marshal, the chief justice had a warrant prepared for apprehending the fugitives, expecting that the evidence tendered would be such as could be judicially received. The only evidence offered was documentary, consisting of indictments, without the evidence upon which they were framed. The act requires that copies of the depositions upon which the original warrant was granted, certified, &c., must be adduced in order to render the provisions of the act available. The chief justice, with his associate judges, were under the necessity of refusing the warrant applied for, chiefly on the following grounds:—"An indictment per se can never be received as evidence: it is not enough for us to know that the American jury thought the parties guilty; we ought to know the grounds upon which they thought them guilty. What may constitute the crime of murder in Florida may be very far from doing so according to the British laws, or even to the laws of the Northern States of America. By issuing a warrant, then, to apprehend the parties in virtue of these indictments, we might be doing so on evidence which would not justify their apprehension by the British law, and should thereby be proceeding in direct violation of the act." (*Parl. Paper,* No. 64, sess. 1844.)

CONVICT. [TRANSPORTATION.]

CONVOCATION, the assembly of the Clergy of England and Wales, under the authority of the king's writ, which takes place at the commencement of every new parliament. The convocation writs issue from the Crown Office, and are addressed to the two primates of Canterbury and York.

The tendency of the western states of modern Europe in political relations to become thrown into the form of which kings, lords, and commons is no inapt type, is apparent in the ecclesiastical constitution of almost every country in which Christianity has been received and professed. The archbishop has had his suffragan bishops, and the bishops each his canons, who formed his council, in some of whom have been vested peculiar functions, as dean, archdeacon, and the like; while the great body of the clergy have had their meetings under the form of diocesan synods or provincial assemblies, in which they have been accustomed to discuss matters pertaining to the common interest and benefit of themselves or of the whole church.

These meetings, resembling as they do in some points the convocation of the English clergy in later times, might easily be supposed to be that assembly in its primordial state. But writers on this subject trace the origin of the convocation to something more special than this. It is supposed that originally the clergy were thus called together by the king's authority for the purpose of assessing themselves in levies of taxes at a time when they contended for exemption from the general taxation of the country imposed by the authority of parliament. Like many other questions in our early constitutional history (we mean by "early" when we ascend beyond the reign of King Edward the First), this is perhaps one of presumption and probability, rather than of evidence and certainty. It is said that the convocation which was summoned in 1295, in the reign of King Edward the First, was for the purpose of obtaining a supply of money from the clergy by means of their representatives. Edward had taxed the clergy very heavily in 1294, and, instead of repeating the experiment, he thought it better to get some money out of them with their own consent.

The clergy were not willing to obey the king's writ which summoned them to convocation, upon which the king issued his writ to the Archbishops of Canterbury and York, who, in obedience to it, summoned the clergy in their respective provinces to grant the king a subsidy. Thus there were two convocations, one for the province of Canterbury and the other for the province of York. The convocation of Canterbury contained two houses, the Upper House of Bishops and Archbishops, and the Lower House of Deans, Archdeacons, and Proctors of the clergy. In the convocation at York, all the members composed (or at present compose) only one house.

From this time to the year 1663, the clergy were taxed in convocation in respect of their benefices and lands; and the grants of subsidies by the clergy in convocation required no confirmation except the assent of the king, who wanted the money. From the time of Henry VIII. the grants were always confirmed by act of parliament. Thus it appears that the origin of the convocation was like the origin of the House of Commons: the first object of the convocation was to grant money. By the 8 Hen. VI. c. 1, all the clergy called to convocation by the king's writ, their servants and familiars, shall enjoy the liberty, in coming, tarrying, and returning, as the commonalty called to parliament enjoy. The two convocations of Canterbury and York were quite independent of one another, and they did not always grant the same or a proportionate amount. In the twenty-second year of Henry VIII. the convocation of Canterbury granted the king 100,000l., in consideration of which an act of parliament was passed which gave the clergy a free pardon for all spiritual offences, with a proviso that the pardon should not extend to the province of York, unless the clergy would show themselves equally liberal.

When such an assembly was called together under the direct authority of the crown, it was natural that ecclesiastical subjects should be introduced, discussed, and in some instances determined by it. The old doctrine was that the convocation had only authority in spiritual matters, and that they had no power to bind the temporalty, but only the spiritualty. (Comyns' *Digest*, 'Convocation.')

The crown, however, had always in its hands the power of controlling this assembly, by possessing the prerogative of proroguing and dissolving. But at the Reformation an act was passed (25 Henry VIII. c. 19), which expressly deprived the convocation of the power of performing any act whatever without the king's licence. The act declares that the "clergy, nor any of them, from henceforth shall presume to attempt, allege, claim, or put in use any constitutions or ordinances, provincial or synodal, or any other canons, nor shall enact, promulge, or exercise any such canons, constitutions, or ordinances provincial, by whatever name or names they may be called in their convocations in time coming, which always shall be assembled by authority of the king's writ, unless the same clergy may have the king's most royal licence."

By an act passed in 1665 (16 & 17 Chas. II. c. 1), the clergy were bound by the act, which was for the raising of a tax, just like the laity, and they were discharged from the payment of the subsidies hitherto granted in convocation. Though this act reserves to the clergy the right of taxing themselves in convocation if they think fit, it has never been attempted, and the clergy and the laity are now precisely on the same footing as to taxation. The clergy, instead of being represented by the lower house of convocation, are now represented in parliament in the House of Commons, not however as an ecclesiastical body, but simply as citizens; they can vote for a member in respect of their ecclesiastical freeholds, or in respect of any other qualification which they may have in common with the laity.

The decisions of the convocation of the province of Canterbury have always had great authority in that of York; and sometimes the two convocations have acted as one, either by jointly consenting, or by the attendance of deputies from the province of York at the convocation of Canterbury. One of the most important of the convocations, that in which the Constitutions and Canons Ecclesiastical were established in 1603 [CONSTITUTIONS and CANONS ECCLESIASTICAL], appears to have been only attended by deputies of the Canterbury convocation; but the king's confirmation of the canons then made extends them to the province of York. No business beyond matters of form has been done in convocation since 1741.

The practical annihilation of the convocation was a considerable change. It may be viewed as completing the victory obtained in England by the civil power over the ecclesiastical. The clergy can now make no canons which shall bind even their own body without the consent of the crown, that is, of the ministers of the crown; and it is certain that whatever canons they might make, even with the licence of the crown, would not bind the laity. In fact, the British parliament now makes canons for the clergy, as we see in the Church Discipline Act. [CLERGY.] The Anglican Church is now completely in the power of parliament, with no other weight there than the bench of bishops in the House of Lords, who may be considered as in some way representing the ecclesiastical estate.

But though the convocation has become a nullity, the practice has been continued, and continues to the present day, of summoning the clergy to meet in convocation whenever a new parliament is called; and the forms of election are gone through in the dioceses, and the meeting for the province of Canterbury is held, usually in St. Paul's Church, when the form is also gone through of electing a prolocutor or speaker. The king's writ, as already stated, is directed to the archbishops, commanding them to summon the bishops and the inferior clergy. The archbishops, in compliance with this writ, summon the bishops, and command them to summon the archdeacons and deans in their respective dioceses, and to command the chapters to elect one proctor each, and the great body of the clergy in each diocese two proctors, to represent them in the convocation. When assembled, they form two houses in the province of Canterbury, but, as stated above, only one house in the province of York. In the upper house of the convocation of Canterbury sit the bishops; in the lower, the other clergy, in all 143; viz. 22 deans, 53 archdeacons, 24 canons, and 44 proctors of the inferior clergy. It is the usual practice for the king to prorogue the meeting when it is about to proceed to any business.

There is no convocation for Ireland. The history of the English convocation may be collected from Gibson's Codex, and Atterbury's Rights, Powers, and Privileges of the English Convocation stated and vindicated, London, 1700; and from a Charge, delivered at a visitation of the Archdeaconry of Oxford, 1841, by Archdeacon Clarke.

The sketch of the history of convocation here given may be tolerably correct as far as it goes, and it pretends to be nothing more. The complicated and inextricable difficulties which beset every attempt to restore the convocation, or to set it to work again, are fully stated in an article in the 'Quarterly Review,' No. 150.

This article makes us acquainted with the strange fact (strange enough it seems to us, who have thus heard of it for the first time), that a parliamentary writ issues from the Petty-Bag Office [CHANCERY, p. 486] concurrently with the convocation writs from the Crown Office.

The parliamentary writs are addressed to the archbishops and bishops of England and Wales, who are commanded to attend the parliament to be holden at Westminster. The same writ also commands the attendance of the dean of the bishop's church of Canterbury, Exeter, and so forth, and the archdeacons to appear also at Westminster in their proper persons; and each chapter by one, and the clergy of each diocese by two meet proctors. A similar notice is sent to the Irish archbishops and bishops. These ecclesiastics are summoned to Westminster at the day appointed, to consent to what shall be advanced by the common counsel of the United Kingdom. According to the summons, the clergy ought to appear at Westminster as a component part of the Imperial Parliament; and the English clergy are required at the same time to appear in convocation at St. Paul's, London, for the province of Canterbury, and at St. Peter's, York, for the province of York. The parliamentary writ was no doubt the original one; and it is suggested by the writer in the 'Quarterly Review,' that the concurrent convocation writ was probably introduced to enable the clergy to save their privileges at the expense of their money. Since the convocation writs have been issued, the practice has been for the clergy to obey the writ of convocation.

CONVOY, in the military service, is a detachment of troops appointed to guard supplies of money, ammunition, provisions, &c., while being conveyed to a distant town, or to an army in the field, through a country in which such supplies might be carried off by the peasantry or by parties of the enemy. In the navy, the name is applied to one or more ships of war which are ordered to protect a fleet of merchant vessels on their voyage.

COPPER, STATISTICS OF. Copper was at first obtained in this country in small quantities in working the tin-mines in Cornwall; but about the close of the seventeenth century mines were set at work purposely for copper. The first application of the steam-engine in drawing water from copper-mines was in 1710, and the quantity of ore raised has increased with each successive improvement in the steam-engine. In 1837 the number of steam-engines employed in the copper-mines in Cornwall was 58. The produce of the Cornish mines is known with tolerable accuracy as far back as 1771, and there are accounts of the produce of other copper-mines since 1821. Improvements in the art of smelting have greatly increased the products of the mines, and ores which produce only three or four per cent. of metal are now smelted.

The number of persons employed in the copper-mines in England and Wales, in 1841, was 15,407; and the number employed in copper manufactures was 2126.

The average annual produce of the Cornish mines at different periods between 1771 and 1837, was as follows:—

1771-75,	3450 tons.
1776-80,	3310
1781-85,	3990
1796 to 1800,	5174
1801-5,	5544
1806-10,	6575
1811-15,	7181
1816-20,	7018
1821-31,	9143
1831-37,	11,637

COPPER.

In 1837 the value of the ore was 908,613*l.*, and the quantity of copper was 10,823 tons.

The value of the produce of all the British copper-mines is in good years about 1,500,000*l.* Four-fifths of the whole quantity is raised from the Cornish mines. The produce of the mines in Devonshire and Staffordshire was 871 tons in 1821, but it has not much exceeded 500 tons since 1827. In 1831 the mines in Anglesey produced 915 tons, which was above the average quantity. In 1843, 176 tons of ore were received from the Isle of Man. The total quantity of copper from all British mines in the following years has been as under:—

Years.	Tons.	Years.	Tons.
1821	10,288	1831	14,685
1822	11,018	1832	14,450
1823	9,679	1833	13,260
1824	9,705	1834	14,042
1825	10,358	1835	14,474
1826	11,093	1836	15,369
1827	12,326	1837	15,360
1828	12,188	1838	13,958
1829	12,057	1839	14,672
1830	13,232	1840	13,022

In the year ending 30th June, 1840, the mining and smelting operations in Cornwall and at Swansea were as follows:—

CORNWALL.

Ore raised	159,214 tons
Value	792,750*l.*
Metallic copper produced	11,056 tons
Produce per cent. of metal	7½

SWANSEA.

Ore smelted	56,285 tons
Value	674,012*l.*
Produce per cent. of metal	15
Quantity of copper	8,476 tons

Of the above, the following portion was foreign ore:—

Quantity of ore	30,367 tons
Metallic copper produced	6,510 „
Produce per cent. of metal	21¾

The copper yielded by the British mines being more than sufficient for the use of the kingdom, a considerable quantity is exported every year, both in its unwrought and in a manufactured state.

The quantity of British copper retained yearly for use, on an annual average of each decennial period during the present century, is calculated by Mr. Porter ('Progress of the Nation.' iii. p. 92), as follows:—

1801-10,	3694 tons.
1811-20,	3472
1821-31,	4912
1831-40,	6290

The exports since 1820 have been:—

Years.	Tons.	Years.	Tons.
1820	6,094	1831	8,530
1821	6,271	1832	9,730
1822	5,683	1833	7,811
1823	5,326	1834	8,886
1824	5,305	1835	9,111
1825	3,931	1836	8,076
1826	4,799	1837	7,129
1827	7,171	1838	7,459
1828	6,206	1839	7,687
1829	7,976	1840	5,926
1830	9,157		

In the accounts of English produce and manufactures exported, the Custom-House statements include brass and copper manufactures together: the total quantity and declared value of these shipments averaged as follows for each year in the four years ending 1831 and 1835:—

Years.	Cwts.	£
1828-31	165,222	790.405
1832-35	213,627	964,321

From 1838 to 1844 inclusive the quantity and declared value of the exports have been as under:—

Years.	Cwts.	£
1838	265,204	1,221,737
1839	272,141	1,280,505
1840	311,153	1,450,464
1842	395,210	1,810,742
1843	364,128	1,644,248
1844	. .	1,735,528

The quantities and declared value of the principal shipments in 1842 were as follows:—

	Cwts.	£
France	155,848	682,833
East India Company's Territories & Ceylon	109,107	514,945
Holland	36,934	163,988
United States of North America	19,097	89,952
Italy and the Italian Islands	13,813	62,691
Belgium	13,166	57,480

COPPER. [633] COPYHOLD.

And the remainder to forty other States and countries.

In the year 1843 the exports of British copper consisted of 8463 tons unwrought, in bricks, pigs, &c., 66 tons of coin, 8386 tons of sheet, nails, &c., 6 tons of wire, 598 tons of wrought copper; making a total of 17,515 tons.

Within the last twenty years a considerable quantity of copper-ore has been brought to England for the purpose of being smelted and re-exported in the metallic state. These importations amounted only to 2 cwts. in 1825, and have gradually but rapidly increased as follows:—

Years.	Tons.	Years.	Tons.
1826	64	1836	18,491
1827	32	1837	19,465
1828	334	1838	30,000
1829	1,212	1839	30,195
1830	1,436	1840	41,925
1831	2,545	1841	34,150
1832	3,955	1842	48,546
1833	5,931	1843	54,391
1834	6,987	1844	55,720
1835	13,945		

The duty on copper-ore is paid after smelting, but it is paid upon the ore: in 1843, 64,445 tons of ore produced 11,640 tons of metal. Since July, 1842, the duty has been charged according to the following proportions of metal which the ore contains.

Ore containing	Tons. in 1843.	Duty per ton.
Under 15 per cent	5,460	£3 3 0
15 and under 20	10,339	4 14 6
Above 20 . .	48,630	6 6 0

The duty on copper-ore from British possessions is 21s. per ton, but only 14 tons from Australia were imported. Copper-mines have been recently discovered in South Australia, which, it is said, are likely to prove very productive. In 1843 we received 31.683 tons of ore from Cuba; 19,829 from Chili; 1200 from Mexico; 1151 from the United States of North America; and smaller quantities from Peru, the British West Indies, Italy, Spain, and some other places.

The value of the foreign copper-ore imported in 1843 was about 900,000l., the freights varied from 2l. 10s. to 6l. per ton. It is a valuable return cargo to vessels trading to the Pacific, Australia, and especially the western coast of South America, which affords few commercial products. A high duty on such a commodity is more especially impolitic, as it may be an inducement to other countries to commence smelting operations on a large scale, and since the increase of duty in 1842 this has taken place in France, Holland, and the United States. Any diminution in the foreign supply, which now amounts to nearly three-sevenths of the copper made in Great Britain, would be seriously felt by the smelters and manufacturers of this country. Although the import of foreign copper is now so much greater than it was ten years ago, the price of British ore has not fallen, but is at present higher than it was in 1832, and the supply from our own mines has also steadily increased.

COPYHOLD, a term in English law applied to lands held by what is called tenure by copy of court roll, the nature of which is thus described by Littleton (§ 73, 4, 5): "Tenant by copy of court roll is as if a man be seised of a manor, within which manor there is a custom which hath been used time out of mind of man, that certain tenants within the same manor have used to have lands and tenements to hold to them and their heirs in fee-simple or fee-tail, or for term of life, at the will of the lord, according to the custom of the same manor. And such a tenant may not alien his land by deed, for then the lord may enter as into a thing forfeited unto him. But if he will alien his land to another, it behoveth him after the custom to surrender the tenements in court into the hands of the lord to the use of him that shall have the estate. And these tenants are called tenants by copy of court roll, because they have no other evidence concerning their tenements, but only the copies of court rolls." From this it appears that the title to copyhold lands is not only modified but altogether constituted by custom; subject to the estates in them which the custom confers, they are held by the lord under the common law as part of the demesnes of his manor. For these customary estates were in their origin mere tenancies at will, though by long usage they have in many instances acquired the character of a permanent inheritance, descendible (except where otherwise modified by custom) according to the rules of the common law; and as tenancies at will they continue to be considered in all questions relating to the *legal* as distinguished from the customary property in the land.

The origin of copyholds is involved in great obscurity. The opinion generally adopted among our lawyers and antiquarians, and supported by the authority of Littleton, Coke, Sir Martin Wright, and Mr. Justice Blackstone, is, that copyholders have gradually arisen out of the villeins or tenants in villeinage who composed the mass of the agricultural population of England for some centuries after the Norman conquest, through the commutation of base services into specific rents either in money or money's-worth. (See Co. Litt., 58 a—61 a; Blackstone's *Comm.*, ii. p. 92; Wright *on Tenures*, 3rd edit., p. 215. See also Hallam's *Middle Ages*, vol. iii., p. 254.) [VILLEINAGE.]

Although the change in the condition of these classes of persons was accomplished gradually, it seems in the middle of the thirteenth century to have begun to assume a more decided character. There are proofs of as early a date as the reign of Henry III. of a limitation of the services of villeins to certain specified acts which were recorded in the lord's book. The descendants of persons so privileged began to claim a customary right to be entered on the court roll on the same terms as their predecessors, and, in process of time, prevailed so far as to obtain a copy of the roll for their security. It is said in the year-book of the 42nd of Edw. III. to be "admitted for clear law that if the customary tenant or copyholder did not perform his services, the lord might seize his land as forfeited," which seems to imply a permanent interest in the copyholder, so long as he performed the services. This view of the law is confirmed by Britton in a passage cited by Lord Coke (Co. Litt., 61 a) and was adopted by the judges in Edward IV.'s time, who held that a copyholder might maintain an action of trespass against the lord for dispossession.

The two great essentials of copyhold tenure, according to Blackstone, are: 1. That lands be parcel of and situate within that manor under which they are held; and 2, That they have been demised or demisable by copy of court roll immemorially. "For immemorial custom," says that author, ii. p. 96, "is the life of all tenures by copy; so that no new copyhold can, strictly speaking, be granted at this day."

The burdens to which a copyhold tenure is liable in common with free tenures, are fealty, services, reliefs, and escheats; besides which it has certain liabilities peculiar to itself in the shape of heriots and fines. A heriot is the render of the best beast or other chattel (as the custom may be) to the lord on the death of a tenant.

Of fines, some are due on the death of a tenant, and others on the alienation of the land; they are sometimes fixed by the custom, sometimes arbitrary; but in the latter case it is an established rule of law that the lord cannot demand by way of fine upon the descent or alienation of the land more than the amount of two years, improved value of the property, after deduction of the quit-rents to which it is liable. The ordinary mode of alienating a copyhold estate in fee-simple is by *surrender and admittance*, which is effected in the following manner:—The copyholder appears in court and professes to surrender or deliver up his land to the lord (either in person, or, which is more usual, as represented by his steward), expressing the surrender to be to the use of A and his heirs; and thereupon A is *admitted* tenant of the land to hold it to him and his heirs at the will of the lord according to the custom of the manor. He then pays a fine, and also (if required) does fealty. All these circumstances, or at least the surrender and admittance, are entered on the court rolls; and the new tenant, paying his fees to the steward, receives a copy of this fundamental document of his title. Surrenders are made in various forms, by the delivery of a rod, glove, or other symbol, to the steward or other person taking the surrender.

Surrenders may also be made to the lord in person out of court; to the steward; and by special custom to the lord's bailiff; to two or three copyholders, or into the hands of a tenant in the presence of other persons. But when a surrender is taken out of court it must be presented by the homage or jury of copyholders at the next general court, except where a special custom authorizes a presentment at some other court. Admittances also may be made out of court and even out of the manor.

The words in the admittance "to hold at the will of the lord" are characteristic of those customary estates to which the term copyhold is in ordinary legal language exclusively appropriated, in contradistinction to what are sometimes called "customary freeholds" (which estates are very common in the north of England), and ancient demesne lands. These are all included under the term copyhold in the statute 12 Car. II. c. 24, which abolished all the old tenures in England except common soccage, copyhold, and some other specified tenures. Though customary freeholds and ancient demesne lands for the most part pass by surrender and admittance, the admittance is expressed to be "to hold according to the custom of the manor."

The Statute of Entails (13 Edw. I.), commonly called the Statute of Westminster the 2nd, does not extend to copyholds; but in most manors a custom of entailing copyholds has prevailed. These entails might formerly be barred by a proceeding in the lord's court, analogous to a common recovery, or, in the absence of a custom authorizing such a proceeding, by a mere statute. And now by statute (3 & 4 Wm. IV. c. 74, § 50-54 inclusive) entails of copyholds may be barred by assurances made in pursuance of the provisions of that act. It is a general rule that no statute relating to lands or tenements in which those of a customary tenure are not expressly mentioned, shall be applied to customary estates, if such application would be derogatory to the customary rights of the lord or tenant. Hence neither the Statute of Uses (27 Henry VIII. c. 10), nor the Statutes of Partitions (31 Henry VIII. c. 1, and 32 Henry VIII. c. 32), nor the statute enabling persons having certain limited interests in lands to grant valid leases (32 Henry VIII. c. 28), nor any of the local Registry Acts, are applicable to copyholds.

Copyholds now descend to the heir-at-law according to the rules that regulate the descent of all other kinds of land, under the 3 & 4 Wm. IV. c. 106.

The Statutes of Wills (32 Hen. VIII. c. 1, and 34 & 35 Hen. VIII. c. 5) do not include copyholds, and therefore it was formerly necessary, in order to enable a person to dispose of copyholds by will, that he should first have surrendered them to the use of his will, as it was called. This ceremony was rendered unnecessary in most cases by the 55 Geo. III. c. 192. This statute, however, did not apply to customary freeholds, nor to cases where there was no custom to surrender to the use of a will, nor did it extend to estates of customary tenure not being copyhold, though the distinction between them is little more than nominal. There were also some customary freeholds which were neither devisable at law nor capable of being conveyed or surrendered to the use of a will; and it was even thought doubtful whether a custom against a surrender of copyholds to the use of a will might not be supported. But though a surrender to the use of a will might be dispensed with, admittance of the devisor before the date of the will was necessary in all cases except that of a person claiming as heir of the person last admitted. In the case of a surrender the legal estate remained in the surrenderor till the surrenderee was admitted, and therefore the surrenderee had nothing to dispose of but his right to admittance, which could not be devised. Also the 12th section of the Statute of Frauds, whereby estates *pur auter vie* were made devisable, did not extend to copyholds. By the 1st section of the 1 Vict. c. 26, the last statute which relates to wills and testaments, the 55 Geo. III. c. 192, and the above-mentioned enactment of the Statute of Frauds, are repealed; and by the 3rd section the power of disposition by will is extended to customary freeholds and tenant right estates, and all estates of a customary or copyhold tenure, without the necessity of any surrender or admittance, and notwithstanding the want of a custom to devise a surrender to the use of a will; and to all estates *pur auter vie*, whether of customary freehold, tenant right, customary, or copyhold tenure. The 4th section provides that where any real estate of the nature of customary freehold, or tenant right, or customary or copyhold, might by the custom of the manor of which the same is holden, have been surrendered to the use of a will, and the testator shall not have surrendered the same, no person claiming to be entitled under his will shall be entitled to be admitted, except upon payment of all such stamp-duties, fees, and sums of money as would have been due in respect of the surrender of such estate, or the presentment, registering, and enrolment of such surrender to the use of his will. And also, that where the testator, being entitled to admission to any real estate, and upon such admission to surrender the same to the use of his will, shall not have been admitted thereto, no person claiming to be entitled to such real estate in consequence of such will shall be entitled to admission, except on payment of all such stamp-duties, fees, fine, and sums of money as would have been due in respect of the admittance of the testator to such real estate, the surrender to the use of his will, the presentment, registering, or enrolment of such surrender; all such stamp-duties, fees, fine, or sums of money, to be paid in addition to the stamp-duties, fees, fine, or sums of money due on the admittance of the person so claiming to be entitled to such real estate.

By the 5th section, when any real estate of the nature of customary freehold, or tenant right, or customary, or copyhold, is disposed of by will, the lord of the manor, or reputed manor, of which such real estate is holden, or his steward, or the deputy of such steward, is to cause the will by which such disposition is made, or an extract thereof, to be entered on the Court Rolls; and when any trusts are declared by the will, it is not to be necessary to enter the declaration of such trusts, but it is to be sufficient to state in the entry on the Court Rolls that such real estate is subject to the trusts declared by the will; and when such real estate could not have been disposed of by will, except by virtue of the act, the same fine, heriot dues, duties, and services are to be paid and rendered by the devisee as would have been due from the customary heir in case of the descent of such real estate. And the lord is, as against the devisee, to have the same remedy for recovering and enforcing such fine, heriot dues, duties, and services as he is entitled to against the customary heir in case of a descent.

By the 6th section, if no disposition by will be made of any estate *pur auter vie* of a freehold nature, the same is to be chargeable in the hands of the heir, if it come to him by reason of special occupancy, as assets by descent, as in the case of freehold land in fee simple; and in case there be no special occupant of any estate *pur auter vie*, whether freehold or customary freehold, tenant right, customary or copyhold, or of any other tenure, and whether a corporeal or incorporeal hereditament, it is to go to the executor or administrator of the party that had the estate by virtue of the grant; and if the estate come to the executor or administrator either by reason of a special occupancy or by virtue of the act, it is to be assets in his hands, and to go and be applied and distributed in the same manner as the personal estate of the testator or intestate. By the 26th section a general devise of the testator's lands is to include copyholds, unless a contrary intention appear by the will; which is an alteration of the old rule whereby copyholds did not pass under a general devise of "lands, tenements, and hereditaments," or other general words descriptive of real estate, unless the copyholds had been surrendered to the use of the will, or the testator had no freehold lands upon which it could operate. And besides the above-mentioned changes relating peculiarly to copyholds, all the other enactments of the act, including that which prescribes the formalities to be observed in making a will, are applicable to estates of copyhold or customary tenure.

Copyholds cannot be seized upon an outlawry, and not being expressly mentioned in the Statute of Westminster which introduced the elegit, could not be taken under it upon a judgment against the copyholder; but by the 11th section of the 1 & 2 Vict. c. 110, copyholds are made subject to execution by judgment creditors in the same manner as freeholds.

Copyhold lands belonging to traders have been subjected to the operation of the bankrupt laws (stat. 6 Geo. IV. c. 16, § 68 and 69; 3 & 4 Wm. IV. c. 74, § 66); and by stat. 3 & 4 Wm. IV. c. 104, customaryhold and copyhold lands which a man has not by his last will charged with or devised subject to the payment of his debts, are rendered assets to be administered in a court of equity for the payment both of specialty and simple contract debts. Copyholds are not liable (except by special custom) to the incidents of curtesy or dower. The latter, where authorized by the custom, is called the widow's "free bench." These estates, being considered continuations of that of the deceased tenant, are perfected without admittance. A purchaser or devisee of copyholds has an incomplete title until admittance, but the customary heir is so far legal owner of the land before admittance, that he can surrender it or maintain an action of trespass or ejectment in respect of it. The lord may by a temporary seizure of the land compel an heir or devisee to come in and be admitted; and he is himself compellable by a mandamus of the Court of King's Bench to admit any tenant, whether claiming by descent or otherwise.

By the general custom of all manors, every copyholder may make a lease for any term of years, if he can obtain a licence from the lord, and even without such licence he may demise for one year, and in some manors for a longer term; and the interest thus created is not of a customary nature, but a legal estate for years, of the same kind as if it had been created out of a freehold interest. But every demise without licence for a longer period than the custom warrants, and in general, every alienation contrary to the nature of customary tenure, as a feoffment with livery of seisin, is followed by a forfeiture to the lord. A copyhold estate may also be forfeited by waste; as by cutting down timber, or opening mines, when such acts are not warranted by the custom. In the absence of such special custom, the general rule seems to be that the right of property both in trees and mines belongs to the lord, while only a possessory interest is vested in the tenant; but neither can the lord without the consent of the tenant, nor the tenant without the licence of the lord, cut down trees, or open and work new mines. In like manner forfeiture may be incurred by an inclosure or other alteration of the boundaries of an estate, refusal to attend the customary courts, or to perform the services, or to pay the rent or fine incident to the tenure. The 9th section of the 1 Wm. IV. c. 65, protects infants, lunatics, and married women from the last-mentioned cause of forfeiture. In case of felony or treason being committed by a copyholder, the lord has the absolute benefit of the forfeiture, unless it has been expressly provided otherwise by act of parliament. In all cases of forfeiture the lord may recover the forfeited estate by ejectment, without prejudice to the rights of the copyholders (if any there be) in reversion or remainder. He may waive the forfeiture by a subsequent act of recognition of the tenure. If he does not take advantage of the forfeiture for twenty years, his right to do so is barred by the act for the Limitation of Actions, 3 & 4 Wm. IV. And if he neglect to take advantage of the forfeiture in his life-time, his heir cannot avail himself of it.

The lord may also become entitled to a customary tenement by escheat for want of heirs. Formerly where a copyhold was surrendered to a mortgagee and his heirs, and no condition was expressed in the surrender, and the mortgagee died intestate and without an heir, the lord was entitled to enter for escheat To remedy this, the 4 & 5 Wm. IV. c. 23, enacts that where a trustee or mortgagee of lands of any tenure whatsoever dies without an heir, the Court of Chancery may appoint a person to convey or surrender the legal estate for the benefit of the persons entitled to the equitable interest in the property, and provides against the future escheat or forfeiture of lands by reason of the attainder or conviction of trustees or mortgagees who have no beneficial interest therein.

If the lord (having acquired a copyhold tenement by forfeiture, escheat, or surrender to his own use) afterwards grant it away by an assurance unauthorized by the custom, the customary tenure is for ever destroyed. And if he makes a legal conveyance in fee-simple of a copyhold tenement to the tenant, the tenement is said to be enfranchised, that is, converted into freehold.

Copyholders were till very lately incapable of serving on juries, or voting at county elections of members of parliament; but the former disability was removed by 6 Geo. IV. c. 50, § 1, and the latter by the 2 & 3 Wm. IV. c. 45, § 19. As to the qualification for killing game under 22 and 23 Chas. II. c. 25, § 3, there seems to be no distinction between freeholders and copyholders.

There are no lands of a copyhold tenure in Ireland.

Still greater changes in the nature of estates of copyhold and customary tenure are gradually taking place under the provisions of the stat. 4 & 5 Vict. c. 35, the principal objects of which are—1. The commutation of certain manorial rights in respect of lands of copyhold and customary tenure; 2. The facilitating the enfranchisement of such lands; and 3. The improvement of such tenure.

1. The enactments with respect to the commutation of manorial rights are partly compulsory and partly permissive. All rents, reliefs, and services (except service at the lord's court), fines, heriots, or money payments in lieu thereof, the lord's rights in timber, and in mines and minerals, may be made the subject of compulsory commutation upon an agreement being entered into between the lord and the tenants of any manor at a meeting called in the way prescribed by the act. As soon as this agreement receives the signatures of the lord or tenants whose interests are not less than three-fourths in value of such manor and lands, and of three-fourths in number of the tenants, it becomes (on receiving the confirmation of the commissioners appointed under the act) compulsory on the lord and all the tenants of such manor. Powers are likewise given to any lord, and any one or more of the tenants, to effect by agreement between themselves a commutation, wholly voluntary, of the above-mentioned rights or any other rights of the lord, such as escheats, waifs, fairs, markets, &c. The lord's rights may be commuted either for an annual rent-charge and a small fixed fine not exceeding 5s. on death or alienation, or for the payment of a fine on death or alienation or any other contingency, or at any fixed period or periods to be agreed upon between the parties: such annual rent charge or such fine, as the case may be, if exceeding the sum of 20s., to be variable according to the price of corn, upon the principle of tithe rent-charges. After the completion of the commutation, the lands are to continue to be held by copy of Court Roll, and to pass by surrender and admittance or other customary mode of conveyance. but the customs of Borough-English, or Gavelkind (except in Kent), or any other customary mode of descent or custom relating to dower, freebench, or curtesy to which the lands may have been subject, are to cease, and they are to be thenceforth subject to the general law of descent, dower, and curtesy relating to lands of freehold tenure.

2. For the purpose of facilitating the enfranchisement of copyhold lands, the act enables lords of manors, whatever may be the extent of their interests, with the consent of the commissioners under the act, to enfranchise all or any of the lands holden of their manors, in consideration of any sum or sums of money payable forthwith or at a future time, according to agreement: and tenants, whatever be the extent of their interests, are in like manner enabled, with the consent of the commissioners, to accept of enfranchisement on the terms agreed upon. After the completion of any such enfranchisement, the lands included in it are to become of freehold tenure, subject to the consideration agreed upon for the enfranchisement, but without prejudice to the tenant's right of common and existing limitations affecting the land.

3. The act contains a clause applicable to cases where commutation or enfranchisement has been effected, and there has

been a reservation of the lord's right in mines and minerals, enabling the tenants to grant to the lord such rights of entry and way, and such other easements, as may be necessary to the enjoyment of the reserved rights. [ENFRANCHISEMENT.]

It also, after stating the doubts entertained as to the power of the courts of equity to decree a partition of lands of copyhold or customary tenure, confers that power to be exercised according to the practice of the court in freehold cases. Formerly a customary court could not be legally constituted unless two or more tenants were present to form the homage; all acts of court were by usage required to be matters of presentment by the homage; and in a great majority of manors grants could not be made nor admissions taken except at courts held within the manors. A remedy is provided for these inconveniences by clauses giving power to hold customary courts though there should be no tenant of the manor holding by copy, or though no such tenant, or not more than one such tenant, should be present; enabling lords and stewards to make grants and take admissions out of court and out of the manor: and requiring the lord forthwith, upon payment of the usual fees, to enter on the rolls all such surrenders, deeds, wills, grants, and admissions as would formerly have required the formality of a court to authorize their entry or to give them legal effect; and also declaring that no presentment of a surrender, will, or other instrument shall be essential to the validity of any such admission. But the operation of these provisions is restrained by a clause providing that wastes and commons are not to be granted or inclosed without the consent of the homage at a court duly constituted.

The act also contains a provision extending the powers of the lords and tenants of certain manors to dispose of and divide ancient tenements held of the manor, subject to a due apportionment of the ancient rent where a tenement is sold in parcels.

There are likewise numerous provisions in the act for defining boundaries, settling disputes, providing for cases of disability, payment of expenses, &c., similar to those in the Tithe Commutation Act, 6 & 7 Wm. IV. c. 71.

The act applies partially to the Duchy of Lancaster, but not otherwise to Crown lands, and not at all to the Duchy of Cornwall.

COPYRIGHT, or, as it was formerly termed, Copy, has been defined by Lord Mansfield, "to signify an incorporeal right to the sole printing and publishing of somewhat intellectual, communicated by letters." By this "somewhat intellectual" is to be understood something proceeding from the mind of the person by whom, or through whom, such a right is claimable. Yet, although mere republications of the compositions of others are no subject for copyright, it is not limited to such productions as contain new or original ideas. Translations both from ancient and modern languages, and notes and additions to existing works, are similarly protected. Further, a right of copy attaches to the authors of ideas expressed by other symbols as well as letters, to musical composers for example.

The origin of copyright must be sought in the general opinion of its justice and expediency. It has been supposed that a common-law right of copy existed in England previously to any statute on the subject. As a legal proposition, however, this cannot be supported by any proper and direct proof of a fair judicial decision before the passing of the first statute relating to copyrigt, 8 Anne, c. 19; inasmuch as it never appears to have been directly controverted up to that time. But, in the absence of positive authority, it may be fairly inferred, from the old charters of the Stationers' Company, and much more from their registers, whence it appears that some thousands of books, even as early as the times of Elizabeth, passed from one owner to another by descent, sale, and assignment; from acts and ordinances of parliament which imply a recognition of it by the nature of their provisions respecting printing; and from decrees of the Star-chamber, which, though not binding precedents, are evidence of the opinion of many learned men as to the then state of the law. The non-existence of express decisions on the point is accounted for down to 1640 by the necessity of obtaining a licence prior to the printing of anything, so that authors had no occasion to apply to civil tribunals for protection, as none but themselves and those claiming under them were so licensed, and he who printed a book without this was subject to enormous penalties.

It has hardly been controverted in the various arguments upon this common-law right of copy that literary compositions in their original state, and the right of the publication of them, are the exclusive property of the author. The argument has been that this property was put an end to by publication: and yet without publication it is useless to the owner, because it is without profit, and property without the power of use or disposal is not property. In that state it is lost to society as a means of improvement, as well as to the author as a means of gain. Publication is therefore the necessary act and the only means to render such a property useful to the public and profitable to the owner. If, says Lord Mansfield, the copy which belonged to the author before publication does not belong to him after, where is the common law to be found which says there is such a property before? All the metaphysical subtleties from the nature of the thing may be equally objected to the property before. It is equally detached from the manuscript or any physical existence whatsoever. There is in fact nothing in the act of publication to vary the nature of the right, so that what is necessary to make a work useful and profitable should be taken as destructive at once of an author's confessed original property against his expressed will. It has accordingly been the almost unanimous opinion of the high authorities who were called on to decide the point, that by the common law of England authors were entitled to copyright, and as there was nothing in statute or custom to determine it, or distinguish this from other species of property, that such right was once perpetual. The arguments for the contrary opinion are collected in the judgment of Mr. Justice Yates in the case of Millar v. Taylor, 4 Burrow, p. 2303. It must be observed that this argument in favour of a common-law copyright is founded on the assumption that copyright is property independently of written law; a proposition which may be denied.

From the above premises arose the question, after the passing of the first statute respecting literary property in 1710, whether by certain of its provisions this perpetual copyright at common law was extinguished for the future. After some less important decisions in the negative on motion in the Court of Chancery and elsewhere, the question was argued before the Court of King's Bench, during the term, when Lord Mansfield presided, in 1769. The result was a decision in favour of the common-law right as unaltered by the statute, with the disapproval, however, of Mr. Justice Yates. Subsequently, in 1774, the same point was brought under the consideration or the House of Lords, and the decision of the court below was reversed by a majority of six judges in eleven, as Lord Mansfield, who adhered to the opinion of the minority, declined to interfere; it being very unusual, from motives of delicacy, for a peer to support his own judgment on appeal to the House of Lords. It is somewhat remarkable, that although this could hardly be termed a decision, as the judges were in point of fact divided equally, it has since been held so important as a precedent and sustained in so many subsequent cases, that it must now be considered as settled law that perpetual copyright is put an end to by the statutes.

The universities of Cambridge and Oxford protected themselves from the consequences of this decree in the case of Donaldsons and Beckett, by obtaining from parliament, in 1775, the following year, an act for enabling the two universities in England, the four universities in Scotland, and the several colleges of Eton, Westminster, and Winchester, to hold in perpetuity their copyright in books given or bequeathed to the said universities and colleges for the advancement of useful learning and other purposes of education. This protection, sanctioned by penalty and forfeiture, so long as such books are printed at the presses of the universities and colleges respectively, is still enjoyed, affected by the general statutes on the subject; and a similar protection is extended to the university of Dublin by 41 Geo. III. c. 107.

The chief provisions of the 8 Anne, c. 19, entitled 'An act for the encouragement of learning, by vesting the copies of printed books in the authors or purchasers of such copies during the times therein mentioned,' as regards the effecting of that purpose, were, that the authors of books already printed, and those claiming under the authors, should have the sole right and liberty of printing them for a term of twenty-one years and no longer; and that the authors of books thereafter to be printed, and their assigns, should have the same right for fourteen years and no longer. The last clause of the statute directed that after the expiration of these fourteen years the same right should return to the authors, if living, for another fourteen years. The persons infringing these provisions were to be punished by forfeiture of the pirated book to the proprietor, and a penalty of one penny for each sheet, one-half to go to the crown and the other half to the informer, provided always the title to the copy of the book had been duly entered with the Stationers' Company.

The 41 Geo. III. c. 107, which extended the same law to Ireland, gave a further protection to authors and their assigns by action for damages and double costs, and raised the penalty per sheet to three pence, to be divided in the same way.

The 54 Geo. III. c. 156, entitled 'An act to amend the several acts for the encouragement of learning by securing the copies and copyright of printed books to the authors of such books and their assigns,' enacted, that the author of any book which should be published after the passing of the act, and his assigns, should have the sole liberty of printing and reprinting such book for the full term of twenty-eight years from the day of publication, and, if the author should be living at the end of that period, for the residue of his natural life; while with regard to books at that time already published, of which the authors were then living, and in which copyright had not expired, if the authors should die before the expiration of fourteen years from publication, their representatives should have the benefit of the second fourteen years; and if the authors should survive till twenty-eight years from publication, they themselves should have the benefit for the remainder of their lives; the rights of all assigns being saved in both cases. The penalties for the infringement of copyrights were the same as in the former statutes, but with the limitation that all legal proceedings under the act must be commenced within one year.

The act 5 & 6 Vict. c. 45 (Lord Mahon's Act), entitled 'An act to amend the law of copyright,' and having for its preamble, "Whereas it is expedient to amend the law relating to copyright, and to afford greater encouragement to the production of literary works of lasting benefit to the world," is the act now regulating literary property. It repeals the three before-mentioned acts, and enacts that, in every book published in the life-time of the author, after the passing of the act (1st of July, 1842), the author and his assigns shall have copyright for the term of the author's life, and for seven years after his death, or if these seven years expire before the end of forty-two years from the time of publication, then for such period of forty-two years; while for books previously published, in which copyright still subsisted at the time of the passing of the act, the copyright should be continued for the full term provided in the cases of books thereafter published, except in cases where the copyright should belong wholly or in part to a person other than the author, "who shall have acquired it for other consideration than that of natural love and affection." In these excepted cases, however, the author, or his personal representative, and the proprietor or proprietors of copyright may agree, before the expiration of the subsisting term of copyright, to accept the benefits of the act; and on a minute of such agreement being entered in a book of registry directed to be kept at Stationers' Hall, the copyright will be continued, as in other cases, for the author's life and seven years after his death, or for forty-two years from the time of publication, and will be the property of the person or persons specified in the minute. The copyright of a book published after the author's death is to endure for forty-two years from the time of publication, and to belong to the proprietor of the manuscript from which it is first published, and his assigns. With regard to encyclopædias, reviews, magazines, periodical works, or works published in a series of books or parts, or any book in which the publisher or projector shall have employed persons to write, on the terms that the copyright shall belong to himself, the copyright shall be in the publisher or projector, after he has paid for it, in the same manner and for the same term as is given to authors of books, except only in the case of essays, articles, or portions forming part of and first published in reviews, magazines, or other periodical works of a like nature, the right of publishing which separately shall revert to the authors at the end of twenty-eight years after publication, for the remainder of the term given by this act; and during these twenty-eight years the publisher or projector shall not have the right to publish any such essay, article, or portion separately, without the consent of the author or his assigns.

The act provides, at the same time, against the suppression of books of importance to the public, by empowering the judicial committee of the Privy Council, on complaint made to them that the proprietor of the copyright in any book, after the death of its author, refuses to republish or allow the republication of the same, to license the complainant to publish the book, in such manner and subject to such conditions as the Privy Council may think fit.

The remedies provided by this act for infringement of copyright are, an action for damages (in which the defendant is required, on pleading, to give notice to the plaintiff of the objections to the plaintiff's title on which he means to rely), and a power given to the officers of customs and excise to seize and destroy all foreign reprints of books in which copyright exists, with a penalty on the importer (if he be not the proprietor of the copyright) of 10l., and double the value of every copy of any book imported, on conviction before two justices of the peace; 5l. of the penalty to go to the officer of customs or excise who shall procure the conviction, and the remainder to the proprietor of the copyright.

The act provides that a book of registry be kept at Stationers' Hall, where entries may be made of proprietorships of copyright, assignments thereof, licences of the judicial committee, and agreemv its as to copyrights subsisting at the time of the passing of the act, on payment in each case of a fee of 5s. The entry of proprietorship of copyright in this book does not affect copyright; but no action can be brought for infringement of copyright, nor any other legal proceedings taken, unless the proprietorship of copyright has been entered. The entry of an assignment in the registry book is to all intents and purposes an effectual assignment. § 13. Certified and stamped copies of entries in the registry book are to be evidence in all courts of justice, and are to be taken as *primâ facie* proof of copyright. The making of a false entry in the registry book, or the production in evidence of any paper falsely purporting to be the copy of an entry therein, is made a misdemeanor. Persons thinking themselves aggrieved by any entry in the registry book, may apply to a court of law in term time, or a judge in vacation, for an order to vary or expunge such entry; and such court or judge may make an order for varying, expunging, or confirming such entry, with or without costs.

It has been said that the exclusive pro perty of authors in their manuscripts has always been recognised by the law. But as this principle only prevented the printing or circulating copies of them without the licence of the owner, it has been found necessary to provide for the peculiar protection of the authors of dramatic and musical compositions. The 3 Will. IV. c. 15, entitled 'An Act to amend the Laws relating to Dramatic Literary Property,' and known as Sir Bulwer Lytton's act, after reciting the 54 Geo. III. c. 156, provided that the author of any dramatic piece, not hitherto printed or published by authority of him or his assigns, should have as his property the sore liberty of representing it, or causing it to be represented, at any place of dramatic entertainment; and the author or assignees of any such work, printed and published within ten years before the date of the act, should have the same privilege, for twenty-eight years from publication, and for the remainder of the author's life, if he lived longer; the penalty for violating these enactments to be enforced by action for damages, with double costs, to be brought within twelve months from the commission of the offence. The 5 & 6 Vict. c. 45, has extended the term of the sole liberty of representing dramatic pieces to the period provided by that act for the copyright of books, and gives the same protection to the authors of musical pieces and their assigns. The remedies provided by the 3 Will. IV. c. 15, in the case of dramatic pieces are confirmed by the 5 & 6 Vict. c. 45, and extended to musical pieces. The 5 & 6 Vict. c. 45, also enacts that no assignment of the copyright of any book consisting of a dramatic piece or musical composition shall convey the right of representing or performing such dramatic piece or musical composition, unless an entry, expressing the intention that such right should pass by the assignment, be made in the registry book at Stationers' Hall.

There are certain works excepted from the benefit of the law of copyright from the nature of their contents. Such are, all publications injurious to morality, inimical to Christianity, or stimulating, either as libellous or seditious, to a breach of the peace. This must however be understood of their general tenor, and not of isolated passages. As far as a rule on the subject can be laid down, it is, that any work containing matter for which a public indictment or private prosecution could be sustained is not protected by the law, but may be pirated by other parties at pleasure, who, if sued for penalties under the act, are allowed to give in evidence the nature of the composition which they have published, in order to defeat the action. This is a remarkable exception to the general rule of law, that none shall take advantage of his own wrong; and its operation is quite as remarkable, the effect of the rule having often been to disseminate more widely that which the law has declared not to merit protection.

The protection given to authors by the statute of copyright is coupled with the condition of presenting five copies of every book to public libraries. A copy of every work, and of every second or subsequent edition which contains any additions or alterations, bound, sewed, or stitched together, and on the best paper on which the same shall be printed, is to be delivered at the British Museum within one month after its first publication, if it is published within the bills of mortality, or within three months if published in any other part of the United Kingdom, or within twelve months if published in any other part of the British dominions; and a copy of every work, or second or subsequent edition, containing additions and alterations, on the paper of which the largest number of copies shall be printed for sale, in the like condition as the copies prepared for sale by the publisher, is to be delivered, if demanded, within twelve months after publication, within one month after demand made, at Stationers' Hall, for the Bodleian Library at Oxford, the Public Library at Cambridge, the Library of the Faculty of Advocates at Edinburgh, the Library of Trinity College, Dublin, under penalty of forfeiting the value of the copy of each book or edition not delivered, and a sum not exceeding 5*l*., to be recovered by the Librarian, or other officer properly authorised, of the Library to which the book should have been delivered, on conviction before two justices of the peace for the county or place where the publisher resides, or by action of debt in any Court of Record in the United Kingdom. Formerly, under the 54 Geo. III. c. 156, an author was obliged to give eleven copies of his work to public libraries. The 6 & 7 Will. IV. repealed the 54 Geo. III. c. 156, so far as related to the delivering of copies to the four universities of Scotland, Sion College, and the King's Inns, Dublin, compensation being given to these institutions upon an estimate of the annual value of books supplied on an average of three years, ending the 30th of June, 1836.

Besides the special copyrights of the universities secured to them as before mentioned by statute, there still exist certain prerogative copyrights attaching to the owners in perpetuity. Of these the chief belong to the king, which were more numerous and considerable formerly than at present. Many are now quite obsolete, such as those of almanacs, law-books, and Latin grammars; and others very questionable, such as that of the exclusive right of the universities of Oxford and Cambridge, and the king's printer in England and in Scotland, to print the English translation of the Bible. The king has a prerogative copyright in the liturgy and other services of the church, in proclamations, orders in council, and other state papers, and in the statutes. It has been decided, that the University of Cambridge shares by letters patent in the king's prerogative of printing acts of parliament. The House of Lords also exercises an exclusive privilege, somewhat fallen into disuse, of publishing its own proceedings as the supreme court of judicature.

The modes of legal proceeding to prevent or punish the infringement of copyright, or as it is more usually termed, piracy, are by action for damages; or more commonly by obtaining an injunction in equity to prohibit the unlawful publication, which affords immediate and summary redress. This is always granted where the legal title of the plaintiff to the work is made out, and the identity of the pirated publication with his own shown to the satisfaction of the court. The proof even of an equitable title has been held sufficient to entitle the plaintiff to this relief. (Mawman v. Tegg, 2 Russ. 385.) Neither will the court refuse to grant the injunction on the ground that the matter pirated forms only a part of the publication complained of, and that what is original will be rendered useless to the defendant and the public by prohibiting its sale. But as this mode of proceeding presses very severely upon defendants, and often inflicts irreparable injury, the court, where any doubt attaches, will either refuse the injunction altogether, or grant it only on condition of the plaintiff's bringing an action immediately, to have the merits of the case decided by a jury with the smallest possible delay; and in the mean time the defendants will be ordered to keep an account of the copies sold.

The strict powers given by the 5 & 6 Vict. c. 45, have been exercised vigorously by the Custom-house authorities, and found very effectual to prevent the importation into this country of the French, Belgian, German, and American reprints of popular English works; but English authors still suffer by the circulation of these reprints abroad; and a practice so destructive of the fair profits of mental labour can only be effectually redressed by prevailing on foreign countries to extend the benefits of their own laws against literary piracy to aliens as well as native authors. Two statutes have been passed in the present reign to enable her Majesty to extend to foreigners the benefits of our laws of copyright. The first of these, 1 & 2 Vict. c. 59, was repealed by 7 Vict. c. 12, the statute which is now in force, and which was substituted in consequence of the alterations in our law of copyright. This act, entitled 'An Act to amend the law relating to International Copyright,' empowers her Majesty by order in council to enable authors of works first published in foreign countries to have copyright in the British dominions for books, prints, articles of sculpture, and the sole liberty of representing dramatic and musical pieces, for periods not exceeding those allowed by the various copyright acts for the respective classes of works when first published in this country, on conditions of registration and delivering of one copy at Stationers' Hall; but no such order in council is to have any effect unless it is stated therein, as ground for issuing the same, that reciprocal protection for British authors has been secured in the foreign country to which the order in council refers. The power given by this act has not yet been exercised in the case of any single foreign country.

A notice of the law of copyright would be incomplete which did not advert to some other compositions which receive from statute a protection analogous to that of literature. Such are engravings, etchings, and prints, maps and charts, designs for articles of manufacture, and sculpture of all kinds. These resemble written works as regards the incorporeal right in them accruing to the author by the exertion of his mental powers in their production, but differ as they also require a good deal of his manual skill and labour, and are therefore his property upon the same general principles as any other manufacture. Such productions therefore are even more plainly entitled to the protection of the law than books.

The chief statutes affecting the copyright in the arts of designing, engraving, and etching prints, are the 8 Geo. II. c. 13, which vests it in the inventor, designer, and proprietor, for fourteen years from the first publication, and enforces this provision against any person pirating the same by forfeiture of the plate and prints, and a fine of 5s. for each print, to be recovered by action within three months of the discovery of the offence. The 7 Geo. III. c. 38, extends the term of copyright to twenty-eight years; and in addition to the subjects of the former statute, includes maps, charts, and plans, under the same conditions. It also extends the time of bringing an action for the penalties to six months. The 17 Geo. III. c. 57, gives the owner of the copyright a further remedy of action for damages and double costs within the same limits of time. The 6 & 7 Will. IV. extends the provisions of the previous acts to Ireland.

With regard to models, casts, and other sculptures, the 38 Geo. III. c. 71, vests the right and property in these for fourteen years in the proprietor, and gives him a special action on the case against the offender, if brought within six months. These provisions were rendered more effectual by 54 Geo. III. c. 56, by which double costs were given, and an additional term of fourteen years superadded in case the maker should be living at the end of the first term.

As to sculpture certainly, but more doubtfully as to prints, for there have been conflicting decisions on the point, the work must bear upon it the name of the maker and the date of publication to entitle it to the protection of the law.

With regard to designs for manufactured articles, the 27 Geo. III. c. 38, continued by 29 Geo. III. c. 19, and confirmed and made perpetual by 34 Geo. III. c. 23, gave the sole right of using a new pattern in the printing of linens, cottons, calicoes, and muslins for three months; and the 2 Vict. c. 13, extended this privilege to designs for printing other woven fabrics besides calicoes. The 2 Vict. c. 17, regulated copyright of designs in all articles except lace, and the articles to which the above-mentioned acts apply. But all these statutes were repealed by the 5 & 6 Vict. c. 100 (Mr. Emerson Tennent's Act), which considerably extended the periods of copyright in designs.

This act distributes articles to which designs may be applied into twelve classes:—

1. Articles of manufacture composed wholly or chiefly of any metal or mixed metals.
2. Articles of manufacture composed wholly or chiefly of wood.
3. Articles of manufacture composed wholly or chiefly of glass.
4. Articles of manufacture composed wholly or chiefly of earthenware.
5. Paper-hangings.
6. Carpets.
7. Shawls, where the design is applied solely by printing, or by any other process by which colours are or may hereafter be produced upon tissue or textile fabrics.
8. Shawls not comprised in class 7.
9. Yarn, thread or warp, the design being applied by printing, or by any other process by which colours are or may hereafter be produced.
10. Woven fabrics, composed of linen, cotton, wool, silk, or hair, or of any two or more of such materials, if the design be applied by printing, or by any other process by which colours are or may hereafter be produced upon tissue or textile fabrics; except the articles included in class 11.
11. Woven fabrics composed of linen, cotton, wool, silk, or hair, or of any two or more of such materials, if the design be applied by printing, or by any other process by which colours are or may hereafter be produced upon tissue or textile fabrics, such woven fabrics being or coming within the description technically called furnitures, and the repeat of the

design whereof shall be more than twelve inches by eight inches.

12. Woven fabrics not comprised in any preceding class.

13. Lace, and any article of manufacture or substance not comprised in any preceding class.

The act gives to the proprietor of a design not previously published the sole right of applying it to ornamenting articles of the first, second, third, fourth, fifth, sixth, eighth, and eleventh classes, for three years; to articles of the seventh, ninth, and tenth, for nine months; and to articles of the twelfth and thirteenth classes for twelve months; whether such design be applicable for the pattern, or for the shape and configuration, or for the ornament of the articles, or for any two or more such purposes, and by whatever means the design may be applicable, whether by printing, or by painting, or by embroidery, or by weaving, or by sewing, or by modelling, or by casting, or by embossing, or by engraving, or by staining, or by any other means whatsoever, manual, mechanical, or chemical, separate or combined. The benefits of copyright of designs are made to depend on registration before publication. Piracy is punished by a penalty of not less than 5l. nor more than 30l., to be paid to the proprietor of the design, and to be recovered by an action of debt or for damages, or by summary proceeding before two justices.

The right of patents in many respects resembles that of copyright. [PATENT.]

The act 'for preventing the publication of lectures without consent' (5 and 6 Wm. IV. c. 65) gives to authors of lectures the sole right and liberty of printing and publishing the same, and imposes a penalty on other persons, including printers and publishers of newspapers, who shall print, or publish, or sell them without the author's leave. The act does not extend to lectures of the delivering of which notice in writing shall not have been given to two justices, living within five miles of the place, two days at least before their delivery, or to any lecture delivered in any university, or public school or college, or any public foundation, or by individuals in virtue of any gift, endowment, or foundation. The act does not extend to sermons.

CORN-LAWS and CORN-TRADE. The history of the corn-laws and corn-trade in this country may be conveniently divided into several periods.

Period I.—*From Early Times to 1688.*

A statute of the thirteenth century, supposed to be of the date of 51 Henry III. (1266-7), shows that the average prices of wheat and other grain had become an object of attention. In 1360 the exportation of corn was prohibited by statute (34 Edw. III. c. 20). In 1393 corn might be exported by the king's subjects "to what parts that please them," except to the king's enemies. "Nevertheless," it is added, "the king wills that his council may restrain the said passage when they shall think best for the profit of the realm." (17 Ric. II. c. 7.) This act was confirmed in 1425 (4 Hen. VI. c. 5). Sufficient grain was raised in England to admit of exportation, but it was the policy of that age to endeavour to retain within the kingdom all those things which were indispensable to its wants, rather than by permitting freedom of export and import to trust to the operation of the commercial principle for an adequate supply.

In 1436 the exportation of wheat was allowed without the king's licence when the price per quarter at the place of shipment was 6s. 8d. or under. In the preamble of the statute (15 Hen. VI. c. 2) restrictions on exportation are loudly complained of: "for cause whereof, farmers and other men, which use manurement of their land, may not sell their corn but of a bare price, to the great damage of all the realm;" and the remedy provided is a freer permission to export the surplus—a regulation which is intended for the profit of the whole realm, but "especially for the counties adjoining to the sea." In 1441 this statute was continued (20 Hen. VI. c. 6), and in 1444-5 it was rendered perpetual (23 Hen. VI. c. 5).

Nearly thirty years after the statute of 1436 occurs the first law to prevent a supply of foreign grain. In the preamble of a statute (3 Edw. IV. c. 2), which was passed in 1463, it is remarked that, "Whereas the labourers and occupiers of husbandry within this realm be daily grievously endamaged by bringing of corn out of other lands and parts into this realm when corn of the growing of this realm is at a low price;" in remedy of which it was enacted that wheat should not be imported unless the price at the place of import exceeded 6s. 8d. per quarter. By the act of 1463, so long as the price of wheat was below 6s. 8d. per quarter, exportation was permitted, and importation was prohibited. The price, therefore, was intended to be sustained at that height; and the benefit of the corn-grower was the sole object of the statute. But in 1474 (eleven years after the statute 3 Edw. IV. c. 2 was passed) we have the authority of the Paston Letters in proof of the suffering experienced from the want of a market for the superabundant supply of grain. Margaret Paston, writing to her son on the 29th of Jan. 1474, after quoting the very low price of corn and grain, says—" There is none outload (export) suffered to go out of this country as yet; the king hath commanded that there should none go out of this land. I fear me we shall have right a strange world: God amend it when his will is." In a letter written in the following year she makes the same complaints about low prices and the scarcity of money. ('Paston Letters,' ii. 91-93. Edit. by A. Ramsay.)

In 1533-4 an end was put to the system of exportation which had been established in 1463, and, with some occasional exceptions, had continued from that time; and thenceforth it was forbidden to export corn and provisions without the king's licence. The statute enacted for this purpose was intended to keep down prices, though the preamble sets out with the rational observation that, "forasmuch as dearth, scarcity, good cheap [good market], and plenty [of victual], happeneth, riseth, and chanceth, of so many and divers reasons that it is very hard and difficult to put any certain prices to any such things." It however ended by enacting that, on complaint being made of high prices, they shall be regulated by the lords of the council, and made known by proclamation; and that farmers and others shall sell their commodities at the prices thus fixed.

During the greater part of the sixteenth century a struggle was maintained by the makers of the laws against the rise of prices which characterised nearly the whole of that period. In September, 1549, a proclamation was issued, directed against dealers in the principal articles of food. According to it, no man was to buy and sell the self-same thing again, except brokers, and they were not to have more than ten quarters of grain in their possession at one time. This proclamation directed " that all justices should divide themselves into the hundreds, and look what superfluous corn was in every barn, and appoint it to be sold at a reasonable price; also, that one must be in every market-town to see the corn bought. Whoso brought no corn to market, as he was appointed, was to forfeit 10l., unless the purveyors took it up, or it was sold to the neighbours." (Turner's *Hist. Eng.* i. 172.) Obedience to these regulations was not confined to the temporary provisions of a proclamation; but in 1551-2 they were, with some modifications, embodied in a statute (5 & 6 Edw. VI. c. 14). By this enactment, engrossers (persons buying corn to sell again) were subjected to heavy penalties. For the third offence they were to be set in the pillory, to forfeit their personal effects, and to be imprisoned during the king's pleasure. Farmers buying corn for seed were compelled to sell at the same time an equal quantity of their corn in store, under penalty of forfeiting double the value of what they had bought. Persons might engross corn, not forestalling it—that is, enhancing the price or preventing the supply—when wheat was under 6s. 8d. per quarter.

In 1562-3 a further attempt was made to restrict the operations of buying and selling in articles of food, as well as many other commodities. The 5 & 6 Edw. VI. c. 14, already quoted, contained a proviso that corn-badgers, allowed to that office by three justices of the peace of the county where the said badger dwelt, could buy provisions in open fair or market for towns and cities, and sell them, without being guilty of the offence of forestalling; but this relaxation was not permitted by a subsequent statute passed in 1562-3 (5 Eliz. c. 12), in the preamble of which the act 5 & 6 Edw. VI. is thus alluded to:—"Since the making of which act such a great number of persons, seeking only to live easily and to leave their honest labour, have and do daily seek to be allowed to the said office, being most unfit and unmeet for those purposes, and also very hurtful to the commonwealth of this realm, as well by enhancing the price of corn and grain, as also by the diminishing of good and necessary husbandmen." Accordingly it was then enacted that the licences to corn-badgers should only be granted once a year by the justices at quarter-sessions, instead of at any period by three justices; and that none were to obtain a licence but resident householders of three years' standing, who are or have been married, and of the age of thirty, and are not servants or retainers to another person. Those who received a licence were to have it renewed at the end of every year. Licensed persons were also required to find security not to forestall or engross in their dealings, and not to buy out of open fair or market, except under express licence. The statute did not apply to the counties of Westmoreland, Cumberland, Lancaster, Chester, and York.

In 1554 a new act was passed (1 & 2 Phil. and Mary, c. 5) which allowed exportation so long as the price of wheat should not exceed 6s. 8d., that of rye 4s., and that of barley 3s. per quarter. The preamble complains that former acts against the exportation of grain and provisions had been evaded, by reason whereof they had grown unto a "wonderful dearth and extreme prices." Under the act of 1554, when prices exceeded 6s. 8d. per quarter for wheat exportation was to cease; and when it was under that price it could not be exported to any foreign country, or to Scotland, without a licence, under penalty of forfeiting double the value of the cargo as well as the vessel, besides imprisonment of the master and mariners of the vessel for one year. The penalty for exporting a greater quantity than was warranted by the licence was treble the value of the cargo, and imprisonment; and a cargo could be taken only to the port mentioned in the licence. The object was to prevent exportation when there was not a sufficient supply in the home market, and to permit it to be sent abroad when it was below a certain price at home.

In 1562, only eight years after the act 1 & 2 Phil. and Mary had been passed, the liberty of exportation was extended, and wheat might be carried out of the country when the average price was 10s. per quarter and under, that of rye, peas, and beans 8s., and that of barley or malt 6s. 8d. per quarter (5 Eliz. c. 5); and to prevent evasion of the law, it was enacted that the corn and grain should only be exported from such ports as her Majesty might by proclamation appoint.

In 1571 a statute was passed (13 Eliz. c. 13) which contains provisions for settling once a-year the average prices by which exportation should be governed. The Lord President and Council in the North, also the Lord President and Council in Wales, and the Justices of Assize, within their respective jurisdictions, "yearly shall, upon conference had with the inhabitants of the country, of the cheapness and dearth of any kinds of grain," determine "whether it shall be meet at any time to permit any grain to be carried out of any port within the said several jurisdictions or limits; and so shall, in writing, under their hands and seal, cause and make a determination either for permission or prohibition, and the same cause to be, by the sheriff of the counties, published and affixed in as many accustomed market-towns and ports within the said shire as they shall think convenient." The averages, when once struck, were to continue in force until the same authorities ordered otherwise; and if their regulations should "be hurtful to the country by means of dearth, or be a great hinderance to tillage by means of too much cheapness," they could make the necessary alterations. All proceedings under this act were to be notified to the queen or privy council. The statute enacted that, "for the better increase of tillage, and for maintenance and increase of the navy and mariners of this realm," corn might be exported at all times to friendly countries when proclamation was not made to the contrary. A poundage or customs duty of 1s. per quarter was charged on all wheat exported; but if exported under special licence, and not under the act, the duty was 2s. per quarter.

The law of 1463, which prohibited importation so long as the price of wheat was under 6s. 8d., that of rye under 4s., and that of barley under 3s. the quarter, appears not to have been repealed, but it must have remained inoperative, from the prices seldom or probably never descending below these rates. The importation of corn, therefore, we may reckon to have been practically free at this time.

In 1592-3 the price at which exportation was permitted was raised to 20s. per quarter, and the customs duty was fixed at 2s. (35 Eliz. c. 7). In 1603-4 the importation price was raised to 26s. 8d. per quarter (1 Jac. I. c. 25); and in 1623 to 32s. (21 Jac. I. c. 28). By the 21 Jac. I. c. 28, unless wheat was under 32s. per quarter, and other grain in proportion, buying corn and selling it again was not permitted. The king could restrain the liberty of exportation by proclamation. In 1627-8 another statute relative to the corn-trade was passed (3 Car. I. c. 5), which, however, made no alteration in the previous statute of James I. In 1660 a new scale of duties was introduced. When the price of wheat per quarter was under 44s. the import duty was 2s.; and when the price was above 44s., the duty fell to 4d. Exportation was permitted at a duty of 1s. per quarter whenever the price of wheat did not exceed 40s. per quarter (12 Car. II. c. 4): the export duty was 1s. per quarter.

In 1663 the corn-trade again became the subject of legislation, and an act was passed (15 Car. II. c. 7). The preamble of this act commenced by asserting that "the surest and effectualest means of promoting and advancing any trade, occupation, or mystery, being by rendering it profitable to the users thereof," and that, large quantities of land being waste, which might be profitably cultivated if sufficient encouragement were given for the cost and labour on the same, it should be enacted, with a view of encouraging the application of capital and labour to waste lands, that, after September, 1663, when wheat did not exceed 48s. per quarter at the places and havens of shipment, the import duty should be 5s., and when the price was above 48s. the duty was to be 4d. By the same act when wheat did not exceed 48s. per quarter, it might be exported, and when it was also at this price "then it shall be lawful for all and every person (not forestalling nor selling the same in the open market within three months after the buying thereof) to buy in open market, and to keep in his or their granaries or houses, and to sell again, such corn and grain," any statute to the contrary notwithstanding. This latter part of the statute abolished in effect the provisions of 5 & 6 Edward VI. c. 14, respecting the buying and selling of corn and grain.

In 1670, by another act (22 Car. II. c. 13), exportation was permitted, although the price of wheat should exceed the price fixed by the act of 1663 (48s.); but a customs' duty of 1s. per quarter was in this case to be charged. Wheat imported from foreign countries was at the same time loaded with duties so heavy as effectually to exclude it, the duty being 16s. when the price in this country was at or under 53s. 4d. per quarter, and 8s. when above that price and under 80s., at which latter price importation became free. The object of this act was to relieve the agricultural interests from the depression under which they were labouring from the low prices of produce which had existed for twenty years, more particularly from 1646 to 1665. Between 1617 and 1621 wheat fell from 43s. 3d. the quarter to 27s., in consequence of which farmers were unable to pay their rents. The low price was occasioned by abundant harvests; "for remedy whereof the Council have written letters into every shire, and some say to every market-town, to provide a granary or storehouse, with a stock to buy corn, and keep it for a dear year." (Contemporary writers quoted by Mr. Tooke in his 'Hist. of Prices.') The cheapness of wheat was attended with the good effect of raising the standard of diet amongst the poorer classes, who are described as "traversing the markets to find out the finest wheats, for none else would now serve their use, though before they were glad of the coarser rye-bread." (Ibid.) The act of 1670 does not appear to have answered its object. Roger Coke, writing in 1671, says—"The ends designed by the acts against the importation of Irish cattle, of raising the rents of the lands of England, are so far from being attained, that the contrary hath ensued" (Ibid); and Coke speaks of a great diminution of cultivation.

The harvests of 1673-4-5 proved defective, and the same result occurred in 1677-8, so that the average price of the seven years ending 1672, during which wheat ranged at 36s. the quarter, was followed in the seven subsequent years, ending 1679, by an average of 46s., being a rise of nearly 30 per cent. But these years of scarcity were followed by twelve abundant seasons in succession (with the exception of 1684, which was somewhat deficient), and the price of corn and grain again sunk very low. In the six years ending 1691 the average price of wheat was 29s. 5d. the quarter, and if the four years ending 1691 be taken, the average price was only 27s. 7d., being lower than at any period during the whole of the century. There was no competition in the English market with the foreign grower during the above-mentioned years of low prices; and exportation was freely permitted on payment of a nominal duty. The means which the landed interest took to relieve themselves will be noticed in the next period.

The mode of taking the average prices of corn and grain established in 1570 (13 Eliz. c. 13) was acted upon till 1685, the necessary provisions for an alteration having been neglected in the Corn Act of 1670. These were made by a statute which enacted that justices of the peace, in counties wherein foreign corn might be imported, may, at quarter-sessions, by the oaths of two persons duly qualified— that is, possessed of freehold estates of the annual value of 20l., or leasehold estates of 50l., and not being corn-dealers, and by such other means as they shall see fit, determine the market price of middling English corn, which is to be certified on oath, hung up in some public place, and sent to the chief officer at the custom-house in each district.

II.—*From* 1689 *to* 1773.

The high prices of the seven years ending 1679 led to an extension of tillage, and this was followed by a succession of favourable seasons which occasioned low prices. Exportation of corn therefore was not only permitted as heretofore, but encouraged by bounties. The statute for granting bounties (1 Wm. and Mary, c. 12) is entitled 'An Act for Encouraging the Exportation of Corn.' The preamble states that it had been "found by experience that the exportation of corn and grain into foreign countries, when the price thereof is at a low rate in this kingdom, hath been a great advantage, not only to the owners of land, but to the traders of this kingdom in general;" and it was enacted that a bounty of 5s. the quarter should be granted on the exportation of wheat, so long as the home price did not exceed 48s., with other bounties of smaller amount upon the exportation of barley, malt, and rye. The growers of corn were in possession of a market the sole supply of which was secured to them by the act of 1670 (22 Car. II. c. 13), and by the Bounty Act it was designed to prevent the overstocking of that market.

The seven years immediately succeeding 1693 were remarkable for a succession of unfavourable seasons. In the four years ending 1691 the price of wheat averaged 27s. 7d. the quarter, but in the four years preceding and including 1699 it reached 56s. 6d. The bounty was inoperative during this period, and was suspended by statute (12 Wm. III. c. 1), from the 9th of February, 1699, to the 29th of September, 1700. The preamble of the act contained an acknowledgment that the statute granting the bounty "was grounded upon the highest wisdom and prudence, and has succeeded, to the greatest benefit and advantage to the nation by the greatest encouragement of tillage." Before this temporary act had expired, another act was passed in 1700 (11 & 12 Wm. III. c. 20), which abolished the export duties of 1s. per quarter for wheat, and a less sum on other corn. "From 1697 to 1773 the total excess of exports over imports was 30,968,366 quarters, upon which export bounties, amounting to 6,237,176*l.* were paid out of the public revenue." (Commons' Report on Agric. Distress, 1821.) In 1750 the sum of 324,176*l.* was paid in bounties on corn. The exports of 1748-49-50 (during which, moreover, the price of wheat fell from 32*s.* 10½*d.* to 28*s.* 10¾*d.* the quarter) amounted to 2,120,000 quarters of wheat, and of all kinds of corn and grain to 3,825,000 quarters. This was the result of a cycle of abundant years and of extended cultivation caused by the bounty. In the twenty-three years from 1692 to 1715, says Mr. Tooke, in his elaborate 'History of Prices,' there were eleven bad seasons, during which the average price of wheat was 45*s.* 8*d.* the quarter; in the fifty years ending 1765 there were only five deficient harvests, and the average price for the whole half-century ranged at 34*s.* 11*d.*; and, taking the ten years ending 1751, during which the crops were constantly above an average, the price of wheat was only 29*s.* 2¼*d.* the quarter.

Adam Smith refers to "the peculiarly happy circumstances" of the country during these times of plenty; and Mr. Hallam describes the reign of George II. as "the most prosperous period that England had ever experienced." "Bread made of wheat is become more generally the food of the labouring people," observes the author of the 'Corn Tracts,' writing in 1765. Referring to the same period, Mr. Malthus remarks:—"It is well known that during this period the price of corn fell considerably, while the wages of labour are stated to have risen." Trade was flourishing, and the exports and imports progressively increasing during this period of abundance.

In twenty-six years, from 1730 to 1755, there had been only one unfavourable season, but from 1765 to 1775 there was a very frequent recurrence of unfavourable years, and the last five years of this period were all of this character. In 1766 the quartern loaf was selling in London at 1*s.* 6*d.*; addresses were sent up from various parts of the country complaining of general distress; and a proclamation was issued suspending exportation, and for enforcing the laws against forestallers and regraters. Exportation was suspended also in the following year, and also in 1770 and 1771. In 1772 importation was allowed duty-free to the 1st of May, 1773; and in this latter year the city of London offered a bounty of 4*s.* per quarter for 20,000 quarters of wheat, to be imported between March and June. The average prices of wheat had risen from 29*s.* 2¼*d.* in the ten years ending 1751, to 51*s.* for the ten years ending 1774, being an advance of 75 per cent. The excess of exports over imports from 1742 to 1751 had been 4,700,509 quarters of wheat, and, including all kinds of grain, 8,869,190 quarters, but from 1766 to 1775 there was an excess of imports to the extent of 1,363,149 quarters of wheat and 3,782,734 of corn and grain of all kinds. The old corn-law of 1689, under which a bounty on exportation had been granted, was now become a dead letter in consequence of the high range of prices in the home market.

After the peace of 1763 population rapidly advanced with the growth of trade and manufactures. In the reign of George I. there had only been sixteen enclosure acts passed; in the succeeding reign there were 226; but the number of such acts from 1760 to 1772 inclusive amounted to 585.

Several acts were passed in the period between 1689 and 1773 relating to the mode of ascertaining the average prices of corn and grain. In one of them, passed in 1729, the preamble states that the justices of the peace had "neglected to settle the price of corn at their quartersessions after Michaelmas last, and to return certificates thereof to the chief officer and collector of the customs residing in the respective ports where the said corn or grain has been or may be imported; by means whereof the said officers were at a loss how to charge the customs and duty due for such corn; which has been, and may be, a great loss to the revenue, and a detriment to the farmers and fair traders." To remedy the negligence of the gentry, the collectors of customs were empowered to settle the averages.

In 1732 another act was passed "for the

better ascertaining the common prices of middling English corn and grain, and for preventing the fraudulent importation of corn and grain." After 1st June, 1732, the justices of the peace, in counties which contained ports of importation, were to charge the grand jury at quarter-sessions to make inquiry and presentment upon oath of the common market-prices, which were to be certified to the officers at the ports specified. The averages were, however, only to be taken four times a year.

In 1766 the authorities of the city of London were empowered to settle the price of middling English corn and grain in January and July, in addition to the former periods of April and October.

It was not until 1770 that returns of prices were directed to be made weekly. In that year an act was passed, on the ground that a "register of the prices at which corn is sold in the several counties of Great Britain will be of public and general advantage." The justices of the peace were to order returns to be made weekly of the prices of British corn and grain from such towns in each county as they thought proper; the number of towns selected in each county not being more than six nor less than two. The Treasury was to appoint a receiver of corn returns, who was to publish an abstract of the weekly returns in the 'London Gazette,' and four times a year certify to the clerks of the peace the prices which were respectively prevalent in each county.

In 1772 an act was passed (12 Geo. III. c. 71) which removed several restrictions in old statutes on the ground that, "by preventing a free trade in the said commodities [corn, flour, cattle, &c.], they have a tendency to discourage the growth and enhance the price of the same, which statutes, put into execution, would bring great distress on the inhabitants of many parts of the kingdom."

III.—*From* 1773 *to* 1791.

In the preamble of the Corn Act of 1773 (13 Geo. III. c. 43) it is acknowledged that previous laws had greatly tended to the advancement of tillage and navigation, but that, on account of the small supplies on hand and scanty crops, it had been frequently necessary to suspend the operation of the laws; and that a permanent law on the corn-trade "would afford encouragement to the farmer, be the means of increasing the growth of that necessary commodity, and of affording a cheaper and more constant supply to the poor." And the act then fixes the following scale of duties, to come into operation on the 1st of January, 1774:—Whenever the price of middling British wheat, at ports of importation, was at or above 48s. per quarter, a duty of only 6d. per quarter was to be taken on all foreign wheat imported during the continuance of that price. When the price was at or above 44s., exportation and the bounty together were to cease; and the carrying of British grain coastwise ceased also. Under this act, corn and grain might be shipped to Ireland when exportation was prohibited from that country. Foreign corn warehoused under bond in twenty-five ports of Great Britain mentioned in the act might be re-exported duty free.

The home market was now opened to foreign supplies of corn under much more advantageous terms than before. Importation was constant and considerable, and prices were steadier on the whole, during the eighteen years from 1775 to 1792—notwithstanding the occurrence of five seasons in which the harvests were deficient—than they had been in the ten years preceding 1773. In the ten years ending 1769 the excess of exports amounted to 1,384,561 quarters; but in the next ten years, ending 1779, the excess was on the side of the imports to the extent of 431,566 quarters; and in the similar ten years ending 1789 there was also an excess amounting to 233,502 quarters. From 1760 to 1780 the number of acres enclosed under local acts was 1,912,350; in the ten years ending 1789 the number of acres enclosed had fallen to 450,180. The average price of wheat was 45s. the quarter in the ten years ending 1779, and 45s. 9d. in the ten years ending 1789. The extension of cultivation in the twenty years from 1760 to 1780, together with the improvement of agriculture, sufficed for the increased demands of the country, without breaking up much fresh land.

It was alleged, however, that the act of 1773 had rendered England dependent upon other countries for the supply of corn. The bounty by which the corn-growers had formerly profited, and which they were led to anticipate would still be secured to them, had never been obtained under this act.

At the commencement of the present period the average prices of corn were struck four times a-year, at the quarter-sessions, and they could not be altered between the interval of one quarter-session and another. In 1774, however, an act was passed (14 Geo. III. c. 64) by which exportation was regulated by the price on the market-day preceding the shipment; thus adopting the real average price at the time, instead of the average which existed three months before.

Six years afterwards, in 1780-1, it was enacted (21 Geo. III. c. 50) that the prices of English corn for the port of London and the ports of Kent and Essex should be determined by the averages taken at the London Corn Exchange. The weekly average was to regulate the exportation; but the importation of foreign corn and grain was regulated by averages struck only once a quarter.

In the session of 1788-9 new regulations were framed (29 Geo. III. c. 58), applying to all parts of the kingdom, which was divided into twelve districts, and in each a number of the principal market-towns was selected, in which, and at the sea-ports, the price of corn was to be ascertained for each district. Weekly returns were to be made to the receiver in London, who, on the 1st of February, May, August, and November, was to compute from the returns of the six preceding weeks the average price of each description of British corn and grain (with the exception of oats, the averages of which were to be computed on the returns of the twelve preceding weeks). The aggregate average price of the six weeks (and for oats of the twelve weeks) was to be transmitted to the principal officer of the customs in each district, and to regulate the importation at each port of the said district. The export-trade was still regulated by the weekly averages. Under this act each of the twelve maritime districts was treated as distinct in itself, and counties on one side of the kingdom might be exporting their surplus produce to a foreign market, while those on the other side might be importing.

IV.—*From* 1791 *to* 1804.

In the new corn-law of 1791 it was enacted that the bounty of 5s. per quarter should be paid when wheat was under 44s., and that, when wheat was at or above 46s., exportation was to cease. The new scale of import duties was as follows:—For wheat under 50s. per quarter, the "high duty" of 24s. 3d. was payable; at 50s., but under 54s., the "first low duty" of 2s. 6d.; at or above 54s., the "second low duty" of 6d. was payable. The duty of 24s. 3d., so long as the price of wheat was under 50s. the quarter, was equivalent to a prohibition.

The thirteen years from 1791 to 1804 form a very eventful period in the history of the Corn Laws. Under the comparatively free system established by the Corn Act of 1773, the excess of imports had been comparatively trifling; but under an act constructed rather to prevent importation, the excess of imports in the thirteen years from 1791 to 1803 amounted to 6,458,901 quarters of wheat and wheat-flour, and enormous sacrifices were made to obtain this quantity.

The harvest of 1793 was below an average, and those of the two following years were still more deficient. The average price of wheat rose from 55s. 7d., in January, 1795, to 108s. 4d. in August. Parliament met in October, when the King's speech alluded to the "very high price of grain" as a subject of "the greatest anxiety." An act was passed, granting a bounty of from 16s. to 20s. the quarter, according to the quality, on wheat from the south of Europe, till the quantity should amount to 400,000 quarters; and from America till it should amount to 500,000 quarters; and 12s. to 15s. from any other part of Europe till it should amount to the same quantity; the bounty to be 8s. and 10s. after that quantity was exceeded. Neutral vessels laden with grain were forcibly seized on the high seas, and the masters compelled to sell their cargoes to the government agents. The members of both houses of parliament bound themselves by a written pledge to observe the utmost frugality in the use of bread in their respective households; and engaged to reduce the consumption of wheat by at least one-third of the usual quantity consumed in ordinary times, unless the average price of wheat should be reduced to 8s. the bushel. The hair-powder tax was imposed at this period, as one means of diminishing the consumption of wheat.

For two or three years after 1795 the harvests were more favourable, until the disastrous season of 1799. The average price of wheat at the commencement of 1799 was 49s. 6d. the quarter, but in December it had risen to 94s. 2d.; and soon after the commencement of the following year the prospects of scarcity had alarmingly increased. Recourse was again had to a bounty; and an act was passed, offering to the importer the difference between the average price of English wheat in the second week after importation and 90s. on wheat from the south of Europe, Africa, and America; 85s. from the Baltic and Germany; and 90s. from Archangel, if imported before the 1st of October, 1800. Lord Hawkesbury also brought in a bill, which was passed through its various stages on the following day, prohibiting the sale of bread until twenty-four hours after it had been baked. Prices, however, continued to advance, and in June, 1800, wheat was 134s. 5d. the quarter. Considerable importations brought down the price to 96s. 2d. in August; but in December it had again advanced to 133s., in consequence of the deficiency of the harvest of 1800. Parliament in consequence met in November, 1800, earlier than had been intended. The speech from the throne alluded to the supposition of combination and fraudulent practices for the purpose of raising the price of grain, but this a committee of the House of Lords denied. A select committee of the Commons was again appointed to take into consideration the existing high prices, and by the end of December this committee had presented six reports to the house, in the first of which the deficiency of the crops was stated to be one-fourth, and that the old supplies were exhausted before harvest. The committee suggested a variety of remedies to meet the emergency. Among other things they recommended the encouragement of the fisheries, the stoppage of the distilleries, a bounty on importation; also a recommendation from persons in authority, pointing out the necessity of the general practice of economy and frugality in all articles of food; and it was proposed to call upon the other house of parliament to join in an address to the throne, requesting his Majesty to issue a proclamation in favour of this suggestion. A royal proclamation was issued accordingly, and was widely circulated by the clergy and magistrates throughout the kingdom. An act was also passed, guaranteeing the difference between the average price of foreign wheat in the third week after importation and 100s. to the importer of *all* wheat weighing 53 lbs. per bushel, if imported within the time limited by the act. The advance of prices continued unchecked in spite of these various plans; and in March, 1801, wheat averaged 156s. 2d. the quarter, or, taking the imperial measure now in use, 20s. the bushel; barley averaged 90s. 7d. the quarter, and oats 47s. 2d. The importations of the year were, wheat, 1,424,766 quarters; barley, 113,966; oats, 583,043. For four weeks the quartern loaf in London was as high as 1s. 10½d. The agricultural districts were again disturbed by riots. The money wages of the agricultural labourer, in order to have been equal to those which he received in the reign of George II., should have risen to about 30s. per week. An advance of wages to a trifling extent was obtained in some trades. The salaries of persons holding official situations under the government were also increased. The misery of the bulk of the people during the years of scarcity is shown by the diminished number of marriages, which, from 79,477 in 1798, were reduced to 67,288 in 1801. The fallacy that wages advance with the price of food was never more glaringly displayed than at this period. This me-

morable dearth was a season of prosperity, as Mr. Tooke states, "to the landlords, who were raising, or had the prospect of soon raising, their rents; and to the farmers, who were realizing enormous gains pending the currency of their leases."
Comparative abundance was restored by a tolerably good harvest in 1801. In the two following years the harvests, though not very abundant, were favourable, and a further depression of prices took place. At the close of 1802 the average price of wheat was 57s. 1d. the quarter; early in 1803, 52s. 3d.; and at a corresponding period in 1804 the average price was as low as 49s. 6d. Meetings were now held by the agriculturists for the purpose of petitioning parliament for additional protection to agriculture, the act of 1790-1, which had raised the free import price (there was merely a nominal duty of 6d.) from 48s. to 54s., not having satisfied them. This brings us to the termination of the fourth period.

The Corn Act of 1790-1 consolidated, amended, and repealed a number of old statutes relating to the corn-trade; amongst the latter, the 15 Charles II. c. 7, which prohibited buying corn to sell again and laying up corn in warehouses. It also permitted foreign corn and grain to be bonded in the king's warehouses, the duty to be payable only when taken out for home consumption. The object of this beneficial clause is stated as follows:—"To promote and extend the commerce of the merchants of this kingdom in foreign corn, and to provide stores which may always be ready for the relief of his Majesty's subjects in times of dearth." Many of the provisions of the act, however, interfered with trade to a vexatious and injurious extent. When foreign exportation was not allowed at any particular port, not even home produce could be carried thence coastwise, even to a port at which exportation was at the time taking place. Foreign vessels might, however, change their destination to any port where importation was permitted, if, on their arrival at that for which their cargo had been shipped, importation had ceased to be allowed. The country was still divided into so many independent sections, and this regulation was introduced into Scotland, which was divided into four districts. For the purposes of exportation, the weekly averages of each district were cited, and, for importation, the average of the six weeks preceding the 15th of February, May, August, and November. Thus the one varied from week to week, and the latter could only be changed four times a-year.

V.—*From* 1804 *to* 1815.

On the 13th of April, 1804, the Chancellor of the Exchequer moved for the appointment of a select committee to inquire into the principle and operation of the Corn Regulation Act of 1791, and to determine whether the scale which it fixed for the regulation of imports and exports was now applicable. On the 14th of May the committee reported that the act alluded to required "very material alteration." On the 14th of June they stated in a second report "that the price of corn from 1791 to the harvest of 1803 has been very irregular; but, upon an average, increased in a great degree by the years of scarcity, has in general yielded a fair profit to the grower. The casual high prices, however, have had the effect of stimulating industry, and bringing into culture large tracts of waste land, which, combined with the two last productive seasons, has occasioned such a depression in the value of grain as it is feared will greatly tend to the discouragement of agriculture, unless maintained by the support of parliament."

A new Corn Act was therefore passed which established the following scale for the admission of foreign corn:—Wheat under 63s. per quarter, the "high duty" of 24s. 3d. payable; at 63s. and under 66s., the "first low duty;" and at or above 66s., the "second low duty," which amounted only to 6d. The free import or nominal duty price was thus raised from 54s., at which it stood in the act of 1790-1, to 66s.—an increase of 12s. The bounty of 5s. on exportation was to be paid when the average price of wheat was at or under 48s.; and when the average rose to 54s. exportation was to be prohibited: these two provisions of the act proved inoperative.

Immediately after the passing of this act prices rose between March and December from 49s. 6d. the quarter to 86s. 2d. The crop of 1804 proved deficient; in the three following seasons the harvests were not abundant; and in the five years from 1808 to 1812 they were very deficient. In August, 1812, the average prices were —for wheat 155s., barley 79s. 10d., and oats 56s. 2d.; and Mr. Tooke says (Hist. of Prices, i. 323) that in Mark-lane the finest Dantzic wheat fetched 180s., and oats in one or two instances were sold at the enormous price of 84s. the quarter.

The war in which we were engaged during the above-mentioned years when the harvests were deficient, added to the expense and difficulty of procuring supplies of grain from abroad; but notwithstanding the anti-commercial spirit which the war had assumed, the French government granted licences under which about 400,000 quarters of wheat, besides other grain, were imported to supply the deficiency of the harvest of 1809. In 1810 we imported 1,500,000 quarters of wheat and flour, and 600,000 quarters of other grain and meal. The expenses of freight, insurance, and licenses amounted to from 30s. to 50s. per quarter on wheat. The enormous charges on importation were added to the natural price of British corn; and this was one of the causes of what were called the "war prices" of this memorable period, and of the extraordinary profits of farmers and landowners

The high prices stimulated cultivation, and from 1804 to 1814 inclusively the number of inclosure bills which received the royal assent was 1084, being considerably more than for any other corresponding period. The state of the agricultural interest at this time has been impartially described by Mr. Tooke:—A great amount of gain had been distributed among the agricultural classes; and as the range of high prices (with an interval of depression between the harvests of 1810 and 1811, so short as not to have been felt at all by the landlord, and very little by the farmer) had been of an unusually long continuance, it was concluded that the causes of that high range were permanent. From 1809 to 1813 was accordingly the period in which rents experienced their greatest rise,—that is, upon the expiration of leases, they were advanced in full proportion to the high range of the prices of produce; and in several instances they were raised threefold or upwards of what they had been in 1792. (Hist. of Prices, i. 323-6.)

A year or two of low prices of agricultural produce again brought to a close another period in the history of the Corn Laws. Wheat, which had been sold as high as 180s. the quarter (for select parcels) in 1812, fell to 73s. 6d. after the abundant harvest of 1813; and after that of 1814, which was rather favourable than otherwise, the average price was reduced to 53s. 7d. the quarter. This fall in prices and the cessation of hostilities led to the reconsideration of the whole question of the Corn Law.

During the present period an important change was made in the mode of striking the average prices of corn and grain. The twelve maritime districts of England, and the four similar districts of Scotland, ceased to be regarded as sixteen separate sections, each of which was regulated by the prices prevalent within its separate limits; but for England, the averages, taken as before, were computed for the whole of the twelve districts at once, and the average price obtained from the computation regulated importation and exportation at sea-ports situate in any part of the country; and for Scotland the same plan was pursued. The six weeks' averages, struck quarterly, regulated the import-duty, and the weekly average the exports.

In 1806 was passed 'An Act to permit the free interchange of every Species of Grain between Great Britain and Ireland' (46 Geo. III. c. 97). Ireland had been previously treated as a colony, but this act placed her on an equality with other parts of the kingdom.

VI.—*From* 1815 *to* 1822.

The real object of the Corn Act of 1815 was to perpetuate high prices and high rents by artificial scarcity. In June, 1814, a committee of the House of Lords on the corn trade was appointed, and in their second report the committee recommended that so long as the average price of wheat was under 80s. the ports should be completely closed against supplies from other countries. The prohibitive price suggested by the agricultural witnesses examined by the committee varied from 72s. to 96s. Out of sixteen witnesses belonging to this class, only four were in favour of the free importation price being below 80s. per quarter. This second report was presented on the 25th of July; but a bill which had been brought in, founded on its recommendations, was strongly opposed, and eventually abandoned. An act was however passed, which repealed the bounty on exportation (54 Geo. III. c. 69). From 1792, the high prices which prevailed in the home market rendered the bounty inoperative. By the new act exportation might take place at any time without reference to prevailing prices.

The average price of wheat for the year 1814 was about 34s. per quarter lower than the average of the preceding year, though the harvest had not been an abundant one. In the month of February, 1815, the average price was under 60s., and before harvest it might rise to 66s., when under the act of 1804 the ports would be open and prices again be depressed, and it was thought to a very low point, in consequence of the obstacles to free intercourse with the continent being removed. Early in the session of 1815, therefore, a bill was brought in, giving effect to the recommendation of the committee of the previous year, and fixing 80s. as the lowest point at which importation should take place. The measure produced great excitement throughout the country, particularly in the manufacturing districts and in all the large towns. In the House of Commons, at an early period, a division took place in favour of 72s. being substituted for 80s., with the following result:—For the motion, 35; against it, 154; majority, 119. On the 3rd of March an attempt was made to throw out the bill:—For the motion, 56; against it, 218; majority, 162. On the 6th of March the vicinity of the House of Commons was thronged by an excited multitude, and several members were stopped, some of them roughly handled, and they were questioned by the mob as to the vote which they intended to give. Ultimately the military were called out, and, with the civil force, kept the streets clear. This evening the gallery of the House of Commons was closed. An attempt was made to render the bill more favourable by substituting 74s. instead of 80s. as the pivot price; and the motion was supported by 77 against 208, being a majority of 131. On the 8th of May, on bringing up the report, an amendment was moved, that the bill be read that day six months, when there voted 50 in its favour, and 168 against it; majority, 118. A final attempt was made to substitute a lower rate than 80s., leaving it to the House to determine the exact price at which prohibition ceased; but only 78 voted for the motion, and 184 in favour of the measure as previously proposed. On the 10th of March, on the third reading, an amendment was moved, that the bill be thrown out, but it was only supported by 77 against 245; majority 168. On the 20th of March the bill passed the Lords by a majority of 107:—128 contents, and 21 non-contents. The measure was opposed with great force and acuteness by several of the most eminent statesmen of the day; and Lord Grenville drew up an excellent protest embodying the views of the minority.

The 23rd of March, 1815, the bill received the Royal assent.

Until the average price of wheat rose to 80s. the ports were now to be effectually closed. Colonial wheat was admitted when the average prices reached 67s. per quarter. Such was the leading feature of the new act (55 Geo. III. c. 26). But the mode in which the average prices were determined greatly increased its stringency. A new average was to be struck quarterly, on the 15th of February, May, August, and November, from the aggregate prices of the six preceding weeks; but it was provided that, if during the six weeks subsequent to any of these dates the average prices, which might be at 80s., fell below that price, no supplies should be admitted for home consumption from any ports between the rivers Eyder and the Bidassoa,—that is, from Denmark to Spain.

It was the general expectation of the

farmers that the act of 1815 would maintain the prices of their produce at a rate somewhat under that of the scale which the legislature had adopted; and which, for wheat, was 80s.; barley 40s.; oats 27s.; and rye, beans and peas, 53s. They entered into contracts with their landlords and others with this conviction. But, as in every measure passed since 1773 prices had risen above the scale which had been fixed as the prohibitive rate, it happened that they now sunk below it. In 1816, 1817, and 1818, three deficient harvests occurred, that of the former year being below an average crop to a greater extent than in any year since the periods of scarcity at the close of the last century. Prices rose above the rate at which foreign supplies were admitted, and in 1817 and 1818 above 2,600,000 quarters of wheat were imported. In 1821 and 1822 the agriculturists endured the severest distress, and the engagements which they had been induced to make under the fallacious hopes excited by the last Corn Act and the range of high prices during the war occasioned them to be swept from the land by thousands. In the week ending December 21st, 1822, the average prices of corn and grain were as follow:—

Wheat.	Barley.	Oats.	Rye.	Beans.	Peas.
s. d.	s. d.	s. d.	s. d.	s. d.	s. d.
38 8	29 4	19 9	23 6	28 10	29 4
Being 41 4	10 8	8 3	29 6	24 2	23 8

lower than the scale which was framed for the farmer's protection. The harvest of 1820 was estimated as one-fourth above an average crop. and by some, who included the extended breadth of wheat under cultivation in consequence of the high prices of 1816-17-18, the surplus was computed at about one-third above the average,—that is, there was a surplus of between 3 and 4 million quarters of wheat, for which there was no demand. The crop of 1821 was large, but of inferior quality; that of 1822 was above an average, and the harvest was unusually early. The cause of the great fall of prices and of its distressing effects on the farmers was sufficiently obvious. They were under leases and rents founded upon an extraordinary conjuncture of bad seasons with a state of war, and upon an act which promised to keep up high prices by excluding supplies of foreign grain.

The fluctuations in price under the corn-law of 1815 were as extraordinary as they were unexpected, and amounted to 199½ per cent.

The cry of agricultural distress never ceased to ring in the ears of the legislature during the years 1820-1-2. Committees of the House of Commons were appointed to inquire into the condition of agriculture. In Parliament Sir Thomas Lethbridge proposed a permanent duty on foreign wheat of 40s. per quarter. Mr. Benett's plan was a permanent duty of 24s. per quarter after the averages had again reached 80s., and a drawback of 18s. per quarter to be allowed on the exportation of wheat of marketable quality. Mr. Curwen suggested that when the average price of wheat reached 80s. the ports should be opened for the admission of 400,000 quarters of foreign wheat, at a duty of 10s.; and if, six weeks after this quantity had been admitted, the average price should still continue above 80s., then to allow of the importation of an additional 400,000 quarters, at a duty of 5s. The late Mr. Ricardo moved resolutions to the effect that when the averages rose to 65s. per quarter all the foreign wheat then in bond should be liberated at a duty of 15s.; and that afterwards, whenever the averages exceeded 70s. the trade in wheat should be free, at a permanent duty of 20s.: one year from that time the duty to be reduced to 19s., and a similar reduction to be made each year until the duty was 10s., at which it should be permanently fixed; at the same time allowing a drawback or bounty on exportation of 7s. per quarter. On the 29th of April, during the agricultural panic of 1822, Mr. Huskisson moved a series of resolutions, the first and second of which affirmed that prices had fallen, although the quantity of corn imported was trifling, and the third resolution showed—" That the excess of the supply above the demand must have arisen either from an extent of corn-tillage more than commensurate to the average consumption of the country, or from a succession of abundant harvests upon the same extent of tillage, or from the coincident effect of both these causes." To prevent the alternate evils of scarcity and redundance, Mr. Huskisson proposed that the trade should be permanently free at a duty of 15s. per quarter, when the averages were under 80s.; and when above 80s. the duty to be 5s.; and above 85s. a nominal duty of 1s. only to be imposed.

The Select Committee of the House of Commons had a still greater variety of projects offered for its consideration. One plan proposed to the Committee of 1821 was to withdraw the permission to warehouse foreign wheat or any other foreign grain in England. The Committee of 1822 had under its serious consideration two plans for the alleviation of agricultural distress:—1. The application of 1,000,000l. in Exchequer bills, to be employed through the agency of government in buying up a certain quantity of British wheat to be placed in store. 2. Advances to be made to individuals on produce deposited in warehouses, to prevent them coming into the market simultaneously. The first plan was rejected by the Committee, but they considered the second was feasible, and were of opinion that "The sum of 1,000,000l. so employed (in loans on stock) would probably be fully adequate to give a temporary check to the excess which is continually poured into the overstocked market." In the House of Lords, the Marquis of Londonderry, on the 29th of April, moved that 1,000,000l. be advanced in Exchequer bills, when the average price of wheat was under 60s.

The fall of prices in 1820-1-2 had fully demonstrated the futility of the corn-law of 1815, and it was therefore proposed to modify it.

VII.—*From* 1822 *to* 1828.

The corn-law of 1815 was suspended by a new act passed in July, 1822, which enacted that, " as soon as foreign wheat shall have been admitted for home consumption under the provisions of the Act of 55 Geo. III. c. 26 [the corn-law of 1815], the scale of prices at which the home consumption of foreign corn, meal, or flour is permitted by the said Act shall cease and determine." The new scale was as follows:—Wheat at or above 70s., duty 12s.; and for the first three months of the ports being open an additional duty of 5s. per quarter, being a duty of 17s. Above 70s., and under 80s., the "first low duty" of 5s., with the addition of 5s. for the first three months; above 80s. and under 85s., the "second low duty" of 1s. was alone to be charged. This act never came into operation. It is justly described as being merely a pretended relaxation of the act of 1815; for, though the limit of total prohibition was lowered from 80s. to 70s., yet the duty would have rendered it more severe than the measure for which it was substituted as an improvement. In 1826, in consequence of the unfavourable harvest, a temporary act was passed, under which a quantity of foreign grain was admitted for home consumption. In 1827 the Government was driven to a still more decisive step. In the spring of the year ministers had stated that it was not their intention to liberate the corn then in bond, upon which prices immediately rose. This was followed by some disturbances in the manufacturing districts, to allay which the Government, on the 1st of May, proposed to Parliament to release the bonded corn, and, as a measure of precaution, required to be invested with powers to admit during the recess of Parliament an additional quantity, not exceeding 500,000 quarters, in case the harvest proved deficient. These powers were acted upon, and on September 1 an Order in Council was issued, admitting certain descriptions of grain for home consumption, until forty days after the next meeting of Parliament, at an almost nominal rate of duty, on the ground that, " if the importation for home consumption of oats and oatmeal, and of rye, peas, and beans, be not immediately permitted, there is great cause to fear that much distress may ensue to all classes of his Majesty's subjects." In the ensuing session of Parliament ministers obtained an act of indemnity for this order.

In 1827 it had become sufficiently evident that some other system must be devised, and Mr. Canning introduced certain resolutions in the House of Commons, the leading principle of which was to permit importation at all times by substituting a graduated scale of duties. A bill was brought in, founded on these resolutions, fixing a duty of 1s. on foreign wheat when the average price was 70s. per quarter. In respect to colonial wheat, the duty was fixed at 6d. when the averages were 65s. per quarter, and when under that sum at 5s. per quarter. The bill was not carried, as the Duke of Wellington moved and carried a clause the effect of which would have been to keep the ports entirely shut so long as the price of wheat was under 66s. the quarter. An act was, however, passed during this session to permit corn, meal, &c., warehoused on the 1st of July, 1827, to be entered for home consumption upon payment of duties according to a fluctuating scale. About 372,000 quarters of wheat and flour were entered for consumption under this act, at a duty averaging above 20s. per quarter. The harvest had not been defective, and this was the very reason why the corn in bond was released notwithstanding the high duty, as there was no prospect of prices advancing.

In 1821 a new act was passed relative to the averages. Instead of "the maritime districts," 148 towns were named, for which the magistrates were to appoint inspectors to make a return of the weekly purchases.

The six weeks' averages still regulated the amount of duty on importation, but they were greatly improved by being every week subject to an alteration. Each week the receiver of corn returns struck out one week's averages, admitting those last received, and thereby affecting the aggregate average, as prices rose or fell from week to week. The introduction of a fluctuating scale of duty was an important step, and its effect will be considered in the next period.

It was impossible to continue any longer a system which, for three successive years, 1825-6-7, had been compelled to bend to the force of temporary circumstances; and like previous measures it was abandoned by its supporters either as inefficient or injurious. Such a state of things brings us to another period in the history of corn-law legislation.

VIII.—*From July 1828 to April 29, 1842.*

In 1828 Mr. Charles Grant (afterwards Lord Glenelg) introduced a series of resolutions slightly differing from those which had been moved by Mr. Canning, and they were eventually embodied in a bill which was carried through both Houses, and received the Royal assent on the 15th of July. The act was entitled, 'An Act to amend the Laws relating to the Importation of Corn,' and it repealed 55 Geo. III. c. 26 (1815); 3 Geo. IV. c. 60 (1822); and 7 and 8 Geo. IV. c. 58 (1827).

The provisions for settling the averages under this act were as follow:—In one hundred and fifty towns in England and Wales, mentioned in the act, corn-dealers were required to make a declaration, that they would return an accurate account of their purchases. [In London, the sellers made the return.] Inspectors were appointed in each of these one hundred and fifty towns, who transmitted returns to the Receiver in the Corn Department of the Board of Trade, whose duty it was to compute the average weekly price of each description of grain, and the aggregate average price for the previous six weeks, and to transmit a certified copy to the collectors of customs at the different outports. The return on which the average prices were based was published every Friday in 'The London Gazette.' The aggregate average for six weeks regulated the duty on importation.

Wheat at 50s. paid a duty of 36s. 8d.; barley at 33s. a duty of 13s. 10d.; oats at 24s. a duty of 10s. 9d.; rye, peas, and beans at 35s., a duty of 16s. 9d. Colonial wheat was admitted at a duty of 6d. when the average of the six weeks was at or above 67s.; and when below 67s. the duty was 5s. the quarter, and for other grain in proportion. Importation was free on payment of 1s. on the quarter when wheat in the home market was 73s.; barley 41s.; oats 31s.; and rye, peas, and beans 46s. the quarter.

In the following Table the scale of duties proposed by Mr. Canning, and that adopted by the legislature in 1828, are placed in juxtaposition:—

Average Prices of Wheat.	Duty according to Mr. Canning's Bill.	Duty fixed by Lord Clevely's Act.
s.	s.	s. d.
73	1	1 0
72	1	2 6
71	1	6 8
70	1	10 8
69	2	13 8
68	4	16 8
67	6	18 8
66	8	20 8
65	10	21 8
64	12	22 8
63	14	23 8
62	16	24 8
61	18	25 8
60	20	26 8
59	22	27 8
58	24	28 8
57	26	29 8
56	28	30 8
55	30	31 8
54	32	32 8
53	34	33 8

After the experience of a few seasons the corn-law of 1828 gave no more satisfaction than those which had preceded it. In December, 1835, the average price of wheat was down to 35s. 4d. per quarter, and in January, 1839, it was as high as 81s., being a difference of 129 per cent. In 1835 and 1836 the distressed condition of the agricultural interest was noticed in the speech from the throne on the opening of parliament, and select committees were appointed in both years to inquire into it. The law had neither prevented great fluctuation in prices nor agricultural distress. This unsteadiness of price was complained of by persons engaged in manufactures and trade; for, assuming the consumption of Great Britain to be 16,000,000 quarters of wheat, the sum paid for a year's consumption would be about 31,000,000l. in 1835, while the same quantity would cost 56,000,000l. in 1839. The difference, amounting to 25,000,000l., was withdrawn from the usual channels of circulation, and created stagnation in the different branches of non-agricultural industry. The new principle of a sliding-scale of duty required time and variety of circumstances fully to develop its effect; but it was at length placed beyond a doubt that the manner in which the scale was arranged tended to give a gambling character to the corn trade, which, instead of being a steady branch of commerce, was subjected to sudden movements and speculative operations. In one year (1838) the duty underwent thirty different changes from January to the end of November, and in the short period of two weeks went up from 1s. to 10s. 8d. the quarter. It was generally believed that, about the period of harvest, fraudulent returns were made of corn sold, with a view of raising the average price, and consequently lowering the duty; and it was quite certain that the scale operated in such a manner as to check the supplies of foreign grain until prices reached their maximum and the duty fell to the lowest point. "The gain of speculators is calculated not only on the advance in the price of corn, but also in the fall in the scale of duty; and as the duty falls in a greater ratio than the price of the corn rises, the duty operates as a bounty to withhold sales." (Salomons, *On the Operation of the Sliding Scale*.) When, for example, the average price in the home market was 66s., the duty was 20s. 8d., and on prices reaching 73s. the duty was only 1s.; the difference of profit to the importer was thus 7s. by the advance of prices, and 19s. 8d. by the fall of duty, making a total of 26s. 8d. When the quantity of wheat in bond had been liberated at the lowest duty the object of the speculators was attained, and to some of them, doubtless, the trade became an object of indifference until another opportunity occurred for availing themselves of the gambling capabilities of the sliding scale. The transactions in the corn trade of the year 1838 exhibited several of the inherent evils of this scale: first, as causing scarcity; secondly, as glutting the market just at the period when home produce was coming in; and, thirdly, by violently disturbing prices and overthrowing all the calculations on which a steady trade must be founded. In the second week of January the duty was 34s. 8d., and it declined gradually until September 13th, when it reached 1s., the lowest point. During this period prices were rising in the home market;

but instead of the foreign corn in bond being gradually admitted for consumption, there were only about 33,000 quarters entered from the beginning of the year up to the end of August, though the average price for that *month* was 74s. 8d. The speculators *waited* until the second week of September, when, by having withheld the supply, the duty became nominal, and in a single week 1,514,047 quarters of foreign wheat were thrown upon the markets. This *sudden* addition to the supply occasioned a decline of prices, and the duty again rose. The progress of the duty in the short space of six weeks was as follows:—

		s.	d.
Week ending Sept.	13th	1	0
,,	,, 20th	2	8
,,	,, 27th	10	8
,,	Oct. 4th	16	8
,,	,, 11th	20	8
,,	,, 18th	21	8
,,	,, 25th	22	8

A cargo which arrived at the end of September, instead of the middle of the month, would have been subject to a duty of 10s. 8d. instead of 1s. per quarter. It would then be bonded, and might remain in the warehouses until actually unfit for use. In a parliamentary paper (No. 46, Sess. 1839) it is stated that 899 quarters of foreign wheat were abandoned and destroyed that year in the port of London.

Another natural effect of the sliding scale was to limit the radius of supply. Buyers rushed into the markets of Hamburg, Danzig, and the Baltic ports, and, by competition within a narrow circle, raised the prices to an excessive height, in reliance upon the profits to be obtained by speculating upon the lowest duty. The unsteadiness of the trade did not encourage that demand for our manufactures which would have sprung up if it had been less subject to impulsive starts. The derangement of monetary affairs was a necessary consequence of a trade conducted under these circumstances; and the value of merchandise of all kinds declined from sales being forced in order to meet engagements at a time when money had been rendered scarce by the drain of remittances for corn.

In years when the crops were of inferior quality another disadvantage of the sliding scale was experienced. There was not in this case a general scarcity, but there was an excessive scarcity of wheat of good quality; and the quantity sold of an inferior quality depressed the average prices, and raised the duty so as to exclude a supply of sound foreign wheat except at the most extravagant prices.

On the 7th of May, 1841, after the injurious operation of the sliding scale had long been obvious, Lord John Russell, as the organ of the government, announced the intention of substituting a fixed duty, which had not hitherto been adopted under any of the numerous acts for regulating the importation of foreign corn. The fixed duties which Lord John Russell proposed were as follows:—

Wheat	.	.	.	.	.	8s.	0d.	per quarter.
Rye, peas, and beans	5	0	,,
Barley	.	.	.	.	.	4	6	,,
Oats	.	.	.	.	.	3	4	,,

The proposed duty of 8s. on wheat exceeded by 2s. 4d. the duty (5s. 8d.) which had actually been paid on all wheat imported during the thirteen years that the sliding scale had been in operation, and by 4s. the duty per quarter paid on the importation of four and a half million quarters imported in 1838 and 1839; but a fixed duty would have rendered the trade steady; the supplies would have come into the market gradually as they were wanted, when the bonus which the sliding scale offered for withholding them was withdrawn; and they would also have been procured at a less cost than when speculators suddenly rushed into the foreign markets. But in the general election which took place in June and July, 1841, the government was defeated, and shortly after the parliament had assembled the ministry resigned office.

The government which had been overthrown at the general election partly in consequence of the plan for the proposed alteration of the corn-law, was replaced by one which was raised to office in a great measure by the agricultural interest, who probably now felt confident that the corn-laws would not be thrown into the "lottery of legislation." The prime minister, however, knew too well that at least such a change as would mitigate the evils of the sliding scale of 1828 was at all events essential; and in the speech from the throne, 3rd February, 1842, her majesty recommended to the consideration of parliament "the state of the laws which affect the import of corn, and of other articles the produce of foreign countries." On the 9th Sir Robert Peel brought forward the government plan, in which a sliding scale of duty was still retained, but instead of the duty successively falling from 10s. to 6s. 8d., 2s. 8d., and 1s., it was proposed to have two stationary points of price, and with these exceptions (52s. to 55s., and 66s. to 69s.), the duty would only fall 1s. for each increase of 1s. in the average price. On the 7th April the new corn bill was read the third time in the Commons; on the 22nd of April it was read the third time in the Lords; and on the 29th of the same month the act (5 Vict. c. 14) came into operation.

Under the act 9 Geo. IV. c. 60, which regulated the foreign trade in corn from the 15th of July, 1828, to the 29th of April, 1842, the total quantity of foreign wheat admitted was 13,562,856 quarters and 4,305,150 cwts. of foreign wheat-flour, and, in addition, at a lower rate of duty, 597,700 quarters of colonial wheat and 1,744,591 cwts. of colonial flour. Nearly one-half of the foreign wheat and flour was admitted at the lowest rate of duty, and comparatively little at the higher rates, as the following statement will show:—

Duty at	Wheat.	Wheat-flour.
1s.	5,788,045 qrs.	1,758,372 cwts.
2s. 8d.	2,880,613	862,262
6s. 8d.	1,997,226	519,123
10s. 8d.	620,342	243,120

The average rate of duty for the period was under 6s. the quarter. For the whole period during which the act was in operation the average price of wheat in England and Wales was 59s. 4d., and the extreme points of fluctuation in the weekly averages were from 36s. 8d. to 81s. 6d., or 122 per cent. The highest yearly average was 70s. 8d., in 1839; and the lowest 39s. 4d., in 1835. The largest quantity of wheat and wheat-flour in the warehouse at the end of any month was 1,006,832 quarters in August, 1840. The year of largest importation was 1839, when 2,711,723 quarters of wheat and wheat-flour were admitted for home consumption. In 1835 the quantity admitted was only 28,554 quarters, and in the following year only 30,107 quarters. In 1839 and 1840 the duties on foreign and colonial corn and grain yielded above a million sterling each year: in 1839 1,098,849l., and in 1840 1,156,660l.

IX.—*From* 1842 *to* 1849.

The following was the scale of prices and rates of duty for foreign wheat under 5 Vict. c. 14:—

Average per Qr.		Duty per Qr.
s.	s.	s. d.
If under	51	20 0
51 ,,	52	19 0
52-3-4 ,,	55	18 0
55 ,,	56	17 0
56 ,,	57	16 0
57 ,,	58	15 0
58 ,,	59	14 0
59 ,,	60	13 0
60 ,,	61	12 0
61 ,,	62	11 0
62 ,,	63	10 0
63 ,,	64	9 0
64 ,,	65	8 0
65 ,,	66	7 0
66-7-8 ,,	69	6 0
69 ,,	70	5 0
70 ,,	71	4 0
71 ,,	72	3 0
72 ,,	73	2 0
73 & upwards.		1 0

The lowest rate of duty (1s. per quarter) occurs for rye, peas, and beans, when the price is 42s. and upwards the quarter; on barley when the price is 37s.; and on oats when the price is 27s. and upwards. The lowest duty for wheat is not reached by jerks, as in the former scale, by which the duty fell at each increase of 1s. in price from 10s. 8d. to 6s. 8d., and next to 2s. 8d. and 1s., and the "rest" between 66s. and 69s. is an important modification. Still, like the preceding scale, the present did not admit of a steady trade with every country which had corn to export;

and it was in fact only a mitigated evil. One hundred and thirty-eight new towns were added by 5 Vict. c. 14, to the one hundred and fifty which returned the average prices under the act of 1828. The average duty for six weeks regulated importation as under the previous act.

From April 29th, 1842, to 5th January, 1844, the quantity of foreign wheat entered for consumption was 3,464,618 quarters; foreign wheat-flour, 554,559. The lowest rate of duty was 8s. per quarter, at which 2,105,484 quarters of wheat and 427,579 cwts. of wheat-flour were entered; 740,149 quarters of wheat were entered at a duty of 14s. In 1844 the quantity of wheat and wheat-flour entered was 1,026,976 quarters, and of barley 1,029,021 quarters. The duty on foreign and colonial corn and grain in 1843 was 758,295*l.*, and in 1844 was 1,098,333*l.*

After the passing of 5 Vict. c. 14, another change was made in the corn law. Under the act of 1826 the duties on colonial wheat was under 67s., and 6d. when at or above 67s. the quarter. The act 5 Vict. c. 14, fixed the duties on colonial wheat as follows:—When the price here was under 55s. the quarter, the duty was 5s.;

55s. and under 56s.		duty	4s.
56s.	,,	57s.	,, 3s.
57s.	,,	58s.	,, 2s.
58s. and upwards		,,	1s.

The above, to 1849, were the rates of duty charged on wheat imported from all other colonies, except Eastern and Western Canada; but the Canadian legislature having, at the suggestion of the home government, agreed to impose a duty of 3s. on all wheat imported into Canada, an act was passed (6 & 7 Vict. c. 29) in 1843, and came into operation 10th Oct., under which wheat from Canada, or flour manufactured there, might be at all times admissible into the United Kingdom at a fixed duty of 1s. per quarter, charged here. For the five years ending January, 1843, the rate of duty on Canadian wheat averaged 2s. 1d. per quarter. The largest quantity of wheat and wheat-flour imported from Canada in any one year previous to this act was 259,600 quarters, in 1841, of which above two-thirds was in the shape of flour. The largest quantity in any one year from 1831 to 1840 was 193,985 quarters in 1832, and the average price of wheat in this country for that year was 58s. 8d.; the smallest quantity imported during the above nine years was 12,742 quarters in 1839, and the average price in England for the year was 70s. 8d. The importations of the three years 1842-4, and the average price of wheat in England, were as follows:—

	Qrs.	Average price for the year.
1842	214,348	57s. 3d.
1843	138,100	50s. 1d.
1844	235,591	51s. 3d.

The quantity of wheat imported from the United States into Canada, at the 3s. duty, was 31,265 quarters, from 11th Oct., 1843, to 31st July, 1844.

This brings our retrospect to the last and most important change in the history of the Corn Laws, and which was effected in 1846, under the administration of Sir R. Peel. The success which had attended the minister's relaxations in the tariff from 1842-4, strongly enforced the policy of the unreserved application to every productive interest, of the great principle of Free Trade. The manufacturers of the North were deeply impressed with the conviction that the most certain mode of widening the mercantile circle abroad, for the reception of their fabrics, was the throwing open the British ports for the free interchange of the products of other countries. Under this impression they continued for years, with extraordinary vigour and great pecuniary sacrifices, their popular agitation against the corn-duties, and no intermediate resting-place seemed left to the government save their entire repeal. Other circumstances tended to accelerate this issue, and smooth the way to the abandonment of what might be considered the corner stone of the protective system. This was the letter from Edinburgh, dated Nov. 22, 1845, addressed by Lord John Russell to his London constituents, in which he informed the electors that he had relin-

CORN-LAWS. [665] CORN-RENT.

quished his former position of a fixed duty in preference to the graduated scale, and declared himself in favour of a total repeal of the Corn Laws. The public renunciation by the opposition leader of a fixed duty on corn, was an example of yielding either to the forcible representations of the Anti-Corn Law League, or other urgencies that opportunely lessened the obloquy of dereliction from past professions in the minister; while contemporary therewith, the dreadful famine impending in Ireland, from the failure of the potato crop, pleaded strongly in favour of the prompt removal of every obstruction to the free importation of food.

Accordingly, on the first day of the parliamentary session of 1846, Sir R. Peel announced his entire conversion; declaring that his opinions on the law which governed the importation of corn had undergone a change, that he could no longer meet the annual motion of Mr. Villiers for the repeal of the duties thereon by a direct negative, and that he now felt that all the grounds on which protection to native industry had been advocated, were untenable.

In conformity with these sentiments, the minister lost no time in bringing forward a measure, first for the immediate reduction of the import duties on corn, and next, their final repeal in 1849. The following is the last scale of duties imposed upon the chief corn article from the passing of the 9 & 10 Vict. c. 22, up to February 1st, 1849:—

Wheat per quarter—	s.	d.
Under 48s. the duty	10	0
48s. and under 49s.	9	0
49s. and under 50s.	8	0
50s. and under 51s.	7	0
51s. and under 52s.	6	0
52s. and under 53s.	5	0
53s. and upwards	4	0

From February 1, 1849, there has been levied on every quarter of wheat, barley, oats, bigg, rye, pease, and beans imported, the nominal or register duty of *one shilling*, and upon every hundred-weight of wheat-meal, barley or oatmeal, &c. a duty of *four-pence half-penny*.

CORN-RENT is a money rent varying in amount according to the fluctuations of the price of corn. In some countries the rent is paid in the produce of the land itself [METAYER RENTS]; but in no part of the United Kingdom does this primitive custom exist. Some landlords in Ireland, indeed, for the accommodation of their tenants, agree to accept corn in payment of their rent, at the price of the nearest market, and ship it to England for sale; but the rent is calculated in money. (See Appendix F to *First Report of Poor Laws* (Ireland) *Commissioners,* 1836, p. 221.)

A corn-rent is founded upon the principle that a farm being assumed to grow, upon an average, a certain quantity of produce, the value of such proportion of that produce as may be agreed upon, shall be paid to the landlord as rent. But as the prices of all produce are liable to considerable variation, and as the profits arising from the land must generally be mainly dependent upon the prices for which the produce is sold, it is supposed to be equitable to the farmer, that the money value of that portion of the produce which he pays as rent should be calculated so as to vary with prices, instead of being determined by any arbitrary or unvarying standard. And it is undeniable, that with long leases a corn-rent is a security against the growth of any serious disproportion between the rent originally agreed upon and the actual value of the produce of the land. If the farmer, under the security of a long lease, lay out capital upon the land and thus increase the quantity of produce, he derives the entire benefit arising from increased production, as the quantity to be paid as rent has already been agreed upon; and he is secured against loss caused by a fall in prices, as the amount of his rent is governed by prices.

For the purpose of assessing a corn-rent the average price of wheat alone, or of wheat and other grain, is taken—sometimes for the last year, and sometimes for a certain number of years. If the price for one year only be taken, the results to the farmer may be thus stated. When prices are low from a limited demand for produce, his rent is reduced; and when they are low from increased production, his rent is still reduced, although he has more produce than usual to sell. When prices are high from an increased demand, he has more rent to pay, but the remunerative prices enable him to pay it easily; but when an advance of prices is caused by scarcity, his rent is raised, while the high prices may be counterbalanced by the diminished quantity of produce which he has to sell. Thus in three cases out of four a corn-rent is favourable to the farmer; and even in the fourth case he is secured from loss by its favourable operation in other years. In some leases, also, a further advantage is given to him by fixing a *maximum* price: and thus if prices should happen to rise beyond that point, he derives the whole profit accruing from the difference. Under this system of annual averages, so advantageous to the farmer, there is a certain degree of unfairness to the landlord, which is sometimes corrected by assessing rent upon the average price of different kinds of produce for a certain number of years; by which means a just proportion is maintained between the money-rent and the average annual value realized from the land. It is upon this principle that the rent-charges are calculated, from the average price of grain for seven years [TITHES]; and corn-rents are sometimes regulated by the scale of average prices published annually for the purposes of the Tithe Commutation Act. In Wiltshire some farms are let in this manner, but their number is inconsiderable. The rent of grazing and dairy farms cannot be regulated by the ordinary system of corn-averages; but in some of the dairy-farms of Cheshire the rent is determined by the average price of wheat and of cheese. In many parts of the south of Scotland corn-rents are paid according to the *fiar* prices of corn, as determined in each county by a jury summoned by the sheriff for that purpose.

The principle of a corn-rent is by no means of recent origin; for by an act 18 Elizabeth, § 6, it was required that in all future leases granted by the colleges in the universities of Oxford and Cambridge, and by the colleges of Winchester and Eton, one-third part, at least, of the old rent shall be reserved and paid in good wheat at 6s. 8d. the quarter or under, and good malt at 5s. the quarter or under: or shall be paid in ready money after the rate of the best wheat and malt sold at the nearest market. (*Journal of the Royal Agricultural Society*, vol. v. p. 84, 177; see also Index to *Report on Agricultural Distress*, 1836.)

CORN-TRADE, ANCIENT. The production of corn, one of the chief necessaries of life, and its commercial exchange, have been a subject of the first importance in all ages. It is proposed here to state briefly the general nature of the trade in corn among two of the states of antiquity to whom we are mainly indebted for our knowledge of the economical condition of antient times. There are few important political questions at the present day to which we cannot find something similar in former times; and the blunders of antient legislation may still be instructive to modern statesmen.

The small and comparatively barren territory of Attica did not produce sufficient corn for the consumption of the inhabitants. Corn was brought into the Piraeus, the port of Athens, from the countries bordering on the Black Sea, Syria, Egypt, and other parts of Africa, and from Sicily. Demosthenes asserted (B.C. 355) that the Athenians imported more grain than any other people. (*Against Leptines*, c. 9.) But the trade in corn between Greece and the Black Sea was of some magnitude at a much earlier date. In B.C. 480, Xerxes, while at Abydos on his way to the invasion of Greece, saw the corn-ships that were sailing from the Black Sea and through the Dardanelles and carrying corn to Peloponnesus and Ægina. (Herodotus, vii. 147.) Some parts of the country on the coast of the Black Sea now export grain, and probably have exported grain ever since the time of Xerxes.

The importation of grain into Attica was a matter that was protected and regulated by the state; and instances are mentioned of armed ships convoying the corn-vessels from the Black Sea to the Piraeus. The exportation of corn from Attica was forbidden; and only one-third of the foreign corn that was imported into the Piraeus could be re-exported to other countries: this law as to importation was enforced by the overseers of the harbour. The law interfered with the trade in corn in other ways also, with the intention apparently of keeping prices low; but with what success it is easy to conjecture. Engrossing or the buying-up of corn was a serious offence: a man could not purchase more than fifty loads (called φορμοί). The amount of these loads cannot be exactly ascertained, nor is it material: the principle is clearly shown by the limitation. The penalty for violating this law was death. Boeckh (*Public Economy of Athens*, Eng. transl.) states the law thus: " in order to prevent the accumulation and hoarding of corn, engrossing was very much restricted; it was not permitted to buy at one time more than fifty such loads as a man could carry." According to this a man might buy fifty loads as often as he pleased at different times. But the meaning of the passage of Lysias appears to be that a man must not buy up corn so as to have on hand more than fifty loads at a time. This interpretation is consistent with the Greek, and the other is not; and it is not open to the same kind of objection that Boeckh's interpretation is.

The absurdity of the Athenian legislation on the trade in corn appears from a speech of Lysias against the corn-dealers (Κατὰ τῶν Σιτοπωλῶν). The corn-dealers were generally aliens, and their business made them objects of popular detestation : it was alleged that they bought up corn and refused to sell it when it was wanted, and thus compelled the buyers to pay them their own price. Yet it is stated by Lysias that the law was, that a dealer must sell his corn only one obolus dearer (the medimnus ?) than he bought it. Thus the law attempted to fix the maximum profit of the dealers. But they evaded the law according to the same authority by selling it a drachma (six oboli) higher on the same day ; the meaning of the orator here is not quite clear. The orator states that the hope of great gain made the dealers run the risk of the extreme penalty of the law. He urges the court which was then sitting for the trial of some of the corn-dealers whom he was prosecuting, to enforce the penalty against them, and so make them mend their manners; and he represents both the consumers and the importers of corn as suffering from the combinations of the dealers. A more signal instance of absurdity and commercial ignorance is not extant than this oration.

To carry the laws as to the sale of corn into effect, the Athenians had Corn Wardens (σιτοφύλακες) who kept an account of the corn that was imported, inspected flour and bread, and saw that they were sold of the weight and at the price fixed by law.

Various enactments were made with a view of securing a supply of corn ; such as that no money should be lent on a vessel which did not bring back to Athens a return cargo of goods, among which corn was mentioned ; and that no person living in Attica should import corn to any place except the port of Athens. The interests of individuals, and ultimately the real interests of the community, were thus set in opposition to the supposed interests of the state, and evasions of the laws are often spoken of. Individuals attempted what they will always do, to sell their grain at the dearest market. (Xenophon, *Œconom*, c. 20.)

There were public corn-warehouses at Athens, in which corn was lodged that had been purchased at the expense of the State, and sometimes as it appears, by private contributions. There were officers appointed to purchase the corn (corn-buyers, σιτῶναι) and persons to give or measure it out (ἀποδέκται). Corn so purchased was probably sold to the people at a low price, and sometimes also there were gratuitous distributions of it, as at Rome ; and occasionally, as at Rome also, presents of grain were received from foreign princes or rich persons, and distributed among the people gratis.

This subject has been investigated by Boeckh, *Public Economy of Athens*, translated by G. C. Lewis, 2nd edition, revised, 1842 ; and these remarks are mainly founded on what is said there. The subject is curious, but unfortunately, as we must collect our information mainly from detached passages of the Athenian orators, who deal largely in falsehood and exaggeration, it is not possible to arrive at certainty on some points.

CORN-TRADE, ROMAN. What we know of the ancient corn-trade of Italy mainly relates to the city of Rome. From an early period it belonged to the administration to see that the city was duly supplied with grain. The immediate neighbourhood of Rome did not supply the wants of the city, and grain was imported into Rome from the country of the Volsci and from Cumae soon after the establishment of the consular government. (Livy, ii. 9.) An importation of corn from Sicily is mentioned by Livy (ii. 41) under the year B.C. 486. As the Romans extended their empire, and provincial governments were formed, such as those of Sicily and Sardinia, supplies of grain were got from foreign parts. After the conquest of Sicily, the proprietors were allowed to keep their lands on condition of paying a tenth of the produce to the Romans, according to the system which had been established by King Hiero. Sardinia, after the conquest, paid the same (Livy, xxxvi. 2). The mode of proceeding, as to the tenths in Sicily, was this. The cultivator gave notice of what quantity of land he intended to sow, and an entry was made of it. The Roman State took the tenth of the produce in kind, which the cultivator was bound to convey to some port in Sicily, where it was embarked for Rome. All the wheat produced by the tenths was entered in the public books, and it was all conveyed to Rome or to the armies; this at least appears to have been the general rule.

Sometimes two-tenths of the produce were claimed by the Roman State (Livy, xxxvi. 2; xxxvii. 2), but in this case the second tenth was paid for out of the Roman Aerarium. Presents of grain from foreign states and princes were sometimes made to the Romans (Plutarch, *C. Gracchus*, c. 2). Thus it appears that the State undertook to provide the chief supply of grain for the city: the grain was sometimes sold, and sometimes distributed gratis among the poor, a practice which became common under the late Republic. Besides these distributions of corn at the public expense, the wealthy Romans who sought popularity sometimes made like distributions of corn among the poorer citizens, as M. Crassus the Rich did in his consulship (Plutarch, *Crassus*, c. 2, 12).

It does not appear, then, that the chief supply of corn for the city of Rome during the Republic was furnished in the regular way of trade. It was the business of the State to keep the proper supply of corn for the city in the public warehouses; but the supply was not always equal to the demand, and it also often happened that many people could not afford to pay the price. Scarcity was not uncommon both under the Republic and the Empire.

In Livy (iv. 12) we have a notice of the creation of a Praefectus Annonae, or Superintendent of Provision, L. Minucius, B.C. 440, in a season of scarcity. He exercised his office in an arbitrary manner, by compelling persons to state what corn they had in their possession, and to sell it; and he endeavoured to raise a popular clamour against the corn dealers; if Frumentarii here means private dealers. Cn. Pompeius Magnus was intrusted with the superintendence of Provision for five years. (Cicero, *Ad. Attic.*, iv. 1.) Augustus, at the urgent importunity of the people, took on himself the office of Praefectus Annonae, such as Pompeius held it. (Dion Cassius, liv. 1.)

Under the early Republic many parts of Italy were well cultivated, and Rome, as already observed, derived supplies of corn from various parts of the Peninsula. But the civil wars which devastated Italy near the close of the Republic were injurious to agriculture. Murder and proscription thinned the numbers of the people, and life and property were insecure. Many of the lands changed owners, and the property of those who were cut off by violence fell into the hands of others, and chiefly of the soldiers. These and other causes made Italy less productive about the time of the Christian aera than it had been some centuries earlier. Even under the peaceable administration of Augustus, 60,000,000 modii of wheat were annually imported into Italy and Rome from Egypt and the Roman province of Africa. The modius is estimated at 1 gallon and 7·8576 pints, English measure. But this did not prevent scarcity: there was a great famine at Rome in the latter part of the administration of Augustus (Dion Cassius, lv. 26; Vell. Paterc. ii. 104; Suetonius, *Augustus*, c. 42). The general administration of Tiberius, the successor of Augustus, is commended by Tacitus (*Annal.* iv. 6). He endeavoured to secure a proper supply of corn by intrusting to the Publicani the management of the tenths of grain from the provinces; but there was a great famine in his time, and the high price of grain almost caused an insurrection. The emperor showed that he had not neglected this important part of the administration: he published a list of the provinces from which corn was brought, and he proved that the importation was larger than in the time of Augustus (Tacit. *Annal.* vi. 13). Again, under the administration of the Emperor Claudius, a famine in Rome occurred (Tacit. *Annal.* xii. 43). Tacitus observes that during the scarcity Claudius was assailed with menaces while he was seated on the tribunal in the forum, and he only escaped by the aid of his soldiers. He adds there were only fifteen days' provisions in the city; and " formerly Italy used to export supplies for the legions to distant provinces; nor is Italy now barren, but men prefer cultivating Egypt and Africa, and the existence of the Roman people is intrusted to ships and the dangers of the sea." Claudius subsequently paid great attention to the supplying of Rome with corn. Under Nero, the successor of Claudius, there was a famine at Rome (Suetonius, *Nero*, c. 45).

The comparison of antient and modern prices of grain is a difficult subject, and the results hitherto obtained are not satisfactory. It is also necessary to be careful in considering the circumstances when any prices are mentioned. P. Scipio on one occasion (B.C. 200) sent a great quantity of corn from Africa, which was sold to the people at four asses the modius (Livy, xxxi. 4). In the same book of Livy (c. 50) another sale is mentioned at the rate of two asses the modius. But on these, as on many other occasions, these prices were not the market prices at which wheat would have sold, but they were the lower prices at which the State sold the grain in order to relieve the citizens. Rome, both under the Republic and the early Empire, suffered occasionally from scarcity or from high prices of grain. It is possible that a supply might have readily been procured from foreign parts if there had been a body of consumers in Rome to pay for it. But the export of grain to Rome was not a regular trade; it was, as above explained, a system by which the Romans drew from their provinces a contribution of corn for the consumption of the capital, and it was not regulated by the steady demand of an industrious class who could pay for it. The reign of Tiberius appears to have been a period of scarcity; the complaints were loud, and the emperor fixed the price of corn in Rome, and he promised to give the merchants a bounty of two sesterces on the modius. This seems to mean that the emperor fixed the prices for all grain, including whatever private merchants might have; but to make them amends for any loss, he paid them part of their prices out of the treasury. After the fire at Rome, in the time of Nero, Tacitus speaks of the price of corn being lowered to three sesterces the modius. Under the reign of Diocletian, the emperor, by an edict, fixed the prices of all articles through the Roman Empire. The reason for this measure is stated, in the preamble to the edict, to be the high market price of provisions, which is attributed to the avarice of the dealers, and was not limited even when there was abundance (Inscription of Stratoniccia; see an Edict of Diocletian, fixing a maximum of prices throughout the Roman Empire, A.D. 303, by Colonel Leake, London, 1826, 8vo.).

It does not appear whether the grain which was brought to Rome from the provinces was brought in public ships, or in private ships, by persons who contracted to carry it. There seems, however, to be no doubt that there was also importation of corn by private persons, and that there were no restrictions on the trade, for the object was to get a full supply. A constitution of Valentinian and Valens (De Canone Frumentario Urbis Romæ, Cod. xi. tit. 23), declares that merchants (nau-tiel) were to make a declaration of the grain which they imported before the governors (of provinces) and the magistrates, and that they had only good corn on board; and it was the business of the authorities to see that the grain was good. The provisioning of Constantinople, Alexandria, and probably other great cities, under the later Empire, was subject to regulations similar to those of Rome, and there were public granaries in these cities.

It is almost impossible to collect from the scattered notices in the Roman writers a just notion of the nature of the trade in grain. So far as concerns Rome, we can hardly suppose that there was a regular trade in our sense of the term. The chief supply of grain was provided by the State. That which is best left to private enterprise was undertaken by the government. It is true that the condition of Rome was peculiar under the late Republic and the Empire. The city was full of paupers, who required to be fed by occasional allowances of corn. The effect, however, of the State purchasing for the people was not a certain supply, but occasional scarcity. Whether a State undertakes to buy for the people what they may want for their consumption, or regulates the trade by interfering with the supply, is immaterial as to the result. In either case the people may expect to be starved whenever corn is scarce. The Roman system was to import all that could be got into Rome, but it was not left to private enterprise. There was no exclusion of foreign grain in order to favour the Italian farmer; nor can it be said that the Italian farmer suffered because foreign grain was brought into Rome and other parts of Italy; he could employ much of his land better than in growing corn for Rome and sending it there. Corn came from countries which were better adapted to corn-growing than many parts of Italy; and besides this, the transport of grain from many foreign parts to Rome, such as Sardinia, Sicily, and the province of Africa, would be as cheap as the transport of grain by sea from the remote parts of Italy, and much cheaper than the transport by land. The English foreign corn-trade is regulated with the avowed purpose of giving the English wheat-grower a high or what is considered a sufficient price, without any consideration of the pecuniary resources of those who have to buy corn. By interfering with the free trade in grain, the English system keeps the price unsettled, and exposes the people in times of scarcity to the danger of famine; for when a bad harvest occurs in England, the deficiency must be made up from abroad, and the price must be paid for it, whatever that price may be, which must always be paid for an article that is suddenly in demand, and is not an article of regular supply. The two systems were equally bad, but bad in a different way. The Roman system was founded on ignorance of the true nature of trade, and it was closely connected with the vices of the political constitution. The English system is founded partly on ignorance, and partly on the wish of the landowners, who possess a preponderating political power, to keep up their rents, which are derived from the lands which their tenants cultivate.

The essay of Dureau de la Malle, 'De l'Economie Politique des Romains,' and the treatise of Vincentius Contarenus, 'De Frumentaria Romanorum Largitione,' in Graevius, Antiq. Rom. Thesaurus, vol. viii., contain most of the facts relating to the supply of corn to Rome; and both have been used for this article.

CORNET, a commissioned officer in a regiment of cavalry. He is immediately inferior to a lieutenant, and his rank corresponds to that of an ensign in a battalion of infantry.

The word is derived from the Italian cornetta, signifying a small flag; and hence, both in the English and French services during the sixteenth and seventeenth centuries, it was applied not only to the officer who had charge of the standard, but to the whole troop, which seems then to have consisted of 100 men and upwards, and to have been commanded by a captain.

The full-pay of a cornet, which is the same in all the regiments of cavalry in the British army, is 8s. per day, or 146l. a year, and the half-pay is 5s. 6d. a day. In 1845 there were on full-pay twenty-four cornets in the household cavalry and one hundred and fifty in the cavalry of the line, constituting a charge of 25,404*l*. a year.

CORONATION, the act of crowning or consecrating a king. This rite is of remote antiquity, as may be gathered from the notices which we have in Scripture, in the first and second books of Kings, of the coronations of Solomon, and of Joash the son of Ahaziah, of the latter of whom it is said that Jehoiada the priest took him, put the crown upon his head, and gave him the testimony, and they made him king, and anointed him.

In England, after the kingdoms of the Heptarchy had become united, we find the ceremony of coronation alluded to in the Saxon Chronicle, under the term "gehalgod," by which is expressed that the king was hallowed or consecrated. Kingston-upon-Thames was the place where the Saxon kings were crowned during nearly the whole of the tenth century. (See Diceto and the other historians in the *Decem Scriptores*.) Edgar, who succeeded to the throne in 959, is said to have been crowned either at Kingston or at Bath. Edward the Confessor was crowned at Winchester in 1042. The copy of the Gospels upon which the Saxon kings were sworn at their coronations is believed to be still preserved amongst the Cottonian Manuscripts in the British Museum, in the volume Tib. A. ii. Harold and William the Conqueror were crowned at Westminster. It was customary with the Norman kings to be crowned more than once. Henry II. crowned his eldest son, and associated him with himself in the administration during his own life.

In one or two instances, in the Norman times, we find the regnal years of our kings dated from their coronations only; the previous time, between the predecessor's death and the performance of the inaugural ceremony, was considered as an interregnum. This is a fact of no small importance to those who would accurately fix the dates of public instruments and transactions in the reigns of Richard I., John, and their successors.

The first English coronation of which we have any detailed account is that of Richard I., in the Histories of Diceto and Bromton. (Twysden, *Script*. x. coll. 647, 1157.) An account of all the formalities observed at that of Richard II., taken from the 'Close Rolls,' is in Rymer's 'Fœdera,' the old edition, vol. vii. p. 157. Froissart has given a short but interesting narrative of the coronation of Henry IV., which is printed in the English edition of his 'Chronicle,' by Lord Berners, 4to., London, 1812, vol. ii. pp. 753, 754. The details of the English coronations of Henry V. and VI., and of that of Henry VI. in France, are contained in the Cottonian Manuscripts, Tib. E. viii. and Nero C. ix. Hall and Grafton have described the ceremonies at the coronation of Richard III. The account of the coronation of Henry VIII., with the king's oath prefixed, interlined and altered with his own hand, is likewise preserved in the Cottonian Manuscript already mentioned, Tib. E. viii. The oath, with its interlineations, is engraved in facsimile in the first volume of the second series of Ellis's 'Original Letters illustrative of English History.' Fuller, in his 'Church History,' and Ellis's 'Letters,' 1st Ser., vol. iii. p. 213, detail particulars of the coronation of Charles I. Several editions of the Form and Order of Charles II.'s coronation at Scone in 1651 were published at the time in 4to. at Aberdeen; reprinted at London in folio, 1660; and the entertainment of Charles II. in his passage through London to his coronation, with a narrative of the ceremony at the coronation, by John Ogilby, with plates by Hollar, fol., London, 1662. Sandford's 'History of the Coronation of James II.,' fol. London, 1687, illustrated with very numerous engravings, is the most complete of all our works upon English coronations published by authority. That of George IV., of which two portions only appeared, was far more splendid, with coloured plates, but remains unfinished.

A very antient MS. of the ceremonial of crowning the German emperors at Aix-la-Chapelle was purchased at the last of the sales of Prince Talleyrand's libraries, by the late Mrs. Banks, and is now among the additional manuscripts in the British Museum. Of foreign published coronations, that of Charles V. at Bologna

CORONATION. [672] CORONER.

as emperor, in 1530, is one of the most curious, engraved in a succession of plates upon a roll of considerable length. The 'Sacre de Louis XV., Roy de France et de Navarre, dans l' Eglise de Reims, 25 Oct. 1722,' is a work of pre-eminent splendour, full of finished engravings. The 'Description of the Ceremonies at the Coronation of Napoleon as Emperor of France, with his Consort Josephine, 2 Dec. 1804,' is a work of equal size, but the engravings are chiefly in outline: folio, Paris, 1807. There is a volume, with engravings, of the coronation of the Empress Anne of Russia, fol. Petersburg, 1731; and many others might be enumerated.

The formulary which has served as the general model for the English coronations since the time of Edward III. is the 'Liber Regalis,' which is deposited in the archives of the dean and chapter of Westminster. It is supposed to have been written for the particular instructions of the prelates who attended at the coronation of King Richard II. and his queen. Copies of this manuscript, without its illuminations, are preserved in one or two of our manuscript libraries. The substance of the ceremonial directed in it is abridged in Strutt's 'Manners and Customs,' vol. ii. p. 22-37.

The following is the form of and ceremonial in administering the *Coronation Oath* to our kings:—Sermon being ended, and the King having made and signed the declaration, the Archbishop goes to the King, and standing before him, administers the Coronation Oath, first asking the King—" Sir, is your Majesty willing to take the Oath ?" and the King answering, " I am willing ;" the Archbishop ministereth these Questions; and the King, having a Copy of the printed Form and Order of the Coronation service in his hands, answers each Question severally as follows :—

Archb. " Will you solemnly promise and swear to govern the People of this United Kingdom of *Great Britain and Ireland*, and the Dominions thereto belonging, according to the Statutes in Parliament agreed on, and the respective Laws and Customs of the same ?"

King. " I solemnly promise so to do."

Archb. " Will you to your Power cause Law and Justice, in Mercy, to be executed in all your Judgments ?"

King. " I will."

Archb. " Will you to the utmost of your Power maintain the Laws of God, the true Profession of the Gospel, and the Protestant Reformed Religion established by Law? And will you maintain and preserve inviolably the settlement of the United Church of *England* and *Ireland*, and the doctrine, worship, discipline, and government thereof, as by Law established within *England* and *Ireland*, and the territories thereunto belonging? And will you preserve unto the Bishops and Clergy of England and Ireland, and to the United Church committed to their charge, all such rights and privileges as by Law do or shall appertain to them, or any of them ?"

King. " All this I promise to do."

Then the King arising out of his Chair, supported as before, and assisted by the Lord Great Chamberlain, the Sword of State being carried before him. shall go to the Altar, and there being uncovered, make his solemn Oath in the sight of all the People to observe the premises: laying his right hand upon the Holy Gospel in the Great Bible, which was before carried in the Procession, and is now brought from the Altar by the Archbishop, and tendered to him as he kneels upon the steps, saying these words:

" The Things which I have here promised I will perform and keep, So help me God."

Then the King kisseth the Book, and signeth the Oath. (See the *Form and Order observed in the Coronation of His Majesty King George IV.*, 4to., London, 1821.)

CORONER. The coroner (*coronator*) is an ancient officer by the common law of England. The name is said by Lord Coke to be derived "*a coronâ*," because he is an officer of the crown, and hath conusance in some pleas which are called *placita coronæ*." In this general sense the chief justice of the Court of King's Bench is by virtue of his office the supreme coroner of all England, and may, if he pleases, hold an inquest, or otherwise exercise the office of coroner, in any part of the kingdom. Lord Coke mentions an instance in which Chief Justice Fineux in the reign of Henry VII. held an inquest on the body of a man slain in open rebellion (5 *Reports*, 51). In this sense also, the Master of the Crown Office in the Court of King's Bench, is styled the " coroner or attorney for the king;" his business being confined to pleas of the crown discussed in that court. But the officers now usually understood by this term are the coroners of counties, who are of high antiquity, being said in one of the oldest treatises on the common law to have been ordained together with the sheriffs to keep the peace of counties when the earls gave up the wardship. (*Mirror*, c. i. § 3.) In early times too, the office appears to have been one of great estimation; for by the statute 3 Edw. I. c. 10, they are required to be knights, and by the 28 Edw. III. c. 6, they must be "of the most meet and most lawful men of the county." By the 14 Edward III. st. 1, c. 8, " no coroner shall be chosen unless he have land in fee sufficient in the county, whereof he may answer to all manner of people." No peculiar qualification is now required, though Serjeant Hawkins seems to express an opinion that the persons chosen, though not knights, must be "of good substance and credit." (Hawkins's *Pleas of the Crown*, book ii. cap. 9.) Most commonly there are three or four coroners in each county; but the number varies, and in some there are six or seven coroners. There have been instances in which, upon a representation made to the lord chancellor by the magistrates, that the existing number of coroners was insufficient for the business of the county, writs have issued for the election of additional coroners. (3 Swanston's *Reports*, 181.)

There are divers coroners for franchises and other separate jurisdictions. The dean of York, as custos rotulorum of the liberty of St. Peter's, in the city of York, appoints two coroners for the liberty. A coroner for the honor of Pontefract is appointed by letters patent under the seal of the duchy of Lancaster. Lords of manors or liberties in some cases appoint a coroner for their lordship. In Huntingdonshire there are five coroners, who are all so appointed. The archbishop of York and bishop of Ely appointed coroners before their secular jurisdiction was extinguished by 6 & 7 Wm. IV. c. 87. The bishop of Durham appointed the coroners for that county before the passing of 1 Vict. c. 64, "for regulating the coroners of the county of Durham." The constable of the Tower of London appoints a coroner for the Tower liberty. The coroner for the city and liberty of Westminster is appointed by the dean and chapter. By a charter of Edward IV. the mayor and commonalty of London may grant the office of coroner to whom they please, and no coroner except the city coroner shall have any power in the city.

Coroners of counties are elected under the direction of the stat. 28 Edw. III. c. 6, by the freeholders in the county court, in the same manner as sheriffs and conservators of the peace formerly were; the election takes place by virtue of an ancient king's writ, *De Coronatore Eligendo*, returnable in chancery. The 58 Geo. III. c. 95, which made provision for conducting these elections, similar to those for the election of knights of the shire, was repealed in 1844 by 7 & 8 Vict. c. 92, which substituted other regulations on the ground that the former mode of election was inconvenient and attended with great and unnecessary expense. This act applies only to county coroners. The coroners of the City of London and Borough of Southwark, of the Queen's Household and the Verge of the Queen's Palace, and Admiralty coroners, are specially exempted from the operation of the act. Counties may be divided by the justices into two or more districts for the purposes of this act, and alterations may be made in existing divisions. The justices, in making such divisions, are in the first place to petition her majesty, and notice is to be given to each coroner by the clerk of the peace of the time when the justices will take such petition into consideration. Any coroner of the county may present a petition to her majesty touching the proposed division or alteration of districts. Her majesty, with the advice of the privy council, may order that such county shall be divided into so many districts as may

2 x

be considered convenient, and determine at what place within each district the court for the election of coroner for such district shall be held. The justices are to direct the clerk of the peace to make out a list of the several parishes, townships, or hundreds in each of the coroner's districts into which the county is divided, specifying the place within each district at which the court for the election of coroner is to be held, the place or places at which the poll is to be taken, and the parishes or places attached to each polling place. The justices may then assign one district to each coroner; and whenever a vacancy occurs the election is to be made in the manner prescribed by the act, which provides that the coroner shall reside in the district for which he is elected, or in some place wholly or partly surrounded by such district, or not more than two miles beyond its outer boundary; that the election must be made in the district; and that the coroner shall be chosen by a majority of persons duly qulified who shall reside in such district: no voter can poll out of the district where his property lies. Within not less than seven or not more than fourteen days after the sheriff shall have received the writ De Coronatore Eligendo, he is required to hold in the district for which a vacancy has occurred a special county court for the election; and if a poll be demanded, it may be kept open for two days, eight hours each day, from eight o'clock in the morning. The sheriff is to erect polling-booths; poll-clerks are to be sworn; and an inspector of poll-clerks is to be appointed on the nomination of each one of the candidates. Electors may be required by or on behalf of any candidate to make oath respecting their qualification. The result of the poll is to be declared by the sheriff. The coroner, although elected for a district, is to be considered as a coroner for the whole county; but he is only to hold inquests within his own district, except in case of the illness or unavoidable absence of the coroner for another district; and his inquisition must certify the cause of his holding such inquest.

Coroners in counties are elected for life; but if they accept an office incompatible with the duties, such as that of sheriff, or dwell in a remote part of the county, or are incapacitated by age or infirmity, they are removable by means of the writ *De Coronatore Exonerando*, and by the stat. 25 Geo. II. c. 29, § 6, they may be removed upon conviction of extortion, wilful neglect of duty, or misdemeanor in their office. The Lord Chancellor has authority, however, independently of the above statute, to remove coroners for neglect of duty, upon petition presented by the freeholders of the county. (1 Jacob and Walker, *Reports*, 451.)

At common law the coroner had authority to hear and determine felonies; but his powers in this respect were expressly abrogated by Magna Charta, cap. 17. The article (G) *Officer* in Comyns' 'Digest' contains a statement of the various duties of the coroner in the king's house, and of the coroner in a county. The most usual duty of a coroner is that of taking inquisitions when any person dies in prison or comes to a violent or sudden death; and though his duties, as well as his authority in this respect, are said to have existed at common law, they are declared by the 4 Edw. I. stat. 2, commonly called the statute *De Officio Coronatoris*. His court is a Court of Record. By the directions of that statute, "the coroner, upon information, shall go to the places where any be slain, or suddenly dead or wounded, and shall forthwith command four of the next towns, or five or six, to appear before him in such a place; and when they are come thither, the coroner, upon the oath of them, shall inquire in this manner; that is to wit, if they know where the person was slain, whether it were in any house, field, bed, tavern, or company, and who were there; who are culpable, either of the act, or of the force; and who were present, either men or women, and of what age soever they be, if they can speak, or have any discretion; and how many soever be found culpable, they shall be taken and delivered to the sheriff, and shall be committed to the gaol; and such as be found and be not culpable, shall be attached until the coming of the judge of assize." And it is declared by the same statute, that "if it fortune any such man be slain, which is found in the fields or in woods, first it is to be inquired whether he were slain in the same place, or not; and if he were brought and laid there, they should do so much as they can to follow their steps that brought the body thither, whether he were brought upon a horse or in a cart. It shall also be inquired if the dead person were known, or else a stranger, and where he lay the night before." It is declared also by the same statute, that "all wounds ought to be viewed, the length, breadth, and deepness; and with what weapons; and in what part of the body the wound or hurt is; and how many be culpable; and how many wounds there be; and who gave the wound." In like manner it is to be inquired by the coroner "of them that be drowned, or suddenly dead, whether they were so drowned or slain, or strangled by the sign of a cord tied straight about their necks, or about any of their members, or upon any other hurt found upon their bodies. And if they were not slain, then ought the coroner to attach the finders and all other in the company." The provisions of this ancient statute are still in force, and are to be followed by coroners in all their particular directions as nearly as possible at the present day in inquisitions of death. In case of a death happening upon the high sea, inquisitions are taken before the Admiralty coroner, who is appointed by the king or the lord admiral; and the county coroners have in such a case no jurisdiction. The inquisitions taken before the Admiralty coroner are returned to the Commissioners of the Admiralty under stat. 28 Hen. VIII. c. 15. Coroners ought to sit and inquire into the cause of death of all persons who die in prison. They have no jurisdiction within the verge of the king's courts. The coroner of the king's household has jurisdiction within the verge of the king's courts.

The coroner has authority to assemble a jury by means of a precept directed to the constables of the hundred or adjoining township, and jurors and witnesses who make default may, under 7 & 8 Vict. c. 92, be fined any sum not exceeding 40s. and their names returned to the clerk of the peace, who is to levy the fine. Before this act the names of jurors who did not attend were returned to the judges of assize, by whom they might be fined. The coroner may also punish witnesses who refuse to give evidence, for contempt of court. When the jury are assembled, they are charged and sworn by the coroner to inquire, upon view of the body, how the party came by his death. The act for the registration of deaths (6 & 7 Will. IV. c. 86) provides that at every inquest "the jury shall inquire of the particulars herein required to be registered concerning the death, and the coroner shall inform the registrar of the finding of the jury." One of the particulars herein required to be registered is the "cause of death." The inquiry assumes therefore something of a medico-jurisprudential character, by being directed to the "cause" of death, instead of being chiefly made with a view to ascertain if death were the result of homicide. That was and is important; but there are other points to be settled which are also important, and in which medical and chemical skill can alone determine whether the cause of sudden death has been natural or whether suicide has been committed. Instances have occurred in which death from opium has been mistaken for apoplexy, until a post-mortem examination has taken place. The Life Insurances have a direct interest in ascertaining the precise cause of death, and to the community generally it is of consequence that there should be as little impunity as possible to crime. The coroner has no authority to take an inquisition of death, except upon view of the body by himself and the jury; and if he does so, the inquisition is wholly void. (Rex v. Ferrand, 3 Barn. and Ald. Reports, 260.) Formerly, it is probable that the whole inquisition was taken in the presence of the body, but it is now sufficient if the coroner and jury together see the body, so far as to ascertain whether there are marks of violence upon it or any appearances which may account for the cause of death. The coroner must sit at the place where the death has happened. If the coroner's inquest finds that any person is guilty of murder or other homicide, it is his duty to commit

2 x 2

them to prison for trial, and he must also inquire what lands, goods, and chattels he may have, which are liable to forfeiture for such murder. He must also inquire whether any deodand has in any case of violent death become due to the king, or the lord of the franchise by the death of the person upon whose body the inquisition is held. If a body liable to an inquest has been buried before the coroner has notice of the circumstances of the death, he has authority to cause it to be disinterred for the purpose of holding the inquest, provided he does so within a reasonable time. The coroner has power to exclude persons from his court. By a recent statute (7 Geo. IV. c. 64, § 4), which repeals an old enactment on this subject, it is provided that "every coroner, upon any inquisition before him taken, whereby any person shall be indicted for manslaughter or murder, or as an accessary to murder before the fact, shall put in writing the evidence given to the jury before him, or as much thereof as shall be material; and shall have authority to bind by recognizance all such persons as know or declare anything material touching the said manslaughter or murder, or the said offence of being accessary to murder, to appear at the next court of oyer and terminer, or gaol delivery, or superior criminal court of a county palatine, or great sessions, at which the trial is to be, then and there to prosecute or give evidence against the party charged; and every such coroner shall certify and subscribe the same evidence, and all such recognizances, and also the inquisition before him taken, and shall deliver the same to the proper officer of the court in which the trial is to be, before or at the opening of the court." It is also a branch of the coroner's business to inquire into shipwrecks, and certify whether it is a wreck or not, and who has got possession of the goods. He also inquires into treasure trove. By a section of the 7 Geo. IV. c. 64, authority is given to the court to which the inquisition ought to be delivered to examine in a summary manner into any offence committed by the coroner against the act, and to punish him by fine. The coroner's inquisition may be removed into the Court of King's Bench, and the facts found may be traversed by the personal representatives of the deceased; or the court may make it for any apparent defect. By 7 & 8 Vict. the coroner is prohibited from acting professionally in any case in which he shall have sat as coroner.

For every inquisition taken in any place contributing to the county rates, the coroner is entitled to a fee of 20s., and by 1 Vict. c. 68, to an addition of 6s. 8d., and also to 9d. for every mile which he is obliged to travel from his usual place of abode to any other place, for the purpose of taking it, to be paid by order of sessions out of the county rates. If he holds two or more inquisitions at the same place at the same time, he is only entitled to one 9d. for each mile of distance; but this rule is not always very strictly observed in some counties. By 7 & 8 Vict. c. 92, the coroner may be paid travelling expenses, although in the exercise of his discretion he may have deemed it unnecessary to hold an inquest. The sum paid to coroners out of the county rates in 1834 was 15,648l. In 1838 and 1839 about 35,000 inquests were held in the two years. The act 1 Vict. c. 68, authorises the justices of the peace in England and Wales, at their quarter-sessions, and the town councils of every borough which has a coroner's court at their quarterly meetings, to make a schedule of the fees, allowances, and disbursements which the coroner is allowed to pay (except the fees payable to medical witnesses, under 6 & 7 Will. IV. c 89), on holding any inquest. This schedule regulates for each county or division of a county the expenses to be paid to the constable for summoning witnesses, &c. There is usually a small sum allowed to each juryman, generally 1s. 6d. in counties and 1s. in boroughs. The following are extracts from the schedule of fees settled by the magistrates of the county of Warwick:—

	At the discretion of the coroner, and not exceeding	
	s.	d.
To the Keeper of any Inn or other public-house for the use of a room for a dead body until the Inquest is held	20	0
To the Keeper of any Inn or other public-house for the use of a room for holding an Inquest . . .	5	0
To a Witness residing in the parish where the Inquest is held, for loss of time in attending to give evidence .	5	0
To a witness who does not reside in the parish, is allowed per mile . . .	0	4
To every Witness in the three professions of law, physic, and divinity, for each day	42	0
To each Juryman residing in the parish where an Inquest is held	1	6
To each Juryman not residing in the parish where the Inquest is held . . .	3	0
To any person for taking a dead body out of the water, extinguishing fire in the case of a person burning, or removing a dead body when found to some convenient place till an Inquest can be held, and giving notice to the proper authorities .	7	6
To a Chemist, Engineer, or other scientific person per day	42	0
For interring the body of a *Felo de se*, including horse and cart, and other trouble (exclusive of burial fees, if any)	10	0
For digging the grave for interring the body of a *Felo de se*	3	6
To bearers of the body of a *Felo de se* . . .	10	0
Coffin for a *Felo de se* . .	7	0

By a recent act of parliament, 6 & 7 Will. IV. c. 89, the coroner is empowered to order the attendance of legally qualified medical practitioners upon an inquisition of death, and to direct the performance of a *post mortem* examination; and if the majority of the jury are dissatisfied with the first examination, they may call upon the coroner to summon a second medical witness, to perform a *post mortem* examination, whether it has been performed before or not. The statute also authorizes the coroner to make an order for the payment of a fee of one guinea to such witness, if he has not performed a *post mortem* examination, and of two guineas if he has performed such examination. Medical practitioners are also liable to a penalty of 5*l*. if they neglect to attend. By 1 Vict. c. 68, the fees of medical witnesses are to be paid at once by the coroner, instead of by an order on the churchwardens, as directed by 6 & 7 Wm. IV. c. 89.

The coroner has also occasionally to exercise a ministerial office, where the sheriff is incapable of acting. Thus where an exception is taken to the sheriff on the ground of partiality or interest, the king's writs are directed to the coroner. This incident to the office of coroner points distinctly to their ancient character as ministerial officers of the crown. For his services when acting for the sheriff, he was not allowed any fees before the passing 7 & 8 Vict., but this statute secures to him the same amount of fees as the sheriff would be entitled to.

By the Municipal Reform Act, 5 & 6 Will. IV. c. 76, § 62, the council of every borough, to which a separate court of quarter-sessions has been granted, is empowered to appoint a fit person, not being an alderman or councillor, to be coroner of the borough, who is to hold his office during good behaviour. The fees and general duties of borough coroners are the same as those of county coroners; but the borough coroners are required by the statute to make an annual return to the secretary of state of all inquests of death taken by them. The number of inquests held in the boroughs of Manchester, Birmingham, Liverpool, and Bristol in 1844, and their proportion to the population, was as follows:—

CORPORATION. [678] CORPORATION.

	One in
Manchester . 259	938
Birmingham 263	741
Liverpool . 432	663
Bristol . . 203	690

The average cost of the coroner's court for the borough of Birmingham, averaged 899*l*. for the five years ending 31st of December, 1844; coroner's fees (20*s*.) under 25 Geo. II. c. 29, and 6*s*. 8*d*. under 1 Vict. c. 68, annually averaged 337*l*. 4*s*.; and the expense of 1416 inquests averaged 3*l*. 3*s*. 5¼*d*. each. The disbursements, independent of coroner's fees, averaged 561*l*. 8*s*. 2¾*d*. a year. [DEODAND.] (Hawkins's *Pleas of the Crown*, book ii. cap. 9; Burn's *Justice*, tit. 'Coroner;' and Jervis's *Practical Treatise on the Office and Duties of Coroners.*)

CORPORAL (in the French service *caporal*), a non-commissioned officer in a battalion of infantry. The word is derived from the Italian *capo*, signifying a head; and the title denotes that the person who bore it was the chief of a small squadron or party. During the reigns of Mary and Elizabeth the corporal was a kind of brigade-major; he superintended the marches of the companies, and commanded the troops who were sent out on skirmishing parties. But at present he is immediately under the sergeant; he places and relieves the sentinels, and at drill he has charge of one of the squads. In the ranks he does the same duty as a private soldier, but his pay is rather higher.

Lance-corporal, originally *lance-spesata*, denoting a broken or spent lance, was a term applied to a cavalry soldier who had broken his lance or lost his horse in action, and was subsequently retained as a volunteer in the infantry till he could be remounted. He is now merely a soldier who does the duty of a corporal, but without the pay, previously to obtaining the full appointment to that grade.

CORPORATION. For the purpose of maintaining and perpetuating the uninterrupted enjoyment of certain powers, rights, property, or privileges, it has been found convenient to create a sort of artificial person, or legal person, not liable to the ordinary casualties which affect the transmission of private rights, but capable, by its constitution, of indefinitely continuing its own existence. This artificial person is called an *incorporation, corporation,* or *body-corporate*. The last of these names is the most correct, as well as the earliest, that occurs in our law. The former express rather the act of creating the body than the body itself, and do not appear to have been used in their modern sense till the fifteenth century. The institution of such bodies under similar or different names was common among the Romans [COLLEGIUM], and it seems probable that bodies possessing all the essential characteristics of modern corporations were known in the Greek polities.

Corporations may be divided into various kinds, according to the mode in which they are viewed. Viewed with respect to number, they are either corporations sole, which consist of a single person and his successors; or they are composed of many persons, who are legally considered as one, and are called corporations aggregate. Viewed with respect to the distinction between things spiritual and things temporal or civil, all corporations are either ecclesiastical or lay corporations. Lay corporations are subdivided into civil corporations and eleemosynary corporations. Civil corporations are those which have purely a civil object, such as administration, commerce, education, and other like purposes. Eleemosynary corporations may have various objects, but they all agree in this, that they have been endowed for the purposes of distributing the alms or bounty of the founder and other donors. Spiritual corporations are divisible into regular and secular corporations.

The idea of a corporation *sole*, formed by a succession of single persons, occupying a particular office or station, and each in virtue of his character succeeding to the rights and powers of his predecessor, has been said to be peculiar to our law, and to be an improvement upon the original notion of a corporation. (4 Blackstone's *Comment*. 469.) The king, a bishop, a parson, the chamberlain of London, &c. are examples of such corporations sole. It may be observed, however, with respect to the supposed novelty of the invention, that similar cases of official succession and representation probably occur in almost every system of law, so that the claim of originality must be restricted to the mere name; and even in this respect, we incline to the opinion of Dr. Wooddesson, "that as so little of the law of corporations in general applies to corporations sole, it might have been better to have given them some other denomination." (1 Wooddes. *Vin. Lect.* 471, 2.) The following notice is chiefly confined to the law of corporations aggregate. The legal incidents of such corporations sole, as bishops and parsons, are mentioned under BISHOP and BENEFICE.

The members of cathedral and collegiate chapters are secular ecclesiastical corporations aggregate. Before the reformation the law recognised a class of ecclesiastical corporations *regular*, consisting of abbots or priors and their respective convents, and apparently the societies of friars or mendicant orders. (Brook's *Abr. Corporations*, pl. 12.) The heads of these conventual bodies were often distinct corporations sole, as is still the case in many of the modern secular ecclesiastical establishments.

The colleges in Oxford and Cambridge, and incorporated schools and hospitals, are instances of eleemosynary corporations; being endowed and established for the purpose of perpetuating the bounty of their respective founders. [COLLEGIUM.]

But the largest class of corporations, and those which are most varied in their object and character, are lay and civil incorporations. Among these are the universities of Oxford, Cambridge, Durham, and London, the municipal corporations of different cities and boroughs, the East India Company, the Bank of England, the Colleges of Physicians and of Surgeons, the Royal Society and Academy, the Society of Antiquaries, and numerous commercial and other companies erected by charter or by act of parliament.

A corporation cannot be created by any authority except that of the king or the parliament. Where any such body has existed from time beyond legal memory, it is presumed to have a legitimate origin in one or the other of the above sources.

Until the Reformation the pope and the bishop of the diocese were considered necessary parties to the foundation of any new society of monks or *regular* clergy. The refusal of the pope to confirm the foundation of Sion Monastery in the reign of Henry VI. is known to have caused an alteration in the original plan of that establishment. (Cotton's *Abridgment*, 589.) The king creates a corporation by letters-patent: the parliament by act of parliament, that is, by a law. Sometimes a corporation is created by implication from the words of an act of parliament; for instance, if certain persons, such as the conservators of a river, are declared to take lands by succession, they are incorporated: for the word "succession" is opposed to "inheritance," and involves the notion of a corporate body. Custom sometimes establishes a corporation, as in the case of churchwardens, who are a corporation with respect to the goods and chattels of the church, and they may purchase goods for the church, but not land, except by the special custom of the city of London. Those corporations which have existed from time beyond legal memory, and have no charter or warrant to show for their authority, are said to be corporations by prescription.

The principal incidents of a corporation aggregate are the following:—

1. It can purchase, convey, and hold land or goods in perpetual succession, notwithstanding the changes and fluctuations that occur among the members successively appointed to fill the vacancies which happen in it.

2. It can become a party to proceedings at law, or to contracts, by the corporate name given to it on its foundation.

3. The act or assent of the majority is binding on all the rest; such at least is the general rule, wherever the instrument of foundation does not otherwise provide.

4. It signifies its assent, and testifies its corporate acts, by a common seal, without which hardly any contract is binding on the corporate body.

5. It is competent to enact regulations called bylaws, which are binding on the members of the corporation, and, in some cases, on strangers also. [BYLAW.]

6. The particular members of the body

are not in general personally responsible for the acts, contracts, or defaults of the corporation, so long as the acts of the corporation are conformable to the powers which are given to it. This exemption from individual liability makes it very desirable for commercial and other trading companies to obtain charters of incorporation, by which the members escape the risk of ordinary partnerships.

7. The personal defaults or misconduct of the members cannot in general be visited on the corporate body.

The capacity of holding land is restrained by the statutes of mortmain, which make it necessary to obtain an express licence to that effect from the crown or the legislature. [MORTMAIN.]

With regard to the exemption from personal responsibility in respect of corporate acts, the members of the body cannot directly authorize an injury to be done to another under the sanction of a corporate act, without incurring the usual personal consequences. Thus, if a corporation should by an instrument under the common seal direct a trespass to be committed on a third person, every member of the majority who was present, and actually assenting to the act, would be liable in his private capacity.

The mode of filling up vacancies which occur in the constituent members of the corporate body, is determined either by the express provisions of the charter of incorporation, or (in the case of immemorial corporations) by ancient usage. The most common and regular method of maintaining the succession is by election. In the case of corporations sole the successor is appointed by the crown, or by a patron or founder. In the case of ecclesiastical corporations the forms of election are in many instances preserved, but the substantial right of nomination has long been exercised either by the crown or by some authority or person independent of the chapter or other corporate body.

With a view to ensure the performance of those duties, and a strict adherence to those regulations which are imposed upon corporate bodies either by the will of their founders or the general tenor of their charters, there are certain persons and courts, whose office it is to exercise a power of superintendence and correction.

In the instance of eleemosynary bodies, as colleges, schools, and hospitals, the person so appointed is called a *visitor*, and is either the heir of the original founder, or some person specially appointed by him, or (in the absence of either of these) the king. [COLLEGIUM.]

In ecclesiastical corporations, the bishop of the diocese is, of common right, the visitor. His right of visitation formerly also extended over all the monastic establishments within the same district, unless the abbot or other head of the convent had purchased a papal bull of exemption, the effect of which was to subject him to the sole superintendence of the pope himself. With regard to lay corporations, such as municipal corporations, trading companies, and similar bodies, their irregularities are left for correction to the ordinary courts of justice, which have sufficient powers for that purpose. The Court of King's Bench exercises the authority by the writ of mandamus of compelling corporate bodies to do acts which they ought to do and neglect to do.

A corporation may be extinguished in various ways.

1. A corporation aggregate may be extinguished by the natural death of all the members.

2. Where a select body of definite number, constituting an integral part of the corporation, is so reduced by death, or other vacancy, that a majority cannot be present at corporate meetings, the whole body becomes incapable of doing any corporate act, and, according to the better opinion, the corporation is thereby extinguished. This is the result of a rule in corporation law,—that every act must be sanctioned, not only by a majority of the number actually present at a meeting, but also at a meeting composed of a majority of each definite body into which the corporation has been subdivided by the charter. Thus, if a corporation consists of a mayor, twelve aldermen, and an indefinite number of burgesses, at least seven aldermen must be present at every meeting; nor can a legal meeting be convened in the absence of the mayor, except

for the purpose of electing a new one. The tendency of the rule is to compel the elective body to fill up vacancies without delay, and to secure the attendance of a competent number when the public business is transacted. The rule is inapplicable to a body of *indefinite* number, such as the general body of freemen; and it is liable to be modified and controlled by the charter, or other fundamental constitution of the corporation. The rule of the civil law, requiring the actual presence of two-thirds of the corporation at elections, seems to have been dictated by a similar policy; but Sir W. Blackstone (*Commentaries*, vol. i. p. 478) is in error, when he supposes that a bare majority of the body so assembled could not bind the rest. (See Pancirollus, *De Magist. Municip. apud Grævium.*)

3. A dissolution may be effected by a surrender to the crown; at least where the incorporation is by charter, and where all the members concur and are competent to concur.

4. A corporation may be forfeited, where the trust for which it was created is broken, and its institution perverted. Such a forfeiture can only be declared by judgment of the superior courts on process issued in the ordinary course of law, called, from the initial words of the writ, *Quo Warranto*, in which the fact of misuser, if denied, must be submitted to a jury.

5. A corporation may be dissolved or remodelled by act of parliament. Having already alluded to the religious corporations of monks and other regular clergy formerly existing in this country, we may observe that the validity of the surrenders obtained by the crown at their suppression was deemed sufficiently doubtful to require the confirmation of an express act of parliament. Even then, in the opinion of the canonists, the *spiritual* incorporations still continued until suppressed by competent spiritual authority, and were capable of perpetuation, although their possessions were lost, and their civil rights extinguished. Hence it was that the Brigettine nuns of Sion, suppressed by Henry VIII., restored by Queen Mary, and again ejected by her successor, continued to maintain a migratory existence for two centuries and a half in Holland, Belgium, France, and Portugal, and still claimed to be the same convent which Henry V. had founded on the banks of the Thames. (See letter of the Abbé Mann, 13 *Archæologia.*)

The corporations established for local administration of towns are now generally called municipal corporations. [MUNICIPAL CORPORATIONS.] Bodies incorporated for the purpose of commerce, or the profitable investment of capital, such as railway companies, mining companies, banking companies, belong to the class of JOINT-STOCK COMPANIES, under which head they are treated of. Any number of individuals associated for purpose of traffic, who are not incorporated, form a partnership, and they are individually liable like the partners of any mercantile firm.

CORPORATIONS, MUNICIPAL. [MUNICIPAL CORPORATIONS.]

CORPORATION AND TEST ACTS. [TEST AND CORPORATION ACTS.]

CORRECTION, HOUSES OF. [TRANSPORTATION.]

CORRUPTION OF BLOOD. [ATTAINDER.]

CORTES, the name of the assembly of representatives of the Spanish nation. These assemblies have been variously constituted in different ages, and in the different kingdoms into which Spain was divided till the time of Ferdinand and Isabella. The cortes of Castile and Leon and those of Aragon were the principal. Considerable obscurity prevails as to the origin and the formation of both. The earliest national assemblies under the Visigothic kings met generally at Toledo; they consisted chiefly of the dignitaries of the church, and were called councils. After deciding all questions of church discipline, they deliberated upon temporal affairs, and in this stage of the discussion the lay lords or barons took an active part, and the king presented his requests. In the acts of the council of Leon, A.D. 1020, ch. vi., the transition from ecclesiastical to temporal affairs is clearly pointed out:—" Judicato ergo ecclesiæ judicio, adeptaque justitia, agatur causa regia, deinde populorum." In the acts of the council of Jaca, 1063, we find that several points of discipline were reformed "with the consent of the nobles and prelates;" and the signatures are those of the king, the infantes, nine bishops, three abbots, and three magnates; but it is added in a note that "all the other magnates had subscribed to the same acts." It is now generally acknowledged, that in that age, and down to the end of the twelfth century, there was no popular representation from the towns or commons of Castile and Leon in those assemblies. (Marina, *Teoria de las Cortes;* Sempere, *Histoire des Cortes;* Dunham, *History of Spain and Portugal.*) The people are said to have occasionally attended these national councils on some solemn occasions, as at the council held at Toledo in 1135, but only as spectators and witnesses, "to see, to hear, and to praise God." By degrees, as the towns rose into importance, and obtained local fueros, or charters, from the kings for their own security, or formed themselves into fraternities for their mutual protection against the Moors or against the violence of their own nobles, some of them obtained at last the privilege of sending deputies to the national councils, which were now styled cortes, because, according to some etymologists, they were held at the place where the king had his court. The cortes held at Salamanca by Ferdinand II., in 1178, consisted only of the nobility and clergy; but at the cortes of Leon, A.D. 1188, we first hear that there were present deputies "of towns chosen by lot;" and in the same year the cortes of Castile assembled at Burgos, where deputies from about fifty towns or villages, the names of which are mentioned, were present. How these places came to obtain this privilege is not known, although it is probable that it was by the king's writ or by charter. The cortes were henceforth composed of three estamentos or states, clergy, lords, and procuradores, or deputies from the enfranchised towns, forming together one chamber, but voting as separate estates. It was a standing rule, that general laws must have in their favour the majority of each estamento. This was the principle of the cortes of the united kingdom of Castile and Leon. The same principle existed in the kingdom of Aragon, only there the cortes were composed of four brazos or estates, namely, the prelates, including the commanders of the military orders, the ricos hombres, or barons, the infanzones, or caballeros, who held their estates of the great barons, and lastly, the universidades, or deputies of the royal towns. These last are first mentioned at the cortes of Monzon, in 1131. The towns and boroughs in Aragon which returned deputies were thirty-one; but the number of deputies returned by each is not stated by the historians, any more than those for the cortes of Castile. We find the same town returning sometimes a greater, sometimes a smaller number, and at other times none at all, and a small town or village sending more deputies than a large one; while many considerable towns never returned any, independently of the seignorial towns, which of course had no representative privilege. How all this was made to agree with the manner of voting, in order to ascertain the opinion of the majority, is not clearly stated. The institutions of the kingdom of Aragon, which have been much extolled by some writers, appear to have been better defined than those of Castile, as the Aragonese, with the exception of the peasant serfs of the nobility, certainly enjoyed a greater share of individual liberty than the rest of the Peninsula.

In Castile, from the end of the thirteenth century, the popular estamento made rapid strides towards increasing its influence, being favoured in this by some kings or pretenders to the crown, such as Sancho IV. and Enrique II., or taking advantage of disputed successions and stormy minorities, to obtain from one of the contending parties an extension of their privileges. In 1295 the deputies of thirty-two towns and boroughs of Castile and Leon assembled at Valladolid, and entered into a confederacy to defend their mutual rights against both the crown and the nobles. Among many other resolutions, one was, that each of the thirty-two constituencies should send two deputies every two years to meet about Pentecost at Leon or some other place, in order to enforce the observance of their agreement. In 1315, during the frightful confusion which attended the minority of Alonso XI., we find another confederacy between the nobles and the procuradores of 100 communities, with a similar clause as to deputies meeting once or twice every year. These meetings of deputies for special purposes ought not to be confounded with the general cortes of the kingdom, which were always convoked by the king, though at no fixed times. Enrique II., having revolted against his brother Pedro the Cruel, courted the support of the municipal towns, which at the cortes of 1367 demanded the admission de jure of twelve deputies into the royal council, which had till then consisted of hereditary nobles and prelates, with occasionally some civilian called in by the king. Enrique promised to comply with their request; but his brother's death having ensured his seat on the throne, he evaded the fulfilment of his promise by creating an Audiencia Real, or high court of appeal, consisting of prelates and civilians, and a criminal court of eight alcaldes chosen from different provinces of the kingdom. Juan I., who succeeded him, after the loss of the battle of Aljubarrota, created a new council in 1385, consisting of four bishops, four nobles, and four citizens, with extensive executive powers. The towns next solicited the dismissal of the bishops and nobles from the council, in order that it should consist entirely of citizens; but Juan rejected the demand. They also contrived at times to exclude the privileged orders from the cortes. Marina says that the privileged orders themselves, having lost much of their influence, abstained from attending the cortes; yet it is certain that although money might be voted without them, for the simple reason that they were exempt from taxation, the third estate alone paying all direct taxes, yet nothing else of importance could be decided without their concurrence. Although members of the privileged orders should not attend, they might be represented by proxy, as was the case in Aragon. Besides, the cortes were not all of one sort; there were general or solemn cortes, and especial cortes, for some particular purpose. Juan appointed by his testament six prelates and nobles as guardians of his infant son

Enrique III., who were not, however, to decide in any important affair without the concurrence of six deputies, one from each of the cities of Burgos, Toledo, Leon, Seville, Cordova, and Murcia. The fourteenth century seems to have been the brightest period of popular or more properly municipal representation in Spain. The cortes were frequent, and the subject of their deliberations of the most important nature. But Spain had never a definite representation; to no meeting of this period did all or half the great towns send deputies; and those which did return them appear to have observed little proportion in the numbers. There can be no doubt that two ought to have been returned from each; yet in the cortes of Madrid, in 1390, we find that Burgos and Salamanca sent eight each, while the more important cities of Seville and Cordova sent only three ; Cadiz only two ; Oviedo and Badajos one ; Santiago, Orense, Mondonedo, and other great cities of Galicia sent none at all. In fact, only forty-eight places returned deputies to these cortes, and the number, at the most, was inconsiderable. Incidentally we learn that in the assemblies of this period the archbishop of Toledo spoke for the ecclesiastical state, and the chief of the house of Lara for the nobles. Some of the deputies contended for the precedence in voting, as well as for that of seats. This rivalry was more conspicuous between Burgos and Toledo, until Alonso XI. found the means of settling it. "The deputies of Toledo," said the king in the midst of the assembly, "will do whatever I order them, and in their name, I say, let those of Burgos speak." The municipal corporations could boast of something more than the honour of returning deputies, an honour to which many of them were perfectly indifferent. Their condition was far superior to that of the seignorial towns, which for the most part groaned under the oppressions of the nobles. (Dunham, *History of Spain and Portugal*, b. iii. sect. 3, ch. ii.)

The remonstrances or petitions of the general cortes to the king generally began as follows:—" The prelates, lords, and caballeros of the kingdoms of Castile and Leon, in the name of the three estates of the kingdom," &c. Remonstrances from the deputies of the towns began:— "Most high and powerful prince! your very humble vassals, subjects, and servants, the deputies of the towns and boroughs of your kingdoms, who are assembled in your presence by your order," &c. (Cortes of Valladolid, June, 1420.)

In the cortes of 1402, Enrique III. demanded for his wars with the Moors a supply of 60,000,000 maravedis, but the deputies granted only 45,000,000. The king then proposed that if the money should be found insufficient, he might be allowed to raise the deficiency by a loan without convoking the cortes afresh for the purpose. To this the majority of the deputies assented. By his testament Enrique excluded the citizens from the Council of Regency during the minority of his son Juan II., and after this they were no longer admitted into the royal council. Thus the municipal towns lost a great advantage which they had gained thirty years before under Juan I. They soon after sacrificed, of their own accord, their elective franchises. The expenses of the deputies to the cortes had been till then defrayed by the towns, but now having lost their influence at court by their exclusion from the royal council, the towns began to complain of their burthen. Juan II. listened attentively to their complaints, and in the cortes of Ocaña, 1422, he proposed that the future expenses of the deputies should be defrayed out of the royal treasury, a proposal which was willingly accepted. Accordingly, in the next cortes, 12 cities only, Burgos, Toledo, Leon, Zamora, Seville, Cordova, Murcia, Jaen, Segovia, Avila, Salamanca, and Cuenca, were summoned to send their deputation; some other towns were informed that they might entrust their powers to any deputy from the above. The privilege was subsequently extended to six more cities; Valladolid, Toro, Soria, Madrid, Guadalaxara, and Granada. These eighteen places constituted henceforth the whole representation of the kingdoms of Castile, Leon, Galicia, and Andalusia. The other communities at last perceiving the advantage they had lost, petitioned to be restored to their right, but found themselves strenuously opposed by the eighteen privileged towns. The influence of the court was openly exercised in the elections of these towns, and although the cortes of Valladolid in 1442, and those of Cordova in 1445, requested the king to abstain from such interference, yet the practice became more barefaced than ever. In 1457 Enrique IV. wrote to the municipal council of Seville, pointing out two individuals fit to be deputies in the next session, and requesting they might be elected. The municipal councils, which elected their own officers as well as the deputies to the cortes, were composed of all the heads of families, but by degrees the crown interfered in the appointment of the municipal officers. [AYUNTAMIENTO.]

Thus long before Charles I. (the emperor Charles V.), who has been generally accused of having destroyed the liberties of Spain, the popular branch of the representation was already reduced to a shadow, for the deputies of the eighteen cities, elected by court influence, were mere registrars of the royal decrees, and ready voters of the supplies demanded of them. Under Ferdinand and Isabella the royal authority became more extended and firmly established by the subjection of the privileged orders; the turbulent nobles were attacked in their castles, which were razed by hundreds, and the Santa Hermandad hunted the proprietors throughout the country. Many of the grants by former kings were revoked, and the proud feudatories were tamed into submissive courtiers.

Charles only finished the work by excluding the privileged orders from the cortes altogether, he and his successors contenting themselves with convoking the deputies of the eighteen royal cities of the crown of Castile on certain solemn occasions, to register their decrees, to acknowledge the prince of Asturias as heir apparent to the throne, to swear allegiance to a new prince. The policy of absolutism has been the same in all countries of Europe: it has used the popular power against the aristocracy, in order to reduce and destroy both in the end.

In Aragon, Valencia, and Catalonia, which formed the dominions of the crown of Aragon, the cortes of each of these three states continued to assemble under Charles I. and his successors of the Austrian dynasty, who convoked them in their accustomed manner by brazos or orders, and they maintained some show of independence, although in reality much reduced in importance after Philip II. had abolished the office of the Justiza. But after the War of the Succession, Philip V. of Bourbon formally abolished the cortes of these states by right of conquest, as he expressed it, because they had taken part with his rival the Archduke Charles.

In 1808, when the Spanish people rose in every province against the invasion of Napoleon, the king was a prisoner in France, after having been obliged by threats to abdicate the crown, and the nation was without a government. Municipal juntas were formed in every province, consisting of deputies taken from the various orders or classes of society, nobles, clergymen, proprietors, merchants, &c. These juntas sent deputies to form a central junta, with executive powers for the general affairs of the country, but a legislature was still wanting. The central junta was called upon to assemble the cortes for all Spain. They at first thought of reviving the ancient cortes by estamentos or brazos, but many difficulties presented themselves. The difference of formation between the old cortes of Aragon and those of Castile; the difficulty of applying those forms to the American possessions of Spain, which were now, for the first time, admitted to equal rights with the mother country, but where the same elements of society did not exist, at least not in the same proportion; the difficulty even in Spain of collecting a legitimate representation of the various orders, while most of the provinces were occupied or overrun by French armies, and while many of the nobility and the higher clergy had acknowledged the intrusive king Joseph Napoleon; all these, added to the altered state of public opinion, the long discontinuance of the old cortes by orders or estates, the diminished influence of the old nobility, and the creation of a new nobility during the latter reigns merely through court favour, made the original plan appear impracticable. The situation of the country was in fact without a parallel in history. The central junta consulted the consejo (reunido) or commission of magistrates, from the old higher courts of the kingdom, who proposed to assemble deputies of the various brazos or estamentos, all to form one house, a proposal extremely vague and apparently impracticable, which looks as if made to elude the question. Jovellanos and others then proposed two houses, constituted as in England; but this would also have been a new creation without precedent in Spain, and surrounded by many difficulties, the state of society being greatly different in the two countries. Meantime the central junta being driven away by the French, first from Madrid, and afterwards from Seville, in January, 1810, took refuge at Cadiz, which became the capital of the Spanish patriots, whither a number of persons from the various provinces and classes had flocked. Before leaving Seville, the central junta issued regulations addressed to the provincial juntas about the manner of electing the deputies to the cortes, stating at the end that "similar letters of convocation would be addressed to the representatives of the ecclesiastical brazo and of the nobility." This, however, was never done.

The central junta soon after arriving at Cadiz resigned its power into the hands of a council of regency composed of five individuals, but before its resignation it issued a decree approving of the plan of Jovellanos for two chambers, and recommending it to the regency. The regency however paid little attention to this recommendation; it seemed to hesitate during several months about convoking any cortes at all, for there was at Cadiz a party of pure absolutists opposed to any representation whatever. The regency again consulted the consejo reunido, the majority of which, departing from its former opinion, gave up the idea of cortes by estamentos, and proposed the election of deputies without distinction of classes. The council of state being likewise consulted by the regency, decided that, owing to the actual state of affairs, it was best to elect the deputies without estamentos, reserving to the "representatives of the nation once assembled to decide whether the cortes should be divided by brazos or into two chambers, after listening to the claims of the nobility and clergy." The regency at length issued letters of convocation for the deputies of all the provinces to assemble in cortes at the Isla de Leon on the 24th September, 1810. The elections for those provinces which were entirely occupied by the French were made at Cadiz by electoral juntas, composed of individuals of those provinces who had taken refuge there. A similar process was adopted with regard to the American provinces. (Arguelles, *Examen historico de la Reforma Constitucional*; Jovellanos, *Memoria a sus Compatriotas*, with *appendix* and *notes* to the same.)

The cortes, styled "extraordinary," sat at Cadiz from September, 1810, till September, 1813. During this time, amidst numerous enactments which they passed, they framed a totally new constitution for Spain, which has become known by the name of "the Constitution of 1812," the year in which it was proclaimed. This constitution established the representative system with a single popular chamber, elected in a numerical proportion of one deputy for every 70,000 individuals. The elections were not direct, but by means of electoral juntas or colleges, as in France: assembled citizens of every parish appointed, by open written votes, a certain number of delegates, who chose, by conference among themselves, one or more parish electors, in proportion to the population. All the parish electors, of every district, assembled together at the head town or village of the same, and there proceeded to elect by ballot the electors for the district. All the district electors of one province formed the electoral junta which assembled in the chief town of that province to appoint the deputies to the cortes, either from among themselves or from among the citizens who were not district electors, provided they were Spanish citizens born, in the full exercise of their civil rights, were more than 25 years of age, and had had their domicile in the province for at least seven years past. By Art. 92, a qualification was inserted of a yearly income, the amount and nature of which were left to the discretion of future cortes to determine. Every district elector, in succession, stepped up to the table where the president and secretary were, and told the name of his candidate, which the secretary wrote down. The scrutiny then took place, and the majority of votes decided the election. The deputies elected received full powers, in writing, from their electors, "to act as they think best for the general welfare, within the limits prescribed by the constitution, and without derogating from any of its articles." They were allowed by the respective provinces a fixed emolument during the time of the sessions. The ordinary cortes assembled once every year, in the month of March, and the session lasted three or, at the utmost, four months. The deputies were renewed every two years.

These were the principles of the formation of the cortes of Cadiz of 1812, which, whatever might have been their merits, had evidently little in common, except the name, with the old cortes of Castile or Aragon. The king had a veto for two years following; but if the resolution were persisted in the third year, his veto ceased.

The extraordinary cortes of Cadiz were succeeded in October, 1813, by the ordinary cortes, elected according to the principle of the Constitution. In January, 1814, they transferred their sittings to Madrid, which had been freed from the French. In March, of that year, King Ferdinand returned to Spain, and soon after dissolved the cortes, abrogated the Constitution, and punished its supporters. In 1820 the Constitution was proclaimed again through a military insurrection; the king accepted it, and the cortes assembled again. The king and the cortes, however, did not remain long in harmony. In 1823 a French army, under the Duke of Angoulême, entered Spain; the cortes left Madrid, taking the king with them to Seville, and thence transferred him by force to Cadiz. Cadiz having surrendered to the French, the cortes were again dispersed, the Constitution was again abolished, and the liberals were again punished. This name of "liberal," which has become of such general use in our days, originated in the first cortes of Cadiz, where it was used to designate those deputies who were favourable to reform, whilst the opposite party were styled "serviles." (Arguelles, end of chap. v.)

The history of the first cortes of Cadiz has been eloquently written by Arguelles; that of the cortes of 1820-23 and of the subsequent royalist reaction is found in numerous works and pamphlets of contemporary history, written with more or less party spirit, among which the least partial is perhaps the *Révolution d'Espagne, Examen Critique*, 8vo., Paris, 1836: it professes to be written by a Spanish emigrant, who, though no great admirer of the Constitution of 1812, speaks with equal freedom of the guilt and blunders of the violent men of both parties.

Ferdinand VII., before his death, in 1833, assembled the deputies of the royal towns, according to the ancient form, not to deliberate, but to acknowledge as his successor his infant daughter Isabella.

On the 10th of April, 1834, the queen regent proclaimed a charter for the Spanish nation, which was called Estatuto Real. It established the convocation of the cortes and its division into two houses, the procuradores, or deputies from the provinces, and the proceres, or upper house, consisting of certain nobles, prelates, and also of citizens distinguished by their merit. The power of the cortes, however, was very limited, the initiative of all laws being reserved to the crown. This charter was in force only to the 14th August, 1836. In the summer of 1836 insurrections broke out at Malaga and other places, where the Constitution of 1812 was again proclaimed; and at last the insurrection spread among the troops which were doing duty at the queen's residence at La Granja, in consequence of which the queen accepted the Constitution, "subject to the revision of the cortes." The cortes were therefore convoked according to the plan of 1812. Early in 1837 they commenced their duties, and finally approved of and decreed a Constitution, which was proclaimed in Madrid on the 16th of June, 1837. This Constitution has since been arbitrarily suspended.

The following were some of the leading provisions of the Constitution of 1837, so far as they related to the powers of the cortes:—The power of enacting the laws is possessed by the cortes in conjunction with the king, who sanctions and promulgates the laws. The cortes is composed of two co-legislative bodies, equal in powers, the Senate and Congress of Deputies. Of the Senate: The number of senators shall be equal to three-fifths of the total number of deputies. They are appointed by the king, from a triple list, proposed by the electors of each province who elect the deputies. To each province belongs the right of proposing a number of senators, proportionable to its population; but each is to return one senator at least. To be a senator, it is necessary to be a Spaniard; to be forty years of age, and to be possessed of the income and other qualifications defined in the electoral law. All Spaniards possessed of these qualifications may be proposed for the office of senator in any of the provinces. The sons of the king and of the immediate heir to the throne are senators of right at the age of twenty-five years. Of the Congress of Deputies: Each province shall appoint one deputy, at least, for every 50,000 souls of the population. The deputies are elected by the direct method, and may be re-elected indefinitely. To be a deputy it is necessary to be a Spaniard, in the secular state, to have completed the twenty-fifth year, and to possess all the qualifications prescribed by the electoral law. Every Spaniard possessing these qualifications, may be named a deputy for any of the provinces. The deputies shall be appointed for three years. The Cortes are to assemble each year. It is the right of the king to convoke them, to suspend and close their meetings, and dissolve the Cortes; but under the obligation, in the case of dissolution, of convoking and reassembling another Cortes within three months. If the king should omit to convoke the Cortes on the 1st of December in any one year, the Cortes are notwithstanding to assemble precisely on that day; and in case of the conclusion of the term of the congress holding office happening to occur in that year, a general election for the nomination of deputies is to commence on the first Sunday of the month of October. On the demise of the crown, or on the king being incapacitated to govern, through any cause, the extraordinary cortes are immediately to assemble. . . . . . The sessions of the senate and of the congress shall be public, and only in cases requiring reserve can private sitting be held. The king and each of the co-legislative bodies possess the right of originating laws. Laws relating to taxes and public credit shall be presented first to the congress of deputies; and if altered in the senate contrary to the form in which they have been approved by the congress, they are to receive the royal sanction in the form definitely decided on by the deputies. The resolutions of each of the legislative bodies are to be determined by an absolute plurality of votes; but in the enactment of the laws, the presence of more than half the number of each of these bodies is necessary. If one of the co-legislative bodies should reject any project of law submitted to them, or if the king should refuse it his sanction, such project of law is not to be submitted anew in that congress. Besides the legislative powers which the cortes exercise in conjunction with the king, the following faculties belong to them:—1st, To receive from the king, the immediate successor to the throne, from the regency or regent of the empire, the oath to observe the constitution and the laws. 2ndly, To resolve any doubt that may arise of fact or of right with respect to the order of succession to the crown. 3rdly, To elect the regent, or appoint the regency, of the empire, and to name the tutor of the sovereign while a minor, when the constitution deems it necessary. 4thly, To render effective the responsibility of the ministers of the crown, who are to be impeached by the deputies, and judged by the senators. The senators and deputies are irresponsible and inviolable for opinions expressed and votes given by them in the discharge of their duties. Deputies and senators who receive from the government, or the royal family any pension, or employment which may not be an instance of promotion from a lower to a higher office of the same kind, commission with salary, honours, or titles, are subject to re-election.

On the 27th of December, 1843, the cortes were suddenly suspended by an arbitrary decree of the ministers. It was rumoured that the cabinet would promulgate certain laws by edict, after which the cortes were again to be assembled to pass a bill of indemnity for this act of usurpation; and that if the cortes did not pass such bill, they would be dissolved. On the 10th of July, 1844, a decree was published in the Madrid Gazette dissolving the cortes and summoning a new cortes for the 10th of October. They were opened at the appointed time by the queen in person, who on that day completed her fourteenth year, and in the speech from the throne some measures of constitutional reform were recommended to their consideration. On the 18th of October a bill for remodelling the constitution was presented to the congress. This bill proposed to suppress the preamble to the constitution of 1837, which asserted the national supremacy. The members of the senate were to be absolutely appointed by the crown for life. The article requiring the cortes to assemble every year was altered, and it was proposed that they should be convoked by the crown only when it thought fit. These important changes in the constitutional law of the state amounted in fact to a revolution. It was moreover proposed by this bill that political offences, including those of the press, were not to be submitted to the jury.

On the 11th of March, 1845, a new electoral law was brought forward in the cortes by the ministry. The qualification of deputies is to be the possession of 12,000 reals (120*l.*) per annum, from real property, or the payment of 1000 reals (10*l.*) in direct taxes. The qualification for electors is to consist in the payment of 400 reals (4*l.*) per annum, in direct taxes; but members of the learned professions, retired officers in the army and navy, and persons in the employment of government or in active service, who have a salary of 15,000 reals (150*l.*) and upwards, are qualified if they pay 200 reals (2£.) a year direct taxes. When the number of electors in a district does not amount to one hundred and fifty, that number is to be made up by adding the highest tax-payers. Both deputies and electors must be twenty-five years of age. The number of persons who pay 400 reals direct taxes is said to be very small in many parts of Spain, and the admission to the electoral franchise of persons in the employment of government with a salary of 150l. a year is calculated to neutralize the independent opinions of the country, and may sometimes have the effect of keeping in power a government adverse to the general interests. By this electoral law the country is to be divided into 300 electoral districts, each to contain about 40,000 inhabitants, and each district will return one member. This is considered an improvement upon the plan of returning the deputies by provinces.

The history of the cortes of Portugal is nearly the same as that of those of Spain, only that the towns which sent deputies were comparatively fewer, seldom more than ten or twelve at a time, and the influence of the privileged orders greater in proportion. The nobles having by degrees become courtiers, as in Spain, the kings reigned in fact absolute. In latter times there were less remains of popular freedom observable in Portugal than in Spain. In 1820, while King João VI. was in Brazil, a military insurrection broke out in Portugal, and a Constitution was framed in imitation of the Spanish one of 1812, but it was soon after upset. For an account of these transactions see Kinsey's *Portugal Illustrated*, 1828. After the death of King João, his son, Don Pedro, gave a charter to Portugal, establishing a system of popular representation, with two houses; this charter was afterwards abolished by Don Miguel, and again re-established by Don Pedro; but some changes have subsequently been made .n it.

The Aragonese, during their period of splendour, extended their representative system by brazos or estamentos to the island of Sardinia, then subject to the crown of Aragon, and the institution, although on a contracted basis, remains to this day in Sardinia under the name of Stamenti, or Estates.

COTTAGE SYSTEM. [ALLOTMENTS.]

COTTON CULTIVATION AND TRADE. Cotton is called, in French, *Coton*; German, *Baumwolle*; Dutch, *Katoen, Boomwol*; Danish, *Bomuld*; Swedish, *Bomull*; Italian, *Cotone Bambagia*; Spanish, *Algodon*; Portuguese, *Algodao*; Russian, *Chlobtschataju Bumaga*; Polish, *Bawelna*; Hindustani, *Rúhi*; Malay, *Kapas*; Latin, *Gossypium*.

The distinctive names by which cotton is known in commerce are, with the following two exceptions, derived from the countries of their production. The finest kind, which commands the highest price, is called sea-island cotton, from the circumstance of its having been first cultivated in the United States of North America, in the low sandy islands on the coast, from Charlestown to Savannah. It is said that its quality is gradually deteriorated in proportion as the plants are removed from "the salutary action of the ocean's spray." The seed is supposed to have come originally from Persia. It was taken from the island of Anguilla to the Bahamas for cultivation and was first sent thence to Georgia in 1786. The annual average crop does not exceed 11,000,000 pounds. Upland or Bowed Georgia cotton, the green-seed kind, has received its name of *upland* to distinguish it from the produce of the islands and low districts near the shores. The expression bowed was given as being descriptive of the means employed for loosening the seed from the filaments, which was accomplished by bringing a set of strings, attached to a bow, in contact with a heap of uncleaned cotton, and then striking the strings so as to cause violent vibrations, and thus open the locks of cotton and cause the seeds to be easily separable from the filaments.

A few years ago Mr. Woodbury, secretary of the United States' Treasury, prepared some tables which showed the cultivation, manufacture, and trade in cotton throughout the world. According to these tables, which must be considered as rough estimates, though probably not far from

2 Y

the truth, the progress of production in the United States was as follows from 1791 to 1831:—

	lbs.		lbs.
1791	2,000,000	1821	180,000,000
1801	48,000,000	1831	385,000,000
1811	80,000,000		

From the season 1832-33 to the season 1843-44 the growth of cotton estimated in bales was as under:—

	Bales.		Bales.
1832-33	1,070,438	1838-39	1,360,532
1833-34	1,205,394	1839-40	2,177,835
1834-35	1,254,328	1840-41	1,634,945
1835-36	1,360,725	1841-42	1,683,574
1836-37	1,422,930	1842-43	2,379,000
1837-38	1,801,497	1843-44	2,030,000

In the ten years preceding 1845 the average annual rate of increase in the growth of cotton in the United States has been about 100,000 bales. The distribution of the cotton crops of the United States was as follows in 1843 and 1844:

	1843. Bales.	1844. Bales.
Great Britain	1,470,000	1,203,000
France	346,000	283,000
Other parts of Europe	194,000	144,000
American consumption	326,000	346,744

The progressive average annual increase in the consumption of American cotton in the ten years from 1835 to 1845 has been about 43,609 bales in Great Britain; 12,448 in the United States of North America; and 27,187 on the Continent of Europe and all other places. In the same period the consumption of cotton from all other countries, except North America, has increased at an annual average rate of 14,107 bales.

The cotton wool imported into Great Britain from Brazil, India, Egypt, &c. in 1843 and 1844 was as under:—

	1843. Bales.	1844. Bales.
Brazil	98,821	112,031
Demerara and Berbice	114	234
Egypt	47,638	66,563
East Indies	181,993	237,559
West Indies, Carthagena, &c.	19,093	17,373

It appears from Mr. Woodbury's tables that in 1834 rather more than two-thirds (68 per cent.) of all the cotton sent away from all the places of production were shipped to England. About five-sixths of all the cotton brought into the United Kingdom is of the growth of the United States of North America. Above one-half in value of the exports of the United States consists of cotton wool—47,090,000 out of a total of 92,000,000 dollars in the year ending 30th September, 1842, and 49,000,000 out of a total of 77,000,000 dollars in the nine months ending June 30th, 1843.

During the period in which the increased production has been going forward with the greatest rapidity in America, the prices have been continually declining. In the table of prices given by Mr. Woodbury as those of the United States, at the places of exportation, and including all kinds of cotton, it is shown that the average price of each period of five years, from 1791 to 1835, has been as follows, viz.:—

per lb.	per lb.
1791 to 1795. 15¾d.	1816 to 1820. 13d.
1796 to 1800. 18¼d.	1821 to 1825. 8d.
1801 to 1805.12½d.	1826 to 1830. 5d.
1806 to 1810. 9¼d.	1831 to 1835. 6d.
1811 to 1815. 7¼d.	

Mr. Woodbury states that "where rich lands and labour were low, as in Mississippi and Alabama a few years ago, two cents (one penny) per pound for cotton in the seed, or eight cents when cleaned, would pay expenses. It is supposed to be a profitable crop in the South-western States at ten cents per pound." Mr. Bates, of the house of Baring and Co., stated before a Parliamentary Committee, in 1833, that "even six cents, or threepence per pound, is a price at which the planters can gain money in the valley of the Mississippi."

Land fresh brought under cultivation in the United States will yield on an average from 1000 to 1200 pounds per acre of cotton with the seed, which will yield of clean cotton from 250 to 300 pounds.

Bengal cotton of inferior quality can, it is said, be raised for three half pence per pound, and delivered in England at an advance of one penny upon that price. Good Surat cotton is said to cost two-pence half-penny per pound, delivered at Bombay. The cost of production in our West India colonies is considerably greater, and the cultivation of cotton has consequently been for the most part abandoned by the British planters.

The relative value of the kinds of cotton most commonly introduced for sale and use in this country, will be seen in the following list of average prices per lb. for the years 1843 and 1844:—

	1843.			1844.		
	d.		d.	d.		d.
Sea Island .	10½	to	21	10	to	22
Bowed .	4½	to	6	3¼	to	5
Orleans, &c. .	4⅝	to	7½	3⅛	to	6
Pernambuco .	5⅝	to	6¾	5	to	6¼
Bahia .	5½	to	6½	4⅞	to	5¾
Maranham .	4¾	to	6¼	4	to	5¾
Egyptian .	6	to	8¼	5	to	8½
Surat .	3¼	to	4½	2¼	to	4

The growth of the cotton trade has been rapid beyond all commercial precedent. In 1786 the total imports were somewhat less than 20,000,000 pounds, no part of which was furnished by North America. Our West India colonies supplied nearly one-third, about an equal quantity was brought from foreign colonies in the same quarter, 2,000,000 pounds came from Brazil, and 5,000,000 pounds from the Levant. In 1790 the importations amounted to 31,447,605 pounds, none of which was supplied by the United States. In 1795 the quantity was only 26,401,340 pounds. In this year a commercial treaty was made between the United States of North America and Great Britain, by one article of which, as it originally stood, the export was prohibited from the United States in American vessels of such articles as they had previously imported from the West Indies. Among these articles cotton was included, Mr. Jay, the American negotiator, not being aware that cotton was then becoming an article of export from the United States. In 1800 the imports had more than doubled, having reached 56,010,732 pounds. This was the first year in which any considerable quantity was obtained from America; the imports from that quarter were about 16,000,000 pounds. The progress of this trade during the present century is shown by the following table, exhibiting the imports at intervals of five years:—

	From all places.	From the United States.
	lbs.	lbs.
1805 .	59,682,406 .	32,500,000
1810 .	132,488,935 .	36,000,000
1815 .	99,306,343 .	45,666,000
1820 .	151,672,655 .	89,999,174
1825 .	228,605,291 .	139,908,699
1830 .	263,961,452 .	210,885,358
1835 .	363,702,693 .	284,455,812
1840 .	592,488,010 .	487,856,504
1842 .	673,193,136 .	574,738,520
1844 .	646,874,816 .	. . .

The quantities actually employed in our manufactories in different years during the same period have been as under:—

	lbs.		lbs.
1800,	51,594,122	1837,	368,445,035
1805,	58,878,163	1838,	455,036,755
1810,	123,701,826	1839,	352,000,277
1815,	92,525,951	1840,	528,142,743
1820,	152,829,633	1841,	437,093,631
1825,	202,546,869	1842,	473,976,400
1830,	269,616,640	1843,	585,922,624
1835,	326,407,692	1844,	558,015,248
1836,	363,684,232		

The average deliveries of cotton per week, for home consumption, from the ports of Great Britain, distinguishing the deliveries at Liverpool, have been as follows since 1835:—

	Liverpool.	Total Great Britain.
	Bales.	Bales.
1835 .	16,806 .	18,127
1836 .	18,495 .	19,851
1837 .	19,271 .	20,785
1838 .	22,934 .	24,320
1839 .	18,888 .	19,935
1840 .	23,037 .	24,837
1841 .	20,041 .	22,133
1842 .	22,142 .	23,749
1843 .	24,738 .	27,004
1844 .	25,213 .	27,255

The rapid increase in the consumption of cotton has altogether resulted from the inventions of Hargreaves, Arkwright, Crompton, and others, in spinning machinery, and more recently from the invention by Dr. Cartwright, since perfected by other mechanicians, of the power-loom. But for these inventions it would have been impossible for our artisans to have competed successfully with the spinners and weavers of India, from which country we previously received our supply of muslins and calicoes. Not only have we ceased to import for use the muslins of India, but have for many years sent great and continually increasing shipments of those goods to clothe the natives of India. In 1814 our looms supplied 818.202 yards of cotton goods to India. Two years afterwards the shipments were doubled. In 1818 they amounted to 9,000,000 yards; in 1835 the markets of India and China took from us 62,994,489 yards, the declared value of which amounted to 1,660,806*l.*, exclusive of 8,233,142 lbs. of cotton yarn, valued at 603,211*l.* In 1842 we exported to India and Ceylon 155,506,914 yards, of the declared value of 2,480,031*l.*, besides 12,050,839 lbs. of cotton yarn, valued at 545,075*l.* Considerable shipments of cotton piece goods are still made from India to this country, but nearly the whole are re-exported.

The duty on cotton wool was wisely abandoned in 1845, although it amounted to only 5-16ths of 1*d.* per lb. This apparently small duty constituted a tax of 10 per cent. on the New Orleans price of middling cotton most extensively used in this country. It placed the English cotton spinner on very unequal terms with the cotton manufacturers of the United States, who were already in possession of advantages arising from contiguity to the cotton-market, saving in freight, and other diminished charges, which were estimated at 14 per cent., making a total difference of 24 per cent. In 1844 the cotton-spinners of the United States of America were larger consumers of the raw material than the spinners of Great Britain in 1815. The duty pressed most heavily on the coarsest kind of manufactures. Comparing it with the wages of the spinners, the duty of 5-16ths of 1*d.* was 50 per cent. upon the wages of the operatives employed in producing the coarsest heavy yarns; on yarn for domestic goods 30 to 45 per cent.; on yarns spun for printed calicoes 25 per cent.; on yarn for ordinary muslin 10 per cent.; while on the finest lace-yarns the fraction of duty upon the wages of labour was almost inappreciable. On No. 100 twist the pressure of the tax was $2\frac{3}{4}$ per cent. on the material, and $1\frac{1}{4}$ on the cost of twist; on No. 12, the coarsest kind, the tax was 12 per cent. on the material and $7\frac{1}{4}$ per cent. on the cost of twist. On a coarse cotton shirt or stout piece of calico, the duty, small as it might really be, was 200 times greater than on fine muslins. In 1843 the gross duty on cotton-wool amounted to 736,546*l.*, and in 1844 to 672,614*l.* (Messrs. Blackburn and Co.'s *Annual Statistics of the Cotton Trade*, 1844.)

COTTON MANUFACTURE AND TRADE. The use of cotton as a material for the production of woven fabrics was known in India and China for many centuries before its introduction into Europe. The earliest mention of cotton by the Greek writers is by Herodotus (iii. 106) in his brief notice of the usages of the Indi: he calls it (iii. 47) by the significant name of tree-wool (εἴριον ἀπὸ ξύλου), apparently not being acquainted with the native name. In the reign of Amasis, B.C. 563—525, cotton was known in Egypt, but it must have been imported, as there is no reason for supposing it was then grown in Egypt. Cotton cloths were, according to Arrian, among the articles which the Romans received from India, and there is no doubt the manufacture had been carried on in many parts of Asia, long before any extant notice of that quarter of the world being visited by Europeans. The perfection to which the weaving of cotton had then been brought by the natives of many parts of India, notwithstanding their rude and imperfect implements, attests at once their patience and ingenuity. In China, this manufacture is supposed not to have existed at all before the beginning of the sixth century of the Christian æra. The cotton plant was indeed known in that country at a much earlier period, but continued till then to be cultivated only as a garden shrub, and was not indeed propagated on a large scale until the eleventh century;

at the present time nearly all the inhabitants of that populous empire are clothed in cotton cloths of home manufacture.

Before the discovery of the passage to India by the Cape of Good Hope, cotton wool is said to have been spun and woven in some of the Italian states, the traders of which were the channels through which the cotton fabrics of India were distributed to the different countries of Europe. Becoming thus acquainted with these goods, and having near at hand the raw material of which they were formed, it was natural that they should apply to the production of similar goods the manufacturing skill they had long possessed.

Mr. Baines has shown ('Hist. of Cotton Manufacture,') that the cotton plant was extensively cultivated, and its produce manufactured, by the Mohammedan possessors of Spain in the tenth century. This branch of industry flourished long in that country. In the thirteenth century, the cotton manufacturers formed one of the incorporated companies of Barcelona, in which city two streets received names which point them out as the quarter in which the manufacturers resided. The cloths made were mostly of coarse texture, and a considerable quantity was used as sailcloth. The name *fustians*, from the Spanish word *fuste*, signifying "substance," was borrowed from the Spanish weavers, and is still used to denote a strong fabric made of cotton. In consequence of religious prejudice, the arts which long flourished among the Mohammedan possessors of Spain did not extend themselves to the Christian inhabitants of other European countries: the traffic of Andalusia was all carried on with Africa and the East.

From Italy the art made its way to the Netherlands, and about the end of the sixteenth or the beginning of the seventeenth century was brought thence to England by protestant refugees. Lewis Roberts, in 'The Treasure of Traffic,' published in 1641, makes the earliest mention extant of the manufacture in England. He says, "The town of Manchester buys cotton wool from London that comes from Cyprus and Smyrna, and works the same into fustians, vermillians, and dimities."

There is abundant evidence to show that in the beginning of the sixteenth century, and probably before that time, cotton was cultivated and converted into clothing in most of the countries occupying the southern shores of the Mediterranean. The European conquerors of Mexico in their first invasion of that country found in use native manufactures of cotton, both unmixed and mixed with the fine hair of rabbits and hares. Some of these fabrics were sent by Cortes to Spain as presents to the Emperor Charles V. Cotton was cultivated and manufactured at an equally early period by different nations on the coast of Guinea, and it is stated by Macpherson in his 'Annals of Commerce,' that cotton cloths were imported into London in 1590 from the Bight of Benin.

Previous to the introduction of Arkwright's inventions the cotton manufacture was of small importance, as is evident from the quantities of the raw material then brought into the country. Arkwright's first patent for the mode of spinning by rollers was taken out in 1769, and the following account of the importations of cotton at different periods preceding and speedily following that event will show how rapid was the progress occasioned by it, and by the other inventions for which it prepared the way:—

1697	. . .	1,976,359 lbs.
1701 to 1705	.	1,170,881 „ average
1710	. . .	715,008 „
1720	. . .	1,972,805 „
1730	. . .	1,545,472 „
1741	. . .	1,645,031 „
1751	. . .	2,976,610 „
1764	. . .	3,870,392 „
1771 to 1775	.	4,764,589 } average
1776 to 1780	.	6,766,613 }
1790	. . .	31,447,605 „
1800	. . .	56,010,732 „

The system under which this manufacture was long carried on was very different from that which is now pursued. It was the custom for the weavers who were dispersed in cottages throughout the district to purchase the material with which they worked, and having converted it into cloths to carry their wares to market and sell them on their own account to the dealers: but about 1760, the merchants of Manchester began to employ the weavers, furnishing them with yarn for warp, and with raw cotton, which was spun by the weaver's family for the weft, and paying a fixed price for the labour bestowed in weaving.

The application of machinery to the preparation and spinning of raw cotton for weft preceded by some years the inventions of Arkwright. In the year 1760, or soon after, a carding engine not very different from that now used was contrived by James Hargreaves, an illiterate weaver, residing near Church in Lancashire; and in 1767 the *spinning-jenny* was invented by the same person. This machine as at first formed contained eight spindles, which were made to revolve by means of bands from a horizontal wheel. Subsequent improvements increased the power of the spinning-jenny to eighty spindles, when the saving of labour which it thus occasioned produced considerable alarm among those persons who had employed the old mode of spinning, and a party of them broke into Hargreaves' house and destroyed his machine. The great advantage of the invention was so apparent, however, that it was soon again brought into use, and nearly superseded the employment of the old spinning-wheel, when a second rising took place of the persons whose labour was thus superseded by it. They went through the country destroying wherever they could find them both carding and spinning machines, by which means the manufacture was for a time driven away from Lancashire to Nottingham.

The cotton-yarn produced both by the common spinning-wheel and spinning-jenny could not be made sufficiently strong to be used as warp, for which purpose linen-yarn was employed. It was not until Arkwright's spinning-frame was brought into successful operation that this disadvantage was overcome. Yarn spun with Hargreaves' jenny continued for some time to be used for weft. At first, the manufacturers of cloths composed of cotton only were subject to much annoyance from the determination of the revenue officers to charge them with double the duty paid upon calicoes woven with linen warp and printed for exportation; and also by prohibiting their use at home. With some difficulty an act of parliament was obtained for removing these obstacles to the development of the manufacture, which from that time was prosecuted with a great and continually accelerated rate of increase.

The earliest attempts at producing muslins were made about the year 1780, but without much success, although India-spun yarn was substituted as weft for that produced by the spinning-jenny: the greatest degree of fineness to which yarn spun with Arkwright's frame had then been brought, was eighty hanks to the pound, and even this degree was not attainable by means of the jenny. This disadvantage was overcome by the invention of Mr. Samuel Crompton, which came into general use about the year 1786, and which partaking of the nature of both Hargreaves' and Arkwright's machines, was aptly called the *mule-jenny*. By means of this piece of mechanism, yarns were produced of a much greater fineness than had before been attained. Mr. Crompton's invention was made several years before it could be openly used, because of its interference with the patented invention of Arkwright: but when this patent was annulled, the mule-jenny was brought rapidly and extensively into use, so that in 1787, 500,000 pieces of muslin were made at Bolton, Glasgow, and Paisley, with yarn of British production. The price paid at that time by the manufacturers for these fine yarns was 20 guineas per lb; but such have been the improvements since made in the machine and the manner of working it, that yarn of the same fineness has been sold at 14 shillings per lb. Mr. Crompton did not secure to himself the benefit of his invention by taking out a patent; he carried on a spinning and weaving business on a small scale at Bolton, and worked his mule-jenny with his own hands in an attic. In a brief memoir of Crompton, Mr. Kennedy has stated, that about 1802 he, in conjunction with Mr. Lee, set on foot a subscription which amounted to 500*l.*, and with this Crompton was enabled to increase his manufacturing establishment, and to set up several looms for fancy work at Bolton. In 1812 he made a survey of all the cotton-manufacturing districts in the kingdom, and ascertained that the number of spindles then at work upon his principle amounted to between four and five millions: since that time the number has been doubled. The kind friends already named assisted him in making an application to parliament for some reward, and the great merit of his invention having been established before a Committee of the House of Commons, he received a grant of 5000*l.*, which was paid to him in full without any deduction for fees or charges. This money was employed by Crompton in putting his sons into business, but they proved unsuccessful, and he was reduced to poverty, when Mr. Kennedy again interfered in his behalf, and raised a second subscription, with the produce of which a life annuity of 63*l.* was purchased. He lived only two years to enjoy this small provision. The first mule-jennies consisted of not more than thirty spindles each, but the number has been progressively increased, and they now frequently contain more than 600 spindles each. With one of these machines, a good workman can produce in a week consisting of sixty-nine working hours, thirty-two pounds of yarn of the fineness of 200 hanks to the pound, and as each hank measures 840 yards, the produce of his week's work if extended in a line would measure 3050 miles. This work, extraordinary as it may seem, does not afford a full conception of the degree of tenuity to which cotton is capable of being reduced, one pound of raw cotton having been converted into 350 hanks, forming a continuous thread 167 miles in length. Mules have been put to work which carry each 1100 spindles. The greatest recent improvement made in the construction of this machine has been effected by Messrs. Sharp, Roberts, and Co., machinists, of Manchester. These machines, which are called self-acting mules, do not require the manual aid of a spinner, the only attendance necessary being that of children, called piecers, who join such threads as may be accidently broken. Self-acting mules were contrived at different times by Mr. William Strutt of Derby, Mr. Kelly of Lanark, Mr. De Jongh of Warrington, and others; but none of these were brought successfully into use, owing no doubt in some measure to the inferior skill of the machine-makers as compared with the perfection which they have since attained.

The first successful attempt to weave by means of machinery was made in 1785 by Dr. Cartwright, who secured the invention by patent. In a commercial point of view Dr. Cartwright did not draw any advantage from his power-loom: but in 1809 he obtained from parliament a grant of 10,000*l.* as a reward for his ingenuity. Mr. Monteith, of Pollokshaws, Glasgow, who fitted up 200 power-looms in 1801, was the first person who brought them to profitable use. A great obstacle to their success was presented by the necessity for the frequent stopping of the machine in order to dress the warp. This difficulty was removed in 1804 by the invention of a machine for dressing the whole of the warp before it is placed in the loom, which was made the subject of a patent by Mr. Radcliffe, the inventor. In the use of this machine the warp in its progress to the weaving beam is passed through a dressing of hot starch; it is then compressed between rollers to free it from the superfluous quantity of starch taken up, and is afterwards, in order to dry it, drawn over a succession of cylinders heated by passing steam through them; during this last part of the operation the warp is "lightly brushed as it moves along, and is fanned by rapidly revolving fanners." The flour used for this dressing operation throughout the cotton factories of this kingdom amounts in the year to at least 650,000 bushels. The number of power-looms used in cotton factories throughout the kingdom at the end of the year 1835 was stated by the inspectors of factories in a return laid before parliament to be 109,626. The number in England was 90,679; Scotland, 17,531; Ireland 1416. In Lancashire the number of spindles was 61,176; Cheshire, 22,491; Lanarkshire, 14,069.

Each of these looms, if of good construction and attended by a skilful weaver, was capable of producing 120 yards of cloth per week, or 6240 yards in the year, at which rate the annual productive power of the whole number of looms amounted to 684 millions of yards.

Hitherto it has not been practicable to produce any but coarse or heavy goods by means of the power-loom; fine calicoes, muslins, and fancy goods are woven by the hand. The number of hand-loom weavers cannot be ascertained with the same correctness as the number of power-looms, the latter being collected together in factories which are under the superintendence of official inspectors, while hand-loom weaving is altogether a domestic manufacture carried on in the cottages of the artisans. Computations of the number of these domestic looms have been made by different intelligent persons conversant with the trade, who have estimated them variously; the lowest at 200,000 and the highest at 250,000.

Mr. Kennedy, who is considered a good authority on this subject, supposed the value of cotton goods made in Great Britain in 1832, when the quantity of the raw material used was about 12 per cent. less than in 1833, was 24,760,000*l.* Mr. Baines, who has taken great pains to test the accuracy of his calculations in every possible way, has made the value amount, in 1833, to 31,338,693*l.* Of this value the part exported amounted to 18,459,000*l.*, and the value of the goods remaining for home consumption would therefore be 12,879,693*l.* (*Hist. of Cotton Manufacture*, p. 412.) Following Mr. Baines's mode of calculation, Mr. Porter estimated the value of the cotton goods manufactured in 1841 at 48,641,343*l.*; and as the exports, including yarn, amounted to 24,668,618*l.*, there would remain for home consumption goods to the value of 23,972,725*l.* The capital invested in the cotton manufacture in Great Britain is variously estimated at from 30,000,000*l.* to 34,000,000*l.*; and Mr. Baines regards the latter estimate as very moderate.

The number of persons returned under the head Cotton Manufacture in the Census Returns of 1841 is 302,376, to which should be added those returned under the heads Hose and Lace, which are branches of the Cotton Manufacture, and also a proportionate number of those who were returned as weavers, spinners, and factory workers ('fabric not specified'), and we have then a total of nearly half a million persons engaged in this great branch of national industry, and this at a time when it was in a very depressed state.

Persons Employed.
Cotton . . 377,662
Hose . . 50,955
Lace . . 35,347

463,964

The ages and sex of the above number (377,662) engaged in the manufacture of cotton fabrics were as follows:—
Males aged 20 and upwards. 138,112
under 20 . . . 59,171
Females aged 20 and upwards . 104,470
under 30 . . . 75,909

The employment of young persons in cotton factories is regulated by statute. [FACTORIES ACT.]

The first cotton-mill built in the United States was set to work in Rhode Island in 1790, and about the same time one was erected at Beverley, Massachusetts, by an incorporated company. The manufacture made at first so little progress in the United States, that up to 1808 not more than 15 spinning-mills had been erected. There was a great increase in 1812, occasioned by the war between England and America; again from 1820 to 1825 much capital was applied to this object; also in 1831 and 1832; and still more since the passing of the tariff of 1842, which imposed higher import duties on cotton and other manufactured goods generally.

In 1840 the number of cotton manufactories in the United States was 1240, which employed 2,284,631 spindles, and produced manufactured articles valued at 46,350,000 dollars. The capital invested was estimated at 51,000,000 dollars; and the number of persons employed, including dyers, printers, &c., was 72,119. The value of goods produced in Massachusetts in 1840 was 16,553,000 dollars; Rhode Island 7,116,000; Pennsylvania, 5,013,000; New Hampshire, 4,142,000; New York, 3,640,000; Connecticut,

2,715,964; New Jersey, 2,086,104; Maryland, 1,150,000 dollars; and in other States in smaller quantities. One-half of the cotton manufacture was carried on in Massachusetts and Rhode Island. The great demand for cotton goods within the States at first prevented any very considerable exportation. Between 1826 and 1832 the total annual value of the shipments made was under 250,000*l.*, the greater part of which were to Mexico and the South American States. The annual value of the exports in the following years was as under:—

Dollars.		Dollars.
1834 . 2,200,000	1837	. 3,758,000
1835 . 2,255,000	1838	. 2,975,000
1836 . 2,831,000	1839	. 3,549,000

In the year ending 30th September, 1842, the exports of cotton manufactured goods from the United States consisted of

	Dollars.
Printed and coloured piece goods	385,040
White	2,297,964
Twist, yarn and thread	37,325
Other cotton goods	250,361
	2,970,690

In the nine months ending 30th June, 1843, the value of the exports of cotton goods was 3,223,550 dollars, and the principal countries to which they were sent were China, Chili, Brazil, and Mexico, which took about four-fifths of the whole: it is stated in the official returns that white cotton goods of the value of 113,694 dollars were exported to the British East Indies. The value of the exports to China was 1,063,285 dollars; to Chili, 550,857 dollars; Brazil, 383,408 dollars; and Mexico, 193,027 dollars.

The quantity of cotton imported into France in 1787, the earliest year as to which any returns are given, was 4,466,000 kilogrammes, or not quite ten millions of pounds. In 1815 the importation was 16,414,606 kilogrammes; in 1820 had reached 20,000,000 kilogrammes; in 1825 it was still below 25 millions; in 1830 it amounted to 29½ millions, and in 1835 reached 38,760,000 kilogrammes, and in 1840 it was 52,942,000 kilogrammes (116,000,000 lbs). In 1840 the quantity of cotton spun in France was about one-fifth of that used in our mills, and the value of the exports from France, nearly one-third of which, according to Mr. Macgregor ('Commercial Statistics') are smuggled into Spain, was between one-fifth and one-sixth part of the value of the shipments from England. In 1820 the value of the exports of cotton manufactured goods was 29,000,000 fr., and in 1840 107,000,000 fr.; and the value of cotton twist exported in 1820 was 397,000 fr., and 593,000 fr. in 1840.

The cotton manufacture is of modern introduction in Switzerland. The first spinning-machine was established at St. Gall, in the year 1800; but Switzerland still imports considerable quantities of foreign-spun yarns for the use of her hand-loom weavers, as well as of power-loom cloths from England, which are dyed and printed, and afterwards exported. So great is the degree of perfection attained in the application of the colour denominated Turkey red, that calicoes and prints of that colour are imported from Switzerland into England: the same may be said of embroidered muslins.

Within the last few years the cotton manufacture has made great progress in the Rhenish provinces of Prussia and in Saxony, and also, though to a smaller extent, in Würtemberg and Baden. It is one of the objects of the German Customs' Union to foster the cotton and other manufactures by high duties on the cheaper products of England.

The cotton manufacture is the most generally diffused of all the branches of industry upon which the production of clothing depends. The greater part of the countries in which it is carried on limit their production of cotton goods to the wants of their own people. The perfection to which the spinning processes have been carried in this country has made the greater part of the world in some measure dependent upon our cotton-mills for the finer descriptions of yarns. In 1844 the exports of cotton goods, hosiery, and twist from England amounted in value to 25,831,586*l.*, or nearly one-half of the total exports. In the following years the declared value was as follows:—

COTTON. [698] COTTON.

£		£
1820 . 16,516,748	1835 .	22,128,304
1825 . 18,359,526	1840 .	24,668,618
1830 . 19,428,664		

The following tables show the countries to which we exported cotton goods, hosiery, and twist and yarn, in 1842:—

I. Account of the Declared Value of British Cotton Manufactured Goods, Hosiery, Lace, and small Wares, and Cotton Yarn and Twist, Exported from the United Kingdom in 1842.

1. Cotton Goods.

Russia	£36,345
Sweden	5,481
Norway	26,231
Denmark	3,766
Prussia	104
Germany	757,771
Holland	475,465
Belgium	78,302
France	72,578
Portugal	602,311
Spain	32,724
Gibraltar	633,817
Italy and the Italian Islands	901,954
Malta	127,570
Ionian Islands	41,339
Morea and Greek Islands	552
Turkey	901,264
Syria and Palestine	240,678
Egypt	124,877
Tripoli, Tunis, Algiers, and Morocco	22,940
Western Coast of Africa	220,564
Cape of Good Hope	79,575
Cape Verd Islands	1,250
St. Helena	1,108
Ascension Island	6
Mauritius	79,887
East India Company's Territories and Ceylon	2,480,031
Sumatra, Java, and other Islands of the Indian Seas	194,173
Philippine Islands	39,360
China	468,539
New Zealand	1,791
British Settlements in Australia	69,312
Do. North America	435,511
Do. West Indies	613,632
Hayti	78,936
Cuba and Foreign W. Indies	283,596
United States of North America	358,573
Texas	1,452
Mexico	147,143
Columbia	128,641
Brazil	786,572
Rio de la Plata	374,451
Chili	555,002
Peru	354,265
Guernsey, Jersey, Man, &c.	47,781
Total	12,887,220

2. Hosiery, Lace, and small Wares.

Germany	£184,341
France	131,136
United States of North America	125,811
Belgium	91,380
Holland	70,282
British North America	49,979
British West Indies	42,549
Rio de la Plata	36,435
E. I. Co.'s Territories and Ceylon	35,366
Brazil	32,958
Italy and the Italian Islands	28,371
Chili	22,706
British Settlements in Australia	20,712
Cuba and Foreign W. Indies	19,639
Peru	19,636
Gibraltar	18,744
To 29 other countries, &c.	90,619
	1,020,664

3. Cotton Yarn and Twist.

Declared Value.

Germany	£2,842,628
Holland	1,609,460
Russia	1,256,172
East India Company's Territories and Ceylon	545,075
Italy and the Italian Islands	480,658
Turkey	319,590
China	245,965
Sweden	124,199
Syria and Palestine	123,174
Norway	30,964
Malta	27,270
Portugal	20,868
Ionian Islands	17,336
Egypt	15,529
All other countries	112,576
	7,771,464

4. Exports of cotton twist and yarn, at various periods from 1820 to 1842:

lbs.	lbs.
1820 . 23,032,325	1835 . 83,214,198
1825 . 32,641,604	1840 118,470,223
1830 . 64,645,342	1842 .137,466,892

COUNCIL OF THE CHURCH, an assembly of prelates who meet, being duly convoked by the legitimate authority, for the purpose of defining questions of doctrine, or making regulations or canons in matters of discipline. There are various sorts of councils:

1. General or Œcumenic councils, which are considered as a representative and legislative assembly of the whole church, and to which all bishops are summoned. In the early ages of the Christian Church the general councils were convoked by the Roman Emperor; they have been since convoked by the Popes, at least for the Western or Roman Church. The authority of general councils is considered as binding on the whole church only in matters of faith when the canon establishes a dogma which it enjoins all the faithful to believe under pain of anathema and heresy. In matters of faith the Roman Church considers a general council to be infallible: some say, however, only after its canons have been confirmed by the Pope. All bishops have a right to attend and vote in a general council; the abbots and generals of monastic orders have also been admitted to vote in most councils by consent of the council. Priests and monks have also attended the councils as theologians and advisers, with a consultative and deliberative vote. In the Western Church the Pope, or his legate for him, presides in the council. For a council to be legitimate it is required that all the bishops should be called, whether they attend or not, except those who are declared by the church to be schismatical or heretical, and all deliberations should be free and unconstrained.

2. National councils, consisting of the bishops of a whole kingdom or state, which can be convoked by the sovereign power of such state; but the authority of such council is limited to the kingdom or state for which it is convened.

3. Provincial councils are convoked by the respective metropolitans, with the consent of the sovereign power, or the king, as in England. A bishop may also convoke a diocesan council, with the consent of his superior. (Benedict XIV. de Synodo diocesana.) The Church of Rome reckons several councils, though not œcumenic, previous to that of Nice, the earliest of which seems to be that held at Jerusalem, about A.D. 50, and which was attended by the apostles Peter, John, James, and Barnabas, and which is mentioned in the fifteenth chapter of the 'Acts of the Apostles.'

COUNCILLORS. [MUNICIPAL CORPORATIONS.]

COUNSEL, an abbreviation of counsellor. In England a counsellor is a barrister [BARRISTER], or one who has kept twelve terms at one of the four inns of court, and has been called to the bar. After keeping his terms a man may act as a conveyancer, special pleader, or equity draftsman, without being called to the bar, but he must take out a certificate under 9 Geo. IV. c. 49. The word counsel has no plural number, and is used to denote either one or more counsel. The duty of counsel is to give advice in questions of law, and to manage causes for clients. They are styled common-law, equity, or chamber counsel, according to the nature of the business they transact. They are supposed to work for nothing, but in fact they are paid. But, according to Mr. Justice Bayley, 1 Chit. R. 351—"they are to be paid beforehand, because they are not to be left to the chance whether they shall ultimately get their fees or not, and it is for the purpose of promoting the honour and integrity of the bar that it is expected all their fees should be paid when their briefs are delivered. That is the reason why they are not permitted to maintain an action for their fees." Though it is expected that all their fees should be paid before the work is done, this is very far from being the general practice; and sometimes the payment is deferred, and sometimes it happens that it is never made. The counsel is paid by the attorney or solicitor of the person whose business he does. Counsel may be retained generally, that is, to advocate any cause in which the retaining party may be engaged, or specially with reference to a pending cause; and generally speaking, a counsel cannot refuse a retainer: there are certain rules, however, by which their practice is regulated.

Counsel in a cause may urge and argue

upon anything which is contained in their instructions, and is pertinent to the matter in question, and it is not considered to be their business to inquire whether it be true or false: they are also at liberty to make comments on the evidence adduced on that part of the case to which they are opposed, and to cross-examine the witnesses of the opposite party.

Formerly, in cases of felony, counsel for the prisoner were not allowed to address the jury on his behalf: they might, however, examine and cross-examine the witnesses, and argue points of law; but now by stat. 6 & 7 Wm. IV. c. 114, all persons tried for felony may make full answer and defence by counsel.

Counsel are punishable by stat. West. 1. 3. Ed. I., c. 28, for deceit or collusion, and are so far under the jurisdiction of the judges, that in the event of malpractice they may be prohibited from addressing the court: there are also certain rules established by each court for the regulation of its own practice, to which counsel are subject.

COUNT, through the French word *comte*, from the Latin *comes, comitis,* meaning companion. The word, though simply meaning Companion, received various particular significations. Young Romans of family used to go out with the governor of a province and commander of armies, under whom they got an insight into public and military matters. They were called comites; Juvenal (*Sat.* viii. 127) speaks of the cohors comitum. Perhaps some of them acted as secretaries to the commander or governor, as in the case of Celsus Albinovanus, the friend of Horace, to whom he addresses the eighth epistle of the first book. With the establishment of the imperial power at Rome, comites were established about the emperor's person; and a great number of functionaries and officers received the title of comes, with some addition to indicate their duty. When the emperor sat as judge he had comites and jurisconsulti (jurists) with him. (Spartian, *Hadrian.* c. 18.) In the time of Constantine, comes became a title, and there were comites of the first and second class, and so forth. The term comes, as a title, was established both in the eastern and the western empire. Some of them were governors of provinces or particular districts. The rank and condition of these comites may be collected from the Theodosian Code, vi. tit. 12-20, with the commentary of Gothofredus (Godefroy). The kingdoms of modern Europe have inherited the tributary spoils of the lower empire. By substituting the word *grand* for that of *count*, which was a title common to all the officers or ministers of the emperors of the East, it is easy to show the analogy of the titles of modern court dignities to the antient. Thus the *comes sacrarum largitionum* has been called *grand almoner;* the *comes curiæ, grand master of ceremonies;* the *comes vestiarius, grand master of the wardrobe;* the *comes domesticorum, grand master of the royal household;* the *comes equorum regiorum, grand equerry,* &c. The *comes marcarum,* counts of the frontiers, which were formerly called *marches* (a denomination still in use in the papal states), took subsequently the title of *marquis;* an innovation which raised long and serious discussions among the learned in feudal right and court etiquette.

Under the first two races of the Frank kings, the counts were, as under the lower empire, officers of various degrees. The count of the palace was the first dignity in the state, after the *maire* of the palace. He presided in the court royal when the prince was absent, and possessed sovereign jurisdiction. He also exercised a great influence in the nomination of the king's delegates, who, under the title of counts, administered the provinces. A count had the government of a small district, often limited to a town and its dependencies. He was at the same time a judge, a civil administrator, and a military commander. In case of war, he led in person the contingent of his county to the army. The learned Dutillet, in his 'Recueil des Rois de France, de leur Couronne et Maison,' &c., expatiates on the functions of antient counts. With the progress of time, the counts, as well as the other officers appointed to govern the provinces, the towns, and the frontiers, succeeded in rendering their places hereditary, and in making themselves sovereigns of the districts of which they had only been created removable and revocable administrators.

COUNT. [701] COUNTY COURT.

At first they contented themselves with securing the reversion to their sons, then to their collateral heirs, and finally they declared those places hereditary for ever, under Hugh Capet, the son of Robert, count of Paris, who himself only obtained the throne partly in consequence of that concession. It was feudalism that introduced inheritance instead of election as a permanent rule in political successions. The supreme chief of the antient Franks, *koning* (Lat. *rex*), was a magistrate, and as a magistrate he was elected, although always from the same family. The inferior chiefs, *heri-zoghe, graven, rakhenberghe* (Lat. *duces, comites, judices*), were also elected. But when the feudal system attained its perfection, when men were no longer ruled by men, but lands by lands, and men by lands or by the legitimate heir of the lands, then no kind of election remained. One demesne made a king, as another made a duke, a count, a viscount, &c.; and thus the son of a count became a count, the son of a duke became duke, and the son of a king became king. Finally, to form a just idea of the formidable power of the feudal counts, we must refer to the period of the erection of the towns of the northern provinces of France into communalties or republics, when their heroic population had to sustain a most deadly struggle, from the eleventh century to the middle of the fourteenth, before they could shake off the iron yoke of the counts and the bishops. The term "count" is now become in France a mere title, conferring no political power. In the papal states, as well as in those of Austria, it may be bought for a moderate sum; and in the other monarchical states of the continent, it is granted as a mark of imperial or royal favour.

The title of *earl*, or, as it was often rendered in official Latin, *comes*, companion, is of very high antiquity in England, being well known to the Saxons under the name of *ealdorman*, that is to say, *elder-man*, and also *shireman*, because each of them had the government of a distinct *shire*, or, as it is now generally called, *county*. The sheriff, under his Latinized name, is called vice-comes, or viscount, which term is now one of the titles of rank in the British peerage. The term count seems not to have been used in England as a title of honour, though the wives of earls from a very early period have been addressed by the title of countess. The king, in mentioning an earl in any writ or commission, usually styles him "trusty and well-beloved cousin"—a peculiarity at least as antient as the reign of Edward III.

COUNTY. [SHIRE.]

COUNTY COURT. Before the superior courts of Westminster were created the County Courts kept by the sheriffs were the chief courts of the kingdom. Their powers were, however, greatly curtailed by Magna Charta, and their ordinary jurisdiction limited to debts under 40s. Specialty debts were not recoverable in them, and the cause must arise within the county. In consequence of the inadequacy of these tribunals, with the dilatory and expensive proceedings of other local courts, there were few courts of inferior jurisdiction in which debts above 40s. could be recovered. To remedy these deficiencies in local administration, the County Court Act of 1846 was passed, and gave increased facilities by a prompt, inexpensive, and simple procedure for the recovery of small debts.

The Act of 1846, the 9 and 10 Vict. c. 95, has been put in force by the Privy Council, who were empowered to divide counties; and any city, borough, or district, if more convenient to be included in an adjoining county. Local courts, already existing, to be held as county courts, and districts assigned them.

Another Act, 13 and 14 Vict. c. 61, extends the jurisdiction of the county courts to the recovery of any demand not exceeding 50l. With respect to fees, it provides that an attorney shall be entitled to a fee not exceeding 1l 10s. for his fees and costs, when the demand shall not exceed 35l. or a fee of 2l. in any other case within the jurisdiction of the Act. No fee, exceeding 2l. 4s. 6d. in amount, to be allowed for employing a barrister in any cause.

By the Act of 1846, the Lord Chancellor appoints the judges of the county courts, each of whom must be a barrister of seven years' standing, or a barrister, attorney, or other person who has presided as judge in a local court; and they are removable for inability, or their district may be changed.

By a reference to section 58, it will be seen what causes of action are within the jurisdiction of the County Courts. These are all pleas of personal actions, where the debt or damage claimed is not above 20*l*., whether on balance of account or otherwise; and with the view of confining suits for small debts to the new tribunals, the 128th section enacts, that "no costs shall be awarded to a plaintiff in a superior court, excepting where the plaintiff or defendant live twenty miles apart, if the verdict be for plaintiff for less than 20*l*. on contract, or 5*l*. on tort, unless the judge will certify that it was a proper action to be tried in a superior court."

A creditor whose debtor owes him above twenty pounds is at liberty to relinquish the difference beyond twenty pounds, and commence a suit for that sum; but if he obtain a judgment it will be a release to the defendant of all the excess that he owed to the plaintiff beyond twenty pounds; and even should the defendant not comply with the order of the court by paying the twenty pounds and costs, the plaintiff cannot afterwards sue him in a superior court for the original larger debt, for he will have made his election to proceed in the County Court, and must abide by its decision.

By the splitting of demands, the jurisdiction of the act has been sought to be extended to *collective debts* which in the whole exceed 20*l*.; but none of the decisions in the County Courts yet go the length of empowering a plaintiff in an arbitrary way to divide a cause of action. For example, if a plaintiff had a running account which amounted to 100*l*., he could not bring an action in the County Court for every item, or more than 20*l*., and the judgment of the court would be a bar to his recovering the remaining 80*l*.; but if it was stipulated between the plaintiff and defendant, prior to the commencement of the credit, that all goods delivered within two three, or six months should be paid for at the expiration of these respective periods, the plaintiff may enter a plaint for each cause of action, if the defendant failed to pay at the time when the credit expired; but the plaintiff could only bring one action against the defendant if the credit was given unconditionally: prohibiting splitting demands, in such a case, appears to be what was contemplated by the act. (Jagoe's *Practice of the County Courts*, p. 193.)

If an account is *settled* by two parties, consisting of several items, each of which separately would be a sufficient cause of action, it has the effect of consolidating them into one, which, if over 20*l*., cannot be sued for in a County Court without abandoning the excess. If there are two or more causes of action, that together do not amount to 20*l*., an action may be brought for each, the judge having no power to compel a plaintiff to consolidate causes of action; and the act gives a right to enter a plaint for each.

The judge has no power to imprison merely for failure of payment, either of the whole debt or any instalment. Imprisonment does not satisfy or extinguish the debt, and is meant only for the punishment of a positive offence by the fraudulent concealment of property, a contempt of court, or other wilful default.

This important act has doubtless effected a great improvement in one branch of the debtor laws. It comprises 143 clauses, and is too long for abridgment; but we shall endeavour to present a condensed analysis of the sections not already referred to.

The judges are not interdicted from acting as justices, if in the commission of the peace. Their salary is not to exceed 1200*l*., nor that of a clerk 600*l*. A barrister or attorney who has presided as a judge in a local court is eligible to a judgeship; but any attorney appointed a judge, who is in partnership, must dissolve such partnership within twelve calendar months. Officers of the court are not allowed to act as attorney or agent in the same court.

The actions for small debts withheld

whether on balance of account or otherwise, may be holden in the county court without writ, and such actions determined in a summary way. On the application of any person desirous to commence a suit, the clerk of the court shall enter in a book a plaint in writing, stating the names and the last known places of abode of the defendants, and the substance of the action intended to be brought; upon which a summons shall be served on the defendant so many days before the day on which the court shall be holden at which the cause is to be tried, as shall be directed by the rules; and delivery of such summons, in manner specified in the rules of practice, shall be deemed good service; no misnomer or inaccurate description of any person or place in any such plaint or summons shall vitiate the same, so that the person or place be therein described so as to be commonly known. Such summons may issue in any district in which the defendant shall dwell or carry on his business at the time of the action brought; or, by leave of the court for the district in which the defendant shall have dwelt or carried on his business, at some time within six calendar months next before the time of the action brought, or in which the cause of action arose.

A plaintiff having a cause of action for more than 50*l*. must not divide the claim for the purpose of bringing two or more actions; but if he has so done, he may abandon the excess, and the judgment of the court will be a full discharge of all demands in respect of such cause of action. Minors may sue under this Act for wages or piece-work, or for work as a servant; and the court has also jurisdiction in cases of partnership or intestacy; executors also may sue and be sued, and no privilege of exemption can be pleaded. Where two or more persons are liable, one may be sued, and on satisfying the judgment when obtained, such person may proceed for contribution against any other person jointly liable with him.

The judge is to determine all questions, whether of fact or of law, unless a jury be summoned; either plaintiff or defendant may demand a jury; or, where t'e amount is under 5*l*., if required, the judge, at his discretion, may grant a jury; the party giving notice of his requiring a jury, and this notice being communicated to the opposite party; and the party requiring a jury is to pay a deposit for payment of the jury, to be considered as costs in the cause. The number of the jury is to be five, and their verdict must be unanimous.

COUNTY RATE. County rates are taxes levied for the purposes of defraying the expenses to which counties are liable. They are levied either under the authority of acts of parliament, or on the principle that as duties are imposed upon a county, there must be a power to raise the money for the costs incurred in the performance of such duties.

The ancient purposes of the county rate "were to provide for the maintenance of the county courts, for the expenses incidental to the county police, and the civil and military government of the county; for the payment of common judicial fines; for the maintenance of places of defence (sometimes, however, provided by a separate tax common to counties and to other districts, called *burgbote*), prisons, gaols, bridges (when these were not provided for by a separate tax common to counties and to other districts, called *brukbote*), and occasionally high roads, rivers, and watercourses, and for the payment of the wages of the knights of the shire. Additions to these purposes, some occasional and some permanent, were made from time to time by statutes. The King's aids, taxes, and subsidies, were usually first imposed on the county, and collected as if they had been county taxes. But the first statute defining any of its present purposes (though now repealed as to the mode it prescribes for imposing the tax) was passed in the 22nd Hen. VIII. From that time up to the present, new purposes have constantly been added, and new and distinct rates were constantly created for purposes of comparatively little importance, and to raise sums of money quite insignificant in amount."— (*Report on Local Taxation*, by the Poor Law Commissioners.)

The assessment and collection of separate county rates was not only very inconvenient and troublesome, but so expensive that the charge of collection and assessment frequently exceeded the sum rated. For remedying this evil the 12 Geo. II. c. 29, was passed, whereby justices of the peace at general or quarter-sessions were enabled to make a general rate to answer the purpose of the distinct rates previously leviable under various acts of parliament for the purposes of bridges, gaols, prisons, and houses of correction, such rate to be assessed upon every town, parish, and place within the county, to be collected by the churchwardens and overseers along with the poor rates of every parish and paid over to the high constables of hundreds, by them to treasurers appointed by the justices, and again by them to whomsoever the justices should direct. The county rate for lunatic asylums is, however, by statute, a special rate, and so is likewise the county rate for shire-halls, assize courts, session-houses, judges' lodgings, &c.; but the provisions of the statutes under which these rates are levied are disregarded, and the justices pay the expenses out of the general county rate. This is the case also with the rate for the county and district police force, where such force is established, though it is directed to be a special rate. There are some other special rates which are required to be separate rates, one of which is the rate for reimbursing to overseers the costs incurred in the burial of dead human bodies found on the shore of the sea. The contributions of a whole parish to this rate would perhaps not amount to a farthing, and the expense is of course defrayed out of the general county rate.

In places where there is no poor's rate the county rate was directed by 12 Geo. II. c. 29, to be levied by the petty constable or other peace officer of the place in the same manner as poor rates are levied, and paid over by him to the high constable of the hundred. The counties of York, Derby, Durham, Lancaster, Chester, Westmoreland, Cumberland, and Northumberland, were excepted from the compulsory direction that the county rate should be levied along with the poor's rate, and it was left discretionary with the justices of those counties at quarter-sessions to direct the county rate to be levied either by the churchwardens and overseers along with the poor rate or by the petty constable, by an assessment after the manner of the poor-rate. The rates so levied are applicable to the repair of bridges, gaols, prisons, or houses of correction, on presentment made by the grand jury at the assizes or quarter-sessions of their wanting reparation. The act gave to the churchwardens and overseers a right of appeal against the rate on any particular parish to the justices at the next sessions. It also contained provisions enabling the justices to contract for repairs, to oblige collectors to account, &c. It was not the object of this act to impose any new rates, nor to vary the obligation to pay, but merely to facilitate the collection of the amounts previously leviable: it therefore contained an exception of places not theretofore liable to the payment of all or any of the county rates referred in the act, and also a provision that the rate should be assessed in every parish or place in such proportions as any of the rates by the former acts therein referred to had been usually assessed. But this last provision is now to be interpreted with reference to the next-mentioned act as applying only to the fair and equal proportionable rates.

By the 55 Geo. III. c. 51, further improvements were made in the assessments to county rates. The justices of counties at quarter-sessions were by it empowered to make a fair and equal county rate when circumstances required, for all the purposes to which the county stock or rate was then or should thereafter be made liable by law, extending to all parts of the county except liberties or franchises having a separate co-extensive jurisdiction. The act contained numerous provisions giving powers for enforcing payment of the rate; for ascertaining the value of property for the purpose of assessment; for regulating the right of appeal given by the former act; extending the provisions of the former act to that act; enabling counties where the rates had been regulated by local acts to make use of that act; extending the provisions of the act to places having commissions of the peace within themselves, &c.

By the 56 Geo. III. c. 49, extra parochial and other places, though not rateable to the relief of the poor, were made subject to county rates, and certain powers were given for the ascertainment of boundaries between counties, ridings, &c., and other places of separate jurisdiction for the purpose of assessing and levying county rates.

By the 57 Geo. III. c. 94, the provisions contained in the 56 Geo. III. c. 49, as to appeals, were repealed and other regulations established in that respect; and it was provided that where there were no high constables the constables of the parish or place might levy the rates on the warrant of the justices.

By 58 Geo. III. c. 70, all such parts of former statutes as provided that rewards should be paid out of the public revenue to prosecutors upon conviction for various crimes were repealed, and it was enacted that in future the county rates were to be charged with the allowances to prosecutors in such prosecutions. By subsequent statutes the costs in the prosecution of certain misdemeanours are paid out of the county rates. By 7 Geo. IV. c. 64, the principle of compensation to witnesses and prosecutors at the expense of the county was carried into effect more extensively. In 1836, however, the government determined that one-half of the expense of prosecutions and the conveyance of prisoners should be defrayed out of the public revenue.

By the 1 Geo. IV. c. 85, the powers of former acts were extended to places where there were no separate churchwardens, and where no separate or distinct poor rate has been made for any place extending into two or more counties, ridings, or other divisions; justices were empowered to appoint persons to tax and assess the county rate in extra-parochial places where no poor rate exists, and certain regulations were made as to distress for rates.

By the 4 & 5 Wm. IV. c. 48, all business relating to the assessment and application of county rate is to be transacted in open court held upon due notice.

By the 5 & 6 Wm. IV. c. 76, § 112, after a grant of a separate court of quarter-sessions has been made to any borough the justices of the county in which such borough is situate are not to assess any property therein to any county rate thereafter to be made, but (§ 113) such boroughs are to bear the expenses of prosecutions at the assizes.

By 7 & 8 Vict. c. 33, high constables are relieved from the duty of collecting the county rate and paying it to the county treasurer, and these functions are to be undertaken by the Boards of Guardians.

Several local acts have been passed from time to time for regulating the county rates in particular counties. On this subject see Burn's 'Justice of Peace,' 29th edit., *County Rate*, where the different purposes for which county rates may be levied are enumerated at length.

The expenditure of county rates in England and Wales in 1792 and 1832 was as follows:—

	1792 £.	1832 £.	Inc. p. Cent.
Bridges	42,237	74,501	76
Gaols, Houses of Correction, &c.	92,319	177,245	92
Prisoners' Maintenance, &c.	45,785	127,297	178
Vagrants	16,807	28,723	70
Prosecutions	34,218	157,119	359
Lieutenancy and Militia	16,976	2,116	
Constables	659	26,688	4338
Professional	8,990	31,103	248
Coroners	8,153	15,254	87
Salaries	16,315	51,401	215
Incidental	17,456	32,931	88
Miscellaneous, Printing, &c.	15,890	59,061	
	315,805	783,441	

The amount disbursed in 1834 under the different heads of expenditure for which provision is made by the county rates was as follows:—

£.
Bridges, Building and Repairs, &c. . . 72,532
Gaols, Houses of Correction, &c., and Maintaining Prisoners, &c. 222,787

COUNTY RATE. [704] COUNTY RATE.

	£
Shire-Halls and Courts of Justice, Building, Repairing, &c.	13,951
Lunatic Asylums	12,371
Prosecutions	131,416
Clerks of the Peace	31,880
Conveyance of Prisoners before Trial	31,030
Conveyance of Transports	10,370
Vagrants, Apprehending and Conveying	7,621
Constables, High and Special	14,007
Coroners	15,648
Debt, Payment of Principal and Interest	78,022
Miscellaneous	52,112
	693,747

The expenditure in the following years was as under:—

	£
1835	705,711
1836	699,845
1837	604,203
1838	681,842
1839	741,407
1840	855,552
1841	1,026,035
1842	1,230,718
1843	1,295,615

In the last three years the county police expenditure, which in 1843 amounted to 243,738l., is included.

From 1830 to 1838 the proportion of five heads of expenditure was 69 per cent. of the total expenditure:—Bridges, 9·3 per cent; Gaols, 9·7; Prisoners' Maintenance, 25·8; Prosecutions, 19·9; Constables and Vagrants, 4·3 per cent.

The county rate is levied on the same description of property as the poor's rate, that is, on lands, houses, tithes impropriate, propriations of tithes, coal-mines, and saleable underwoods: the term "lands" includes improvements of lands, by roads, bridges, docks, canals, and other works and erections not included under the term "houses." Under "houses" is comprehended all permanent erections for the shelter of man, beast, or property. Mines, other than coal-mines, are exempted, and the exemption extends to limestone and other stone quarries, or to other matter that is obtained by quarrying. The county rate is to be assessed upon parishes " rateably and equally according to the full and fair annual value of the messuages, lands, tenements, and hereditaments liable, or which might be liable, to be rated to the relief of the poor." The sum assessed in 1833 was about 8¾ per cent. (or rather more than one-twelfth) of the levy for the poor, out of which fund it is paid, and in 1843 the proportion was between one-sixth and one-seventh. About five-eighths of the assessment is paid by land, and three-eighths by houses, mills, manors, canals, &c. The act 55 Geo. III. c. 51, already mentioned, has not been found very successful in correcting unfair valuations, as the overseers on whom the revaluation depends have no interest in a low rateable value. "In some counties the contribution to the Land Tax serves as a scale for the proportionate contribution. In these cases the proportion has been unchanged since the year 1792, notwithstanding the subsequent alterations in the value of property. In other counties the valuation to the Property Tax made in the years 1814-1815 determines the scale of contribution. In other counties some ancient scale, of which the origin is unknown to the respective clerks of the peace, determines the proportion. In other counties the nominal valuation to poor's rate, uncorrected by the application of the powers of 55 Geo. III. c. 51, and made in some counties in or very early after the year 1739, and in other counties at various periods between that date and the present time, serves as the basis of the contribution to the county rate. All these various practices are alike complained of as unequal in the counties in which they are adopted." (Report on Local Taxation.)

In the session of 1845 a bill was brought in to amend the law relating to the assessing, levying, and collecting of county rates. It provided for the appointment by the justices at general or quarter sessions of a committee to consist of not more than eleven nor less than five justices, whose duty it should be to prepare a fair and equal county rate, with power to alter and amend it from time to time as circumstances might require. By § 4 the words "full and fair valuation" shall be taken to mean " the net annual value of any rateable property, that is to say, the rent at which the same might reasonably be expected to let for from year to year free of all tenants' rates and taxes, and tithe commutation rent-charge (if any), and deducting therefrom the probable average annual cost of the repairs, and insurance, and other expenses (if any), necessary to maintain them in a state to command such rent." The fate of this bill is not at present (May, 1845) known.

The proportion in the £ to the county rate valuation in England and Wales and for several of the counties is as follows:—
England, 3¼d.; Wales, 3½d.; Northumberland, 1¼d.; Bedford, 12½d.; Westmoreland, 2¼d.; Middlesex, 3½d.; Lancaster, 1¼d.; Anglesey, 2¼d.; Pembroke, 1d.

COURT BARON. [MANOR.]

COURT-MARTIAL, a tribunal occasionally instituted for the purpose of trying military and naval men for the commission of offences affecting discipline in either of those branches of the public service.

Courts for the trial of rebels by martial law appear to have early existed in this country; and in the time of Henry VIII. the Marshal of England held one regularly for the trial of causes connected with military discipline. In the reigns of Elizabeth and her successor, those courts of war, as they were called, were superintended not by the marshal, but by a president chosen for the purpose. This president was probably a general or field-officer, but captains of companies were allowed to sit as members. The colonel of each regiment was charged with the duty of preparing the evidence relating to offences which fell under his cognizance, and of bringing it before the court. But courts-martial in their present form were instituted in the reign of James II.; and in the ordinances of war published in 1686 they are distinguished as general or regimental. Subsequently to the revolution, their powers have been expressly regulated by parliament, and are fully detailed in what is called the Mutiny Act, which is revised and renewed every year. Naval courts-martial are regulated by the statute 22 Geo. II. c. 33.

General courts-martial are assembled under the authority of the king, or of an officer having the chief command within any part of his majesty's dominions to whom such authority may be delegated. Regimental courts-martial are held by the appointment of the commanding officer of the regiment. The East India Company's Mutiny Act empowers the governor-general in council, and the governor in council, at the presidencies of Fort William, Fort St. George, and Bombay, and at St. Helena, to appoint general courts-martial, or to authorize any military man not below the rank of a field-officer to do so. What are called detachment courts-martial may be either general or regimental, and their appellation is derived from the nature of the command with which the officer convening the court is invested.

The chief crimes of which a general court-martial takes cognizance are mutiny, abandonment of a fortress, post, or guard committed to the charge of an officer or soldier, disobedience of orders, and desertion: these crimes, if proved to their greatest extent, are punishable with death; and the penalty extends to any military man, being present, who does not use his best endeavours to prevent them. In desertion is included the fact of enlisting in any regiment without having had a regular discharge from that in which the offender may have last served. The practice of sending challenges between commissioned officers is punished with cashiering; between non-commissioned officers and privates, with corporal punishment: and, in all cases, seconds and accessories are held to be equally guilty with the principals. Self-mutilation, theft, making false returns of stores, and neglect of ordinary duty, in non-commissioned officers and privates, are usually punished by the infliction of a certain number of lashes, not exceeding one thousand; and men of the former class may, in addition to other punishments, be suspended, or degraded to the ranks. There are many offences which might tend to the subversion of discipline, but which are hardly capable of being precisely defined, as immoralities, and behaving in a manner unbecoming an officer and a gentleman; of these the courts-martial take cognizance, and on conviction the offender may be

2 z

dismissed from the service. At home, military men are not, in general, amenable to courts-martial for civil offences; but abroad, where there may be no civil courts, the case is different.

The provisions of the Mutiny Act affect not only the cavalry and infantry of the regular army, but extend to the officers and privates in the corps of artillery, engineers, and marines; to all troops in the employment of the East India Company, or serving in the colonies; to the militia during the time that it is assembled and being trained; and, lastly, to the yeomanry and volunteer corps. All are subject, without distinction, to trial and punishment by courts-martial.

The rules of the service require that the president of every general court-martial should be a field-officer, if one of that rank can be obtained; but, in no case, must he be inferior in rank to a captain. And it should be observed, that none of the members are to be subalterns when a field-officer is to be tried. As the president has the power of reviewing the proceedings, it is prescribed, and the propriety of the regulation is manifest, that he be not the commander-in-chief or governor of the garrison where the offender is tried. A judge-advocate is appointed to conduct the prosecution in the name of the sovereign, and act as the recorder of the court.

No general courts-martial held in Great Britain or Ireland are to consist of less than thirteen or nine commissioned officers, as the case may require; but in Africa and in New South Wales the number may be not less than five; and, in all other places beyond sea, not less than seven. Commonly, however, a greater number are appointed, in order to guard against accidents arising from any of the members being found disqualified or falling sick. An uneven number is purposely appointed, in order that there may be always a casting vote; and the concurrence of two-thirds of the members composing the court is requisite in every capital sentence. No officer serving in the militia can sit in any court-martial upon the trial of an officer or soldier in the regular army; and no officer in the regulars is allowed to sit in a court-martial on the trial of an officer or private serving in the militia. Likewise, when marines, or persons in the employment of the East India Company, are tried, the court must be composed of members consisting in part of officers taken from the particular service to which the offender belongs. The members both of general and regimental courts-martial take rank according to the dates of their commissions; and there is a particular regulation for those who hold commissions by brevet. [BREVET.] They are always sworn to do their duty, and witnesses are examined upon oath.

In the accusation the crime or offence must be clearly expressed, and the acts of guilt directly charged against the accused; the time and place must be set forth with all possible accuracy; and, at a general court-martial, a copy of the charge must be furnished by the judge-advocate to the accused, that he may have full opportunity of preparing his defence. The accused has the power of challenging any of the members, but the reason of the challenge must be given, and this must be well founded, otherwise it would not be admitted; for the ends of justice might be often defeated from the impossibility of getting members to replace those who were challenged.

The court must discuss every charge brought against the accused, throwing out only such as are irrelevant; and judgment must be given either upon each article separately, or the decision of the court upon all may be included in one verdict. The evidence is taken down in writing, so that every member of the court may have the power occasionally of comparing the proceedings with his own private notes; and he is thus enabled to become completely master of the whole evidence before he is required to give his opinion. At the last stage of the trial the decisions of the several members are taken in succession, beginning with the junior officer on the court: a regulation adopted obviously in order to insure the unbiassed opinions of those who might otherwise be influenced by deference to the members who are superior to them in age or rank.

Regimental or garrison courts-martial are appointed by the commanding officer, for the purpose of inquiring into criminal matters of the inferior degrees; and they are empowered to inflict corporal punishments to a certain extent only. The articles of war require that not less than five officers should constitute a court of this nature, or three when five cannot be obtained. The practice is to appoint a captain as president, and four or two subalterns as the case may be; the court has no judge-advocate to direct it; therefore the members must act on their own responsibility. The proceedings are to be taken down in writing, and the sentence cannot be put in execution till it has been confirmed by the commanding officer, or by the governor of the garrison.

No commissioned officer is amenable to a regimental court-martial; but if an inferior officer or private should think himself wronged by such, he may, on application to the commanding officer of the regiment, have his cause brought before a regimental court-martial, at which, if the complaint is judged to be well founded, he may on that authority require a general court-martial to be held.

An appeal may be made from the sentence of a court-martial by the party who conceives that he has suffered injustice: the appeal lies from a regimental to a general court-martial; and from this to the supreme courts of law in the kingdom. It is easy to imagine, however, that the superior court will refuse to receive the appeal unless there should be very satisfactory evidence that the merits of the case have not been fairly discussed.

After the sentence of the court-martial has been pronounced, it is transmitted to the king, who may either confirm it, or, if sufficient reason should exist, may, on the ground that the process is not complete till the royal sanction has been given to the judgment, return it to the court for revision; or again, by virtue of his prerogative, he may remit the punishment awarded.

The chief distinction between the trial by court-martial and by jury is, that in the latter the verdict must be unanimous, while in the former the concurrence of a majority only in opinion determines the verdict. The writers on military law have endeavoured to show that the advantages in this respect are on the side of the court-martial: they contend that every member of such court delivers the opinion which he has formed from the evidence before him; while it may frequently happen in other courts that, in order to procure unanimity, some of the jury must surrender their own opinions. It may be observed, however, that in such a case the decisions are at least of equal value, since, in the event of a concession of private judgment, the verdict is in fact formed on the opinion of the majority.

(Grose, *Military Antiquities*; Tytler, *Essay on Military Law*; Samuel, *Historical Account of the British Army*; Simmons, *On the Practice of Courts-Martial*, with *Supplement*.)

COURTESY OF ENGLAND is the title of a husband to enjoy for life, after his wife's decease, lands of the wife of which she and the husband were seised in deed in the wife's right, for an estate of inheritance, and to which issue of the marriage is born which by possibility may inherit. It is said to be called courtesy of England as being peculiar to this country. In the law of Scotland however it is known under the title of "jus curialitatis," and it is also stated in the laws of the Alemanni, Lindebrog, ' Codex Legum Antiquarum,' 1613, p. 387, 'Lex Aleman.' c. 92; though by the law of the Alemanni the husband took the inheritance under circumstances similar to those that establish the title to a life estate only in the English law. This title of the husband's tenancy of the estates of his wife depends upon a valid marriage, the seisin of the husband and wife in right of the wife during marriage of the same estate respecting which courtesy is claimed, issue born alive during the wife's life which is capable of inheriting, and the previous death of the wife. Lands held by the wife descendible only to her sons would not, in case of the birth of a daughter, be subject to this claim of the husband; nor would a child brought into the world by the cæsarean operation, after the mother's death, establish it. It differs from the similar right of the wife to dower in several respects. [DOWER.]

By the custom of Gavelkind, a man

2 z 2

may be tenant by the courtesy without having had issue by his wife; but he has only half of the lands, and he loses them if he marries again. There is no tenancy by the courtesy of copyhold lands except by special custom, and the customs are various. (Cruise, *Digest* i. 'Copyhold.')

COURTESY OF SCOTLAND, otherwise called in the law of that kingdom 'jus curialitatis,' or right of courtship, is substantially the same with the courtesy of England. As in the latter kingdom, five things are necessary to it; namely, marriage, that the wife is an heiress and infeft, issue, and the death of the wife.

As to the marriage, it must indeed be a lawful marriage, but it is not necessary that it be regular and canonical; it is sufficient that it is valid in law, whatever be the precise form in which it became so. According to the ancient borough laws, c. 44, the courtesy extended only to such lands as the woman brought in tocher; but afterwards it was the lands to which she had right by inheritance, as the law still is. It was always the law that the wife must be heritably infeft and seised in the lands. The fourth requisite is, inheritable issue born alive of the marriage; that is to say, the child born must be the heir of the mother's estate, and it must have been heard to cry; for though it be otherwise in England, crying is in Scotland the only legal evidence of life. In the last place, by such issue the husband has during the life of the wife only *jus mariti*, as Skene says (*De verb. signif.* voce *Curialitas*); after her decease he has *jus curialitatis*; or as Blackstone speaks, with reference to the law of England, the husband by the birth of the child becomes tenant by the courtesy *initiate*, but his estate is not *consummated* till the wife's death; which is the fifth and last requisite to give the complete right of courtesy, the husband needing no seisin or other solemnity to perfect his title.

COURT OF RECORD. [COURTS.]

COURTS. The word court has come from the French *cour*, which is from the Latin *curia*. The Roman citizens were originally distributed into thirty curiæ, which were political divisions; but the name curia was also given to the buildings in which the curiæ met. The place of assembly of the Roman Senate was also called curia, and the name is often used to signify the senate or body of senators. The name curia was in fact given to a place either for the celebration of religious observances or the transaction of civil business. The French word cour is defined to be "a part of the house which is not built upon, and is immediately behind the carriage entrance or other entrance, and in the better sort of houses is paved." (Richelet, *Dictionnaire*.) It also signifies the residence of a prince (Aula); the government of a country, as la cour de la France; the judges of a supreme court, or the court itself, as la cour de parlement. These various significations occur in the English language: we speak of the court of a house, of the king's court, of the high court of parliament, and of the courts of law and equity.

The courts of common law in this country, like most other branches of our constitution, have grown up gradually with the progress of the nation, and may be traced back, partly to the institutions of our Anglo-Saxon forefathers, and partly to the more artificial systems introduced under the government of the Normans.

From the earliest times of which we have any account, we find the tribunals of the Germanic nations consisting of a presiding officer, called graf reeve or earl, comes or count; together with certain assessors, whose denominations (and probably their functions also) were different among different tribes and at different periods. Of this nature were the earliest tribunals with which we are acquainted in this country. The most important of these was that whose jurisdiction extended over a shire or county, in which the presiding officer was at first the earl, alderman, or count; and subsequently, his deputy the vice-count or sheriff (shire-reeve). This tribunal exercised ecclesiastical as well as civil jurisdiction, and the bishop sat as an associate to the earl or sheriff.

The judicial functions of this court were divided into four distinct branches. The first included all ecclesiastical offences; and in these the bishop was judge, and the count or sheriff his assistant, and if the delinquent disregarded the censures of the church, he enforced the sentence by imprisonment. The second branch (in which the sheriff was judge) included all temporal offences, such as felony, assaults, nuisances, and the like. The third head included all actions of a purely civil nature: here the sheriff was the presiding officer, and executed the judgment; but the judges were the freeholders who did suit to the court. And, fourthly, the sheriff's court held an inquest yearly of frank pledge. One branch of the jurisdiction of this tribunal was abolished by William the Conqueror, who separated the ecclesiastical from the civil power, and the bishop was no longer associated with the civil magistrate. The view of frank pledge now exists only as a form, but the other two branches of jurisdiction still subsist, though with diminished power and importance.

In order to exercise his criminal jurisdiction, the sheriff was required twice in every year to make a tour or circuit of his county. The power of determining felonies was taken away by Magna Charta, but the remains of this tribunal are still known as the sheriff's tourn, in which cognizance is taken of false weights, nuisance, and other misdemeanors. The civil jurisdiction of the sheriff still continues in the county court, the powers of which were limited to cases under forty shillings, at least as early as the reign of King Edward I.: and that sum now (except in case of replevin) limits the ordinary jurisdiction of the county court.

The land over which the jurisdiction of the sheriff extended, is said to have been distinguished as reve land. The thanes or nobles had, in the lands granted to them, a similar jurisdiction of their own, both civil and criminal. (1, Reeve's *Hist. of English Law*, 7.) The limits between the jurisdiction of the sheriff and that of the lord were strictly preserved. But when the lord had no court, or refused to do justice, or when the parties were not both subject to his jurisdiction, the suit was referred to the tribunal of the reeve; and a suit commenced before the lord might be removed by the defendant before the higher tribunal.

The civil tribunal of the lord was similar to the county court in its constitution and its powers, except that the presiding officer was not a public functionary (as the reeve was), but the bailiff of the lord. This court still exists under the style of the court baron, and is incident to every manor in the kingdom. The judges are the freeholders who owe suit and service to the lord of the manor, and if there are not at least two such freeholders in the manor, the court is lost. This was formerly the proper court in which to commence real actions to try the title to lands within the manor. The lord's court in criminal cases, in which he had the same powers that the sheriff exercised in his turn, was called the Leet.

The same powers which were exercised over a particular manor by the court baron and court leet, were also exercised over particular hundreds by the hundred court and the leet of the hundred. But the number of these courts was much diminished by stat. 14 Edward III., by which all hundreds, except such as were of estate in fee, were rejoined (as to the bailiwick of the same) to the counties at large.

Besides these courts of inferior jurisdiction, there was also a Supreme Court in which the king presided. In the Saxon age, and for some time after, the legislative, the administrative, and the judicial functions of the government had not been separated; and the Wittenagemote, or meeting of the wise, was consulted by the king in all these departments indiscriminately. The Anglo-Saxon king had the same jurisdiction over his thanes that they had over their own vassals. He punished all enormous crimes committed against the king's peace. His court was likewise open to all those to whom justice had been refused in the inferior courts; and he had the power of punishing the judges if they pronounced an iniquitous sentence. It also seems probable that the king's court was a court of appeal, in which the judgments of all other tribunals, if erroneous, might be reversed.

The Norman Conquest does not seem to have produced any immediate change in the constitution of this national assembly, which thenceforth became more known as the Great Council. The members exercised the same varied functions as under the Saxons; but when they sat in their judicial capacity, they had the assistance of the great officers of state and certain persons learned in the law, styled justiciars, or justices. William the Conqueror also created an officer to preside over judicial business, under the title of chief justiciar. The functions of this court thus became gradually separated from the general business of the grand council; and from being held in the hall of the king's palace, it was distinguished by the style of Aula Regis. A great distinction was drawn between this and all the courts of Saxon origin, from the mode of authenticating its proceedings. There were at this time no written memorials of legal proceedings, and indeed of few other public acts; and when it was necessary to establish any judgment or statute which had been made by the king assisted by his council, it was usual to call the testimony of some of the nobles who were present, to bear *record* of the fact. In progress of time, all such proceedings were written down at the time on parchment, the nobles present signing their names as witnesses, and so bearing record of the truth of what was there alleged. The writing itself was called a Record; and it was held to be evidence so conclusive, that when produced, nothing was allowed to be alleged in derogation of it. The entry of proceedings on record was adopted in the judicial, as well as in the other departments of the great council, and hence the Aula Regis became distinguished as *a court of record*. The power and importance of the Aula Regis rapidly increased. It not only maintained the former powers of the council in punishing offences against the public, in controlling the proceedings of inferior courts, and in deciding on questions relating to the revenue of the king, but it engrossed also a great portion of the "common pleas," or causes between party and party. And though we may suppose that it was only the more important causes that were taken into the Aula Regis, yet as early as the reign of Edward I., when the jurisdiction of the county courts was confined to 40s., all actions above that amount were brought into the king's courts. The Aula Regis seems at a very early period to have been distinguished as exercising three several functions, according to the different natures of the causes that were brought before it, which are treated of in our earlier legal writers as Pleas of the King, Common Pleas, and Pleas of the Exchequer. The bond of connexion between these several jurisdictions was the chief justiciar, who presided over all of them. But in the reign of Edward III. this office was abolished, and thus were finally destroyed the unity of the Aula Regis and its connexion with the grand council, which became henceforth essentially a legislative body; and though it still retains traces of its original functions in its title of the *High Court* of Parliament, yet it has ever since ceased to exercise any judicial powers, except in cases of impeachment, or as a court of ultimate appeal. On the dissolution of the Aula Regis, the three courts of the King's Bench, the Common Pleas, and the Exchequer, had each of them a perfectly distinct and separate existence. The Court of King's Bench had the control of all inferior courts, and the cognizance of all trespasses against the king's peace; the Court of Exchequer had cognizance of all cases relating to the revenue; and the Court of Common Pleas was the only court for causes of a purely civil nature between private persons. The Courts of King's Bench and Exchequer still retain each of them its peculiar jurisdiction; and the Common Pleas is still the only court in Westminster in which the three real actions that remain since the passing of 3 & 4 Wm. IV. c. 27 can be tried; but the great mass of causes between party and party may now be brought indiscriminately in any of the three courts. The King's Bench and the Exchequer originally contrived by fictitious proceedings to appropriate to themselves a share in the peculiar jurisdiction of the Common Pleas.

There was likewise another court, of a more limited character, which, though held in the Aula Regis, does not appear ever to have been under the control of the chief justiciar, the Court of the Marshalsea, which had jurisdiction where one of the parties at least was of the king's household. Charles I. created by letters patent a new court, styled the Court of the Palace, with jurisdiction over all personal actions arising within the verge of the palace, that is, within twelve miles of Whitehall. These courts are now held together every Friday. The Court of Marshalsea is, in fact, disused, but the Palace Court is in active operation.

The Saxon kings had been in the habit of making progresses through their dominions for the purpose of administering justice. This practice was not continued by William the Conqueror; but he annually summoned his great council to sit at the three feasts of Easter, Whitsuntide, and Christmas, in three different parts of the kingdom—Winchester, Westminster, and Gloucester. But when the great mass of the legal business of the country was brought into the king's courts at Westminster, it became necessary to take some more efficient measures for the trial of causes in the country.

The first expedient adopted was to appoint itinerant judges, justices in Eyre, who travelled through the kingdom, holding plea of all causes civil or criminal, and in most respects discharging the office of the superior courts. These itinera, or Eyres, usually took place every seven years.

About the end of the reign of Edward III. this system was wholly discontinued, except as to pleas of the king's forests, the functions of the justices in Eyre being superseded by the justices of Nisi Prius. This system was first established by a statute of Edward I., which, in order to prevent the expense of bringing up the juries to the king's courts at Westminster, provided that certain judges of those courts should be appointed to make circuits twice a year for the trial of issues upon which judgment was to be given in the court above. This system is still in operation. The justices of Nisi Prius also receive commissions of Oyer and Terminer and of gaol delivery, to authorize them to try criminals; and a commission of assize under which they used to try a peculiar species of action called assizes. These actions have long been obsolete; but the name of assizes is still given to the sittings of the justices on circuit under their several commissions.

Under the Norman kings the fines, amerciaments, and forfeitures in the king's courts constituted a considerable portion of the revenue, and the administration of justice was an important branch of the royal prerogative; but, like other branches of the prerogative, we sometimes find it in the hands of a subject, either by grant from the crown, or by prescription, which, according to legal notion, supposes a grant, though such supposition is often at variance with probability: within the counties Palatine and other royal franchises, the earls or lords had regal jurisdiction, saving the supreme dominion of the king. They had the same right as the king to pardon offences; they appointed judges of eyre, assize, and gaol delivery, and justices of the peace; all legal proceedings were made in their name, and offences were said to be committed against their peace, as in other places against the peace of the king. These royal prerogatives were, for the most part, re-annexed to the crown by stat. 27 Hen. VIII.; but the form of the judicial establishment still remained. [PALATINE COUNTIES.] But besides these palatinate jurisdictions, created to increase the power and gratify the pride of the nobles on whom they were conferred, the crown has also from time to time created courts, with a jurisdiction united in point of territory, and always under the control of the king's superior courts. If, in the Saxon times, the boroughs had courts similar to those of the hundreds, there are now no traces to be found of their existence; but however that may be, it is certain that when commerce increased, it was found of the utmost importance to the boroughs to be relieved from the jurisdiction of the feudal lord, and at the same time to have some court of justice to apply to, less distant, dilatory, and expensive than the king's courts at Westminster; and accordingly there has, at some time or other, been granted to almost every borough of any importance a civil and criminal jurisdiction within certain prescribed limits. These courts were in all cases courts of record, but in other respects were not modelled on any uniform system. There was the greatest possible variety in their constitution and the extent of their powers; but the mode of proceeding in all of them was founded on the common law and the practice of the superior courts, and a writ of error lay into the King's Bench, except from the courts of London and the Cinque Ports. By far the greater number of these courts have fallen into disuse. One of the causes of their inefficiency, the want of competent judges and juries, has been partially removed by the Municipal Corporations Act, and a greater uniformity has been introduced by giving to all of them jurisdiction as far as 20*l*. But in order to bring these courts into active operation, it still remains for the legislature to provide some more simple means for carrying on their ordinary proceedings; to give them better means of executing process, and of compelling the attendance of witnesses; to secure the efficiency and responsibility of the inferior ministers, and to restrict the power of removing trifling suits into the superior courts. The general incompetency of inferior courts in carrying on the ordinary proceedings in a cause is attested by a plan which has lately been introduced by the legislature. Any of the courts at Westminster is authorized, when a cause commenced there has been carried through all its preliminary stages, to send it by writ of trial, to be tried before any inferior judge, and, after trial, the cause is returned, and judgment given in the superior court. If the borough courts should ever be brought into a state of activity, the system of writs of trial, which is merely a substitute for local tribunals, would probably fall to the ground.

Whenever that time shall arrive, it will be a curious thing to trace the history of the administration of justice, which, under the Saxons, essentially local, rising from the smaller jurisdiction gradually to the higher, became, under the Norman dynasty, centered in one point, the king being the fountain of justice.

This system of centralization, connected as it was with the principles of feudalism, which so long prevailed in this island with peculiar force, was elaborated, in the course of centuries, to a high state of perfection; it absorbed the remains of the ancient local jurisdictions, and stunted all attempts at the establishment of new. But as the artificial systems and feudal associations, which owed their establishment here to the Normans, gradually wear away, people are prepared to revert to the simpler and more popular institutions which existed ages ago among our forefathers, and which seem to be peculiarly adapted to the character of the Germanic nations.

There is a great distinction between Courts of Record and courts not of record: courts of record are the king's courts of common law, and have power to fine and imprison, which is not the case with courts not of record. From the judgment of a court of record there lies an appeal to the superior courts by writ of error: in courts not of record this is effected by a writ of false judgment. The county court, court baron, and hundred court, are courts not of record. The other courts of common law which we have mentioned are courts of record.

The great mass of the litigation of the kingdom is carried on by means of the superior courts of Westminster. In each of these courts there is a chief justice and four puisne judges. In the Exchequer these are styled the chief baron and barons, a title which points to the time when their office was filled by the lords of parliament. Another remnant of the original constitution of the courts appears in the judges being addressed as "my lord," which is always given to the judges in their official character.

The number of puisne judges has varied at different times. During the reigns of the Stuarts there were frequently four, but after the revolution the number seems to have been constantly three in each court, constituting, together with the two chief justices and the chief baron, the twelve judges of England. By an act of parliament of the year 1830, a fourth puisne judge was added to each court, making the total number of the superior judges of common law fifteen instead of twelve. But the five judges never sit all together, the full court consisting, as formerly, of four only.

During the terms, which are four periods in the year of about three weeks each, the three courts sit at Westminster for the determination of all questions of law; and twice a year fourteen of the judges make their circuits through England and Wales, to try, with the assistance of juries, all disputed questions of fact that arise in the country. Actions brought in Middlesex or London are tried in the same manner at the sittings which are held on certain days in and immediately after every term.

From each of the three courts there lies an appeal by writ of error to the Court of Exchequer Chamber. This is not a permanent court, consisting always of the same members; but from whichever of the three courts the appeal is made, it is brought before the judges of the other two. From the constitution of this tribunal, it is evident that where any considerable difference of opinion exists among the fifteen judges, it is incapable of effecting one of the chief purposes of a court of appeal—that of producing uniformity of decision; and, accordingly, a further appeal lies by writ of error to the House of Lords.

For the history of the courts, see Reeve's *History of the English Law*; Maddox's *History of the Exchequer*; Palgrave's *Progress of the English Commonwealth*; Allen's *Inquiry into the Prerogative*.

COURTS CUSTOMARY. [COPYHOLD.]

COURTS ECCLESIASTICAL. [ECCLESIASTICAL COURTS.]

COURTS OF RECORD. [COURTS.]

COVERTURE. [WIFE.]

CREDENTIALS. [AMBASSADOR.]

CREDIT, in commerce and in political economy, signifies the trusting or lending of one man's property to another. The man who trusts or lends is said to give credit, and he who is trusted is said to obtain it. The one is called a creditor, and the other a debtor.

Credit is given either in goods or in money. By the former mode goods are supplied to a purchaser, for which the payment is deferred for some fixed period, or indefinitely, and the person who supplies them indemnifies himself for the delay by an increased price. By the latter mode, money is advanced, upon security or otherwise, and interest is charged upon the loan. [INTEREST; MORTGAGE.] Both these modes are used, in conjunction with each other, in the large transactions of commerce. A manufacturer, for example, sells to a merchant, for exportation, goods to the value of a thousand pounds. The merchant, however, is unable to pay for them until he has received remittances from abroad; and the manufacturer, aware of his solvency, is contented to receive in payment a bill of exchange, due at some future period. [EXCHANGE, BILL OF.] But in the mean time he is himself in need of money to carry on his business; and instead of waiting for the payment of the bill when it shall become due, he gets it discounted by a banker or other capitalist. Thus having given credit to one person in goods, he obtains credit from another in money. In this and other ways capital is circulated and applied to the various purposes for which it is required. But without entering further upon the practical methods by which the mercantile system of credit is conducted, it is proposed to inquire into its causes and into its economical uses and results.

There can be no system of credit until there has been a considerable accumulation of capital; for when capital first begins to be accumulated, those who possess it apply it directly in aid of their own labour. They have no superfluity which they can afford to lend to others; and they are generally engaged in some business in which their savings can be profitably employed. As a country increases in wealth, many persons acquire capital which they cannot employ in their own business, or can only employ by offering inducements to purchase in the shape of deferred payments. Others, again, inherit capital from which they wish to derive an income without the trouble of personally superintending its application. It is from these classes of persons that lenders of capital arise; and they have no difficulty in finding borrowers. Setting aside that countless class of mankind whose maxim it is to get money or money's worth, honestly if they can, but at all events to get it—who will borrow whenever others will lend, and reckon the loan as so much money earned, most men have an instinctive perception that the next best thing to having capital of their own is to have the use of the capital of others. The efficacy of capital is very soon discovered as an instrument for the production of wealth, and those who have it not are willing to pay for its use; or, in other words, to share with a capitalist the profits of their own industry, on condition that he intrusts to them such funds as they require for making it productive. Thus as soon as a sufficient capital exists, a system of credit has a natural tendency to arise, and will continue to grow with the increase of capital, unless it be checked by a general insecurity of property, by imperfect legal securities for the payment of debts, or by a want of confidence in the integrity of the parties who desire to borrow. When the society and laws of a country are in a sound state, and capital is abundant, credit comes fully into operation.

The precise use of credit as an agent in the production of wealth is that it gives circulation to capital, and renders it available wherever it can be most profitably employed. It does for capital what division of employments does for labour. Without augmenting its quantity it increases its utility and productiveness. Credit, in fact, may be best understood by regarding it as one of the many forms in which the division of employments facilitates the production of wealth. Without the aid of capital, the labour of man is comparatively ineffectual; and credit, by circulating capital among those who are engaged in the productive employment of labour, promotes the most essential of all divisions of industry—that which uses and makes effective the ingenuity of men in those pursuits for which they are adapted. [DIVISION OF EMPLOYMENTS.]

To employ capital productively is a business requiring great knowledge, skill, and industry; and is rendered more effective by a division of superintendence, as manual labour is facilitated by a judicious distribution of employments among several hands. Every man who borrows money for the legitimate purposes of industry, and applies it with judgment, is really the agent of the capitalist, in executing duties which the capitalist himself would be unable to perform. A man's capital would be comparatively useless without an active superintendence, and a union of skill and industry in a particular business. These qualities are placed at his disposal by the system of credit, and stimulated to exertion by a share in the profits arising from the use of his capital. If the capitalist should trust persons improvidently, these useful results will not follow; but it is his peculiar province, as it is his interest, to exercise caution and judgment in the investment of his own capital; and if he fail to do this, his fortune will suffer in precisely the same manner as if he superintended a factory himself without understanding the business, and employed idle and ignorant foremen and unskilled operatives.

These illustrations will suffice to explain the nature and uses of credit: but it must always be borne in mind that in circulating capital and making it available in aid of industry, it calls no new capital into existence. It makes the existing capital of a country more productive, and consequently accelerates the accumulation of fresh capital; but credit cannot be, in itself, a substitute for capital. A man without any capital of his own may carry on business by the aid of credit; but he is merely using the capital of another. No man can lend his money, and still use it himself. It is not ubiquitous—nor can it serve two purposes at once. If a man does not use his own capital, he may lend it to another to use; but it is impossible that he can both use it himself and allow another to use it at the same time. He cannot use it in person and by proxy.

Stated in this manner, the truth of these principles is obvious; yet so great is the influence of credit in stimulating enterprise, that it is constantly mistaken for a distinct productive agency. Thus it is said, for example, that wherever credit is freely obtained in a country, great prosperity is the result; and it is undeniable that facilities in obtaining credit and prosperity are ordinary concomitants; but they are both equally the results of an abundance of capital seeking employment, under circumstances favourable for its profitable use. If credit be granted too freely for the amount of capital by which it is supported, or if it be forced beyond the natural demands of trade, speculations and improvidence are encouraged which are ruinous to the parties concerned, and deeply injurious to society. An apparent prosperity exists for a time, but when the day of reckoning arrives, it is discovered that credit, instead of creating capital, has merely diverted it from one investment to another more speculative and hazardous, which at best can only be made ultimately profitable by a continuance of the credit by which it was encouraged. But if this credit be limited or withdrawn, what becomes of the fictitious capital upon which so much reliance had been placed? Without any failure of the enterprise, the capital by which it was conducted is gone at once. This could not happen if credit created capital; but it is perfectly accounted for when it is understood that capital, however it may be circulated and made accessible by credit, in order to be applied to any new object must have been withdrawn from another, to which it is liable to revert. As one of the forms in which capital is distributed, a system of credit is of the highest value; but if relied on as an independent equivalent of capital, it is delusive or fraudulent. [MONEY.]

As yet that description of credit which consists in defined payments for goods has only been generally adverted to; but we cannot close this article without a special notice of its peculiar character and effects. This system of credit is generally resorted to by tradesmen to increase their business; and it is undeniable that deferred payments offer a strong temptation to purchase. We are always eager to possess, and the cost of possession appears small in remote perspective. When a customer buys an article for which he is not to pay for twelve months, he becomes indebted for its value, and he has also, in fact, borrowed that amount of the tradesman, to whom he must ultimately repay—1st, the cost price of the article; 2ndly, the profit upon the sale; and, 3rdly, the year's interest upon the amount advanced. The tradesman, if he have capital, and can rely upon ultimate payment, is very glad to encourage purchases, and not only to sell his goods, but to charge a high rate of interest for deferred payments. If he have not a sufficient capital, he must borrow money from others to enable him to give credit; and, of course, he will charge to his customers a higher interest than he has paid himself. In either case he runs considerable risk, for the debts contracted in this manner are devoid of all security. The goods are supplied and consumed; and if the parties fail in payment, there can be no restitution or compensation. When the system is fully established, many persons avail themselves of it dishonestly; others are improvident, and without intentional fraud, exceed their means, and become insolvent; and various accidental circumstances may prevent the tradesman from recovering his debts. His risk, therefore, is exceedingly great; and in charging interest for his loans, he must cover all his losses. He consequently charges not only a reasonable interest for the risk which he runs in each case, but also an insurance against all the losses which he may incur in his business. Thus a customer pays the price of his own purchases, a high rate of interest for his loans, and a portion of the unpaid debts of other people. Nor can any check be placed upon the creditor, as in other forms of credit. No specific sum is advanced with a stipulated interest; but a gross amount is due, in which the rate of interest is concealed. It may be exorbitant, and out of all proportion to the value of the article supplied, and the accommodation given; but it is not separable from the delusive price. This circumstance is an obvious encouragement to fraud; and it has a tendency to raise prices injuriously to the consumer; an evil which even extends itself, in a great measure, to purchases paid for in ready money.

It is the abuse, however, or the excessive use of this form of credit, which is mischievous. If properly used, and within reasonable limits, it is as useful as credit in any other form. A few examples will suffice to illustrate this position. The receipts of different consumers are irregular; their consumption constant. Within the year their receipts and expenditure may be about the same; but in point of time, they cannot be accurately balanced and adjusted one to the other. This system of credit enables them to provide for themselves and their families without privation, and at the cost of no one else. By an operation scarcely perceptible, their receipts and expenses are adjusted. If, instead of satisfying their wants, they had suffered privation, trade would have been injured and capital employed less fully. Again, a man who pays for everything he consumes a year hence practically adds to his capital a sum equal to the value of his consumption. He gains a whole year of productive industry in advance of his own subsistence. It is true that he will ultimately have to pay for it, together with a high interest; but if he has been able, in the meantime, to apply this additional capital so productively as to leave a balance in his favour, he has enriched himself and the community. The tradesmen who have trusted him, and the capitalists by whom they have been aided, will have made a profit upon his consumption, and have realized the interest upon their loans; while he will have given more employment to capital and to labour than he would have been able to give if he had been compelled to pay for his own subsistence from day to day.

In various other ways credit, in this form, is a valuable auxiliary to capital and industry; but whenever it is injudiciously given or accepted it becomes injurious. In this respect it does not differ from other forms of credit. The precise uses of credit in general have been already explained. In whatever form it is judiciously and honestly applied it is an efficient agent in the circulation and productive use of capital; but whenever it is used without judgment or fraudulently abused, it becomes injurious, and wastes capital instead of encouraging its growth. All great means conducive to social good are, unhappily, liable to perversion and abuse. The public credit of nations and mercantile credit have too often been abused, as recently, in the most signal manner, by the Americans; and the system of tradesmen's credit has also been shamefully perverted; but all alike are conditions inseparable from the application of capital to the infinite purposes for which it is required. The advantages of credit are so great that it will always be extensively used in every form of which it is susceptible; but its evils may be mitigated by the judgment and experience of capitalists, and by improved laws for adjusting the relations between debtor and creditor. [DEBTOR AND CREDITOR; NATIONAL DEBT.]

CREDIT, LETTER OF, is an order given by bankers or others at one place, to enable a person to receive money from their agents at another place. The person who obtains a Letter of Credit may proceed to a particular place, and need only to carry with him a sum sufficient to defray his expenses; and it gives him some of the advantages of a banking account when he reaches his destination, as he may avail himself of it only for part of the sum named in it. If it were not for the convenience which a Letter of Credit affords, a person who was intending to make a tour on the Continent, for example, would be under the necessity either of taking with him the whole of the sum which he would require during his absence, or of receiving remittances from home, addressed to him at particular places.

A Letter of Credit is not transferable. By a strict interpretation of a clause in the Stamp Act (55 Geo. III. c. 184), an instrument of this nature would seem to be liable to the same duty as on a bill of exchange payable to bearer or order; but in practice the duty is openly evaded. If the law were more stringently acted upon, evasion of the duty could be easily practised, as a banker, instead of granting a written instrument, could advise his agent privately to pay certain sums to certain parties, according as the agent might be advised.

CRIME AND PUNISHMENT [TRANSPORTATION.]

CRIMINAL CONVERSATION. [ADULTERY.]

CRIMINAL LAW. [LAW, CRIMINAL.]

CROWN SOLICITOR. In state prosecutions in England the solicitor to the treasury acts as solicitor for the crown in preparing the prosecution. In Ireland there are officers called crown solicitors attached to each circuit, whose duty it is to get up every case for the crown in criminal prosecutions. They are paid by salaries. There is no such system in England; where prosecutions are conducted by solicitors appointed by the parish or other persons bound over to prosecute by the magistrates on each committal; but in Scotland the still better plan exists of a crown prosecutor in every county, who prepares every criminal prosecution whatever.

CURATE, PERPETUAL. [BENEFICE, p. 343.]

CURA'TOR, from the Latin Cura, 'care.' Curators in ancient Rome were public officers of various kinds, particularly after the time of Augustus, who established several officers with this title. (Suet., *Augustus*, cap. 37.)

1. Curatores viarum, that is, curators who superintended the laying out and repairing of the public roads. This office existed under the Republic (Cicero, *Ad Attic.* i. 1), but it was only held as an extraordinary office, and was conferred only for special purposes.

2. Curatores operum publicorum, aquarum, cloacarum, who had the superintendence of the public buildings, theatres, bridges, aqueducts, and cloacæ.

3. Curatores alvei Tiberis, who were the conservators of the Tiber.

4. Curatores frumenti populo dividundi, whose duty was to distribute corn among the people. Under the emperors we find other officers with the name of curatores; as, for instance, the curatores ludorum, who had the superintendence of the public amusements: and curatores reipublicæ, also called logistæ, whose duty it was to administer the landed property of municipia.

Curator is also the name of a person who was appointed to protect persons in their dealings who were above the age of puberty and under the age of twenty-five years. On attaining the age of puberty, which was fourteen according to some authorities, a youth acquired full legal capacity, and he could act without the intervention of a tutor. But though he had thus attained full legal capacity, it was considered that he still required protection, and this was given him by a Lex Plætoria, the date of which is uncertain, but it is as old as the time of Plautus, who alludes to it. The effect of this law was to divide all males into two classes, those above twenty-five years of age and those below, who were sometimes called minores or minors. The object of the law was to protect minors against fraud, for the minor, if he had been cheated in a contract, might plead the Lex Plætoria against an attempt to enforce it. Probably, also, a man who dealt with a minor might protect himself against any risk of the dealing being called in question, by requiring the minor to have a curator for the occasion. It would not be the business of the curator to assent to the contract of the minor, who had full legal capacity, but to prevent his being cheated. The prætorian edict extended the principle of the Lex Plætoria by setting aside all transactions by a minor which might be injurious to him; but it was necessary for the minor to apply to the prætor for redress during his minority, or within one year after he had attained his majority. The remedy that the prætor gave to the minor was the "in integrum restitutio," which means restoring the applicant to his former position by setting aside the contract or dealing.

Till the time of the Emperor Marcus Aurelius, it appears that a minor only had a curator on special occasions, as when he wished to make a contract. In this case he applied to the prætor, and stated the grounds on which he applied. The prætor then gave him a curator if he thought proper. We must suppose that the application would only be made when the matter was of some importance. The object of the application was the security of the person who dealt with the minor, and the benefit of the minor also; for a prudent person would not deal with him without such security. The Emperor

Aurelius established it as a general principle that all minors should have curators. The subject of the Roman curators is fully investigated by Savigny. (*Von dem Schutz der Minderjährigen, Zeitschrift für Geschichtliche Rechtswissenschaft*, x.) If a man was wasting his property imprudently (prodigus), his next of kin (agnati) were his curators; and the same was the rule as to a man who was out of his mind (furiosus). The law of the Twelve Tables fixed this rule; and in cases to which the law of the Twelve Tables did not apply, the prætor named a curator or committee.

It may be just as well to warn people not to confound a Roman Curator with a Roman Tutor [TUTOR].

CURRENCY. [MONEY.]

CURSITOR BARON, an officer of the Court of Exchequer, is appointed by patent under the great seal to be one of the barons of the Exchequer. He attends at Westminster to open the court prior to the commencement of each of the four terms, and on the seal day after each term to close the court. He administers the oaths to all high-sheriffs and under-sheriffs who are sworn by the court, and to several officers of revenue. Prior to 1833 he had various other duties to perform; but since the passing of the act 3 & 4 Will. IV. c. 99, much of the business of his office has entirely ceased; and the commissioners appointed under the 1 Will. IV. c. 58, in reporting on the consolidation of the offices in the Courts of Queen's Bench and Common Pleas, recommended the abolition of the office of cursitor baron. This recommendation however has not been carried into effect. (*Report of Commissioners on offices of Courts of Justice*, 1822; *Parl. Paper*, No. 125; *Parl. Paper*, 1835, No. 314.)

CUSTOMARY FREEHOLD. [COPYHOLD.]

CUSTOMS, or USAGES (consuetudines), are either general or local. The first kind consist of those usages which have prevailed throughout England from time immemorial: their origin is unknown, but having been recognized by judicial decision,* they form that common law, or lex non scripta, which is the foundation of English Law. To like immemorial usage is to be ascribed the existence of such parts of the Roman and canon laws, as from the earliest times have formed the rule in the king's ecclesiastical, military, and admiralty tribunals, and also in the courts of the two English universities. These laws of foreign origin subsist however only as inferior branches of the customary law, subject to control by the superior temporal courts, and to a strict adherence to the rules of construction observed by these courts in the interpretation of statute law.

These general customs of the realm, which form the common law, properly so called, alone warrant the existence and jurisdiction of the king's superior courts; and can only be drawn into question there. These general customs, as originally methodized by the Saxon kings, and in some cases modified in the early Norman reigns, supplied those fundamental rules by which, in cases not otherwise regulated by statute, the law of inheritance, the interpretation of acts of parliament, and most of the remedies for civil and criminal injuries are regulated. Numerous axioms essential to the administration of justice have no other binding force than antient and uninterrupted usage, which has obtained the force of law by the recognition of the courts. [COMMON LAW.]

Among these general customs are those rules which prevail among the particular bodies of men to which they relate; merchants, innkeepers, carriers, owners of lands adjoining the sea-coast, &c. &c., as well as the inhabitants of particular counties or boroughs, in the particular instances of gavelkind and Borough Eng-

---

* Bracton's definition of a custom is this— 'Consuetudo vero quandoque pro lege observatur, in partibus ubi fuerit more utentium approbata, et vicem legis obtinet, longævi enim tem poris usus et consuetudinis non est vilis authoritas.' (Bracton. fol. ii., ed. Lond. 1569.) This is no inapt definition of a custom observed as if it were law, by those who find it convenient and reasonable; but we can hardly conclude from this passage that this excellent old writer clearly saw that custom could not be law till made so by the sovereign power, or those to whom the sovereign power has delegated parts of its authority.

lish. That custom called the law of the road, by which riders and drivers are expected to keep the left hand, as well as that respecting servants hired at yearly wages, by which either master or servant may determine the contract at a month's warning, or on paying a month's wages, have been recognized by the courts from time to time as parts of the common law. These, like the rest, originated in general convenience, and being gradually drawn more into notice by frequent recurrence, have been finally sanctioned by judicial authority. For the principle of immemorial customs may be extended to things and circumstances which arise at the present times. Thus a custom from time immemorial that all officers of a court of justice shall be exempt from serving other offices includes offices created within the time of legal memory, but cannot be enlarged beyond the extent to which the use has been carried; for that, and not the reason of the thing, determines the courts in declaring what the law is in such cases. Yet, though the judges in such a case as this declare the law to be what they do declare it, they do in fact make a new rule of law; they legislate by analogy to the rule that subsists.

The customs by which the king's superior courts of Westminster Hall regulate their administration of justice, are termed their practice. These rules are founded on antient usage, and, in respect of their universality, form a part of the common law without its being necessary to allege custom or prescription to warrant them.

Where a custom is already part of the common law, the superior courts take notice of its existence as such, without requiring it to be stated in the written pleadings. Thus each of these tribunals takes notice of its own customs or practice as well as of that the rest; whereas the practice of inferior courts, as well as local customs, extending to certain persons or districts only, being therefore different from and contrary to the common law, must, with the exception of gavelkind and Borough English, be set forth with due precision.

This, though an observation apparently technical only, forms in its application the test by which we distinguish general from the local or particular customs just described. Particular customs must have had their origin in the peculiar wants of their respective districts, and are the remains of that multitude of similar usages from which Alfred and his Saxon successors collected those laws which may be considered as forming the common law of the nation at the time.

Many of these customs, for reasons now forgotten, have remained in some counties, cities, and manors, in their former vigour, though at variance with the laws of the rest of the nation, and are confirmed by Magna Charta and other acts of parliament. Such are the customs of gavelkind (abolished in Wales by stat. Henry VIII.), by which all the sons inherit alike, of Borough English, by which lands held in burgage tenure descend to the youngest, instead of the eldest son; and of some boroughs, that widows shall have dower of all, instead of a third of their husbands' lands. A more striking instance is that custom in many cities and towns to hold courts for trial of causes without royal grant. The particular customs of manors as to descent were also of this kind, and bind the copyhold and customary tenants; but the law of descent is now made uniform. The existence of every such local custom, with the exceptions above noticed, as well as its application in each particular case, must be alleged in the pleadings, and proved, like any other fact, before a jury: sometimes they are open to evidence without being pleaded. Under no circumstances can these questions be entertained by an ecclesiastical court without the consent of the party who impugns the custom.

Such customs of London as do not concern the property of the corporate body itself are proved by a peculiar mode, that of a certificate to the superior courts of law from the lord mayor and aldermen, conveyed by the mouth of their recorder in a solemn ceremonial; without this certificate these courts will not take judicial notice of them.

A custom to be valid must have been used "from time whereof the memory of man runneth not to the contrary." This is "prescription," or "title by prescription;" and more accurately describes what is commonly called "time immemorial," which means, says Littleton, "that no living witness hath heard any proof or had any knowledge to the contrary," and as Lord Coke adds, "that there is no proof by record or writing or otherwise to the contrary." It has been doubted whether a prescription (in its proper sense) and a custom can coexist. There is some curious learning on this point collected in the arguments and judgment in Blewett v. Tregoning, 3 Ad. and Ellis. It has been held that a custom in a particular market that every pound of butter sold in it should weigh 18 oz. was bad, being directly contrary to 13 & 14 Charles II. c. 26, which enacted that every pound avoirdupois throughout the kingdom should weigh 16 oz. only. The right to a particular custom must have been continued within time of memory peaceably and without lawful interruption, and will not be lost by mere disuse for ten or twenty years; though in such case it becomes more difficult to establish it by proof. But it cannot stand against an express act of parliament to the contrary, for that itself proves a time when the right to such a custom could not exist. It must also be so far reasonable, according to the standard warranted by authority of law, that though no particular origin can now be assigned for it, or though the state of things in which it is known to have arisen has been altered, no good legal reason can be given against its continuance. If it may have had a legal and reasonable origin, it shall be presumed that it actually had it; and its varying from the general law forms no objection, for that is the very essence of a particular custom: but if it be so contrary to any known rule or principle of law, or to the good of the public, or of a multitude of persons, that it cannot be presumed to have had a reasonable commencement in voluntary agreement for some beneficial object, as for securing possessions, promoting trade, or suppressing fraud, it will be void. Thus no length of usage would render good a custom of the secretary of state's office to issue warrants in general terms against the authors, printers, and publishers of a libel, without naming them; that course is contrary to clear and well-settled principles of law, which will not suffer a mere officer to decide on the individuals who are to be imprisoned. Again, a custom in an inferior court to try causes by six jurors was held bad, as contrary to the common law, though saved in Wales in some instances by a statute of Henry VIII., which confirmed such custom where it then existed. But long usage and acquiescence in one uniform payment, or in exempting persons particularly situated from contributing to it, are cogent evidence that it is reasonable; for, as Lord Mansfield once said, it cannot be presumed that during a long period of years one-half the parties were knaves in wrongfully receiving that to which they were not entitled, and the other fools for submitting to an unjust demand. It belongs to the judges of the courts to decide what is reasonable when the question arises in any matter that comes before the court.

Where a custom is harmless and affords recreation to a number of persons, though to the temporary inconvenience of an individual, it will be upheld and referred to a legal origin. Thus a custom for the inhabitants of a parish to play at cricket, or dance, on private property in the parish, was held good, as the lord might have annexed this condition to his original grant of the land. A custom must also be certain as to the description of parties benefited, and compulsory, without its depending on the caprice of any third person whether it can be acted on or not. It must also be consistent; for repugnancy to any other local custom would be plainly contrary to that origin in common consent on which alone it stands: and lastly, it must be strictly pursued, being derogatory from the common law.

Local custom varies from prescription in this: local custom is alleged in legal forms as existing not in any person certain, but within a certain named district, without showing any legal cause or consideration for it; whereas prescription must have a presumed legal origin, and is either a personal right, always claimed in the name of a person certain and his ancestors, or those whose estate he has, or by a body politic and their predecessors, or else is in a *que* estate; that is, a right attached to the ownership of a particular estate, and only exercisable by those who are seised of it. All customs of cities, towns, and boroughs, by which persons not freemen were prevented from keeping shops or using trades or handicrafts within them, were abolished by 5 & 6 Wm. IV. c. 76, § 14, except in the case of the customs of the city of London.

Customs of traders, or seamen, as also of agriculture, mining, and other branches of industry, will be followed in the construction of contracts, unless they are inconsistent with their express terms, and, subject to that condition, they are admissible even to annex incidents to them as to which they are silent. The "custom of the country" means the custom of all parts of the country to which it can in its nature be applied. Thus a custom that land accruing imperceptibly to the seashore belongs to the owners of the shore, applies to all such parts of the realm as adjoin the sea, unless limited in terms to a particular district.

The immemoriality of a particular local custom may be sufficiently proved by living witnesses who can attest its continued existence for twenty years, unless contradicted by contrary proof. Upon this doctrine will be found to depend a great variety of public as well as private rights to ancient offices, estrays, treasure trove, wreck, nomination of juries, &c.; as well as to tolls of markets, port duties, tithes, ancient rents, &c., and to exemptions from those burdens. The numerical amount of instances in which the privilege can be proved to have existed must be considerable or not according to the frequency or the rarity with which according to the nature of the case they may be expected to recur.

Reiterated facts of user make a custom of trade; but the mere opinion of merchants is not sufficient for that purpose; nor can any course of action pursued under colour of a custom of merchants alter a general rule of common law when established by judicial decisions.

A long continued usage for exempting particular persons from a local burden, will, if necessary, be supported by presuming that it originated in an act of parliament now lost, though no length of usage will avail against the terms of a statute to the contrary.

CUSTOMS-DUTIES consist for the most part of taxes levied upon goods and produce brought for consumption from foreign countries; such duties are sometimes collected upon exports made to foreign countries, and upon goods and produce passing from one port to another of the same country. Of this nature were the duties on coals, slate, and stone, carried coastwise from one port in the United Kingdom to another, which duties were repealed in 1831. Since the abolition of the export duty on coal in 1845, the only duties outwards consist of an *ad valorem* duty of one-half per cent. on the shipment of some articles of British production, and it will not produce so much as 1500*l*. a year.

The earliest statute passed in this country whereby the crown was authorised to levy customs-duties, was the 3rd of Edward I. The mode long employed in the collection of these duties was to affix a certain rate or value upon each kind or article of merchandise, and to grant what was called a *subsidy* upon these rates. This subsidy was generally one shilling of duty for every twenty shillings of value assigned in the book of rates. The early acts which grant these duties speak of them as subsidies of tonnage and poundage. The word tonnage was applied to a specific duty charged on the importation of each tun of wine and the exportation of each tun of beer; and the word poundage was applied to other articles valued as already explained.

The first "book of rates agreed upon by the House of Commons," is believed to be that compiled by a committee in 1642, during the reign of Charles I., and published under the authority of the House by Lawrence Blaiklock. The next book of rates of which we have any record was also published by order of the House of Commons in 1660, the year of the restoration of Charles II. In the fifteenth and twenty-second years of the reign of that king, the principle of poundage was altered as respected some articles, and upon those articles specific duties were charged instead, though the system was

3 A

still followed with regard to the great bulk of articles. But in the reigns of William III. and Anne many additional specific rates were imposed, in place of the valuation for the subsidy. This course of substitution was continued from time to time, and some other innovations were adopted, by which the simplicity of the ancient plan was destroyed; so that in a work of authority, published by Mr. Henry Saxby, of the Custom-House, London, in 1757, we find as many as thirty-nine principal branches of customs-duties, with subdivisions applying to different kinds of goods, whereby a degree of complication was introduced into the subject which must have caused great embarrassment to traders.

The difficulties here mentioned were increased by the great number of acts of parliament passed from year to year for altering the duties or regulations of this branch of the revenue; and the great bulk and intricacy of the customs-laws had caused such inconvenience that about the year 1810 the lords of the Treasury employed Mr. Jickling to prepare a digest of those laws. Five years were employed in completing this task, and some idea may be formed of the laborious nature of the work, and of the necessity for its performance, from the fact that the digest forms a large octavo volume of 1375 pages. The work is entitled 'A Digest of the Laws of the Customs, comprising a Summary of the Statutes in force from the earliest period to the 53rd George III. inclusive.' The effect of numerous fresh enactments to impair the usefulness of this exposition of the revenue laws was very soon apparent, and in 1823 Mr. Hume, the secretary of the Board of Trade, then comptroller of the Customs in the port of London, was appointed by the Treasury "to undertake the preparation of a general law or set of laws for the consolidation of the Customs of the United Kingdom." In the performance of this duty, Mr. Hume prepared eleven bills, which received the royal assent in July, 1825, and came into operation 1st of January, 1826. These acts were 6 Geo. IV. caps. 106, 107, 108, 109, 110, 111, 112, 113, 114, 115, 116. The first of these acts repealed 443 statutes, many of which were obsolete. In 1833 eight of Mr. Hume's acts were repealed or altered by 3 & 4 Wm. IV. caps. 50, 51, 52, 53, 54, 55, 56, 57. These acts no doubt effected great improvements in the management of the Customs, but cap. 56 enumerated no fewer than 1150 different rates of duty chargeable on imported articles, all other articles paying duty as " unenumerated." In 1840 Mr. Porter, of the Board of Trade, in his evidence before the Parliamentary committee on import duties, showed that out of a total amount of 22,962,610l. of Customs-duties received in 1839,

17 articles produced 94½ per
    cent. or . . £21,700,630
29 articles produced $3\frac{8}{10}$ per
    cent. or . . . 898,661
—
46 articles produced $98\frac{3}{4}$ per
    cent. or . . £22,599,291

In 1842 Sir Robert Peel effected some improvements in this system, which were carried into effect by 5 & 6 Vict. c. 47. This act reduced the duty on about 750 different articles on which the receipts had amounted to about 270,000l. The general principle of the measure was to reduce the duty on raw materials to about 5 per cent., to limit the highest duty on partially manufactured materials to 12 per cent., and on complete manufactures to about 20 per cent. The number of articles in the tariff was now reduced to 813. Foreign horned cattle, sheep, goats, swine, salmon, soles, and other fish, and fresh beef and pork, which had been prohibited formerly, were admitted on paying a duty under the tariff of 1842. In 1844 the duty on foreign wool was abolished. In 1845 Sir Robert Peel effected further improvements in the tariff by abolishing the duty on cotton wool (about 680,000l.) and on 430 other articles, on which the duty amounted to 320,000l. By this plan expenses of warehousing are saved [WAREHOUSING SYSTEM], and a number of troublesome accounts and impediments to business are got rid of; but for statistical purposes the Customs department retains the power of examining articles which do not pay

CUSTOMS-DUTIES. [723] CUSTOMS-DUTIES.

duty. The paramount object of the tariff reform of 1845 was to encourage the abundance and cheapness of raw materials of manufacture.

The following is an abstract from an official 'Expository Statement,' showing the net annual produce of the duties of Customs on all articles imported into the United Kingdom in two years preceding and in two years following the establishment of the new tariff (5 & 6 Vict. c. 47).

Articles producing under the New Tariff.	Old Tariff. £	New Tariff. £
Under 100l.	19,037	8,040
£100 to 500	71,972	34,461
500 to 1,000	69,032	36,258
1,000 to 10,000	570,718	317,492
10,000 to 50,000	706,991	511,570
50,000 to 100,000	389,006	395,603
100,000 & upwards	20,810,542	21,417,462
Exempt from duty or prohibited	196	„
	22,637,494	22,720,886

On 598 articles, the duties on which were altered in 1842, 1843, and 1844, the receipts were 3,851,259l. in 1840 and 1841, and 2,478,306l in 1843 and 1844.

On 214 articles, the duties on which were not altered in 1842, 1843, and 1844, the receipts were 18,114,525l. in 1840 and 1841, and 19,094,890l. in 1843 and 1844.

In 1844 the gross receipt on the following five articles was 15,728,857l. :—

Sugar	£4,758,415
Tea	3,884,726
Tobacco	3,093,217
Foreign Spirits	2,193,067
Wine	1,799,430

The net amount of duties collected in the United Kingdom on imported articles, after the deduction of drawbacks, repayments, &c. in the several years from 1828 to 1844, both inclusive, was as follows:—

	£	On Corn (included in the preceding column). £
1828	21,691,613	193,251
1829	21,359,802	898,794
1830	21,622,683	790,110
1831	21,272,263	544,792
1832	21,714,524	307,988
1833	20,892,902	35,342
1834	21,282,080	97,987
1835	21,873,814	234,576
1836	22,758,369	149,662
1837	21,849,109	583,271
1838	22,121,038	186,759
1839	22,958,254	1,098,849
1840	23,153,958	1,156,660
1841	23,302,152	568,341
1842	22,356,324	1,363,978
1843	22,450,074	758,295
1844	23,864,494	1,098,383

The following table shows the nature of the tariff previous to the alterations in 1845:—

Articles each producing in 1843-44.	Articles in a raw state for Manufactures.	Articles partially manufactured.	Articles wholly manufactured.	Articles of Food.	Not comprehended under the preceding heads.	Total.
	No.	No.	No.	No.	No.	No.
Under £100	144	54	113	46	91	448
£100 to 500	45	19	31	15	27	137
500 to 1,000	16	5	17	6	6	50
1,000 to 10,000	28	11	27	28	15	109
10,000 to 50,000	6	5	5	7	2	25
50,000 to 100,000	2	—	—	3	—	5
100,000 and upwards	3	1	1	12	—	17
Exempted from duty or prohibited	8	—	2	4	8	22
Total.	252	95	196	121	149	813

The charges of collection on the gross receipt of Customs-duties (24,277,477l.) for the United Kingdom were 1,264,996l. in 1844, or 5l. 4s. 2½d. per cent. On a

3 A 2

CUSTOMS-DUTIES. [724] DAMAGES.

gross receipt of 2,358,543*l.* for Ireland the charges of collection were 215,223*l.*, or 9*l.* 2*s.* 6*d.* per cent., or nearly double the per centage for Great Britain. The great heads of expenditure of the Customs establishment are—797,910*l.* civil department; preventive water-guard, 345,226*l.*; cruisers, 97,401*l.*; land-guard 19,058*l.* The sum of 797,910*l.* for the civil department consists of 429,147*l.* salaries and allowances; 128,201*l.*, day-pay; 121,017*l.*, superannuation allowances; 16,711*l.* for compensation and allowances for offices and fees abolished; 17,789*l.* law charges; special services and travelling charges, 19,208*l.*, besides some other heads under which the disbursements were of smaller amount. Besides the actual charges of collection, the Customs revenue is charged with the following payments:— Quarantine and warehousing establishments, &c., 148,070*l.*; payments in support of the civil government of Scotland, 108,640*l.*; compensation to naval officers in the coast-guard, &c., and to officers of the late tax-department in Ireland, 44,139*l.*; payments on account of the difference of Trinity light and pilotage dues between British and foreign vessels, and on account of compensation to the South Sea Guarantee Fund, 14,220*l.*; and some other sums, making a total of 315,624*l.*

The management of the revenue of Customs is committed to a board of nine commissioners, acting as a subordinate department of the Treasury. The commissioners receive a salary of 1200*l.* : the chairman receives 800*l.* in addition, and the deputy-chairman 500*l.* In 1845 two of the commissioners were young men of twenty-six years of age. The total number of persons in the Customs establishment of the port of London in 1844 was 1881, and the total expense thereof was 259,632*l.*

Nearly one-half of the Customs revenue of the United Kingdom is collected in the port of London, and about one-fifth of the whole in the port of Liverpool. In 1843 the amounts collected at five principal ports was as under:—

London . . . £11,354,702
Liverpool . . . 4,121,522
Bristol . . . £996,750
Dublin . . . 977,890
Hull 525,418

CUSTOS BRE'VIUM. Officers so called existed until lately both in the Court of Queen's Bench and the Court of Common Pleas. They received and had the custody of all the writs returnable in their respective courts, filed warrants of attorney, and various other documents connected with the business of the courts. By virtue of the act 1 Will. IV. c. 58, these offices (of which the duties were performed by deputy) were abolished in both courts, and compensation granted to their possessors. The office in the Court of Queen's Bench was held by Lords Kenyon and Ellenborough jointly, and the compensation granted them was 2089*l.* 17*s.* 4*d.* per annum. In the Court of Common Pleas the compensation granted to the custos brevium was 60*l.* 10*s.* 6*d.* per annum. (*Parl. Papers*, 1835, No. 314; 1844, No. 413.)

CUSTOS ROTULO'RUM is the chief civil officer of the county, to whose custody are committed the records or rolls of the sessions. He is always a justice of the peace and *quorum* in the county for which he is appointed. The lord-lieutenant has the chief military command of the county, and his office is quite distinct from that of custos rotulorum; but it is the invariable practice to appoint the same person to both offices, in whom is united the highest military and civil authority within the county. By statute 37 Hen. VIII. c. 1, and 1 Wm. III. c. 21, he is appointed under the queen's sign manual. As he has the custody of the rolls of the sessions, he should attend there in person or by deputy; and this duty is performed by the clerk of the peace as his deputy. [CLERK OF THE PEACE.] (Blackstone's *Comm.*; Burn's *Justice of the Peace*; Dickinson, *Guide to Quarter Sessions.*)

D.

DAMAGES, for which the Law Latin uses the word Damna, signifies a compensation in money which a man gets by the verdict of a jury for some wrong that he has sustained. The damages in any action in which compensation for a wrong may be got are assessed by a jury, and when judgment is given, the plaintiff is entitled to get these damages from the defendant.

The plural word "damages" in this sense appears to be a technical use of the word "damage," damnum in the Law Latin, which means the loss that one man sustains by the act of another. The loss may be either a loss that affects his property or it may arise from an act which affects only his person, as assault, and imprisonment. There is a legal maxim that a man cannot recover damages when there is a "damnum absque injuria," a loss without an injury, that is, when one person sustains a loss by the act of another, but the act is not an illegal act. The word "injury" is here used in the proper sense of the Latin word "injuria," from which it comes: "injuria" signifies that which is "non jure factum," or done contrary to law. Damages then may be got when the act which causes the damage is an "injury" or "legal wrong," but not otherwise, however great may be the loss caused by the act of another. If one comes and sets up a shop by the side of another and takes away all his custom, he has caused him loss enough, but the sufferer can have no compensation, for it is legal for a man to set up a shop, even if he thereby ruins all other shopkeepers.

The kind of acts which are considered injuries is fixed by law; but sometimes cases arise in which it is difficult to determine how far the act which causes loss is an act which is permitted, or should be permitted, for the administrators of the law sometimes determine what shall be law by an appeal to what should be.

The word "damnum," damage, is used in the Roman Law. There might be "damnum sine injuriâ facientis," which was called Pauperies, a term which signified some damage caused by a quadruped, for which the owner was liable. The word "injuria" implied that the doer must be a rational agent; and therefore in the case of an animal, the mischief was said to be done without "injuria." When the loss or damage was caused by the act of a human being, it was "damnum injuria." (*Dig.* 9, tit. 1 and 2.)

A man may receive great loss from the wrongful act of another, and have no compensation by the law of England. He may have damages for loss to his property caused by an illegal act; and he may have compensation in some cases for damage to his body caused by the wrongful act of another. But as wrongs in the English law are distributed into private and public, and private wrongs are called civil injuries, and public wrongs are called crimes and misdemeanors, so there is a private, that is, an individual compensation in case of a private wrong, and a public compensation (if we may use the term) in the case of a public wrong. A man cannot recover compensation in respect of being robbed, for robbery is a public wrong, and the punishment that is inflicted is not inflicted with a view to compensate the injured person. A man may recover compensation if he is beaten by another, when the case is an assault; but if he should be half killed by a man who intended to kill him outright, this is a public wrong, and the sufferer gets no private compensation. Thus, says Blackstone, "Robbery is an injury to private property, but were that all, a civil satisfaction in damages might atone for it: the *public* mischief is the thing for the prevention of which our laws make it a capital offence. In these gross and atrocious injuries the private wrong is swallowed up in the public: we seldom hear of any mention made of satisfaction to the individual; the satisfaction to the community being so very great." It seems that the amount of satisfaction to the community, that is, to all the members of the state, is so great that the individual who sustains the loss may be well satisfied to go without anything except his share of the public satisfaction.

The extension of the principle of recovering damages, that is, pecuniary compensation, to other cases than those in which they may now be had, is a subject that deserves the attention of legal reformers.

Blackstone (iv. c. 1) has stated generally the cases in which a man may get damages and may not: but, as usual, he is not satisfied with stating the law; he will give a foolish and insufficient reason to show that it is good.

DAMNUM. [DAMAGES.]

DEACON, an ecclesiastical term of Greek origin, from Διάκονος (Diáconus, literally, *a servant*), introduced into the Saxon vocabulary, and continued in use to the present time.

It designates one of the *orders* in the Christian priesthood, the lowest of the three—bishops, priests, and deacons.

The first institution of the order is particularly set forth in the sixth chapter of the Book of Acts. The administration of charities in the Church of Jerusalem was complained of as partial by the Grecian converts. The apostles, in whom the administration had been vested, thought it expedient to divest themselves of this duty, and to devolve it on other persons, that they might devote themselves to prayer and to the ministry of the word. Seven persons were selected for the office, and by prayer and the imposition of hands ordained deacons.

It appears by the First Epistle of St. Paul to Timothy, that there were deacons in other Christian churches, and probably in all where such an officer was needed. He gives instructions (chap. iii. 8-13) respecting the character which became persons who should be admitted into the office. See also *Phil*. i. 1. There were also deaconesses in the primitive church, one of whom, Phœbe, is mentioned, *Rom.* xvi. 1. This female officer may be traced to the eleventh or twelfth century.

The peculiar office of both deacons and deaconesses was to attend to works of mercy, to be the administrators of the alms of the more opulent members of the church.

In the English church the name continues, and the peculiar form of ordination, but the peculiar duties of the office seem to be lost sight of. In fact the Poor Laws, by creating certain civil officers whose duty it is to attend to the poor, have perhaps rendered the services of the deacon in this his characteristic capacity less necessary.

In some dissenting communities there are deacons who still discharge the duties for which the office was instituted: they collect the alms of the people at the sacrament, and distribute them among the poor. But they are always laymen, or persons who have not gone through the forms, generally few and slight, of ordination as practised among the dissenters.

There is a form for the ordination of deacons in the English church: some clergymen never take priests' orders. It appears by the Rubric that a person in deacon's orders is empowered to read publicly the Scriptures and homilies, to catechise, to preach when licensed to do so by the bishop, and to assist a priest in divine service, and especially in the communion. When contemplated in the light in which this form places him, he appears as an assistant to a priest, for he is to seek out the sick and poor, and report them to the priest, and in the absence of the priest to baptize. This latter permission has led to the introduction of the performance of other ecclesiastical duties, namely, the celebration of matrimony and the burial of the dead. In fact the deacon performs all the ordinary offices of the Christian priesthood, except consecrating the elements at the administration of the Lord's Supper and pronouncing the absolution.

A person may be ordained deacon at twenty-three. He may then become a chaplain in a private family; he may be a curate to a beneficed clergyman, or lecturer in a parish church, but he cannot hold any benefice, or take any ecclesiastical promotion. For this it is requisite that he take priest's orders.

DEADWEIGHT. [NATIONAL DEBT.]

DEAN (French *Doyen*, and in Latin *Decanus*), a word which, at first sight, would appear to be allied to DEACON, but which has probably a different origin. Etymologists seem not to be agreed concerning the origin of the word; but the most usual origin assigned to it is the word *decem*, ten, as if a dean were a person who presided over collective bodies of men or things, in number *ten*. The word *Dean* is generally used as an ecclesiastical term. The French word Doyen is applied both to ecclesiastical and lay personages. Richelet (*Dict.*, art. *Doien*) says, that when applied to other than ecclesiastical bodies, it signifies the oldest of the body; thus the French used to speak of the Doien des Conseillers du Parlement. The Italian word *Decano* also signifies the head of a lay corporation, as well as an ecclesiastical dignitary. In Scotland it is used for the head of lay communities, but in England we believe it is generally confined to promotions or presidencies spiritual. It is, however, used in some colleges, as in University College, London, to signify the chief or head of a faculty chosen for a limited period. Deans in the Colleges of Oxford and Cambridge are persons appointed to superintend the religious service in the College chapels, to enforce the attendance of the students there, and to exercise some control over them in other respects.

In England there are three classes of ecclesiastical presidencies to which the title Dean belongs.

1. *Deans rural.* The dioceses are divided into archdeaconries, and the archdeaconries into deaneries, below which there is no other subdivision till we come to parishes, the minutest of the proper ecclesiastical divisions of the country. The whole country is thus divided, with the exception of certain districts of no great extent, which claim to be exempt jurisdictions.

Those who contend for the derivation of the word dean, whence deanery, from decem, suppose that originally there were *ten* churches or parishes forming each of these deaneries. This is a very obscure point, and it is equally uncertain at what time this distribution of the dioceses was made. It appears, however, that there were deaneries before the Norman Conquest.

In each of these deaneries there was a clergyman who was dean; he was usually a beneficed clergyman within the deanery. His duties were to exercise a superintendency over the clergy, to preside at their assemblies, and to be the medium of their communication with their spiritual superiors. He had his public seal. He appears also to have discharged those duties which are now performed by clergymen called surrogates.

By degrees this office in the English church fell into disuse. The history or the reason of its decline is not very well known, for the advantage of having such an officer, especially where the archdeaconries were extensive, must have been always evident. The office, however, did by degrees disappear in one diocese after another, till it became totally lost. There was a dean of Chalke, in the diocese of Salisbury, as late as the reign of Charles the Second; and a dean of Doncaster, in the diocese of York, in the reigns of George the First and Second. Attempts have been made to revive it. Berkeley, bishop of Cloyne, tried to establish the office again in Ireland; and soon after the late Dr. Burgess was made bishop of Salisbury, he did actually revive the office in that diocese, appointing Mr. Dansey, the rector of Donhead St. Andrew, rural Dean of Chalke: this was in 1825. The Report of the Ecclesiastical Commissioners, 1835, under the head Territory, recommends that each parish shall be assigned to a deanery, and each deanery to an archdeaconry. There is a work, in two volumes quarto, entitled 'Horæ Decanicæ Rurales,' which is an attempt to illustrate by a series of notes and extracts, the name and title, the origin, appointment, and functions, personal and capitular, of Rural Deans, by William Dansey, &c. 1835.

The office existed in other parts of Christendom.

2. *Dean in a Cathedral Church.* The canons who formed the bishop's council were presided over by a dean; this has been the case from the remotest times. [CANON.] *Decanus et Capitulum* is the form in which all the acts of such communities run.

Anciently the deans were elected by the chapters; but here, as in other points, the royal power has encroached on the privileges of the church. Now the form is for the crown to issue a *congé d'elire*, naming the person whom the chapter is to choose, in the bishoprics of ancient foundation; but in the bishoprics founded by Henry the Eighth, the king names the dean by his letters patent merely. In the former case the bishop is called in to confirm the election, and he issues his mandate for the installation of the person

DEBENTURE. [728] DEED.

elected. In the bishoprics of St. David's and Llandaff the office of bishop and dean is united in the same person.

3. *Deans in Peculiars.*—There are in England certain ecclesiastical promotions, in which the person holding them is called by the name of dean, and they seem to have all had anciently, as some of them have now, capitular bodies connected with them, and in all there is something peculiar in reference to their spiritual superiors, and in the jurisdiction exercised by them. The principal of them are—the dean of Westminster; the dean of the chapel of St. George, of Windsor; the dean of Christ Church, Oxford; the dean of the Arches; the dean of the King's Chapel; the dean of Battel; the dean of Bocking; the dean of Middleham, &c. If the history of these foundations were traced to their origin, it would be seen that they were ecclesiastical establishments, mostly of royal foundation, possessing peculiar privileges and a peculiar jurisdiction, which escaped dissolution when the framework of the ecclesiastical institutions of England underwent some alteration at the time of the Reformation. There are also *Honorary Deans*, as the dean of the Chapel Royal of St. James's Palace. The Bishop of London is dean of the province of Canterbury, and the Archbishop of Canterbury sends to him his mandate for summoning the bishops of his province in Convocation.

DEBENTURE (Latin, *debentur*, from *debeo*, to owe), formerly written debentur, is a kind of certificate used at the Customhouse, which entitles a merchant who exports goods upon which a drawback or bounty is allowed to receive payment. Goods on which drawback or bounty is allowed are called Debenture goods (3 & 4 Wm. IV. c. 58, §§ 86, 87, 88, &c.). The forging of a Custom-house debenture is simple felony (41 Geo. III. c. 75, § 7). The 7 & 8 Geo. IV. c. 29, § 5, makes it felony to steal any debenture or other security for money.

The word has been used in some acts of parliament to denote a bond or bill, by which the government is charged to pay a creditor or his assigns the money due on auditing his account. Debentures were used to secure the arrears of pay to the soldiery during the Commonwealth, and are mentioned in the Act of Oblivion, 12 Car. II. c. 8. They are in use now in the receipt of Exchequer and Board of Ordnance, and, it is believed, in the king's household. (Cowel's *Interpreter.*)

Debentures are often issued by various associated bodies.

DEBT. [INSOLVENT.]

DEBT, NATIONAL. [NATIONAL DEBT.]

DEBTOR AND CREDITOR. [INSOLVENT.]

DECLARATION. [OATH.]

DECLARATION OF RIGHT. [BILL OF RIGHTS.]

DECREE, DECRETAL. [CANON LAW, p. 445; CATHOLIC CHURCH, p. 459.]

DECREE [EQUITY.]

DEED, an instrument in writing or print, upon paper or parchment, comprehending the terms of an agreement between parties able to contract, duly sealed and delivered. The name for a deed in the Law French of Littleton and others is *fait*, that is, *factum*, a thing done; of which *deed* is the translation. Deeds are of two kinds, indented and poll: a deed indented is called an indenture, and has a waving line cut teeth-fashion on one of the edges of the material upon which it is written, usually the top edge; and when the deed consists of more sheets than one, on the first sheet only. The term indenture implies that the deed is of two parts, that is, two parts or copies exactly alike, and that the two parts were divided by the line in order to afford additional means of authentication; but, except in the cases of leases, marriage settlements, partnership deeds, and some few others, there are seldom more parts than one. The expense of stamps on deeds is so heavy, that frequently, where two or more parties are equally interested in a deed, it is deposited with some person for their joint use. Hence the term indenture, in common acceptation, now implies little more than that the deed is made by and between two or more parties. Anciently some word, as for instance "chirographum" (whence "chirograph"), was written in capital letters upon the part where the parchment or paper was to be divided, and afterwards cut in an indented or, in some cases, a straight line.

A deed poll is cut even, or polled at the edges, and is usually of one part only, that is, the deed of one party, or of several parties of the same part. The form commences in the mode of a declaration, "Know all men by these presents, that," &c.: the form appropriated to an indenture or a deed among several parties is "This indenture, made, &c. between, (here the parties to the deed are named), &c. Witnesseth," &c. A deed between several persons is not necessarily indented, except in those cases where an indenture is required by statute, and except in the working of what is called an estoppel. The indenting is not essential, even though the instrument should commence "This indenture," &c. It has been said that the indenting may be supplied after the deed is executed, and even in court; but in all cases where the indenting is essential to the validity of the deed, it seems clear that this must be a mistake. Since the passing of the act 7 & 8 Vict. c. 76, § 11, entitled 'An Act to simplify the Transfer of Property,' it is not necessary to indent a deed.

A deed. to be absolute and irrevocable, must be founded on a valuable or good consideration, untainted by anything immoral, illegal, or fraudulent, though a gift or voluntary conveyance will be effectual as between the parties, and is only liable to be questioned in certain cases by creditors or subsequent purchasers; and a voluntary deed may become irrevocable by a subsequent sale by the grantee of the subject-matter conveyed by it. [CONSIDERATION.]

Ancient deeds were short, and suited to the simplicity of the times. When transactions became more complicated, it was customary to divide deeds into several formal parts; but it is not necessary that a deed should be so divided: it may be a good deed, if there are sufficient words to show the meaning and intention of the parties to it.

Previous to its execution, the deed should be read, if any of the parties to the deed require it. The modern mode of executing deeds is by signing, sealing, and delivery. Signing is not essential to the validity of a deed, though it is required as to less formal instruments by the Statute of Frauds, 29 Ch. II. c. 3; but sealing is absolutely necessary, which is the most ancient mode of authentication, and has been in use from the earliest times. At present the seal is no real security against fraud, for any impression upon wax or other substance employed is sufficient; indeed it is generally affixed by the stationer who engrosses the deed, and it is not even necessary that there should be a seal for each party; one is sufficient for all. In some of the American States the impression upon wax has been disused, and a flourish with the pen at the end of the name, or a circle of ink, or a scroll, is allowed to be a valid substitute for a seal. The last essential to the due execution of a deed is delivery, except in the case of a corporation, where sealing by the common seal has the effect of delivery. The usual manner of delivering a deed is for the executing party to say, " I deliver this as my act and deed ;" but any less formal mode by which the party signifies his intention to deliver it will be effectual. The delivery means that the person whose deed (act) the instrument is to be, and who is to be bound by it, delivers it to the person who is to receive some benefit from this deed, or to some person acting for him, and thereby declares that the act is complete. All the parties whose deed (act) the instrument is to be, must deliver it as their deed. A deed may also be delivered as an escrow, i. e. to a third person to keep till something is done by the grantee: when the condition is performed, the deed becomes effectual. A deed takes effect from the delivery, and not from the date, and therefore if it has no date, or a date impossible, the delivery ascertains the time from which it is to take effect. Evidence is admissible also of delivery on a day different from the date written. The execution is usually attested. Enrolment and registration are rendered necessary in some cases by statutory enactment, and the revenue laws have imposed certain stamps upon every description of deeds, the absence of which prevents them from being admissible in evidence.

After execution, a deed may become void by erasure, interlineation, or other alteration in any material part; but, generally speaking, such alterations will be presumed to have been made before the execution, if nothing appear to the contrary, or there be no cause to suspect that it has been done in a clandestine manner. A grantee may also disclaim the grant or disagree thereto; and a deed may be destroyed or cancelled, but such destruction or cancellation will not revest the thing granted in the grantor, though all personal engagements established by the deed between the parties will be put an end to. If the seal is broken from the deed, the covenants contained in it are void. If the deed has transferred property from one person to another, the property continues transferred, just as if the deed existed; but if the seal is any way destroyed, the covenants which are to be executed are destroyed, because when any legal proceeding is taken upon the deed, it must be pleaded as a deed, and it is not the deed of the party whose deed it professes to be, if that mark is destroyed which is the legal evidence of its being his deed. But as long as the seal is on a deed, and the deed exists entire, so long is the party, whose deed it is, bound by the covenants. In the case of a bond, which is a deed by which a man binds himself, his heirs, executors, and administrators, to pay a certain sum of money to another at a time named, length of time was formerly no legal bar to an action upon it; yet it was a ground for a jury presuming that it had been satisfied. But by the 3 & 4 Will. IV. c. 42, actions upon specialties, that is, founded upon instruments which are deeds, must be brought within twenty years after the cause of action has arisen.

The effect of the seal remaining is sometimes an unexpected surprise to a man. If a man has taken a lease for a term of years of premises, with covenants to repair, and at the expiration of the lease should agree with his landlord to become tenant from year to year, he should get the seal off the lease in the landlord's hands. If he does not, the landlord may still make him repair by virtue of the seal, if he brings his action within the time fixed by law, for the judges have decided that, though tenant from year to year, he is bound by the original covenants. (Butler, n. Co. Litt. 295 b.; Shepherd, *Touchstone*; Dixon; Co. Litt.; Cruise's *Digest*.)

DEER-STEALING. [GAME LAWS.]
DEFAMATION. [SLANDER.]
DEGREE. [UNIVERSITY.]
DEL CREDERE COMMISSION. [AGENT.]

DELEGATES, COURT OF, was the great court of appeal in ecclesiastical causes, and from the decisions of the Admiralty Court. It was so called because the judges were delegated or appointed by the king's commission under the great seal; they usually consisted of judges of the courts at Westminster and doctors of the civil law, but lords spiritual and temporal might be joined. This court was established by the statute 25 Henry VIII. c. 19, which was passed in consequence of the practice of appealing to the pope at Rome from the decisions of the English courts in the above-mentioned matters.

Appeals lay to the court of delegates in three cases—1, where sentence was given in any ecclesiastical cause by the archbishop or his official; 2, where any sentence was given in an ecclesiastical cause in place exempt; 3, where sentence was given in the admiralty, in suits civil and marine, according to the course of the civil law. After sentence by the delegates, the king might grant a commission of review; but the power was rarely exercised, except upon the ground of error in fact or in law, and it was usual to refer the memorial praying for a commission of review to the chancellor, before whom the expediency of granting the prayer was argued.

By statute 2 & 3 William IV. c. 92, the Court of Delegates was abolished, and its powers and functions were transferred to the king in council, and by the same statute it is enacted that the decision of the king in council shall be final, and that no commission of review shall in future be granted. (Cowell's *Interpreter*; Blackstone, *Com.*) [ADMIRALTY COURTS; ARCHES COURT OF; PRIVY COUNCIL.]

DEMAND AND SUPPLY are terms used in political economy to express the relations between consumption and production—between the demand of purchasers and the supply of commodities by those who have them to sell. The relations between the demand for an article and its supply determine its price or exchangeable value [VALUE]: the relations between the demand for labour and its supply determine the amount of wages to be earned by the labourer [WAGES]. For causes explained elsewhere, the price of an article will rarely vary, for any length of time, very much above or below its cost of production;* nor will the wages of labour, for any length of time, much exceed or fall below the amount necessary to maintain labourers and their families in such comforts as their habits of life have accustomed them to believe necessary for their subsistence; but bearing in mind that, in the prices of commodities and labour, there is a certain point, determined by causes independent of demand or supply, above or below which prices cannot materially vary for any considerable time: all variations of price, if the medium in which they are calculated remains unchanged, may be referred to the proportion which exists between the demand for commodities and the supply of them—between the quantities which purchasers are willing and able to buy, and the quantities which producers are able and willing to sell.

To have any influence upon prices a demand must be accompanied by the means of purchasing. A demand is not simply a want—a desire to obtain and enjoy the products of other men's labour; for if this were its meaning, there would never be the least proportion between demand and supply: all men would always want everything, and production could not keep pace with consumption. But an "effective demand," as it is termed by Adam Smith, exists wherever one man is anxious to exchange the products of his own labour for that of other men. It is, therefore, of an effective demand only that political economists are speaking when they examine the circumstances of demand and supply in connexion with prices.

But although a demand, without the means of purchase, cannot affect prices, the universal desire of mankind to possess articles of comfort and luxury suggests other important considerations. As this desire is natural to man, and too often is so strong as to tempt him even to commit crime, it obviously needs no encouragement; men will always gratify it whenever they have the means, and these means consist in the products of their own labour. Hence all that is required to convert this desire of acquisition into an effective demand is ample employment for industry. Increase the production of all commodities and an increased consumption of them is the certain result; for, men having larger products of their own labour to offer in exchange for the products of other men's labour, are enabled to purchase what they are always eager to acquire. Production, therefore, is the great object to be secured, not only as furnishing a supply of commodities necessary and useful to mankind, but also as creating an effective demand for them. When trade is depressed by a languid demand, it is commonly said that increased consumption is all that is required to restore its prosperity. But how is this consumption to be caused? The desire to consume is invariable, and thus any falling off in consumption must be attributed to a diminished production in some departments of industry which causes an inability to consume. When production is restored, an effective demand for all articles will immediately follow; but until the productive energies of the consumers are in a state of activity it is in vain to expect from them an increased demand.

These considerations lead us to the conclusion that a universal glut of all commodities is impossible. The supply of particular commodities may easily exceed the demand for them, and very often does exceed it; but as the constant desire

---

* "Cost of production" is used by political economists in a sense different from that of commerce, and includes profits. (See M'Culloch's edition of Adam Smith, c. 7.) It means, in fact, the price below which no man would continue to sell his goods. An ordinary profit is a part of the cost of production in an enlarged sense, as much as the expense of wages and materials.

DEMAND AND SUPPLY.

to obtain commodities needs nothing but the power of offering other commodities in exchange, to become an effective demand, it is evident that a universal increase of production is necessarily accompanied by a proportionate increase of consumption. Men are stimulated by no love of production for its own sake, but they produce in order to consume directly, or because by exchanging their produce with others they are able to enjoy the various comforts and luxuries which they are all desirous of obtaining. Active production, therefore, in all departments of industry causes a general and effective demand for commodities, which will continue to be equal to the supply unless it be checked by war, by restrictions upon commerce, or by other circumstances which prevent a free interchange of commodities.

A country is in the highest prosperity when there is an active and steady demand for commodities and labour, and a sufficient supply of them. Any disturbance of the proportion between one and the other is injurious to the community; and the injury is greater or less according to the extent and duration of such disturbance. When the proportion is well adjusted, the whole community derive benefit from the circumstance, both as producers and consumers; when it is disturbed, they are injured in both capacities.

Having described thus generally the nature and causes of demand, and its intimate connexion with supply, it becomes necessary to examine the influence of demand and supply upon one another, and upon production, consumption, prices, and profits. This influence varies according to the circumstances of the market, and the nature of the commodities to which its laws may be applied. These may be best understood by considering, 1st, the effects of a demand exceeding the supply; and, 2ndly, of a supply exceeding the demand.

1. The first effect of a demand exceeding the supply of a commodity, is to raise its price. As more persons want to buy the commodity than the producers are able or willing to supply, they cannot all obtain what they desire; but must share the supply between them in some manner. But their wants are very much regulated by the cost of gratifying them. One man would purchase an article for a shilling for which he may be unwilling or unable to pay two; while others, rather than forego the purchase, will consent to pay that amount. Those who have commodities to sell, finding that they have more customers than they can satisfy, immediately infer that they are selling them too cheaply, and that they could dispose of all their stock at a higher price. The price is accordingly raised, when the sale becomes limited to those who are not restrained from buying by the increased price. In principle, though not in outward form, the market is in the nature of an auction. The sellers endeavour to obtain the highest price for their goods; the price rises with the eagerness of those who wish to buy, and the highest bidders only secure the prizes. In the market, however, the competition of the buyers is not perceptible amongst themselves except through the prices demanded. Their competition determines the prices, but the sellers judge of its extent, and regulate their demands so as to obtain the greatest possible advantage from it.

Some commodities are positively necessary for the support of the people, of which the supply may fall very short of the demand and be incapable of increase. This is the case when there is a bad harvest in a country which is excluded from a foreign supply by war or by fiscal restrictions. Here the price rises in proportion to the deficiency of the crops. The competition for food is universal. Some, indeed, may be driven to the consumption of inferior articles of food, and others to a diminished consumption; but all must eat. The number of consumers is not diminished, while the supply is reduced; and the price must, therefore, rise and continue high until a fresh supply can be obtained. In a siege the competition is still greater. The prices of provisions become enormous: the rich alone can buy; the poor must starve or plunder.

A similar effect is produced if the supply, without being deficient, be confined to the possession of a small number of persons, who limit it to the consumers in order to secure higher prices. However abundant corn might be in a besieged town, if one man were exclusively authorised by law to sell it, it might rise to a famine price, unless the people broke into the granaries, or the government interfered with the monopoly. Less in degree but similar in principle is the effect upon prices of every limitation of the market by fiscal restrictions. When any sellers are excluded, the others are enabled to raise their prices.

These are cases in which the supply cannot be increased to meet the demand, or in which the supply is monopolized. But the greater number of commodities may be increased in quantity, and the supply of them is not artificially limited. The price of these also rises when the demand exceeds the supply: but the increased price raises the profit of the producer and attracts the competition of others in the market. Fresh capital and labour are applied to the production of the profitable article, until the supply is accommodated to the demand or exceeds it. The prices gradually fall, and at length the profits are reduced to the same level as the profits in other undertakings, or even lower. The encouragement to further production is thus withdrawn, and prices are adjusted so as to secure to the producers the ordinary rate of profits, and no more.

But sometimes the demand for a commodity is diminished, if the supply fall short of it for any considerable time. There are various articles useful and agreeable to mankind but not essential to their existence, which they are eager to enjoy as far as they can, but for which they are not prepared to make great sacrifices. When the price of an article of this description is raised by a deficient supply, continuing for some length of time, it is placed beyond the reach of many persons who learn to regard it with indifference. They would buy it if it were cheap; but as it is dear, they go without it or are satisfied with a substitute. In this manner the number of consumers is diminished. Others again, who will not be deprived of an accustomed luxury, enjoy it more sparingly, and consume it in less quantities. But so long as the supply is not increased, the price will continue high, because the consumers who still purchase the article, notwithstanding its price, keep up an effective demand equal to the whole supply; while there is still a dormant demand, only awaiting a reduction of price to become effective.

For the same reasons a demand for articles is diminished when their price is artificially raised by taxation. The demand is gradually confined to a smaller number of persons, and many consume more sparingly. [TAX, TAXATION.]

In these various ways demand and supply become adjusted through the medium of price, whenever the one exceeds the other. This is the result of natural laws, the operation of which is of the highest value to mankind. If the supply be incapable of increase, it economises consumption: if the supply can be increased, it encourages production. In either case it is of great benefit to the consumer. To revert, for a moment, to the example of a bad harvest in a country excluded from all foreign supply. Suppose that prices did not rise, but remained precisely the same as if the harvest had been abundant, what would be the consequence? The whole population would consume as much bread as usual, and use flour in every way that luxury points out, unconscious of any scarcity. Farmers might even feed their cattle with wheat. By reason of this improvidence the whole of the corn would be consumed before the next harvest, and the horrors of famine would burst, without any warning, upon a people living as if they were in the midst of plenty. This evil is prevented by a rise of prices, which is a symptom of scarcity, just as pain is a symptom of disease. By timely precaution the danger is averted. A high price renders economy and providence compulsory, and thus limits consumption. The supply, therefore, instead of being exhausted before the next harvest, is spread over the whole year. In the case of food it is true that such economy is painful and presses heavily upon the poor: but this evil is a mercy compared with famine. If no privation had been endured before scarcity became alarming, none but rich men could buy a loaf: for every one who had a loaf to sell would be risking his own life if he sold it.

These observations are also applicable in some measure to cases in which prices are raised by the supply being confined to one or to a few persons, who have contrived to buy up the whole or nearly the whole of any commodity. But such exclusive possession (sometimes improperly called a monopoly) cannot exist, for any length of time, in articles of which the supply is capable of increase. The extreme case has been put of a besieged town in which the whole supply of corn was monopolized by one man. Under those circumstances he would of course demand a high price; but unless his exclusive supply were upheld by law, it does not follow that the inhabitants would suffer on that account. A most provident consumption of food is absolutely necessary for the defence of a town, and no organization could distribute provisions according to the wants of the people so well as a system of purchase restrained by a high price. It must also be recollected that, without any such exclusive possession, the fact of the siege alone must raise prices by cutting off fresh supplies. If the siege continue, provisions are more likely to last out by the instrumentality of prices than by any other means. At the same time the sole possessor of the corn would be restrained from keeping back the supply beyond the actual necessity of the occasion by many considerations. He would know that if a popular tumult arose, if the town were relieved, the siege raised—a capitulation agreed to or the place suddenly carried by assault —the value of his exclusive property would be destroyed. His own interest, therefore, is coincident with that of the people. It is better for both that the supply should be meted out with parsimony; it is dangerous to both that it should be immoderately stinted.

In circumstances less peculiar than these, very little evil can arise from an exclusive possession of any commodity not protected directly or indirectly by law. If the supply be capable of increase, and the demand be sufficient to enable the owner to secure a high price, for reasons already explained, the market would rapidly be supplied from other quarters.

If the supply cannot be increased, that fact alone would raise the price; and it is probable that the supply would not have been so great without the extraordinary activity of the capitalist who had been able to secure for his country the whole accessible supply to be collected from the markets of the world.

A monopoly, properly so called, is of a totally different character: for however abundant the supply of an article may be, it may, nevertheless, be inaccessible to the consumer. [MONOPOLY.] Such monopolies were properly condemned so far back as the reign of James I. (21 James I. c. 3), although vast monopolies are still indirectly maintained by our fiscal laws. [TAX, TAXATION.] The legislature of this country, however, did not observe any distinction between a legal monopoly and the great speculative enterprises of commerce, miscalled monopolies; and severe penalties were inflicted both by the common and statute laws against offences called "badgering, forestalling, regrating and engrossing." The impolicy of such laws was gradually perceived. If prices were occasionally raised by speculations of this kind, yet the restraints upon commerce, which resulted from these laws, were infinitely more injurious to the consumer. Many of the statutes were therefore repealed by act 12 Geo. III. c. 71; but the common law, and all the statutes relating to the offences of forestalling, regrating, and engrossing, were not erased from our commercial code until the year 1844 (act 7 & 8 Vict. c. 24).

When prices are high by reason of the demand exceeding the supply, it is by no means necessary that the profits of those who sell the dear commodities should always be greater than the profits in other branches of trade. It must always be recollected, that where scarcity is the cause of the high price, the sellers who demand it have the less to sell. Where scarcity is not the cause, but the demand is great because the supply, notwithstanding the exertions of producers, cannot keep pace with it, the profits are undoubtedly greater than usual, until the supply has been increased.

II. It is now time to consider the

effects of a supply exceeding the demand, and this division of the inquiry will require less elucidation, as the effects of such a condition of the market may be stated to be the very reverse of those which we have just been examining. When there is more of a commodity than people are prepared to buy, its price must fall. Its sellers must offer it for sale at the price at which they can induce people to purchase. All is now in favour of consumers. They are no longer bidding against each other: but the sellers are competing among themselves to get rid of their goods. The price falls generally in proportion to the excess of the quantity, but this result is very much qualified by the nature of the article. If there be an excess of supply in perishable goods, there is nothing to prevent the natural fall of prices. When fish is unusually abundant, it must be cheap, or a great part of it will be destroyed: it must be eaten at once, or not at all; and to induce people to eat it, it must be offered to them at a low price. But with articles which may be held back, in expectation of higher prices, their value may be partially sustained. Production may be reduced, and the stock gradually brought into the market, until the supply has been equalized with the demand; and wherever the article is such as to admit of voluntary increase or diminution, the natural result of an excessive supply is to reduce production, until the balance of supply and demand has been restored. This mutual adjustment is in perpetual operation, and is ordinarily effected with such precision, that it may be said, without exaggeration, that a large city is supplied exactly with everything its inhabitants require—even down to an egg or a pint of milk. There is always enough of everything, and rarely too much.

Whenever there is an excessive production of any commodity, it is an evil almost as great as scarcity. It is true that the consumer derives benefit from it, but the producing classes are most injuriously affected. In order to raise the value of the produce of their labour, they must cease to produce, or must produce in less quantities. The workmen are thus either deprived of employment altogether for a time, or are employed for a portion of their time only, at reduced wages; while their employers are disposing of their goods at low prices, which scarcely repay the outlay of their capital. Nor does the penalty of overproduction fall exclusively upon those engaged in the trade in which supply has exceeded the demand. Their distresses extend to other classes. It has been shown already that it is to production we must look as the cause of sustained consumption, and thus the pressure upon any considerable branch of productive industry must be sensibly felt by those who have the produce of their own labour to sell. Production has failed, and consumption must therefore be diminished.

The ruinous consequences of gluts, in particular staples of trade and manufacture, are too well known, especially in this country, to require any further illustration; but their causes are not always agreed upon. Such gluts are often attributed to the facility with which manufactures are produced by machinery, but we have shown that overproduction in all branches of industry is impossible, and if that be true, it is evident that when partial gluts are produced by the aid of machinery, that powerful agent must have been misapplied. It is not contended that nothing can be produced in too great abundance. Whether machinery be used or not, production must be governed by the same laws of demand and supply. Those things only must be produced for which there is a demand, and they must not be produced in greater abundance than the demand warrants. But the more generally machinery is used, the more abundant will be the products which men will have to exchange with each other, and therefore the better will be the market. It follows that machinery can only cause a glut when applied excessively to particular objects, precisely in the same manner as an excessive quantity of labour would cause one if applied where it was not needed by the demands of commerce.

The supply of markets is a very speculative business, and is often conducted with more zeal than discretion. When a particular trade is supposed to be more prosperous than others, capitalists rush into it in order to secure high profits; and in this country the abundance of capital, the perfection of our machinery, and the skill of our workmen, enable them to produce with extraordinary facility. Over-production in that particular trade is the consequence, and all engaged in it suffer from the depreciation in the value of their goods; but if, instead of rushing into the favourite trade, they had distributed their enterprises more widely, their own interest and that of the community would have been promoted. When a ship is wrecked, if all the crew precipitate themselves into one boat, they swamp it; but if they wait till all the boats are lowered, and apportion their numbers to the size of each, they may all reach the shore in safety. And so it is in trade: one trade may easily be glutted, while there is room in other trades for all the capital and industry that need employment.

In proportion to the extent of the market and the variety and abundance of commodities to be exchanged, will be the facility of disposing of the products of capital and labour; and this consideration points out as the most probable antidote to gluts a universal freedom of commerce. When the free interchange of commodities is restricted, not only is a glut caused more easily, but its causes are more uncertain, and dependent upon unforeseen events. With the whole world for a market, the operation of the laws of demand and supply would be more equable, and the universality of the objects of exchange would make gluts of rare occurrence. The market would still be liable to disturbance by bad harvests, by errors in the monetary system, by shocks to public credit, and by war; but apart from these causes of derangement, demand and supply would be adjusted, and the productive energies of all nations called into full activity.

(Adam Smith, *Wealth of Nations*, book i.; M'Culloch, *Principles of Political Economy*, part i. ch. 7, and part ii. ch. 1, 2; Malthus, *Principles of Political Economy*; Ricardo, ch. 30; Mill, *Essays on Unsettled Questions of Political Economy*, Essay ii.)

DEMESNE. [MANOR.]
DEMISE, from the Latin Demissio, is commonly used to express an estate for years. The word *demisi*, 'I have demised,' is a term that is or may be used in the grant of a lease for years. The word demise may also signify an estate granted in fee or for term of life; but the most common signification is that which has been stated.

The term demise, as applied to the crown of England, signifies the transmission (demissio) of the crown and dignity by the death of a king to his successor.

DEMOCRACY (δημοκρατία), a word taken from the Greek language, like aristocracy, oligarchy, monarchy, and other political terms.

The third book of Herodotus (chap. 80—82) contains what we may consider to be the views of the oldest extant Greek historian on the merits and defects of the three respective forms of government as they are called, democracy, oligarchy, and monarchy. It would be difficult to extract from the chapters referred to an exact definition of democracy, but still we learn from them what were considered to be essentials: first, complete political equality (ἰσονομίη); secondly, the election of magistrates by lot (πάλῳ)—which, coupled with the first condition, implies that public offices must be accessible to all; thirdly, responsibility or accountability in public functionaries (ἀρχὴ ὑπεύθυνος), which implies a short term of office and liability to be ejected from it; fourthly, the decision by the community at large of all public matters (τὸ βουλεύματα πάντα ἐς τὸ κοινὸν ἀναφέρειν).

It is unnecessary to discuss the merits and defects of a democracy as pointed out in the above chapters, the defects being only certain consequences supposed to flow from, and the merits certain advantages incident to, a democratical institution, and neither being essentially parts of the fundamental notion of a democracy.

In forming a notion of a democracy as conceived by the Greeks, and indeed in forming any exact notion of a pure democracy, it is convenient to consider a small community, such as a single town with a little territory, and to view such a community as an independent sovereignty. The institutions which in modern times have approached most nearly to the form of a pure democracy are some of the Swiss cantons. The boroughs of England, as existing in their supposed original purity, and as partly restored to that supposed original purity by the late Municipal Corporations Act, may help to explain the notion of a democracy, though they are wanting in the necessary element of possessing sovereignty. Further, to conceive correctly of a Greek democracy and of some of the democracies of the North American Union, it must be remembered that the whole community in such States consisted and consists of two great divisions, freemen and slaves, of whom the slaves form no part of the political system.

In most Greek communities we find two marked divisions of the freemen, the 'few' (ὀλίγοι) or 'rich' (δυνατοί, πλούσιοι), and the 'many') οἱ πολλοί, ὁ δῆμος) or 'not rich' (ἄποροι), between whom a fierce contest for political superiority was maintained. This contest would often end in the expulsion of the 'few,' and the division of their lands and property among the many; sometimes in the expulsion of the leaders of the 'many,' and the political subjugation of the rest. Thus the same state would at one time be called a democracy; at another, an oligarchy, according as one or the other party possessed the political superiority; a circumstance which evidently tended to confuse all exact notions of the meaning of the respective terms used to denote the respective kinds of polities. Under the circumstances described, what was called an oligarchy might perhaps be appropriately so called; what was called a democracy was not appropriately so called, even according to the notions entertained by the Greeks themselves of a democracy; for such so-called democracy was only a 'raction of the community that had obtained a victory over another fraction of ne community, less numerous and individually more wealthy: for the 'few' and the 'rich' were always united in idea; it being, as Aristotle remarks, incident to the 'rich' to be the 'few,' and the rest to be the 'many.'

Aristotle felt the difficulty of defining what a democracy is. He observes (*Politik.* iv. 4) that neither an oligarchy nor a democracy must be defined simply with reference to the number of those who possess the sovereign power: if a considerable majority, he says, are rich, and exclude the remaining body of freemen, who are poor, from political power, this is not a democracy. Nor, on the contrary, if the poor, being few, should exclude the rich, being more numerous, from all political power, would this be an oligarchy. Indeed such a supposition as the latter is impossible in a sovereign community, except during a short period of revolutionary change.

Aristotle, after some preliminary remarks, concludes by defining a democracy to be, when the freemen and those not the rich, being the majority, possess the sovereign power; and an oligarchy, when the rich and those of noble birth, being few, are in possession of the sovereign power. This definition of an oligarchy necessarily implies that the majority are excluded from participating in the sovereign power. It might be inferred, on the other hand, that in this definition of a democracy the few are excluded from the sovereign power; and such in this passage should be the meaning of the author, if he is consistent with himself. In another passage (iv. 4), where he is speaking of the different kinds of democracy, he speaks of the first kind as characterized by *equality* (κατὰ τὸ ἴσον); and by this equality he understands when the law (ὁ νόμος) of such a democracy declares that "the not rich have no more political power than the rich, neither body being supreme, but both equal, and all participating equally in political power." Such in fact approaches very near the exact notion of a pure democracy, or at least a democracy as pure as. we have any example of; for all women, persons of unsound mind, males not adult, and slaves, are excluded from political. power even in democracies. Aristotle adds: "But as the popular party (δῆμος) is the majority, and that which is the will of the majority is supreme, such a consti-

3 B

tution must be a democracy. Aristotle then mentions a second kind of democracy, in which the offices of the state are only open to those who have a property qualification, but it must be a small amount of qualification; and a third, in which all citizens have access to the offices of the state, unless they are under some special disability. But Aristotle still supposes that this second and third kind of democracy, as he defines it, is subordinate to the law (ὁ νόμος); he supposes something like what we call a Constitution, or certain fundamental laws, in conformity to which the state is administered. For, after enumerating the various species of democracies, he says, "There is another kind of democracy which in all other respects is the same as these, except that the people are sovereign and not the law; and this happens when the enactments of the people are supreme and not the law." His exposition is founded on the nature of the democratic assemblies in the Greek States, in which all the people met in the assembly individually and not by representatives, and were guided by their leaders. He does not explain what the law is which in some democracies is supreme, and here his exposition is deficient in fullness and clearness. But it appears that he means that there can be no stability, unless there are certain fundamental rules which are respected and regarded as unchangeable. Where a small community is sovereign, and every question can at any time be proposed to the assembly, and any law can be changed and altered, it is clear, as Aristotle observes, that if Democracy is a Polity, such a government, in which everything is liable to be changed at any moment, is not properly a Democracy. Still it is a Democracy; but if a Polity is a stable thing, such Democracy is not a Polity. The Canton of Schwyz in its constitution comes very near to the notion of such a Democracy. Modern Democracies by virtue of the representative system are secured against perpetual change, for the people legislate by deputy, and continual change is practically made impossible.

A pure democracy then is where every male citizen, with the exceptions above mentioned, forms an equal and integral part of the sovereign body; or, as Aristotle expresses it, where he is speaking of a democracy in which the people are supreme and not the Law, the democracy is "monarch, one compounded of many for the many are supreme, not as individuals, but all collectively." This is the fundamental notion of a democracy; every other institution incident to or existing in a democracy is either a necessary consequence from this notion or a positive law enacted by the universal sovereign.

Thus it is absolutely necessary, in order that a democracy should exist and continue to exist, that the whole body should recognize the principle that the will of the majority must always bind the minority. There must therefore be some means of ascertaining the will of every individual, who is a member of the sovereign body, and there must be no interference with the free expression of his will, so far as such interference can be prevented. Whenever the persons who compose a democracy give their opinion on any subject, they express it by what is called a vote, which is recorded, and the majority of the votes is the will of the democracy. The vote may be given either openly by word of mouth or in writing; or it may be given secretly, which is called vote by ballot, and the vote by ballot is considered by many political writers essential to secure the voter from all interference with the free expression of his opinion. Every freeman, being an equal part of the sovereign, has no responsibility in the proper sense of that term, such as some persons dream of: the many who compose the sovereign are no more responsible than when the sovereign is one; and the notion that the vote of those who possess sovereign power should be open and notorious, on the ground of their being responsible, is inconsistent with the notion of their possessing sovereign power. The only way in which the universal sovereign can be so made responsible to a positive morality (for there is nothing else that such sovereign can be made responsible to) must be by the universal sovereign making such open voting a constitutional rule, which rule the same body that made may repeal when it pleases. But if such rule is inconsistent with the free exercise by each individual of his share of sovereignty, it would be an act of suicide in the body politic.

If the democracy consider a constitution [CONSTITUTION] to be useful for carrying into effect the will of the sovereign, such constitution, when made by the expressed will of the majority, whatever may be the terms of such constitution, does not affect the principle of the democracy. Such constitution can be altered or destroyed by the same power that made it. If a representative body is necessary for effecting the purposes of the sovereign, such body may be elected and invested with any powers by the sovereign body, always provided that the representative body is responsible to the sovereign whose creature it is. Whatever institutions are created, and whatever powers are delegated by the sovereign many, the principle of democracy still exists so long as every individual and every body of individuals who exercise delegated power are responsible to the sovereign body by whom the power is delegated. Hence if property be made a qualification for certain offices, as in one of the forms of democracy mentioned by Aristotle, by the universal sovereign, such requisite qualification does not in itself alter the nature of the democracy, being only a rule or law fixed by the sovereign. It is, however, a rule or law of that class, the tendency of which, where the sovereign power is possessed by the many, is to undermine and ultimately destroy the power that made it.

Experience has shown that even where the universal people are sovereign, if the political community is large and spread over a great surface, every delegation of power, however necessary, is accompanied with danger to the existence of the sovereign power. The more complicated the machinery of administration becomes, and the more numerous are the administering bodies interposed between the sovereign and the accomplishment of the object for which the sovereign delegates part of his power, the greater is the risk that those who have had power delegated to them will make themselves the masters of those who have conferred the power. In a democracy the great problem must be to preserve unimpaired and undisputed the vital principle of the sovereign power being in all and in every individual, and to combine with this such a system of delegated powers as shall in their operation always recognize that principle to which they owe their existence. Aristotle (*Pol.* iv. 5) well observes that a Polity may not be democratic according to the Laws, that is, the fundamental Laws or Constitution, but that by opinion and usage it may be administered democratically: in like manner a democratic constitution may come to be administered oligarchically; and he explains how this may come to pass.

It may happen that other persons besides those enumerated may be excluded from participation in the sovereign power in a government which is called a democracy. The suffrage may be given only to those who have a certain amount of property, which resembles one of the cases mentioned by Aristotle. If the amount of property required should exclude a great number of the people, the government might still be called democratical rather than by any other name, if the persons excluded were a small minority compared with the majority. If they were nearly equal in numbers to the majority, they would find out some name for the majority which would express their opinion of the form of government: and the word that they would now use would be aristocratical, a word which would imply dislike and censure. If the portion of the people who were thus excluded from the suffrage should be a majority, the ruling body would be properly called an aristocracy.

A democracy has been here defined as it has existed in some countries and as it exists in others. No attempt is made to ascertain its origin, any more than the origin of society. It is here viewed as a form of government that may and does exist. The foundation of the notion of a democracy is that the sovereign power is equally distributed, not among all the people in a state, but among all the freemen who have attained a certain age, which is defined. Democracy therefore, if we derive the notion of it from all democracies that have existed, instead of from certain wild theories of natural rights, is based upon the principle that it is for the general interest that some persons should be excluded from the possession of that political power which others enjoy. A democracy also like a monarchy can only give effect to its will through the medium of forms and agents. Practically there cannot always be a reference to the will of the majority on every occasion, no more than there can be in a monarchy. A monarch must govern by the aid of others, and the sovereign democracy must carry its purposes into effect by the aid of members of its body, to whom power sufficient for the purpose is given. The agent of a democracy is a representative body for the purpose of legislating. For the usual purposes of administration a democracy must have agents, officers, and functionaries, as well as a monarchy. The mode in which they are chosen and the tenure of office may be different, but while they act, they must have power delegated of a like kind to that which a monarch delegates. A form of government may be such that there shall be an hereditary head, a class with peculiar privileges, and also a representative body. The existence of a representative body chosen by a large class of the people has led to the appellation of the term democratical to that portion of such governments which is composed of a representative body and to those who elect such body. But the use of the terms democracy and democratical as applied to such bodies tends to cause confusion. It is true that such mixed governments present the spectacle of a struggle between the different members of the sovereign power, and as it is often assumed that the popular part aims at destroying the other parts, and as many speculators wish that it should ultimately destroy them, such speculators speak of such so-called democracy as a thing existing by itself, as if it were a distinct power in the state; whereas, according to the strict notion of sovereignty, there is no democracy except when there is no other power which participates in the sovereignty than individuals possessed of equal political power.

When the popular member of a sovereign body has destroyed all the other members, the popular member becomes the sovereign body, and it is a democracy, if it then corresponds to the description that has been given of a democracy.

A curious article by M. Guizot, entitled 'Of Democracy in Modern Society,' has been translated and published in England. It is written with reference to the condition of France and in opposition to the assertion made by some French writers "that modern society, our France, is democratical, entirely democratical; and that her institutions, her laws, her government, her administration, her politics, must all rest on this basis, be adapted to this condition." M. Guizot successfully combats certain hypotheses and assumptions, most of which however have either been exploded by all sound political writers or would be rejected by any man of reflection. His essay contains, as we might expect from his attainments and long experience in the world, many just remarks, but it is disfigured and often rendered almost unmeaning by the lax use of political terms and a tone of mysticism and obscurity which are better adapted to confuse than to convince.

DEMURRAGE, the term used in commerce to denote the money payable to the owner of a ship on the part of the shippers or consignees of goods, as compensation for detention beyond the time stipulated for her loading or discharge, as the same is expressed in the charter-party or bills of lading. It is usual to insert in all charter-parties the number of working days allowed for the loading of the ship, and also for her unloading, and likewise the sum *per diem* which may be claimed for delay beyond those periods in either case, in addition to the stipulated freight. Sometimes the number of working days for loading and unloading are stated together, so that any delay in the one case may be compensated by greater speed in the other. When the owners of the ship enter her outwards for any port, to receive such goods as may offer, and consequently where no charter-party exists, there is no stipulation for demurrage in the part of loading, but in this case it is common to insert on the face of the bill of lading a statement of the number of days after her arrival at her destined port in which time the goods must be taken from on board the ship, and also the rate of demurrage chargeable daily for any exceeding that time. No claim for demurrage can be set up where a ship is detained by contrary winds or stress of weather, nor where the government interferes to lay an embargo, nor where the port is blockaded by a hostile force.

DENIZEN, an alien born, who has been constituted an English subject by letters of denization granted by the crown through the home secretary of state. The facilities for an alien becoming naturalized, which the act 7 & 8 Vict. c. 66, provides, will render it easier for aliens to obtain naturalization than it was previously to obtain the lesser privilege of denizenship; and therefore, speaking of the future, denization will probably not be resorted to. Before this act was passed the number of aliens who became denizens was about twenty-five annually, and the number who were naturalized was about seven. The cost of letters patent of denization was 120*l*., and it was the practice for the Home Office to insert several names in one patent for the purpose of diminishing the expense. A denizen is in a kind of middle state between an alien and a natural-born subject. [ALIEN.] He may take lands by purchase or devise, which an alien cannot; but he cannot take by inheritance, for his parent through whom he must claim, being an alien, had no inheritable blood. A denizen cannot transmit real property to those of his issue who were born before his denization. By 11 & 12 Wm. III. c. 6, a natural-born subject may derive a title to inheritance through alien parents or ancestors; the statute 25 Geo. II. c. 39, provided that the person who claimed under the statute of William III. must be in existence at the time of the death of the person to whom he claims as heir; but if the claimant be a female and have afterwards a brother or sister born, the estate will descend to the brother, or she and her sister will take it as coparceners. A denizen, when otherwise qualified, may vote for members of parliament. Naturalization gives the same privileges as denization and something more. [NATURALIZATION.] A denizen cannot be a member of the privy council, or sit in either House of Parliament, or hold any office of trust, civil or military, or be capable of any grant of lands or other thing from the crown.

DEODAND (*deodandum*, what is due to God). The word deodand expresses the notion of a thing forfeited, because it has been the immediate cause of death. The thing forfeited is sometimes called deodand, which signifies any personal chattel which is the immediate cause of the death of a human being. In England deodands are forfeited to the king, to be applied to pious uses and distributed in alms by his high almoner; but the crown most frequently granted the right to deodands, within certain limits, either to individuals for an estate of inheritance or as annexed to lands, in virtue of which grants they are now claimed.

Blackstone supposes "that the custom was originally designed in the blind days of popery as an expiation for the souls of such as were snatched away by sudden death, and for that purpose ought properly to have been given to holy church, in the same manner as the apparel of a stranger who was found dead was applied to purchase masses for his soul." But it is perhaps more reasonable to imagine that it was a civil institution intended to produce care and caution on the part of the owners of cattle and goods, and that the subsequent application of the things forfeited has been mistaken for the origin of the law itself. The custom was also a part of the Mosaic Law. (*Exod.* xxi. 28.) In England it has prevailed from the earliest period, and there is no trace of the deodands having been applied to pious uses. The custom is thus mentioned by Bracton, one of the earliest writers on English law, who lived in the reign of Henry III.: 'Omnia quæ movent ad mortem sunt deodanda,' which is Englished in the 'Termes de la Ley,'

What moves to death, or killed the dead,
Is deodand, and forfeited.

A different rule prevails when the thing which occasions accidental death is at rest, and is composed of several parts. For instance, if a man, in climbing up the wheel of a cart, falls and is killed, the wheel only is forfeited; but if the cart is driven against the man, and the wheel goes over and kills him, not only the wheel but the cart and its loading are forfeited. In cases of homicide, the instrument of death is forfeited, even if it belongs to an innocent party, for which reason, in all indictments for homicide, a value is placed on the weapon used in killing, that the king or his grantee may claim the deodand, for it is no deodand unless it be presented by a jury of twelve men. Accordingly, when the coroner's jury find the cause of death, they ought also to find the value of the thing which was the immediate cause of a death. It is common for the coroner's juries to award a given amount as a deodand less than the value of the chattel; and though it is said that this finding is hardly warrantable by law, yet the Court of King's Bench has usually refused to interfere on behalf of the lord of the franchise to assist his claim.

The general rule, then, is, that all personal chattels in motion which kill a human being are forfeited. But the subject has ceased to be of interest since 1846, the 9 & 10 Vict. c. 62 declaring that the law respecting chattels which have moved to or caused the death of man, and respecting deodands, is unreasonable and inconvenient; and subsequent to September 1, 1846, it is enacted that there shall be no forfeiture of any chattel in respect of homicide, nor inquiries by any coroner's inquisition relative to deodands.

DEPARTMENT (or in French DÉPARTEMENT), a territorial division of France, introduced by the States-General in the reign of Louis XVI.

A commune is the smallest territorial division in the present system of France. In the rural districts and in the smaller towns a commune may be considered as equivalent in area and population to our ordinary parishes, or to the townships into which our more extensive parishes are divided. It is only in respect of area and population that we compare the communes of France with our own parishes: the two divisions were made for different purposes, the parish being an ecclesiastical division, which existed in France as well as in England, while the commune was for civil or military purposes. There is moreover this difference, that while our larger towns and cities (especially those whose extent and importance are of an ancient date, such as Norwich, Exeter, Bristol, or York) consist of several parishes, the larger towns of France, with the exception of Paris. form but one commune. The term commune, which is nearly equivalent to corporation, is of ancient date. When Louis VI. (le Gros) sought to raise from the towns of the royal domain a burgher militia as a substitute for the troops of his rebellious and disorderly vassals, and in order to form an alliance between the crown and the commons by sheltering the latter against feudal oppression, he formed the freemen inhabiting the towns into communautés (in the Latin of the middle ages communitates) or corporations, gave them power to raise troops from among themselves, and conferred upon a municipal body, constituted for the purpose, an authority over these troops similar to that which had been exercised over the baronial levies by the great lords themselves, and by their subordinates, the counts, or governors of towns, the viscounts, castellans, &c. These are not to be regarded as the first municipal corporations which had existed in France. Under the Roman dominion there were many; but during the distracted reigns of the later Carlovingian princes, these corporations had mostly, if not entirely, become extinct. The militia of the towns was designated in the Latin of the middle ages communiæ (communes), communitates parochiarum (the commonalties of the parishes), or burgenses (the burghers or burgesses). Where the town consisted of several parishes the troops were formed into smaller bodies according to their parishes, and marched into the field in those divisions, the parochial clergy accompanying their respective parishioners, not to join in the conflict, but to discharge their spiritual duties of preaching to them, confessing them, and administering religious rites to the dying. Some communes consisted of a number of small towns united under one corporation charter. In process of time the greater barons followed the example of the king, in order to become independent of their vassals, among whom the like insubordination existed as among the vassals of the king.

The municipal officers were generally designated Scabini or Echevins, and the principal of them had the title of Major or Maire (Mayor). The communes enjoyed many rights and exemptions; they fortified their respective towns, and were, in fact, so many municipal republics scattered over the kingdom, constituting the most substantial bulwark both of the public liberty and the rights of the crown against the encroachments of the nobility. As, however, the regal power gained strength, the influence and importance of the communes declined. Their militia came into disuse when the kings of the race of Valois began to form a standing army; and upon various causes or pretexts many of the incorporated towns lost their charters, and returned under the jurisdiction of their feudal lords. (For the history of the communes see Raynouard, *Hist. du Droit Municipale en France*, 1829.)

Under the present system of provincial organization the whole of France, the country as well as the towns, is divided into communes. As the plan has been to assimilate the divisions for civil and ecclesiastical purposes, we believe that the communes may in the rural districts and the smaller towns be regarded as ecclesiastically equivalent to our parishes. Each has its church and its curé or clergyman. Some have also succursales or chapels of ease. The larger towns have several churches.

The local administration and the revenues of each commune are placed in the hands of a municipal body, which consists of a mayor and one or more assistants (adjoints), and a certain number of councillors. The number of adjoints and of councillors varies with the population. In the larger communes the mayor and his assistants were appointed by the king, and in those of smaller size by the prefect; but they must be selected from among the councillors elected by the inhabitants. This gave the central government the nomination of about 90,000 functionaries. In a commune which contains a population not exceeding 500, the number of councillors is 10; and when the population is 30,000 and upwards, the number is 36. The term of office for mayors and adjoints is three years; and though they may be temporarily suspended in their functions by the prefect, they can only be dismissed by the king. The members of the municipal body are elected by the inhabitants who pay the largest amount of direct taxes, and, consequently, there is no fixed qualification. In communes with a population not exceeding 1000 inhabitants, one-tenth are eligible as electors, which proportion is increased 5 per cent. for communes exceeding 1000 and not exceeding 5000 population; and by 4 and 3 per cent. according to the further extent of the population. The number of communal electors in France is 2,795,000, and they elect 426,000 communal councillors. In communes with a less population than 2000, the council are elected by the voters assembled in one body; but those of larger population are divided into sections as nearly equal as possible, and each section returns its own councillors, as in this country where a town is divided into wards. In communes of 500 inhabitants and upwards, near relations, as a father and brothers, cannot be at the same time members of the communal council. Provision is made by the law for the meeting of the council four times a-year, and each sitting may be continued for ten days. On the requisition of the mayor, or of one-third of the council, the prefect or sub-prefect may call an extraordinary meeting. Communal councils are prohibited from corresponding with other councils, or issuing protestations, proclamations, or addresses. The king may dissolve a municipal council, but the ordonnance must make provision for a new election. According to the terms of the law of 21st March, 1831, the mayor acts under the authority and surveillance of the prefect or sub-prefect. The duties which devolve upon him may be compared generally to those which are severally discharged by the overseers of the poor and the churchwardens and overseers of the highways in an English parish; but as he is a ministerial officer of the prefect, and executes the orders of the prefect or those which are transmitted through him by the central government, the mayor has duties for which there is no analogy in the administrative system of the rural parts of England. The mayor of a French commune has the absolute right of appointing local officers in some cases; but in others he must have the approbation of the council and the sanction of the prefect. The municipal council "determines" matters relating to the public property of the commune, and executes its decisions, provided that within thirty days they are not annulled by the prefect as contrary to the law or to the routine of the administration. The council "deliberates" on a variety of other subjects affecting the immediate interests of the commune; gives its "advice" on a number of others; and is authorized to express its views and wishes generally on all objects of local interest. The sittings of the council are not public, and its discussions cannot be published officially without the sanction of the prefect. On the demand of any three members the votes may be taken by ballot. The budget of the commune is open to inspection, and in the communes which have a revenue of 10,000f. and upwards it is required to be printed. A certain class of expenses, which are enumerated in the municipal law, are obligatory; such as the payment of municipal officers, the keeping in repair the town-hall, a portion of the expenses of public instruction and the national guard, the cost of foundlings, of public cemeteries, &c. Every commune is bound to maintain a primary school, or to unite with another commune for that purpose. These schools are supported by a government grant and by a communal tax. A law of 25th June, 1841, gives to the prefect of a department the power of fixing, with the advice of the council of arrondissement, the minimum of the monthly contributions of a commune to the primary schools, and a maximum for the number of free scholars. All other expenses are "optional." In case of a council refusing to provide for the discharge of obligatory expenses, the necessary sum may be constituted a part of the communal budget by a royal ordonnance for the larger communes, and by an arrêt of the prefect for the smaller communes. By the same authority an extraordinary contribution may be levied, the proportion of which is, however, limited by the law of 25th June, 1841.

A department consists of several arrondissements, usually four or five: some departments have only three arrondissements; others have as many as six. There are eighty-six departments. These departments have been divided into
363 arrondissements,
2835 cantons,
37,021 communes.

A canton is a division consisting of several communes (the average is nearly fifteen); over each a judicial officer entitled juge de paix (justice of the peace) is appointed. These functionaries receive a small salary; they decide civil suits if the amount in question is under 50 fr.: and all suits whatever must be heard by one of them (in order that he may if possible bring the parties to an agreement) before the cause is carried into a higher court. The number of juges de paix is 2846. They are appointed by the government, but are not removable at pleasure. Each juge has a greffier (clerk), and to each court are attached one or two huissiers (bailiffs).

An arrondissement (circle) comprehends several cantons, seven on the aver age of France. The arrondissements may be compared to the Hundreds or Wapentakes of English counties. Each arrondissement is under the administration of a sous-préfet (sub-prefect), subordinate to the prefect of the department, to whom he addresses a memorial on anything of importance to the arrondissement, assigning the reasons on which his opinions are founded. He receives and settles the accounts of the maires of the several communes. He is assisted by a conseil d'arrondissement (council of the arrondissement), which consists of not fewer than nine members, and otherwise as many as there are cantons in the arrondissement. They are elected for six years, and their qualifications consist in the payment of 150fr. a year direct taxes. The electors are the highest taxed inhabitants of the canton, in the proportion of 1 to 100. This council, like that of the department, meets at a time fixed by the government. It holds two ordinary sittings annually, one before and the other after the sitting of the Council general of the department. In the first of these sittings the Council deliberates on the allocation of the contingent of direct taxes for the arrondissement and listens to the claims of communes who ask for a reduction of their proportion. In the second part of its sittings the Council apportions the amount of direct taxes amongst the different communes. Should it fail to do this, the prefect is authorized to supply the omission on the basis of the preceding repartition. The sub-prefect has the right of speaking at the sittings of the council. Councils of arrondissement are authorized to make a report to the prefect of the wants and condition of the arrondissement, similar to that which the departmental council addresses to the minister of the interior. As the capital of the department is also the chief place of an arrondissement, the prefect and the prefectorial (not the departmental) council discharge in that arrondissement the duties which in the other arrondissements are assigned to their respective sub-prefects and councils.

At the head of each department is an officer entitled préfet (prefect), who has alone the administration of the local government. His usual residence is at the departmental capital; but he makes every year a circuit of inspection through his department, and gives an account of the result of his circuit to the minister of the interior. The prefect is assisted by a conseil de préfecture (prefectorial council), consisting of three, four, or five members, which decides upon individual appeals for an entire exemption or a reduction of the direct taxes; and upon questions arising from the execution of public works, whether between the government and the contractors as to the particulars of the contract, or between the contractors and parties who complain of injuries sustained at their hands, and upon the indemnity due to individuals whose possessions have been required for carrying on public works. The prefect when present at the sittings of this council acts as chairman, and in case of an equal division has a casting vote.

In each department there is a council general with as many members as the department contains cantons, but the number must not exceed thirty. Each canton elects a member whose qualification consists in the payment of 200fr. a-year direct taxes. He is elected for nine years, but a third of the council is renewed every three years. The electors are the highest taxed inhabitants, in the proportion of 1 to 1000. The council assembles annually by virtue of a royal ordonnance which fixes the time and duration of its sittings, which are private; and on the demand of four members the votes may be taken by ballot. The council cannot deliberate except in the place assigned for its sittings, and on matters within its jurisdiction as determined by the law of 23rd June, 1833; nor can it put itself in correspondence with the council of another department or of an arrondissement. On an infraction of these articles the council is suspended by the prefect; and printers or others who publish the proceedings of a council which commits either of these infringements is liable to imprisonment for a period of from two to six months, to the loss of civil rights and of all public employment for ten years. The powers and functions of both the councils of a department and of an arrondissement are regulated by a law of 10th May, 1838. Their powers are not near so extensive as those of county magistrates in England assembled at quarter-sessions. The central authority of the government pervades every part of the local administration from the commune to the department. The chief business of the council is to apportion between the arrondissements the direct taxes which are required by the general government; to hear and determine upon appeals made by the councils of arrondissements against this assessment; to levy, within certain limits fixed by law, an additional tax, destined, like our county rates, to meet the expenses of the local administration; to audit the account yearly rendered by the prefect of the expenditure of this local revenue; and to express, in a report addressed to the minister of the interior, an opinion upon the condition and wants of the department.

The number of members of councils-general is 2300, and of councils of arrondissements 3200.

The departments and arrondissements are electoral divisions. The members of the National Assembly are chosen for the departments, not for single towns, however important or populous; so that the deputies are all, according to our phrase, county members. [CHARTE.]

Each arrondissement has a court of justice, entitled tribunal de première instance, which, except in a very few cases, has its sittings at the capital of the arrondissement. These courts commonly consist of three or four ordinary and two or three supplementary judges: a few arrondissements which include large towns, such as Marseille or Bordeaux, have a considerably greater number of judges, who are divided into two or more sections. To each court there is a procureur du roi, or attorney-general; and where the court consists of two or more sections there are deputy attorneys. Each department has a tribunal criminel (criminal court), or cour d'assize (assize court), consisting of a president, who is a counsellor of the cour royale, to the jurisdiction of which the department is subject, two ordinary and two supplementary judges: to each court is attached a procureur du roi, or attorney-general, and a greffier, or registrar. These courts, except in a few instances, have their seat at the capital of the department. Besides these courts, there are in different parts of France twenty-seven higher tribunals, called cours royales, consisting of from twelve to thirty-three salaried judges. Each of these courts has under its jurisdiction several departments. There is an appeal from these courts on questions of law, not of fact, to the supreme court, cour de cassation, at Paris. The departments are also formed into twenty divisions militaires, or military districts: the head-quarters of these districts are fixed at some important town, usually at the capital of one of the included departments. The departments are also grouped into divisions for other objects of central government: 1, as to bridges and highways; 2, forests; 3, mines.

A department usually constitutes an ecclesiastical diocese. In a few instances two departments are comprehended in one diocese; and in one or two cases a department is divided between two dioceses. The dioceses of France amount to eighty, of which fourteen are archbishoprics and sixty-six bishoprics.

The instruction of youth in France being under the surveillance of government, has occasioned an arrangement of territory with a view to this object.

DEPORTATION. [BANISHMENT.]

DEPOSIT. The term is applied to the sum of money which under 43 Geo. III. c. 46 a man might deposit with the sheriff after he was arrested, instead of putting in special bail. The amount of the deposit was the sum sworn to on the back of the writ. (Blackstone's *Comm.* iii. 290.)

Deposit is also used for any sum of money which a man puts in the hands of another as a kind of security for the fulfilment of some agreement, or as a part payment in advance.

The Roman word depositum signified anything which a man put in the hands of another to keep till it was asked back, without anything being given to the depositarius for his trouble. The depositor was called deponens or depositor. The depositary was bound to take care of the thing, and to make good any damage that happened to it through fraudulent design (dolus) or gross neglect (lata culpa). The depositor could recover the thing by action; but the depositary was entitled to satisfaction for any loss that he sustained in the matter of the deposit by any default (culpa) on the part of the depositor. The depositary could make no use of the deposit, except with the permission of the depositor, either given in express words or arising from implication. If a man refused to return a deposit, and was condemned in an action of deposit (actio depositi), infamy (infamia) was a consequence of the condemnation. (Dig. 16, tit. 3; Juvenal, *Sat.* xiii. 60.)

DEPOSITION, in its extended sense, means the act of giving public testimony, but as applicable to English law the word

DEPOSITION.

is used to signify the testimony of a witness in a judicial proceeding reduced to writing. Informations upon oath and the evidence of witnesses before magistrates and coroners are reduced into writing in the very words used by the witnesses, or as near as possible thereto. Evidence in the Court of Chancery is taken in written answers to interrogatories, which are also in writing, either by commissioners appointed for that purpose in the particular cause, if the witness resides at a greater distance from London than twenty miles, or if he resides nearer or is otherwise willing to appear, before the examiners of the Court of Chancery. These depositions are the evidence which is read at the hearing of the cause. The course of the Ecclesiastical Court is also by written interrogatories and answers. The Court of Chancery has power to grant a commission for the examination of witnesses residing abroad; and by the 1 Wm. IV. c. 22, which extends the provisions of the 13 Geo. III. c. 64, the courts of law at Westminster, in actions pending before them, have power to order the examination of witnesses residing in any of his Majesty's foreign dominions. By the 13 Geo. III. c. 63, § 40, in cases of indictments in the King's Bench for misdemeanors or offences committed in India, that court may award writs of mandamus to the judges of the courts in India to examine witnesses concerning the matters charged in such indictments and offences, and the depositions so taken may be read at any trial for such misdemeanors or offences. Sections 41 and 42 provide for taking the depositions of witnesses on any information or indictment in the King's Bench against the judges of the Supreme Courts in India, and in proceedings in parliament for offences committed in that country. By section 44, when an action or suit in law or equity, the cause whereof shall arise in India, is commenced in any of the courts of Westminster, such court on motion may award a writ in the nature of a mandamus to the judges of the courts in India for the examination of witnesses, and such examination may be read at any trial or hearing between the parties in such action or suit. The 1 Wm. IV. c. 22, § 1, extends the power and provisions

of the 13 Geo. III. c. 63, to all colonies and places under the king's dominion, and to all the judges of the same, and to all actions depending in the courts of law of Westminster. The fourth section of this act empowers the courts at Westminster, and also the Court of Common Pleas of the County Palatine of Lancaster and of Durham, and the several judges thereof, in every action depending in such courts, upon the application of any of the parties to such action, to order the examination upon oath, upon interrogatories or otherwise, before the master or prothonotary of such court, or person or persons named in such order, of any witnesses within the jurisdiction of the court where the action shall be depending, or to order a commission to issue for the examination of witnesses on oath in places out of such jurisdiction by interrogatories or otherwise. But (§ 10) no examination or deposition to be taken under this act shall be used as evidence at any trial without the consent of the party against whom the same may be offered, unless it shall appear to the satisfaction of the jury that the examinant or deponent is beyond the jurisdiction of the court, or dead, or unable, from permanent sickness or other permanent disability, to attend the trial.

When a witness is above the age of 70, or very infirm, or about to go abroad, so that his testimony may be lost before the regular period for his examination arrives, the Court of Chancery will order him to be examined *de bene esse*, as it is termed; that is, his examination is received for the present, and will be accepted as evidence when the proper time for taking the other evidence in the cause arrives, if the witness cannot be then produced. Courts of law do not possess similar power without the consent of both parties, but in order to enforce consent they will put off the trial at the instance of a defendant, if the plaintiff will not consent; and if the defendant refuse, will not give him judgment in case of nonsuit.

The Court of Chancery will also, upon bill filed by a person in the actual and undisturbed possession of property, and who has therefore no means of making his title the subject of judicial investigation, but which nevertheless may be inaterially affected by the evidence of living witnesses, allow the witnesses to be examined in *perpetuam rei memoriam*, that is, to perpetuate testimony. This is done in order that if any of the witnesses should die before the title to the property is disputed, their evidence may be preserved; otherwise a claimant might lie by until all the evidence against him was lost.

Depositions are not admitted as evidence in courts of law, unless the witness is either dead, or from some cause beyond the control of the party seeking to read the deposition, cannot be produced, or against any other persons than the parties to the proceeding in which they were taken, or claimants under them, and who had the opportunity of cross-examining the witness. In cases, however, relating to a custom, prescription, or pedigree, where mere reputation would be good evidence, a deposition may be received as against a stranger.

Depositions taken in Chancery *de bene esse* before answer put in, unless the defendant is in contempt for refusing to answer, are not admissible as evidence in a court of law, because until the defendant has answered he could not have an opportunity of cross-examining the witness; but the Court of Chancery will sometimes direct such depositions to be read. Such order, however, while it concludes the parties, is not binding upon the court of law; of course, however, if the depositions be not read and the decision should be contrary to justice, the Court of Chancery would interfere as between the parties.

DEPRIVATION. [BENEFICE, p. 351.]
DEPUTY. [CHARTE, p. 393.]
DESCENT, in English law (from *discent*, Norman French, and so written in our older law books), may be defined to be the rule of law pursuant to which, on the death of the owner of an estate of inheritance, without making any disposition thereof, it descends to another as heir. Inheritance is sometimes used in the same sense as descent, though it rather signifies that which is, or may be, inherited, or taken by descent. (Littleton, sect. 9.)

The law of inheritance with respect to descents which have taken place since or shall take place after the 1st of January, 1834, is now regulated by the Act 3 & 4 Wm. IV. c. 106. The object here is merely to explain the general notion of descent.

All modes of acquiring property in land by the English law are either Descent or Purchase. Descent, or hereditary succession, signifies the title by which a man acquires an estate in land as the heir-at-law of a person deceased.

The death of the owner of the estate of inheritance is the occasion of the descent of it. In his lifetime there can be no descent, and therefore no heir, though there may be an "heir apparent," or "heir presumptive." An heir apparent is he who must be the heir, if he lives till the inheritance descends; an heir presumptive is he who may be forestalled by the birth of a nearer heir.

The person who dies must be at his death owner of the estate of inheritance, or no descent of it will then take place.

Inheritances, otherwise called *hereditaments*, things which may be *inherited* or *taken by descent*, are various. The principal of these is the Crown, or royal title, dignity, and power of the king of the British Empire, the descent of which differs in one material respect from that of a private inheritance, inasmuch as where there are no sons of the king, an elder daughter takes the whole of the inheritance, in exclusion of the younger sisters. In the case of the descent of private land, when there are several daughters, they all take alike in equal shares, and are called parceners, or coparceners. Dignities and honours, as baronies and other peerages, are descendible, according to the limitations contained in the patents by which they were created. If created by summons in the first instance, they are called dignities in fee, and are descendible to females. [BARONY.] Finally, all the subjects of real property, and all annuities, offices, and whatever other things may be "held in fee," are "descendible," and this whether they are in possession, reversion, remainder, or expectancy. So are all rights and titles to things that may be held in fee, and the expectancy of an heir apparent or presumptive. There are also "descendible freeholds," that is, estates created by leases for lives, which, though not estates in fee, may during their continuance be inherited as if they were. It has been already noticed [CHATTEL] that the large class of things called chattels are not generally the subject of descent, but that some of them are.

Upon the death of the owner, the inheritance devolves upon the heir, without any act done by him, or price paid for his acquisition: in both these respects, the present law of descent differs from the old feudal customs from which it is derived. According to the old feudal customs, upon the death of the tenant of a fee, the lord of whom it was held was entitled to take and retain it till the heir, for whom proclamation was made, appeared, and paid a sum of money called a relief [RELIEF] as the consideration for his admission into the tenancy; whereupon "seisin" or possession was given him, and he took the "oath of fealty" [FEALTY], and if the tenancy was by "knight's service," "did homage" [HOMAGE] also to the lord. All this was more like a new donation, than the present quiet succession of an heir. The descent of copyholds, however, is still regulated much in the manner described. The heir was not, however, formerly, to the same extent as now, subject to the charges and debts of the deceased tenant, in respect of the property that descended to him. [ASSETS]. The present law of descents qualifies materially in one respect the title of the heir to the inheritance descended. Though it makes him as completely the owner of it as if he had purchased it, that is, acquired it otherwise than by descent, as to right of enjoyment and power of alienation, it does not allow it at his death to descend as if he had purchased it, but, on the contrary, declares that it shall descend as if he had never had it. Such at least is the new law. (§ 1, 2, of the Act.) The heir of an inheritance must be always the heir of the last "purchaser" of it, that is, of the last person who acquired the property "otherwise than by descent, or than by an escheat partition or inclosure, by the effect of which the land shall have become part of, or descendible, in the same manner as other land acquired by descent." The practical importance of this rule cannot be understood without knowing who the person is who in any case is designated by the law as the "heir" to another.

As to descents in fee simple, the fundamental rule is, that any person of *kin* to another, that is, descended from the same ancestor, however distant, may be his heir, but that no person connected with him by marriage or affinity only, can inherit to him. [CONSANGUINITY; AFFINITY.] If the son inherits to the father, his mother cannot succeed to him, for though she may be heir to the son, she cannot be heir to the father, from whom, and not from the son, "the descent is to be traced." On the other hand, if the father inherits to the son, the mother may succeed to him, for though she cannot be the heir of the father, she may be the heir of the son. The fee, fief, or feud, which may thus now descend to the kindred of the purchaser *in infinitum*, was once nothing more than a life-interest given to the tenant or holder of it in consideration of the military services to be rendered by the tenant to the donor. The fee was afterwards permitted to descend to the issue of the original grantee, and in process of time to his *collateral* heirs. This was only effected by means of a fiction; for so firmly settled was the notion that "the blood" (descending) alone of the purchaser or original grantee could be allowed to inherit, that the feudal law was never brought to allow collateral heirs, as such, to be heirs. But when a feud was granted *ut antiquum*, that is, to be held by the donee as if it had descended to him from some remote unknown ancestor, then the law permitted collateral relations however distant, that is, relations descended from any common ancestor, however remote, to inherit. For it was not known how far distant the ancestor was who was supposed to have been the purchaser, nor who he was, and it was sufficient that the heir *might* be a descendant of his. (See for the early history of inheritable fiefs, Robertson's *Charles V.*, Sullivan's *Lectures*, Wright's *Tenures*, Gilbert *on Tenures* by Watkins, Butler's *Coke upon Littleton*, 191, a. v. 4, where there is a comparison of the Roman and feudal laws of inheritance.)

While the law, however, went thus far,

it did not, for reasons which some writers have attempted to explain, allow the *lineal ancestors* of the purchaser of the *quasi* ancient feud to inherit it, nor his relations by the half blood, that is, persons descended not from the same father and mother as the purchaser, or any lineal ancestor of his, but from one of them only. Still further exclusions followed from the rule which was afterwards established, that the heir of the fee must be the heir of the person last *seised* or possessed of it, as well as a kinsman of the whole blood to the actual purchaser. Among the practical consequences of this rule were the following: that if the child of the actual purchaser inherited to him, and became seised, the purchaser's child by another wife could not succeed, because only half brother to the person last seised; and that if the father's brother inherited to the son and became seised, the mother's brother could not succeed, because only related by marriage to the person last seised. All these exclusions and the fictions of the ancient feuds are done away with by the new act, the effect of which is, as before said, to admit among the heirs of the purchaser all his kindred, both of the whole and the half blood, and notwithstanding any previous descent to any heir of his. This it does by enacting that every lineal ancestor shall be capable of being heir to any of his issue (§ 6); that any person related to the purchaser by the half blood shall be capable of being his heir (§ 9), and that in every case descent shall be traced from the purchaser (§ 2). Still, however, the wife or her kin cannot inherit to the husband, nor the husband or his kin to the wife. But the hardship of these exclusions is at least mitigated by the law of dower and curtesy, which must be read together with the law of descent as one law. The order in which the kindred of the purchaser inherit is a matter purely legal. The practical difficulty in finding who is heir, is not the difficulty of understanding the law, but in ascertaining the facts upon which the law of descent operates. The new act declares that the last owner of the land shall be presumed to be the purchaser, unless it can be proved that he is not; and this rule diminishes the difficulty of tracing the descent.

The English word *heir* comes from the Roman *heres;* but the Roman word heres had two significations. It signified either the person or persons to whom a testator gave his property by testament; or the person or persons who took the property of a deceased person in case of his dying intestate. The heres by testament corresponds to the English devisee, and to the person or persons to whom a man bequeaths his personal estate for the purpose of distribution, that is, his executors. Further, the Roman law made no distinction between land and other property, as to descent or testamentary disposition. The Roman heres, therefore, who succeeded in case of intestacy (ab intestato) filled the place of the English heir at law, and also of the person who obtains the administration of an intestate's personal estate. Again, in the case of intestacy among the Romans, all persons were heredes, and took the property in equal portions, who were in the same degree of consanguinity to the intestate: sons and daughters who were in the power of their father inherited alike, whether the real children of the intestate or his adopted children; and the wife who was in the hand of her husband (in manu) inherited with the brothers and sisters of the intestate, for such wife was considered as a daughter. If a man left children living, and there were also children of a son deceased, these grandchildren took the share which their father would have had if living: thus the division among the grandchildren in this case was not *in capita*, but *in stirpes*. In fact, the Roman law of succession, in case of intestacy, should be compared with the English law of succession to the personal estate of an intestate, which is founded on the Roman law; and it should not be compared with the English law of descent, which is of a feudal character. The law of Roman intestacy is stated by Gaius, lib. iii.

The rule of descent, which makes the eldest son, brother, &c. sole heir, exclusive of the other children, or the other nephews and nieces, &c., is well known by the name of 'the law of primogeniture.' [PRIMOGENITURE.] It is almost peculiar to our country, not having been observed by the ancients, and being generally abolished where it existed on the Continent and in the United States of America. For the history of this rule, see Hale's *History of the Common Law;* Sullivan's *Lectures;* Robinson *On Gavelkind;* 2 Blackstone's *Com.;* Wright's *Tenures;* and for observations on its expediency, Smith's *Wealth of Nations.* The preference of males to females is not so peculiar. The Jews, Athenians, and Arabians, though not the Romans, gave the inheritance to sons exclusive of daughters. (For the Athenian law of inheritance, see Jones's *Isæus;* for that of the Jews, Selden, *De Successionibus apud Hebræos.*) This is not however the case among most foreign nations at present. The preference of the child of the elder son dead in the purchaser's lifetime to the younger son has some interesting historical associations. The law on this point seems not to have been settled till after most of the other rules of descent. It was still somewhat doubtful when King John kept his nephew Arthur from the throne by disputing it. (2 Blackstone's *Com.;* Sullivan's *Lectures,* lect. 14. In Robertson's *Charles V.,* vol. i. p. 272, there is a curious story of the trial by combat of this point of law.)

The descent of estates tail (regulated by stat. 3 Ed. I. c. 1) differs from that of fees simple principally in this, that only the descendants of the first donee can inherit; and of these only males claiming exclusively through males can be heirs when the estate is in ' tail male:' when it is in tail female (a mode of gift which is quite obsolete), only females claiming exclusively through females. [ENTAIL.] The limited descent of the estates, together with other qualities of them, makes them the best representatives at present existing (excepting indeed copyholds) of the ancient fiefs.

(On the law of descent, as it existed before the late act, see Sir Matthew Hale's *History of the Common Law,* chap. xi.; 2 Blackstone, *Com.,* chap. xiv.; Cruise's *Digest,* vol. iii. Watkins *On Descents* principally treats of curious points, many of which have ceased to be important. As to the reasons for the new alterations, see *First Report, Real Property Commissioners.*)

DESERTER, an officer or soldier who either in time of peace or war, abandons the regiment, battalion, or corps to which he belongs, without having obtained leave, and with the intention not to return. The word deserter is from the Roman *Desertor,* which had various meanings. A soldier who did not give in his name (dare nomen) when duly summoned to service might be treated as a Desertor. (Liv. iii. 69.) The soldier who fled in battle and left the standard was called Desertor, and the punishment was death: sometimes every tenth man was taken by lot and put to death. (Livy. ii. 59; Plutarch, *Crassus,* c. 10.) Desertion among the Romans was a general term for any evasion of military duty: the old punishment was death, or loss of citizenship, as the case might be. He who went over to the enemy was transfuga or perfuga, and was always put to death. Under the Empire there were various classifications of desertion with their several punishments. (*Dig.* 49, tit. 15, "De Re Militari.")

As the last-mentioned circumstance distinguishes the crime of desertion from the less grave offence of being absent without leave, it becomes necessary, before the conviction of the offender, that evidence should be apparent of such intention. This evidence may be obtained generally from the circumstances under which the deserter is apprehended; for example, he may have been found in a carriage or vessel proceeding to a place so distant as to preclude the possibility of a return to his corps in a reasonable time; or letters may have been found in which an intention to desert is expressed; or some offer may have been made by him of enlisting in another corps, or of entering into some other branch of the service.

The civil courts of law in this country have ever had authority to try offenders accused of desertion; but they have long since ceased to exercise such authority, and they now interfere only in the rare case of an appeal from the decision of the court-martial which is held for the purpose of investigating the charge and awarding the punishment. The courts-martial exercise, to a certain extent, a discretionary power in proportioning the punishments to the criminality in the accused; and this power is generally considered as more likely to promote the ends of justice than the inflexibility of the law in civil courts, where, since no middle course can be taken between condemnation and acquittal, the criminal frequently escapes through the compassion of the jury, when the punishment which by law must follow a verdict of guilty appears disproportionate to the crime. The leniency which has invariably characterised the sentences of courts-martial, and the custom of not awarding the punishment in its full extent till after a repetition of the crime, sufficiently justifies the confidence reposed in those courts.

The practice of deserting from one regiment or corps, and of enlisting in another, either from caprice or for the sake of a bounty, having been very frequent, a particular clause has been inserted in the Articles of War, in order to prevent this abuse. It declares that any non-commissioned officer or soldier so acting shall be considered as a deserter, and punished accordingly; and that any officer who knowingly enlists such offender shall be cashiered. It is also declared that if any soldier, having committed an offence against military discipline, shall desert to another corps, he may be tried in the latter corps, and punished for such offence; and his desertion may be stated before the court as an aggravation of his guilt. Any officer or soldier who may advise or encourage another to desert is also punishable by a general court-martial.

Absconding from a recruiting party within four days after having received the enlisting money is also considered as desertion; and an apprentice who enlists, representing himself as free, if he afterwards quits the corps, is esteemed a deserter unless he deliver himself up at the expiration of his apprenticeship. Vagrants also, who, pretending to be deserters, give themselves up as such with a view of obtaining money or provisions, are, by a clause of the Mutiny Act, to be considered as soldiers whether enlisted or not.

A non-commissioned officer or soldier who simply absents himself from his corps without leave is exonerated from the graver part of the charge, if any circumstances can be adduced from which it may be inferred that the absence was intended to be only for a short time. Such circumstances are, goods of value being left behind, the occupation in which the absentee is found to be engaged being in its nature temporary, an intention of returning having been expressed, or again, the offender suffering himself to be brought back without resistance. Simple absence without leave is referred to regimental courts-martial merely, and these award the punishment discretionally.

The Mutiny Act authorises general courts-martial to condemn a culprit to death, if his crime should be found to deserve the extreme punishment; in other cases they may sentence him to be transported as a felon, either for life or for a term of years, or to serve in the ranks for life, or for a length of time exceeding that for which he had originally engaged to serve. In some cases, also, corporal punishment is awarded, and an offender may be sentenced to lose the increased pay or the pension to which he would have been entitled if the guilt had not been incurred.

Desertion is justly considered one of the greatest offences that can be committed by any man who has adopted the profession of arms. The officer or soldier who has undertaken to assist in the defence of his country, and steals away from the duties he is called upon to perform, violates a sacred engagement. Whether he withdraw through caprice, or to escape the privations to which the soldier is occasionally exposed, he sets an example of discipline infringed, he deprives the army of his services at a time perhaps when he can with difficulty be replaced; and while he basely seeks his own ease, he throws an additional burthen upon his companions in arms. If he pass over to the enemy, he becomes the vilest of traitors; and, should he escape the retribution which awaits him from his injured country, he must submit to

live dishonoured, an exile from its bosom.
DESPOTISM. [MONARCHY; TYRANT.]
DEVISE. [WILL.]
DIFFEREATION. [MARRIAGE.]
DIFFERENTIAL DUTIES. [TAXATION.]
DIGEST. [JUSTINIAN'S LEGISLATION.]
DIGNITIES. [TITLES OF HONOUR.]
DILAPIDATION, ECCLESIASTICAL. [BENEFICE, p. 349.]
DIOCESE. [BISHOPRIC.]
DIPLOMACY is a term used either to express the art of conducting negotiations and arranging treaties between nations, or the branch of knowledge which regards the principles of that art and the relations of independent states to one another. The word comes from the Greek diploma, which properly signifies any thing doubled or folded, and is more particularly used for a document or writing issued on any more solemn occasion, either by a state or other public body, because such writings, whether on waxen tablets or on any other material, used anciently to be made up in a folded form. The principles of diplomacy are to be found partly in that body of recognized customs and regulations called public or international law, partly in the treaties or special compacts which one state has made with another. The superintendence of the diplomatic relations of a country has been commonly entrusted in modern times to a minister of state, called the Minister for Foreign Affairs, or, as in England, the Secretary the Foreign Affairs. The different persons permanently stationed or occasionally employed abroad, to arrange particular points, to negotiate treaties commercial and general, or to watch over their execution and maintenance, may all be considered as the agents of this superintending authority, and as immediately accountable to it, as well as thence deriving their appointments and instructions. For the rights and duties of the several descriptions of functionaries employed in diplomacy, see the articles AMBASSADOR and CONSUL.

DIPLOMATICS, from the same root as Diplomacy, is a term used to express the acquaintance with ancient documents of a public or political character, and especially of the determination of their authenticity and their age. But the adjective, diplomatic, is usually applied to things or persons connected not with diplomatics, but with diplomacy. Thus by diplomatic proceedings we mean proceedings of diplomacy; and the *corps diplomatique*, or diplomatic body, at any court or seat of government, means the body of foreign agents engaged in diplomacy that are resident there.

Some of the most important works upon the science of diplomatics are the following:—'Ioannis Mabillon de Re Diplomatica,' lib. vii., fol., Paris, 1681-1709, with the 'Supplementum,' fol., Paris, 1704; to which should be added the three treatises of the Jesuit, Barthol. Germon, addressed to Mabillon, 'De Veteribus Regum Francorum Diplomatibus,' 12mo., Paris, 1703, 1706, and 1707:— Dan. Eber. Baringii 'Clavis Diplomatica,' 2 vols. 4to., Hanov., 1754; Ioan. Waltheri 'Lexicon Diplomaticum,' 2 vols. fol., Götting., 1745-7; 'Nouveau Traité de Diplomatique,' par les Bénédictins Tassin, &c., 6 vols. 4to., Paris, 1750-65; 'Historia Diplomatica,' da Scipione Maffei, 4to., Mant., 1727; Io. Heumann von Teutschenbruun 'Commentarii de Re Diplomatica Imperiali,' 4to., Nurem., 1745; Dom de Vaines, 'Dictionnaire Raisonné de Diplomatique,' 2 vols. 8vo., Paris, 1774; J. C. Gatterer, 'Abriss der Diplomatik,' 8vo., Götting., 1798; and C. T. G. Schoenemann 'Versuch eines vollständigen Systems der allgemeinen besonders ältern Diplomatik,' 8vo., Götting., 1802.

DIRECTOIRE EXE'CUTIF was the name given to the executive power of the French republic by the constitution of the year 3 (1795), which constitution was framed by the moderate party in the National Convention, or Supreme Legislature of France, after the overthrow of Robespierre and his associates. [COMMITTEE OF PUBLIC SAFETY.] By this constitution the legislative power was intrusted to two councils, one of five hundred members, and the other called "des anciens," consisting of 250 members.

The election was graduated: every primary or communal assembly chose an elector, and the electors thus chosen assembled in their respective departments to choose the members for the legislature. Certain property qualifications were requisite for an elector. One-third of the councils was to be renewed every two years. The Council of Elders, so called because the members were required to be at least forty years of age, had the power of refusing its assent to any bill that was sent to it by the other council. The executive power was intrusted to five directors chosen by the Council of Elders out of a list of candidates presented by the Council of Five Hundred. One of the five directors was to be changed every year. The directors had the management of the military force, of the finances, and of the home and foreign departments; and they appointed their ministers of state and other public functionaries. They had large salaries, and a national palace, the Luxembourg, for their residence, and a guard.

The project of this constitution having been laid before the primary assemblies of the people, was approved by them. But by a subsequent law the Convention decreed that two-thirds of the new councils should be chosen out of its own members. This gave rise to much opposition, especially at Paris, where the sections, or district municipalities, rose against the Convention, but were put down by force by Barras and Bonaparte, on the 13th Vendemiaire (4th of October, 1795). After this the new councils were formed, two-thirds being taken out of the members of the Convention, and one-third by new elections from the departments. The councils then chose the five directors, who were Barras, La Réveillière-Lépaux, Rewbell, Letourneur, and Carnot; all of whom, having voted for the death of the king, were considered as bound to the republican cause. On the 25th of October the Convention, after proclaiming the beginning of the government of the laws, and the oblivion of the past, and changing the name of the Place de la Révolution into that of Place de la Concorde, closed its sittings, and the new government was installed. Upon Bonaparte's gaining the ascendancy, the constitution of the year 3 and the Directory were overthrown, after four years' existence. (*Histoire du Directoire Exécutif*, 2 vols. 8vo., Paris, 1802.) The law of the conscription was passed under the administration of the Directory. [CONSCRIPTION.]

DISABILITY is a term used to denote a legal incapacity in a person to inherit lands or enjoy the possession of them, or to take that benefit which otherwise he might have done, or to confer or grant an estate or benefit on another. All persons who are disabled from taking an estate or benefit are incapable of granting or conferring one by any act of their own, but many persons who are incapable of disposing of property may take it either by inheritance or gift.

This legal disability may arise in four ways, which are expressed by the English law in the following terms: By the act of the ancestor; by the act of the party himself; by the act of the law; or by the act of God.

By the act of the ancestor, as where he is attainted of treason or murder, for by attainder his blood is corrupted, and his children are made incapable of inheriting. But by the stat. 3 & 4 Wm. IV. c. 106, § 10, this disability is now confined to the inheriting of lands of which the ancestor is possessed at the time of attainder: in all other cases a descent may be traced through him. [ATTAINDER.]

By the act of the party himself, as where a person is himself attainted, outlawed, &c., or where, by subsequent dealings with his estate, a person has disabled himself from performing a previous engagement, as where a man covenants to grant a lease of lands to one, and, before he has done so, sells them to another.

By the act of law, as when a man, by the act of law, without any default of his own, is disabled, as an alien born.

By the act of God, as in cases of idiotcy, lunacy, &c.; but this last is properly a disability to grant only, and not to take an estate or benefit, for an idiot or lunatic may take a benefit either by deed or will.

There are also other legal disabilities, as infancy, and coverture, or the state of a married woman [WIFE]; but these disabilities are confined to the conferring of interests, for infants and married women are capable of receiving gifts of land or other property.

Married women, acting under and in conformity to powers, since the 3 & 4 Wm. IV. c. 74, by deed executed under the provisions of that statute, may convey lands. Infants, lunatics, and idiots, being trustees, and having no beneficial interest in the property vested in them, are by various statutes enabled to do the necessary legal acts as to such property under the direction of the Court of Chancery.

Particular disabilities also are created by some statutes; as, for instance, Roman Catholics, by the 10 Geo. IV. c. 7 (the Emancipation Act), are disabled from presenting to a benefice; and foreigners (although naturalized) cannot hold offices or take grants of land under the crown. (Cowel's *Interp.*; *Termes de la Ley.*)

DISCOUNT, a sum of money deducted from a debt in consideration of its being paid before the usual or stipulated time. The circumstance on which its fairness is founded is, that the creditor, by receiving his money before it comes due, has the interest of the money during the interval. Consequently he should only receive so much as put out to interest during the period in question, will realize the amount of his debt at the time when it would have become due. For instance, 100*l*. is to be paid at the end of three years; what should be paid now, interest being 4 per cent.? Here it is evident that if we divide the whole debt into 112 (or 100+3×4) parts, 100 of these parts will make the other 12 in three years (at simple interest), whence the payment now due is the 112th part of 10,000*l*., or 89*l*. 5*s*. 9*d*. The rule is, *n* being the number of years (a fraction or number and fraction), *r* the rate per cent., and D the sum due,

$$\text{Present value} = \frac{100 \, D}{100 + nr};$$

$$\text{Discount} = \frac{D \, nr}{100 + nr}.$$

In practice, it is usual not to find the real discount, but to allow interest on the whole debt in the shape of abatement. Thus it would be considered that, in the preceding example, three years' discount upon 100*l*. at 4 per cent. is 12*l*., or 88*l*. would be considered as the present value.

In transactions which usually proceed on compound interest, as in valuing leases, annuities, &c., the principle of discount is strictly preserved. The present value in the preceding case is, in its most usual form,

$$\frac{D}{(1+\varrho)^n}, \text{ and the discount } D - \frac{D}{(1+\varrho)^n};$$

where ϱ is the rate per pound (not per cent.: thus it is ·04 for 4 per cent.). But recourse is usually had to the tables of present values which accompany all works on annuities or compound interest.

The name of discount is also applied to certain trade allowances upon the nominal prices of goods. In some branches of trade these allowances vary according to the circumstances which affect the markets, and what is called discount is in fact occasioned by fluctuations in prices which it is thought convenient to maintain nominally at unvarying rates. This system is practised in some branches of wholesale haberdashery business, and we have now before us a list of prices furnished to his customers by a manufacturer of tools at Sheffield, in which the nominal price of each article is continued the same at which it has stood for many years, while to every different species of tool there is applied a different and a fluctuating rate of discount, this fluctuation constituting in fact a difference of price between one period and another: the rates of discount in this list vary from 5 to 40 per cent. upon the nominal prices of the different articles.

The term discount is also employed to signify other mercantile allowances, such for example as the abatement of 12 per cent. made upon the balances which underwriters, or insurers of sea risks, receive at the end of the year from the brokers by whom the insurances have been effected. The word discount is further used, in contradistinction to premium, to denote the diminution in value of securities which are sold according to a fixed nominal value, or according to the price they may have originally cost.

3 c 2

If, for example, a share in a canal company upon which 100*l.* has been paid is sold in the market for 98*l.*, the value of the share is stated to be at 2 per cent. discount.
DISCOUNT BROKER. [BROKER.]
DISCOVERY. [EVIDENCE.]
DISPENSATION. [BENEFICE.]
DISSEISIN. [SEISIN.]
DISTRESS, "districtio," in the jurisprudence of the Middle Ages, denotes legal compulsion generally, whether ecclesiastical or civil. One mode of compulsion extensively adopted among the nations of Teutonic origin was the taking possession of the whole or a part of the property of the offender or defaulter, and withholding it from him until the requirements of the law had been complied with. This species of distress was called "naam," from nyman, nehmen, to take—a verb common to the Anglo-Saxon, German, and other cognate languages. The modern distress is the "naam," restricted in the taking of *personal* chattels; and in its most simple form it may be stated to be—the taking of personal chattels out of the possession of an alleged defaulter or wrong-doer for the purpose of compelling him, through the inconvenience resulting from the withholding of such personal chattels, to perform the act in respect of which he is a defaulter, or to make compensation for the wrong which he has committed.

Some rights to which the law annexes the remedy by distress, have been considered too important to be left to the protection afforded by the mere detention of the *distress* (by which term the thing taken is also designated), and more efficacious means of dealing with it have been introduced; and in certain cases a sale of the property taken by way of distress is allowed, if, after a certain interval, the party distrained upon continues to be unwilling or unable to do the act required.

Distresses are either for some duty omitted, some default or nonfeasance,—or they are in respect of some wrongful act done by the distrainee. The subject of distress is one of great extent, and in the English law involves a great number of particular cases. Under the head of Distress for Omissions, the most important among the feudal duties for which a distress may be taken is Rent. Rent, in its original and still most usual form, is a payment agreed to be made by the tenant to his landlord as an equivalent or a compensation for the occupation of land or a house. Such rent is denominated rent-service. It comes in lieu of and represents the profits of the land granted or demised, and is therefore said to *issue* out of the land. To rent-service the law annexes the power of distress, although there may be no agreement between the parties as to distress. But a rent reserved upon a grant or demise ceases to be a rent-service if it be separated from the ultimate property in the land, generally called the reversion. Thus, if the owner of land in fee demises it for a term of years, reserving rent, and afterwards assigns the rent to a stranger, retaining the reversion, or grants the reversion, retaining the rent, the rent being disconnected from the reversion is considered as a branch severed from the trunk, and is called a dry rent or rent-seck, to which the common law annexed no power of distress. In like manner, if the owner of the land, without parting with the land, grants to another a rent out of the land, the grantee having no reversion had only a rent-seck, unless the grant expressly created a power of distress, in which case the rent would be a rent-charge. But now, by statute 4 Geo. II. c. 28, § 5, the like remedy by distress is given in cases of rent-seck, as in the case of rent reserved upon lease.

All rents, though distinguished by a variety of names derived from some particular circumstance attached to them, are resolvable into Rent-service, Rent-seck, or Rent-charge, and there may now be a distress for every species of rent, though a practical difference still subsists as to the mode of dealing with distresses taken for the one or for the other.

There may also be distress for Heriots and Tolls.

There is also Distress for Damage done, which is called Distress for Damage-feasant. Cattle or dead chattels may be taken and be detained to compel the payment of a reasonable sum of money by way of satisfaction for the injury sustained from such cattle or dead chattels being wrongfully upon property in the occupation of the party taking them, and doing damage there, either by acts of spoliation or merely by incumbering such property. This is called a distress of things taken damage-feasant (doing damage).

The occupier of land is allowed not only to defend himself from damage by driving out or removing the cattle, but also to detain the thing which did the injury till compensation be made for the trespass. Upon referring to Spelman and Ducange, it will be seen that a similar practice obtained on the Continent amongst the Angli, Werini, Ripuarii, and Burgundians.

The right to distrain damage-feasant is given to all persons who have an immediate possessory interest in the soil or in its produce, and whose rights are therefore invaded by such wrongful intrusion. Thus, not only the occupier of the land trespassed upon, but other persons entitled to share in the present use of the land or of the produce, as commoners, &c., may distrain. But though a commoner may always distrain cattle, &c. of a stranger found upon the common, it would seem that he cannot, unless authorized by a special custom, distrain the cattle, &c. of the person who has the actual possession of the soil. Nor can he distrain the cattle of another commoner who has stocked beyond his proportion, unless the common be stinted, *i.e.* unless the proportion be limited to a certain number. In the more ordinary case of rights of common in respect of all the cattle which the commoner's enclosed land can support during the winter, cattle exceeding the proportion cannot be distrained.

Cattle found trespassing may be distrained damage-feasant, although they have come upon the land without the knowledge of their owner and even through the wrongful act of a stranger. But if they are there by the default of the occupier of the land, as by his neglecting to repair his fences, or to shut his gates against a road or a close in which the cattle lawfully were, such negligent occupier cannot distrain unless the owner of the cattle suffer them to remain on the land after notice and time given to him to remove them; and if cattle trespass on one day and go off before they are distrained, and are taken trespassing on the same land on another day, they can be detained only for the damage done upon the second day.

Cattle, if once off the land upon which they have trespassed, though driven off for the purpose of eluding a distress, cannot be taken even upon immediate pursuit. The occupier must get satisfaction for the damage by action.

Things necessary for the carrying on of trade, as tools and utensils,—or for the maintenance of tillage, as implements of husbandry, beasts of the plough, and sheep as requisite to manure the land, are privileged from Distress whilst other sufficient distress can be found. But this rule does not extend to a distress for a toll or duty arising in respect of the thing taken as a distress, or of things connected with it; as a distress of two sheep for market-toll claimed in respect of the whole flock, or of the anchor of a ship for port-duty due in respect of such ship.

For the protection of tradesmen and their employers, property of which the distrainee has obtained the possession with a view to some service to be performed upon it by him in the way of his trade, is absolutely privileged from distress; as a horse standing in a smith's shop to be shod, or put up at an inn, or cloth sent to a tailor's shop to be made into clothes, or corn sent to a mill or market to be ground or sold. The goods of a guest at an inn are privileged from distress; but this exemption does not extend to the case of a chariot standing in the coach-house of a livery-stable keeper; nor does it protect goods on other premises belonging to the inn but at a distance from it; and even within the inn itself the exemption does not extend to the goods of a person dwelling there as a tenant rather than a guest. Goods in the hands of a factor for sale are privileged from distress; and also goods consigned for sale, landed at a wharf, and placed in the wharfinger's warehouse.

Beasts of the plough may be distrained where no other distress can be found;

and it is sufficient if the distrainor use diligence to find some other distress. A distress is not said to be found unless it be accessible to the party entitled to distrain, by the doors of the house being open, or the gates of the fields unlocked. Beasts of the plough may be distrained upon where the only other sufficient distress consists of growing crops, which though now subjected to distress, are not, as they cannot be sold until ripe, immediately available to the landlord.

A temporary privilege from distress arises when the chattel is in actual use, as an axe with which a man is cutting wood, or a horse on which a man is riding. Implements in trade, as frames for knitting, weaving, &c., are absolutely privileged from distress whilst they are in actual use, otherwise they may be distrained upon if no other sufficient distress can be found.

Rent is not due until the last moment of the day on which it is made payable. No distress therefore can be taken for it until the following day.

A distress for rent or other duties or services can be taken only between sunrise and sunset; but cattle or goods found damage-feasant may be distrained at any time of the day or night.

No distress can be taken for more than six years' arrears of rent; nor can any rent be claimed where non-payment has been acquiesced in for twenty years (3 and 4 Wm. IV. c. 27).

A distress for rent or other service could at common law be taken only upon the land charged therewith, and out of which such rent or services were said to issue.

But this restriction did not apply to the king, who might distrain upon any lands which were in the actual occupation of his tenant, either at the time of the distress or when the rent became due.

The assumption of a similar power by other lords was considered oppressive, and it was ordained by the statute of Marlbridge, that no one should make distress for any cause out of his fee, except the king and his ministers thereunto specially authorized. The privilege of distraining in all lands occupied by the party chargeable, is communicated by 22 Car. II. c. 6; 26 Geo. III. c. 87; 30 Geo. III. c. 50; and 34 Geo. III. c. 75, to the purchasers of certain crown rents.

Under 8 Ann. c. 14, and 11 Geo. II. c. 19, where a lessee fraudulently or clandestinely carries off his goods in order to prevent a distress, the landlord may within five days afterwards distrain them as if they had still continued on the demised premises; provided they have not been (*bonâ fide*) sold for a valuable consideration.

And by the 7th section of the latter statute, where any goods fraudulently and clandestinely carried away by any tenant or lessee, or any person aiding therein, shall be put in any house or other place, locked up or otherwise secured, so as to prevent such goods from being distrained for rent, the landlord or his bailiff may, in the day time, with the assistance of the constable or peace officer (and in case of a dwelling-house, oath being also first made of a reasonable ground to suspect that such goods are therein), break open and enter into such house or place, and take such goods, for the arrears of rent, as he or they might have done if such goods had been put in an open field or place.

To entitle the landlord to follow the goods, the removal must have taken place after the rent became due, and for the purpose of eluding a distress. It is not however necessary that a distress should be in progress, or even contemplated: nor need the removal be clandestine. Although the goods be removed openly, yet if goods sufficient to satisfy the arrears are not left upon the premises, and the landlord is turned over to the barren remedy by action, the removal is fraudulent and the provisions of these statutes may be resorted to. These provisions apply to the goods of the terant only. The goods of a stranger or of an under-tenant may be removed at any time before they are actually distrained upon, and cannot be followed.

The landlord may enter a house to distrain if the outer door be open, although there be other sufficient goods out of the house. It is not lawful to break open outer doors or gates; but if the outer door be open, an inner door may be forced.

If the landlord, having distrained, is forcibly expelled, he may break open outer doors or gates in order to retake the distress. If a window be open, a distress within reach may be taken out at it.

At common law a distress might be taken for rent in a street or other highway being within the land demised. But now, by the statute of Marlbridge, private persons are forbidden to take distresses in the highway. This statute applies only to distresses for rent or for services, and not to toll. Nor does the statute make the distress absolutely void; for though the tenant may lawfully rescue cattle distrained in the highway, or may bring his action on the case upon the statute, yet if he brings trespass or replevin, it seems to be no answer to a justification or an avowry made in respect of the rent.

A distress may be made either by the party himself or his agent, and as distresses in manors were commonly made by the bailiff of the manor, any agent authorized to distrain is called a bailiff. The authority given to the bailiff is usually in writing, and is then called a warrant of distress; but a verbal authority, and even the subsequent adoption of the act by the party on whose behalf the distress is made, is sufficient. In order that the distrainee may know what is included in the distress, an inventory of the goods should be delivered, accompanied, in the case of a distress for rent, by a notice stating the object of the distress, and informing the tenant that unless the rent and charges be paid within five days, the goods and chattels will be sold according to law. This notice is required by 2 W. & M. sess. i. c. 5, § 2, which enacts, "where any goods shall be distrained for rent due upon any demise, lease, or contract, and the tenant or owner of the goods shall not, within five days next after such distress taken, and notice thereof with the cause of such taking, left at the chief mansion house, or other most notorious place on the premises, replevy the same, with sufficient security to be given to the sheriff,—that after such distress and notice and expiration of the five days, the person dis-training shall and may, with the sheriff or under-sheriff, or with the constable of the place, cause the goods to be appraised by two sworn appraisers, and after such appraisement may sell the goods distrained towards satisfaction of the rent, and of the charges of distress, appraisement, and sale, leaving any surplus in the hands of the sheriff, under-sheriff, or constable, for the owner's use."

At common law, goods distrained were, within a reasonable time, to be removed to and confined in an enclosure called a pound, which is either a pound covert, *i. e.* a complete enclosure, or a pound overt, an enclosure sufficiently open to enable the owner to see, and if necessary, to feed the distress, the former being proper for goods easily removed or injured, the latter for cattle; and by 5 & 6 Will. IV. c. 59, § 4, persons impounding cattle or animals in a common open or close pound, or in enclosed ground, are to supply them with food, &c., the value of which they may recover from the owner. By 11 Geo. II. c. 19, § 10, goods distrained for any kind of rent may be impounded on any part of the tenant's ground, to remain there five days, at the expiration of which time they are to be sold, unless sooner replevied. The landlord is not however bound to remove the goods immediately after the expiration of the five days; he is allowed a reasonable time for selling. After the lapse of a reasonable time he is a trespasser if he retain the goods on the premises without the express assent of the tenant, which assent is generally given in writing.

The 1 & 2 Ph. & M. c. 12, requires that no distress of cattle be removed out of the hundred, except to a pound overt in the same county, not above three miles from the place where such distress is taken, and that no cattle or other goods distrained at one time be impounded in several places, whereby the owner would be obliged to sue out several replevins.

The 2 Will. & Mary, sess. 1, c. 5, § 3, directs that corn, grain, or hay distrained be not removed, to the damage of the owner, out of the place where the same shall be found or seized, but be kept there until replevied or sold· and 11

Geo. II. c. 19, which gives a distress for rent-service upon growing crops, directs, §§ 8 and 9, that they shall be cut, gathered, and laid up, when ripe, in the barn or other proper place on such premises, or if none, then in some other barn, &c., to be procured for that purpose, and as near as may be to the premises, giving notice within one week of the place where such crops are deposited; and if the tenant, his executors, &c., at any time before the crops distrained are ripe and cut, pay or tender the rent, costs, and charges, the goods distrained are to be restored. In all other cases, if the rent or other duty be paid, or performed, or tendered to be paid or performed before the distress is impounded, a subsequent detainer is unlawful, and a subsequent impounding or driving to the pound is a trespass.

The statutes authorising the sale of distresses extend only to those made for rent. At common law distresses cannot in general be either sold or used for the benefit of the party distraining. But a distress for fines and amerciaments in a court leet, or for other purposes of public benefit, may be sold; and a special custom or prescription will warrant the sale of a distress in cases where the public has no immediate interest.

A distress made by a party who has no right to distrain, or made for rent or other service which the party offers to pay or perform, or made in the public highway, or upon goods privileged from distress either absolutely or temporarily, is called a *wrongful distress*. Where no right to distrain exists, or where the rent or duty is tendered at the time of the distress, the owner of the goods may rescue them or take them forcibly out of the possession of the distrainer, or bring either an action of replevin, or of trespass. In replevin, the cattle or goods taken are to be redelivered to the owner upon his giving security by a replevin bond, for returning them to the distrainer, in case a return shall be awarded by the court; and therefore in this action damages are recovered only for the intermediate detention and the costs of the replevin bond. In the action of trespass the plaintiff recovers damages to the full value of the goods; because upon such recovery, the property in the goods is transferred to the defendant.

The 2 W. & M. sess. i. c. 5, § 5, provides "that in case of any distress and sale for rent pretended to be due, where in truth no rent is due, the owner of the goods so distrained and sold may, by action of trespass or upon the case, recover double the value of such goods, with full costs of suit."

Whether goods are rightfully or wrongfully distrained, to take them out of the pound is a trespass and a public offence. The proceeding by action is a more prudent course than making a rescue, even before an impounding, where any doubt exists as to the lawfulness of the distress. Independently of the danger of provoking a breach of the peace by the rescuer's thus taking the law into his own hands, he will be liable to an action for the injury sustained by the distrainor by the loss of the security of the distress; should the distress ultimately turn out to be lawful; and in such action, as well as in the action for poundbreach, the rescuer will be liable, under 2 W. & M. sess. i. c. 5, § 4, to the payment of treble damages and treble costs.

A distress for more rent, or greater services than are due, or where the value of the property taken is visibly disproportionate to the rent or other appreciable service, is called an *excessive distress*, for which the party aggrieved is entitled to recover compensation in an action on the case; but he cannot rescue, nor can he replevy or bring trespass.

Upon a distress rightfully taken being afterwards irregularly conducted, the subsequent irregularity at common law made the whole proceeding wrongful, and the party was said to be a trespasser "ab initio." But now, by 11 Geo. II. c. 19, where distress is made for rent justly due, and any irregularity or unlawful act is afterwards done by the party distraining or his agent, the distress itself is not to be deemed unlawful nor the party making it a trespasser; but the person aggrieved by such irregularity, &c. may recover satisfaction for the special damage sustained. (Bradby *On Distresses*, Gilbert, *Distr.*; Bracton; Fleta; Coke upon Littleton; Bacon, Comyns, and Viner's *Abridgments;* Willes's *Reports;* 6 Nevile and Mann, 606.)

DIVIDEND, in commerce, is a word which has two distinct meanings. In its more general employment it is understood to express the money which is divided, *pro rata,* among the creditors of a bankrupt trader, out of the amount realised from his assets. [BANKRUPT.]

The other meaning attached to the word dividend is not so appropriate as that which has just been explained. It is used to signify the half-yearly payments of the perpetual and terminable annuities which constitute the public debt of the country, and does not therefore strictly express that which the word is made to imply. The payment of those so-called dividends is managed on the part of the government by the Bank of England, which receives a compensation from the public for the trouble and expense attending the employment. The exact number of individuals who are entitled to receive these half-yearly payments is not known, as the number of annuitants is not nearly so great as the number of distinc warrants, because many individuals are possessed of annuities due at the same periods of the year, which are included under different heads or accounts in the books of the bank, as bearing different rates of interest, or being otherwise under different circumstances; and besides, many persons hold annuities which are payable at both half-yearly periods. It is certain, however, that the greater part of the public creditors are entitled to annuities for only small sums, more than nine-tenths of the payments being for sums not exceeding 100*l.*, and nearly one-half for sums not exceeding 10*l.* The number of warrants issued for the payment of dividends at each quarter of the year ending 5th January, 1843, was as follows:—5th April, 89,560; 5th July, 191,980; 10th October, 89,379; 5th January, 192,970.

DIVISION OF EMPLOYMENTS, in political economy, is an important agent in increasing the productiveness of labour. It is by labour alone that wealth is produced. It is a law of man's nature that "by the sweat of his face he shall eat bread;" and in return for his labour he acquires various sources of enjoyment. The ingenuity with which he has been endowed, and the hard necessities of his condition, lead him to discover the most effective means of applying his labour to whatever objects he may be seeking to attain. He desires first to work no more than is necessary, and secondly to obtain the largest return—the most abundant enjoyment, for his industry. He soon finds that his own unaided labour will scarcely provide for him the barest necessaries, and that ease or enjoyment is unattainable. Thus instead of each man labouring separately, and independently of all others, many men combine together for securing the various objects of life, by means of their joint labour; and this combination of labour leads to division of employments. Labour is naturally exerted in these two forms in the very earliest stages of society. The first pair whom God's ordinances and their own instinct united, must have combined for the support of themselves and their common family, and diversity of sex alone must have produced distinct employments. Among savages the man engages in the chase, for which he has a natural predilection, and for which his strength adapts him, while his mate rears their children and executes those functions which are suited to her sex, but which are as conducive to the comfort of both as if both performed them. In this manner a division of employments naturally arises, and each family affords an example of its origin and character.

This combination for a common object, succeeded by a division of employments, pervades every process of human industry, and increases in variety and complexity with the growth of civilization. One of the earliest forms of industry is that of fishing, and none, perhaps, exemplifies more aptly the mode in which labour is necessarily applied to the purposes of life. A man desirous of building a fishing-boat may cut down a tree, without any assistance from others, and may even hew it into shape: but if it be larger than a mere canoe he cannot, by his own strength, remove it from the spot on which the tree had fallen, and launch it upon the sea. To effect this, others must combine their strength with his. To manage a boat the labour of more than one man is ordinarily required, and the larger the boat the greater must be the number who combine to navigate it. If they paddle or row it, their labour is simply combined for one purpose and in one manner, except that one, instead of rowing, may probably steer the boat. As the art of navigation improves and its objects become multiplied, in addition to a more extensive combination of men in pursuit of the same objects, a diversity of employments ensues. In a deep-sea fishery, some attend to the nets, others to the sails; and on their return to land, some arrange the nets to dry and repair them, while others are engaged in disposing of the fish.

From these illustrations it is evident that the cause of a division of employments is to be sought in the nature and circumstances of man. It is not the result of extraordinary foresight, but is suggested by the most common exigencies of life: its convenience is obvious, but the feeling which prompts men to adopt it is spontaneous and, as it were, intuitive. It is a social necessity, and the very foundation of any social system whatever, yet it is practised almost unconsciously by the greater part of mankind. Its existence, however, lies so open to observation that it is scarcely to be ranked as a discovery of political economy; but that science, having noted the facts of a combination of labour and a division of employments, explains their uses and results; and in pursuing these inquiries it developes some of the most important principles connected with the production and distribution of wealth. To these inquiries we must now devote our attention.

As labour is the lot of man, it is desirable that his labour should be as productive as possible, in order that the sum of his enjoyments should exceed that of his endurance. This result is attained by several men combining their labour for one object, and pursuing different employments for their reciprocal benefit, instead of each man labouring independently for himself and employing himself in the same manner as all other men. A division of employments, therefore, is not only a natural incident of labour, but is an important auxiliary of human enjoyment. The means by which it adds to the efficacy of labour are described by Adam Smith to be—1st. an "increase of dexterity in every particular workman;" 2ndly. " the saving of the time which is commonly lost in passing from one species of work to another;" and, 3rdly. " the invention of a great number of machines which facilitate and abridge labour, and enable one man to do the work of many:" to which may be added, 4thly, the separation which it causes between labour and the direction of labour; 5thly, the power which it gives of using machinery effectually, when invented; 6thly, the opportunities of exchange which it affords and the means of availing ourselves of the enjoyments arising from the natural capabilities of the soil, climate, situation, or mineral productions of different parts of the world, and of the peculiar aptitude of their inhabitants for various kinds of industry.

1. The superior dexterity of workmen engaged exclusively in one occupation is universally known. " Use is second nature," and when a man has been long accustomed to a particular employment, not only has he acquired great dexterity, but his mind appears to be endowed with faculties specially adapted to his business. The jockey seems to have been born for the saddle; the sailor for the ship: both are active, intelligent, dexterous: but fancy their occupations exchanged or combined! the sailor in the saddle, the jockey at the helm; or both alternately riding the favourite horse at Newmarket and furling the top-gallants of a threedecker at Spithead! The constant exercise of the faculties in any act or business gives them an aptitude for it, which to others is a matter of astonishment. The eye and the hand perform their offices with such precision and rapidity, that their work seems spontaneous, as it were, and independent of the will of the workman. Without deliberation, almost without care, the business is done; and done better than others could do it with the greatest pains. All processes of art and manufacture, and the daily experience of all

DIVISION OF EMPLOYMENTS.

men, confirm this statement as an unquestionable fact (Babbage, *Economy of Machinery and Manufactures*). The advantages of peculiar skill are that men can work better and faster, that the products of their labour are more valuable and more abundant, and that their contributions to the general stock of the world's enjoyments are multiplied. By following out these advantages through all their relations, they will be found to be the primary source of wealth; and, in a moral point of view, the main cause of social progress and of the development of the highest faculties of man.

2. "The saving of time which is commonly lost in passing from one species of work to another" enables a man who is constantly engaged in one process to perform more work than he would have been able to get through in the course of a day, if he had been required to change his employment. For this reason, as well as on account of his skill, a division of employments makes his labour more productive.

3. The invention of tools and machinery is the most effective auxiliary of labour, and it is necessarily promoted by a division of employments. Those who are constantly attending to one business or description of labour must become best acquainted with its requirements—their observation and experience are concentrated upon it—their interest urges them to facilitate their own exertions. How many inventions are due to workmen employed in manual labour the history of the steam-engine and of the cotton manufacture will furnish examples: but it is not in the case of workmen alone that division of employments facilitates invention. Their employers also have their whole minds bent upon improving their business; and amidst the multiplication of trades arise engineers and machinists, whose sole business it is to construct, improve, and invent machinery, aided by all the lights of theoretical science. And this leads us to the fourth advantage of a division of employments.

4. If all men were doing the same thing, and working for themselves unaided by others, their condition would never be improved; but by following particular occupations those who exert most skill and industry produce more than they require for their own subsistence, and reserve a fund for the employment of others. [CAPITAL.] And thus there grows up from the midst of the people a class of employers who direct the labour of others. Until labour is so directed and maintained by the previous accumulation of capital, it is comparatively ineffectual; and while a division of employments is a powerful agent in producing capital, the latter, in its turn, facilitates a further subdivision. Without it, indeed, a system of division can only be carried out imperfectly and to a very small extent. The growth of capital also gives to many men the glorious privilege of leisure, exempts them from the necessity of labour, and leaves them free to study, to reflect, to observe, to reason and investigate. From this class arise men of science and of letters—philosophers, statesmen, historians, poets. And even with these the apportionment of a peculiar province gives power to their minds, and expands their knowledge. Their natural talents are developed, and their aptitude for particular pursuits becomes as conspicuous in intellectual industry as that of other men in manual operations.

5. Adam Smith speaks of the importance of a division of employments as leading to the invention of machinery, but passes over its utility in using machinery effectually, when invented. Every part of a large machine requires workmen whose sole business it is to work in unison with its peculiar movement. So distinct are these various processes—so diverse their character—that in all large manufactures there is an extensive vocabulary of names by which operatives working in the very same factory are distinguished.* Without such a subdivision of peculiar employments the most ingenious machinery would be useless: and thus while machinery multiplies distinct operations of labour, they are, in their turn, essential to its efficacy.

---

* A curious example will be found in the glossary annexed to the 'Report of the Commission on Frame-Work Knitters,' 1845: and numerous others in the Occupation Abstract of the Census Commissioners—counties of Lancaster, Leicester, West Riding of Yorkshire, &c.

6. Adam Smith assigns the origin of a division of employments to the "trucking disposition" of mankind—to their "propensity to truck, barter, and exchange one thing for another" (book i. ch. ii.). This love of barter, however, is only a secondary cause: men have no natural taste for it; but use it as a means of obtaining the various objects which they desire. If they could obtain them without the trouble of barter, they would unquestionably not follow barter as an amusement, any more than they would work if they could get what they wanted without labour. So far, then, from the trucking disposition of men being the cause of a division of employments, it would appear that a division of employments is rather the proximate cause of commerce. For if all men worked in the same manner and produced the same things, there would be nothing to exchange: but as soon as men learn to devote themselves to the production of one commodity, the whole of which they cannot consume, they must exchange the produce of their labour with others, who have been producing objects which they desire to possess. This is an intelligible origin of barter and commerce—consistent with the natural propensities of mankind, and not requiring for its support the strained hypothesis that men have an innate disposition to truck. But a division of employments, like barter, is itself but a secondary cause; and both alike must ultimately be referred to the one original cause of all forms of industry—the desire of mankind to possess various enjoyments which are only to be gained by labour.

This would appear to be the natural course of social progress. First, a man applies himself to a particular business because he has facilities for following it. One man lives by the sea and is a fisherman: another lives near the forest and hunts game. Each could obtain more of this particular food than he requires for his own use, and may desire some little variety. Under these circumstances it is very natural that they should effect exchanges with each other—not for the mere love of barter—but for the love of food. But such an exchange could not be made between two men who both lived by fishing—nor between two others who both lived by hunting: for under such circumstances neither party would have anything to offer but that of which the other already had enough. It is perfectly true that without barter no extensive division of employments can exist: but it is clear that barter is the immediate effect rather than the cause of such division. Of the influence of commerce upon the division of employments we shall have to speak presently; but, in this place, it is sufficient to show that the production of different commodities beyond the immediate wants of those who produce them enables men to barter, by giving them something to offer in exchange: and, that afterwards, the advantages derived from barter are an encouragement to further production of the same kind. When this state of things has been once established, men avail themselves of all the natural advantages of their several positions, and apply themselves to the production of those commodities for which they have peculiar facilities. In one country minerals can be drawn from the bowels of the earth in unlimited abundance: in another the fruits of the earth teem upon its surface—fostered by a genial climate and a fertile soil. The inhabitants of these countries naturally seek to develop the resources of the earth which are within their reach. They labour effectively and produce abundance of their particular commodities, which they give in exchange for other things which they cannot produce themselves, but which they desire to enjoy. And thus a division of employments, by the aid of an extended commerce, distributes over the whole world, the advantages of soil, climate, situation, and mineral productions, obtained by the experience and skill of men who have adapted their talents to the circumstances of each country.

Having thus hastily enumerated the several ways in which a division of employments adds to the efficacy of human labour, and increases the enjoyments of men, let us inquire in what manner it is restrained and limited. It may be collected from several of the preceding remarks, that the power of distributing men into particular employments must be limited by the extent of the market in which the produce of their labour may be exchanged. When there are no means of exchanging, men must provide everything for themselves that they require; and there is no further division of employments than that which necessarily takes place in families, and in the most simple forms of industry. So in every degree in which the situation and circumstances of men give facilities of exchange, do particular employments become assigned to individuals. A village draper sells all kinds of drapery, together with hats, shoes, coats, smock-frocks: nay, in some villages there is but one shop, in which nearly every kind of trade is carried on. In a populous city, on the other hand, trades are almost indefinitely subdivided. And why is this? Solely because of the extent of the market. In the one case, if a man sold nothing but hats, he could not gain a livelihood, and therefore he sells coats, smock-frocks, shoes, and all kinds of drapery—everything, in fact, which the people round about him are likely to buy. In the other case, there is so large a demand for hats, that a man can gain a better livelihood by the exclusive sale of them, than by a heterogeneous trade like that of the village shopkeeper.

But while, by means of exchange, employments are thus subdivided, the labour of many men is most efficiently combined in producing particular results. The combinations of industry for one object are often truly wonderful, while the employments of those who are really co-operating with one another are so distinct, that they are wholly unconscious of any combination at all; nor is their combination at once perceptible to others. If you ask a man "who made his coat?"—he will naturally answer "his tailor." But ask him to enumerate the persons who had contributed to its production, and he will pause long before he attempts any answer, however incomplete. He will be reminded of the grazier, the shepherd, the wool-salesman, the various workmen in the cloth factory—the button-makers, the manufacturers of silk, and thread, and needles: but still the catalogue will be imperfect. In producing the raw materials, and in conveying, selling, and manufacturing them, the diversity of occupations is extraordinarily great. Each man attends to his own business, and scarcely thinks of its relations to the business of other people; and yet all are co-operating in the most effectual manner, for the most perfect and economical manufacture of this finished work of varied art.

The general operation of the principles of a combination of labour and division of employments has now been sufficiently explained, so far as it relates to the efficiency of human industry. Of its effects upon the distribution of wealth (another important branch of political economy) no more need be said, than that by multiplying the modes in which industry is made productive, it is the main cause of the various grades of society which exist in all civilized countries. The different employments of men determine their social position as labourers or employers of labour; and the wealth arising from the effective employment of labour is distributed, through the several classes, as rent, profits, and wages.

It has been urged as an objection to an extended division of employments, that it unfits men for any change of business which altered circumstances may require; and that, on that account, great misery is caused when the demand for any particular kind of labour is reduced. Of this position the hand-loom weavers of England and Scotland are a familiar example, who are said to have been thrown out of employment by the extension of machinery. That they have been reduced to great distress is certain; but in their employment there was nothing to unfit them from engaging in power-loom weaving. On the contrary, the transition from one employment to the other would have been perfectly natural; but they preferred their independent life to the discipline of a factory, and for that and other reasons persisted in continuing in their old trade. In the mean time thousands of agricultural labourers and their families, whose occupations had been totally dissimilar, flocked into the manufacturing districts, and readily learned their new business. This example, therefore, instead of sustaining the objection, proves that a division of employments does not disable men, so much as might be expected, from transferring their labour to other departments of industry, whenever a sufficient inducement attracts them. But any interruption or change in the ordinary course of industry is necessarily productive of temporary suffering to the working classes, from whatever cause it may arise; and an alteration in the forms of applying labour is but one out of many such causes. Yet much as this evil must be deplored, it is a satisfaction to know that it is only occasional, temporary, and partial in its operation, while the permanent welfare of mankind is promoted by all those means which render industry most productive and multiply the sources of human enjoyment.

Another objection to a minute subdivision of employments is, that it reduces vast masses of men to the condition of organized machines, uses them like tools, and uses them as such merely because machines have not yet been invented to do their work. From these facts, which are, to a certain extent, undeniable, it is inferred that the moral and intellectual character of men is degraded. This inference, however, is not supported by experience. Agricultural employments are less subdivided than trades and manufactures; but no one will contend that the farm labourer is ordinarily more intelligent than the operative, nor that his morals are decidedly superior. In comparing their relative condition, we shall be led into error if we confine our attention to the influence of a division of employments. In the lower departments of labour the work is rarely of a kind to enlarge the understanding, whether it consist of a combination of several occupations or of one only; and in either case the greater part of a man's time is engaged in his daily work. It is, therefore, to the circumstances by which he is surrounded, rather than to the nature of his work itself, that we must generally refer his condition. In thinly peopled countries there can be comparatively little division of employments, and in populous cities the principle of division, for reasons already explained, is carried ve the one case the intercourse with each other is very confine enlivened with scarcely any v the other case persons are crow ther, and brought into contin course. These opposite circ produce different results for go evil. The intelligence of mank questionably increased by exten course with one another: their the same time, are more liable tion. In large cities they are e more temptations—they are t restraint; and, above all, tl almost universally, higher wag enable them to indulge their pl more freely. Much of the il disparity of rural and town pe might be removed by an efficie of education, by which men better qualified to observe an upon the objects by which the surrounded. And great woul moral influence of education in high wages innocuous, by offeri sources of recreation to the opera attractive than the temptations

But to all objections it may be that a division of employments perative law of civilization. powering is the necessity of a tion of labour with a distributi tinct employments, for the proc wealth, that Mr. Wakefield niously ascribed to it the origin o in countries where labour has accessible by means of wages. (to Adam Smith, book i. ch. 1. land is abundant, families natur ter themselves over it, and pr themselves nearly all that th More than they want they do no as there is no market; and the capital, under such circumstanc possible. One man has no indu offer to another for his labour; the strongest men, with domin finding the necessity of combin try for any extensive producti war upon their weaker neighb compel them to work by fo where land becomes scarce a men are forced into other emp distinct from agriculture; capit wages are offered as an inducement to work, and the more wealthy and populous a country becomes, the more extensive must be the distribution of separate employments. To object to a division of employments, therefore, is no less than to object to civilization altogether; for the two conditions are inseparable. It is deeply to be lamented that many evils have hitherto clung to the progress of civilization, which are not its necessary accompaniments. Many of them may be referred to the slow growth of political science, and might be corrected by the application of sound principles of government; many may be attributed to the neglect of the religious and moral culture of an *increasing* population: but short indeed must be the sight of any man who would seek to correct them by applying to a civilized state the rude expedients of barbarism.

(Adam Smith's *Wealth of Nations*, book i. chapters 1, 2, 3, with Notes by M'Culloch and Wakefield; M'Culloch's *Principles of Political Economy*, &c.)

DIVORCE (from the Latin word divórtium, a divertendo, from diverting or separating), the legal separation of husband and wife. In England, divorce is of two kinds: à mensâ et thoro, from bed and board; and à vinculo matrimonii, from the bond of the marriage. The divorce à mensâ et thoro is pronounced by the spiritual court for causes arising subsequent to the marriage, as for adultery, cruelty, &c.: it does not dissolve the marriage, and the parties cannot contract another marriage. [BIGAMY.] In fact it is equivalent only to a separation.

The divorce à vinculo matrimonii can be obtained in the spiritual courts for causes only existing before the marriage, as precontract, consanguinity, impotency, &c. This divorce declares the marriage to have been null and void, the issue begotten between the parties are bastardized, and the parties themselves are at liberty to contract marriage with others.

From the curious document preserved by Selden ('Uxor Ebraica,' c. xxx., vol. iii. 845, folio ed. of his Works), whereby John de Cameys, in the reign of Edward I., transferred his wife and her property to William Paynel; and also, from the reference to the laws of Howel the Good, at the end of this article, it would seem that in the early periods of English law a divorce might be had by mutual consent; but all trace of such a custom is lost. We know however (3 Salk. *Rep.* 138) that, until the 44 Eliz., a divorce à vinculo matrimonii might be had in the ecclesiastical courts for adultery; but in Foljambe's case, which occurred in that year in the Star Chamber, Archbishop Bancroft, upon the advice of divines, held that adultery was only a cause of divorce à mensâ et thoro.

The history of the law of divorce in England may perhaps be thus satisfactorily explained. Marriage, being a contract of a civil nature, might originally be dissolved by consent; and probably the ordinary courts of justice asserted their jurisdiction over this as well as every other description of contract. At length, the rite of marriage having been elevated to the dignity of a sacrament by Pope Innocent III., A.D. 1215, the ecclesiastical courts asserted the sole jurisdiction over it. In the course of time the power of these courts was again controlled, and the sole jurisdiction for granting divorces for matter arising subsequently to the marriage was vested in the superior court of the kingdom, the House of Lords, where it was less likely to be abused than by the ecclesiastical authorities, who used to grant these and other dispensations for money.

Marriage is now, by the law of England, indissoluble by the decree of any of the ordinary courts, on account of any cause that arises subsequently to the marriage; but divorce à vinculo matrimonii may still for adultery, &c. be obtained by act of parliament. For this purpose it is necessary that a civil action should have been brought by the husband in one of the courts of law against the adulterer [ADULTERY], and damages obtained therein, or some sufficient reason adduced why such action was not brought, or damages obtained, and that a definitive sentence of divorce à mensâ et thoro should have been pronounced between the parties in the ecclesiastical court. But this sentence cannot be obtained for the adultery of the wife, if she recriminates, and can prove that the husband has been unfaithful to the marriage vow; and further, to prevent any collusion between the parties, both houses of parliament may, if necessary, and generally do, require satisfactory evidence that it is proper to allow the bill of divorce to pass.

The first proceeding of this nature was in the reign of Edward VI., and bills of divorce have since greatly increased. Where the injured husband can satisfy both houses of parliament, which are not bound in granting or withholding the indulgence by any of those fixed rules which control the proceedings of ordinary courts, a divorce is granted. The expenses of the proceeding are so considerable as to amount to an absolute denial of the relief to the mass of society; indeed from this circumstance divorce bills have not improperly been called the privilege of the rich. There is an order of the House of Lords that, in every divorce bill on account of adultery, a clause shall be inserted to prohibit the marriage of the offending parties with each other; but this clause is generally omitted; indeed it has been inserted only once, and that in a very flagrant case. But it is not unusual for parliament to provide that the wife shall not be left entirely destitute, by directing a payment of a sum of money, in the nature of alimony, by the husband, out of the fortune which he had with the wife. By the divorce à vinculo matrimonii the wife forfeits her dower. [DOWER.]

A Parliamentary return (354, Sess. 1844) gives the number of matrimonial suits instituted in each metropolitan and diocesan court in England, Wales, and Ireland, for the four years 1840-1-2-3; the number in the Court of Session, Scotland; the number of appeals before the Judicial Committee of Privy Council, or the House of Lords; and the number of divorce acts passed in the same four years. The following is an abstract of this return:—

	Suits.
England	160
Wales	2
Ireland	57
Scotland	169

	Appeals.
Judicial Committee	6
House of Lords	4

	Divorce Acts.
1840	8
1841	5
1842	9
1843	5

In the Court of Arches the average expense of 32 suits was 168*l*.; in the Consistorial and Episcopal Court of London the average expense of 87 suits was 120*l*. In appeals before the Judicial Committee the average expense of 6 suits was 586*l*.; in appeals before the Lords (4 cases, all from the Court of Session, Scotland) the expenses varied from 23*l*. to 53*l*. The average expense (fees, House of Lords), of each act (27 acts) was 87*l*. 16*s*. 10*d*.

The causes admitted by various codes of law as grounds for the suspension or dissolution of marriage are various, and indicative of the state of society.

According to the law of Moses (24 *Deut.* i.), "When a man hath taken a wife and married her, and it come to pass that she find no favour in his eyes, because he hath found some uncleanness in her, then let him write her a bill of divorcement and give it in her hand, and send her out of his house." After 90 days, the wife might marry again. But after she had contracted a second marriage, though she should be again divorced, her former husband might not take her to be his wife. About the time of our Saviour, there was a great dispute between the schools of the great doctors Hillel and Shammai as to the meaning of this law. The former contended that a husband might not divorce his wife except for some gross misconduct, or for some serious bodily defect which was not known to him before marriage; but the latter were of opinion that simple dislike, the smallest offence, or merely the husband's will, was a sufficient ground for divorce. This is the opinion which the Jews generally adopted, and particularly the Pharisees, which explains their conduct when they came to Jesus "tempting him, and saying unto him, Is it lawful for a man to put away his wife for every cause?" (*Matth.* xix.) The answer was, "Moses, because of the hardness of your hearts, suffered you to put away your wives, but from the beginning it was not so." From this it is evident that Christ considered that the law of Moses allowed too great a latitude to the husband in his exercise of the power of divorce, and that this allowance arose from "the hardness of their hearts;" by which we may understand that they were so habituated to the practice, that any law which should have abolished such practices would have been ineffectual. All it could do was to introduce such modifications, with the view of diminishing the existing practice, as the people would tolerate. The form of a Jewish bill of divorcement is given by Selden, *Uxor Ebraica,* lib. iii., ch. 24; and see Levi's *Ceremonies of the Jews,* p. 146.

It is probable that the usages in the matter of divorce now existing among the Arabs, are the same, or nearly so, as they were when Mohammed began his legislation. An Arab may divorce his wife on the slightest occasion: he has only to say to her "Thou art divorced," and she becomes so. So easy and so common is that practice, that Burckhardt assures us that he has seen Arabs not more than 45 years of age who were known to have had 50 wives, yet the Arabs have rarely more than one wife at a time.

By the Mohammedan law a man may divorce his wife orally and without any ceremony; when this is done, he pays her a portion, generally one-third of her dowry. He may divorce her twice, and take her again without her consent; but if he divorce her a third time, or put her away by a triple divorce conveyed in the same sentence, he cannot receive her again until she has been married and divorced by another husband, who must have consummated his marriage with her.

By the Jewish law it appears that a wife could not divorce her husband; but under the Mohammedan code, for cruelty and some other causes, she may divorce him; and this is the only instance in which Mohammed appears to have been more considerate towards women than Moses.

(Sale's *Koran;* Lane's *Modern Egyp-* tians; Hamilton's *Hedaya,* and the *Mishcat ul-Masâbih;* Selden's *Uxor Ebraica;* and see the case of *Lindo* v. *Belisario,* 1 Hagg. 216, before Lord Stowell.)

Among the Hindoos, and also among the Chinese, a husband may divorce his wife upon the slightest grounds, or even without assigning any reason. Some of the rules mentioned by the Abbé Dubois, as laid down in the 'Padma Purana,' one of the books of highest authority among the Hindoos, show their manner of thinking concerning the conduct of their wives. "In every stage of her life, a woman is created to obey. At first she yields obedience to her father and mother; when married, she submits to her husband and her father and mother-in-law; in old age, she must be ruled by her children. During her life she can never be under her own control. If her husband laugh, she ought to laugh; if he weep, she will weep also; if he is disposed to speak, she will join in conversation. When in the presence of her husband, a woman must not look on one side and the other; she must keep her eyes on her master, to be ready to receive his commands. When he speaks, she must be quiet, and listen to nothing besides. When he calls her, she must leave every thing else, and attend upon him alone." And in the Hindoo code it is said, "The Creator formed woman for this purpose, viz., that children might be born from her." The reasons for which, according to the Brahmanic law, a man may divorce his wife, may be seen in Colebrooke's *Digest of Hindoo Law,* vol. ii. p. 414, &c., 8vo. edit.; and Kalthoff, *Jus Matrimonii veterum Indorum* (Bonn. 1829, 8) p. 76, &c.

The laws in the several Grecian states regarding divorce were different, and in some of them men were allowed to put away their wives on slight occasions. The Cretans permitted it to any man who was afraid of having too great a number of children. Among the Athenians either husband or wife might take the first step towards dissolving the marriage. The wife might leave the husband, or the husband might dismiss his wife. Adultery on the part of the wife was apparently in itself a divorce; but the adultery, we may presume, must have been legally proved first. The Spartans seldom divorced their wives; indeed the ephori fined Lysander for repudiating his wife. Ariston (Herod. vi. 63) put away his second wife, but it seems to have been done rather to have a son, for his wife was barren, than according to the custom of the country. Anaxandrides (Herod. v. 39) was strongly urged by the ephori to divorce his barren wife, and on his not consenting, the matter was compounded by his taking another wife: thus he had two at once, which Herodotus observes was contrary to Spartan usage.

The common Roman term for Divorce is Divortium. It is said that the word Repudium, corresponding to which we have the word "repudiate," applied only to the dissolution of a contract of marriage (sponsalia), and not to an actual marriage (*Dig.* 50, tit. 16, s. 101): but Divortium and Repudium are sometimes used indifferently. Plutarch states (*Romulus*, c. 22) that originally the husband alone had the power of effecting a divorce, which may be true, but it was not so in the late period of the Republic and under the Empire. When the wife was *in manu viri*, a technical term that implied she was in the relation of a daughter to her husband, it is not easy to conceive how the wife could effect a divorce. In other cases, it is easily conceivable. The essence of the nature of a Roman marriage was abiding consent, and if either party expressed a dissent to the union, it followed that it was at an end. The first instance of a divorce at Rome, according to Gellius (iv. 3), was the case of Sp. Cervilius Ruga, who put away his wife because she was barren. As to this story, see Savigny, *Zeitschrift der Geschichthe Rechtswissenschaft*, v 269. Divorces were common at Rome in the time of Cicero, as we may collect from his writings; and Cicero himself divorced his aged wife Terentia and took a young wife in her place. The portion (dos) which the wife brought with her to support part of the matrimonial expenses, was as a general rule returned to the wife when she was divorced by the husband, or when they separated by consent: this condition tended somewhat to check a husband from divorcing his wife on light grounds.

As the children of a Roman marriage were in the power of the father, and belonged to him alone, there was no difficulty in divorce as to this point. Whether the marriage continued to subsist or not, the children were alone at the disposal of the father. But a constitution of Diocletian and Maximian empowered a competent judge to declare whether the children should stay with the father or with the mother (*Cod.* v. tit. 24). In some cases, where the wife was to blame, as for instance if she had committed adultery, a sixth part of the dos might be retained by the husband.

As to the form of divorce, it was necessary that there should be some distinct declaration of the intention of the husband or wife, or of both, to separate. In some cases, a written notice was delivered. The Lex Julia de Adulteriis required seven witnesses to the divorce, and a freedman of the person who made the divorce. One object of the Lex Papia et Poppæa, which, as well as the Lex Julia de Adul teriis, was passed in the time of Augustus, was to impose some restraint on divorces. The practice of divorce continued under the Christian Emperors, but subject to the observance of certain forms, and certain penalties.

Among the antient Britons, it may be collected from the laws of Howel the Good that the husband and wife might agree to dissolve the marriage at any time; in which case, if the separation took place during the first seven years of the marriage, a certain specified distribution of the property was made, but after that period the division was equal. No limit was set to the husband's discretion in divorcing his wife, but the wife could only divorce her husband in case he should be leprous, have bad breath, or be impotent, in which cases she might leave him and obtain all her property. The parties were at liberty to contract a fresh marriage; but if a man repented of having divorced his wife, although she had married another man, yet if he could overtake her before the consummation of the marriage, or, as the law expresses it, "with one foot in the bed of her second husband, and the other outside," he might have his wife again.

The law of Scotland relating to divorce differs widely from that in England: there, a divorce à vinculo matrimonii is a civil remedy, and may be obtained for adultery, or for wilful desertion by either party, persisted in for four years, though to this a good ground of separation is a defence. But recrimination is no bar to a divorce, as it is in England.

In the Dutch law there are only two causes of divorce à vinculo matrimonii, adultery and desertion.

In Spain the same causes affect the validity of a marriage as in England, and the contract is indissoluble by the civil courts, matrimonial causes being exclusively of ecclesiastical cognizance. (*Instit. Laws of Spain.*)

The law of France, before the Revolution, following the judgment of the Catholic Church, held marriage to be indissoluble; but the legislators of the early Revolutionary period permitted divorce at the pleasure of the parties. where incompatibility of temper was alleged. In the first three months of the year 1793, the number of divorces in the city of Paris alone amounted to 562, and the marriages to 1785, a proportion not much less than one to three; while the divorces in England for the previous century did not amount to much more than one-fifth of the number. (Burke's *Letters on a Regicide Peace.*) Burke further states that he followed up the inquiry through several subsequent months till he was tired, and found the results still the same. It must be remembered however that Burke wrote in the spirit of an advocate; that the period he chose was that immediately following the promulgation of the law, when all couples previously discontented with each other obtained divorces; and that if his calculations had fully borne out his statement, he would have given them in his pamphlet, which was written for a political purpose, and he would not have rested satisfied with indefinite allegations. It was generally admitted however that the licence was too great. The Code Napoleon accordingly restricted the liberty, but still allowed either party to demand a divorce on the ground of adultery committed by the other; for outrageous conduct, or illusage; on account of condemnation to an infamous punishment; or to effect it by mutual consent, expressed under certain conditions. By the same code a woman could not contract a new marriage until the expiration of ten months from the dissolution of the preceding.

On the restoration of the Bourbons a law was promulgated (8th May, 1816), declaring divorce to be abolished; that all suits then pending for divorce, for definite cause, should be for separation only, and that all steps then taken for divorce by mutual consent should be void; and such is now the law of France.

In the United States, marriage, though it may be celebrated before clergymen as well as civil magistrates, is considered as a civil contract. The causes of divorce, and the facility or difficulty of obtaining it, are by no means the same in the several States. The more general causes of a divorce à vinculo matrimonii are, former marriage, physical incapacity, or consanguinity; by the Connecticut law, fraudulent contract; and by the New York code, idiotcy and insanity, and either party being under the age of consent. Adultery is also a cause of divorce à vinculo matrimonii; and the laws of some of the States prohibit the guilty party from marrying again. If the husband or wife is absent seven years, or by the laws of some States, three years, and not heard from, the other is at liberty to marry again; and in some States, if the husband desert the wife, and make no provision for her support during three years, being able to make such provision, the wife can obtain a divorce. Extreme cruelty in either party is also generally a cause of divorce à vinculo matrimonii. In many of the States applications to the legislature for divorce, in cases not provided for by the statutes, are very frequent. In New York and New Jersey divorce is a subject of Chancery jurisdiction, from which, as in other cases, questions of law may be referred to a jury for trial. In New Hampshire, joining the religious society of Shakers, who hold cohabitation unlawful, and continuing in that society for three years, is sufficient ground for a

3 D 2

divorce. But in most of the States the courts of law have cognizance of divorce. The laws prescribe the provision to be made for the wife in case of divorce, confiding to the courts however some degree of discretion in fixing the amount of alimony.

It is very questionable, says Chancellor Kent, whether the facility with which divorces can be procured in some of the States be not productive of more evil than good: and he states that he has had reason to believe, in the exercise of a judicial cognizance over numerous cases of divorce, that adultery was sometimes committed on the part of the husband for the very purpose of the divorce.

(Kent's *Commentaries*; *Ency. Americ.* Upon the general advantages of indissolubility, as opposed to unlimited divorce, see Hume's *Essay on Polygamy and Divorce*; Paley's *Moral Philosophy*; and the judgment of Lord Stowell in Evans v. Evans, 1 Hagg. *Repts.*, 48; Milton, in his famous treatise, advocates the increased facility of obtaining a divorce; and see also Gibbon, *Decline and Fall*, c. 44.)

DIWAN is a Persian word familiar to readers of works relating to the East, in the sense of—1st, a senate, or council of state; and, 2nd, a collection of poems by one and the same author. The earliest acceptation, however, in which we find it employed is that of a muster-roll, or military pay-book.—The Arabic historian, Fakhreddin Râzi, informs us that when, in the caliphat of Omar, the second successor of Mohammed, the conquests of the Mussulmans assumed an extensive character, the equal distribution of the booty became a matter of great difficulty, A Persian marzbân, or satrap, who happened to be at the head-quarters of the caliph at Medinah, suggested the adoption of the system followed in his own country, of an account-book, in which all receipts and disbursements were regularly entered, along with a list, duly arranged, of the names of those persons who were entitled to a share in the booty. With the register itself, its Persian appellation (dîwân) was adopted by the Arabs. (Freytag, *Locmani Fabulæ et plura loca ex add. historicis selecta*, &c., pp. 32, 33;

Henzi, *Fragmenta Arabica*, St. Petersburg, 1820, p. 36, et seq.) Whether a council of state was subsequently called dîwân, as having originally been a financial board appointed to regulate the list (dîwân) of stipendiaries and pensioners, or whether it was so called as being summoned according to a list (dîwân) containing the names of all its members, we are unable to determine. The opinion that a body of councillors should have received this appellation, as has been asserted by some, in consequence of the expression of an ancient king of Persia, *inân diwân end*, "these (men) are (clever like) devils," will scarcely be seriously entertained by any one. The word 'dîwân' is also used to express the saloon or hall where a council is held, and has been applied to denote generally a state chamber, or room where company is received. Hence probably it has arisen that the word 'divan,' in several European languages, signifies a sofa. Collections of poems in Persian, Arabic, Turkish, Hindustani, &c., seem to have received the appellation 'dîwân' from their methodical arrangement, inasmuch as the poems succeed one another according to the alphabetic order of the concluding letters of the rhyming syllables, which are the same in all the distichs throughout each poem.

DOCKET. [BANKRUPT.]

DOCTOR, one that has taken the highest degree in the faculties of Divinity, Law, Physic, or Music. In its original import it means a person so skilled in his particular art or science as to be qualified to teach it.

There is much difference of opinion as to the time when the title of Doctor was first created. It seems to have been established for the professors of the Roman law in the University of Bologna, about the middle of the twelfth century. Antony à Wood says, that the title of Doctor in Divinity was used at Paris, after Peter Lombard had compiled his Sentences, about the year 1151. (*Hist. and Antiq. Univ. of Oxford*, 4to. Oxf. 1792, vol. i. p. 62.) Previously those who had proceeded in the faculties had been termed Masters only. The title of Doctor was not adopted in the English Universities earlier than the time of John or Henry the Third. Wood cites several instances of the expense and magnificence which attended the early granting of the higher degrees in England in the reigns of Henry III. and Edward I. (Wood, ut supr. pp. 65, 66.)

In Oxford the time requisite for the Doctor of Divinity's degree, subsequent to that of M.A., is eleven years: for a Doctor's of Civil Law, five years from the time at which the Bachelor of Laws' degree was conferred. Those who take this degree professionally, in order to practise in Doctors' Commons, are indulged with a shorter period, and permitted to obtain it at four instead of five years, upon making oath in convocation of their intentions so to practise. For the degree of M.D., three years must intervene from the time of the candidate's having taken his Bachelor of Medicine's degree. For a Doctor's degree in Divinity or Law three distinct lectures are to be read in the schools, upon three different days: but by a dispensation, first obtained in convocation or congregation, all three are permitted to be read upon the same day; so that by dispensation a single day is sufficient in point of time for these exercises. For a Doctor's degree in Medicine, a dissertation upon some subject, to be approved by the Professor of Medicine, must be publicly recited in the schools, and a copy of it afterwards delivered to the Professor.

In Cambridge a Doctor of Divinity must be a Bachelor of Divinity of five, or an M.A. of twelve years' standing. The requisite exercises are one act, two opponencies, a Latin sermon and an English sermon. A Doctor of Laws must be a Bachelor of Laws of five years' standing. His exercises are one act and one opponency. Doctors of Physic proceed in the same manner as Doctor of Laws. For a Doctor's degree in music, in both Universities, the exercise required is the composition and performance of a solemn piece of music, to be approved by the Professor of the Faculty. (*Oxf. and Camb. Calendars.*)

Coloured engravings of the dresses worn by the doctors of the several faculties of Oxford and Cambridge will be found in Ackermann's *History of the Univ. of Oxford*, 4to., 1814, vol. ii. p. 259, *et seq.*; and in his *History of the Univ. of Cambridge*, 4to., 1815, vol. ii. p. 312, *et seq.*

DOCTORS' COMMONS, the College of Civilians in London, near St. Paul's Churchyard, founded by Dr. Harvey, Dean of the Arches, for the professors of the civil law. The official residences of the judges of the Arches' Court of Canterbury, of the judge of the Admiralty, and the judge of the Prerogative Court of Canterbury, are situated there. It is also the residence of the doctors of the civil law practising in London, who live there (for diet and lodging) in a collegiate manner, and common together, and hence the place is known by the name of Doctors' Commons. It was burnt down in the fire of London, and rebuilt at the charge of the profession. (*Chamberlayne Mag. Brit. Notitia.*) To the college belong a certain number of advocates and proctors. [BARRISTER, p. 317; PROCTOR.]

In the Common Hall are held all the principal spiritual courts, and the High Court of Admiralty.

DOMESDAY BOOK, the register of the lands of England, framed by order of King William the Conqueror. It was sometimes termed *Rotulus Wintoniæ*, and was the book from which judgment was to be given upon the value, tenures, and services of the lands therein described. The original is comprised in two volumes, one a large folio, the other a quarto. The first begins with Kent, and ends with Lincolnshire; is written on three hundred and eighty-two double pages of vellum, in one and the same hand, in a small but plain character, each page having a double column; it contains thirty-one counties. After Lincolnshire (fol. 373), the claims arising in the three ridings of Yorkshire are taken notice of, and settled; then follow the claims in Lincolnshire, and the determination of the jury upon them (fol. 375): lastly, from fol. 379 to the end there is a recapitulation of every wapentake or hundred in the three ridings of Yorkshire: of the towns in each hundred, what number of carucates and ox-gangs are in every town, and the names of the owners placed in very small character above them. The second volume in quarto, is written upon four hundred and fifty double pages of vellum, but in a single column, and in a large fair character, and contains the counties of Essex, Norfolk, and Suffolk. In these counties the " liberi homines" are ranked separate: and there is also a title of " Invasiones super Regem."

These two volumes are preserved, among other records of the Exchequer, in the Chapter House at Westminster: and at the end of the second is the following memorial, in capital letters, of the time of its completion: " Anno Millesimo Octogesimo Sexto ab Incarnatione Domini, vigesimo vero regni Willielmi, facta est ista Descriptio, non solum per hos tres Comitatus, sed etiam per alios." From internal evidence there can be no doubt but that the same year, 1086, is assignable as the date of the first volume.

In 1767, in consequence of an address of the House of Lords, George III. gave directions for the publication of this Survey. It was not, however, till after 1770 that the work was actually commenced. Its publication was intrusted to Mr. Abraham Farley, a gentleman of learning as well as of great experience in records, who had almost daily recourse to the book for more than forty years. It was completed early in 1783, having been ten years in passing through the press, and thus became generally accessible to the antiquary and topographer. It was printed in fac-simile, as far as regular types, assisted by the representation of particular contractions, could imitate the original.

In 1816 the commissioners upon the Public Records published two volumes supplementary to Domesday, which now form one set with the volumes of the Record: one of these contains a general introduction, accompanied with two different indexes of the names of places, an alphabetical index of the tenants in capite, and an " Index Rerum." The other contains four records; three of them, namely, the Exon Domesday, the Inquisitio Eliensis, and the Liber Winton., contemporary with the Survey; the other record, called ' Boldon Book,' is the Survey of Durham, made in 1183, by Bishop Hugh Pudsey. These supplementary volumes were published under the superintendence of Sir Henry Ellis.

Northumberland, Cumberland, Westmorland, and Durham were not included in the counties described in the Great Domesday; nor does Lancashire appear under its proper name ; but Furness, and the northern part of that county, as well as the south of Westmorland and part of Cumberland, are included within the West Riding of Yorkshire : that part of Lancashire which lies between the rivers Ribble and Mersey, and which at the time of the Survey comprehended six hundreds and a hundred and eighty-eight manors, is subjoined to Cheshire. Part of Rutlandshire is described in the counties of Northampton and Lincoln ; and the two ancient hundreds of Atiscross and Existan, deemed a part of Cheshire in the Survey, have been since transferred to the counties of Flint and Denbigh. In the account of Gloucestershire we find a considerable portion of Monmouthshire included, seemingly all between the rivers Wye and Usk. Kelham thinks it probable that the king's commissioners might find it impossible to take any exact survey of the three counties northernmost of all, as they had suffered so much from the Conqueror's vengeance. As to Durham, he adds, all the country between the Tees and Tyne had been conferred by Alfred on the bishop of this see, and at the coming in of the Conqueror he was reputed a count-palatine.

The order generally observed in writing the Survey was to set down in the first place at the head of every county (except Chester and Rutland) the king's name, *Rex Willielmus*, and then a list of the bishops, religious houses, churches, any great men, according to their rank, who held of the king in capite in that county, likewise of his thains, ministers, and servants ; with a numerical figure in red ink before them, for the better finding them in the book. In some counties the cities and capital boroughs are taken notice of before the list of the great tenants is entered, with the particular laws or customs which prevailed in each of them ; and in others they are inserted promiscuously. After the list of the

DOMESDAY BOOK.

tenants, the manors and possessions themselves which belong to the king, and also to each owner throughout the whole county, whether they lie in the same or different hundreds, are collected together and minutely noted, with their under tenants. The king's demesnes, under the title of *Terra Regis*, always stand first.

For the adjustment of this Survey certain commissioners, called the king's justiciaries, were appointed. In folios 164 and 181 of the first volume we find them designated as "Legati Regis." Those for the midland counties at least, if not for all the districts, were Remigius, bishop of Lincoln, Walter Giffard, Earl of Buckingham, Henry de Ferrers, and Adam, the brother of Eudo Dapifer, who probably associated with them some principal person in each shire. These inquisitors, upon the oaths of the sheriffs, the lords of each manor, the presbyters of every church, the reves of every hundred, the bailiffs and six villains of every village, were to inquire into the name of the place, who held it in the time of King Edward, who was the present possessor, how many hides in the manor, how many carucates in demesne, how many homagers, how many villains, how many cotarii, how many servi, what free-men, how many tenants in socage, what quantity of wood, how much meadow and pasture, what mills and fish-ponds, how much added or taken away, what the gross value in King Edward's time, what the present value, and how much each free-man or soc-man had or has. All this was to be triply estimated: first, as the estate was held in the time of the Confessor; then as it was bestowed by King William; and thirdly, as its value stood at the formation of the Survey. The jurors were, moreover, to state whether any advance could be made in the value. Such are the exact terms of one of the inquisitions for the formation of this Survey, still preserved in a register of the monastery of Ely.

The writer of that part of the Saxon Chronicle which relates to the Conqueror's time, informs us, with some degree of asperity, that not a hide or yardland, not an ox, cow, or hog was omitted in the census. It should seem, however, that the jurors, in numerous instances, framed returns of a more extensive nature than were absolutely required by the king's precept, and it is perhaps on this account that we have different kinds of descriptions in different counties.

From the space to which we are necessarily limited, it is impossible to go more minutely into the contents of this extraordinary record, to enlarge upon the classes of tenantry enumerated in it, the descriptions of land and other property therewith connected, the computations of money, the territorial jurisdictions and franchises, the tenures and services, the criminal and civil jurisdictions, the ecclesiastical matters, the historical and other particular events alluded to, or the illustrations of ancient manners, with information relating to all of which it abounds, exclusive of its particular and more immediate interest in the localities of the country for the county historian.

As an abstract of population it fails. The tenants in capite, including ecclesiastical corporations, amounted scarcely to 1400; the under-tenants to somewhat less than 8000. The total population, as far as it is given in the record itself, amounts to no more than 282,242 persons. In Middlesex, pannage (payment for feeding) is returned for 16,535, in Hertfordshire for 30,705, and in Essex for 92,991 hogs; yet not a single swineherd (a character so well known in the Saxon times) is entered in these counties. In the Norman period, as can be proved from records, the whole of Essex was, in a manner, one continued forest; yet once only in that county is a forester mentioned, in the entry concerning Writtle. Salt-works, works for the production of lead and iron, mills, vineyards, fisheries, trade, and the manual arts, must have given occupation to thousands who are unrecorded in the survey; to say nothing of those who tended the flocks and herds, the returns of which so greatly enlarge the pages of the second volume. In some counties we have no mention of a single priest, even where churches are found; and scarcely any inmate of a monastery is recorded beyond the abbot or abbess, who stands as a tenant in capite. These remarks might be extended, but they are sufficient for their purpose. They show that, in this point of view, the Domesday Survey is but a partial register. It was not intended to be a record of population further than was required for ascertaining the geld.

There is one important fact, however, to be gathered from its entries. It shows in detail how long a time elapsed before England recovered from the violence attendant on the Norman Conquest. The annual value of property, it will be found, was much lessened as compared with the produce of estates in the time of Edward the Confessor. In general, at the survey, the king's lands were more highly rated than before the Conquest; and his rent from the burghs was greatly increased: a few also of the larger tenants in capite had improved their estates; but, on the whole, the rental of the kingdom was reduced, and twenty years after the Conquest the estates were, on an average, valued at little more than three-fourths of the former estimate. An instance appears in the county of Middlesex, where no Terra Regis, however, occurs. The first column, headed T. R. E., shows the value of the estates in the time of King Edward the Confessor; the second, the sums at which they were rated at the time of the survey, *tempore Regis Willielmi*:—

	T.R.E.			T.R.W.		
	£	s.	d.	£	s.	d.
Terra Archiep. Cant.	100	14	0	86	12	0
Terra Episc. Lond.	190	11	10	157	19	6
Eccl. S. Pet. West.	114	0	0	86	16	6
Eccl. Trin. Rouen	25	10	0	20	10	0
Geoff. de Mandeville	121	13	0	112	5	0
Ernald de Hesding	56	0	0	24	0	0
Walter de St. Waleri	120	0	0	111	0	0
Terr. alior. Tenent	204	0	0	147	8	0
	932	8	10	746	11	0

We shall now say a few words on the uses and consequences of the Survey. By its completion the king acquired an exact knowledge of the possessions of the crown. It afforded him the names of the landholders. It furnished him with the means of ascertaining the military strength of the country; and it pointed out the possibility of increasing the revenue in some cases, and of lessening the demands of the tax-collectors in others. It was moreover a register of appeal for those whose titles to their property might be disputed.

Appeals to the decision of this Survey occur at a very early period. Peter of Blois notices an appeal of the monks of Croyland to it in the reign of Henry I. Others occur in the Abbreviatio Placitorum from the time of John downward. In later reigns the pleadings upon ancient demesne are extremely numerous; and the proof of ancient demesne still rests with the Domesday Survey. Other cases in which its evidence is yet appealed to in our courts of law, are in proving the antiquity of mills, and in setting up prescriptions *in non decimando*. By stat. 9 Edw. II., called Articuli Cleri, it was determined that prohibition should not lie upon demand of tithe for a *new* mill. The mill, therefore, which is found in Domesday must be presumed older than the 9th Edw. II., and is of course discharged, by its evidence, from tithe.

On the discharge of abbey-lands from tithes, as proved by Domesday, it may be proper to state that Pope Paschal II., at an early period, exempted generally all the religious from paying tithes of lands in their own hands. This privilege was afterwards restrained to the four favoured orders, the Cistercians, the Templars, the Hospitallers, and the Premonstratensians. So it continued till the fourth Council of Lateran, in 1215, when the privilege was again restrained to such lands as the abbeys had at that time, and was declared not to extend to any after-purchased lands. And it extends only to lands *dem propriis manibus coluntur*. From the paucity of dates in early documents, the Domesday Survey is very frequently the only evidence which can be adduced that the lands claiming a discharge were vested in the monastery previous to the year expressed in the Lateran Council.

Although in early times, Domesday, precious as it was always deemed, occasionally travelled, like other records, to distant parts, till 1696 it was usually kept with the king's seal, at Westminster, by the side of the Tally Court in the exchequer, under three locks and keys, in the charge of the auditor, the chamberlains, and deputy chamberlains of the exchequer. In the last-mentioned year it was deposited among other valuable records in the Chapter House, where it still remains.

DOMICILE. [777] DOMICILE.

The two most important works for the student of the Domesday Survey are Kelham's *Domesday Book illustrated*, 8vo., London, 1788, and the *General Introduction* to the Survey, reprinted by command of his Majesty under the direction of the Commissioners on the Public Records, 2 vols. 8vo., 1833, accompanied by fresh indices. A translation of the whole, under the title of 'Dom-Boc,' was undertaken early in the present century by the Rev. William Bawdwen, Vicar of Hooton Pagnell, in Yorkshire, who published Yorkshire, with the counties of Derby, Nottingham, Rutland, and Lincoln, in 4to., Doncaster, 1809, followed by the counties of Middlesex, Hertford, Buckingham, Oxford, and Gloucester, 4to., Doncaster, 1812; but the work went no further. County portions of this record will be found translated in most of our provincial histories; the best are undoubtedly those in Dugdale's Warwickshire, Nichols's Leicestershire, Hutchins's Dorsetshire, Nash's Worcestershire, Bray and Manning's Surrey, and Clutterbuck's Hertfordshire. Mr. Henry Penruddocke Wyndham published Wiltshire, extracted from Domesday Book, 8vo., Salisb., 1788, and the Rev. Richard Warner, Hampshire, 4to., Lond., 1789. Warwickshire has been published recently by Mr. Reader. There are numerous other publications incidentally illustrative of Domesday topography, which the reader must seek for according to the county as to which he may desire information.

DOMICILE. In the Roman law Domicile (*Domicilium*) was defined to be that place which a person " makes his family residence, and principal place of business; from which he does not depart unless some business requires: when he leaves it he considers himself a wanderer, and when he returns to it he deems himself no longer abroad." (Cod. lib. 10, tit. 39, 1, 7.) Similar definitions of the term are given by modern jurists.

The constitution of domicile depends on the concurrence of two elements—1st, residence in a place; and, 2nd, the intention of the party to make that place his home. Domicile cannot be established except it be *animo et facto*, that is, actually and in intention also. It is sometimes not very easy to determine in what place a person actually has his domicile. It is obviously a question depending upon the evidence in each particular case, which is of course capable of every variety both in nature and degree. The evidence as to the place of residence is frequently far from clear; while the intention of the party has to be gathered from circumstances yet more difficult to come to a conclusion upon.

The following rules appear to comprise the generally adopted principles on the subject:—

1. The domicile of the parents is the domicile of the child. " *Patris originem unusquisque sequitur.*" (Cod. lib. 10, tit. 31, 1, 36.) This is usually called the domicile of origin or nativity, and is in most cases the same with the place of birth. But the mere accident of birth in a place where the parents may happen to be *in itinere*, or on a visit, will have no effect in determining the domicile of origin. An illegitimate child, having no father in contemplation of law, follows the domicile of his mother.

2. Minors are generally considered incapable of changing, by their own act, the domicile of origin during their minority. If the father change his domicile, that of the children follows it; and if he dies, his last domicile will be that of his infant children. It has been much questioned whether the guardians of minors, idiots, or lunatics can change their domicile. It has been held in England that a mother, being guardian, might change the domicile of her children, provided it was not done for a fraudulent purpose, which would be presumed in the absence of any reasonable motive. In Scotland a minor, after the age of puberty, is not personally under the control of his guardian, and may change his domicile by his own act.

3. A married woman follows the domicile of her husband.

4. A widow retains the domicile of her late husband till she acquires another.

5. The place where a man resides is, for a great many purposes, to be considered his domicile, and, *primâ facie*, is to be taken to be so till other facts establish the contrary.

6. Every person of full age, who removes from one place to another, with the intention of making the latter his place of residence, immediately constitutes it his domicile.

7. The domicile of origin must be considered to prevail till the party has not only acquired another, but manifested and carried into effect an intention of abandoning his former domicile, and abiding by another as his sole domicile. But the domicile of origin cannot be preserved by a mere floating intention of returning to it at some fut re period, or revived by a mere abandonment of the acquired domicile, unless perhaps where the party dies *in itinere* towards the intended domicile. "It is to be remembered," says Sir Wm. Scott (Lord Stowell), "that the native character easily reverts, and that it requires fewer circumstances to constitute the domicile in the case of a native subject than to impress the national character on one who is originally of another country."

8. An acquired domicile is not lost by mere abandonment, but continues until a subsequent domicile is acquired, which can be done only *animo et facto*.

9. A married man's domicile is generally to be taken to be where the residence of his family is; unless this conclusion is controlled by circumstances, such as proof that he has altogether abandoned his family, or that their place of residence is temporary: but

10. If a man, whether married or not, has two places of residence at different times of the year, that will be esteemed his domicile which he himself selects, describes, or deems to be his home, or which appears to be the centre of his affairs; *e. g.* that of a nobleman or country gentleman, his residence in the country— that of a merchant, his residence in town.

11. Residence in a place, to produce a change of domicile, must be voluntary. Thus, if it be produced by constraint, as by banishment, arrest, or imprisonment, it cannot affect the domicile. For the same reason a person abroad in the service of the state does not change his domicile. But it has been held that a Scotchman entering the service of the East India Company acquires a domicile in India, which (like a domicile acquired in any of the colonies) is in legal effect the same as a domicile in England.

12. It was held in the Roman law that a man might, under certain circumstances, be said to have no domicile, as when he quits one place of residence with the intention of fixing himself in another. But this is not admitted in our law, in which, as before stated, it is held that the former domicile is not lost till the new one is acquired *animo et facto*. And in the possible case of a man of unknown origin acquiring two contemporaneous domiciles under the same circumstances, the *lex loci rei sitæ* would probably prevail *ex necessitate* in questions as to his personal property.

Thus it appears that domicile, considered in relation to the civil status of the person, is of three kinds—1st, domicile of origin, depending on that of the parents at the time of birth; 2nd, domicile of choice, which is voluntarily acquired by the party; and, 3rd, domicile by operation of law, as that of a wife, arising from marriage.

The word domicile is sometimes used in another sense, as signifying the length of residence required by the law of some countries for the purpose of founding jurisdiction in civil actions. In England every person, whether native or foreigner, who is for the time being within England, is amenable to the jurisdiction of its courts, and may sue or be sued in them; but in Scotland a residence of at least forty days within the country is necessary to establish jurisdiction *ratione domicilii*.

(On the subject of Domicile, see Story's *Commentaries on the Conflict of Laws*, c. iii.)

DONA'TIO MORTIS CAUSA, a gift made in prospect of death. The doctrine is derived from the Roman law, and a donation of this kind is defined in the Institutes (ii., tit. 7) as "a gift which is made under an apprehension of death, as when a thing is given upon condition that, if the donor die, the donee shall have it, but that the thing given shall be returned if the donor shall survive the danger which he apprehends, or shall repent that he has made the gift; or if the donee shall die before the donor." The definition of a "donatio mortis causa" in Fleta

(ii. 57, *De Testamentis*) agrees almost word for word with that of Ulpian (*Dig.* 39, tit. 6, s. 2). Fleta's definition is, perhaps, taken from Bracton (ii. 26), who has adopted the words of Ulpian. In the English law it is necessary to the validity of this gift that it be made by the donor with relation to his dying by the illness which affects him at the time of the gift, but it takes effect only in case he die of that illness. There must be a delivery of the thing itself to the donee; but in cases where actual transfer is impossible, as, for instance, goods of bulk deposited in a warehouse, the delivery of the key of the warehouse is effectual. This principle is expounded by Lord Hardwicke, in the case of Ward *v.* Turner (2 Vez. 431). A donatio mortis causâ partakes of the nature of a legacy so far as to be liable to the debts of the donor, and, by 36 Geo. III. c. 53, §. 7, to the legacy duty; but as it takes effect from the delivery, and not by a testamentary act, it is not within the jurisdiction of the ecclesiastical courts, and neither probate or administration is necessary, nor the assent of the executors, as in the case of a legacy.

The English law of Donations, "mortis causa," is explained in Roper *On Legacies,* vol. i.; and in the judgment of Lord Hardwicke already referred to. See also Edwards *v.* Jones, 1 M. & C. 226; Duffield *v.* Elwes, 1 S. & S. 239.

Ulpian (*Dig.* 39, tit. 6, s. 2) quotes Julian as laying down three forms of "donatio mortis causa:" first, when a man under no present danger of death, but solely influenced by a consideration of his mortality, makes a gift; second, when a man, moved by imminent danger of death, makes a gift, so that the thing becomes forthwith the property of the receiver; third, when a man, moved by danger, gives not so that the thing shall forthwith become the property of the receiver, but only in case of the death of the giver. But the third was the only proper kind of "donatio mortis causa." Any thing might be the subject of a "donatio mortis causa," as a piece of land, an agreement that a sum of money should be paid to the donee after the death of the giver, or a slave. It follows from the nature of the things that might be the subjects of a "donatio mortis causa," that the Roman law did not require delivery, as the English law does, a circumstance which restrains the power of making a "donatio mortis causa" by the English law. It was long disputed whether "donationes mortis causa" should be considered as legacies, or as other gifts; but a constitution of Justinian (*Cod.* viii. tit. 57, s. 4) assimilated them in all respects to legacies, and declared that they might be either made orally or in writing, but it required four witnesses.

DONATIVE. [BENEFICE, p. 344]

DOWAGER is a widow who is endowed [DOWER]; but the term is often applied to ladies of rank, whether they may be endowed or not.

The Queen Dowager is the widow of a king, and she has many of the privileges of a queen-consort. But it is not high treason to conspire to kill her; nor is it high treason to have sexual intercourse with her, as in the case of a queen-consort. The reason of the distinction in this second case is, that the succession to the crown is not endangered by sexual connection with her. It is said that a man cannot marry a queen-dowager without a licence from the king, under pain of forfeiting his lands and goods; but this may not be so now.

By the Regency Bill of 1830 (1 Wm. IV. c. 2), the queen of William IV. would, if she had survived him, have been Regent of the United Kingdom, in case of his Majesty's demise and his leaving issue by the queen.

The queen-dowager has now, by act of parliament (1 & 2 Wm. IV. c. 11), a pension of 100,000*l.*, and also Marlborough House and the rangership of Bushy Park for life.

DOWER is that part of the husband's lands, tenements, or hereditaments to which the wife is entitled for her life upon the husband's death.

Prior to the reign of Charles II. five, and, until the passing of the act 3 & 4 Wm. IV. c. 105, there were four kinds of dower known to the English law.
1. Dower at the common law.
2. Dower by custom.
3. Dower ad ostium ecclesiæ.
4. Dower ex assensu patris.
5. Dower de la plus beale.

This last was merely a consequence of tenure by knight's service, and was abolished by stat. 12 Charles II. c. 24; and the 3rd and 4th having long become obsolete, were finally abolished by the above-mentioned statute of Wm. IV.

By the old law, the right called dower extended to all the lands of which the husband was seised at any time during the marriage, and which a child of the husband and wife might by possibility inherit; and they remained liable to dower in the hands of a purchaser, though various ingenious modes of conveyance were contrived, which in some cases prevented the attaching of dower; but this liability was productive of great inconvenience, and frequently of injustice. The law, too, was inconsistent, for the wife was not dowable out of her husband's equitable estates, although the husband had his courtesy in those to which the wife was equitably entitled. To remedy these inconveniences the statute above mentioned was passed, and its objects may be stated to be—1, to make equitable estates in possession liable to dower; 2, to take away the right to dower out of lands disposed of by the husband absolutely in his life or by will; 3, to enable the husband, by a simple declaration in a deed or will, to bar the right to dower.

"The law of dower," say the Real Property Commissioners, in their Second Report, upon which this statute was founded, "though well adapted to the state of freehold property which existed at the time when it was established, and during a long time afterwards, had, in consequence of the frequent alienation of property which takes place in modern times, become exceedingly inconvenient." In short, dower was considered and treated as an incumbrance, and was never, except in cases of inadvertency, suffered to arise. The increase of personal property, and the almost universal custom of securing a provision by settlement, afforded more effectual and convenient means of providing for the wife. Dower at the common law is the only species of dower which affects lands in England generally; dower by custom is only of local application, as dower by the custom of gavelkind and Borough Enlish; and freebench applies exclusively to copyhold lands. The former is treated of in Robinson's 'History of Gavelkind,' the latter in Watkins on 'Copyholds.'

As to dower at common law, every married woman who has attained the age of nine years is entitled to dower by common law, except aliens, and Jewesses, so long as they continue in their religion. From the disability arising from alienage, a queen, and also an alien licensed by the king, are exempt.

The wife is entitled to be endowed, that is, to have an estate for life in the third part of the lands and tenements of which the husband was solely seised either in deed or in law, or in which he had a right of entry, at any time during the marriage, of a legal or equitable estate of inheritance in possession, to which the issue of the husband and wife (if any) might by possibility inherit.

By Magna Charta it is provided, that the widow shall not pay a fine to the lord for her dower, and that she shall remain in the chief house of her husband for forty days after his death, during which time her dower shall be assigned. The particular lands and hereditaments to be held in dower must be assigned by the heir of the husband, or his guardian, by metes and bounds if divisible, otherwise specially, as of the third presentation to a benefice, &c. If the heir or his guardian do not assign, or assign unfairly, the widow has her remedy at law, and the sheriff is appointed to assign her dower; or the widow may enforce her rights by bill in equity, which is now the usual remedy.

A woman is barred of her dower by the attainder of her husband for treason, by her own attainder for treason, or felony, by divorce à vinculo matrimonii, by elopement from her husband and living with her adulterer, by detaining the title-deeds from the heir at law, until she restores them, by alienation of the lands assigned her for a greater estate than she has in them; and she might also be barred of her dower by levying a fine, or suffering a recovery during her marriage, while those assurances existed. But the most usual means of barring dower are by jointures, made under the provisions of the 27 Hen. VIII. c. 10; and by the act of the husband. Before the stat. 3 & 4 Will. IV. c. 105, a fine or recovery by the husband and wife was the only mode by which a right to dower which had *already attached* could be barred, though, by means of a simple form of conveyance, a husband might prevent the right to dower from arising at all upon lands purchased by him. By the above-mentioned statute, it is provided that no woman shall be entitled to dower out of any lands absolutely disposed of by her husband either in his life or by will, and that his debts and engagements shall be valid and effectual as against the right of the widow to dower. And further, any declaration by the husband, either by deed or will, that the dower of his wife shall be subjected to any restrictions, or that she shall not have any dower, shall be effectual. It is also provided that a simple devise of real estate to the wife by the husband shall, unless a contrary intention be expressed, operate in bar of her dower. This statute, however, affects only marriages contracted, and only deeds, &c., subsequent to the 1st of January, 1834.

Most of these alterations, as indeed may be said of many others which have recently been made in the English real property law, have for some years been established in the United States of America. An account of the various enactments and provisions in force in the different States respecting dower may be found in 4 Kent's *Commentaries*, p. 34-72. (Blackstone, *Comm.*; Park *On Dower*.)

DRAMATIC LITERARY PROPERTY. [COPYRIGHT.]

DRAWBACK is a term used to signify the sum paid back on the re-exportation of goods, upon the importation of which an equal sum has already been paid as duty. A drawback is also allowed on the exportation of articles which are subject to excise duties. The object of this repayment is to enable the exporter to sell his goods in foreign markets unburthened with duties; and it is clear that if duties are required to be paid on the first importation, no transit trade can possibly be carried on unless

drawback is allowed by the government. Payments of this nature are in principle essentially different from bounties, which enable the exporter to sell his goods at less than they cost; but a drawback does not interfere with the natural cost. [BOUNTY.] Previous to the establishing of the warehousing system in this country in 1803, and when the payment of duties on all foreign and colonial merchandise, with the exception of tobacco and East India goods, was required on the first importation, drawbacks were in all cases allowed upon re-exportation. This course was injurious to trade, because of the larger capital which was necessarily employed, and it was prejudicial to the revenue because it gave rise to numerous and ingenious fraudulent expedients, by means of which greater sums were received for drawback than had been originally paid by the importers; besides which, the machinery required for the collection and repayment of duties was more complicated and expensive than would otherwise have been necessary. The amount of customs' duty collected in Great Britain before the passing of the Warehousing Act in 1803 was usually from twice to three times as great as the sum paid into the exchequer, the greater part of the receipts being absorbed by drawbacks, bounties, and charges of management.

The only articles upon which drawback was paid at our Custom-houses, and the amount of repayment in 1844, were as follows:—

	£
Coffee	146
Rice in the husk	3,937
Thrown silk	30
Sugar	892
Timber	1,115
Tobacco and Snuff	20,058
Wine	65,489
Total	91,669

The drawback on timber is not indeed a payment made on its re-exportation, but an allowance upon such quantities as are used in the mines. The quantities of thrown silk, sugar, and tobacco entitled to drawback had already paid duty previous to their undergoing a manufacturing process, and drawback on wine is only paid when exported in bottles, for transferring it to which from the cask it was, until lately, necessary to pay the duty. In 1830 the sum paid for various drawbacks amounted to 3,300,000*l.*; and in 1836 to 781,154*l.* The reduction has been obtained by totally repealing many duties, and by affording greater opportunity of exportation from the warehouses.

DRAWER. [EXCHANGE, BILL OF.]

DROITS OF ADMIRALTY are the perquisites attached to the office of Admiral of England (or Lord High Admiral). Prince George of Denmark, the husband of Queen Anne and Lord High Admiral, resigned the right to these droits to the Crown for a salary, as Lord High Admiral, of 7000*l.* a year. When the office was vacant they belonged of right to the Crown. Of these perquisites the most valuable is the right to the property of an enemy seized on the breaking out of hostilities. Large sums were obtained by the Crown on various occasions in the course of the last war from the seizure of the enemy's property, most of which however was eventually given up to the public service. In the arrangement of the Civil List, during the last two reigns, it was settled that whatever Droits of Admiralty accrued were to be paid into the Exchequer for the use of the public. The Lord High Admiral's right to the tenth part of the property captured on the seas has been relinquished in favour of the captors.

DUCHIES OF CORNWALL AND LANCASTER. [CIVIL LIST, p. 515.]

DUELLING. The rise of the practice of duelling is to be referred to the trial by battle which obtained in early ages, jointly with the single combat or tournament of the age of chivalry, which again most probably owed its own existence to the early trial by battle. The trial by battle, or duel (as it was also called), was resorted to, in accordance with the superstitious notions of the time, as a sure means of determining the guilt or innocence of a person charged with a crime, or of adjudicating a disputed right. It was thought that God took care to see that, in every case, innocence was vindicated and justice observed. The trial by battle was introduced into England by William the Conqueror, and established in three cases; viz., in the court-martial or court of chivalry, in appeals of felony, and in civil cases upon issue joined in a writ of right. Once established as a mode of trial, the duel was retained after the superstition which had given rise to it had died away, and was resorted to for the purpose of wreaking vengeance, or gaining reputation by the display of courage. Then came the age of chivalry, with its worship of punctilio and personal prowess, its tilts and tournaments, and the duel, originally a mode of trial established by law, became in time (what it now is) a practice dependent on fashion or certain conventional rules of honour.

It is an instance of the length of time for which abused and improper obsolete laws are often allowed to encumber the English statute-book, that the trial by battle in appeals of felony and writs of right was only abolished in 1818. An appeal of felony had been brought in the previous year, in a case of murder, and the appellee had resorted to his right of demanding wager of battle (Ashford *v.* Thornton, 1 Barn. and Ald. 405). The appeal was not proceeded with, so that the barbarous encounter did not take place. [APPEAL.]

The law of England makes no distinction between the killing of a man in a duel and other species of murder: and the seconds of both parties are also guilty of murder. But the practice of duelling is maintained by fashion against laws human and divine; and it may be well to enter a little into the reasons of this practice, without reference to its illegality, or to its variance, which no one will dispute, with Christianity.

The professed object of a duel is *satisfaction*. The affronter professes to have satisfied the man whom he has affronted, and the challenger professes to have been satisfied by the man whom he has challenged, after they have fired, or have had an opportunity of firing, pistols at one another. That this satisfaction is of the nature of *reparation*, is of course out of the question. Satisfaction in this its most obvious sense, or reparation for an injury, cannot be effected by the injured man firing at his injurer, and being fired at in return.

The satisfaction furnished by a duel is of a different sort, and of a sort which, were it distinctly comprehended, would at once show the absurdity of the practice; it is a satisfaction occasioned by the knowledge that, by standing fire, the challenger has shown his courage, and that the world cannot call him coward. Now it is clear that there would be no reason for dissatisfaction on this point, previous to the fighting of the duel, and therefore no reason for seeking satisfaction of this sort, were it not that the practice of duelling existed. Were men not in the habit of fighting duels, and therefore not expected to expose themselves to fire after having received an affront, there would be no ground for calling their courage into question, and therefore no necessity for satisfying themselves that the world thinks them courageous. The practice of duelling thus causes the evil which it is called in to remedy,—the injury for which it is required to administer satisfaction. And every one who saw this would immediately see the absurdity of the practice. But the word *satisfaction* is conveniently ambiguous. When one speaks of it, or hears it spoken of, one thinks of that satisfaction which means reparation for an injury, and which is not the satisfaction furnished by the duel. Thus are men the dupes of words.

The real object then of the duel is, in most cases, to satisfy the person who provokes it, or who sends the challenge, that the world does not suspect him of a want of courage: and it will be useful to observe, in passing, that the duel furnishes this sort of satisfaction as well to the man who gave the affront, as to him who was affronted. Its object also, in certain cases, is doubtless to gratify the vengeance of the man who has received an affront. But in all cases the object which is professed, or generally understood to be professed, of satisfaction in the sense of reparation for the affront, is no more than a pretence.

But though the practice of duelling cannot effect the good of repairing an injury, it may very possibly effect other sorts of good. The advantage of the practice of duelling is generally said to consist in its tendency to increase courtesy and refinement of manners; as it will be a reason for a man to abstain from giving an affront, that he will be subjected in consequence to the fire of a pistol.

Now it is clear, in the first place, that all the affronts which are constituted reasons or grounds of duels by fashion, or the law of honour or public opinion, are so constituted because they are judged by public opinion deserving of disapprobation. If then the practice of duelling did not exist, public opinion, which now constitutes these affronts grounds of a duel, as being deserving of disapprobation, would still condemn them, and, condemning them, provide men with a reason to abstain from them. Thus there would still exist a reason to abstain, in all cases in which the practice of duelling now provides a reason. But, in the second place, the practice of duelling itself depends on public opinion alone. A man fights because public opinion judges that he who in certain cases refuses to challenge or to accept a challenge is deserving of disapprobation: he fights from fear of public opinion. If he abstain from giving an affront on account of the existence of the practice of duelling, it is because the fear of public opinion would oblige him to fight; he abstains then from fear of public opinion. Now we have seen that there would be the fear of public opinion to deter him from the affronts which now lead to duels, if the practice of duelling did not exist. Thus the practice of duelling does not in any case provide a reason to abstain, which public opinion would not provide without its aid. As a means then of increasing courtesy and refinement of manners, the practice of duelling is unnecessary; and inasmuch as its tendency to polish manners is the only advantage which can, with any show of probability, be ascribed to it, there will be no good effects whatever to set against the evil effects which we now proceed to enumerate. There will be no difficulty in striking the balance between good and evil.

First, the practice of duelling is disadvantageous, inasmuch as it often diminishes the motives to abstain from an affront. We have seen that the existence of this practice leads public opinion to employ itself concerning the courage of the two persons, who (the one having affronted and the other having been affronted) are in a situation in which, according to custom or fashion, a duel takes place. Public opinion then is diverted by the practice of duelling from the affront to the extraneous consideration of the courage of the two parties. It censures the man who has given the affront only if he shrinks from a duel; and even goes so far as to censure the man who has received the affront for the same reason. Thus in a case where a man, reckless of exposing his life, is disposed to give affronts, he is certain that he can avert censure for an affront by being ready to fight a duel; and in a case where a bold or reckless man is disposed to affront one who is timid, or a man expert with the pistol one who is a bad shot, he can reckon on the man whom he affronts refusing to fight, and on censure being thus diverted from himself who has given an affront to him who has shown want of courage. It is well observed in a very ingenious article on this subject in the 'Westminster Review:'—" It is difficult to conceive how the character of a bully, in all its shades and degrees, would be an object of ambition to any one, in a country where the law is too strong to suffer actual assaults to be committed with impunity, where public opinion is powerful, and duelling not permitted; but where duelling is in full vigour, it is very easy to understand that the bully may not only enjoy the delight of vulgar applause, but the advantages of real power" (vol. iv. p. 28).

Secondly, the practice of duelling is disadvantageous, as increasing the amount of injury which one man can do to another by an affront.

Thirdly, the practice of duelling affords means for the gratification of vengeance; and thus tends to hurt the characters of individuals, by the encouragement both of that feeling, and of hypocrisy in those who, thirsting for vengeance, and daring not to own it, profess (in the common ambiguous phrase) to be seeking for satisfaction.

Fourthly (which is the most important consideration), there are the evils entailed by the deaths which the practice of duelling brings about—evils entailed both on the persons dying, and on their surviving relatives and friends. It is an evil that a man should be cut off from life, "unhouseled, unappointed, unaneled." It is an evil that he should be taken from relatives and friends to whom his life is, in different ways and degrees, a source of happiness; from parents who have centred in him their hopes, and to whom, in their declining years, he might be a comfort, or from a wife and children who look to him for support.

Such are the evil effects of the practice of duelling; and there being no list of good effects to set against them, it follows immediately that the tendency of the practice is, on the whole, evil. There arises, then, the question, how is it to be got rid of?

A mild and judicious legislation—one which takes into account, and does not set itself violently against, public opinion, may do much. The punishment assigned to the crime of duelling should be *popular*. It should be a punishment which does not tend to excite sympathy for the criminal, and thus defeat its own object; for where an opinion prevails that a punishment is too severe, witnesses, jurors, judges are provided by the punishment itself with motives to shield the criminal. It is clear that the punishment of death, which the law of England now assigns, is not popular; and it is clear further that, in consequence of this, it is almost entirely nugatory. Public opinion, which favours duelling, sets itself against the punishment of death, and renders legislation vain.

Were a man who had killed his antagonist in a duel compelled by the law to support, or assist in supporting, some of his surviving relatives, this, so far as it would go, would be a punishment popular and efficacious. Public opinion would then infallibly be against the man who, having incurred the penalty, should endeavour to avoid it. And such a punishment as this would furthermore be superior to the punishment of death, as being susceptible of graduation—as furnishing reparation to a portion of those who have been most injured, and as preserving the offender, that he may have all those opportunities, which his natural life will afford him, of improving himself and of benefiting others.

A mild and judicious legislation would tend to guide and improve public opinion; whereas such a legislation as the present tends only to confirm it in its evil ways.

And as legislation may and should assist the formation of a right public opinion, so is it possible and desirable to operate independently on public opinion, either that the absence of good legislation may, as far as is possible, be compensated for, or that good legislation may be assisted. This operation on public opinion must be brought about by the endeavours of individuals. It is the duty of each man to oppose this practice to the utmost extent of his power, both by precept and example,—to abstain from challenging when he has received an affront, and to refuse a challenge when he is considered to have given one, making public in both cases, so far as his situation allows, his reasons for the course which he takes, and thus producing an impression against the practice as widely as he can. In the second of these two cases, he must either be able to defend, or he must apologize for, that which was considered an affront. If he can defend it, or show that the evil to the person insulted was overbalanced by the good accruing to others, he refuses rightly to be fired at for having been the author of a benefit; or, if unable to defend the affront, he apologizes for it, he performs a manly and a rational part in refusing to fire at a man whose feelings he has wantonly injured.

This duty is peculiarly incumbent on public men, whose sphere of influence is larger, and whose means of producing good effects by example are therefore greater, than those of others. A public man who should at all times refuse to challenge or to accept a challenge, resting his refusal on the ground of the evil tendency of duelling, not of the infraction of some other duty which an accident has in his case connected with it (as the violation of an oath), and who should at the same time preserve himself from suspicion or reproach by circumspection in speech, by a manly defence, where it is possible, and, where it is not, by a manly apology, would be a mighty aid for the extirpation of this practice.

The following three new articles of war were issued in the course of the year (1844), with a view to the abatement of duelling in the army:—

1. Every officer who shall give or send a challenge, or who shall accept any challenge to fight a duel with another officer, or who, being privy to an intention to fight a duel, shall not take active measures to prevent such duel, or who shall upbraid another for refusing or for not giving a challenge, or who shall reject, or advise the rejection, of a reasonable proposition made for the honourable adjustment of a difference, shall be liable, if convicted before a general court-martial, to be cashiered, or suffer such other punishment as the court may award.

2. In the event of an officer being brought to a court-martial for having acted as a second in a duel, if it shall appear that such officer had strenuously exerted himself to effect an adjustment of the difference on terms consistent with the honour of both parties, and shall have failed through the unwillingness of the adverse parties to accept terms of honourable accommodation, then our will and pleasure is, that such officer shall suffer such punishment as the court may award.

3. We hereby declare our approbation of the conduct of all those who, having had the misfortune of giving offence to, or injured or insulted others, shall frankly explain, apologize, or offer redress for the same; or who, having had the misfortune of receiving offence, injury, or insult from another, shall cordially accept frank explanations, apology, or redress for the same; or who, if such explanations, apology, or redress are refused to be made or accepted, shall submit the matter to be dealt with by the commanding officer of the regiment or detachment, fort or garrison; and we accordingly acquit of disgrace, or opinion of disadvantage, all officers and soldiers who, being willing to make or accept such redress, refuse to accept challenges, as they will only have acted as is suitable to the character of

3 E

honourable men, and have done their duty as good soldiers, who subject themselves to discipline.

DUKE, the title given to those who are in the highest rank of nobility in England. The order is not older in England than the reign of king Edward III. Previously to that reign those whom we now call the nobility consisted of the barons, a few of whom were earls. Neither baron nor earl was in those days, as now, merely a title of honour; the barons were the great tenants in chief, and the earls important officers. It does not appear that in England there was ever any office or particular trust united with the other titles of nobility, viscount, marquis, and duke. They seem to have been from the beginning merely honorary distinctions. They were introduced into England in imitation of our neighbours on the Continent. Abroad however the titles of duke and marquis had been used to designate persons who had political power, and even independent sovereignty. The czar was duke of Russia or Muscovy. There were the dukes of Saxony, Burgundy, and Aquitaine: persons with whom the earls of this country would have ranked, had they been able to maintain as much independence on the king as did the dukes on the continent of the Germanic or Gallic confederacy.

The English word duke is from the French duc, which originally was used to signify "a man of the sword (a soldier) and of merit, who led troops." The remote origin is the Latin dux, a "guide," or a "military commander." The word is used by the Latin writers to signify generally any one who has military command, but sometimes "dux," as an inferior officer, is contrasted with "imperator," commander in chief. Under the Lower Empire, dux was the title of a provincial general, who had a command in the provinces. In the time of Constantine there were thirty-five of these military commanders stationed in different parts of the empire, who were all duces or dukes, because they had military command. Ten of these dukes were also honoured with the title of comtes [COUNT] or counts. (Gibbon, *Decline and Fall*, &c., cap. 17.)

The German word *herzog*, which corresponds to our duke, signifies "a leader of an army."

The first person created a duke in England was Edward, Prince of Wales, commonly called the Black Prince. He was created duke of Cornwall in parliament, in 1335, the eleventh year of king Edward III. In 1350, Henry, the king's cousin, was created duke of Lancaster, and when he died, in 1361, his daughter and heir having married John of Gaunt, the king's son, he was created duke of Lancaster, his elder brother Lionel being made at the same time duke of Clarence. The two younger sons of king Edward III. were not admitted to this high dignity in the reign of their father: but in the reign of Richard II. their nephew Edmund was made duke of York and Thomas duke of Gloucester.

The dignity was thus at the beginning kept within the circle of those who were by blood very nearly allied to the king, and we know not whether the creation of the great favourite of king Richard II., Robert Vere, earl of Oxford, duke of Ireland, and marquis of Dublin, is to be regarded as an exception. Whether, properly speaking, an English dignity or an Irish, it had but a short endurance, the earl being so created in 1385 and attainted in 1388.

The persons who were next admitted to this high dignity were of the families of Holland and Mowbray. The former of these was half-brother to king Richard II.; and the latter was the heir of Margaret, the daughter and heir of Thomas de Brotherton, a younger son of king Edward I., which Margaret was created duchess of Norfolk in 1358. This was the beginning of the dignity of duke of Norfolk, which still exists, though there have been several forfeitures and temporary extinctions. Next to them, not to mention sons or brothers of the reigning king, the title was conferred on one of the Beauforts, an illegitimate son of John of Gaunt, who was created by king Henry V. duke of Exeter. John Beaufort, another of this family, was made duke of Somerset by king Henry VI.

In the reign of Henry VI. the title was granted more widely. There were at one time ten duchesses in his court. The families to whom the dignity was granted in this reign were the Staffords, Beauchamps, and De la Poles. In 1470, under the reign of Edward IV., George Nevil was made duke of Bedford, but he was soon deprived of the title, and Jasper Tudor was made duke of Bedford by his nephew king Henry VII. in the year of his accession.

King Henry VIII. created only two dukes, and both were persons nearly connected with himself; one was his own illegitimate son, whom he made duke of Richmond, and the other was Charles Brandon, who had married the French queen, his sister, and who was made by him duke of Suffolk. King Edward VI. created three dukes; his uncle, Edward Seymour, the Protector, duke of Somerset (from whom the present duke of Somerset derives his descent, and, by reversal of an attainder, his dignity), Henry Grey, duke of Suffolk, and John Dudley, duke of Northumberland.

Queen Elizabeth found on her accession only one duke, Thomas Howard, duke of Norfolk, attainder or failure of male issue having extinguished the others. He was an ambitious nobleman, and aspiring to marry the queen of Scotland, Elizabeth became jealous of him: he was convicted of treason, beheaded, and his dignity extinguished in 1572; and from that time there was no duke in the English peerage except the sons of king James I., till 1623, when Ludovick Stuart, the king's near relative, was made duke of Richmond. which honour soon expired. In 1627 George Villiers was created duke of Buckingham, and he and his son were the only dukes in England till the civil wars, when another of the Stuarts was made duke of Richmond, and the king's nephew, best known by the name of Prince Rupert, duke of Cumberland.

In the first year after the return of Charles II. from exile, he restored the Seymours to their rank of dukes of Somerset, and created Monk, the great instrument of his return, duke of Albemarle. In 1663 he began to introduce his illegitimate issue into the peerage under the title of duke, his son James being made in that year duke of Monmouth. In 1664 he restored to the Howards the title of duke of Norfolk; and in 1665 he created a Cavendish, who had held a high military command in the civil war, duke of Newcastle. In 1682 he created the marquis of Worcester duke of Beaufort. As for the rest the dignity was granted only to issue of the king or to their mothers. The only duke created by king James II. was the duke of Berwick, his natural son.

Of the families now existing, beside those who are descended from king Charles II., only the Howards, the Seymours, and the Somersets date their dukedoms from before the Revolution. The existing dukedoms originally given by Charles II. to his sons are Grafton, Richmond, and St. Albans. To the duke of Richmond Charles granted letters patent which entitled him to a tonnage duty on coal. In 1799 this duty was commuted for an annuity of 19,000l. a-year. The duke of Grafton is still paid a pension of 5843l. a-year out of the Excise revenue, and 3407l. out of the Post-office revenue. The duke of St. Albans is Hereditary Grand Falconer of England. Under king William and queen Anne several families which had previously enjoyed the title of earls were advanced to dukedoms, as Paulet duke of Bolton, Talbot duke of Shrewsbury, Osborne duke of Leeds, Russell duke of Bedford, Cavendish duke of Devonshire, Holles duke of Newcastle, Churchill duke of Marlborough, Sheffield duke of Buckinghamshire, Manners duke of Rutland, Montagu duke of Montagu, Douglas duke of Dover, Gray duke of Kent, Hamilton duke of Brandon; besides members of the royal family and Marshal Schomberg, who was made an English peer as duke of Schomberg. This great accession gave an entirely new character to the dignity. King George I., besides the dukedoms in his own family, made Bertie duke of Ancaster, Pierrepoint duke of Kingston, Pelham duke of Newcastle, Bentinck duke of Portland, Wharton duke of Wharton, Brydges duke of Chandos, Campbell duke of Greenwich, Montagu duke of Manchester, Sackville duke of Dorset, and Egerton duke of Bridgewater. George II. created no duke out of his own family, and the only addition he can be said to have made to this branch of the peerage was by enlarging the limitation of the Pelham dukedom of Newcastle so as to comprehend the Clintons, by whom the dukedom is now possessed. From 1720 to 1766 there was no creation of an English duke except in the royal house. In that year the representative of the ancient house of Percy was made duke of Northumberland, and the title of duke of Montagu, which had become extinct, was revived in the Brudenels, the heirs. The same forbearance to confer this dignity existed during the remainder of the reign, and during the reign of George IV. no dukedom was created out of the royal house, till the eminent services of the duke of Wellington marked him out as deserving the honour of the highest rank which the king has it in his power to confer. His dukedom was created in 1814, forty-seven years after the creation of a duke of Northumberland. The marquis of Buckingham was advanced to the rank of duke of Buckingham and Chandos in 1822, so that for a hundred years, namely from 1720 to 1822, only four families were admitted to this honour.

During the reign of William IV. two dukedoms were created, Gower duke of Sutherland, and Vane duke of Cleveland.

The whole number of dukes in the English peerage is at present twenty, exclusive of the blood royal. There are seven Scottish dukes (Argyll, Atholl, Buccleuch, Hamilton, Lennox, Montrose, and Roxburghe), of whom one (Hamilton) is also an English duke. The only Irish duke is the duke of Leinster.

All the dukes of England have been created by letters patent in which the course of succession has been plainly pointed out. Generally the limitation is to the male heirs of the body.

DUTY. [RIGHT.]

E.

EARL. The title of count or earl, in Latin *comes*, is the most ancient and widely spread of the subordinate or subject titles. This dignity exists under various names in almost every country in Europe. By the English it is called earl, a name derived to us from the ealderman of the Anglo-Saxons and the eorle of the Danes. By the French it is called *comte*, by the Spaniards *conde*, and by the Germans *graf*, under which title are included several distinct degrees of rank:— landgraves or counts of provinces, palsgraves, or counts palatine, markgraves, or counts of marches or frontiers (whence marchio or marquess), burggraves, or counts of cities, counts of the empire, counts of territories, and several others. [COUNT; BARON.]

After the battle of Hastings, William the Conqueror recompensed his followers with grants of the lands of the Saxon nobles who had fallen in the battle, to be held of himself as strict feuds; and having annexed the feudal title of carl to the counties of the Saxon earls (with whom the title was only official), he granted them to his principal captains.

These earldoms were of three kinds, all of which were by tenure. The first and highest was where the dignity was annexed to the seisin or possession of a whole county, with "jura regalia." In this case the county became a county palatine, or principality, and the person created earl of it acquired royal jurisdiction and seigniory. In short, a county palatine was a perfect feudal kingdom in itself, but held of a superior lord. The counties of Chester, Pembroke, Hexham, and Lancaster, and the bishopric of Durham, have at different times been made counties palatine; but it does not appear that the title of earl palatine was given to the most ancient and distinguished of them, the earl of Chester, before the time of Henry II., surnamed Fitz-Empress, when the title of palatine was probably introduced from the Germanic Empire. The earls of Chester created barons and held parliaments, and had their justiciaries, chancellors, and barons of their exchequer. This county palatine reverted to the crown in the reign of Henry III.

The second kind of earls were those whom the king created earls of a county, with civil and criminal jurisdiction, with a grant of the third part of the profits of the county court, but without giving them actual seisin of the county. The third kind was where the king erected a large tract of land into a county, and granted it with civil and criminal jurisdiction to be held *per servitium unius comitatûs.*

Under the early Norman kings, all earls, as well as barons, held their titles by the tenure of their counties and baronies; and the grant, or even purchase, with the licence of the king, of an earldom or a barony, would confer the title on the grantee or purchaser; but with the solitary exception of the earldom of Arundel, earldoms by tenure have long since disappeared, and in late times the title has been conferred by letters patent under the great seal. Earls have now no local jurisdiction, power or revenue, as a consequence of their title, which is no longer confined to the names of counties or even of places; several earls, as Earl Spencer, Earl Grey, and others, have chosen their own names, instead of local titles.

The coronet of an English earl is of gold surmounted with pearls, which are placed at the extremity of raised points or rays, placed alternately with foliage. The form of their creation, which has latterly been superseded by the creation by letters patent, was by the king's girding on the sword of the intended earl, and placing his cap and coronet on his head and his mantle on his shoulders. The king styles all earls, as well as the other ranks of the higher nobility or peerage, his cousins. An earl is entitled right honourable, and takes precedence next after marquesses, and before all viscounts and barons. When a marquess has an earldom, his eldest son is called earl by courtesy; but notwithstanding this titular rank, he is only a commoner, unless he be summoned to the House of Lords by such title. So the eldest sons of dukes are called earls where their fathers have an earldom but no marquisate, as the duke of Norfolk.

The number of earls in the House of Lords is at present 116.

EARL MARSHAL OF ENGLAND, one of the great officers of state, who marshals and orders all great ceremonials, takes cognizance of all matters relating to honour, arms, and pedigree, and directs the proclamation of peace and war. The *curia militaris*, or court of chivalry, was formerly under his jurisdiction, and he is still the head of the heralds' office, or college of arms. Till the reign of Richard II., the possessors of this office were styled simply Marshals of England: the title of Earl Marshal was bestowed by that king in 1386 on Thomas lord Mowbray, Earl of Nottingham. The office is now hereditary in the family of Howard, and is enjoyed by the duke of Norfolk. (Chamberlaine's *State of England;* Dallaway's *Inquiries into the Origin and Progress of Heraldry in England,* 4to. Glouc. 1793, pp. 93-95.)

EARTHENWARE. According to the census of 1841, the number of persons in Great Britain employed in this important and most useful manufacture ('Pottery, China, and Earthenware,') was 24,774, of whom 17,442 were returned for Staffordshire, which is the great seat of the manufacture. The district in this county known as 'The Potteries' is about a mile from the borders of Cheshire, and extends through a distance of more than seven miles, in which there are towns and villages so close to each other, that to a stranger, the whole appears like one straggling town. There are likewise extensive manufacturers of earthenware and porcelain in Yorkshire and Worcester, and the commoner kinds of ware are made in many parts of England.

Earthenware is a general term applicable to all utensils composed of earthen materials, but it is usual to distinguish them into three different kinds: the brown stone-ware, red pans and pots, and articles of a similar kind are called pottery; and porcelain is distinguished from earthenware as being a semi-vitrified compound, in which one portion remains infusible at the greatest heat to which it can be exposed, while the other portion vitrifies at a certain heat, and thus intimately combines with and envelopes the infusible part, producing a smooth, compact, shining and semi-transparent substance well known as the characteristic of porcelain.

Until the beginning of the eighteenth century the manufacture of earthenware was confined to a few coarse articles, which were devoid of taste. Earthenware was largely imported from Holland, and superior kinds from Germany and France. Even till nearly the close of the century the porcelain of China was still in common use on the tables of the wealthy, as the home manufacture, generally speaking, had not established its reputation. The improvement of the earthenware manufacture originated with Mr. Wedgwood, who carried it to great perfection. He availed himself of the services of artists and men of taste; and by this association of the manufacture with the fine arts it has been still further improved.

In the five years from 1831 to 1835, the declared value of earthen manufactures exported gradually rose from 461,090l. in 1831 to 540,421l. in 1835. The value of the exports to the United States of North America in 1835 was 246,220l. The number of pieces of earthenware exported and the real value of the same for the last four years were as under:

	Pieces.	£.
1841	53,150,903	600,759
1842	52,937,454	555,430
1843	55,597,705	629,148
1844	. . . .	751,279

The countries to which the largest quantities were exported in 1842 were as follows:—

	£.
United States of North America	168,873
Brazil	38,976
British North America	35,152
Germany	34,445
East India Company's territories and Ceylon	28,891
British West Indies	26,155
Holland	24,645
Cuba and Foreign West Indies	18,024
Italy and Italian Islands	17,201
Rio de la Plata	15,946
Chili	14,414
Denmark	12,434
Peru	11,421
Sumatra, Java, and Indian Archipelago	11,198

The earthenware manufacture in France is far inferior to that of England. (M'Gregor's Statistics.) In the United States of North America, the number of potteries in 1840 was 659; but no earthenware is exported.

EASEMENT (from the French words aise, aisement, ease) is defined by the old law writers as a service or convenience which one neighbour hath of another by charter or prescription without profit; as a way through his ground, a sink, or the like. It includes rights of common, ways, water-courses, antient lights, and various other franchises, issuing out of corporeal hereditaments, and sometimes, though inaccurately, the term is applied to rights of common.

At the common law these rights (which can only be created and transferred by deed) might be claimed either under an immemorial custom or by prescription; but twenty years' uninterrupted and unexplained enjoyment of an easement formerly constituted sufficient evidence for a jury to presume that it originated in a grant by deed; except in the city of London, where the presumption of a grant from twenty years' possession of windows was excluded by the custom which required that there should exist "some written instrument or record of an agreement." Nonuser during the same period was also considered an extinguishment of the right, as raising a presumption that it had been released.

By the statute 2nd & 3rd William IV. cap. 71, several important alterations have been made with regard to this description of property: forty years' enjoyment of any way or other easement, or any watercourse, and twenty years' uninterrupted "access and use of any light to and for any dwelling-house," &c., now constitute an indefeasible title in the occupier, unless he enjoys "by some consent or agreement expressly given or made for that purpose by deed or writing." The same statute also enacts that nonuser for the like number of years (according to the description of the particular right) shall preclude a litigating party from establishing his claim to it.

The easements of the English correspond to the Servitutes of the Roman and the Servitudes of the French law. (*Code Civil*, liv. ii. tit. 4, *Des Servitudes ou Services Fonciers*.)

The Roman Servitutes comprehended those rights which a man had in the property of another, and in a corporeal thing. The subject of easements forms a large head in the Roman Law, which was so far elaborated as to form a basis on which modern decisions may repose. The title De Servitutibus in the eighth book of the Digest contains the chief rules of Roman law on this subject, which have been discussed by various modern writers, as Mühlenbrach, *Doctrina Pandectarum*, p. 268, &c.; Savigny, *Das Recht des Besitzes*, p. 525, 5th ed.; Dirksen, *Zeitschrift für Geschichtliche Rechtswissenschaft*, vol. ii.; Puchta, *Cursus der Institutionen*, ii. 739, &c.

EASTER OFFERING. [OFFERINGS.]

EAST INDIA COMPANY. This association originated from the subscriptions, trifling in amount, of a few private individuals. It gradually became a commercial body with gigantic means, and next, by the force of unforeseen circumstances, assumed the form of a sovereign power, while those by whom it was directed continued in their individual capacities to be without power or political influence, thus presenting an anomaly without a parallel in the history of the world.

The Company was first formed in London in 1599, when its capital, amounting to 30,000*l*., was divided into 101 shares. In 1600 the adventurers obtained a charter from the crown, under which they enjoyed certain privileges, and were formed into a corporation for fifteen years, with the title of "The Governor and Company of Merchants of London trading to the East Indies." Under this charter the management of the company's affairs was intrusted to twenty-four members of a committee chosen by the proprietors from among their own body, and this committee was renewed by election every year.

The first adventure of the association was commenced in 1601. In the month of May of that year five ships, with cargoes of merchandise and bullion, sailed from Torbay to India. The result was encouraging, and between 1603 and 1613 eight other voyages were performed, all of which were highly profitable, with the exception of the one undertaken in the year 1607. In the other years the clear profits of the trade varied from 100 to 200 per cent. upon the capital employed.

At this time the trading of the company was not confined to the joint stock of the corporation, but other adventurers were admitted, who subscribed the sums required to complete the lading of the ships, and received back the amount, together with their share of the profits, at the termination of every voyage.

The charter of the Company was renewed for an indefinite period in 1609, subject to dissolution on the part of the government upon giving three years' notice to that effect.

In 1611 the Company obtained permission from the Mogul to establish factories at Surat, Ahmedabad, Cambaya, and Goga, in consideration of which permission it agreed to pay to that sovereign an export duty upon all its shipments at the rate of $3\frac{1}{2}$ per cent.

After 1612 subscriptions were no longer taken from individuals in aid of the joint-stock capital, which was raised to 420,000*l*., and in 1617-18 a new fund of 1,600,000*l*. was subscribed. This last capital, although managed by the same directors, was kept wholly distinct from the former stock, and the profits resulting from it were separately accounted for to the subscribers.

The functions of government were first exercised by the Company in 1624, when authority was given to it by the king to punish its servants abroad either by civil or by martial law, and this authority was unlimited in extent, embracing even the power of taking life.

In 1632 a third capital, amounting to 420,700*l*., was raised, and its management, although confided to the same directors, was also kept distinct from that of the first and second subscriptions. It is uncertain whether the capitals here severally mentioned were considered as permanent investments, or were returned to the subscribers at the termination of each different adventure.

A rival association, formed in 1636, succeeded in obtaining from the king, who accepted a share in the adventure, a licence to trade with India, notwithstanding the remonstrances of the chartered body. After carrying on their trade for several years in a spirit of rivalry which was fatal to their prosperity, the two bodies united in 1650, and thenceforward carried on their operations under the title of "The United Joint-Stock."

In 1652 the Company obtained from the Mogul, through the influence of a medical gentleman, Mr. Boughton, who had performed some cures at the Imperial Court, the grant of a licence for carrying on an unlimited trade throughout the province of Bengal without payment of duties.

Some proprietors of the Company's stock, becoming dissatisfied with the management of the directors, obtained from Cromwell, in 1655, permission to send trading vessels to India, and nominated a committee of management from their own body, for which they assumed the title of "The Merchant Adventurers." The evils to both parties of this rivalship soon became apparent, and in about two years from the commencement of their operations the Merchant Adventurers threw their separate funds into the general stock under the management of the directors. On this occasion a new subscription was raised to the amount of 786,000*l*. In April, 1661, a new charter was granted to the Company, in which all its former privileges were confirmed, and the further authority was given to make peace or war with or against any princes and people "not being Christians;" and to seize all unlicensed persons (Europeans) who should be found within the limits to which its trade extended, and to send them to England.

The first factory of the English was at Bantam, in Java, established in 1602. In 1612 the Mogul granted certain privileges at Surat, which was for a long time the centre of the English trade. In 1639 permission was obtained to erect a fortress at Madras. In 1652 the first footing was obtained in Bengal through the influence of Mr. Boughton, as already mentioned. In 1668 the Company obtained a further settlement on the western coast of the peninsula by the cession in its favour of the island of Bombay, made by Charles II., into whose hands it had come as part of the marriage portion of the Princess Catherine of Portugal. At the same time the Company was authorized to exercise all the powers necessary for the defence and government of the island.

At the close of the seventeenth century the three presidencies, Bengal, Madras, and Bombay, were distinguished as they still are, but it was not until 1773 that Bengal became the seat of the supreme government.

The first occasion on which the Company was brought into hostile collision with any of the native powers of India occurred in the beginning of 1664, when Sevajee, the founder of the Maharatta States, found occasion, in the prosecution of his plans, to attack the city of Surat. On this occasion the native inhabitants fled; but the members of the British factory, aided by the crews of the ships in the harbour, made a successful resistance, and forced Sevajee to retire. To show his satisfaction at the conduct of the Europeans upon this occasion, the Mogul accompanied the expression of his thanks with an extension of the trading privileges enjoyed by the Company. Another attack made upon Surat by the Maharattas in 1670 was repelled with equal success.

The right given to the Company by the charter of 1661 of seizing unlicensed persons within the limits above mentioned, and sending them to England, was exercised in a manner which, in 1666, produced a very serious dispute between the two houses of parliament.

For several years following the junction with the Merchant Adventurers about 1657, the trade of the Company was carried on without any serious rivalry, and with considerable success. Sir Joshua Child, who was one of the directors of the Company, in his 'Discourses on Trade,' published in 1667, represents that trade as the most beneficial branch of English commerce, employing from twenty-five to thirty sail of the finest merchant ships in the kingdom, each manned with from sixty to one hundred seamen.

In 1677-78 the whole adventure of the Company to India was 7 ships, with an investment of 352,000*l*. In 1678-79 the number of ships was 8, and the amount employed 393,950*l*. In 1679-80 there were despatched 10 ships with cargoes valued at 461,700*l*. In 1680-81, 11 ships, with the value of 596,000*l*.; and in 1681-82 there were 17 ships employed.

and the investment amounted to 740,000*l*.

In 1682-83 a project was set on foot for establishing a rival company, but it failed to obtain the sanction of the government. As one means for discouraging similar attempts in future, the Company ceased to give any detailed statements concerning the amount of the trade. This caused the public to entertain an exaggerated opinion concerning it, and tempted many private adventurers to set the regulations of the Company at defiance. These *interlopers*, as they were called, were seized by the Company's officers wherever they could be found, and under the pretext of piracy or some other crimes, they were taken before the Company's tribunals. Sentence of death was passed upon several, and the Company boasted much of the clemency that was shown in staying execution until the king's pleasure could be known; but they kept the parties meanwhile in close confinement.

A new charter, to have effect for twenty-one years, was granted in 1693, in which it was stipulated that the joint-stock of the Company, then 756,000*l*., should be raised to 1,500,000*l*., and that every year the corporation should export British produce and manufactures to the value of 100,000*l*. at least. The power of the crown to grant the exclusive privileges given by this charter was questioned by the House of Commons, which passed a declaratory resolution to the effect "that it is the right of all Englishmen to trade to the East Indies, or any part of the world, unless prohibited by act of parliament." The House of Commons directed an inquiry to be made into the circumstances attending the renewal of the charter in 1693, when it was ascertained that it had been procured by a distribution of 90,000*l*. amongst some of the highest officers of state. The duke of Leeds, who was charged with receiving 5000*l*., was impeached by the Commons; and it is said that the prorogation of parliament, which occurred immediately afterwards, was caused by the tracing of the sum of 10,000*l*. to a much higher quarter.

The resolution of the House of Commons just recited, acted as an encouragement to new adventurers, many of whom, acting individually, began to trade with India; but a still more formidable rival arose in a powerful association of merchants, whose means enabled them to outbid the old Company for the favour of the government. The old Company, which had now been in existence nearly a century, was dissolved, and three years were allowed for winding up its business. In 1700 the old Company obtained an act which authorized them to trade under the charter of the new Company, of which privilege it availed itself to the amount of 315,000*l*. The existence of two trading bodies led to disputes which benefited neither. In 1702 an act was passed for uniting them, and seven years were allowed for making preparatory arrangements for their complete union. Before the expiration of these seven years various differences which had arisen between the two bodies were settled by reference to Lord Godolphin, then Lord High Treasurer, whose award was made the basis of the act 6 Anne, c. 17, which was the foundation of the privileges long enjoyed by the Company. The united bodies were entitled "The United Company of Merchants of England trading to the East Indies;" a title which was continued until 1834.

The capital stock of the Company, which in 1708 amounted to 3,200,000*l*., was increased, under successive acts of parliament, as follows:—in 1786, 800,000*l*.; 1789, 1,000,000*l*.; 1794, 1,000,000*l*.; making its total capital 6,000,000*l*.; and upon this sum dividends are now paid: the later subscriptions were made at rates considerably above par, so that the money actually paid into the Company's treasury has been 7,780,000*l*.

The home government of the Company consists of—1st. The Court of Proprietors; 2nd. The Court of Directors; and 3rd. The Board of Control, the origin and functions of which body will be hereafter explained.

The Court of Proprietors elect the directors of the Company, declare the amount of dividend, and make bye-laws, which are binding upon the directors for the management of the Company in all respects which are not especially regulated by act of Parliament. The votes of the proprietors are given according to the amount of stock which they possess. The lowest sum which entitles a proprietor to vote is 1000*l.* of stock; 3000*l.* stock entitles to two votes; 6000*l.* to three votes; and 10,000*l.* to four votes, which is the largest number of votes that can be given by any one proprietor. In 1825 the number of proprietors entitled to vote was 2003; in 1833 the number was 1976; and in 1843 there were 1880; of whom 44 were entitled each to four votes, 64 had each three, 333 had two votes, and 1439 had single votes. In 1773, when all owners of stock amounting to 500*l.* had each one vote, and none had a plurality, the number of proprietors was 2153.

The Court of Directors consists of 24 proprietors elected out of the general body. The qualification for a seat in the direction is the possession of 2000*l.* stock. Six of the directors go out of office every year; they retire in rotation, so that the term of office for each is four years from the time of election. The directors who vacate their seats may be re-elected, and generally are so, after being out of office for one year. The chairman and deputy chairman are elected from among their own body by the directors, thirteen of whom must be present to form a court.

The power of the directors is great: they appoint the governor-general of India and the governors of the several presidencies; but as these appointments are all subject to the approval of the crown, they may be said to rest virtually with the government. The directors have the absolute and uncontrolled power of recalling any of these functionaries; and in 1844 they exercised this power by recalling Lord Ellenborough, the governor-general. All subordinate appointments are made by the directors, but, as a matter of courtesy, a certain portion of this patronage is placed at the disposal of the President of the Board of Control.

The Board of Control was established by the act of parliament passed in August, 1784, and which is known as Mr. Pitt's India Bill. This board was originally composed of six privy councillors, nominated by the king; and besides these, the chancellor of the exchequer and the principal secretaries of state are, by virtue of their office, members of the board. By an act passed in 1793 it is no longer necessary to select the members from among privy councillors. In practice the senior member, or president, ordinarily conducts the business, and on rare occasions only calls upon his colleagues for assistance. It is the duty of this board to superintend the territorial or political concerns of the Company; to inspect all letters passing to and from India between the directors and their servants or agents which have any connexion with territorial management or political relations; to alter or amend, or to keep back, the despatches prepared by the directors, and, in urgent cases, to transmit orders to the functionaries in India without the concurrence of the directors. In all cases where the proceedings of the directors have the concurrence of the Board of Control, the court of proprietors has no longer the right of interference. The salaries of the president and other officers of the Board, as well as the general expenses of the establishment, are defrayed by the East India Company.

The act 6 Anne, c. 17, already mentioned, conferred upon the Company the exclusive privilege, as regarded English subjects, of trading to all places eastward of the Cape of Good Hope to the Straits of Magalhaens; and these privileges, with some unimportant modifications, which it is not necessary to explain, were confirmed by successive acts of parliament, and continued until 1814. By the act 53 Geo. III. c. 155, passed in 1813, the Company's charter was renewed for twenty years, but received some important modifications, the trade to the whole of the Company's territories and to India generally being thrown open to British subjects under certain regulations; the trade between the United Kingdom and China was still reserved as a monopoly in the hands of the East India Company. It was also provided by the act of 1813 that the territorial and commercial accounts of the Company should be kept and arranged so as to exhibit the receipts and expenditure of each branch distinctly from those of the other branch.

The act of 1833, by which the charter was renewed for twenty years, took away from the Company the right of trading either to its own territories or the dominions of any native power in India or in China, and threw the whole completely open to the enterprise of individual merchants.

The progress of the Company's trade at different periods has not been regularly published. The following particulars, showing the annual average amount of the Company's trade in the forty years between 1732 and 1772, are from the report of the select committee of 1773 :—

Exports of goods and bullion . £742,285
Bills of exchange paid . . 247,492
Total cost of goods received . 989,777
Amount of sales of goods . . 2,171,877

The average annual profit amounted, from 1733 to 1742, to 116 per cent.; in the second ten years, to 90 per cent.; in the third, to 84 per cent.; in the fourth, to 132 per cent.; and embracing the whole forty years, the gross profit amounted to 119¼ per cent. It must be borne in mind, however, that this was *gross* profit, and that the expenses of carrying on the trade according to the method employed of establishing factories were necessarily very great. In fact, they were such as to absorb the profits and to bring the Company considerably into debt: a result which it would be more correct to attribute to the political character of the Company than to its necessary commercial expenditure. In 1780 the entire value of the export goods and bullion amounted to only 401,166*l.*, a large part of which must have consisted of military stores and supplies required by the various factories and establishments of the Company. In 1784 Mr. Pitt made a great reduction in the duty on tea, and this gave a stimulus to the exports; but in each of the three years which preceded the renewal of the charter of 1793 they did not exceed one million sterling. Under the provisions of this new charter, the Company was bound to provide 3000 tons of shipping every year for the accommodation of private traders, and under this apparently unimportant degree of competition the trade of the Company increased rapidly and greatly. During the last four years of its existence, from 1810-11 to 1813-14, the average annual exports of the Company to the three Presidencies, Batavia, Prince of Wales's Island, St. Helena, and Bencoolen, and to China, amounted to 2,145,365*l.* Of this sum 102,585*l.* consisted of exports to China, and 397,481*l.* of military and other stores.

On the occasion of the renewal of its charter, viz. in 1813, the Company was obliged to make a further cession of its exclusive privileges, and stipulating only for the continuance of its monopoly in the importation of tea into this country, to allow the unrestricted intercourse of British merchants with the whole of its Indian possessions. Under these circumstances the Company found it impossible to enter into competition with private traders, whose business was conducted with greater vigilance and economy than was possible on the part of a great company; its exports of merchandise to India fell off during the ten years from 600,000*l.* in 1814-15, to 275,000*l.* in 1823-24, and to 73,000*l.* in the following year, after which all such exportation of merchandise to India on the part of the Company may be said to have ceased. The shipments to China were still continued, and large quantities of stores were also sent to India for the supply of the army and other public establishments.

In the twenty years from 1813 to 1833 the value of goods exported by the private trade increased from about 1,000,000*l.* sterling to 3,979,072*l.* in 1830, while the Company's trade fell from 826,558*l.* to 149,193*l.* The actual returns of the trade at the commencement, middle, and termination of the above twenty years, were as follows :—

	By the East India Company.	By Private Traders.
1814	£826,558	£1,048,132
1815	996,248	1,569,513
1822	606,089	2,838,354
1823	458,550	2,957,705
1831	146,480	3,488,571
1832	149,193	3,601,093

The impossibility, as thus shown, of the Company's entering into competition with private merchants had a powerful influence with parliament when it was last called

EAST INDIA COMPANY.

upon to legislate upon the affairs of India, and in the charter of 1833 not only was the monopoly of the China trade abolished, but the Company was restricted from carrying on any commercial operations whatever upon its own account, and was confined altogether to the territorial and political management of the vast empire which it has brought beneath its sway. The title of the Company is now simply "The East India Company." Their warehouses and the greater part of the property which was required for commercial purposes were directed to be sold. The real capital of the Company in 1832 was estimated at 21,000,000*l.* The dividends guaranteed by the act which abolished trading privileges is 630,000*l.*, being 10½ per cent. on a nominal capital of 6,000,000*l.* The dividends are chargeable on the revenues of India, and are redeemable by parliament after 1874.

It would extend this notice to an unreasonable length if we attempted to trace the successive wars and conquests which mark the annals of the Company. All that it appears requisite to give under this head will be found in the following chronological table of the acquisitions of the British in India and other parts of Asia.

Date.   Districts.
1757 Twenty-four Pergunnahs
1759 Masulipatam, &c.
1760 Burdwan, Midnapore, and Chittagong
1765 Bengal, Bahar, &c.
— Company's Jaghire, near Madras
1766 Northern Circars
1775 Zamindary of Benares
1776 Island of Salsette
1778 Nagore
— Guntoor Circar
1786 Pulo Penang
1792 Malabar, Dundigul, Salem, Barramahal, &c.
1799 Coimbatore, Canara, Wynaad, &c.
— Tanjore
1800 Districts acquired by the Nizam in 1792 & 1799 from Sultan of Mysore
1802 The Carnatic
— Gorruckpore, Lower Doab, Bareilly
— Districts in Bundelcund
,804 Cuttack and Balasore
— Upper part of Doab, Delhi, &c.
1805 Districts in Gujerat
1815 Kumaon and part of the Terraie
1817 Saugur and Huttah Darwar, &c.
— Ahmedabad Farm
1818 Candeish
— Ajmeer
— Poonah, Concan, Southern Mahratta Country, &c.
1820 Lands in Southern Concan
1822 Districts in Bejapore and Ahmednuggar
1824 Singapore
1825 Malacca
1826 Assam, Aracan, Tarvi, Tenasserim
1828 Districts on the Nerbudda, Patna, Sumbhulpore, &c.
1832 Cachar
1834 Coorg, Loudhiana, &c
1835 Jynteeah
1839 Aden
1840 Kurnoul
1843 Scinde
1849 Punjaub.

It has always been felt to be highly anomalous than an association of individuals, the subjects of a sovereign state, should wage wars, make conquests, and hold possession of territory in foreign countries, independent of the government to which they owe allegiance. At a very early period of the Company's territorial acquisitions, this feeling was acted upon by parliament. By the act 7 Geo. III. c. 57 (1767), it was provided, that the Company should be allowed to retain possession of the lands it had acquired in India for two years, in consideration of an annual payment to the country of 400,000*l.* This term was extended by the 9 Geo. III. c. 24, to February, 1774. The sums paid to the public under these acts amounted to 2,169,398*l.* The last of these payments, which should have been made in 1773, was not received until 1775, and could not then have been paid but for the receipt of 1,400,000*l.*, which was lent to the Company by parliament. This loan was afterwards discharged, and the possession of its territory was from year to year continued to the Company until 1781, and was then further continued for a period to terminate upon three years' notice to be given after 1st March, 1791. Under this act the Company paid to the public 400,000*l.*

in satisfaction of all claims then due. In 1793 the same privileges were extended until 1814, the Company engaging to pay to the public the sum of 500,000*l.* annually, *unless prevented by war expenditure;* but owing to the contests in which it was engaged throughout that period, two payments of 250,000*l.* each, made in 1793 and 1794, were all that the public received under this agreement.

The act of 1813, by which the charter was renewed for twenty years from 1814, continued the Company in the possession of its territory, without stipulating for any immediate payment to the public. It contained provisions which established the right of parliament to assume possession of the Company's territories and of the revenues derived from them.

Throughout the whole of the territories held in absolute sovereignty by the East India Company, it exercises the right of ownership in the soil, not by retaining actual possession in its own hands, but by levying assessments.

The executive government of the Company's territories is administered at each of the presidencies by a governor and three councillors. The governor of Bengal is also the governor-general of India, and has a control over the governors of the other presidencies, and if he sees fit to proceed to either of those presidencies, he there assumes the chief authority. The governors and their councils have each in their district the power of making and enforcing laws, subject in some cases to the concurrence of the supreme court of judicature, and in all cases to the approval of the court of directors and the board of control. Two concurrent systems of judicature exist in India, viz., the Company's courts, and the king's or supreme courts. In the Company's courts there is a mixture of European and native judges. The jurisdiction of the king's courts extends over Europeans generally throughout India, and affects the native inhabitants only in and within a certain distance around the several presidencies: it is in these courts alone that trial by jury is established. Every regulation made by the local governments affecting the rights of individuals must be registered by the king's court in order to give it validity.

The constitution, in other respects, of the East India Company is shown by the following brief analysis of the principal clauses of the act 3 & 4 Will. IV., c. 85, which received the royal assent, 28th August, 1833, and under which its concerns are at present administered:—

The government of the British territories in India is continued in the hands of the Company until April, 1854. The real and personal property of the Company to be held in trust for the crown, for the service of India. (§ 1.)

The privileges and powers granted in 1813, and all other enactments concerning the Company not repugnant to this new act, are to continue in force until April, 1854. (§ 2.)

From 22nd April, 1834, the China and tea trade of the Company to cease. (§ 3.)

The company to close its commercial concerns and to sell all its property not required for purposes of government. (§ 4.)

The debts and liabilities of the Company are charged on the revenues of India. (§ 9.)

The governor-general in council is empowered to legislate for India and for all persons, whether British or native, foreigners or others. (§ 43.)

If the laws thus made by the governor-general are disallowed by the authorities in England, they shall be annulled by the governor-general. (§ 44.)

Any natural-born subject of England may proceed by sea to any part or place within the limit of the Company's charter having a custom-house establishment, and may reside thereat, or pass through to other parts of the Company's territories to reside thereat. (§ 81.)

Lands within the Company's territories may be purchased and held by any persons where they are resident. (§ 86.)

No native nor any natural-born subject of his majesty resident in India, shall, by reason of his religion, place of birth, descent, or colour, be disabled from holding any office or employment under the government of the Company. (§ 87.)

Slavery to be immediately mitigated, and abolished as soon as possible. (§ 88.)

EAST INDIA COMPANY.

Previously to the passing of this act, the Company possessed the power of arbitrary deportation against Europeans without trial or reason assigned, and British-born subjects were not only restricted from purchasing lands, but were prohibited from even renting them. Under the 87th section, if fairly carried into execution, a greater inducement than had hitherto been offered, is held out to the natives of India to qualify themselves for advancement in the social scale; a circumstance from which the best moral effects upon their characters are expected to result.

The revenue of the Indian government is not confined to its collections from the land, but consists likewise of customs' duties, stamp-duties, subsidies, and tribute from certain native states, some local taxes, and the profits arising from the monopolies of salt and opium. The following is an abstract of the principal revenues and charges of the Indian government for 1839-40:

	£.
Gross Revenue	17,577,244
Charges of Collection	2,238,507
Net Revenue	15,338,737
Indian Debt	30,703,778
Interest on Debt	1,447,453
Other Principal Charges:—	
Army	7,932,268
Civil and Political Establishments	2,018,205
Judicial Establishment	1,428,777
Provincial Police	283,440
Total Charges, exclusive of Interest on Debt and Allowances, paid under Treaties	11,663,638
Allowances and Assignments payable out of the Revenues in accordance with Treaties or other Engagements	1,596,377

Principal Charges defrayed in England in 1841-42.

	£.
Dividends to Proprietors of India Stock	632,545
Interest on Home Bond Debt	61,373
Furlough and Retired Pay to Officers	535,608
Payments on account of Her Majesty's Troops in India	400,000
Retiring Pay to ditto	60,000
Total Charges defrayed in England	2,848,618

In 1830, the total number of the military force employed at the three presidencies and subordinate settlements in India amounted to 224,444 men, and its expense to 9,474,481*l.*; but in several years subsequently a larger force has been employed.

The progress of the trade with India since the abolition of the East India Company's privileges is shown generally in the following tables:

1. Average annual number of ships and their tonnage which entered and cleared the ports of the United Kingdom, from and to the East India Company's territories and Ceylon, in the six years ending 1836, and in the six years ending 1842:

	1831-36.	1837-42.
Ships Inwards	188	329
Tons	79,204	149,064
Ships Outwards	202	323
Tons	88,920	156,141

2. Ships entered inwards and cleared outwards in the years 1838 and 1844 between the ports of the United Kingdom and Calcutta, Bombay, Madras, Ceylon, Singapore and Penang, and China:—

	1838.	1844.
Ships Inwards	318	534
Tons	128,087	247,087
Ships Outwards	307	540
Tons	143,458	239,368

The increase has been almost uniformly gradual in each year between 1838 and 1844.

3. Ships inwards and outwards in 1838 and 1844 between the ports of the United Kingdom and the following places:

	Inwards.		Outwards.	
	1838.	1844.	1838.	1844.
Calcutta	118	226	117	228
Bombay	57	109	73	132
Madras	13	22	11	39
Ceylon	16	35	14	29
Singapore & Penang	16	43	31	34
China	52	99	48	78

The proportion per cent. of the shipping

ECCLESIASTICAL [799] COMMISSIONERS.

employed to and from the ports of the United Kingdom and the Cape of Good Hope, and places eastward thereof, was as follows, in 1839 and 1844:—

Inwards.	1839.	1844.
London	74·1	66·8
Liverpool	20·5	27·2
Hull & Bristol	1·95	1·9
Clyde, &c.	3·45	41
Outwards.		
London	61·7	50
Liverpool	25·5	31·9
Hull and Bristol	2·0	1·9
Clyde, &c.	10·8	16·2

4. Value of British and Irish Produce and Manufactures exported to the East India Company's Territories, and Ceylon, and to China, in the undermentioned years.

	East Indies. £.	China. £.
1834	2,576,229	842,852
1835	3,192,692	1,074,708
1836	4,285,829	1,326,388
1837	3,612,975	678,375
1838	3,876,196	1,204,356
1839	4,748,607	851,969
1840	6,023,192	524,198
1841	5,595,000	862,570
1842	5,169,888	969,381
1843	6,404,519	1,456,180

In the last of the above years, the exports to the East Indies and China (7,860,699l.) were between one-sixth and one-seventh of the whole of our exports, and more than double the value exported in 1834. In 1844 the exports to China were considerably more than double the value of the exports of 1843. In the ten years from 1834 to 1844 the value of the exports to the West Indies has rather declined; and to British North America the increase is not very great.

ECCLESIASTICAL COMMISSIONERS FOR ENGLAND. On the ground that it was "expedient that the fullest and most attentive consideration should be forthwith given to ecclesiastical duties and revenues," a royal commission was issued, dated 4th February, 1835, which appointed certain commissioners, and directed them " to consider the state of the several doiceses in England and Wales, with reference to the amount of their revenues and the more equal distribution of episcopal duties, and the prevention of the necessity of attaching, by commendam, to bishoprics benefices with cure of souls;" and the commissioners were further directed "to consider also the state of the several cathedral and collegiate churches in England and Wales, with a view to the suggestion of such measures as may render them conducive to the efficacy of the Established Church; and to devise the best mode of providing for the cure of souls, with special reference to the residence of the clergy on their respective benefices." The commissioners were required to report their "opinions as to what measures it would be expedient to adopt" on the several points submitted to their consideration.

The commissioners were the archbishops of Canterbury and York, the bishops of London, Lincoln, and Gloucester, the lord chancellor, the first lord of the Treasury (Sir Robert Peel), and several members of the government, with other laymen. A change in the cabinet having occurred a few months afterwards, a new commission was issued on the 6th of June, 1835, for the purpose of substituting the names of members of the new cabinet.

The four Reports presented by the commissioners were respectively dated 17th March, 1835, and 4th March, 20th May, and 24th June, 1836. A fifth Report was prepared, but it had not been signed when the death of king William IV. occurred, and it was presented as a parliamentary paper (Sess. 1838 (66), xxviii. 9).

The First Report related to the duties and revenues of bishops. The commissioners recommended various alterations of the boundaries of dioceses, the union of the sees of Gloucester and Bristol, the union of the sees of Bangor and St. Asaph, and the erection of sees at Ripon and Manchester. They calculated the net income of the bishoprics of England and Wales at 148,875l., but from the unequal manner in which this revenue was distributed, the income of one-half of the bishoprics was below the sum necessary to cover the expenses to which a bishop is unavoidably subject; and to remedy this state of things, and with a view of doing away with commendams and diminishing the motives for translations, they recommended a different distribution of episcopal revenues.

The Third Report also related to episcopal matters.

The Second and Fourth Reports, and the draft of the Fifth Report, related to the cathedral and collegiate churches and to parochial subjects. They recommended the appropriation of part of the revenues of the cathedral and collegiate churches, and the entire appropriation of the endowments for non-residentiary prebends, dignities, and officers, and that the proceeds in both cases should be carried to the account of a fund out of which better provision should be made for the cure of souls.

The Commissioners stated in their Second Report that they had prepared a bill for regulating pluralities and the residence of the clergy; and in 1838 an act was passed (1 & 2 Vict. c. 106) relating to these matters. The chief provisions of the act are given in BENEFICE, p. 347 and p. 351.

On the 13th of August, 1836, an act was passed (6 & 7 Wm. IV. c. 77) which established the ecclesiastical commissioners as "one body politic and corporate, by the name of the 'Ecclesiastical Commissioners for England.'" The number of commissioners incorporated was thirteen, of whom eight were ex-officio, namely, the archbishops of Canterbury and York, the bishop of London, the lord chancellor, the lord president of the council, the first lord of the Treasury, the chancellor of the exchequer, and such one of the principal secretaries of state as might be nominated under the sign manual. There were five other commissioners, of whom two were bishops; and these five were removable at the pleasure of the crown. The laymen who were appointed were required by the act to subscribe a declaration as to their being members of the United Church of England and Ireland by law established.

By an act passed 11th August, 1840 (3 & 4 Vict. c. 113), the constitution of the Ecclesiastical Commission was considerably modified by increasing the number of ex-officio members, and by other alterations. In addition to the members constituted ex-officio commissioners under the act 6 & 7 Wm. IV. c. 77, the following were by this act also appointed:—all the bishops of England and Wales, the deans of Canterbury, St. Paul's, and Westminster, the two chief justices, the master of the rolls, the chief baron, and the judges of the Prerogative and Admiralty Courts. By this act the crown is empowered to appoint four, and the archbishop of Canterbury two laymen as commissioners in addition to the three appointed under the former act. Under the former act the commissioners were removeable by the crown; but now each commissioner continues a member of the corporation "so long as he shall well demean himself in the execution of his duties." Lay members are required as before to subscribe a declaration that they are members of the Established Church.

Five commissioners are a quorum at meetings of which due notice has been given. The chairman, who has a casting vote, is the commissioner present first in rank; and if the rank of all the commissioners present be equal, the chair is to be taken by the senior commissioner in the order of appointment. Two of the episcopal commissioners must be present at the ratification of any act by the common seal of the corporation; and if they, being the only two episcopal commissioners present, object, the matter is to be referred to an adjourned meeting. The commissioners may summon and examine witnesses on oath, and cause papers and documents to be produced before them.

The act (6 & 7 Wm. IV. c. 77) empowers the ecclesiastical commissioners to prepare and lay before his majesty in council such schemes as shall appear to them to be best adapted for carrying into effect the recommendations contained in the five Reports already mentioned, with such modifications or variations as to matters of detail and regulation as shall not be substantially repugnant to any or either of those recommendations. The king, by an order in council, ratifies these schemes, and appoints a time for their coming into operation. This order must be registered by the diocesan registrar of the diocese within which the place or district affected by the order is situated, and it must also be published in the London Gazette.' A copy of all the orders issued during the preceding twelve months must be presented annually to Parliament within a week after its meeting. As soon as an order is registered in the diocese, and gazetted, it has the same force as if it had been included in the acts for carrying into effect the Reports of the Commissioners.

By special enactments, and by the joint authority of the Queen in council and the Ecclesiastical Commissioners, changes of great importance have been made in relation to ecclesiastical revenues and duties.

The first act (6 & 7 Wm. IV. c. 77) is entitled 'An Act for carrying into effect the Reports of the Commissioners appointed to consider the state of the Established Church in England and Wales, with reference to Ecclesiastical Duties and Revenues, so far as they relate to Episcopal Dioceses, Revenues, and Patronage.' By this act the dioceses of England and Wales have been re-arranged, four sees have been consolidated into two, two new sees have been created, the patronage of the several bishops has been more equally divided, commendams are abolished, and the revenues of the different sees have been also more equally apportioned. [BISHOP, p. 385.] The jurisdiction of archdeacons was also settled by the Act. [ARCHDEACON, p. 180.]

The second act (3 & 4 Vict. c. 113) was passed 11th August, 1840, and is entitled 'An Act to carry into effect, with certain modifications, the Fourth Report of the Commissioners of Ecclesiastical Duties and Revenues;' but its enactments also comprehend some of the propositions of the Second Report and of the draft Fifth Report. The main subject of the act is the cathedral and collegiate churches, and the application of parts of their revenues to spiritual destitution in parishes. The act made some change in the constitution of deans and chapters, suspended a large number of canonries, founded honorary canonries [CANON, p. 443], abolished non-residentiary deaneries and sinecure rectories in public patronage; deprived non-residentiary prebends and other non-resident offices in cathedral and collegiate churches of the endowments formerly attached to such offices. Self-elected deans and chapters are abolished: deans are to be appointed by the crown, and the canons by the bishops. Sinecure rectories in private patronage may be bought by the Commissioners and suppressed. The profits of these dignities and offices, and sinecure rectories, are vested in the Ecclesiastical Commissioners, and are carried to a common fund, out of which additional provision is to be made for the cure of souls in parishes where such assistance is most required. Thus the act provided that a portion of the proceeds of prebends suppressed in Lichfield Cathedral should be devoted to making provision for the rector of St. Philip's, Birmingham, and for the perpetual curate of Christ Church in the same town; that the endowments belonging to the collegiate churches of Wolverhampton, Heytesbury, and Middleham should be applied to making better provision for the cure of souls in the districts with which those places are connected; and that the endowments of the collegiate church of Wimborne minster should be applied with a like object to the parish of Wimborne minster. The act empowers the Commissioners to annex the whole or any part of the endowments of sinecure rectories abolished by the act or purchased to the vicarages or perpetual curacies dependent on them, when the extent of the population or the incompetent endowment of such vicarages or curacies may render it expedient. Sinecure preferments may be annexed to benefices with cure of souls. Benefices may be divided or consolidated with consent of patrons. Arrangements may be made for a better provision for the spiritual duties of ill-endowed parishes by exchange of advowsons or other alterations in the exercise of patronage. When two benefices belong to the same patron, the income may be differently apportioned with his consent.

A third Act was passed 21st June, 1841 (4 & 5 Vict. c. 39). Its chief object was to amend and explain the two former acts, but it contains various enactments calculated to carry out the principle of the first two acts as to various regulations and details.

In each of the acts for carrying into effect the recommendations of the Ecclesiastical Commissioners, vested interests are specially protected.

From a return presented to Parliament, it appears that, down to May 1st, 1844, the number of benefices and churches whose incomes had been augmented by the Ecclesiastical Commissioners for England, was 496, and that the annual augmentation amounted to the sum of 25,779*l*.

There is in Ireland a body styled the Ecclesiastical Commissioners, who were appointed under the act 3 & 4 Wm. IV. c. 37 ('Church Temporalities Act'), and are empowered to receive the incomes of bishoprics on their becoming extinct in pursuance of the abovementioned act.

ECCLESIASTICAL COURTS. Courts in which the canon law is administered [CANON LAW], and causes ecclesiastical determined. Coke, in treating of the distinction between temporal and spiritual causes, says:—" And as in temporal causes, the king, by the mouth of his judges in his courts of justice, doth judge and determine the same by the temporal laws of England; so in causes ecclesiastical and spiritual, as, namely, blasphemy, apostacy from Christianity, heresies, schisms, ordering admissions, institutions of clerks, celebration of divine service, rights of matrimony, divorces, general bastardy, subtraction and right of tithes, oblations, obventions, dilapidations, reparation of churches, probate of testaments, administration and accounts upon the same, simony, incests, fornications, adulteries, solicitation of chastity, pensions, procurations, appeals in ecclesiastical causes, commutation of penance, and others, (the cognizance whereof belongeth not to the common laws of England,) the same are to be decided and judged by ecclesiastical judges according to the king's ecclesiastical laws of this realm."

In July, 1830, a Commission was appointed to inquire into the Practice and Jurisdiction of the Ecclesiastical Courts in England and Wales. The Report of the Commissioners, which was presented in 1831, was signed by the archbishop of Canterbury, and three of the bishops, the two chief justices, the chief baron, and several other persons of authority and eminence. This report gives the most correct and authentic account which exists of: 1, The nature of the ecclesiastical courts. 2, Of the course of proceeding in ecclesiastical suits; and 3, The nature of the processes, practice and pleadings of the ecclesiastical courts. The report in question has been almost solely used in the present article with such abridgment and slight alterations, as were necessary to bring it within the requisite space which could be devoted to the subject.

The ordinary ecclesiastical courts are—
1. The *Provincial Courts*, being, in the province of Canterbury, the Court of Arches, or Supreme Court of Appeal, the Prerogative or Testamentary Court, and the Court of Peculiars; and in the province of York, the Prerogative or Testamentary Court, and the Chancery Court; 2. the *Diocesan Courts*, being the consistorial court of each diocese, exercising general jurisdiction; the court or courts of one or more commissaries appointed by the bishop, in certain dioceses, to exercise general jurisdiction, within prescribed limits; and the court or courts of one or more archdeacons, or their officials, who exercise general or limited jurisdiction, according to the terms of their patents, or to local custom. 3. There are also *Peculiars* of various descriptions in most dioceses, and in some they are very numerous: royal, archiepiscopal, episcopal, decanal, sub-decanal, prebendal, rectorial and vicarial; and there are also some manorial courts, which exercise testamentary jurisdiction.

The Provincial courts of the archbishop of Canterbury, and the archbishop of York, are independent of each other; the process of one province does not run into the other, but is sent by a requisition from the court of one province to the local authority of the other, for execution, when it is necessary. The appeal from each of the provincial courts lies to the Judicial Committee of Privy Council; but before the passing of the statute 2 & 3 Wm. IV. c. 92, the appeal was to the king, and a commission issued under the Great Seal in each individual case of appeal, to certain persons or delegates, to hear and determine the matter in contest. [DELEGATES, COURT OF.]

Of the three Archiepiscopal Courts of Canterbury, the Arches Court is the first. [ARCHES, COURT OF.] This court exercises the appellate jurisdiction from each of the diocesan and most of the peculiar courts within the province. It may also take original cognizance of causes by letters of request, from each of those courts; and it has original jurisdiction, for subtraction of legacy given by wills proved in the Prerogative Court of Canterbury.

The Prerogative Court has jurisdiction of all wills and administrations of personal property left by persons having *bona notabilia*, or effects of a certain value, in divers ecclesiastical jurisdictions within the province. A very large proportion, not less than four fifths of the whole contentious business, and a very much larger part of the uncontested, or as it is termed commonform business, is dispatched by this court. Its authority is necessary to the administration of the effects of all persons dying possessed of personal property to the specified amount within the province, whether leaving a will or dying intestate; and from the very great increase of personal property, arising from the public funds and the extension of the commercial capital of the country, the business of this jurisdiction, both as deciding upon all the contested rights, and as registering all instruments and proofs in respect of the succession to such property, is become of very high public importance.

The Court of Peculiars, which is the third Archiepiscopal Court of Canterbury, takes cognizance of all matters arising in certain deaneries: one of these deaneries is in the diocese of London, another in the diocese of Rochester, another in the diocese of Winchester, each comprising several parishes; and some others, over which the archbishop exercises ordinary jurisdiction, and which are exempt from and independent of the several bishops within whose dioceses they are locally situated.

The province of Canterbury, includes twenty-one dioceses, and therein the diocese of Canterbury itself, where the ordinary episcopal jurisdiction is exercised by a commissary, in the same manner as in other dioceses.

The province of York includes five dioceses, besides that of Sodor and Man, and the archiepiscopal jurisdiction is exercised therein much in the same manner as in the province of Canterbury.

The Diocesan Courts take cognizance of all matters arising locally within their respective limits, with the exception of places subject to peculiar jurisdiction. They may decide all matters of spiritual discipline; they may suspend or deprive clergymen, declare marriages void, pronounce sentence of separation à mensâ et thoro, try the right of succession to personal property, and administer the other branches of ecclesiastical law.

The Archdeacon's Court is generally subordinate, with an appeal to the bishop's court; though in some instances it is independent and co-ordinate.

The archdeacons' courts, and the various peculiars already enumerated, in some instances take cognizance of all ecclesiastical matters arising within their own limits, though the jurisdiction of many of the peculiar courts extends only to a single parish: the authority of some of them is limited to a part only of the matters that are usually the subject of ecclesiastical cognizance; several of the peculiars possess voluntary, but not contentious, jurisdiction.

The total number of courts which exercise any species of ecclesiastical jurisdiction in England and Wales is 372, which may be classed as follows:—

Provincial and diocesan courts	36
Courts of bishops' commissaries	14
Archidiaconal courts	37
PECULIAR JURISDICTIONS.	
Royal	11
Archiepiscopal and episcopal	44
Decanal, subdecanal, &c.	44
Prebendal	88
Rectorial and vicarial	63
Other peculiars	17
Courts of lords of manors	48

In 1843 the gross fees, salaries, and emoluments of the judges, deputy judges, registrars, deputy-registrars, and all other officers in the ecclesiastical courts of England, Wales, and Ireland, amounted to 120,513*l.*, as follows:—

	£.
England	101,171
Wales	4,882
Ireland	14,459

The ecclesiastical jurisdiction comprehends causes of a civil and temporal nature; some partaking both of a spiritual and civil character, and, lastly, some purely spiritual.

In the first class are testamentary causes, matrimonial causes for separation and for nullity of marriage, which are purely questions of civil right between individuals in their lay character, and are neither spiritual nor affect the church establishment.

The second class comprises causes of a mixed description, as suits for tithes, church-rates, seats, and faculties. As to tithes, however, the courts of common law can restrain the ecclesiastical courts from trying any cases of modus or prescription, if either of the parties apply for a prohibition.

The third class includes church discipline, and the correction of offences of a spiritual kind. They are proceeded upon in the way of criminal suits, pro salute animæ, that is, for the safety of the offender's soul, and for the lawful correction of manners. Among these are offences committed by the clergy themselves, such as neglect of duty, immoral conduct, advancing doctrines not conformable to the articles of the church, suffering dilapidations, and the like offences; also by laymen, such as brawling, laying violent hands on any person, and other irreverent conduct in the church or churchyards, violating churchyards, neglecting to repair ecclesiastical buildings, incest, incontinence, defamation; all these are termed "Causes of Correction," except defamation, which is of an anomalous character. These offences are punished by monition, penance, excommunication, formerly, and now in place of it imprisonment for a term not exceeding six months [EXCOMMUNICATION], suspension ab ingressu ecclesiæ, suspension from office and deprivation.

The canon law has been practised in the Ecclesiastical courts as a distinct profession for upwards of three centuries. The rules for the admission of advocates are given in BARRISTER, p. 317. The residence of the judges and advocates, and the proper buildings for holding the Ecclesiastical and Admiralty Courts, are at Doctors' Commons, the site of which was purchased by some members of this body in 1567. [DOCTORS' COMMONS.] The members of the society were incorporated in 1768 by a royal charter, under the name of " The College of Doctors of Laws exercent in the Ecclesiastical and Admiralty Courts." The proctors discharge duties similar to those of solicitors and attorneys in other courts. [PROCTOR.]

The course of proceeding in these courts is as follows:—The mode of commencing the suit, and bringing the parties before the court, is by a process called a Citation, or summons. This citation, in ordinary cases, is obtained as a matter of course, from the registry of the court, and under its seal; but in special cases, the facts are alleged in what is termed an act of court, and upon those facts the judge or his surrogate decrees the party to be cited; to which, in certain cases, is added an intimation, that if the party does not appear, or appearing does not show cause to the contrary, the prayer of the plaintiff, set forth in the decree, will be granted. The party cited may either appear in person, or by his proctor, who is appointed by an instrument, under hand and seal, termed a proxy. The proctor thus appointed represents the party, acts for him and manages the cause, and binds him by his acts.

In Testamentary causes, the proceeding is sometimes commenced by a Caveat, which may be entered by a party interested in the effects of the deceased person, against the grant of probate of will or letters of administration, without notice being first given to him who enters the caveat. This caveat is then *warned* by the party who claims the representation either as executor or administrator, which is in effect a notice to the proctor who enters the caveat, that he must appear and take further steps, if he intends to continue his opposition. Both parties are then assigned by order of court to set forth their respective claims, and the suit thus commences, either to try the validity of an alleged will, or the right to administration, either under an intestacy or with a will annexed. [ADMINISTRATION; EXECUTOR.]

There is another process in testamentary matters, extremely useful and frequently resorted to. The executor, or other person who claims the grant of probate of a will or other testamentary instrument, may cite the next of kin and other parties interested in case there should be an intestacy or under a former will, to appear and see the will propounded and proved by witnesses; and if the parties cited do not appear and oppose the probate, they are barred from afterwards contesting its validity, unless on account of absence out of the kingdom, or some other satisfactory cause.

So again, the next of kin, or other parties entitled either to the grant of letters of administration or under a former will, may cite the executor or other person apparently benefited under a suggested will or testamentary instrument, to appear and propound it; or otherwise show cause why probate should not be granted of the suggested will of the deceased, on the ground of his having died intestate, or why probate should not be granted of a former will; and the parties cited, not appearing, are barred from afterwards setting up the will. But if probate or administration be taken in common form, without citing persons who have an adverse interest, the grant may afterwards be called in, and the executor or administrator cited, and put upon proof of his right, as if no such common form grant had issued. Again, where no grant is applied for by the person primarily entitled to it, such as an executor, residuary legatee, or next of kin, process may be taken out by any person who claims an interest in the effects of the deceased, such as a legatee, a party entitled to a distributive share of the estate, or a creditor, but he must call upon the persons primarily entitled to accept or refuse the grant, or otherwise show cause why it should not pass to such person who claims an interest. Or if a person be dead intestate, without leaving any known relations, a creditor may obtain letters of administration, upon advertising for next of kin in the Gazette and a morning and evening newspaper, provided he serves a process on the Royal Exchange and on the king's proctor, but the Crown has a right to take the grant, if it makes the claim.

In all these and similar cases, the facts must be supported by affidavit, all due notice is required to be given, and the grant is moved for before the court, at its sitting.

The mode of enforcing all process, in case of disobedience, is by pronouncing the party cited to be contumacious; and if the disobedience continues, a significavit issues, upon which an attachment from Chancery is obtained, to imprison the party till he obeys. In cases where some act is required to be done by the party cited, to exhibit an inventory and account, for instance, or to pay alimony, the compulsory process is enforced; but in some cases, where no act is necessary to be done by the party cited, the plaintiff may proceed in pœnam contumaciæ, and the cause then goes on ex parte, as if the defendant had appeared. The party cited, to save his contumacy, may appear under protest, and may show cause against being cited; such as, that the court has no jurisdiction in the subject-matter, or that he is not amenable to that jurisdiction: this preliminary objection is heard upon petition and affidavits; and either the protest is allowed, and the defendant dismissed, or the protest is overruled, and the defendant is assigned to appear absolutely; and costs are generally given against the unsuccessful party. Either party may appeal from the decision on this preliminary point; or the defendant, in case the judge decides against him on the question of jurisdiction, and on some other questions, may apply to a court of law for a prohibition.

Some other points, such as the claim to administration among persons of admitted equal degree of kindred, objections to an inventory and account, and other similar matters, may be heard upon petition and affidavit, where the facts are not of such a nature as to require investigation in the more formal proceeding of regular pleadings and depositions, with the benefit of cross-examining witnesses.

The form of the pleadings is next to be described. These are intended to contain a statement of the facts relied upon and proposed to be proved by each party in the suit, the real grounds of the action, and of the defence.

Causes, in their quality, are technically classed and described as plenary and summary, though in modern practice there is substantially little difference in the mode of proceeding. All causes in the Prerogative Court are summary.

The first plea bears different names in the different descriptions of causes. In criminal proceedings, the first plea is termed the Articles; in form, it runs in the name of the judge, who articles and objects the facts charged against the defendant; in plenary causes, not criminal, the first plea is termed the Libel, and runs in the name of the party or his proctor, who alleges and propounds the facts founding the demand; in testamentary causes, the first plea is termed an Allegation. Every subsequent plea, in all causes, whether responsive or rejoining, and by whatever party given, is termed an Allegation.

Each of these pleas contains a statement of the facts upon which the party founds his demand for relief, or his defence; they resemble the bill and answer in equity, except that the allegation is broken into separate positions or articles: the facts are alleged under separate heads, according to the subject-matter, or the order of time in which they have occurred. Under this form of pleading the witnesses are produced and examined only to particular articles of the allegation, which contain the facts within their knowledge; a notice or designation of the witnesses is delivered to the adverse party, who is thereby distinctly apprised of the points to which he should address his cross-examination of each witness, as well as the matters which it may be necessary for him to contradict or explain by counter-pleading.

Before a plea of any kind, whether articles, libel, or allegation, is admitted, it is open to the adverse party to object to its admission, either in the whole or in part: in the whole, when the facts altogether, if taken to be true, will not entitle the party giving the plea to the demand which he makes, or to support the defence which he sets up; in part, if any of the facts pleaded are irrelevant to the matter in issue, or could not be proved by admissible evidence, or are incapable of proof. These objections are made and argued before the judge, and decided upon by him, and his decision may be appealed from. For the purpose of the argument, all the facts capable of proof are assumed to be true: they are, however, so assumed merely for the argument, but are not so admitted in the cause; for the party who offers the plea is no less bound afterwards to prove the facts, and the party who objects to the plea is no less at liberty afterwards to contradict the facts. If the plea is admitted, the further opposition may be withdrawn: if the plea is rejected, the party who offers it either abandons the suit, or appeals against the rejection, in order to take the judgment of a superior tribunal. When a plea has been admitted, a time, or term probatory, is assigned to the party who gives the plea, to examine his witnesses; and the adverse party is assigned, except in criminal matters, to give in his answers upon oath, to his knowledge or belief of the facts alleged. The defendant may proceed then, if he thinks proper, or he may wait until the plaintiff has examined his witnesses, to give an allegation controverting his adversary's plea. This responsive allegation is proceeded upon in the same manner; objections to its admissibility may be taken, answers upon oath be required, and witnesses examined. The plaintiff may, in like manner, reply by a further allegation; and on that, or any subsequent allegation, the same course is pursued.

In taking evidence the witnesses are either brought to London to be examined, or they are examined by commission near their places of residence. Their attendance is required by a Compulsory, somewhat in the nature of a subpœna, obedience to which is enforced in the same way as in other cases of contumacy. The examination is by depositions taken in writing and in private by examiners of the court, employed for that purpose by the registrars. The examination does not take place upon written interrogatories previously prepared and known; but the allegation is delivered to the examiner, who, after making himself master of all the facts pleaded, examines the witnesses by questions which he frames at the time, so as to obtain, upon each article of the allegation separately, the truth and the whole truth, as far as he possibly can, respecting such of the circumstances alleged as are within the knowledge of each witness. The cross-examination is conducted by interrogatories addressed to the adverse witnesses, and when the deposition is complete, the witness is examined upon the interrogatories delivered to the examiner by the adverse proctor, but not disclosed to the witness till after the examination in chief is concluded and signed, nor to the party producing him till publication passes; and each witness is enjoined not to disclose the interrogatories, nor any part of his evidence, till after publication. In order that the party addressing the interrogatories may be the better prepared, the proctor producing the witness delivers, as before stated, a designation, or notice of the articles of the plea on which it is intended to examine each witness produced.

The examination and cross-examination of witnesses is kept secret until publication passes, that is, until copies of the depositions may be had by the adverse parties, after which either party is allowed to except to the credit of any witness, upon matter contained in his deposition. The exception must be confined to such matter, and not made to general character, for that must be pleaded before publication; nor can the exception refer to matter before pleaded, for that should be contradicted also before publication. The exception must also tend to show that the witness has deposed falsely and corruptly. The exceptive allegations are proceeded upon, when admitted, in the same manner as other pleas. They are not frequently offered, and are always received with great caution and strictness, as they tend more commonly to protract the suit and to increase expense than to afford substantial information in the cause. It is always, however, in the power of the court to allow further pleading in a cause; and if new circumstances of importance are unexpectedly brought out by the interrogatories, the court will, in the exercise of its discretion, allow a further plea after publication. This may also be permitted in cases where facts have either occurred or come to the knowledge of the party, subsequently to publication having passed.

The evidence on both sides being published, the cause is set down for hearing. All the papers, the pleas, exhibits (or written papers proved in the cause), interrogatories, and depositions are delivered to the judge for perusal before hearing the case fully discussed by counsel. All causes are heard publicly in open court; and on the day appointed for the hearing, the cause is opened by the counsel on both sides, who state the points of law and fact which they mean to maintain in argument: the evidence is then read, unless the judge signifies that he has already read it, and even then particular parts are read again, if necessary, and the whole case is argued and discussed by the counsel. The judgment of the court is then pronounced upon the law and facts of the case; and in doing this the judge publicly, in open court, assigns the reasons for his decisions, stating the principles and authorities on which he decides the matters of law, and reciting or adverting to the various parts of the evidence from which he deduces his conclusions of fact, and thus the matter in controversy between the parties becomes adjudged.

The execution of the sentence, in case there be no appeal interposed, is either completed by the court itself, according to the nature of the case—such as by granting probate or letters of administration, or signing a sentence of separation—or remains to be completed by the act of the party, as by exhibiting an inventory and account, by payment of the tithes sued for, and other similar matters, in which cases execution is enforced by the compulsory process of contumacy, significavit, and attachment. The question of costs in these courts is, for the most part, a matter in the discretion of the judge, according to the nature and justice of the case; and the reasons for granting or refusing costs are publicly expressed at the time of giving the judgment.

Attempts were made more than three centuries ago, to remedy the defects of the ecclesiastical courts. The earliest efforts of this kind were directed to the peculiar jurisdictions. Some of these jurisdictions extend over large tracts of country, and embrace many towns and parishes; others comprehend several places lying at a great distance apart from each other; and some only include one or two parishes. The jurisdiction to be exercised in these courts is not defined by any general law, and it is often difficult to ascertain to what description of cases the jurisdiction of any particular court extends. The commissioners appointed to revise the ecclesiastical laws, in the reigns of Henry VIII. and Edward VI., recommended that the power of the bishop, in matters of discipline, should extend to all places in the diocese, notwithstanding the exemptions and privileges of Peculiars. In the reign of Queen Elizabeth, it was proposed or talked of in convocation that parliament should be applied to, to subject peculiar and exempt rites and jurisdictions of what had belonged to monasteries to the diocesan. Nothing, however, appears to have been done.

In 1812, Sir W. Scott (Lord Stowell) brought a bill into parliament which passed the House of Commons, but was afterwards dropped in the Lords, which provided that "the power of hearing and determining contested causes of ecclesiastical cognizance should be exercised only by ecclesiastical courts sitting under the immediate commission and authority of the archbishops and bishops, and not by inferior or other ecclesiastical courts."

In 1832, the commissioners appointed to inquire into the practice and jurisdiction of the ecclesiastical courts, recommended a number of important changes in these courts. In 1833 the real property commissioners expressed an opinion in favour of their extensive reform. In the same year a select committee of the House of Commons made a report in which similar views were urged, and in 1836 a select committee of the House of Lords adopted the same course. From 1836 until the present time several bills have been brought in for amending the ecclesiastical courts, none of which were carried. In 1836 Lord Cottenham brought in an ecclesiastical courts bill. On opening the session of parliament in 1842 a measure for the improvement of the ecclesiastical courts was announced in the speech from the throne; but the bill brought in by the government, lingered through the session and was finally abandoned. In 1843 and 1844, other bills with the same object were equally unsuccessful. In the session of 1845 Lord Cottenham brought in an ecclesiastical courts' bill, and as it had received the concurrence of the Lord Chancellor, hopes were indulged that it might pass. Lord Cottenham's bill was identical with that which he brought in in 1836. It proposed the establishment of a central court in London to which all wills were to be sent. Surrogates were to act in the towns where there are now diocesan courts, who were to grant probates where the amount of property was small; but in every case the will was to be sent to London to be registered. The central court was to retain the power of the old courts in questions of divorce. In matters relating to church-rates, there was to be an appeal to quarter sessions, where the rate had been illegally levied; and in that of tithes the power of the ecclesiastical courts was to be abolished altogether. But this bill shared the fate of its predecessors, and all anterior efforts at reform; and the spiritual courts remain an unredressed grievance.

By a clause in 6 & 7 Will. IV. c. 77, which was an act for carrying into effect the Reports of the Ecclesiastical Commissioners of 1835, it was enacted that future appointments in any of the ecclesiastical courts in England and Wales (except the Prerogative Court of Canterbury) were not to give a vested interest in any office, nor any claim or title to compensation in case of the abolition of offices.

E'CHEVIN, the name given under the old French monarchy to the municipal magistrates of various cities and towns. At Paris there were four échevins and a prévôt des marchands, whose jurisdiction extended over the town and adjacent territory; in the other towns there was a maire and two or more échevins. In the south of France the same officers were called by other names, such as consuls in Languedoc and Dauphiné, capitouls at Toulouse, jurats at Bordeaux. The last name, that of jurats, was used in some of the English municipalities. They tried minor suits, laid the local duties or octroi upon imports, had the inspection of the commercial revenues and expenditure, as well as the superintendence of the streets, roads, and markets, the repairs of public buildings, &c. The name échevins seems to have been derived from scabini, a Latin word of the middle ages, which was used in Italy under the Longobards, and in France, Flanders, and other countries under the Carlovingian dynasty. In Holland they are called schepens. The scabini were the assessors to the counts, or missi dominici, appointed by the monarch to administer a province or district; and they were chosen among the local inhabitants. Afterwards, when charters were given to the communes, the municipal magistrates elected by the burgesses assumed also the name of scabini or échevins. (Ducange, *Glossarium*.)

ECONOMISTES. [POLITICAL ECONOMY.]

EDICTA, EDICTS. [EQUITY.]

EDUCATION. In every nation, even those called uncivilized, there are, and necessarily must be, certain practices and usages according to which children are instructed in those things which are to form the occupation of their future life; and every civilized nation, and, we may presume, nations also called uncivilized, have some general term by which they express this process of instruction. In the European languages derived from the Latin, and in others that have a mixture of that language, this general term is Education. It is not important to consider the more or less precise notions attached to this or any other equivalent word, but it is enough to observe, that, as the language of every nation possesses such a term, it is a universal truth that all nations admit that there is something which is expressed by the comprehensive term education, or by some equivalent term. But like all other general terms which have been long in use, this term Education comprehends within the general meaning already assigned to it a great number of particulars, which are conceived by various people in such different modes and degrees and in such varying amount as to the number of the particulars, some nations or individuals conceiving a certain set of particulars as essential to the term, others conceiving a different set of particulars as essentials, and others again conceiving the same particulars in such different ways, that two or more persons who agree in their general description of the term might very probably, in descending into the enumeration of the particulars, find themselves completely at variance with one another. This remark possesses no claim to novelty, but it is not on that account the less important. The discrepancy just stated is apparent not only as to such general terms as Education, Government, Right, Duty, and numerous other such words; but it is perceived and occurs even in things obvious to the senses, which consist of a number of parts, such as a machine, or any other compound thing. The general use of a machine, as a mill, for instance, is conceived in the same way by all, by the miller and by persons who knew nothing more about the mill than that it is used for grinding corn. As to the particulars, there may be all imaginable discrepancies among the persons who are only acquainted with the general purpose of the mill. But discrepancies as to the mode in which the several parts of a thing and the uses of the several parts are conceived, are generally discrepancies to be referred to the inaccuracy of the conceptions; they are, in fact, only errors, not the same but about the same thing. The more completely a large number of persons approach to harmony in their whole views as to this machine, the nearer, as a general rule, do their several views approach to accuracy; it being of the nature of truth to produce a harmony of opinion, the truth being one and invariable; and it being of the nature of error to admit of more varieties than man has yet conceived, inasmuch as men yet unborn will conceive errors never conceived before.

The same holds good as to Education which holds good of the machine. The general use, the general object of Education is roughly and rightly conceived by all persons to whom the name is familiar; but the great contrariety which exists among mankind as to the particulars which they conceive as entering into and forming a part of this term, and as to their mode of conceiving the same, proves either that all are still wrong as to their particular conceptions of this term, or that hitherto no means have been discovered of producing a general harmony of opinion, or in other words, of approaching to the truth. And here there is no person, or class of persons, who, as in the case of the miller, is or are allowed to be an authority competent to decide between conflicting opinions.

In every society, Education (in what particular manner conceived by any particular society is of no importance to our present inquiry) is, as a general rule, and must necessarily be, subjected to the positive law of the society, and to that assemblage of opinions, customs and habits which is not inappropriately called by some writers the Positive Morality of Society, or the Law of Opinion. This truth, or truism, as some may call it, is the basis of every inquiry into Education. In no country can there exist, as a general rule, an Education, whether it be good or bad, not subordinate to the law as above explained: for if such Education did exist, the form of that society or political system could not co-exist with it. One or the other must be changed, so that on the whole there must at last result a harmony, and not a discord. In every country then there does exist Education, either directed by and subordinate to the Positive Law and Positive Morality of that country, or there is an Education not so directed and subordinate, and consequently inconsistent with the continuance of that political system in which it exists. But such an anomaly, if found anywhere, should not be allowed to exist, because it is inconsistent with the continued existence of the society in which it has established itself; and if such an Education does exist, and can maintain itself in a society, against the will of that society, such a society is not a sovereign and independent society, but is in a state of anarchy. Education then should be in harmony with and subordinate to the political system: it should be part of it; and whether the political system is called by the name good or bad, if that political system is to continue, Education must not be opposed to it, but must be a part of it. From this it follows that the question, What is the best education? involves the question, What is the best political system? and that question again cannot be answered without considering what are the circumstances of the particular nation or society as to which we inquire what is the best political system. Recollecting however that the question of the best education and of the best political system cannot be discussed apart, because, as we have shown, Education is a part of the system, still we can consider several important questions as to Education, without determining what is the best political system.

One is, the political system being given, what ought the Education to be?

And, how far is it the business of the state to direct, control, and encourage that Education?

A man (under which term we include woman) has two distinct relations or classes of relations towards the state: one comprehends his duties as a citizen, wherein he is or ought to be wholly subordinate to the state; the other comprehends all his functions as a producer and enjoyer of wealth, wherein he has or ought to have all freedom that is not inconsistent with the proper discharge of his duties as a citizen. It is barely necessary to state this proposition in order to perceive that his Education as a citizen should be directed by the state. To suppose any other directing power, any power for instance which may educate him in principles opposed to the polity of which he is to form a part, is to suppose an inconsistency which, in discussing any question involving principles, we always intend to avoid.

His Education then as a citizen, it must be admitted, ought to be under the superintendence of the state: but How ought the state to exercise this superintendence? It is not our purpose to attempt to answer this question, which involves the consideration of some of the most difficult questions in legislation. It is our object here to present the questions which it belongs to the civilization of the present and future ages to solve; to show What is to be done, not How it is to be done.

But we may answer the question so far as this: the state having the superintendence of the citizen's Education, must have the superintendence of those who direct that Education; in other words, must direct those who are to carry its purposes into effect. The body of teachers therefore must be formed by, or, at least, must be under the superintendence of the state. Unless this fundamental truth is admitted and acted on, the state cannot effectually direct or superintend the Education of its citizens.

Every branch of this inquiry into Education runs out into other branches almost innumerable, till we find that the solution of this important question involves the solution of the greater part of those questions which occupy or ought to occupy a legislative body. For this reason, as above stated, we cannot attempt to answer in its full extent, How the state must direct the Education of its citizens, because this question involves the consideration of How far the direction and control of the state should be a matter of positive law imperative on all, how far and with respect to what particular matters it should encourage and give facilities only, how far it should act by penalties or punishment, how far it should allow individuals or associations of individuals to teach or direct teaching according to their own will and judgment, or, to express the last question in other words, whether and to what extent the state should allow competition in Education?

To these questions, and more especially to the last, the answer is in general terms, that the general interest, considered in all its bearings, must determine what and how much the state must do. This answer may be said to determine nothing. It is true it determines no particular thing, but it determines the principle by which all particular measures must be tested; and it would not be difficult to select instances from our own legislation, where enactments relating to places of education have been made with a view to particular interests only, without a reference to all the bearings of the question, and which, consequently, if tried by the test above given, would be found to be mischievous. As to the last question, the answer more particularly is,—that individual competition must not be destroyed. It is possible to reconcile the two principles of state direction and control and individual competition. The state may allow no person to teach without being examined and registered: such register will show if he has been trained under the superintendence of the state or not. This fact being established, it may be left to individuals or associations of individuals to employ what teachers they please. In all the schools founded by the state, in all schools under the superintendence of the state (to which latter class belong nearly all charitable foundations; and all such foundations which are not under the superintendence of the state ought, consistently with the general principles already laid down, to be brought under that superintendence), it follows as a matter of course that none but teachers trained under the superintendence of the state should be appointed. The selection of the teachers, out of the whole authorized body, for any particular school of the class just described, may be safely left to the local authorities who have the immediate superintendence of these schools.

If the principle that a state ought to exercise a superintendence over the Education of its citizens as citizens be admitted, it may be asked, how far and to what branches of knowledge does this extend? To this we reply that a precise answer can only be given by the legislature of each country, and the question cannot be answered without many years of labour and perhaps without many experiments. But it follows from the principles already laid down that no citizen ought to exercise any function of government, or be intrusted with the exercise of any power delegated by the state, without having received some (what, we cannot here say) Education under the superintendence and direction of the state.

When the sovereign is one, it is clear how he will and ought to direct the Education of his people. His first object must be to maintain his own power. It is an absurdity to suppose any Education permitted in any state which shall be inconsistent with the existence of that state; and consequently in a monarchy, the first object is and must be the preservation of the monarchy. It is unnecessary to show that the attainment of this object is by no means inconsistent with good Education, and Education which is good when considered with reference to other objects than the conservation of the monarchy.

In a democracy [DEMOCRACY] the business of the state is also plain and easy. It is not plain how far and to what classes of subjects the superintendence of the state should extend, for that may be as difficult to determine in a democracy as in any other form of government; but it is plain to what objects the superintendence of the state in such a community should extend. Its objects should be to maintain in all its purity the principle of individual political equality, that the sovereign power is in all and every person, that the will of the majority declared in the form prescribed by the constitution, is the rule which all must obey, and that the expression of opinion on all subjects, by speaking or writing, should be perfectly free. If any checks are wanting on the last head, they will always be supplied in a democracy by the positive morality of the society in a degree at least great as is required, and certainly in a greater degree than in any other form of government; and when opinion is ineffectual, law must supply its weakness.

What must the state do in a political system which is neither a monarchy nor a democracy; in a system where there are contending elements, and none has yet obtained the superiority? The answer is, it must do what it can, and that which it does, being the will of the stronger part for the time, must be considered right. But such a political system, though it may continue for a long time, is always moving (at least it is only safe when it is moving) in the direction impressed upon it by one or other of the contending powers which exist in the state. Still, so long as the struggle continues, there can be no Education in the sense which we are considering, no Education which has the single, clear, and undivided object proposed to it in a monarchy and in a democracy. Such a political system then would appear to be wanting in one of the chief elements of a political system, which we have explained to be the bringing up of the citizens in such a manner as to secure the stability of that system under which they live. In such a system as we here imagine, there being no unity in the object, there can be no unity of means with reference to any object; and such a system might be more properly called an aggregation of political societies, than one political society; what is implied by the word aggregation being the existence of something just strong enough to keep the whole together. Such a society, in spite of its incongruity, may be kept together by several things: one may be, that the positive morality of the whole society is favourable to order, as characterized by a love of wealth, and impressed with a profound conviction of the necessity of leaving free to every individual the pursuit of wealth and the enjoyment of it when it is acquired. Another may be, that in this same society, though there are contending elements, there may be a slow and steady progress, and a gradual change, tending in one direction only; such a gradual progress in such a system may be regarded as the only security against its destruction.

If the history of the world has ever presented, or if it now presents, such a phenomenon as we have attempted to describe; further, if such a society contains the greatest known number of instances of enormous individual wealth opposed to the greatest amount of abject poverty; the highest intellectual cultivation and the greatest freedom of thought, side by side with the grossest ignorance and the darkest superstition; thousands in the enjoyment of wealth for which they never laboured, and tens of thousands, depending for their daily bread upon the labour of their hands and the sensitive vibrations of the scale of commerce; political power in appearance widely diffused, in effect confined to the hands of a few; ignorance of the simplest elements of society in many of the rich and those who have power; ignorance not greater in those who are poor and have none—such a society, if it exists, is a society in which every reflecting man must at moments have misgivings as to its future condition and as to the happiness of those in whom he is most nearly interested. But if such a society contains a class, properly and truly denominated a middle class, a class neither enervated by excessive wealth and indolence nor depressed by poverty; a class that is characterized by industry and activity unexampled; a class that considers labour as the true source of happiness, and free inquiry on all subjects as the best privilege of a free man—such a society may exist and continue to be indefinitely in a state of progressive improvement. Such a society, with its monstrous anomalies and defects, offers to a statesman of enlarged mind and vigorous understanding the strongest motive, while it supplies him with all the means, to give to the political system an impulse that shall carry it beyond the region of unstable equilibrium and place it at once in a state of security.

In such a society the simple enunciation by one possessed of power, that Education is a part of the business of the state, would be considered as the forerunner of some measure which should lay the foundation of that unity without which the temporary prosperity of the nation can never become permanent and its real happiness can never be secured.

The particular questions that the philosophic legislator has then to solve with respect to the education of the citizens, are—1. How are teachers to be taught, and what are they to be taught? 2. How is the body of teachers to be directed, superintended, rewarded, and punished? 3. What schools and what kinds of schools are to be established and encouraged for the Education of the people? 4. What are the teachers to teach in those schools? 5. Where is the immediate government of such schools to be placed? 6. And where the ultimate and supreme direction and control of such schools? The word Schools is here used as comprehending all places of Education.

It remains to consider those other relations of a man to the state in which we view him as a producer of wealth for his own enjoyment. Here the general principle is, that the pursuit and enjoyment of wealth must be left as free as the public interest requires; and this amount of freedom will not depend in any great degree on the form of government. To this head, that of the production of wealth, belong all the divisions of labour by which a man, to use a homely but expressive phrase, gets his living, or what in other words are called the professions, trades, and arts of a country. The only way in which the state can with any advantage direct or control the exercise of any profession, trade, or art, is by requiring the person who undertakes to exercise it to have been trained or educated for the purpose. Whether this should be done in all cases, or in some and what cases, and to what extent, and how, are questions for a legislature guided by a philosopher to answer.

In all countries called civilized this has been done to a certain extent. The legislation of our own country offers instances of great errors committed by legislating where no legislation was wanted, or by legislating badly. Perhaps instances may also be noted in all countries where evil has arisen for want of legislation on the subject. We may explain by example.

Perhaps it is unnecessary for a state to require that a shoemaker, or a tailor, or a painter, or a sculptor, should be required to go through a certain course of training before he exercises his art. The best shoemaker and best tailor will be sure to find employment, and individual shoemakers and tailors have as ample means of giving instruction in their craft as can be desired. It may be true or not true, that the best painters and sculptors will meet with most employment; but is it unnecessary or is it necessary for a state to offer facilities and encouragement to those who design to educate themselves as painters and sculptors? Most civilized nations have decided this question by doing so, and there are many reasons in favour of such a policy.

Ought the state to require the professor of law, of medicine, or of religious teaching, to undergo some kind of preliminary Education, and to obtain a certificate thereof? Nearly all civilized countries have required the lawyer and physician to go through some course of Education. There are strong reasons in some countries, our own for instance, both for and against such a requisition; but on the whole, the reasons seem to preponderate in favour of requiring such Education from him who designs to practise law, and still more from him who designs to practise the art of healing. Most civilized countries, perhaps all, except two (so far as we know), require all persons who profess the teaching of Religion to have received some Education, to be ascertained by some evidence. But in both the nations excepted, any person, however ignorant, may preach on subjects which the mass of the community believe or affect to believe to be of greater importance both for their present and future welfare than any other subjects. Professing to maintain, as we hope they always will do, the principle of religious freedom, these two nations have fallen into the greatest inconsistencies. They have checked the free expression of individual opinion by word of mouth, and fettered it in the written form, in the one country by the severe penalties of positive law, and the no less severe penalties of positive morality; and in the other by the penalties of positive morality carried to an excess which is destructive to the interests of the society itself. (See Attorney General *v.* Pearson, 3 Merrivale, 353.) But both nations allow any person, if he professes to be a teacher of religion, however ignorant he may be, to become the weekly, the daily instructor of thousands, including children, who derive and have derived no instruction of any kind except from this source. Such a teaching or preaching, if it only assumes the name and form of religious teaching, is permitted to inculcate principles which may be subversive of the political system; and it may and often does inculcate principles the tendency of which is to undermine the foundations of all social order; for it should never be forgotten that all religious teaching must include moral teaching, though moral teaching is quite distinct from religious teaching. And though it must be admitted that no teacher of religion recommends a bad thing *as* bad, he may recommend a bad thing as good, solely because he knows no better. We have endeavoured to point out an anomaly which exists in certain political institutions, and which can only be allowed to exist so long as it protects itself under a specious and an honoured but misunderstood name. For though it be admitted that such anomaly exist, it may be said that it cannot be remedied without interfering with the important principle of religious freedom. But what is religious or any other freedom? Is it the individual power of doing or saying what a man likes? Certainly not. It means no more than a freedom not inconsistent with the public welfare. Still it may be urged that this is precisely the kind of freedom with which no state, where the principle of religious freedom is admitted, can safely interfere. But this is only bringing us round again to the question, What is religious freedom? To say that it cannot be interfered with is to assume an answer to the question. Does what is called religious freedom, as the same is now understood, admitting it to produce much good, produce also any evil? If it does, can the evil be remedied? Is the free practice of any art or profession, medicine or law, for instance, or the art of instructing children in general knowledge, or perfect freedom in teaching and expounding religious doctrines, inconsistent with the condition of qualification? How the qualification is to be ascertained, and what it is to be, is the question; and it is a question which may be answered.

It may be asked: If a man should not be a teacher of Religion without complying with some previous conditions, why should he be allowed to write on Religion without some like qualification, for he may do mischief by his writing as well as his oral preaching? This is true; and if it were possible, consistently with religious freedom, as here understood, to prevent persons from writing on Religion who have not had a competent Education, it would be a good thing to prevent them. So would it also be a good thing to prevent persons from writing on many other subjects, who know little or nothing about them, if it could be done consistently with letting those write who do understand what they are writing about. But it cannot be done; and as the free expression of opinion is essential to the full development of a nation's powers, both physical and intellectual, we must be content to take the bad with the good. Writing, however, is different from teaching and preaching. Oral instruction reaches thousands whom a book, however small or cheap, never can reach. If a man should propound doctrines destructive to all social organization in a learned and extensive work, it might be most prudent to take no notice of him. If he should propound them in a form adapted for universal circulation, the case is different; and if his doctrines are such as tend to overthrow the political system under which he lives, it would be a gross inconsistency to allow them to be circulated. Still more, if he should go about preaching them, would it be the business of the state to quench such a firebrand by any means, however severe, that are required for the purpose.

In a Monarchy, such an evil is stopped by the monarch or his agents; but there is the danger that the interference may extend to cases when no real harm could be done by the circulation of the book or the preaching of the doctrine, and to cases in which good would follow. In a free state, no man is convicted of the offence of writing or teaching what is bad without the judgment of his fellow-citizens—in England by a jury; and though a jury is neither always wise nor always impartial, no better means have yet been discovered of reconciling the free expression of opinion with the restraint of opinions which cannot be broached without danger to the state.

The relation of Religion to the State is a question of vital importance to all nations, but to none is it of so great import ance as to those of a Republican form, those in which political power is distributed among many individuals, and extends to a large part of the people in general, as distinguished from a privi leged class.

He who views a state rightly views it as a Unity: the sovereign power, whether it is lodged in one or in many, is that which gives a unity to all the members of the social body. In the middle-age history of Europe, we see two contending bodies in a state, a body Political and a body Ecclesiastical, and the consequence was anarchy. The states of Europe have long been Christian States, and the Christian Religion is inseparably blended with all European systems, and those of America, which have arisen out of them. In one state in Europe, the Papal State, the constitution is Ecclesiastical, and the Political is merged in it. In some other states of Europe the Ecclesiastical body is now completely subjected by the Political; in others the Ecclesiastical body still possesses large political power. The paramount importance of Religion leads many persons to conclude that the Ecclesiastical Estate should have political power, or at least that it should have the sole power of regulating all its own concerns. Those who maintain this proposition must admit that a state is not a Unity: it is a divided body, one member of which is to some extent independent of the whole body; a monstrous anomaly which can only breed confusion and stop all social improvement.

If the state is to be One, must it be One as a Political body, or as a body Political and Religious? If there is only one religion in the state, and no other allowed, the state may be Politically and Religiously one. Such a state may be perfect in theory, but, in fact, its movements will not be towards improvement, but retrograde. Experience has shown that the free exercise of the understanding on all matters of speculation, on all matters of belief, on all matters that extend beyond the limits of sense, is as necessary to the development of the understanding, as freedom from unwise restrictions on trade and industry is necessary to the increase of national wealth. If a state then allows each man to think, speak, and so write as he pleases, subject only to the condition that he shall not speak, write, or act, as to attempt to overthrow the power which gives him this freedom, the state must consistently declare, the sovereign body by its acts of legislation must declare, that it is neither a Religious nor an Anti-religious body. The state is neither Christian nor not-Christian. But it is objected—it has been admitted that all European nations are now Christian, and that Christianity is intimately blended with them. True; and for this reason,—the state need not occupy itself about the matter. It is admitted that Christianity has rooted itself in all our social systems deeper than any legislation can do. It pervades all society, its influence is above law. Christianity is therefore recognised by all; for as to the few speculative thinkers who do not recognise its truths, and as to the still larger number who are indifferent, they do not affect the great mass. It is a truth indisputable, a truth which no man in his senses can deny, that modern civilization is Christian; and that if all state establishments of religion were abolished, Christianity would exist in the minds of the great mass of a nation, and would be taught and propagated by zealous teachers. Nay, were a state to oppose itself to all religion, to persecute those who profess and those who teach it, Christianity would only flourish the more. For a state is directed by a comparatively small number, and this small number, if it opposed Christianity, would be precisely in the same position as if one man should attempt to control by force a million.

If then Christianity pervades the mass of a nation, the political system, the Government, cannot oppose Christianity, and it need not be identified with it. Christianity, though one thing as contrasted with Mohammedanism or other religions, is not one in itself. There are numerous sects: all profess Christianity, but all differ among themselves in some matters of faith and ceremony. If all are allowed to differ, and all are allowed to profess Christianity as they choose, it is an idle thing to speak of a Christian State, if we understand thereby that the state is to be considered both a Political and a Religious body. It involves a contradiction, for the state can not be Christian in any given form, without being opposed to those who are Christians in a different form. It follows that in a state where all forms of Christianity are allowed, the state is not Christian, and it gives, or ought to give, no more encouragement to one form of Christianity than to another. It allows to all the free exercise of their religion, it subjects all alike to the same rules and restraints, it gives its aid and encouragement to all on equal terms. How far it shall give its aid, and in what form, is a matter that it is not necessary to determine here. It is enough to show that in a state which allows all forms of Christianity, the state as such is not Christian, and that when the principle of the free profession of any form of Christianity is once acknowledged, from that time the state has abandoned the character of being Christian as a state. The practical consequences of this must be that whatever remains there may be in an old state of this identity of a Church and a state, or, as it is sometimes expressed, union of church and state, the course of events, if it proceeds onwards in the same direction, must in time efface every trace of this union.

If a state, besides allowing the profession of Christianity in any form, shall likewise allow the open profession of any other faith, that is not Christian, it is still more absurd to speak of the state, as such, being Christian. It is, as a state, as much non-Christian as Christian; and it must, to be consistent, give its protection to those who are not Christians as much as to those who are Christians, and as a state it must make no distinction between those who are not Christians and those who are.

If the number of those who profess some faith which is not Christian should increase and approach to the number of those who are Christian, such a State would be threatened with anarchy or a revolution. But the amount of risk of this kind is not great; for as the world stands at present, there seems little danger of a Christian country becoming Mohammedanized, and not much prospect of a Mohammedan country becoming Christianized.

The practical conclusion is, that in a State where perfect religious freedom, as it is termed, exists, the State treats all religious associations or communities alike: it shows no favour, extends no aid, and gives no countenance to one more than to another. This is the true conclusion that is deduced where a State which had once one religion, and only one, and allowed no other, has so changed this its fundamental polity as to allow all religions to be professed openly, freely, without penalty, persecution, or restraint.

In all that we have said on Education as a subject of legislation, it is assumed either that the state can enforce, if necessary, that which it enacts; or that the enactments of the state will be only the expression of the public will; or that they will be founded on reasons so clear and convincing as to receive, when promulgated, the assent and support of a majority large enough to secure their being carried into effect. If some one of these conditions cannot be fulfilled, the legislation is premature, and will probably be injurious.

The extent of that department of Education with which the legislature should not interfere can only be fixed with precision by ascertaining the extent of its proper, that is, its useful interference. We may state, however, in general terms, that the early and domestic Education of the young of both sexes is in nearly all, perhaps all, modern political systems, placed beyond the reach of direct legislative control by the constitution of modern society. But inasmuch as one of the great functions of government is the instruction, direction, and superintendence of the teaching body, even the domestic Education is not beyond its influence, but will be subjected to it in precisely the same degree as the state shall succeed in forming a body of good teachers. For the importance and value of Education (in some sense or other: it matters not here in what sense) are universally admitted. The objects of Education, it is true, are often misunderstood by parents and those who have the charge of youth, and the means are as often ill-calculated for the end proposed. But this is only a consequence of ignorance, not an indication that Education is undervalued. When better objects and better means are proposed, whether by individual example or by associations of individuals called societies, or by the state, such objects and means will be readily embraced by all who can comprehend them. It being assumed that the objects and means thus presented are desirable in themselves, there can be no obstacle to the reception of them, so far as the state allows the reception to be voluntary, except the ignorance and prejudices (which are, in fact, only ignorance under another name) of those to whom they are proposed. But till this obstacle which ignorance presents is overcome, nothing can be effected in the way of improvement; and it being admitted, that as to the department of education under consideration, direct legislation is not the proper means, some other means must be adopted. Individuals and societies often effect their benevolent objects by example, and by the authority of their name and character. The state may do the same. The influence of authority and example is in all countries most efficient when the sovereign power calls them in to its aid. Individuals may do much; societies have done more; but Society (the whole, in its collective power) is the body from which all improvements must come that are calculated to operate on the mass. From these considerations we conclude that if any state seriously and anxiously apply itself to the business of forming a body of teachers, it is impossible to foresee how far the beneficial influence of such a body, well organized, may extend. It may penetrate into the house of the wealthy, where the child who is born to the possession of wealth is not thereby secured in the enjoyment of it, or against any one calamity of human life. His wealth may be wasted by improvidence; his health may be enfeebled by indolence and debauchery; his under-

3 G

standing may be cramped and corrupted by vicious Education and bad example; and he may become an object of detestation and contempt, though born to the command of wealth sufficient to purchase all the luxuries that combined ingenuity and industry can produce. This influence may also reach, and perhaps sooner and more effectually reach, the hovels and the garrets of the poor, where thousands of children are now brought up under such circumstances, that to be unhealthy, vicious, criminal, and unhappy, are the only results which, as a general rule, can follow from the given conditions of their existence. When the unhappy wretch, who cannot be other than what he is, has at last transgressed the limits of the positive morality of society, and got within the verge of the penalties of the law, his crimes are blazoned forth by the public prints, the respectable part of society are shocked at the disclosures, and are only relieved from their pain when the criminal is hid in a prison, or his life is taken by the executioner. But the example is soon forgotten, and misery and vice fester in the very heart of society unheeded, till some new warning again startles it from its lethargy.

Some zealous promoters of education set great value on books as a means of improvement, and much has been done towards supplying all classes of society with better elementary works. This is a department that perhaps should not be overlooked by the State; for good books are of course better than bad. But no elementary books for learners will ever effect any great change. If the teachers are made what they ought to be, books are of little importance for learners; and if the teachers are not well trained, a good book in their hands will not be much more efficacious than a bad one. The kind of elementary books most wanted are books for the use of teachers. Those who lay so much stress on books for learners, and especially for the children of the poor, speak as men who know little of practical education.

It may appear almost superfluous to state that the true interest of the sovereign power, considered in all its bearings, must coincide with the interest of the governed; the difference in forms of government or in the distribution of the sovereign power being mainly to be considered a difference in the instruments or means by which an end is to be obtained. But still this difference is important. Where the sovereign power is in all those who as individuals are subject to it, the coincidence of power and of interest is complete; and the nearer any form of government approaches to this distribution of power, the more obvious and the stronger is the principle laid down. The principle may express a common-place truth; but the consequences that flow from it are numerous and important. When it is clear that the state can promote the general good by its regulations, its business is to make regulations. If regulations will not promote the general good, that is a reason for not making them. Now, to protect a man in the enjoyment of his property, and to preserve him from the aggressions of others, is a main part of the business of governing. For this purpose restraints and punishments are necessary: immediately, to protect the injured, and give compensation, when it can be given; remotely, to prevent others from being injured, and, so far as it can be done, to reform the offender. But the punishment of any offender, in its extremest shape, can do little more than prevent the same person from offending again. Those who are deterred from crime by his example can at any rate only be those to whom the example is known, and they are a small portion even of the actual society. Generally, then, those who do not offend against the laws, do not offend, either because they have been sufficiently educated to avoid such offence, or because the opportunity and temptation have not been presented to them, or because they know that punishment may follow the crime. But a large class of offenders have not been sufficiently educated to enable them to avoid the commission of crime; a very large number are brought up amidst the opportunities, the temptations, and the example of crime, to oppose all which the single fact of knowing that the crime *may* be punished (and even that amount of knowledge is not always possessed by the criminal) is all the means of resistance that such persons are armed with. In societies which boast of their wealth, their civilization, and their high intellectual cultivation, such is the feeble barrier opposed by those who have the government of a people between thousands of their fellow-citizens and the commission of crimes the penalties of which are always severe and often cruel.

If the general considerations which we have urged are of any weight, there is no branch of legislation which comprehends so many important questions as are comprehended in the word Education, even when taken in its ordinary acceptation; but when viewed in all its bearings, it is of all questions most peculiarly that which it concerns the present age and the present state of society to determine. That Education was an integral, an essential part of legislation, was clearly seen by the Greeks, to whom belongs the merit of having approached, and often having solved, nearly all the important questions that affect the constitution of society. It was their good fortune to contemplate many truths from a nearer point of view and in a clearer light than we can do now. The relations of modern society are so numerous and complicated, that the mind is bewildered amidst the multiplicity and variety of facts, the claims of opposing interests, and the number and magnitude of the objects which are presented for its consideration. It is only by keeping ourselves as free as possible from mere party influences, and steadily looking to the general welfare as the end to be attained by and the true test of all political institutions, that we can hope to discover and apply the principles which shall secure, so far as such a thing can be secured, the universal happiness of a nation.

"That the legislator should especially occupy himself with the education of youth, no one can dispute; for when this is not done in states, it is a cause of damage to the polity (form of government). For a state must be administered with reference to its polity; and that which is the peculiar characteristic of each polity is that which preserves and originally constitutes it; as, for instance, the democratical principle in a democracy, and the oligarchical in an oligarchy; and that which is the best principle always constitutes the best polity. Further, in every occupation and art a person must receive previous instruction and discipline, in order to the exercising of the occupation or art; consequently also to the enabling him to the exercise of virtue. Now, since the end of every state is one, it is evident that the education must be *one*, and of necessity the same for all, and that the superintendence of the education must be with the public and not with individuals, as it now is, when each individual superintends his own children singly, and teaches them what he chooses. But when things are matter of public concern, the discipline pertaining to them must also be matter of public concern; and we must not consider any citizen as belonging to himself, but all as belonging to the state; for each is a part of the state, and the superintendence of each part has naturally a reference to the superintendence of the whole. In the matter of education, as well as in other matters, the Lacedæmonians deserve praise; for they take the greatest pains about the education of their children, and that, too, as a public concern. That, then, a state ought to legislate on education and make it a public concern, is clear; but what education is, and how education must be conducted, is a subject for consideration." (Aristotle, *Politick*, viii. c.)

EFFENDI is a Turkish word, which signifies 'Master, Monsieur,' and is subjoined as a title of respect to the names of persons, especially to those of learned men and ecclesiastics, e. g. *Omar Effendi*, *Ahmed Effendi*, in the same manner in which *Agha* is placed after the names of military and court officers. The word Effendi occurs also as part of some titles of particular officers, as *Reis Effendi*, the title of the principal secretary of state and prime minister of the Ottoman empire, which is properly an abbreviation of *Reis-al-Kottáb, i. e.*, 'the head or chief of secretaries or writers.'

EGG-TRADE. The supply of apparently insignificant products of rural industry is often a branch of trade of considerable importance in this country. All these products must be obtained through the medium of dealers or shopkeepers by the non-agricultural part of the population; and even those who are employed in agriculture are, generally speaking, supplied with the products which they raise in the same way as those who have no connexion with the soil. There is no large class of persons who consume the products of their labour.

In 1835 the value of eggs exported from Ireland to Great Britain was 68,687*l*.; and perhaps at the present time it may exceed 100,000*l*. At 4*d*. per dozen the number of eggs which this sum would purchase would be 72,000,000. From France and Belgium we imported 96,000,000 eggs in 1840; on which the duty of one penny per dozen produced 34,450*l*. Nine-tenths of the foreign eggs are from France. The departments nearest to England, from the Pas de Calais to La Manche, are visited by the dealers, and their purchases often produce a scarcity in the country markets. At most of the ports of these departments, from Calais to Cherbourg, some vessels are employed in the egg-trade. The weight of 80,000,000 eggs will not be far short of 2500 tons. In the last three years the importations of foreign eggs were as follows:—

1842 . . . 89,548,747
1843 . . . 70,415,931
1844 . . . 67,487,920

The consumption of eggs at Paris is estimated at one hundred millions a-year.

A hen of the Polish breed will lay 175 eggs in one year. Their weight will be between 13 and 14 lbs.

ELECTION is when a man is left to his own free will to take or do one thing or another which he pleases (*Termes de la Ley*); and he who is to do the first act shall have the election. If A covenants to pay B a pound of pepper or saffron before Whitsuntide, it is at the election of A at all times before Whitsuntide which of them he will pay; but if he does not pay either before the time fixed, then it is at the election of B to sue for which he pleases. If a man give to another one of his horses, the donee may take which he chooses; but if the donation be that he will give one of his horses (in the future tense), then the election is in the donor.

Courts of equity frequently apply the principle of election in cases where a party has inconsistent rights, and compel him to elect which he will enforce: as, if A by his will assumes to give an estate belonging to B to C, and gives other benefits to B, B cannot obtain the benefits given to him by the will unless he gives effect to the testator's disposition to C. It does not appear to be quite settled whether the party who elects to retain his own property in opposition to the instrument is bound to relinquish only so much of the property given to him as will be sufficient to compensate the disappointed parties, or whether his election will be followed by absolute forfeiture of the whole. The arguments on both sides are ably stated 1 Roper, Husband and Wife, 566 n.; 1 Swanst. Reports, 441; 2 Coke's Repts., 35 b., Thomas's note. The principle of election is equally recognized in courts of law, though they are seldom called to deal upon it, except where the alternative is very distinct, or the party has already elected. Indeed this principle is of universal application, and prevails in the laws of all countries; it is applicable to all interests, whether of married women or of infants; to interests immediate, remote, or contingent; to copyhold as well as to freehold estates; to personalty as well as to realty; to deeds as well as to wills.

Courts of equity also will compel a plaintiff suing at law as well as in equity, or in a foreign court as well as in the court in England, for the same matter, at the same time, to elect in which court he will proceed, and will restrain him from pursuing his rights in all others. There are some exceptions to this doctrine, as in the case of a mortgagee, who may proceed in equity for a foreclosure, and on his bond or covenant at law at the same time; but this arises from the difference of the remedy, and from the original agreement to give the concurrent remedies: and even in such a case a court of equity will restrain a mortgagee from enforcing his judgment at law upon the bond or covenant, if he is not prepared to deliver up the mortgaged property and the title-deeds belonging to it.

On Election under a will in the Roman

Law see *Dig.* xxxiii. tit. 5, De Optione vel Electione Legata: and as to the French Law, see the *Code Civil*, art. 1189, &c., Des Obligations Alternatives. The term Election is borrowed from the Roman Law. The word *optio* often occurs in the Roman writers to express that a man may choose of two or more things or conditions, which he will take. The instances of election and option given in the title of the Digest, above referred to, are limited to options given by way of legacy, which is the subject treated of in that part of the Digest. Probably the legal meaning of election and option was limited to election under a testament.

ELECTION-COMMITTEES. The course of elections of members of the House of Commons from the issuing of the writs to the returns made to the Clerk of the Crown is briefly sketched under the head HOUSE OF COMMONS. The Clerk of the Crown certifies the returns made to him to the House [CLERK OF THE CROWN.] The mode of adjudicating election-petitions is the subject of the present article.

Till 1770, when the act well known as the Grenville act was passed, questions of controverted elections were decided by the whole House of Commons: and every such question was made a party contest. The Grenville act introduced a plan, which, with several modifications, continued till 1839, of appointing committees for the trial of election petitions by lot. Since 1839 a different system has been in operation, under which the choice of members of election-committees has not been left to chance, and their individual responsibility has been increased by diminishing the number of members. By the 7 & 8 Vict. c. 103 (passed the year, 1844) the number of members of an election-committee was reduced from seven to five, including the chairman.

The 7 & 8 Vict. c. 103, now regulates the constitution and the proceedings of committees on controverted elections.

At the commencement of every session, the Speaker appoints by warrant six members of the House to be a General Committee of Elections. The General Committee of Elections, when appointed, proceed to select, "in their discretion, six, eight, ten, or twelve members, whom they shall think duly qualified, to serve as chairmen of election-committees;" and the members so selected for chairmen are formed into a separate panel, called the Chairmen's Panel. The members of the General Committee of Elections are excused from serving as members of election committees, and all members of the House of Commons above the age of sixty are also excused from this service. The House also allows other special grounds of exemption; the principal ministers for instance are excused from serving on election-committees, so long as they hold their offices, on account of their official duties. After the General Committee of Elections have appointed the Chairmen's Panel, they divide the remaining members of the House who are not exempted from service, into five panels; and members are chosen to serve on elections from these panels, in an order of succession determined by lot. All election-petitions are referred by the House to the General Committee of Elections; and this General Committee give notice, as provided by the act, of the days on which particular election-committees will be appointed, and of the panel from which members will be taken. "The General Committee shall meet at the time appointed for choosing the committee to try any election-petition, and shall choose from the panel then standing next in order of service, exclusive of the chairmen's panel, four members, not being then excused or disqualified for any of the causes aforesaid, and who shall not be specially disqualified for being appointed on the committee to try such petition for any of the following causes; (that is to say) by reason of having voted at the election, or by reason of being the party on whose behalf the seat is claimed or related to the sitting member or party on whose behalf the seat is claimed by kindred or affinity in the first or second degree, according to the canon law." (§ 55.) At least four members of the general committee must agree in the appointment. On the same day on which the general committee choose the members of an election-committee, the chairmen's panel choose from themselves a chairman for the committee, and communicate the name of the chairman selected to the general committee. The names of the chairman and members selected are thus communicated to the petitioners and sitting member or members, who may object to any of the members on any ground of disqualification specified in the 55th section of the act, but on no other ground. If any member is shown to be disqualified, the general committee select another; or if the chairman is disqualified, they send back his name to the chairmen's panel, who proceed to choose another chairman. The five members finally chosen are afterwards sworn at the table of the House " well and truly to try the matter of the petitions referred to them, and a true judgment to give according to the evidence."

Such is a general sketch of the present mode of constitution of election-committees: for other details the reader must refer to the act itself, or to Mr. May's Treatise on the Law of Parliament, pp. 341-373. It is a matter of practice for the General Committee of Elections to take the four members of an election committee equally from the two sides of the House.

The second section of the act defines election-petitions, and specifies by whom they must be signed. Election-petitions are petitions complaining, 1. Of an undue election, or, 2. That no return has been made to a writ on or before the day on which the writ was returnable, or, 3. If the writ be issued during any session or prorogation of Parliament, that no return has been made within fifty-two days after the date of the writ, or, 4. That a return is not according to the requisition of the writ, or 5. Of special matters contained in the writ; and they must be signed by some person claiming therein to have had a right to vote at the election, or to have had a right to be returned, or alleging himself to have been a candidate at the election.

All election-committees are empowered to send for persons, papers, and records, and to examine any one who may have signed the petition, unless it shall appear that he is an interested witness, and to examine all witnesses upon oath, which is to be administered by the clerk attending the committee. Election-committees are the only committees of the House of Commons in which evidence is taken upon oath. Any one giving false evidence is made liable to the penalties of wilful and corrupt perjury.

Parties complaining of or defending a return are required to deliver in to the clerk of the General Committee of Elections lists of the voters intended to be objected to, with the several heads of objections, not later than six in the afternoon of the sixth day next before the day appointed for choosing the committee to try the petition: and the election-committee cannot enter into evidence against any vote, or upon any head of objection, not included in the lists.

The committee are required to decide " whether the petitioners or the sitting members or either of them be duly returned or elected, or whether the election be void, or whether a new writ ought to issue." Their decision on these points is final between the parties: and the House carries it into execution.

ELECTOR. [COMMONS, HOUSE OF; MUNICIPAL CORPORATIONS.]

ELOPEMENT. [DOWER.]

EMANCIPATION. [PARENT AND CHILD.]

EMBARGO, the word used to denote the act by which any government lays an arrest on ships to prevent their leaving its ports. On the breaking out of war with any nation it has been usual for the government of each country to lay an embargo upon such of the enemy's ships as are within reach, with a view to their being declared good and lawful prize. During the progress of war, when any expedition is on foot against the enemy, and it is desirable to keep the circumstance from the knowledge of the party to be attacked, it is usual to lay an embargo upon all private vessels, as well those under the national flag as foreign vessels, until the object to be attained by secresy is accomplished. An embargo may also be laid by the government upon ships belonging to its subjects with a view to their employment for the service and defence of the nation. In all these cases it is clear that embargoes are detrimental to commerce; the only case in which they have an opposite character is when a foreign vessel of war or privateer frequents a neutral port, and is restrained from quitting the same until a certain time shall have elapsed after the departure from the port of any vessel of which it might otherwise make prize.

EMBEZZLEMENT. [AGENT.]

EMIGRATION may be defined to be a man's leaving his native country with all his property to settle permanently in another. Emigration is therefore necessarily implied in the word Colonization, and it is by the terms of our definition easily distinguished from a man's temporary absence from his native country, and from the kind of absence specially called Absenteeism.

Though a man may be properly called an emigrant who leaves Great Britain or Ireland, for instance, and settles in France or Germany, or elsewhere in Europe, the term has in modern times come to have a more restricted and particular sense. By the term emigrant we generally understand one who leaves an old and thickly peopled country to settle in a country where there is abundance of land that has never been cultivated before, and where the native population is thinly scattered, and the foreign settlers are yet either few compared with the surface or none at all. The countries to which emigration is mainly directed at present are the British possessions in North America, the United States of North America, and the great island of Australia, with Van Diemen's Land and New Zealand.

An emigrant to any of these remote countries must be either a capitalist or a labourer, or he may combine in himself both conditions; but even a mere labourer cannot emigrate without some capital, though the amount may be only enough to convey him to the spot where his labour and skill will be in demand. It was long a prevalent notion among nations, or perhaps we may rather say with those possessed of power at the head of nations (who have generally been slower in learning any great practical truth than the mass of the people, whose understanding is sharpened by a nearer view of their own interest), that emigration should be discouraged or prevented, as tending to weaken a nation. The objection, we believe, was generally founded rather on a notion that the nation lost by its diminished population, than that it suffered from the abstraction of capital. As to the matter of population, however, some observers even then could not fail to remark, that emigration did not seem to diminish the population, but that on the contrary it seemed to be soon followed by an increase. This was observed with respect to Portugal at the time when she was extending her conquests and colonies, and is a fact confirmed by more recent experience, the explanation of which presents no difficulty. The abstraction of capital, skill, and industry might seem, and indeed is primarily, so much good taken from the mother country; but inasmuch as the emigrants retain in their new settlements, through the medium of commercial exchange which is daily becoming more rapid and easy, a connexion with the parent state, it may be and often is the fact, that they ultimately contribute more to the wealth of the mother country when in the new settlements than they could have done at home. Many of those, for example, who settle in the western states of America or in Canada with no capital beyond their hands, by their industry become the possessors of a well-cultivated piece of land, and ultimately consume more of the products of British industry, for which they must give something in exchange, than if they had remained in their native country: and as, in order that emigration to new countries may be a successful undertaking to those who emigrate, and ultimately advantageous to the mother country, there must be an emigration both of capitalists and labourers, it would seem to follow that a state, if it consult the happiness of its citizens, should place no impediments to the emigration either of capitalists of all kinds or of labourers or artisans of any kind, but should on the contrary give reasonable facilities.

If a state then should be wise enough not to discourage emigration, it may be asked, should it aid and direct it? So far as a state should aid and direct emigration, there must be two distinct objects kept in view by the state; one must be to benefit the parent country, the other to benefit those who emigrate. On the contrary, as to the individual who emigrates, whether he emigrates under the protection and direction of the government or not, his sole object is of course to better his own condition.

One cannot well conceive why a state, or any section or part of a nation, should make any contribution or raise any fund for the purpose of aiding emigration, except it be with the view of bettering the condition of some who cannot find employment at home, and at the same time adopting some systematic plan for improving the condition of those who are left behind. Yet any system of emigration thus conducted by government, or by societies, or by the inhabitants of particular districts, would fail in its primary object, relief to the emigrants, unless a corresponding amount of capital should be taken out of the country by other emigrants who might settle in the same place to which the emigrant labourers were sent. To effect such an adjustment between capital and labour, not only should both these elements of wealth in due proportion be transported to the new country, but such proportion should, for some time at least, be maintained by the body which superintends such system of emigration; an arrangement which seems impracticable, except by some such provisions as are hereinafter mentioned.

It is further to be observed that, as no persons can ever succeed as emigrants who are not sober, intelligent, and industrious, and as such alone are consequently fit people to go to a new country, such alone should be sent out by a state or a society, if it interferes in the matter of emigration. But if a large number of the most industrious labourers should emigrate from a given district, and leave behind them the worthless and idle, though the emigrants might better their condition and improve the settlement of which they go to form a part, the mother country would be no gainer by this change. We are not inclined to consider that any advantage, at all commensurate to the expense, would result from any emigration, however extensive, from districts where there is a superabundant and pauperized, or a pauperized and not superabundant population. If the idle, the ignorant, and the vicious were exported wholesale, they would only die a few years sooner in the land of their new settlement, without conferring any benefit on it, and those of the same kind who were left behind would hardly be more susceptible of improvement in consequence of the removal of any part of their numbers which did not amount to pretty nearly the whole number; while the industrious and the intelligent, who, by the supposition, remain at home and are willing to labour whenever it is in their power, would hardly derive any benefit by this removal of the bad from among them, at all commensurate to the amount of capital which must be expended on such wholesale exportations. Besides, as already observed, unless a proper supply of emigrant capitalists can be secured, all general plans for the emigration of labourers can only lead to disappointment and starvation. Any plan, therefore, which shall have for its object the amelioration of a population sunk in ignorance or debased by pauperism, must be one of an internal character, one which must gradually and on certain fixed principles aim at removing the evils which exist in the social system. Emigration must be left to the free choice of individuals, and must be recommended to the young, the sober, and industrious solely on the grounds of offering to them a reasonable prospect of bettering their condition in a new country.

The disadvantages of emigration however, when there is no plan, no controlling or directing power, are obvious. Emigrants often go to a new country without any definite or clear notion of what they are going to. Dissatisfied or unhappy at home, imagination pictures to them a remote and unknown country as an asylum from all the evils of life; or if they have any distinct idea of the new kind of existence which they are going to adopt, they often underrate the difficulties of the undertaking, or form a false estimate of their own capabilities to meet them. It is no wonder then that so many, on landing in the New World, are startled at the obstacles which then stare them in the face, and shut their eyes to the real advantages, such as they are, which a fertile unoccupied soil presents to a hardworking industrious man.

We have stated that any system of emigration for labourers without a corresponding emigration of capitalists would be fruitless; it is also obvious that if capitalists only were to emigrate without being able to secure a supply of labour, the result would be equally unfortunate.

Considerations like these led to the formation of a scheme of emigration which was first brought into operation in the colony of South Australia. "The distinguishing and cardinal principles of the colony of South Australia are, that all public lands shall be sold, and that the proceeds of the sale shall be employed in conveying labourers to the colony." Further: "It is essential to the prosperity of a new colony in which there are neither slaves nor convicts, that there should be a constant supply of free labourers willing to be employed for wages. No productive industry worthy of the name can be undertaken, unless several hands can be put on the same work at the same time; and if there be not, in a colony in which the compulsory services of slaves or convicts cannot be obtained, a constant supply of labour for hire, no extensive farm can be cultivated, no large and continuous work can be carried on, and the capital imported must perish for want of hands to render it reproductive." (*First Annual Report of South Australian Commissioners*, 1836.)

It was therefore the object of the commissioners to prevent the labourers, for some time after their arrival in the colony, from purchasing land. This was done by fixing the price of land sufficiently high to prevent the labourer from being tempted too soon to exchange that condition which is for the time the most profitable both to himself and the body of emigrants for the apparently higher character of a landowner.

It is justly remarked in the Report that the result of such premature purchases " would be alike disastrous to the capitalist and to the labourer; as the supply of labour for hire being thus diminished, improvements requiring the co-operation of many hands would be suspended, and capital would waste and perish for want of means to use it; and the labouring population becoming separated upon small patches of land, each family would be obliged to perform every species of work for themselves; and the absence of all division of employment and combination of labour would so reduce the efficacy of their industry, that instead of advancing in wealth and civilization, they would fall back to a semi-barbarous state." Such a result has already been witnessed in numerous new settlements, and such a result must inevitably follow the dispersion of small capitalists and labourers who aspire to be land-holders over a large uncultivated surface, however rich it may naturally be.

The mode in which unoccupied Land is disposed of in the colonies has, it will be seen, a most important influence on the condition and welfare of immigrants. By the application of a general principle of law the waste lands in the British colonies were considered to be vested in the Crown, and that every private title must rest upon a royal grant as its basis. But since 1831 another principle has been acknowledged and observed: that the Crown holds the lands in question in trust for the public good, and cannot, without a breach of that trust on the part of the responsible ministers of the government, be advised to make to any person a gratuitous donation of any such property. It is held in trust, not merely for the existing colonists, but for the people of the British empire collectively. It must be appropriated to public uses and for the public benefit. (Instructions addressed by Lord John Russell when Secretary of State for Colonial Affairs, 14th Jan. 1840.) The Land Sale Act for the Australian Colonies (5 & 6 Vict. c. 36) prohibits land being alienated by her Majesty, or by any one acting under her authority, except by sale, and in the manner directed by the act.

Down to the year 1831 no regular or uniform system of selling land appears to have been adopted in the British colonies. In place of such system conditions were attached to the occupation of land under the name of Quit-Rents, money payments, or the cultivation of the soil; but these conditions were not effectually enforced, and in fact it was generally found impossible to enforce them. Land was profusely granted to individuals in large tracts, and as cultivation was not enforced, and no roads were made through these tracts, they interrupted the course of improvement. Under the old system lands in the colony of the Cape of Good Hope, amounting to upwards of thirty-one million acres, have been disposed of for less than 46,000*l.* In Prince Edward's Island the whole of the land was granted in one day to absentee proprietors upon terms which have never been fulfilled. The influence of these proprietors with the Home Government prevented such measures being adopted as were calculated to enforce the settlement of the grants, and consequently the greater part of them remained chiefly in a wild state. (*Report of Mr. C. Buller, M.P., to the Earl of Durham, on Public Lands in British North America*, 1838.) This Report contains an account of the system of granting lands in each of the provinces of British North America; and in all of them it appears to have been injurious to the public interests.

In 1831 the Earl of Ripon framed certain regulations which required that all land in the colonies should be disposed of at a minimum upset price for ready money only. In 1842 an act was passed (5 & 6 Vict. c. 36), already noticed, "for regulating the sale of waste lands belonging to the Crown in the Australian colonies." The chief provisions of this statute are given in a subsequent part of this article under the head "Australian Colonies and New Zealand," to which islands the act also applies. The expense of making surveys, which are usually from 4*d*. to 4½*d*. an acre, and other expenses connected with the sale of the land, are, under this act, the primary charges on the land fund. The rest of the proceeds are applicable to the public service of the colony, after one-half at least has been appropriated to the purposes of immigration.

The select committee of the House of Commons on the disposal of lands in the British colonies, which sat in 1836, recommended that the whole of the arrangements connected with the sale of land, including both the price and the precise mode of sale, should be placed under the charge of a land board in London.

In January, 1840, commissioners were appointed under the royal sign manual to act as a Land and Emigration Board. The sale of the waste lands of the Crown throughout the British colonies is regulated by the commissioners, and they apply the proceeds of such sales towards the removal thither of emigrants from this country, when the land-fund is appropriated to this object. This board is a subordinate department of the Colonial Office.

In none of the British colonies is the disposal of unoccupied lands conducted in such a systematic and perfect manner as in the United States of North America. The unoccupied lands within the limits of the Union are vested in the Federal government. There is a General Land Office at Washington, under which there are above forty district land-offices in other parts of the Union. Connected with the Land Office is a Surveying Department. The surveys are founded upon a series of true meridians. The greatest division of land marked out by a survey is called a township, and it contains 23,040 acres, being a square of six miles to the side. The township is divided into thirty-six equal portions, or square miles. These portions are called sections, and they are subdivided into quarter sections of a hundred and sixty acres each. The quarter sections are finally divided into two parts, called half-quarter sections. Section sixteen (one square mile) in every township is reserved for schools in the township. All salt springs and lead-mines are also reserved, and are let on lease by the general government. In 1820 purchasers of land were no longer allowed to obtain land on credit: and in the same year the minimum price of land was reduced from two dollars to one and a quarter dollar per acre. The mode of sale is by public auction, and lands not sold on the day fixed may be bought by private contract at the minimum price. Squatters, or persons who settle on the land without a title, have pre-emptive rights. [SQUATTER.]

Of the public lands of the United States there had been sold up to 1843, 107,796,536 acres, and the amount received for the same was 170,940,942 dollars (36,000,000*l.*). In the year 1836, the receipts from land sales amounted to 25,167,833 dollars. The net residue of the proceeds of lands are distributed amongst the different states under an act passed in 1841. In 1843 the estimated quantity of land remaining to be sold within the limits of the union was 1,084,064,993 acres, and of this quantity 272,646,356 acres had been surveyed.

The following is an abstract of the regulations at present in operation in the British colonies for the disposal of waste lands:—

Canada.—By a provincial act of 1841 Crown lands are to be sold at a price to be from time to time fixed by the governor in council. The proceeds of the land sales are not specially appropriated, but form part of the general colonial revenue. The prices fixed for the present are as follows:

For Canada, West (Upper Canada), 8s. currency (about 6s. 7d. sterling) per acre; for Canada, East (Lower Canada), in the county of Ottawa, and south of the river St. Lawrence, to the west of the Kennebec road, 6s. currency (about 4s. 11d. sterling); and elsewhere in that division of the province, 4s. currency (about 3s. 3¼d. sterling) per acre. These prices do not apply to lands resumed by government for non-performance of the conditions of settlement on which they were granted under a former system now abolished, nor to lands called Indian Reserves, and Clergy Reserves; which three classes are, as well as town and village lots, subject to special regulations.

The size of the lots of country lands is usually 200 acres; but they are sold as frequently by half as whole lots.

The following are the conditions of sale at present in force:—1st. The lots are to be taken at the contents in acres marked in the public documents, without guarantee as to the actual quantity contained in them.—2d. No payment of purchase-money will be received by instalments, but the whole purchase-money, either in money or land scrip,* must be paid at the time of sale.—3rd. On the payment of the purchase-money, the purchaser will receive a receipt which will entitle him to enter on the land which he has purchased, and arrangements will be made for issuing to him the patent without delay. The receipt thus given not only authorizes the purchaser to take immediate possession, but enables him, under the provisions of the Land Act, to maintain legal proceedings against any wrongful possessor or trespasser, as effectually as if the patent deed had issued on the day the receipt is dated.

Government land agents are appointed in the several municipal districts, with full power to sell to the first applicant any of the advertised lands which the return open to public inspection may show to be vacant within their districts.

Nova Scotia.—The public lands are here also sold at a fixed price of 1s. 9d. sterling per acre, payable at once. The smallest regular farm lot contains one hundred acres. Any less quantity of land may be had, but the cost would be the same as for one hundred acres, viz. 8l. 15s., the minimum sum for which a deed of grant is issued.

New Brunswick.—The mode of sale in this province is by auction. The upset price is generally about 2s. 8d. sterling (3s. currency), but varies according to situation, &c. The average price of ordinary country lands has been from 4s. 6d. to 9s. sterling (5s. to 10s. currency) per acre, according to situation, &c. Fifty acres is the smallest quantity usually sold.

Prince Edward's Island.—In this colony the Crown has little land at its disposal, namely, about 8400 acres. Sale by auction prevails, and the average price realized for ordinary country lands has been from 10s. to 14s. currency per acre.

Newfoundland.—There exists no official return of the surveyed and accessible

---

* This is Scrip issued by the local government in satisfaction of certain old militia claims.

land at the disposal of the Crown in this colony. The area has been estimated at about 2,300,000 acres, of which about 23,000 have been appropriated. Although the agriculture of the province is progressively increasing, there are yet comparatively few persons exclusively employed in it, the population being nearly all engaged in the fisheries.

The Falkland Islands.—The lands in this colony are now open for sale. The mode of sale is the same as that adopted in the Australian colonies. The upset price of country lands is, for the present, 8s. per acre. Town lots of half an acre each, and suburban lots of fifty acres each, will be put up at 50*l*. Deposits of purchase-money may be made in this country, in the mode prescribed for the Australian colonies, but the depositors will be entitled to nominate for a free passage six, instead of four, adult labourers, for every 100*l*. deposited.

Cape of Good Hope.—Applications for the purchase of Crown lands must be made to the governor, if the lands are situated in the western division ; and to the lieutenant-governor if in the eastern division of the province. The application must pass through the surveyor-general to the land board, and if the land be unsurveyed, the applicant must deposit an amount equal to the probable expense of inspection and survey. If on inspection it be decided that the land ought not to be alienated, the deposit for survey will be returned ; otherwise, the land will be surveyed and offered for sale at public auction. Should the applicant not become the purchaser at the sale, he will be entitled to a return of the preliminary expenses, which must in that case be borne by the actual purchaser ; but should the lands be not then sold, the deposit will be retained until they are sold. The upset price will in no case be less than 2*s*. per acre, and should it become necessary to ascertain the amount which ought to be demanded for lands under peculiar circumstances, such amount is to be ascertained by valuation, and made the upset price at auction.

Ceylon.—In this colony the Crown lands are sold by auction, at an upset price, which is to be fixed by the governor, but which is not to be less than 1*l*. per acre. Before being put up to auction, the lands are surveyed by the government, and duly advertised.

Hong Kong.—The Crown lands will not be alienated in perpetuity, but let on leases, which are to be offered for sale at public auction. The duration of the leases will not exceed 21 years for country lands ; but land for building purposes will be let on leases for 75 years, not renewable of right, but at the option of the government, and on the holder's paying an increased rent. Powers will be reserved, when necessary, for regulating the character of the buildings to be erected in particular situations.

The rent to be paid for lands designated as marine, town, or suburban lots, will be determined exclusively by public auction ; but leases of country lots, if they have been once exposed to auction and not sold, may be afterwards sold by private agreement at the upset price.

The governor will decide whether there is sufficient demand to call for public sales at fixed periods, or whether the leases should only be advertised and brought into the market as they may be applied for.

The colonies in which military and naval officers are allowed privileges in the acquisition of public lands are the following:—New South Wales, Van Diemen's Land, South Australia, Western Australia, New Zealand, Ceylon, Nova Scotia, and Cape Breton, the only province in North America where privileges are still allowed. In the different Australian settlements, and in Ceylon, land is disposed of by sale only; but officers purchasing land are allowed a remission of the purchase-money. Thus field-officers of twenty-five years' service and upwards are entitled to a remission of 300*l*.; and in proportion for different periods of service and according to the rank of the officer. Subalterns of seven years' service and upwards are entitled to a remission of 100*l*.; but subalterns under seven years standing are not entitled to any remission in the purchase of land. Regimental staff officers and medical officers of the army and navy are allowed the benefit of this rule.

In Nova Scotia and Cape Breton, allotments of land are granted to officers on the following scale and conditions, viz.— To a lieutenant-colonel, 1200 acres; to a major, 1000 acres; to a captain, 800 acres; to a subaltern, 500 acres. Military chaplains, commissariat officers, and officers of any of the civil departments of the army; pursers, chaplains, midshipmen, warrant officers of every description, and officers of any of the civil departments of the navy, are not allowed any privileges in respect of land. Although members of these classes may have been admitted formerly, and under different circumstances, they are now excluded. Mates in the royal navy rank with ensigns in the army, and mates of three years' standing with lieutenants in the army, and are entitled respectively to corresponding privileges in the acquisition of lands.

Australian Colonies and New Zealand. —These colonies are the principal field for the operations of the Land and Emigration Commissioners, as it is in them that the principle of devoting the proceeds of the sale of waste lands to emigration is capable of application on a large scale. In the colony of New South Wales the sales of land from 1831 to 1842 inclusive realized the sum of 1,090,583*l.*, out of which 951,241*l.*, or more than 87 per cent., was expended on immigration. In 1840 land was sold in the Port Philip district which produced 218,020*l.* In 1843, when the colony of New South Wales was in a very depressed state, the sum arising from the sale of land was only 11,030*l.* Immigration is therefore under a self-regulating principle: when capital is abundant, and purchases of land are made on a large scale, a fund is supplied for introducing labourers; and when the fund from the sale of land diminishes, a check is given to the introduction of redundant labour. In South Australia, from 1835 to 1840 inclusive, land was sold to the amount of 272,878*l.* In Western Australia there is scarcely any revenue from public lands, in consequence of the large grants of land which were made to individuals when the colony was established.

The following are the regulations now in force under the provisions of the Australian Land Act, 5 & 6 Vict. c. 36, for the disposal of the waste lands in the colonies of New South Wales (including the Sydney and Port Philip districts, and any other districts that may hereafter oc opened), Van Diemen's Land, South Australia, Western Australia, and New Zealand:—1. All lands will be disposed of by sale alone, and must have once at least been exposed to public auction. 2. The lowest upset price will be not less than 1*l.* per acre; but the government will have power to raise the same by proclamation, though not again to reduce it. 3. The lands will be distinguished into three different classes, viz., town lots, suburban lots, and country lots. 4. Upon town and suburban lots, as well as upon a proportion not exceeding one-tenth of the whole of the country lots offered for sale at any auction, the governor will have the power of naming a higher than the general or lowest upset price; the country lots on which such power is exercised to be designated "Special Country Lots." 5. Town and suburban lots will in no case be disposed of except by public auction, but country lots which have already been put up to public auction and not sold, may be disposed of afterwards by private contract at the upset price. 6. No lands will be sold by private contract except for ready money. When sold by public auction, one-tenth at least of the whole purchase-money must be paid down, and the remainder within one calendar month, or the deposit will be forfeited. 7. Lands will be put up for sale in lots not exceeding one square mile in extent. 8. As an exception to the general regulations, and subject to certain restrictions laid down in the Australian Land Act, the governor will have it in his discretion to dispose, by private contract, at a price not less than the lowest upset price for the district, of blocks comprising 20,000 acres or more. 9. Persons will be at liberty to make payments for colonial lands in Great Britain, for which payment or deposit they will receive an order for credit to the same amount in any purchase of land they may effect in the colony, and will have the privilege of naming a proportionate number of emigrants for a free passage, as explained in article No. 10. The deposits must be made in one or more sums of 100*l*. each at the Bank of England, to the account of Edward Barnard, esq., agent-general for crown colonies, No. 5, Cannon-row, Westminster; and the depositor must state at the time the colony in which the land is to be selected, and give notice to Mr. Barnard, and to the colonial land and emigration commissioners, of the deposit. Upon receiving Mr. Barnard's certificate that the money has been duly paid in, the commissioners will furnish the depositor with a certificate, which states the amount which he has paid, and entitles him to obtain credit for that sum in any purchase which he may effect in the colony, subject to all rules and regulations then in force. 10. For every sum of 100*l*. deposited as above, the depositor will be entitled, for six months from the date of payment, to name a number of properly qualified emigrants, equal to four adults, for a free passage. Two children between one and fourteen are to be reckoned as equal to one adult. The emigrants are required to be chosen from the class of mechanics and handicraftsmen, agricultural labourers, or domestic servants, and must be going out with the intention to work for wages. They are to be subject to the approval of the commissioners, and must, in all respects, fall within their general regulations on the selection of labourers.

In New South Wales, and in others of the Australian colonies, though to a smaller extent, a system prevails of granting licences to use lands for pasture. In New South Wales it had long been an established regulation of the government that no land should be sold beyond the part of the country laid out into counties. Beyond these boundaries, therefore, licences are granted for the occupation of such tracts as may be desired for pasture by proprietors of stock. The cost of a licence is 10*l*. a-year. The stock depastured is subject to a fixed assessment per head, the proceeds of which are applied to the maintenance of a border police. The licence is not for any determined quantity of land, and hitherto the extent of each station or "run" "has only been limited by the moderation of the parties, or the mutual pressure of the neighbouring squatters." (*Report of Land and Emigration Commissioners*, 1845.) The extent of a run usually varied from 3000 to 5000 acres. In 1843 the number of licences issued in New South Wales for the use of land beyond the boundaries was 852, "the space over which they were to take effect being unsurveyed and the extent unknown." The land occupied on these terms in New South Wales extends through fourteen degrees of latitude; from Harvey's Bay on the north to South Australia the diagonal line is 1100 miles. This large tract is divided into fifteen districts, and contained in 1844 a population of nearly 10,000 persons; and the stock consisted of 15,000 horses, 570,000 cattle, and upwards of 3,000,000 sheep. The assessment on the stock was, on sheep ½*d*., cattle 1½*d*., and horses 3*d*. per head. In 1844 the governor of New South Wales proposed regulations which he intended should come into operation in July, 1845, which will not leave the extent of the "runs" to the discretion of persons who hold occupation licences, but a limit will be fixed in each case. This limit is not to exceed twenty square miles (12,800 acres), or sufficient land to depasture 500 cattle or 4000 sheep; and it is proposed to define in other respects what shall be accounted a separate station or run. The proposed regulations excited great opposition in the colony. The official correspondence on this subject, accompanied with a number of documents, is published as a parliamentary paper. (Session, 1845, 267, iii.)

There are some difficulties attending the occupying of waste lands under crown licences. Without some pre-emptive rights the squatters could not be expected to make any improvements, and the consequence might be that a large population would be growing up under circumstances disadvantageous to their civilization. On the other hand, the crown is liable to lose its control over the public lands unless the pre-emptive rights which it concedes are carefully guarded. The difficulty has been met in New South Wales by the following arrangement: persons who have already been five years in the occupation of a station are permitted to buy any part of their run, not being less than 320 acres. The land must be put up at the upset price of 20s. an acre, to which will be added the value of the improvements made, which are assessed according to the government regulations; and on a sale taking place, the government will receive the price which the land fetches, and the value of the improvements will be returned to the occupant if he becomes the purchaser; and if he does not, it will be paid to him out of the gross purchase-money.

Land is also occupied under licences within the colonial boundaries of New South Wales. In 1843 the number of licences issued for land thus situated was 237, and the quantity of land over which they extended was 183,859 acres. The sum paid for this limited occupation was at the rate of from 5l. to 6l. per square mile.

The pasture licence system has been adopted in South Australia, Van Diemen's Land, and New Zealand. In South Australia the licence is lower, and the assessment on stock higher, than in New South Wales. The licence costs only 10s. 6d.; but the assessment is, on sheep 1d., cattle 1s., and horses 2s. 6d. per head.

West Indies.—In the West Indies Crown lands are to be sold by auction at an upset price of not less than 1l. per acre.

In the Bahamas the mode of sale is also by auction, but the lieutenant-governor is, from time to time, to name the upset price, which is never to be less than 6s. per acre. Land once exposed to auction may, in the discretion of the lieutenant-governor, be afterwards sold by private contract, at not less than the upset price of such land. The ordinary size of the lots in the Bahamas is to be twenty acres, but lots of five acres may, if thought expedient, be disposed of.

The salt ponds in the Turks' Islands (within the government of the Bahamas) have been the subject of recent regulation by the Land and Emigration Commissioners. These ponds are an important public property, but they were divided annually amongst all persons, without distinction, who happened to be resident on the spot, and these shares had no real value. Instead of this plan, the ponds will in future be granted on leases, which will give the lessees a durable interest, and encourage them to make the outlay requisite for their improvement. It has already been stated that in the United States of North America salt springs are reserved by the federal government, and leased for the public benefit.

The plan under which the great land companies dispose of their lands may be ascertained by application to the secretaries of each company. The principal companies are, the Upper Canada Company, the British American Land Company, the New Zealand Company, and the New Brunswick and Nova Scotia Land Company. The first of these companies has a plan of leasing their lands, which is very advantageous to small capitalists. The South Australian Company have lands which they dispose of both by lease and sale.

The business of regulating emigration has been undertaken to some extent by the government. First an agent-general for emigration was appointed. This officer introduced many judicious plans for rendering the passage of emigrants across the ocean as free as possible from discomfort, and a code of rules was framed to secure this and other objects. The functions of the agent-general for emigration are now exercised by the Land and Emigration Commissioners. Emigrants are also protected by the Passengers' Acts, namely, the 5 & 6 Vict. c. 107, amended by 10 & 11 Vict. c. 103, and in respect to passengers to North America, by the 11 Vict. c. 6. The general scope of these statutes are to regulate the number of passengers in each ship, and to provide for their proper accommodation on board; to ensure a proper supply of provisions and water for their use; to provide for the seaworthiness of the vessels; and to protect emigrants from the numerous frauds to which their helplessness and inexperience expose them. If the ship does not sail on the day mentioned in the agreement, the Passengers' Act compels the captain to victual the emigrants just the same as if the voyage had commenced; and they are entitled to remain on board forty-eight hours after the ship reaches her destination.

As a further protection to emigrants and to enforce the provisions of the Passengers' Act, government emigration agents are appointed for the ports of London, Liverpool, Plymouth, Glasgow and Greenock, Dublin, Cork, Belfast, Limerick, Sligo, and Londonderry. These officers act under the immediate directions of the Colonial Land and Emigration Commissioners. They procure and give gratuitously information as to the sailing of ships, and means of accommodation for emigrants; and whenever applied to for that purpose, they see that all agreements between ship-owners, agents, or masters, and intending emigrants, are duly performed. They also see that the provisions of the Passengers' Act are strictly complied with, viz., that passenger-vessels are sea-worthy, that they have on board a sufficient supply of provisions, water, medicines, &c., and that they sail with proper punctuality. They attend personally at their offices on every weekday, and afford gratuitously all the assistance in their power to protect intending emigrants against fraud and imposition, and to obtain redress where oppression or injury has been practised on them.

In the colonies there are government immigration agents. The duties of these officers are to afford gratuitously to emigrants every assistance in their power by way of advice and information as to the districts where employment can be obtained most readily, and upon the most advantageous terms, and also as to the best modes of reaching such districts. In Canada there are immigration agents at Quebec, Montreal, Kingston, Bytown, Port Hope and Cobourg, Toronto, and Hamilton; in New Brunswick at St. John's and Fredericton; and the deputy-treasurers act as immigration agents at St. Andrew's, Bathurst, Dalhousie, and Chatham (Miramichi). There are also government immigration agents for the colonies of New South Wales (at Sydney and Port Philip) and for Van Diemen's Land, Western Australia, Southern Australia, and New Zealand.

Emigration is one of the "modes of relief" contemplated by the Poor Law Amendment Act (4 & 5 Wm. IV. c. 76). In some years a large number of persons have emigrated with the assistance of funds obtained under the act. In 1835-6 the number of emigrants was 5141, and the sum borrowed, either from the Exchequer Loan Office or from private persons, amounted to 28,414l. By § 62 of the Poor Law Act owners and rate-payers are empowered to raise money on security of the rates for purposes of emigration, under the authority of the Poor Law Commissioners. The sum so raised must not exceed half the average yearly rate of the preceding three years, and it must be repaid within five years. The money is advanced to emigrants by way of loan, and is recoverable against persons above the age of twenty-one, who, having consented to emigrate, refuse to do so after the expenses of emigration have been incurred; and the loan is also recoverable if persons who emigrate shall return to this country.

By the act 7 & 8 Vict. c. 101, for the amendment of the Poor Laws, it is provided that the boards of guardians are exclusively to apply money raised or borrowed for the purpose of emigration.

Under the Irish Poor Law Act money may be raised for enabling poor persons to emigrate to British colonies; but the money so raised must not exceed one shilling in the pound on the net annual value of rateable property.

The Bounty System derives its name from the mode in which the proceeds of land sales are applied in obtaining immigrants. In this case persons who introduce persons into the colony receive so much per head, according to the terms of agreement. The contractors engage to find persons willing to emigrate, and undertake to land them in the colony. This system is in force only in some of the Australian colonies. In New South Wales 51,736 persons were introduced from 1831 to 1842 under bounties.

The Land and Emigration Commissioners are required by their official instructions to prepare and issue "a distinct and compendious account of whatever relates to the agriculture, the commerce, the natural products, the physical structure, and the ecclesiastical and political institutions of each of the colonies" in which they offer lands for sale. Lord John Russell issued these instructions, in the hope that the office of the Land and Emigration Commissioners would become the depository of information "for the assistance, not of private adventurers only, but of this (the colonial) and of every other department of the state." The Commissioners in pursuance of this object have published in a cheap form " Information for Emigrants to British North America;" a similar pamphlet relating to the Falkland Isles; and they issue occasionally a "Colonization Circular" which contains matter calculated to be of use to emigrants or persons who intend at some time to settle in the colonies. The Annual Reports of the Commissioners presented to parliament are also reprinted in a convenient form for general use. These useful matters are published by Knight & Co., London; and may be procured through any bookseller.

The average annual number of persons who emigrated in the ten years from 1825 to 1834 was 50,304; and in the ten years from 1835 to 1844 inclusive 75,293. The largest number who emigrated in any one year, in the first ten years, was 103,140, in 1832. The number in each of the last ten years was as follows:—

1835	. . 44,478	1840	. . 90,743
1836	. . 75,417	1841	. . 118,592
1837	. . 72,034	1842	. . 128,344
1838	. . 33,222	1843	. . 57,212
1839	. . 62,207	1844	. . 70,686

A variety of circumstances affect the extent of emigration and its particular direction. In some years the stream is increased by distress at home; in others, by the activity caused by the bounty system, and the amount raised by the sales of land in the Australian colonies; an insurrection in Canada diverts the current of emigrants to other colonies; a massacre in New Zealand, and the effects of misgovernment there, have their influence. The fluctuation in the average annual number of emigrants during the following periods is curious.

	Average annual number of emigrants.
In the 4 years ending 1828	. 22,500
In the 6 years ending 1834	. 69,000
„ 5 years ending 1839	. 57,500
„ 3 years ending 1842	. 112,500
1843 and 1844	. 64,000

The numbers who proceeded to the United States, British North America, the Australian Colonies, and New Zealand, in each of the following years was as under:—

	British North America.	United States.	Australia and New Zealand.
1835	15,573	26,720	1,860
1836	34,226	37,774	3,124
1837	29,884	36,770	5,054
1838	4,577	14,332	14,021
1839	12,658	33,536	15,786
1840	32,293	40,642	15,850
1841	38,164	45,017	32,625
1842	54,123	63,852	8,534
1843	23,518	28,335	3,478
1844	22,924	43,660	2,229

The destination of the emigrants who left the United Kingdom, in 1844, is more minutely given in the following table:—

Destination.	
United States	. 43,660
Texas	1
Central and South America	. 710
Canada	. 18,747
New Brunswick	. 2,489
Nova Scotia and Cape Breton	. 747
Newfoundland	. 684
Prince Edward's Island	. 257
Jamaica	. 126
British Guiana	. 142
Trinidad	. 60
Other settlements in British West Indies	. 168
Foreign West Indies	. 39
East Indies	. 176
Hong Kong	. 18
China	. 9
Mauritius	. 13
Cape of Good Hope	. 161
Western Africa and Madeira	. 250
Sydney	. 1,179
Port-Philip	. 934
South Australia	. 47
Van Diemen's Land	. 1
New Zealand	. 68
Grand Total	. 70,686

In 1844 the number of persons who emigrated from ports in England was 50,257; Scotland, 4504; Ireland, 15,925. The number of emigrants who embarked at Liverpool was 44,427, and from London only 2303. The number of cabin passengers was 4889, of whom 4070, or 1 in 12½, were from England; 663, or 1 in 7, were from Scotland; 156, or 1 in 102, were from Ireland. The destination of the English, Scotch, and Irish emigrants is shown in the subjoined table.

Went to	English.	Scots.	Irish.
United States	39,070	1,597	2,993
Central and South America	668	43	—
North American Colonies	8,058	2,470	12,396
British West Indies	283	197	16
Foreign do.	38	1	—
East Indies	131	45	—
Hong Kong	17	1	—
China	9	—	—
Mauritius	9	4	—
Western Africa and Madeira	240	10	—
The Cape	153	8	—
Australian Colonies	1,581	128	520

The emigration of native labourers from China and India, and of liberated and other Africans from Sierra Leone to the Mauritius and to the British Colonies in the West Indies, it may be sufficient to mention, is under the regulation of the Land and Emigration Commissioners.

The various political questions which arise from the connexion between a parent state and colony are treated of in "An Essay on the Government of Dependencies," by George Cornewall Lewis, London, 1841.

EMPANNEL. [PANEL.]

EMPEROR, from the Latin *Imperator*. Among the early Romans the title of Imperator was bestowed by the acclamations of his soldiers in the camp on a commander-in-chief who had signalized himself by a victory. (Tacit. *Annal.* iii. 74.) In the case mentioned by Tacitus, Tiberius is said to have allowed the soldiers to salute Blæsus by the title of Imperator (Compare Velleius, ii. 125). But the word Imperator was properly applied to him who had what the Romans called Imperium, which on the Roman kings by th riata (Cicero, *De Repub.* was the case with Tullus his predecessor Numa, and Ancus Marcius. Under th title was sometimes conferr vidual for the occasion (*Livy*, xxvi. 21; xlv. (*Philipp.* ix. 16), defines be "that power without v affairs cannot be carried commanded, or a war cond formably to this we have Livius, in which the Sen acknowledge a general as because he had not recei rium in due form (xxvi. 2) tion on the Lex Manilia, C a single Imperator was re duct the war against Mith The name used by the Gr of Rome to express Impera tor (αὐτοκράτωρ), one who l from which is derived the which is sometimes appliec ror of Russia. C. Julius (the name Imperator as a title (Imperator C. Julius (tice which was followed by as we may observe on thei tonius, *Cæsar*, 76.) There of this title in the coins Aurelius, and other Ron On the reverse of the co we observe Imp. VIII., or octavum, or imperator the which shows, as indeed (from a variety of example man emperors often assum special occasions when the nerals had obtained some This term Imperator, un emperors, cannot be cons noting any sovereign pov this distinction was obser peror, when the title was : in his sovereign capacity, Imperator prefixed, as Im Augustus; but the indivic the honorary distinction some particular occasion after his name, Iunius Blæ as in the Republican perioc After the time of the term Imperator seems gradually to have grown into common use as one of the titles which expressed the sovereign of the Roman world, though the name Princeps was also long used as indicating the same rank and power. (See the Dedication of J. Capitolinus to Constantine.) It may be difficult to state when this term Imperator became exclusively the designation of the Roman sovereign. In the introduction to the Digest (De Conceptione Digestorum), Justinian assumes the title of Imperator Cæsar Flavius Justinianus, &c., semper Augustus. In the proemium to the Institutes, Justinian uses the terms Imperatoria Majestas to express his sovereign power, and yet in the same paragraph he calls himself by the name of Princeps, a term which dates from the time of the so-called Republic, and expressed the precedence given to one particular member of the Senate. The term Princeps was adopted by Augustus as the least invidious title of dignity, and was applied to his successors.

From the emperors of the West this title, in the year 800, devolved to Charlemagne, the founder of the second or German empire of the West. Upon the expiration of the German branch of the Carlovingian family, the imperial crown became elective, and continued so until the last century. The title of Emperor of Germany now no longer exists: Francis II. laid it aside, and assumed the title of Emperor of Austria. The only other European potentate who uses the style of emperor is the autocrat of Russia, the monarchs of which country, about the year 1520, exchanged their former title of duke or great duke of Russia, for that of Czar or Tzar. In early times it was asserted by the civilians that the possession of the imperial crown gave to the emperors of Germany, as titular sovereigns of the world, a supremacy over all the kings of Europe, though such was never attempted to be exercised; and they denied the existence of any other empire: but in spite of this denial it is certain that several of the kings of France of the second race, after they had lost the empire of Germany, styled themselves Basileus and Imperator. Our own King Edgar, in a charter to Oswald bishop of Winchester, styled himself "Anglorum Basileus omnium que regum insularum oceani que Britanniam circumjacentis cunctarum que nationum quæ infra eam includuntur *Imperator et Dominus.*" Alfonso VII. also, in the 12th century, styled himself Emperor of Spain. It might be easily shown how the title and rank of king and emperor have been feudalized, as it were, in passing through the ordeal of the middle ages.

ENDOWMENT. [DOWER; BENEFICE; USES, CHARITABLE.]

ENEMY. [ALIEN, p. 102.]

ENFEOFFMENT. [FEOFFMENT.]

ENFRANCHISEMENT. The Third Annual Report of the Copyhold Commissioners, dated 22nd June, 1844, gives the following information respecting the progress of enfranchisement of manors under the Copyhold Act. The Commissioners state that "enfranchisemen. of church property is now proceeding to a considerable extent, and there is every reason to suppose that in manors held by ecclesiastical persons the disposition to avail themselves of the act will become general." Enfranchisements had also increased in other manors, but not in the same proportion, and that the act had encouraged building, especially in the neighbourhood of London. They suggested, as an improvement, that, without being in any way compulsory on the lord, enfranchisements might be made binding on the other tenants, if two-thirds of the tenants, in number and value, agreed. At present it may happen that the lord is willing to enfranchise, and he can make arrangements with the principal tenants; but if there is a difficulty in agreeing with the smaller tenants, enfranchisement is hindered, as the lord might be left with the dregs of the manor.

ENGROSSING. [FORESTALLING.]

ENLISTMENT, an engagement to serve as a private soldier either during an unlimited period or for a certain number of years, on receipt of a sum of money. Enlistment differs from enrolment, inasmuch as it is a voluntary act, whereas the latter is, under some circumstances, rendered compulsory: as in the case of men who are selected by ballot for the militia in this country, or by the conscription, for military service generally, on the continent.

The practice of impressing men to serve as soldiers, on sudden emergencies, was formerly very common in England; and it is well known that within the last half century young men were entrapped and secretly conveyed away to recruit the armies employed in the east. The discovery of this illegal and disgraceful method of obtaining soldiers was speedily followed by its abolition; and now, the East India Company's troops, as well as those of the regular army, are obtained by voluntary engagement.

The number of young men who are induced to enlist by the ambition of entering upon a course of life which appears to hold out a prospect of distinguishing themselves by gallant achievements in the field is, however, too small for the wants of the military service; and the allurement of a bounty must necessarily be presented in order that the ranks of the army may be filled. But the profession of a soldier can never possess such advantages as might induce an industrious man who can obtain a subsistence in another way to embrace it; and it is to be regretted that too frequently those who enter the service are thoughtless youths or men of indolent habits or desperate fortunes. Some attention, however, to the character of a person offering himself for enlistment is necessary if it be desired to render the service honourable; for it is found that idle and dissipated men are with difficulty brought to submit to the necessary restraints of discipline; their frequent desertions entail heavy losses on the government, and they often corrupt those who are compelled to associate with them. When circumstances render it necessary to enlist such men, it is obvious that they ought to be distributed in small numbers among the different regiments, and quartered in places remote from those from which they were taken.

By the 34th clause of the Mutiny Act, every person who has received enlisting-money from any military man employed in the recruiting service is considered as having enlisted; but within forty-eight hours afterwards notice is to the recruit, or left at his place of his having so enlisted: within four days from the 1 ceiving the money, the recrui by any person employed as is to appear before a magistra ing a military man), when, il that he has voluntarily enlist gistrate is to question him con name, age, and condition, a larly to inquire of him whe then serving, or whether he served, in the army or navy. gistrate is then to read to the articles of war relating to r desertion, and administer to h of allegiance, of which a form a schedule to the act: if refuse to take the oath, he r prisoned till he do so. But as the young and simpl sometimes inveigled by ill mises, or persuaded, while (judgment by intoxication, to recruit, on reflection, wish to from the engagement into wh have been surprised, it is prov 35th clause of the Mutiny Act taken before the magistrate a shall be at liberty to declare from such enlistment; on ma declaration and returning the money, with 20s. in additio charges which may have bee on his account, he shall be for charged. But if he omit wit four hours after so declaring to pay such money, he is to be as enlisted, as if he had giver before the magistrate.

If a recruit, after receiving ment-money, and after notice enlisted has been left at hi abode, shall abscond, he may hended and punished as a dese being absent without leave; a discovered that he is unfit for vice, in consequence of any which he had not declared magistrate, he may be transfer garrison, or veteran or invalid though he may have enliste particular regiment. If it be the recruit concealed the fact (

a discharged soldier, he may be sentenced to suffer punishment as a rogue or vagabond; and if, at the time of enlisting, he falsely denied being in the militia, he may be committed to the house of correction for a period not exceeding six months; and, from the day in which his engagement to serve in the militia ends, he is to be deemed a soldier in the regular forces.

An apprentice who shall enlist, denying himself to be such, is deemed guilty of obtaining money under false pretences; and, after the expiration of his apprenticeship, if he shall not deliver himself up to some officer authorised to receive recruits, he may be taken as a deserter. A master is not entitled to claim an apprentice who may have enlisted unless the claim be made within one month after the apprentice shall have left his service.

In the third clause of the Mutiny Act it is stated that no man enlisted as a soldier is liable to be arrested on account of any process for leaving a wife or child chargeable to a parish, or on account of any engagement to work for an employer (except that of an apprenticeship), or on account of any debt under 30*l.* And in the 41st clause it is declared that negroes, purchased on account of the crown and serving in any of the regular forces, are deemed to be free, and are considered as soldiers having voluntarily enlisted. Every military officer acting contrary to the provisions of the Mutiny Act, in what regards enlisting recruits, is liable to be cashiered, and disabled to hold any civil or military office or employment in her Majesty's service.

During the reign of Queen Anne it was the custom to enlist recruits for three years; but this period seems too short, considering the time unavoidably spent in training the men, to afford the government an advantage adequate to the expense of maintaining them; and the present practice is regulated by 10 & 11 Vict. c. 39. By this act no person can be enlisted for longer than ten years in the infantry, or twelve years in the cavalry, artillery, or other ordnance corps; the term of service to be reckoned from the day of attestation, or day on which the party, if under eighteen years of age, attains that age. The term of enlistment in the marine forces is limited to twelve years. The enlistments for the Honourable East India Company's service are either for unlimited periods, or for twelve years, provided the recruit be not less than eighteen years of age.

The advantages of a limited period of service are, that a greater number of recruits are obtained under that condition, probably because men are more willing to engage themselves for a certain number of years than for life; and that, during the period, opportunities are afforded of discovering the character of a man. Should this be such as to render it not advisable to retain him, he may be discharged at the end of his time of service; while an additional bounty, strengthened by the unwillingness of most men to leave the comrades with whom they have been long accustomed to associate, will probably induce a good soldier to re-enlist should the continuance of his services be desired.

By an act passed in 1835 a man is allowed to enlist in the navy for a period not exceeding five years, after which he is entitled to his discharge and to be sent home, if abroad, unless the commanding officer should conceive his departure to be detrimental to the service; such officer is then empowered to detain the man six months longer, or until the emergency shall cease, in which case the man is entitled, during such extra service, to receive an increase of pay amounting to one-fourth of that which he receives according to his rating. At the end of his time of service a seaman may re-enlist for a like period, and he will then be allowed the same bounty as at first. Seamen entering as volunteers within six days after a royal proclamation calling for the services of such men receive double bounty. In the year 1819 was passed that which is called the Foreign Enlistment Act, by which British subjects are forbidden to engage in foreign service without licence from the crown. This act for several years was suspended in favour of the British troops employed in the service of the present Queen of Spain. Lastly, a bill has recently passed, confirming the act of 55 Geo. III., by which her majesty is empowered to grant the rank of field and general officers to foreigners; and to allow foreigners to enlist and serve as non-commissioned officers and soldiers in the British service in the proportion of one foreigner for every fifty natural born subjects.

ENSIGN, a commissioned officer, the lowest in degree, and immediately subordinate to the lieutenants in a regiment of infantry. One of this rank is appointed to each company, and the junior ensigns are charged with the duty of carrying the colours of the regiment. Ensigns in the regiments of foot guards have also the rank of lieutenants. In the rifle brigade, and in the royal corps of artillery, engineers, and marines, in place of an ensign, a second lieutenant is attached to each company.

Among the Spaniards and Italians, in the seventeenth century, it appears that no officer existed like the lieutenant of a company, whose rank is between that of a captain and ensign, any such being considered superfluous, and as tending to diminish the importance which was attached to the post of the officer who had the charge of the colours, on the preservation of which, in action, the honour of the regiment was made greatly to depend.

When, as formerly, a battle partook far more than at present of the nature of a mêlée, the loss of a standard, which served as a mark for the soldiers under each leader to keep together in the fight, or to rally when dispersed, must have been a serious misfortune, and probably was often attended by the total defeat and destruction of the party; and hence, no doubt, arose the point of honour respecting the colours. A French military author, who served and wrote in the time of Charles IX., intending to express the importance of preserving the colours to the last, observes that, on a defeat taking place, the flag should serve the ensign as a shroud; and instances have occurred of a standard-bearer who, being mortally wounded, tore the flag from its staff and died with it wrapped about his body. Such a circumstance is related of Don Sebastian, king of Portugal, at the battle of Alcazar, and of a young officer named Chatelier at the taking of Taillebourg during the wars of the Huguenots.

In the ancient French service, the duty of carrying the oriflamme at the head of the army was confided to a man of rank and also of approved valour and prudence; the post was held for life.

The price of an ensign's commission in the foot guards is 1200*l.*, and his daily pay is 5*s.* 6*d.*; in the regiments of the line the price is 450*l.*, and the daily pay 5*s.* 3*d.*

ENTAIL. [ESTATE.]

ENVOY, a diplomatic minister or agent, inferior in dignity to an ambassador, but generally invested with equal powers. [AMBASSADOR.]

EPISCOPACY. [BISHOP.]

EQUALITY. [LIBERTY.]

EQUERRIES (from the French *écurie* a stable), the name given to certain officers of the household of the King of England in the department of the master of the horse, the first of whom is styled chief equerry and clerk-marshal. Their duties fall in rotation. When the king or queen ride abroad in state, an equerry goes in the leading coach. They formerly rode on horseback by the coach side. Officers of the same denomination form a part of the established household of the Prince Consort, the Duke of Cambridge and the Queen Dowager.

EQUITY, according to the definition given by Aristotle, is "the rectification of the law, when, by reason of its universality, it is deficient; for this is the reason that all things are not determined by law, because it is impossible that a law should be enacted concerning some things so that there is need of a decree or decision; for of the indefinite the rule also is indefinite: as among Lesbian builders the rule is leaden, for the rule is altered to suit the figure of the stone, and is not fixed, and so is a decree or decision to suit the circumstances." (*Ethics*, b. v. c x. Oxford trans.) "Equity," says Blackstone, "in its true and genuine meaning is the soul and spirit of all law; positive law is construed and rational law is made by it. In this respect, equity is synonymous with justice; in that, to the true and sound interpretation of the rule."

According to Grotius, equity is the correction of that wherein the law, by reason of its generality, is deficient.

It is probable that the department of law called equity in England once deserved the humorous description given by Selden in his 'Table Talk:' "Equity in law is the same that spirit is in religion, what every one pleases to make it: sometimes they go according to conscience, sometimes according to law, sometimes according to the rule of court. Equity is a roguish thing: for law we have a measure, know what to trust to; equity is according to the conscience of him that is chancellor; and as that is larger or narrower, so is equity. It is all one as if they should make the standard for the measure we call a foot a chancellor's foot; what an uncertain measure would this be! One chancellor has a long foot, another a short foot, a third an indifferent foot: it is the same thing in the chancellor's conscience."

This uncertainty has however long ceased in that branch of our law which is expressed by the term Equity, and, from successive decisions, rules and principles almost as fixed have been framed and established in our courts of equity as in our courts of law. New cases do indeed arise, but they are decided according to these rules and principles, and not according to the notions of the judge as to what may be reasonable or just in the particular case. Nothing in fact is more common than to hear the chancellor say, that whatever may be his own opinion, he is bound by the authorities, that is, by the decisions of his predecessors in office and those of the other judges in equity, that he will not shake any settled rule of equity, it being for the common good that these should be certain and known, however ill-founded the first resolution may have been.

In its enlarged sense, equity answers precisely to the definition of justice, or natural law (as it is called), as given in the 'Pandects' (i. tit. 1, s. 10, 11); and it is remarkable that subsequent writers on this so-called natural law, and also the authors of modern treatises on the doctrine of equity, as administered in the English courts, have, with scarcely any exception, cited the above passage from Aristotle as a definition of equity in our peculiar sense of a separate jurisdiction. But according to this general definition every court is a court of equity, of which a familiar instance occurs in the construction of statutes, which the judges of the courts of common law may, if they please, interpret according to the spirit, or, as it is called, the equity, not the strict letter.

It is hardly possible to define Equity as now administered in England and Ireland, or to make it intelligible otherwise than by a minute enumeration of the matters cognizable in the courts in which it is administered in its restrained and qualified sense.

The remedies for the redress of wrongs and for the enforcement of rights are distinguished into two classes, those which are administered in courts of law, and those which are administered in courts of equity. Accordingly rights may be distributed into Legal and Equitable. Equity jurisdiction may therefore properly be defined as that department of law which is administered by a court of equity as distinguished from a court of law, from which a court of equity differs mainly in the subject matters of which it takes cognizance and in its mode of procedure and remedies.

Courts of common law proceed by certain prescribed forms of action alone, and give relief only according to the kinds of actions, by a general and unqualified judgment for the plaintiff or the defendant. There are many cases, however, in which a simple judgment for either party, without qualifications or conditions, will not do entire justice. Some modifications of the rights of both parties may be required; some restraints on one side or the other, or perhaps on both; some qualifications or conditions present or future, temporary or permanent, ought to be annexed to the exercise of rights or the redress of injuries. To accomplish such objects the courts of law in this country have no machinery: according to their present constitution they can only adjudicate by a simple judgment between the parties. Courts of equity, however, are not so restrained; they adjudicate by decree pronounced upon a statement of his case by the plaintiff, which he makes by a writing called a bill, and the written answer of the defendant, which is given in upon oath, and the evidence of witnesses, together, if necessary, with the evidence of all parties, also given in writing and upon oath. These decrees are so adjusted as to meet all the exigencies of the case, and they vary, qualify, restrain, and model the remedy so as to suit it to mutual and adverse claims, and the real and substantial rights of all the parties, so far as such rights are acknowledged by the rules of equity.

The courts of equity bring before them *all* the parties interested in the subject matter of the suit, and adjust the rights of all, however numerous; whereas courts of law are compelled by their constitution to limit their inquiry to the litigating parties, although other persons may be interested; that is, they give a complete remedy in damages or otherwise for the particular wrong in question as between the parties to the action, though such remedy is in many cases an incomplete adjudication upon the general rights of the parties to the action, and fails altogether as to other persons, not parties to the action, who yet may be interested in the result or in the subject matter in dispute.

The description of a court of equity, as given by Mr. Justice Story in the 'Encyclopædia Americana,' which he has filled up in his recent Treatise on Equity, is this. A court of equity has jurisdiction in cases where a plain, adequate, and complete remedy cannot be had in the common law courts. The remedy must be plain, for if it be doubtful and obscure at law, equity will assert a jurisdiction. It must be adequate, for if at law it fall short of what the party is entitled to, that founds a jurisdiction in equity; and it must be complete, that is, it must attain the full end and justice of the case; it must reach the whole mischief and secure the whole right of the party present and future, otherwise equity will interpose and give relief. The jurisdiction of a court of equity is sometimes concurrent with the jurisdiction of the courts of law; sometimes assistant to it; and sometimes exclusive. It exercises concurrent jurisdiction in cases where the rights are purely of a legal nature, but where other and more efficient aid is required than a court of law can afford. In some of these cases courts of law formerly refused all redress, but now will grant it. For strict law comprehending established rules, and the jurisdiction of equity being called into action when the purposes of justice rendered an exception to those rules necessary, successive exceptions on the same grounds became the foundation of a general principle, and could no longer be considered as a singular interposition. Thus law and equity are in continual progression, and the former is constantly gaining ground upon the latter. Every new and extraordinary interposition is by length of time converted into an old rule; a great part of what is now strict law was formerly considered as equity, and the equitable decisions of this age will unavoidably be ranked under the strict law of the next. (Prof. Millar, *View of the Eng. Govt.*) But the jurisdiction having been once acquired at a time when there was no such redress at law, it is still retained by the courts of equity.

The most common exercise of the concurrent jurisdiction is in cases of account, accident, dower, fraud, mistake, partnership, and partition. In many cases which fall under these heads, and especially in some cases of fraud, mistake, and accident, courts of law cannot and do not afford any redress: in others they do, but not in so complete a manner as a court of equity.

A court of equity is also assistant to the jurisdiction of the courts of law in cases where the courts of law have no like authority. It will remove legal impediments to the fair decision of a question depending at law, as by restraining a party from improperly setting up, at a trial, some title or claim which would prevent the fair decision of the question in dispute; by compelling him to discover, upon his own oath, facts which are material to the right of the other party, but which a court of law cannot compel him to disclose; by perpetuating, that is, by taking in writing and keeping in its custody, the testimony of witnesses, which is in danger of being lost before the matter can be tried; and by providing for the safety of property in dispute pending litigation. It will also counteract and control fraudulent judgments, by restraining the parties from insisting upon them.

The exclusive jurisdiction of a court of equity is chiefly exercised in cases of merely equitable rights, that is, such rights as are not recognised in courts of law. Most cases of trust and confidence fall under this head. This exclusive jurisdiction is exercised in granting injunctions to prevent waste or irreparable injury; to secure a settled right, or to prevent vexatious litigation; in appointing receivers of property which is in danger of being misapplied; in compelling the surrender of securities improperly obtained; in preventing a party from leaving the country in order to avoid a suit; in restraining any undue exercise of a legal right; in enforcing specific performance of contracts; in supplying the defective execution of instruments, and reforming, that is, correcting and altering them according to the real intention of the parties, when such intention can be satisfactorily proved; and in granting relief in cases where deeds and securities have been lost.

Various opinions have been expressed upon the question whether it would or would not be best to administer justice altogether in one court or in one class of courts, without any separation or distinction of suits, or of the forms or modes of procedure and relief. Lord Bacon, upon more than one occasion, has expressed his decided opinion that a separation of the administration of equity from that of the common law is wise and convenient. "All nations," says he, "have equity, but some have law and equity mixed in the same court, which is worse, and some have it distinguished in several courts, which is better;" and again, "In some states, that jurisdiction which decrees according to equity and moral right, and that which decrees according to strict right, is committed to the same court; in others, they are committed to different courts. We entirely opine for the separation of the courts; for the distinction of the cases will not long be attended to if the jurisdictions meet in the same person; and the will of the judge will then master the law."

Lord Hardwicke held the same opinion. Lord Mansfield, it is to be presumed, thought otherwise, for he endeavoured to introduce equitable doctrines into the courts of law. The old strictness has however been restored. His successor, Lord Kenyon, made use of these expressions: "If it had fallen to my lot to form a system of jurisprudence, whether or not I should have thought it advisable to establish different courts, with different jurisdictions, and governed by different rules, it is not necessary to say; but influenced as I am by certain prejudices that have become inveterate with those who comply with the systems they find established, I find that in these courts, proceeding by different rules, a certain combined system of jurisprudence has been framed most beneficial to the people of this country, and which I hope I may be indulged in supposing has never yet been equalled in any other country on earth. Our courts of law only consider legal rights; our courts of equity have other rules, by which they sometimes supersede strict legal rules, and in so doing they act most beneficially for the subject." In this country the principle of separating jurisdictions has been largely acted upon. We have our courts of equity and law; our bankrupt and insolvent courts, and courts of ecclesiastical and admiralty jurisdiction; indeed until lately our several courts of law had, in principle, jurisdiction only over certain specified classes of suits. In countries governed by the civil law, the practice has in general been the other way. But whether the one opinion or the other be most correct in theory, the system adopted by every nation has been mainly influenced by the peculiarities of its own institutions, habits, and circumstances, and the original forms of giving redress for wrongs.

In some of the American states, the administration of law and equity is distinct; in others the administration of equity is only partially committed to distinct courts; in a third class the two jurisdictions are vested in one and the same tribunal; and in a fourth there are no courts that exercise equitable jurisdiction.

In most of our colonies the governor is invested with the jurisdiction of chancellor; but in some of the most important colonies, where a judicial establishment of some magnitude is maintained, the chief or supreme court is invested with the chancery jurisdiction.

This attempt at the exposition of the general principles of what in this country is called Equity, seems to be better suited to a work of this nature than a full description of the practice of, that is, the course of proceeding in a suit in a court of equity. The practice or procedure of any court can hardly be made intelligible to any person except one who knows something of it by experience; and any technical description of it is useless unless it is minutely and circumstantially exact. It is desirable, however, that in addition to some knowledge of the subjects which belong to the jurisdiction of a court of equity, all persons should have some clear notion of the way in which the matters in dispute between parties to a suit in equity are brought before the court, and by what kind of proof or evidence they are established. It may also be useful that persons should have a general and, so far as it goes, a correct knowledge of the different modes in which such questions of fact are put in issue, and proved in our courts of law and equity. The following short outline of the course of proceeding in a suit of chancery, taken in connection with other articles in this work, such as CHANCELLOR, CHANCERY, DEPOSITION, and EVIDENCE, may probably give somewhat more information on the subject of equity jurisdiction that is found in books not strictly professional.

A suit on the Equity side of the courts of chancery is commenced by presenting a written petition to the lord chancellor, containing a statement of the plaintiff's case, and praying for such relief as he may consider himself entitled to receive. This petition is technically called a Bill, and is in the nature of the Declaration at common law; but if the suit is instituted in behalf of the crown, or a charity, or any of the objects under the peculiar protection of the crown, the petition is in the form of a narrative of the facts by the attorney-general, and is called an Information. There is also a petition termed an information and bill, which is, where the attorney-general, at the relation (that is, the information) of a third person (thence called the relator), informs the court of the facts which he thinks are a fit subject of inquiry. The practice in all these proceedings is the same. At the end of the statement in a bill, there is added what is called the interrogating part, which consists of the statements of the bill thrown into the form of distinct questions, and often expressed in terms of great length and particularity. The statements in the bill are not made upon oath: and further, in order to obtain a full and complete discovery from the defendant, both as regards the complaint and the supposed defence, various allegations are made in many cases from mere conjecture, a practice which tends to the due administration of justice; for though many frivolous suits are instituted, yet, from the nature of cases of fraud and concealment, the plaintiff is often ignorant of the precise nature of his own case, and frames his bill in various forms so as to elicit from the defendant a full discovery of the truth. Bills of this nature are called original bills, and either may be for Discovery and Relief, or for Discovery merely.

When the bill is placed on the records of the court it is said to be *filed*, and the writ of subpœna issues which commands the defendant to appear and answer the allegations of the bill within a certain time.

If, upon the face of the bill, it should appear that the plaintiff is not entitled to the relief prayed for as against the defendant, the defendant may demur, that is, demand the judgment of the court upon the statement made by the plaintiff, whether the suit shall proceed; and if any cause, not apparent upon the bill, should exist why the suit should be either dismissed, delayed, or barred, the defendant may put in a plea, stating such matter, and demanding the judgment of the court as in the case of a demurrer. But if neither of these modes of defence are applicable, and the defendant cannot disclaim all knowledge of the matters contained in the bill, he must answer upon oath the interrogatories in the bill according to the best of his *knowledge, remembrance, information,* and *belief.* This mode of defence is styled an Answer. All or any of these several modes of defence may be used together, if applied to separate and distinct parts of the case made by the plaintiff.

In the successive stages of a suit, references as to the pleadings, and as to facts, may be made to the Masters of the court of Chancery: as for instance, if any improper statements be made reflecting upon the character of any party, which are not necessary to the decision of the suit, the pleadings may be referred to the master for scandal; if there be long and irrelevant statements, not concerning the matter in question, a reference may be made for impertinence, and the matter so complained of as scandalous or impertinent may be expunged at the expense of the party in fault. Again, if the defendant does not answer the bill with sufficient precision, the plaintiff may except to the answer for insufficiency, and this question is decided by the masters in Chancery. If the answer is decided to be insufficient, the defendant must answer further.

It frequently happens that during the progress of the suit, from the discovery of new matter, the deaths and marriages of parties, and other causes, the pleadings become defective, and in these cases it is necessary to bring the new matter, or parties becoming interested, before the court. This is done by means of further statements, which refer to the previous proceedings, and are in fact merely a continuation of them, which are called supplemental bills, bills of revivor, or bills of revivor and supplement, according to the nature of the defect which they are intended to supply. These bills are called bills not original.

There is also a third class, called bills in the nature of original bills, which are occasioned by former bills, such as cross bills, which are filed by the defendant to an original bill against the plaintiff who files such bill, touching some matter in litigation in the original bill, as where a discovery is necessary from the plaintiff in order that the defendant may obtain complete justice. There are also bills of review, to examine a decree upon the discovery of new matter, &c., and several others. Upon both these latter descriptions of bills the same pleadings and proceedings may follow as to an original bill.

Pleas and demurrers are at once argued before the court: if allowed, the suit, or so much of it as is covered by the demurrer or plea, is at an end, though the court will generally permit the plaintiff to amend his bill where it is not apparent from his own statement that he cannot make any case against the defendant; otherwise the only object attained by the demurrer or plea would be to drive the plaintiff to file a new bill, in which he would omit or amend the objectionable part. But if the demurrer or plea is overruled, the defendant is compelled to answer fully, just as if he had not demurred or pleaded. When the answer is filed, the plaintiff, if from the disclosures made he deems it advisable, may amend his bill, that is, erase such part of his statements as he no longer considers necessary, and insert other statements which may appear necessary to sustain his case; and the defendant must answer to this new matter.

In cases where the bill is for discovery only, and in some others, the answer puts an end to the suit; and when the object of the bill is to obtain an injunction, which is granted either upon affidavits before answer or in default of an answer, the suit is also ended, unless the defendant desires to dissolve the injunction. But where a decree is necessary, the cause must come on to be heard either upon evidence taken in writing before the examiners of the court or commissioners appointed for the purpose [DEPOSITION; EVIDENCE]; or where the plaintiff considers the disclosures in the answer sufficient, the cause is heard upon bill and answer alone, without further evidence, and this is at the plaintiff's discretion.

The cause is heard in its turn by the master of the rolls or the vice-chancellors, for the lord chancellor rarely hears causes in the first instance. [CHANCERY.] If the nature of the suit admits, a final decree is made; or if any further inquiry be necessary, or any accounts are to be taken, references are made to a master in Chancery for those purposes.

The master, being attended by the parties or their agents, makes his report; and the cause again comes on in its turn to be heard upon further directions (as it is called), when the like practice prevails as at the hearing.

This is the form of the simplest suit in equity, and is sufficient to point out the successive steps necessary to be taken; but generally suits are of a far more complicated character. Many special applications to the court may become necessary at various stages before the cause is ready for hearing; and when reference is made to the master, the inquiries to be prosecuted before him may be entangled in the greatest confusion; and even when he has made his report, either party may except to it, and have his exceptions argued before the court. Also when the cause is heard on further directions, that is, further instructions given by the court to the master to whom the cause has been already referred, other references to the master may be found to be necessary, or may arise out of the circumstances stated in his report; the subject matter of the suit may be such as to prevent an immediate and final decree; a party may be entitled for life to the interest of money, and the persons to take after him may not be born or may be infants. In these and many other cases the court makes such decree as may be necessary, and retains the suit, giving liberty to any parties interested to apply to the court for directions as may become necessary from time to time. It is impossible here to give an adequate notion of the various and complicated operations performed by decrees, by which the interests and rights of all parties are settled, and the most embarrassed affairs are arranged. A very valuable collection of decrees has been published by Mr. Seton.

Those who wish for a more accurate knowledge of the proceedings in a suit in Chancery may consult Lord Redesdale's *Treatise on Pleading*; Beames *On Pleas*; and the various books on Chancery Practice.

The principal English treatises on Equity are those of Mr. Maddock and Mr. Fonblanque: the former treats of his subject under heads devoted to the several subject matters cognizable in courts of equity; the latter considers it with reference to the jurisdiction exercised by courts of law, as concurrent, assistant, exclusive. The American treatise of Mr. Justice Story unites these two modes.

The English Equity has some resemblance to the Roman Edictal Law, or Jus Prætorium or Honorarium, as it is often called. All the higher Roman magistrates (magistratus majores) had the Jus Edicendi or authority to promulgate Edicta. These magistratus majores were Consuls, Praetors, Curule Aediles, and Censors. By virtue of this power a Magistrate made Edicta or orders, either temporary and for particular occasions (edicta repentina); or upon entering on his office he promulgated rules or orders, which he would observe in the exercise of his office (edicta perpetua). These Edicta were written on a white tablet (album) in black letters; the headings or titles were in red: the Alba were placed in the Forum, in such a position that they could be read by a stander-by. Those Edicta which related to the administration of justice had an important effect on the Roman law; and especially the Praetoria Edicta and those of the Curule Aediles. That branch of law which was founded on the Praetorian Edicta was designated Jus Praetorium, or Honorarium, because the Praetor held one of these offices to which the term Honores was applied. The Edicta were only in force during the term of office of the Magistratus who promulgated them; but his successor adopted many or all of his predecessor's Edicta, and hence arose the expression of "transferred edicts" (tralaticia edicta); and thus in the later Republic the Edicta which had been long established began to exercise a great influence on the law, and particularly the forms of procedure. About the time of Cicero many distinguished jurists began to write treatises on the Edictum (libri ad edictum). Under the Emperors new Edicta were rarer, and

EQUITY [845] ESCHEAT.

in the third century of our aera they ceased. Under the Empire we first find the Edicta of the Praefectus Urbi mentioned; but these must be considered as founded on the Imperial authority (majestas principis), and to have resembled the Imperial Constitutions. Under the reign of Hadrian, a compilation was made by his authority of the Edictal rules by the distinguished jurist Salvius Julianus, in conjunction with Servius Cornelius, which is spoken of under the name of Edictum perpetuum. This Edictum was arranged under various heads or titles, such as those relating to Marriage, Tutores, Legata (legacies), and so on.

By the term Praetorian Edict the Romans meant the Edicts of the Praetor Urbanus, who was the chief personage employed in the higher administration of justice under the Republic. The Edicta which related to Peregrini (aliens) were so named after the Praetor Peregrinus; and other edicta were called Censoria, Consularia, Aedilicia, and so on. Sometimes an Edict of importance took its name from the Praetor who promulgated it, as Carbonianum Edictum. Sometimes the Honorariae actiones, those which the Praetor by his Edict permitted, were named in like manner from the Praetor who introduced them. Sometimes an Edict had its name from the matter to which it referred. The Romans generally cited the Edicta by parts, titles, chapters, or clauses of the Edictum Perpetuum by naming the initial words, as Unde Legitimi, and so on; sometimes they are cited by a reference to their contents. Examples of these modes of citing the Edictum occur in the titles of the forty-third book of the 'Digest.' (See the title 'Quorum Bonorum.') In our own law we refer to certain forms of proceedings and to certain actions in a like way, as when we say Quo Warranto, Quare Impedit, and speak of Qui tam actions.

The Jus Praetorium is defined by Papinian (*Dig.* i., tit. i. 7) as the law which the Praetors introduced for the purpose of aiding, supplying, or correcting the law (jus civile), with a view to the public interest. The edict is called by Marcianus "the living voice of the jus civile,"

that is, of the Roman law. (*Dig.* i., tit. i. 8.) The Praetorian Law, as thus formed, (Jus Praetorium) was a body of law which was distinguished by this name from the Jus Civile, or the strict law; the opposition resembled that of the English terms Equity and Law. In its complete and large sense Jus Civile Romanorum, or the Law of the Romans, of course comprehended the Jus Praetorium; but in its narrower sense Jus Civile was contrasted, as already explained, with the Jus Praetorium.

The origin of the Roman edictal Law is plainly to be traced to the imperfections of the old Jus Civile, and to the necessity of gradually modifying law and procedure according to the changing circumstances of the times. It was an easier method of doing this than by direct legislation. Numerous modern treatises contain a view of the origin and nature of the Roman Jus Praetorium, though on some points there is not complete uniformity of opinion.

(Böcking, *Institutionen*, vol. i.; Puchta, *Cursus der Institutionen*, vol. i. p. 293; Savigny, *Geschichte des Röm. Rechts*, vol. i.; Heffter, *Die Oeconomic des Edictes, Rhein. Mus. für Juris.* i. p. 51; E. Schrader, *Die Prätorischen Edicte der Römer*, 1815.)

ESCHEAT is from the Norman French *eschet*, which is from the word *eschier* or *eschoir*, 'to fall;' for an escheat is a casual profit, which comes to the lord of a fee.

An escheat may happen in two ways, as it is stated by the old law writers, *Per defectum sanguins*, for want of heirs, or *Per delictum tenentis*, for the crime of the tenant. There can only be an escheat of the whole fee; and this happens when the tenant of lands in fee simple dies intestate and without an heir: the lands, if freehold, escheat to the king, or other lord of the fee; if copyhold, to the lord of the manor. All such lands therefore either escheat to the king as the supreme lord, or to the intermediate lord, if there is one. Lands which have descended to the last tenant from a paternal or maternal ancestor, escheat, if there are no heirs on the part of that ancestor from whom the lands descended.

ESCHEAT. [846] ESQUIRE.

Since the 1st day of January, 1834, there can be no escheat on failure of the whole blood, wherever there are persons of the half-blood capable of inheriting under 3 & 4 Wm. IV. c. 106, § 9.

If a bastard dies intestate and without issue, his lands escheat to the lord of whom they are held [BASTARD, p. 330]. Escheats propter delictum may happen in consequence of a man being attainted for treason or felony, by which he becomes incapable of inheriting from any of his next of kin, or transmitting an inheritance to them. This is the consequence of Attainder and the legal corruption of blood. The 3 & 4 Wm. IV. c. 106, § 10, which is referred to under ATTAINDER, somewhat modifies the old law, so as to prevent escheat in some cases.

By the 4 & 5 Wm. IV. c. 23, no property vested in any trustee or mortgagee shall escheat or be forfeited by reason of the attainder or conviction for any offence of such trustee or mortgagee, except so far as such trustee or mortgagee may have a beneficial interest in the property.

In 1838 an act was passed (1 & 2 Vict. c. 69) for removing doubts which had arisen respecting the acts 1 Wm. IV. c. 60, and 4 Wm. IV. c. 23, with reference to mortgagees; and it enacts that these acts shall extend only to cases where any person seised of any land by way of mortgage shall have died without having been in possession of such land, or in receipt of the rents and profits, and the money due thereon shall have been paid to his executor, and the devisee or heir of such mortgagee shall be out of the jurisdiction of the Court of Chancery, or it shall be uncertain whether he be living or dead, or who are his heirs; or when such mortgagee, or devisee, or heir shall have died without an heir, or such devisee, &c., neglect or refuse to convey for twenty-eight days after tender of a deed. In any of these cases the court may direct any person to convey such land as directed by 1 Wm. IV. c. 60.

The words Escheat and Forfeiture are carelessly used even by law writers. Escheat arises solely because there are no heirs to take the land, for one or the other of the two reasons stated above. Forfeiture is a direct consequence of an illegal act: it is a punishment of feudal origin inflicted on a tenant who breaks his fealty (fidelity) to his lord. The doctrine of escheat seems to have been adopted in every civilized country to avoid the confusion which would otherwise arise from the circumstance of any property becoming common; and the sovereign power, or those who claim under it, are consequently the ultimate heirs to every inheritance to which no other title can be found.

ESCUAGE. [FEUDAL SYSTEM.]

ESQUIRE (from the French *écuier*, or shield-bearer) is the next title or dignity to that of knight. The esquire was the second in rank of the aspirants to chivalry, or knighthood, and had his name from carrying the shield of the knight, whose bachelor, or apprentice in arms, he was. The gradations of this service, or apprenticeship to arms, were page, esquire or bachelor, and knight, who, in his turn, after the formation of degrees of knighthood, was called a knight bachelor, as aspiring to the higher honours of chivalry. The esquire was a gentleman, and had the right of bearing arms on his escutcheon or shield: he had also the right of bearing a sword, which denoted nobility or chivalry, though it was not girded by the knightly belt; he had also a particular species of defensive armour which was distinguished from the full panoply of the knight. This is the esquire of chivalry, which order is only preserved in the almost obsolete esquires for the king's body, whom antiquaries have pronounced to be the king's esquires in chivalry (that is, his esquires, as being a knight), and in the esquires of knights of the Bath.

There was also another class, who may be called feudal esquires, and consisted of those tenants by knight's service who had a right to claim knighthood, but had never been dubbed. They were in Germany called *ritters*, or knights, but were distinguished from the actual knights, who were called dubbed knights, or *Ritter Geschlagen*, and had many of the privileges of knighthood. This distinction still exists in many of the countries which formed part of the German empire. In Hainault, Brabant, and other provinces of what was Austrian Flanders, the antient untitled nobility, or gentry as they are called in England, to this day are styled collectively the *Ordre Equestre,* or knightly order. It also existed in England until James the First had prostituted the honour of knighthood, for Camden frequently speaks of knightly families (*familias equestres,* or *familias ordinis equestris*), where the heads of them were not, at the time, actual knights. Writers on precedence make mention of esquires by creation, with investiture of a silver collar or chain of ss, and silver spurs: but these seem to have been only the insignia of the esquires for the king's body, which being preserved in a family as heir-looms, descended with the title of esquire to the eldest sons in succession. The sons of younger sons of dukes and marquesses, the younger sons of earls, viscounts, and barons, and their eldest sons, with the eldest sons of baronets, and of knights of all the orders, are all said to be esquires by birth, though their precedence, which differs widely, is regulated by the rank of their respective ancestors. Officers of the king's court and household, and of his navy and army, down to the captain inclusive, doctors of law, barristers, and physicians, are reputed esquires. A justice of the peace is only an esquire during the time that he is in the commission of the peace, but a sheriff of a county is an esquire for life. The general assumption of this title by those who are not, in strictness, entitled to it, has virtually destroyed it as a distinct title or dignity. It is now usual to address most people as esquires on the outside of a letter; but even in this practice and other cases, the title is not generally given to inferior tradesmen and shopkeepers. The heads of many old families are, however, still deemed esquires by prescription.

ESTABLISHED CHURCH. United Church of England and Ireland. [SCOTLAND, CHURCH OF.] The history of the Protestant Episcopal Church in England, now called the United Church of England and Ireland, commences in the reign of Henry VIII., when that king abjured the ecclesiastical supremacy of the Pope and declared himself head of the church.

[SUPREMACY.] The object of this notice is to show the nature of the connexion which exists between the united church of England and Ireland and the state. Whoever shall come to the possession of the crown of England shall join in communion with the church of England as by law established. (12 & 13 Wm. III., c. 2, § 3.) The Regency act, 3·& 4 Vict. c. 52, which appoints Prince Albert Regent of the United Kingdom in case of Her Majesty dying before her next lineal successor is eighteen years of age, provides that in case of his marrying a Roman Catholic the guardianship of the heir to the crown and regency should thenceforth cease.

At the coronation of the king or queen regnant of England, one of the archbishops or bishops is required by 1 Wm. III.,.c. 6, to administer an oath, that they will, to the utmost of their power, maintain the Protestant reformed church established by law, and will preserve unto the bishops and clergy of this realm, and to the churches committed to their charge, all such rights and privileges as by law do or shall appertain unto them or any of them. By 5 Anne c. 5, § 2, the king at his coronation is required to take and subscribe an oath to maintain and preserve inviolably the settlement of the church of England, and the doctrine, worship, discipline, and government thereof, as by law established.

The religious tenets of the United Church of England and Ireland, are contained in the Thirty-nine Articles; and the services of the church [FRANKALMOIGNE] are set forth in the Book of Common Prayer. The Thirty-nine Articles and the Rubric of the Book of Common Prayer, "being both of them established by act of parliament, are to be esteemed as part of the statute law." (Burn, Preface, *Ecc. Law.*) Articles of Religion were published by order of Henry VIII. in 1536. In 1552, Edward VI. promulgated Forty-two Articles which had been drawn up and signed by the Convocation. These Articles were set aside in the reign of Queen Mary. In 1562 Queen Elizabeth confirmed the Thirty-nine Articles which had been agreed upon by the Convocation.

They were published in Latin, but when they were revised in 1571 the Convocation signed an English as well as the Latin copy.

The act 13 Eliz. c. 12, requires that all persons who are admitted to holy orders, shall subscribe the Thirty-nine Articles.

The Thirty-nine Articles include some which are of a political character, or relate to the government of the Established Church. Article 39 recognizes the Queen's supremacy as head of the Church. Article 37 asserts the power of the Church to decree rites and ceremonies.

The promulgation of the Thirty-nine articles by Queen Elizabeth was accompanied by a 'Declaration' which set forth Her Majesty's powers as head of the Church, and defined the powers of the clergy in Convocation. The Queen declared herself "the supreme governor of the Church; and that if any difference arise about the external policy, concerning the injunctions, canons, and other constitutions whatsoever thereto belonging, the clergy in their Convocation is to order and settle them, having first obtained leave under our broad seal so to do; and we approving their said ordinances and constitutions, providing that none be made contrary to the laws and customs of the land." In like manner the clergy in convocation might settle matters of doctrine and discipline, which were, however, only to be authoritative after the queen had given her assent; and this being done, the declaration says: "we will not endure any varying or departing in the least degree." It is declared of the articles that "no man hereafter shall either print, or preach, to draw the article aside any way, but shall submit to it in the plain and full meaning thereof; and shall not put his own sense or comment to be the meaning of the article, but shall take it in the literal and grammatical sense;" also "That if any public reader in either of our Universities, or any head or master of a college, or any other person respectively in either of them, shall affix any new sense to any article, or shall publicly read, determine, or hold any public disputation, or suffer any such to be held either way, in either the Universities or colleges respectively; or if any divine in the Universities shall preach or print anything either way other than is already established in convocation with our royal assent, he or they, the offenders, shall be liable to our displeasure and the church's censure in our commission ecclesiastical, as well as any other; and we shall see there be due execution upon them."

The Constitutions and Canons Ecclesiastical were framed by the Convocation of the province of Canterbury in 1603, and assented to by King James (who confirmed them for the province of York also). These Canons maintain the king's supremacy over the Church of England, and subject to the punishment of excommunication whoever shall affirm the following things: "That the Church of England, by law established under the King's Majesty, is not a true and apostolical church, teaching and maintaining the doctrine of the apostles" (Canon 3). "That the form of God's worship in the Church of England, established by law and contained in the Book of Common Prayer and Administration of Sacraments, is a corrupt, superstitious or unlawful worship of God, or containeth anything that is repugnant to the Scriptures" (Canon 4). "That any of the Thirty-nine Articles are in any part superstitious or erroneous, or such as he may not with a good conscience subscribe to" (Canon 5). "That the rites and ceremonies of the Church of England are wicked, anti-christian or superstitious, or such as being commanded by lawful authority, men who are zealously and godly affected, may not with any good conscience approve them, use them, or as occasion requireth, subscribe unto them" (Canon 6). "That the government of the Church of England under his Majesty by archbishops, bishops, deans, archdeacons and the rest that bear office in the same, is anti-christian or repugnant to the word of God" (Canon 7). "That the form and manner of consecrating and ordering archbishops, bishops, &c., containeth anything in it that is repugnant to the word of God; or that they who are thus made are not truly either bishops, priests, &c., 'until they have some other calling to those divine offices.'" Schismatics were directed by the canons to be excommunicated. [NONCONFORMISTS.]

The reign of Queen Elizabeth is a most important period in the history of the Established Church. On the queen's accession an act was passed (stat. 1, Eliz. c. 1), which conferred on her the supremacy over the church as fully as it had been enjoyed by Henry VIII. and Edward VI. There is a clause in this act which empowered the queen to name and authorise by letters patent, as often as she shall think meet, for such time as she shall please, such person or persons, being natural born subjects, as she shall think fit, to execute all jurisdiction concerning spiritual matters within the realm, and to visit, reform, redress, order, correct, and amend all errors, heresies, schisms, abuses, offences, contempts, and enormities whatsoever, which by any ecclesiastical authority might be lawfully ordered or corrected. This was the origin of the Court of High Commission, which exercised a sort of jurisdiction equivalent to that of the Inquisition or Holy Office in some other countries One of the clauses for regulating the proceedings of this court, authorised the commissioners to make inquiry by juries and witnesses, "and all other means and ways which they could devise, which seems," observes Reeves (*Hist. English Law*), "to authorise every inquisitorial power—the rack, the torture, and imprisonment." By the same act the oath of supremacy was directed to be taken by all persons holding any office, spiritual or temporal, on pain of deprivation, and also by all persons taking degrees in the Universities, and by all persons wearing livery or doing homage: writing or preaching against the queen's supremacy was made punishable for the first offence with forfeiture of goods and one year's imprisonment, for the second with the pains of præmunire, for the third as high treason. In 1563, by an act (5 Eliz. c. 1) "For the assurance of the Queen's Majesty's royal power over all estates and subjects within her highness's dominions," the oath of supremacy was required also to be taken by all persons taking holy orders, by all schoolmasters, barristers, teachers, and attorneys, by all officers of any court of common law or other court whatever, and by all members of the House of Commons; and the refusing it, or upholding the jurisdiction of Rome, was made punishable with the pains of præmunire for the first offence, and for the second with those of high treason. The penal enactments against the Roman Catholics in this and other reigns are noticed under the head ROMAN CATHOLICS.

Another act (1 Eliz. c. 2) was passed on the accession of Elizabeth, entitled "An Act for the Uniformity of Common Prayer and Divine Service in the Church, and the Administration of the Sacraments." By this act, clergymen who refused to use King Edward's Book of Common Prayer were ordered to be punished, for the first offence, with forfeiture of one year's profit of their benefices and six months' imprisonment; for the second, with one year's imprisonment and deprivation; for the third, with deprivation and imprisonment for life: all persons, either speaking anything against the said service-book, or causing any other forms than those it prescribed to be used in any church or other place, in the performance of prayer or the administration of the sacraments, were subjected to a fine of 100 marks, and for the third offence to forfeiture of goods and imprisonment for life.

The course of legislation throughout the whole of Elizabeth's reign was designed to enforce religious uniformity, and it was consistent with this idea to punish nonconformity with various pains and penalties. These are specifically noticed under NONCONFORMISTS and ROMAN CATHOLICS. The same policy was pursued in the succeeding reign. Penal enactments were multiplied ; but they only hastened a crisis in which the fabric and polity of the Established Church were overthrown.

The disputes between King Charles I. and the parliament, which resulted in a civil war, brought on the overthrow of the Established Church, which occurred several years before Charles was beheaded, A.D. 1649. The Court of High Commission was abolished by statute (16

Car. I. c. 11), A.D. 1641. In 1642 bishops were deprived of their seats in parliament, and their lands were subsequently seized for the expenses of the civil war. Parliament passed numerous ordinances by which many hundreds of clergymen were turned out of their livings. The cathedral service was everywhere put down, and the clergy were left to read the Liturgy or not, as they pleased, and to take their own way in other things. Marriage was made a civil rite, and was performed by justices of the peace. In 1643 the Assembly of Divines was called together by an order of the two Houses of Parliament, to give their advice respecting a new system of ecclesiastical polity. [WESTMINSTER ASSEMBLY OF DIVINES.] The majority of the assembly were Presbyterians; and, in place of the suppressed Liturgy, they formed a Directory of Public Worship, which was established by an ordinance of the parliament on the 3rd of February, 1645. The assembly also laid down a Confession of Faith, which comprehended a Presbyterian form of ecclesiastical polity, and was at once received by the Scottish Church; but it was never distinctly sanctioned by the English legislature. On the 6th of June, 1646, an act was passed which partially established the Presbyterian form of church government in England; but this was confessedly done by way of experiment, as the preamble of the act expressly declares, "that if upon trial it was not found acceptable it should be reversed or amended;" and to this law a further effect was afterwards given by several additional ordinances of the House of Commons; till at last, in 1649, it was declared, without qualification, by the House, that Presbyterianism should be the established religion. The Presbyterian form of church government, however, never obtained more than a limited and imperfect establishment. The clergy were not exclusively Presbyterians: some benefices were retained by their old Episcopalian incumbents; a few were held by Independents; and some by persons belonging to the minor sects, which increased so abundantly at this time. At last, in March, 1653, Cromwell, by an ordinance of council, appointed a Board of Triers, as they were termed, in all thirty-eight in number, of whom part were Presbyterians, part Independents, and a few Baptists, to which was given, without any instructions or limitations whatever, the power of examining, approving, or rejecting all persons that might thereafter be presented, nominated, chosen, or appointed to any living in the church. This was tantamount to dividing the church livings amongst these different religious bodies; but the measure was designed by Cromwell to restrain the excessive liberty that had previously existed, when any one who chose might set up as a preacher, and so give himself a chance of obtaining a living in the church. The Board of Triers continued to sit and to exercise its functions at Whitehall, till a short time after the death of Cromwell.

As soon as the Restoration of Charles II. was effected in 1660, the work of reconstructing the Established Church was commenced. The convention parliament passed an act (12 Car. II. c. 17) " for the confirming and restoring of ministers;" and the next parliament, which met in May, 1661, repealed the act which disabled persons in holy orders from exercising any temporal jurisdiction or authority, the effect of which was to restore the bishops to their seats in the Upper House.

The Book of Common Prayer, which had been revised by a commission appointed by Charles II. after his restoration, was unanimously adopted by both houses of convocation, and having been approved of by the king, was transmitted to the House of Peers on the 24th of February, 1662, with a message from his majesty, recommending that the book so altered should be that "which in aud by the intended Act of Uniformity shall be appointed to be used by all that officiate in all cathedrals and collegiate churches and chapels, and in all parish churches of England and Wales, under such sanctions and penalties as the parliament shall think fit." The act here alluded to received the royal assent on the 19th of May (14 Car. II. c. 4), and was entitled "An Act for the Uniformity of Public Prayers and Administration of Sacraments, and other Rites and Ceremonies, and for establishing the form of making, ordaining, and consecrating Bishops, Priests, and Deacons, in the Church of England." It provided that all ministers should henceforth use the amended Book of Common Prayer, and that all persons who enjoyed any ecclesiastical benefice or promotion should publicly declare their assent to the use of the same, and their approval of everything contained in it: and, besides the oath of canonical obedience, the terms of conformity were now made to include the abjuration both of the solemn league and covenant, and of the lawfulness of taking up arms against the king, or any commissioned by him, on any pretence whatsoever.

During the reign of Charles II. many acts were passed for the punishment of persons who did not conform to the Established Church. Some of them were even more severe than those passed in the reigns of Elizabeth and James I. [NONCONFORMISTS.]

William III. was more tolerant than most of his subjects, and soon after his accession he proposed a repeal of the Test Act, the statute most obnoxious to the Nonconformists; but the House of Lords rejected a motion to this effect. Eventually, however, an act was passed (1 Wm. III. c. 18) which mitigated the enactments against all sects except the Roman Catholics. We must again refer to the article NONCONFORMISTS, for a brief notice of the Toleration Act, and some other statutes of a like character. Between this act of Wm. III. and the reign of Geo. IV. little was done to relieve Nonconformists or Roman Catholics from any of the penalties against those who did not conform to the doctrines and discipline of the Protestant Established Church of England and Ireland.

In 1828 an act was passed (9 Geo. IV. c. 17) "for repealing so much of several acts as imposes the necessity of receiving the sacrament of the Lord's Supper, as a qualification for certain offices and employments." This act, which repeals the Test Act, provides another security in lieu of the tests repealed: "And whereas the Protestant Episcopal Church of England and Ireland, and the Pro-

testant Presbyterian Church of Scotland, and the doctrine, discipline, and government thereof respectively, are by the laws of this realm severally established, permanently and inviolably: and whereas it is just and fitting, that on the repeal of such parts of the said acts as impose the necessity of taking the sacrament of the Lord's Supper, according to the rite or usage of the Church of England, as a qualification for office, a declaration to the following effect should be substituted in lieu thereof, it is therefore enacted, that every person who shall hereafter be placed, elected, or chosen in or to the office of mayor, alderman, recorder, bailiff, town clerk, or common councilman, or in or to any office of magistracy, or place, trust, or employment relating to the government of any city, corporation, borough, or cinque port within England and Wales, or the town of Berwick-upon-Tweed, shall within one calendar month next before or upon his admission into any of the aforesaid offices or trusts, make and subscribe the declaration following:—'I, A. B., do solemnly and sincerely, in the presence of God, profess, testify, and declare, upon the true faith of a Christian, that I will never exercise any power, authority, or influence which I may possess, by virtue of the office ————————, to injure or weaken the Protestant Church as it is by law established in England, or to disturb the said church, or the bishops and clergy of the said church, in the possession of any rights or privileges to which such church, or the said bishops and clergy, are or may be by law entitled.'" The 7th section of the act provides that no naval officer below the rank of rear-admiral, and no military officer below the rank of major-general in the army, or colonel in the militia, shall be required to make or subscribe the above declaration; and no commissioner of customs, excise, stamps, and taxes, or any person holding any of the offices concerned in the collection, management, or receipt of the revenues which are subject to the said commissioners, or any persons subject to the authority of the postmaster general, shall be required to make or describe such declaration.

In 1829, when the Roman Catholic Relief Act (10 Geo. IV. c. 7) was passed, a provision was made for the security of the Established Church; and the oath to be taken by Roman Catholic peers on taking their seat in the House of Lords, and Roman Catholic persons upon taking their seat as members of the House of Commons, contains the following pledge, which is sworn to "on the true faith of a Christian:" "I do hereby disclaim, disavow, and solemnly abjure any intention to subvert the present Church Establishment as settled by law within this realm." Other acts have also been passed which have further departed from the old principle of requiring uniformity of religious faith. The act 6 & 7 Wm. IV. c. 85, enables persons to be married according to the rites of their own sect, instead of those of the Established Church only; and the same act permits the marriage contract to be made by a merely civil ceremony, in which respect the law now resembles in effect that which was established during the Commonwealth. In the act 3 & 4 Vict c. 72, which is an act relating to marriages, the recent acts on the same subject are alluded as being framed with the view of enabling marriage to be "solemnized according to the form, rite, or ceremony the parties see fit to adopt." The act for the registration of births, marriages, and deaths renders baptism unnecessary for civil purposes, and establishes a lay department for the registration of births, marriages, and deaths. The act 3 & 4 Vict. c. 92, enabled courts of justice to admit non-parochial registers as evidence of births or baptisms, deaths or burials, and marriages. In England the chaplains of gaols must be clergymen of the Church of England, but in Ireland there may be appointed for each union workhouse three chaplains, one Roman Catholic, one of the Established Church, and one Protestant dissenter.

Rates are levied in England and Wales called CHURCH RATES, which Nonconformists are required to pay as well as churchmen. In Ireland the churches are kept in repair out of funds in the hands of the Ecclesiastical Commissioners, which are derived from extinguished sees and other sources.

The principle of the state maintaining an exclusive system of education in accordance with the principles and doctrines of the Established Church has been partially abandoned both in England and Ireland. The parliamentary grants for education are enjoyed by dissenters as well as churchmen. In Ireland the state supports schools which are established on the plan of not permitting the inculcation of the peculiar doctrines of any religious body as a part of the regular course of teaching, but religious instruction is given by the ministers of different religious bodies to the scholars of each denomination separately. In the government plan for founding provincial colleges in Ireland the same principle has been adopted. Lastly, parliament has annually voted funds for the maintenance of an institution (Maynooth) for the education of Roman Catholic priests; and in 1845 this annual vote was converted into a fixed annual payment.

The King and Queen of England must be members of the Established Church, and may not marry a Roman Catholic; but the only other offices from which Roman Catholics are now excluded are the offices of guardians and justices of the United Kingdom, or Regent of the same, the office of Lord High Chancellor of Great Britain or Ireland, the Lord Lieutenant of Ireland, and the office of High Commissioner to the General Assembly of the Church of Scotland. With these exceptions the members of the cabinet council, privy councillors, the judges and magistrates, all offices in the state and in the army and navy, may be filled by Roman Catholics or dissenters from the Established Church. The repeal of the Corporation and Test Acts opened the Municipal Corporations to Roman Catholics and Dissenters. Jews are the only class of persons who are excluded from the Houses of Lords and Commons, and from municipal corporations; but a bill under the superintendence of the government is at present passing through parliament which contains a form of oath to be taken by Jews who are elected to municipal offices in corporate boroughs. There are at present instances of persons of the Jewish religion who fill the office of high sheriff, and are in the commission of the peace. [JEWS.]

The connection between the Church and State has been brought within comparatively narrow limits by the course of recent legislation. The Established Church is in possession of revenues from land, a large part of which are enjoyed under the old law of Frankalmoigne. [FRANKALMOIGNE.] The clergy also receive certain customary payments for the performance of marriages, christenings, and interments. Its form of polity is also guaranteed by the State. Parliament may alter the distribution of the property of the Church, as it has recently done by uniting and suppressing bishoprics, creating new sees, abolishing sinecures, and disposing of some parts of the revenues of the church for other church purposes [ECCLESIASTICAL COMMISSIONERS; BISHOPRIC]; but it has not yet sanctioned the diversion of the revenues of the Church to other purposes, though it has been on the point of doing so in the case of the revenues of the Established Church in Ireland.

On the 25th of April, 1836, Lord Morpeth, who was then Secretary for Ireland, brought in a measure which contained a clause known as the "Appropriation Clause," by which it was intended. after supplying the legitimate wants of the Irish Church, to apply 97,612*l*. out of the revenues of the Church to the moral and religious instruction of the Irish people. The principle of the appropriation clause was affirmed by the House of Commons after three nights' discussion, by a majority of 300 to 261. In the House of Lords the clause was rejected by 138 against 47.

The clergy of the Established Church constitute a distinct order. [CLERGY.] No person can be ordained to holy orders who does not subscribe to the Liturgy and the Thirty-nine Articles. which latter comprehend his assent to the doctrine of the king's supremacy. No person can hold any benefice without taking the oath of canonical obedience to the bishop. The constitution of the Universities of Oxford, Cambridge, Durham and Trinity College, Dublin, is such as to exclude persons who do not belong to the Established Church from a full participation in the advantages of these endowed seats of learning. [UNIVERSITY.]

The revenues of the Established Church in England and Wales, as returned to the Ecclesiastical Commissioners in 1831, were as follows.

	Gross. £	Net. £
Archbishops and bishops	181,631	160,292
Cathedral and collegiate churches and ecclesiastical corporations aggregate	284,241	208,289
Prebends and other preferments in cathedral and collegiate churches	54,094	44,705
Renewals of leases (average of three years)	21,760	21,760
Benefices* (10,718)	3,251,159	3,055,451
	£3,792,885	3,490,497

The following is an account of all payments from the public monies to the Established Church of England and Ireland, or to the commissioners of Queen Anne's Bounty, from 1801 to 1840, both inclusive:—

ENGLAND. £
Commissioners for building new churches . . 1,500,000
Grants from 1809 to 1820 inclusive, to governors of Queen Anne's Bounty for poor clergy . . . 1,000,000
Drawback on materials used in building new churches . 153,000

IRELAND.
Grants for building churches from 1801 to 1820 . . 749,551
Grants for Protestant charter-schools from 1801 to 1829 741,048
Grant for relief of tithe arrears 1,000,000

Total . . £5,193,599

In reference to the history of the Established Church in Ireland, it will be sufficient here to quote the fifth article of the act for the Union of Great Britain with Ireland (40 Geo. III. c. 67), passed July 2nd, 1800, which enacts, "That it be the

---
* See the article Benefice, pp. 854-5-6-7.

fifth article of union, that the Churches of England and Ireland, as now by law established, be united into one Protestant Episcopal Church, to be called the United Church of England and Ireland; and that the doctrine, worship, discipline, and government of the said united church shall be and shall remain in full force for ever, as the same are now by law established for the church of England; and that the continuance and preservation of the said united church, as the established church of England and Ireland, shall be deemed and taken to be an essential and fundamental part of the union."

There is this, amongst other peculiarities in the Established Church in Ireland, that it is the church of only about a tenth part of the population. When a special census of the population was taken in 1834, with the object of ascertaining the religious persuasion of the people, it was found that out of a total population of 7,954,760 there were—

		Proportion per cent.
Roman Catholics	6,436,060	80·9
Established Church	853,160	10·7
Presbyterians	643,658	8·4
Other Dissenters	21,882	·2

In England and Wales, on the contrary, the majority of the population belong to the Established Church, and it is not placed in that anomalous position which the church occupies in Ireland. There is no authentic account of the number of persons who belong to the Established Church in England and Wales, and the number of marriages which are celebrated at dissenting places of worship is not an index of the numbers of the population who are dissenters; but it is indicative of the fact that the church has a considerable hold on the respect of a large mass even of those who do not belong to it, while its rites and ceremonies and doctrines contain so little to repulse men who are not churchmen, that we find in 1842, out of 118,825 marriages, only 6200 (representing a population of 806,000, out of a total of nearly sixteen millions) were celebrated in registered places of worship, under the act of the 6 & 7 Wm. IV. c. 86; and in only 2357 cases was the ceremony celebrated without any religious service. The number of dissenting places of worship registered pursuant to 6 & 7 Wm. IV. is 2232, while the number of marriages at each place does not on an average amount to three in the course of a year.

It is stated (*App. to First Report of the Commissioners of Public Instruction, Ireland*, 1834) that of the 1387 benefices in Ireland there were 41 which did not contain any Protestants; 20 where there were less than or not more than 5; in 23 the number was under 10; in 31 under 15; in 23 under 20; and in 27 benefices the number of Protestants was not above 25. There were 425 benefices in Ireland in which the number of Protestants was below 100. There were 157 benefices in which the incumbent was non-resident, and no service was performed. The number of parishes or ecclesiastical districts is 2468, and of this number 2351 possess a provision for the cure of souls; but the total number of benefices is only 1387, as before mentioned, of which 908 are single parishes, and 479 are unions of two or more parishes. Parishes are permanently united by act of Parliament, by act of Council, or by prescription, and they may be temporarily united by the authority of the bishop of the diocese. Latterly, perpetual curates, a new order in the Irish Church, have been appointed to a portion of a parish especially allotted to them, the tithe of which they receive and are not subject to the incumbent of the remaining portion of the parish, but hold their situations for life.

The episcopal revenues in Ireland are chiefly derived from lands let upon lease for twenty-one years, and renewed from time to time at the original rent, on payment of a fine on renewal, which fluctuates according to the altered value of the land. In 1831 the income of the episcopal establishment was 151,128*l*. This amount will in the course of a short time be reduced to 82,953*l*., under the operation of the Church Temporalities Act [BISHOP; ECCLESIASTICAL COMMISSIONERS]; and the surplus of 68,175*l*. will be applied to the purposes of ecclesiastical discipline and education. Some of the leases belonging to the suppressed sees in Ireland have been converted into perpetuities by the Irish ecclesiastical commissioners under the powers of the Church Temporalities Act, and have consequently been in so far alienated. The beneficed clergy derive their income chiefly from tithes, which have been placed on a better footing within the last few years. Glebe-houses are attached to 851 benefices. They have been built partly by donations and partly by loans from the Board of First-Fruits, and partly at the cost of the incumbent, repayable by instalments from his successors. The total quantity of glebe-land attached to benefices is 91,137 acres, but it is very irregularly distributed, and the proportion to each benefice is considerably greater in the province of Armagh than in other parts of Ireland. In cities and towns the parochial clergy are paid by an assessment called minister's money, which is levied on every house of a certain value. Some of these particulars are taken from Dr. Phillimore's edition of Burn's ' Ecclesiastical Law.'

By Lord Morpeth's (government) bill, introduced in 1836, and which was thrown out on the question of appropriation, as already stated, it was proposed to reduce the number of benefices in Ireland to 1250, and to give each incumbent an average income of 295l., which would have been a higher average income than the incumbents enjoy in England and Wales. A table, which shows the number of benefices at different rates of income, as arranged under the Church Temporalities Act, will be found at p. 353, article BENEFICE. The extensive powers which the Irish ecclesiastical commissioners possess in relation to benefices are noticed in BENEFICE, p. 353.

The annual revenue of the Established Church in Ireland, during the three years ending 1831, was returned to parliament as follows:—

Archbishops and bishops . £151,128
Deans and Chapters . 1,043
Economy estates of cathedrals 11,056
Other subordinate corporations 10,526
Dignities (not episcopal) and prebends without cure of souls 34,482
Glebe-lands . . . 92,000
─────
Carried forward . 300,235

Brought forward . £300,235
Tithes 555,000
Ministers' money . . . 10,300
─────
£865,535

The incomes of the parochial clergy in Ireland are subject to some deductions, as payments towards diocesan and parochial schools, repairs of certain parts of churches, and repairs of glebe-houses. Diocesan schools ought to be maintained by annual contributions from the bishop and the beneficed clergy; but the levy drawn from this source is little more than nominal. The parochial schools are supposed to be maintained by an annual stipend from the incumbent, which is estimated by custom at two pounds per annum: in many cases this has not been paid. (Phillimore's Burn, vol. i. p 415.) The First-Fruits have been abolished by recent acts. They were designed to be the amount of the first year's income of every benefice, which was to be employed in the building and repairing of churches and glebe-houses, and the purchase of glebe-land; but the assessment was made on the value of benefices in the reigns of Henry VIII., Elizabeth, and James I., and yielded only a trifling sum.

In the British colonies the Episcopal Church is not established on an exclusive footing: other churches are supported or aided out of the public funds either furnished by the colony or the mother country. Some of the bishoprics in the colonies have been created by act of parliament, and their incomes are derived from the public revenues; but other colonial bishops are consecrated by the heads of the church, and appointed by them to colonial dioceses simply with the sanction of the government for the time.

The expression—Church and State, which is in common use, is apt to mislead. There was a time when the connection of Church and State in England was that which it is not now. At present the relationship of the State to the Established Church of England and Ireland is this. The King is the head of the United Church of England and Ireland,— a notion which is expressed by the term the King's Supremacy. A compound body makes laws for the British Empire,

—the King, the House of Lords, and the House of Commons; and of these three members the two last have no connection as legislative bodies with the Established Church, except so far as the bishops of England and Wales, and certain bishops of Ireland who sit in a certain rotation, have seats in the House of Lords. But the other members of the House of Lords and all the members of the House of Commons may profess any form of Christianity that they please. The property of the Church (a phrase also apt to mislead) is either enjoyed by ecclesiastical bodies, as deans and chapters, or collegiate churches, or it is enjoyed by individuals, as archbishops, bishops, rectors, and vicars. The ecclesiastical patronage, or the right to name those persons who shall enjoy the emolument arising from this property, is either in the Crown, that is, it is exercised by the Lord Chancellor in some cases, and in other cases by the prime minister for the time; or it is vested in private individuals. The Crown, that is, the minister, appoints to bishoprics and other ecclesiastical dignities. The Lord Chancellor has the patronage of many benefices at his disposal; and that of a very large number is in the hands of private individuals. The legislature has of late years interfered with the emoluments attached to bishoprics and ecclesiastical corporations, so as to make a different distribution of the revenues, but no emoluments have been applied to other purposes than purposes ecclesiastical. The legislature has not interfered with the revenues appropriated to benefices which are in the gift of the crown, at least not by any general measure, nor to those that are in the gift of private individuals. Benefices which belong to private individuals are appropriated to ecclesiastical purposes, and certain services [FRANKALMOIGNE] must be performed by those ecclesiastics who are nominated to such benefices. The right to present to vacant benefices is a kind of property; and benefices are things that may be bought and sold [ADVOWSONS], and have so far the characteristics of other private property, from which they differ only in this, that the annual proceeds of such benefices can only be enjoyed by ecclesiastical persons, who must perform the services of the Established Church. Tithes are due both to spiritual persons and in many cases to laymen; and accordingly they are property. Those tithes, which are due to laymen or civil corporations, are exactly on the footing of any other private property, and so are those which are due to spiritual persons, except that ecclesiastical services must be rendered for them, and they are set apart for the support of ecclesiastics. There can be no interference with this kind of property which would not justify any like interference with the property which Roman Catholics and other nonconformists hold for religious purposes. Tithes are often found to be an injurious charge upon lands; but those who own tithes own them by as good a title as he who owns the land which is charged with them; and under several recent acts provision is now made for commuting tithes into money payments. If Church Rates were abolished, there would be no reason for any member of the community, whether of the Established Church or not, to complain of the Established Church in England and Wales as a grievance, so far as concerns the property from which the revenues of ecclesiastical persons in the Church of England are derived. The case of the Church of Ireland is peculiar, and it is stated in this article.

If persons are allowed to form associations for the purposes of religion, which must be allowed in all states where every form of Christianity is allowed to be professed, they must also be allowed to hold property for religious purposes, unless the state pays all the preachers of religion. Whatever restraints, if any, should be put on the acquisition or holding of property for religious purposes, ought to be put on all religious bodies alike. That part of the land in England and Wales which is appropriated to the revenues of those ecclesiastics who are appointed by the Crown, must be considered as so much property held by the Crown for the purposes of the Church of England; and those benefices to which private individuals appoint must be considered as so much perty held by pri-

ESTATE. [857] ESTATE

vate persons for the same purposes. Any alteration in either of these two kinds of property in England and Wales, by which any part of it would be applied to other purposes than those to which it is at present applied, does not seem to be recommended by any measure of policy at present; and if it were, the same reasons would equally apply to all other property which is held by any person or body of persons in England and Wales, for the purposes of any other form of religion.

ESTATE. An estate signifies that title or interest which a man has in lands, tenements, hereditaments, or other property. It is either Real Estate, which comprises lands, tenements, and hereditaments held or enjoyed for an estate of freehold; or Personal Estate, which comprises interests for terms of years in lands, tenements, and hereditaments, and property of every other description. Personal Estate [CHATTELS] goes to the executors, and is liable for payment of debts before Real Estate.

This is the legal signification of Estate, which, as already shown, is not a piece of land or other property, but signifies the relationship of ownership between a man and property. The word was also used in former times to signify men's station (status) or condition in life. It was also used, and is still sometimes used, to signify a class or order in a state.

Real Estate may be considered under three heads:—(1) the quantity of estate, i. e. the amount of interest in the owner; (2) the time when that interest is to commence; and (3) the quality of estate, or the mode in which it is to be enjoyed.

1. All real estates not being of copyhold tenure [COPYHOLD], or what are called customary freeholds, are either of Freehold or less than Freehold. Freeholds may be divided into two kinds; freeholds of inheritance, and freeholds not of inheritance. Freeholds of inheritance admit of a further subdivision, into inheritances absolute, called fees simple, and inheritances limited, called qualified or base fees, and fees conditional. A freehold of inheritance absolute or Fee Simple is the largest estate which a man can have: the owner may freely dispose of it to whom he pleases in his lifetime by deed or by will, and if he dies without making any disposition, it descends to his heir. [DESCENT.]

A qualified or Base Fee has some qualification or limit annexed, which may determine the estate, as in the instance of a grant to A and his heirs *tenants of the manor of Dale*. Whenever A or his heirs cease to be tenants of that manor, their estate is determined, that is, is at an end, though during its continuance the proprietor has the same rights as if he were absolute tenant in fee simple.

A Conditional Fee at common law was a fee restrained to some particular heirs exclusive of others, as to a man and the heirs male of his body, by which limitation his lineal heirs female and collaterals were excluded; and this is the origin of Estates Tail. It was held that if the donee, in the case supposed, had no heirs male of his body, or if, after a male child was born, no alienation were made, the land should revert to the donor on the failure of heirs male of the donee's body: in fact, for all purposes of alienation it was a fee simple, on condition that the donee had male issue. The nobility, however, being anxious to preserve their estates in their own families, procured the Statute of Westminster the Second, 13 Ed. I. c. 1, commonly called Statute de Donis Conditionalibus, to be made, which enacted that the will of the donor should be observed, and that the land should go to the heirs specified, if there were any, or if none, should revert to the donor. Thus the donor acquired an estate in reversion. which could only be allowed, consistently with the nature of estates in reversion, by considering the conditional fee to be changed into a limited, or, as it is called in technical language, a particular estate. This kind of estate was called an estate *tail*, from the word *talliare*, to cut, being as it were a portion cut out of the whole fee. Means were soon however discovered by the ingenuity of the lawyers to enable the donee and his heirs of the specified description to cut off the Entail, as it was called.

A Freehold, not of inheritance, is an estate which the owner has for his own life only, or the life of some other person, or until the happening of some uncertain event. The following are instances :— a gift to A until B returns from Rome; but if the gift had been to A and his heirs until B returns from Rome, the estate would have been a qualified or base fee; and if B had died without returning from Rome, would have become a fee simple absolute. Some freeholds not of inheritance, arise from operation of law, as tenant in tail after possibility of issue extinct, which is where an estate is limited to A and the heirs of his body to be begotten on the body of B his wife, which is called an estate tail special, as distinguished from an estate tail general, that is, to A and the heirs of his body, without specifying the woman from whom they must spring. If B dies without children, A is no longer tenant in tail, but tenant in tail after possibility of issue extinct, and, as to the duration of his estate, he is simple tenant for life. As to tenant by courtesy and tenant in dower, see COURTESY and DOWER.

Of estates less than freehold there are three kinds—estates for years, at will, and by sufferance. An estate for years (which includes an estate from year to year) is personal property, and, like other chattels [CHATTELS], upon the death of the owner, without having disposed of it in his lifetime, devolves upon his executors or administrators. An estate at Will arises where a man lets lands to another expressly at the will of both parties, or without limiting any certain estate; either party may put an end to the tenancy, though, for the sake of general convenience, the courts as far as possible consider them as tenancies from year to year, for the purpose of rendering a six months' notice necessary to their determination. An estate by Sufferance arises where a tenant, who has entered by lawful title, continues in possession after his interest has determined: this estate may be put an end to at any time by the lawful owner, though, after acceptance of rent, the law would consider it as a tenancy from year to year, as in the case of a tenancy at will.

All these estates, real and personal, freehold or less than freehold, freeholds of inheritance or not of inheritance, may become subject to another qualification, and be called estates upon condition, being such whose existence depends upon the happening or not happening of some uncertain event whereby the estate may be either originally created or enlarged, or finally defeated.

2 Estates are either in possession or in expectancy.

An estate in possession requires no explanation here. Estates in expectancy involve some of the nicest and most abstruse learning in English law : they are divided into estates in remainder and reversion, and by executory devise or bequest; and again, remainders are divided into estates in remainder vested or contingent. An executory devise or bequest is such a limitation of a future estate or interest in lands or chattels as the law admits in the case of a will, though contrary to the rules of limitation in conveyance by deed.

3. Estates may be enjoyed in four ways; in severalty, in joint tenancy, in coparcenary, and in common.

An estate in severalty is when one tenant holds it in his own right without any other person being joined with him.

An estate in joint tenancy is when an estate is granted to two or more persons at the same time, in which case they are joint tenants, unless the words of the grant expressly exclude such construction; they have unity of interest, of title, of time of vesting, and of possession, and upon the decease of one, his whole interest, unless disposed of by him in his lifetime, remains to the survivor or survivors.

An estate in coparcenary is when an estate of inheritance descends from the ancestor to two or more persons, who are called parceners, and amongst parceners there is no survivorship. If a man dies seized of an estate of inheritance in land, and have no male heir, it descends to the female heir, and if there is more than one of them in the same degree of kin, it descends to them in equal shares, and they are called parceners or coparceners.

An estate in common is when two or more persons hold property, by distinct titles and for different interests, but by unity of possession.

All these three last-mentioned modes of joint and undivided possession may be put an end to by the parties interested, either by certain modes of conveyance or by partition.

Estates are also Legal or Equitable. It is a legal estate when the owner is in the actual seisin or possession, and also entitled to the beneficial interest himself, or in trust for some other person. An Equitable estate is when some other person, not the person who is the actual and legal owner, is entitled to the beneficial interest of the property of which that other is in possession. The power of the beneficial owner over his equitable estate is as complete as if he were possessed of the legal estate.

EVIDENCE. Legal evidence denotes the means by which facts are ascertained for judicial purposes. The practical importance of the subject is obvious from this definition; and it has accordingly not only attracted much attention from judicial writers, but has formed a prominent part of the jurisprudence of most civilised countries, though the particular rules of evidence have been different in different systems of law. The Roman law contains (so far as we now know it) few regulations respecting evidence, the whole subject being comprised in one short chapter of the Digest, which lays down several positive rules for the exclusion of witnesses within prescribed degrees of consanguinity to the litigant parties. In the common law of England, where facts are ascertained by juries, the body of rules and restrictions denominated the law of evidence has been gradually established within the last two centuries. Previously to that time, in the infancy of the trial by jury, as we understand that institution, the only positive rules respecting evidence were those which related to the two witnesses in treason required by statutes passed in the reign of Edward VI. This gradual development of restrictions upon the admission of testimony seems to show that, in this country at least, the tendency has been to contract and not to enlarge (as some writers have supposed) the rules of judicial evidence. The accounts of our earlier judicial proceedings contained in the state trials sufficiently prove that it was the practice formerly to admit without scruple or question every species of testimony; whereas the present law of evidence is almost wholly composed of restrictive rules.

In giving a compendious view of the principles of the English law of evidence (which are the same at equity as at common law, and in criminal and civil proceedings) it is proposed—1. To enumerate the limitations which it prescribes to the competency of witnesses; 2. To give a brief summary of the principal rules by which the reception of oral evidence is governed; and 3. To state the principal rules which relate to written evidence.

1. *Of the competency of witnesses.*—The general rule of English law upon this subject is, that all persons may be witnesses in courts of justice who have sufficient understanding to comprehend the subject of their testimony, and sufficient religious principle to ensure a right sense of the obligation of an oath to speak the truth. Thus very young children are admissible as witnesses, if they have a competent knowledge of the nature of an oath, and a religious apprehension of the consequences of falsehood. All testimony, by the law of England, must be given under the sanction of an oath, or affirmation in the case of Quakers and Moravians; but the form of the oath is immaterial, and nothing is required beyond a persuasion upon the mind of the witness that in swearing to the truth of what he states he is appealing to a Divine Being who will punish him for falsehood. A Christian is sworn upon the Gospels; a Jew, upon the Old Testament; and a Mohammedan or other person not a Christian, in such form as he considers binding. [OATH.]

To the general rule of the admissibility of all persons of sufficient intellect and religious belief there are several important exceptions. In the first place, a husband cannot be a witness for or against his wife, nor a wife for or against her husband; a rule which is said to arise from the identity of interest subsisting in such a connexion. However, in criminal prosecutions founded upon personal violence committed by either of these parties upon the other, such testimony is admitted upon the ground of necessity. Secondly, in actions at the common law, a party to the suit cannot be examined as a witness; but in courts of equity defendants in a cause may be made witnesses upon a special application for that purpose; and in those courts, if a plaintiff consents to be examined as a witness his evidence may be admitted. Thirdly, a person cannot be a witness who has been convicted of treason or felony, or of any offence which involves the *crimen falsi* (such as perjury or cheating), or which is liable to a punishment which the law considers infamous, as whipping, branding, or the pillory. This principle of exclusion, which is derived from the Roman law (*Digest* ii., tit. " De Testibus"), is now of little practical importance, as the recent statutes have enacted that a pardon in felons, or the actual endurance of the punishment of felony or misdemeanour, excepting perjury or subornation of perjury, shall have the effect of restoring the competency of the party as a witness. Fourthly, the law of England excludes the evidence of those who have a direct interest in the result of the proceedings in which they are called to testify. The indefinite state of the rule respecting the nature of the disqualifying interest led to much perplexity in its practical application. These rules are, however, now altered by a recent act, which will presently be mentioned.

The nature of the interest which disqualified a witness was this: either he must be directly and immediately benefited by a result of the proceeding favourable to the party who called him, by exonerating himself from a liability to costs, or to some process founded upon the decision of the cause in which he was called to testify; or he must be in such a situation as to be able to avail himself of the decision of the cause, by giving it in evidence in support of his own interest in some future litigation. With the view of removing the practical difficulties arising from the rule as to a witness being able to avail himself of the decision of the cause, by giving it in evidence in support of his own interest in some future litigation, it was enacted by the stat. 3 & 4 Will. IV. c. 42. § 26, that "if any witness shall be objected to as incompetent, on the ground that the verdict or judgment in the action on which it shall be proposed to examine him would be admissible in evidence for or against him, such witness shall nevertheless be examined; but in that case a verdict or judgment in that action in favour of the party on whose behalf he shall have been examined, shall not be admissible in evidence *for* him; nor shall a verdict or judgment against the party on whose behalf he shall have been examined be admissible in evidence *against* him. By the 27th section, it was enacted that the name of every witness objected to as incompetent, on the ground that the verdict or judgment in the cause in which he is examined would be admissible in evidence for or against him, shall, at this trial, be indorsed on the record on which the trial shall be had, together with the name of the party on whose behalf he was examined, and shall be afterwards entered on the record of the judgment; such indorsement or entry to be sufficient evidence that such witness was examined in any subsequent proceeding in which the verdict or judgment shall be offered in evidence. The act 6 & 7 Vict. c. 85, entitled ' An Act for improving the Law of Evidence,' enacts, " That no person offered as a witness shall hereafter be excluded by reason of incapacity from crime or interest from giving evidence, either in person or by deposition, according to the practice of the court, on the trial of any issue joined, or of any matter or question or on any inquiry arising in any suit, action, or proceeding, civil or criminal, in any court, or before any judge, jury, sheriff, coroner, magistrate, officer, or person having, by law or by consent of parties, authority to hear, receive, and examine evidence; but that every person so offered may and shall be admitted to give evidence on oath, or solemn affirmation in those cases wherein affirmation is by law receivable, notwithstanding that such person may or shall have an interest in the matter in question, or in the event of the trial of any issue, matter, question, or injury, or of the suit action, or proceeding in which he is offered as a witness, and notwithstanding that such person offered as a witness may have been previously convicted of any crime or offence: provided that this act shall not render competent any party to any suit, action, or proceeding individually named in the record, or any lessor of the plaintiff, or tenant of premises sought to be recovered in ejectment, or the landlord or other person in whose right any defendant in replevin may make cognizance, or any person in whose immediate and individual behalf any action may be brought or defended, either wholly or in part, of the husband or wife of such persons respectively; provided also, that this act shall not repeal any provision in a certain act passed in the session of parliament holden in the seventh year of the reign of his late majesty and in the first year of the reign of her present majesty, intituled 'An Act for the amendment of the Laws with respect to Wills:' provided that in courts of equity any defendant to any cause pending in any such court may be examined as a witness on the behalf of the plaintiff or of any co-defendant in any such cause, saving just exceptions; and that any interest which such defendant so to be examined may have in the matters or any of the matters in question in the cause shall not be deemed a just exception to the testimony of such defendant, but shall only be considered as affecting or tending to affect the credit of such defendant as a witness." This act does not extend to Scotland.

11. *The principal general rules by which the reception of oral evidence is regulated.* —The first general rule (which applies equally to written as to oral testimony) is that all evidence produced must be relevant to the point at issue between the parties. The object of special pleading by the common law is to reduce controversies between parties to particular issues, or propositions of fact affirmed by one and denied by the other, which are to be decided by the jury; and the rule of evidence, that the proofs in the cause must be strictly confined to these issues, is founded upon obvious reasons of justice as well as convenience. Secondly, the affirmative of every issue is to be proved; that is, the party who asserts the affirmative of a proposition must prove it. Thirdly, in proving a fact, the best evidence of it must be given of which the nature of the thing is capable. Thus, a party is not permitted to prove the contents of a deed by a copy, and still less by oral testimony, where the deed itself may be produced; nor to prove the execution of a deed by any other person than a subscribing witness, when he is living and producible. This rule is justified by the presumption which the offer of secondary evidence raises, that the production of the best evidence might have prejudiced the party in whose power it is, had he produced it. This rule is not, however, to be understood as requiring that all the evidence which can be given upon the fact in dispute should be produced; as, for instance, if there are several attesting witnesses to a deed or other contract, it is not necessary that more than one should be called. Fourthly, hearsay testimony, which is a statement on oath of what an absent person has said respecting a fact to be proved, is, in general, excluded both on the ground that the witness to the actual fact does not declare his knowledge upon oath, and also because he is absent from the cross-examination of the party who is to be affected by what he states. To this rule, however, there are the following exceptions:—1. The declarations of persons who are in imminent danger and under the apprehension of immediate death, and who are therefore considered to be speaking under as powerful a religious sanction as the obligation of an oath; 2. The declarations of deceased persons, and made against their interest; as, for instance, charging themselves with the receipt of money on account of third persons, or acknowledging the payment of money due to themselves; 3. The declaration of deceased persons respecting rights of a public nature, such as the boundaries or general customs of a manor or district; 4. The declarations of deceased persons on questions of pedigree, or family occurrences of ancient date before the memory of living witnesses, such as births, deaths, or marriages. With respect to the two last exceptions, however, evidence of declarations of this kind is inadmissible, if they have been made *post*

litem motam, that is, after the matter to which they relate has become the subject of litigation.

III. *Written evidence consists of records, documents under seal, as charters and deeds, and writings not under seal.*—Acts of parliament are records of the highest nature, being the memorials of the legislature; but a distinction is made with respect to evidence between public and private statutes. A public statute requires no express proof in courts of justice, every one being presumed to know the law which he is bound to observe; as to them, therefore, the citation of the statute itself is in all cases sufficient. But private acts of parliament are considered as documents relating to individuals, and must therefore be proved by copies compared with the original roll of parliament. A second and inferior species of records is the proceedings of courts of justice, which are proved by exemplifications, sworn copies, and office copies. Exemplifications are transcripts of the records of different courts, accredited by having the seals of such courts attached to them. Sworn copies are transcripts made by individuals who authenticate them upon oath, when they are produced in evidence. Office copies are copies certified to be true and accurate by an officer expressly intrusted for that purpose by an officer of the court to which the records belong. Charters and deeds are proved by the production of the instrument and proof of the execution by the party to be charged with it; but where the document is more than thirty years old, the execution need not be proved. The general rule is that the original deed must be produced, on the principle already alluded to of its being the best evidence; but this is subject to the following exceptions:—1. Where it has been lost or destroyed by accident; 2. Where it is in the possession of a party to a suit against whom it is sought to be produced, and who refuses to produce it: in either of which cases the contents of the document may be proved by a copy, or, if no copy exists, by oral testimony. Deeds attested must, in general, be proved by one at least of the subscribing witnesses; but if the attesting witnesses be dead, or are not to be found after a diligent search, or for any other reason incompetent to give evidence, the execution of the deed may be proved by proof of the hand-writing of the party. The proof of hand-writing, by the law of England, is peculiar. The testimony of persons skilled in hand-writing is wholly excluded, comparison of hands being inadmissible for the purpose. The course is, that a witness acquainted with the writing of the individual in question, and who has seen him write, or who has had a written correspondence with him, shall testify to his belief that the document to be proved is in his handwriting.

From the above summary of the principal rules of evidence existing in the English law, it will be observed that the system is extremely exclusive. Upon the subject of interested witnesses, the law has lately been altered in the way already explained. With respect to the reception of secondary and hearsay evidence, it sanctions no degree or kind of testimony at second-hand (except in the cases above enumerated), but excludes it under all varieties of circumstances. It is true that we ought not to attach so much weight to hearsay evidence as to direct testimony, because it is beyond all doubt that the certainty of obtaining the truth is diminished, and that the means and causes of error are multiplied, in proportion as you remove from the actual observer and add links to the chain of testimony. But it may still be questioned whether the absolute and unconditional rejection of hearsay evidence is useful. Also with respect to the mode of proving hand-writing, it might be unsafe wholly to rely upon the evidence of comparison of hands by persons of experience in that occupation, but there seems no good reason why such proof should not be *admissible* in aid of the present vague and unsatisfactory mode of proof by the general belief of a witness.

The most plausible reason for the exclusiveness of the English law of evidence is derived from the nature of the trial by jury, with reference to which it is contended to be safer to withdraw doubtful evidence altogether from their consideration, than to leave it to persons who are often uninstructed, and incapable of drawing correct distinctions upon the subject of testimony, to form a proper estimate of its credibility. But this reason is founded upon an assumption not justified by the fact, namely, that the means of proof actually legalized are infallible guides to truth; whereas the truth is, that many of them are quite as liable to lead to a false conclusion as those which are excluded. In this state of things, therefore, there seems no good reason why all practicable means of attaining to truth, however various in their degrees of effectiveness, should not be committed to juries. This seems indeed to be the growing impression in the profession; the inclination of the courts of late years being to let in as much light to a cause as possible, and to regard objections to evidence rather as matters of *credibility* upon which juries may exercise their judgment, than of *competency* to be wholly withdrawn from their consideration.

Witnesses in proceedings in Equity are examined upon written interrogatories, as explained in the article EQUITY. The interrogatories are drawn by counsel, according to the instructions which he receives as to the facts which a witness is considered able to prove; but it frequently happens that the instructions are very defective, and the counsel is obliged to frame his interrogatories as well as he can, in order to elicit the proof of facts favourable to the party for whom he is employed. Though each several interrogatory, when well drawn, is framed for the purpose of establishing some single and distinct fact, or connected facts, written interrogatories cannot from their nature be otherwise than long and somewhat difficult to comprehend. In the oral examination of a witness, it necessarily happens that several questions must be asked consecutively for the purpose of completing the investigation into and the establishment of every important fact to which the examination is directed. Written interrogatories must be framed on the same principle, and therefore every subsequent part of an interrogatory must be framed on the supposition of every previous part being answered in some way; and, consequently, it is hardly possible in written interrogatories to avoid what is called making them *leading*, and at the same time verbose and cumbrous. These long interrogatories, it is proved by experience, are often imperfectly comprehended by the witnesses, and consequently their evidence is in some respects either incomplete or inaccurate, or both. The interrogatories which either party proposes to his witnesses are not known to the adverse party until the examination of all the witnesses on both sides is concluded, when *publication* is passed, as it is termed, and copies of all the depositions are delivered to the litigating parties under an order of the court.

Witnesses in courts of law are produced before the court, and examined by counsel; after which they may be cross-examined by the counsel for the other side. In the equity system there is of course no cross-examination, in the proper sense of the term; for one party does not know what the witnesses examined by the opposite party have deposed, and cannot therefore effectually examine them, as in a court of common law, where the cross-examination of a witness follows, and is founded upon what the witness has stated in his examination in chief. If a party to a suit in chancery will cross-examine a witness who is produced by his adversary for examination, he must examine him on written interrogatories, without knowing what interrogatories have been proposed to him by the opposite party, and without knowing what he has said in his depositions in chief. Such a cross-examination must be in general altogether useless, and often dangerous to the interest of the party making it; unless the witness is one whom he would himself have examined in chief. Under the 32nd order of the 21st of December, 1833, the last interrogatory before that date commonly in use is in future to be allowed as follows: "Do you know or can you set forth any other matter or thing which may be of benefit or advantage to the parties at issue in this cause, or either of them," &c. A party, however, is not bound to insert this interrogatory; and, indeed, no great harm will result if it is never used. Owing to various causes, such as disinclination on the part of a witness to give himself further trouble, particular affection to one of the litigating parties, or forgetfulness, it might have been anticipated that this general interrogatory would fail in its object; and so far as it has been used, such is said to be the case.

This mode of ascertaining facts in suits in equity is evidently very defective, and has been the subject of considerable complaint and of lengthened inquiry; but hitherto nothing has been done to amend the system.

(See *Minutes of Evidence taken before the Chancery Commissioners, annexed to their Report of* 1826; and a pamphlet (1837), by W. A. Garratt, entitled *Suggestions for Reform in Proceedings in Chancery.*)

Those who may be inclined to follow this subject further will find it discussed at great length in Bentham's *Rationale of Judicial Evidence*, a work which has certainly contributed to the formation of more correct opinions on evidence; but it has neither exhausted the subject, nor is it free from great defects. The rules of the English law of evidence are contained in the treatises of Mr. Phillipps and Mr. Starkie.

EXCHANGE. [DIVISION OF EMPLOYMENT; DEMAND AND SUPPLY; BALANCE OF TRADE.]

EXCHANGE, BILL OF, may be described as a written order or request addressed by one person to another, directing him to pay on account of the writer to some third person or his order, or to the order of the person addressing the request, a certain sum of money at a time therein specified. The person who gives the direction is called the drawer of the bill, he to whom it is addressed the drawee, and he in whose favour it is given the payee, or, occasionally, the remitter. Bills of exchange are ordinarily divided into two classes, foreign and inland; foreign bills comprehend such as are drawn *or* are payable abroad; inland, those which are drawn *and* payable in England. Thus, a bill drawn in France, or even in Scotland or Ireland, upon a party in England, or conversely, is a foreign bill; and this is a distinction that has important legal consequences.

The origin of bills of exchange is unknown. It is probable or almost certain that the Greeks and Romans were acquainted with some modes of remitting money and paying debts, similar to those effected by a bill of exchange. Instruments of this kind were current among the commercial states of Italy in the early part of the fourteenth century, and it is probable they were not unknown at the close of the same century in England.

It is certain that bills of exchange were originally employed solely as media of remittance, and the circumstances which brought them into use may be explained as follows:— A., at Hamburg, consigned goods to B., in London, either in execution of an order, or as his factor for sale. B, thereupon, being debtor to A. for the invoice amount, or the proceeds of the sale, as the case might be, was desirous of remitting to A. accordingly. The remittance could only be made in money or in goods; but A. might not want a return cargo of English commodities, and the sending out of specie would be inconvenient and hazardous. Now suppose that some third person, C., were about to go from Hamburg to London, mutual accommodation would suggest the following arrangement:— A. would deliver to C. an open letter addressed to B., requesting him to pay to C. the amount intended to be remitted; and C. on receiving the letter would pay to A. the value of it in money current at Hamburg, and having carried it over to London would there receive from B. the sum specified. Thus much of the expense, and all the risk and trouble of remittance would be saved to B. or A.; and C., besides having a more convenient sign of wealth, would probably receive some advantage for the accommodation. It is obvious, however, that to bring this exchange into operation several things would be wanting: first, the knowledge by the two parties of the mutual want; secondly, confidence on the part of C. that the money would be paid by B. on presentment of the letter of request, or that in default of payment by him he would be repaid by A.; and, thirdly, the determining how much C. ought to give A. in ready money of Hamburg for the sum specified in the letter, to be paid at a future day in money of England. Now the adjustment of the comparative value of different currencies, fell directly within the province of the money-dealers or bankers, and as all persons about to remit or to proceed to foreign countries resorted to them for the requisite coin, they would furnish the merchants with information as to the other particulars also, and would thus become the negotiators of this sort of exchanges.

But there were other cases in which the like operation might take place, for although A. might not want goods from England in return for those shipped by him from Hamburg, other Hamburg merchants might, and so it might happen that at the time of the intended remittance B. had money owing to him at Hamburg in respect of goods so shipped. Let it be supposed then that C., instead of going to London, were about to remit money to B., in that case the whole or a portion, as well of B.'s debt to A. as of C.'s debt to B., might be settled by a simple arrangement of the same kind as that before described. B. would write a letter addressed to C., requesting him to pay a specified sum to A., or, in merc. ntile phrase, would draw upon C. in favour of A.; this letter or draft he would remit, as payment, to A., who, upon presentment to C. would receive from him the amount, and would give credit to B. accordingly.

Now, as the trade between two countries never, unless under very unusual circumstances, consists solely of shipments of goods on the one part, and solely of remittances of money on the other—it might happen that if B. had not a debtor at Hamburg other London merchants would have sums of money owing from Hamburg. B. would endeavour to find out some such merchant, from whom he might procure an order upon his debtor; in other words, he would buy a bill on Hamburg for remittance to A. For the reasons before mentioned, recourse would be had for this purpose to the money-dealers; and it is not difficult to conceive by what steps the procuring and supplying of bills soon became in their hands a distinct business.

Indeed, without the intervention of such dealers, the system could never have become extensively useful; because in the commercial intercourse of two countries the commodities exchanged will never be exactly balanced. There is at times a scarcity of bills upon one country and an excess of those upon some other: but this inequality is equalized by the care of those persons whose business it is to deal in bills; for they send or procure the superfluous bills in one market to meet the demand in another.

The instrument of transfer, or bill of exchange, now assumed a concise and permanent form. At first the order would probably be, to pay on presentment to the drawee, or as it was expressed in the instrument, "on sight." But, as the intervals between drawing and presentment would be variable, it became the practice to fix them by a definite scale; and hence probably arose what was called the *usance* between two ports or countries, or the period fixed by *usage*, at which, with reference to the date, a bill was presentable for payment. Afterwards these usances came to signify the periods at which the merchants of any particular country or port were in the practice of paying the bills so drawn upon them, and these customary periods being universally known, the word usance soon came to signify a specific term of days, and it was formerly not uncommon, when by agreement the time of payment was determined, to draw foreign bills payable at one, two, or more usances. In modern times, the more frequent practice has been to make them payable at so many days after sight, or at so many months or days after date. In course of time the practice was also established of granting what was termed *days of grace*, or a short time to the drawee for providing the requisite cash: these days of grace, though varying as to limits in different communities, are generally recognised as part of the custom of merchants.

Originally, as we have supposed, the bill was a letter addressed by B. to C., directing him to pay A. But as it might not be convenient to A. to present the letter in person, it became usual to give him authority to appoint another, by whom the presentment might be made and the money received. It assumed therefore the form of a direction to pay A., or such

3 K

other person as A. should appoint, expressed with the conciseness of mercantile language, thus: "Pay A., *or order*." But if the letter or bill in the hands of A. were assignable, that is transferable by him to another person, there was no reason why it should not be so in the hands of his assignee, and thus by the operation of the words "or order," it obtained the character of a negotiable instrument or sign of value, transferable from one person to another. The assignment might be in such form as this: "Pay the within to D., or his order—signed A.," and by a similar superscription D. might in like manner assign the bill to E., and E. to F., and so on. But as the bill was of course *delivered* to each successive assignee, possession was of itself a sufficient voucher for payment, and the special superscription therefore was soon frequently dispensed with as unnecessary, the assignment of the prior holder being indicated by his signature alone. In England, and in some other countries, it has long been the practice to write the assignment on the back of the instrument, and it has thence received the name of an *indorsement*: the form first described, in which the assignee is named, is termed a *special* indorsement, or an indorsement *in full*; and the mere signature of the assigner is called an indorsement *in blank*.

When bills were drawn payable at some future day, one might suppose that the first holder who had the opportunity of doing so should, during the currency of the specified period, shew the bill to the drawee, and procure from him an undertaking to pay it at maturity. If he refused, the bill was protested for non-acceptance, and notice of the dishonour was immediately communicated to the drawer. If he gave the undertaking either verbally or in writing upon the bill or otherwise, he was said to have *accepted* it, and became thenceforth liable, as the acceptor, for the amount specified. For the effect of the acceptance was this: the drawee thereby affirmed the right of the drawer to call upon him for payment of the money, and he assented to the transfer of the right. If, therefore, after acceptance, he refused to pay the bill when due, he was responsible to the drawer as having acknowledged himself to be his debtor, and to the payee or other party in possession of the bill, in respect of his express engagement. But the right of the holder was not confined to the acceptor; for although, after acceptance, the drawee became the principal debtor, to whom recourse must be had in the first instance, yet if upon regular presentment the drawee did not pay, the holder was not bound to take measures against him alone, but might resort to all prior parties whose names appeared upon the instrument. For as the indorsement gave the right to receive the money, it was to be presumed that it had not been made without an equivalent, and it was but justice, therefore, that on the dishonour of the bill by the drawee, the holder should receive back the value which he had given: and as every person, whose signature, whether as drawer or indorser, appeared upon the bill, acknowledged himself by the act of signing to have received value for the delivery of the order, it was not unreasonable that the reimbursement should be claimed, not merely from the party from whose hands the bill had been received, but also from the drawer and every other party whose name preceded that of the holder. The result therefore was this: if the drawee paid the bill, the matter was settled; but if he dishonoured it, by a refusal either to pay or to accept on due presentment, a notification of the dishonour was conveyed by the holder to all parties preceding him, or to such as he thought fit to call upon for indemnity; if then the drawer paid the money, or as it was termed *took up the bill*, all the other parties were exonerated, and the drawer had his remedy against the drawee, upon the bill if accepted, or upon the original consideration in respect of which it was drawn, if the acceptance had been refused. In like manner, whoever satisfied the bill by payment, thereby discharged all parties posterior to himself, and obtained a right against all who preceded him. Thus each successive indorsee had the accumulated security of all the parties whose signatures were upon the instrument as acceptor, drawer, or indorser, when it came into his hands.

The party who remits a bill is by the supposition debtor to him to whom the remittance is made; and after the explanation just given, it will be obvious that it would be required of him to acknowledge his liability by making himself a party to the instrument. The bill therefore purchased by him would not be, as has been above supposed, a direction to pay the remittee, but to pay the remitter or his order; and hence it happens, as was said in the commencement, that the party to whom the bill is made payable, is sometimes called the *remitter*.

To obviate the inconvenience that may result from bills being lost, it became usual to draw them *in sets;* that is to say, two or more parts of each bill were drawn, and described as the 1st, 2nd, 3rd, and so on, each containing a condition that it should be payable only while the others remained unpaid. But this practice of drawing in sets is made available for another purpose. The payee having indorsed and paid away one part, frequently remits another part to some agent or correspondent at the place of the drawee's residence, to be by him presented for acceptance, with a direction added, by way of memorandum, to the bill, that, when accepted, it is to be held for the use of the person who shall duly present the other part or parts for payment at maturity. The advantage of this arrangement is obvious: if the bill be accepted, it is held, according to the direction, till maturity: if refused, it is protested, and notice is given to the drawer. Upon this protest the drawer may be called upon to give security for the due payment of the bill at the expiration of its currency; or, as occasionally happens, some correspondent of the drawer at the place upon which the bill is drawn accepts it for his honour, and thereby places himself in the situation of the original drawee, being liable as acceptor to all parties subsequent to the drawer. Such an acceptance is called an acceptance *supra protest*, or *for honour*, and may be made at any time during the currency of the bill, and on behalf of any party who is liable upon it after default made by the drawee. The following illustration will show the use of a Bill of Exchange.

A person in London has a payment of 1000*l*. to make in Paris. Instead of remitting the money, he goes to an exchange-broker, and purchases from him a bill on Paris equivalent to that sum. The bill will be payable in francs; and it will be necessary to ascertain how many francs are equal to 1000*l*. By the mint regulations between England and France, 1*l*. sterling of English money is equal to 25 francs, 20 cents, which is therefore the nominal or standard *par* of exchange between the two countries. According to this scale, then, 1000*l*. in London would be worth 25,200 francs in Paris. But the par is fixed on the supposition that the currencies of the two countries respectively are uniformly of the weight and purity established by the Mint, whereas the coin is often debased by alloy or attrition, and the relative value undergoes a corresponding alteration. This deviation however is well known, and may be regarded as comparatively constant. But other circumstances, which are not constant, affect the ratio of value. When, for instance, any considerable portion of the circulating medium of either of the two countries between which the exchange is to be effected consists of a paper currency, the standard is materially affected by the quantity of paper in circulation. A redundancy of paper money has invariably the effect of depreciating the standard, or, in other words, of raising the value of the *standard coin* as compared with the same nominal sum in *paper money*. This effect is temporary only when the paper is convertible into specie on demand; if inconvertible, it is both permanent and considerable. Thus at one period of the late war, the English guinea was worth 26*s*. in money, estimated according to the value of the 1*l*. sterling in bank notes. At that time therefore the English pound would fall far below the Mint standard of 3*l*. 17*s*. 10½*d*. per ounce, and a proportionate effect would be produced on the rate of exchange with any other country in which the standard was maintained. Taking, as before, the instance of France, the par would vary, other things remaining constant, from 25 francs to somewhere about 19 francs, or 1000*l*., in a Bank of England note, would buy a bill on Paris, not for 25,200 francs, but for about 19,000 francs only. But the same cause might be operating in France also, in which case the calculation would be still further complicated by a *comparison* of the depreciation in the one country with that in the other. The variation here taken for an example is an extreme case, but fluctuations the same in kind, though less in degree, are still of continual occurrence, and must be carefully taken into account in all calculations as to the price of bills.

But there are other causes in operation which materially affect the rate of exchange and the price of bills. The accommodation of a remittance in the form of a bill of exchange is worth a calculable sum, the maximum being the compound of the labour, expense, and risk of the transmission of money in specie. Suppose this maximum to be one per cent., it is evident it is worth the while of the remitter to pay any sum short of 10l. for the purchase of a bill equivalent to 1000l. Now the market price of bills is mainly dependent on the relation of the supply to the demand, and this again is primarily regulated by the state of trade between two given countries. When the value of the exports to any country in a given period is equal to the value of the imports from the same country in the same period, the trade is said to be balanced: the bills drawn in each country upon the other will be equal in amount, and this equilibrium constitutes what is called the *real par of exchange*. But this state of things can never actually exist. Even where, upon the average of years or months, the trade is nearly even, there will be disturbing circumstances which will have a temporary effect upon the exchanges. There will consequently be occasional scarcity and occasional abundance of foreign bills in the market. When scarce, their price of course is higher, or, as it is ordinarily expressed, they bear a *premium*. At such times the imports exceed the exports, and the exchanges are said to be *against us*. Suppose that, in the trade between England and France, the value of our imports from France exceeds that of our exports to France by about three-fourths. The effect of this, if matters were left to themselves, would be, that of the remittances to France three-fourths must be made in specie, and that the bills in which the remaining one-fourth was made would be at the maximum price, that is to say, taking the scale before adopted, would bear a premium of all but one per cent. But it is an established fact, that in every trading community the value of the whole of the exports taken together is, upon an average, very nearly balanced by the value of the whole of the imports, or, in other words, that ultimately all commodities imported are paid for directly or indirectly in commodities exported. Therefore, the bills drawn in England upon foreign countries nearly balance the bills drawn in foreign countries upon England in the same period. Thus, although there may be a deficiency in London, to the extent of three-fourths, of bills upon France, there may be an excess, in nearly the same ratio, of bills upon Belgium, and in like manner there may be an excess in Belgium, to the same extent, of bills upon France. The London bill-merchant by means of his agent will buy bills upon Paris at Antwerp, where they are cheapest, and bring them for sale to London, where they are dearest. The cost of procuring, and the profit of the bill-merchant, therefore, upon this transaction, constitute the third element in the calculation. Supposing then the bill to be a *good* one, that is to say, guaranteed by names of known and established credit, the only remaining operation is to estimate the discount according to mercantile practice, or, in other words, the interest of 1000l. in money for the time which will elapse before payment of the bill; and the combined result will give the sum in francs for which the bill is to be drawn, or the amount of bills already drawn to be given in exchange for 1000l.

Bills of exchange are also in frequent use for the purpose of remittance from one part of the United Kingdom to another. Thus the trader in Manchester, Leeds, or Birmingham, who has a payment to make in London, remits bills of his customers in the country. These are discounted by the moneyed capitalists through the intervention of bill-brokers. A few of the London bankers also discount for the accommodation of their customers, and the Bank of England deals extensively in that department. The bills so cashed are transmitted to the provincial banks to be presented at maturity for payment. Conversely, in the provincial towns the country bankers discount bills on London, and transmit them to their correspondents there for payment. The rate of discount varies according to the demand for money, and the character of the particular bills; but it is seldom, upon regular transactions, more than four, or less than two and a half per cent.

Bills of exchange are also much used as follows:—A tradesman may not be able to pay ready money, but he can give the seller an order for payment on some other person, receiving or paying the difference, as the case may be, and making an allowance by way of interest, or, which is the same thing in other words, paying an extra price, in proportion to the time of the bill's currency. To the seller this mode of dealing is better than the giving of a naked credit, as he gets an additional chance of payment, and a written acknowledgment of his debt. When the negotiability of inland bills was admitted, they served all the purposes of actual money, because in the same manner as the original seller had taken the order in payment, another would receive it from him in the purchase of other commodities, or it might be at once discounted or converted into cash by application to a money-dealer.

The drawing of a bill supposes that the drawee either has in his possession funds of the drawer, or is his debtor to the amount specified in the order: it was therefore an easy step in the transactions of wholesale dealing for the seller to draw upon the buyer, for the price of the goods, a bill payable to his (the seller's) own order at some future day. This bill the buyer immediately accepted, and thus in effect acknowledged himself to be the debtor of the drawer to the amount specified, and engaged to pay the holder at maturity. By this arrangement, now very general, the buyer obtains credit for the term at the expiration of which the bill is made payable, and the seller has the advantage of a fixed day for payment being named in the bill, and a means of procuring cash if he chooses to negotiate the bill.

Bills of Exchange are also frequently drawn and accepted under such circumstances as follow:—There are in most of the principal trading ports of the world, merchants who carry on the business of general factors or agents for sale, and whose establishments are known among mercantile men under the name of commission-houses. The course of dealing with such houses is, for the most part, this:—A., a manufacturer at Manchester, consigns a cargo of cotton pieces to B. and Co., a commission-house at Mexico, for sale on his account. The English correspondents of B. and Co. are Messrs. C. and Co. of London. By an arrangement among these several parties A. draws on C. and Co. for half or two-thirds, as may be agreed, of the invoice price of the goods consigned, and by discounting the bill with his banker obtains at once an instalment in money, which immediately returns into his capital, and becomes useful in producing more goods. Ultimately, account sales are furnished by the Mexican house, and A. again draws on C. and Co. for the balance in his favour. Annual balances are struck between B. and Co. and C. and Co., and remittances by bills for the adjustment of the account complete the transaction. Now the advantages of this anticipatory part-payment are obvious, more especially in the trade with distant countries, as South America or the East Indies. But the practice has degenerated into something of an abuse; for it has of late been frequent with the consigners of goods to make out invoices with prices artificially high, and so to procure a remunerating return even from the proportion for which they are authorized to draw in advance. The effect is to throw upon the consignees the whole risk, which was formerly shared between the two, and proportionately to impair the steadiness and security of commerce.

Good bills, as already observed, may be always discounted. Accordingly, any man whose credit is good may at any time raise money upon a bill drawn, accepted, or indorsed by himself. If his credit be doubtful he may still procure cash by the same expedient, but he will have to pay a premium or rate of discount proportioned to the increased risk. Among needy men instances are not unfrequent of discounts procured by these means at the exorbitant rate of 20 or 30 per cent. But a still more common practice is the negotiation of what are called by the significant name of *accommodation* bills. A trader unable to meet his liabilities applies to a friend whose credit is better than his own, to accept, or in some other way to become a party to, a bill drawn for the purpose : the trader undertakes to provide the funds necessary for paying it when due, and generally gives in return his own acceptance of another like bill, known in the mercantile world as a cross acceptance. When one or more names have thus been obtained sufficient to give currency to the bill, it is discounted, and the money applied to the necessities of the trader. As this bill falls due, the same operation is repeated in order to raise money, until the system of expedients failing at last, as sooner or later it inevitably must, the ruin of the insolvent trader himself is accomplished, and not unfrequently draws along with it others who, unfortunately or imprudently, may have become parties to these unsubstantial representatives of value. Of the more serious mischiefs of this dangerous practice, such as the temptation to forgery by the use of fictitious names as drawers or payees, it is perhaps useless to speak, because few men at first seriously contemplate the commission of a crime, but are rather drawn into it by circumstances not foreseen or not appreciated ; but the reflection that it is a foolish and improvident practice—that, in addition to the loss of credit, which, once perceived (and how can it fail to be perceived ?), it is sure to occasion, there is the certain expense of stamps and higher rates of discount, and moreover a *double liability* in respect of every shilling for which cross acceptances are given—may perhaps have some effect in deterring honest men, however necessitous, from having recourse to this fatal expedient.

Viewed as a legal instrument, a bill of exchange, as well in its original formation as in its successive transfers, is an assignment of a debt, by which the right of the original creditor to sue for and obtain payment is transferred to the holder for the time being. The Roman law presented no obstacles to such a substitution ; and in those countries therefore which had adopted the civil law, the negotiation of bills found no impediment. But it was a principle of the common law of England, that the assignment of things not in possession, such as a debt of right, being in truth the assignment of suits at law, might be converted into a means of oppression, and the validity of such transfers was not recognised by it. But in the case of bills of exchange the principle of law yielded to general convenience ; and the negotiability of foreign bills was recognised by the English law. It was not, however, until three centuries later, that the negotiability of inland bills was recognised by the courts, unless on proof of some special custom of trade ; but expediency finally prevailed, and at the present day, as well by the common law as by the statutes of 9 & 10 Wm. III. c. 17, and 3 & 4 Anne, c. 9, they stand on the same general footing as foreign bills.

It is this assignability, vesting in the holder a right of action against the original parties, which chiefly distinguishes a bill of exchange from every other form of legal contract. Another and scarcely less important privilege is, that though a simple contract debt, and as such requiring a *consideration* to give it legal efficacy, the consideration is presumed until the want of it be shown. It is available therefore in the hands of a *bonâ fide* holder, upon merely formal proof of title by the signature of the party to be charged . that is to say, it is unnecessary to prove value given, unless it be first shown on the other side that the bill is in some stage or other tainted with an illegality, and the *bonâ fides* is assumed until it shall be made to appear that the holder was, at the time of taking it, privy to that illegality. From this rule an exception is made as to bills given for a gambling debt, which by statute are void even in the hands of an innocent holder. The rules of law applicable to bills of

EXCHEQUER COURT.　[871]　EXCHEQUER COURT.

exchange have been settled by numerous decisions, and it is of great importance to mercantile men to be acquainted with them; but the consideration of them properly belongs to a legal treatise.

EXCHANGE BROKER. [BROKER.]
EXCHEQUER BILLS. [NATIONAL DEBT.]
EXCHEQUER CHAMBER. [EXCHEQUER, COURT OF; COURTS.]
EXCHEQUER COURT is a superior court of record established by William the Conqueror as part of the Aula Regis, and reduced to its present order by Edward I.

It is the lowest in rank of the four great courts of law which sit at Westminster Hall, although in ancient times one of the first in importance, as all causes relating to the rights of the crown were there heard and determined, and the revenues of the crown were supposed to be received there.

The Latinized form of the word Exchequer is *Scaccarium*. Camden says it was so called from the covering of the table at which the barons sat being party-coloured or *chequered*, and on which, when certain of the king's accounts were made up, the sums were marked and scored with counters.

The judges of the court of exchequer are the chancellor of the exchequer for the time being [CHANCELLOR, p. 482], the chief baron, and four other barons, who are created by letters patent, and are so called from their having been formerly chosen from such as were barons of the kingdom, or parliamentary barons (Selden's *Titles of Honour*).

The Court of Exchequer was formerly held in the king's palace. Its treasury was the great deposit of records from the other courts; writs of summons to assemble the parliaments were issued by its officers; and its acts and decrees, as they related almost entirely to matters connected with the king's revenue, were not controlled by any other of the king's ordinary courts of justice.

It now consists of two divisions, one of which exercises jurisdiction in all cases relating to the customs and excise, and over revenue matters generally. The other division is a court of common law, in which all personal actions may be brought: the exchequer court of equity was abolished by 5 Vict. c. 5.

A plaintiff, when bringing an action in this court, previously to the Act for Uniformity of Process in personal actions (2 Wm. IV. c. 39), fictitiously alleged himself to be the king's debtor, in order to give the court jurisdiction in the cause; but since the passing of that act it is no longer necessary to resort to this fiction in order to bring an action in the Court of Exchequer, as that statute assimilates the practice of all the common law courts, and the operation as well as the name of the processes issued from them are the same.

The number of officers on the plea side of the Court of Exchequer, and their several duties were regulated by 2 & 3 Wm. IV. c. 110. By 3 & 4 Wm. IV. c. 99, the following officers in the Court of Exchequer were abolished:— the lord treasurer's remembrancer, the filacer, secondaries, deputy remembrancer, and sworn and other clerks and bag-bearer belonging thereto; clerk of the pipe, deputy-clerk of the pipe, controller and deputy-controller of the pipe, secondaries, attornies, or sworn and other clerks and bag-bearer in the said office of the pipe; clerk of the estreats; surveyor of the green wax; the foreign apposer, and deputy foreign apposer, and clerk of the nichills. By 5 & 6 Vict. c. 86, certain officers on the revenue side of the court were abolished, and the office of remembrancer of the court was regulated.

An appeal lies from this court by writ of error to the justices of the courts of king's bench and common pleas sitting in the exchequer chamber, who alone have power to review the judgments of the barons: and from their decision a further appeal may be brought before the House of Lords.

The Court of Exchequer chamber was first erected in England by stat. 31 Edward III., to determine causes upon writs of error from the common law side of the Court of Exchequer. The judges of the three superior courts occasionally sit here to hear arguments in important criminal cases, and upon causes of great weight and difficulty, in which the judges of the courts below have not given their judgment.

As a court of error, the Court of Exchequer chamber underwent considerable alterations by the passing of the 11th Geo. IV. and 1st. Wm. IV. c. 70, and its constitution is now regulated by that statute. [COURTS.]

The *Court of Exchequer in Scotland* was established by the 6th Anne. c. 26. This court was abolished in 1832 by 2 & 3 Wm. IV. c. 54. The judges were the high treasurer of Great Britain, with a chief baron, and four other barons.

The *Court of Exchequer in Ireland* was established by the 40th Geo. III. c. 39, and consists of the chief justices, chief baron, and the rest of the justices and barons, or any nine of them.

EXCISE DUTIES, the name given to taxes or duties levied upon articles of consumption which are produced within the kingdom. This description, which has usually been given of excise duties, is more strictly applicable now than it was formerly, when the commissioners of excise revenue were also charged with the collection of duties upon various articles imported from foreign countries. Among these foreign articles were wine, spirits, tobacco, glass, and tea. The last named of these was the last that was withdrawn from the management of the Excise and transferred to the Board of Customs. There are still, it is true, certain duties to which the name of excise is applied which can hardly be called duties upon consumption, such as the sums charged for licenses to permit persons to carry on certain trades, the post-horse duties, and the duty on sales by auction abolished in 1845.

Excise duties are said to have had their origin in this country in the reign of Charles I., when a tax was laid upon beer, cider, and perry, of home production. The act by which these duties were authorised was passed by the long parliament in 1643. This act contains also a list of foreign articles, and among others tobacco, wine, raisins, currants and loaf sugar, upon which excise duties were imposed in addition to duties of customs already chargeable. This act was adopted and enforced under the protectorate of Oliver Cromwell; and by the statute 12 Charles II. c. 24, the duties of excise were granted to the crown as part of its revenue.

For a long time this class of duties was viewed with particular dislike by the people, on account of its inquisitorial interference with various industrial pursuits; and it certainly forms a very strong ground of objection against excise duties, that the security of the revenue is held to be incompatible with the perfect freedom of the manufacturer as to the processes which he may apply in his works. In every highly taxed country where consumption duties form part of the public revenue, it would seem however to be hardly possible to avoid the adoption of this class of duties. In France there is, for example, a customs duty upon foreign-made sugar; and it is clearly necessary for the protection of the revenue that an excise duty should be imposed upon sugar produced at home from beet-root, otherwise the producer of indigenous sugar would charge the consumer nearly as much as he would pay to the importer of foreign sugar, and would for a time pocket the amount of the duty. By such means a branch of industry would be fostered, unprofitable to the country at large, and profitable only to the few persons by whom the indigenous sugar is produced, but whose profits would not long continue greater than the usual profits upon the employment of stock obtainable in the same country from other branches of industry. In this country sugar manufactured from beet-root or potatoes is subjected to an excise duty. For the same reason it would be unfair to permit malt to be imported without imposing on it a duty corresponding in amount to the excise duty. There are consequently "countervailing duties" on the importation of articles subject to excise duty; and a drawback is allowed on the exportation of domestic articles which are subject to excise duty.

Excise duties are liable to this among other very serious objections, that the regulations under which they are collected interfere with processes of manufacture, so as to prevent the adoption of improvements. Upon the same premises, with the same capital, and the same amount of labour, double the quantity of cloths has been printed which could have been printed previous to the repeal of the duty and the consequent abolition of the excise regulations. The abolition of the excise duty on glass was avowedly made with the object of facilitating improvements in the manufacture. The excise regulations respecting the manufacture of soap have prevented our soap manufacturers from entering into competition with the manufacturers of other countries.

Another great objection that may be urged against excise duties is, the facilities which they offer for the commission of frauds against the revenue. In the Seventeenth Report of the Commissioners appointed to inquire into the management and collection of the excise revenue, it is stated as a striking proof of the extent to which frauds are committed by manufacturers of soap, that "there are in England fifty that take out licenses, for which they pay 4*l*. per annum, each of which makes, or rather brings to charge, less than one ton of soap per annum, from which it is obvious that as the profits of such a sale would not pay for the licence, the entry is made in order to cover smuggling." With regard to malt, another article of great consumption which is subject to excise duties, the commissioners state it to be their opinion, founded upon the evidence given by several respectable maltsters, "that malt is sold throughout the season, and in large quantities, for a price that is insufficient to pay the expense of making it and duty; and that the duty is evaded to a great amount."

In 1797 the number of articles subject to excise duties was 28; 15 in 1833; 10 in 1835; and now, June, 1845, there are only 9, including sugar. The Post-horse duty is under the management of the Board of Excise, and in Ireland the duty on game certificates. In the following list of the articles which paid Excise duties in 1797, the first eight are still subject to these duties, and with sugar made here constitute all the articles on which the Excise duty is now collected:

Bricks.
Hops.
Licences.
Malt.
Paper.
Soap.
Spirits, British.
Vinegar.

Salt,	repealed	1825.
Wire,	do.	1826.
Beer,	do	1830.
Cyder and Perry,	do.	1830.
Hides and Skins,	do.	1830.
Printed Goods,	do.	1831.
Candles,	do.	1832.
Tiles,	do.	1833.
Starch,	do.	1834.
Stone Bottles,	do.	1834.
Sweets and Mead,	do.	1834.
Auctions,	do.	1845.
Glass,	do.	1845.
Tea,	transferred to Customs.	
Coaches,	transferred to Stamps.	
Cocoa and Coffee, transferred to Customs.		
Pepper,	do.	
Spirits, Foreign,	do.	
Tobacco and Snuff,	do.	
Wine,	do.	

In 1822 the Excise duties yielded for the United Kingdom twice as much as the Customs duties. The receipts from Customs were 14,384,710*l*. and from the Excise 31,196,948*l*. In 1797 the Excise duties collected in England amounted to 11,069,668*l*., and in 1821 they reached to 27,400,300*l*., which is the highest sum they ever attained. In 1845 they are again reduced to the amount at which they stood in 1797. In 1829 the large sum of 6,013,159*l*. was paid at the chief office for the London "collection," and in 1835, only 1,462,919*l*.: the boundary of the "collection," it may be as well to state, does not comprise the whole of the metropolis. In 1825 several articles were transferred to the Customs, and in the same year the salt duty was repealed. This example was followed in the case of many other articles, so that between 1825 and 1834 the duties transferred to the Customs amounted to 11,238,300*l*. and the duties altogether repealed to 6,782,000*l*., making a total of 18,020,300*l*., Two articles alone on which the duty was taken off produced upwards of 5,000,000*l*. annually, namely, beer 3,100,000*l*. and printed cottons 2,104,000*l*.

In 1835 the number of traders in the

United Kingdom who were surveyed periodically by Excise officers was 588,000. They were divided into five classes: 1. Persons visited for the purpose of charging the "growing" duties, as maltsters, soap-makers, &c. 2. Persons who paid a licence according to the extent of their business, as brewers and some others. 3. Innkeepers and retailers of beer and others, who dealt in articles upon which an Excise duty was levied. 4. Persons who were dealers in articles upon which Customs duties had been paid. 5. Persons who did not pay duties, but were subject to cautionary surveys; tallow-melters, for example, as a check upon soap-makers. The cost of these surveys in England only amounted to 533,902*l*. In a single year the number of surveys of dealers in tea, wine, and tobacco has been about fifteen millions; 1,657,957 permits were required before goods in certain quantities could leave their premises; and 778,988 books were supplied to these dealers in which to keep an account of their stock and sales. Since 1835 several of the surveys have been abolished, and it has generally been found that they were of little or no value so far as the revenue was concerned, while they were a vexatious hinderance to business. These and some other improvements in the Excise department are in a great measure the result of the Seventeen sound, able, and elaborate Reports of the Commissioners of Excise Inquiry, appointed 27th of March, 1833, and which embraced each of the articles subject to Excise duties.

The gross receipt collected by the Excise on each article of duty in 1844 was as follows:—

	England.	Scotland.	Ireland.
Auctions	£275,177	£20,025	£13,427
Bricks	435,336	11,379	
Glass	785,869	54,714	6,575
Hops	245,668		
Licences	835,430	105,460	95,504
Malt	4,285,887	546,345	161,003
Paper	542,907	135,649	30,762
Post-Horse Duty	146,195	16,966	
Post-Horse Licences	4,166	357	55
Soap	1,092,690	97,962	
Spirits	2,694,049	1,533,028	1,014,505
Sugar	6,867		93
Vinegar	17,805	127	269
	11,368,054	2,522,017	1,133,775*

The gross receipt, charges of management, and the rate per cent. for which the gross revenue of Excise was collected in 1844 were as follows:—

	Great Britain.			Ireland.		
	£	s.	d.	£	s.	d.
Gross Receipt	13,905,022	0	0	1,339,394	0	0
Repayments, Allowances, Drawbacks, &c.	773,468	0	0	1,612	0	0
Charges of Collection	809,038	0	0	166,671	0	0
Rate per cent. of Charges of Collection	5	16	4¼	12	8	10½
Paid into the Exchequer	12,160,111	0	0	1,402,986	0	0

Prior to 1823 there were separate and independent Boards of Excise for England, Scotland, and Ireland, and the total number of Excise commissioners was twenty-one. The business is now better conducted by seven commissioners and by one board in London. The chairman has a salary of 2000*l*., the deputy-chairman 1500*l*., and each of the other commissioners 1500*l*. a year. The commissioners hold courts and decide summarily in case of the infraction of the Excise laws. The number of persons employed at the chief Excise-office in London is about five hundred. In 1797 Mr. Pitt pointed at the Excise establishment as a model for other public departments on account of its efficiency and good management. In 1797 the number of officers belonging to the department in England was 4777, and their salaries amounted to 323,671*l*.; in 1815 the number of officers was 7986, and their salaries 904,922*l*.; and in 1835 there were 4190 officers, and their salaries amounted to 518,620*l*.

For the management of the business of the Excise department the whole of the United Kingdom is divided into Collections, and these are subdivided into Districts, Rides, and Divisions. There are fifty-five collections in England and

* This sum includes 11,575*l*. on account o game certificates.

Wales, exclusive of the London collection, and at the head of each is a collector, who visits the principal towns in his circuit eight times a year to receive the duties and transact other business connected with the department; besides which he is required to have an eye generally upon the discipline and efficiency of the service. The number of officers in a collection varies from forty to ninety. The next subdivision of a collection is the district, at the head of which is a supervisor. Next come the subdivisions of the districts into rides and divisions, or foot-walks. Where the traders are scattered, the officer is obliged to keep a horse, and his circuit is called a ride; but if a larger number of traders reside in a smaller circuit, they are visited by the officer on foot, and then the subdivision is termed a division or foot-walk. Before going out each day, the officer leaves a memorandum at his home which states the places he intends to survey, and the order in which he will visit them; and the exact time at which he commences each must be entered in his journal. The supervisor re-surveys some of the officer's surveys, but which they will be the officer is of course ignorant; and if errors are discovered, they must be entered in the supervisor's diary. These diaries are transmitted to the chief office every two months, and no officer is promoted unless the diaries show him to be efficient. The periodical removal of officers from one part of the country to another was Mr. Pitt's suggestion, and is still acted upon: about 1100 officers change their residence yearly. The Commissioners of Excise Inquiry doubt the advantage of this system to the public service; and it is injurious to the officers by interfering with the comfort of their families and interrupting the education of their children. At the chief office in London there is a department of Surveying-General Examiners, who are despatched to any district without previous intimation, as a check upon the accuracy and integrity of the supervisors. Promotions take place in the Excise department after a certain fixed period in each grade, and only then when the officer petitions for advancement. This involves a rigid examination into his qualifications, which is termed "taking out a character." To take the case of a supervisor, for exampl., who petitions for promotion: the whole of his books for one year and the books of the officers under him for a quarter of a year, are examined in the office of the country examiners; all the accounts are re-cast, and errors in the books of the subordinate officers are reckoned to the supervisor's disadvantage. When this has been done, a surveying-general examiner carries the investigation further, and ascertains whether the supervisor has discharged his duties judiciously or not; amongst other things, whether he has been longer employed on a duty than he ought to have been if fully competent for his office. The whole examination occupies about two months; and when the final report is laid before the commissioners the name of the officer is not given.

EXCOMMUNICATION is the highest ecclesiastical censure which can be pronounced by a spiritual judge. The person against whom it is pronounced is for the time excluded from the communion of the church. This punishment, according to some opinions, has its origin in the advice given by St. Paul when reproving the early Christians for scandalizing their profession by prosecuting law-suits against each other before heathen judges; and the apostle accordingly recommended them to leave all matters in dispute between them to the decision of the Ecclesia, or the congregation of the faithful.

The bishop and his clergy, and afterwards the bishop alone, became sole judge in these disputes; but possessing no coercive powers to enforce their decrees, they were obliged to adopt the only means of which they could avail themselves, to bring the refractory to submission, namely, by excluding them from the rites of the Church, and warning other Christians from their company and presence. A Christian thus shut out from the fellowship of his own brethren could not do otherwise than submit.

This censure, although instituted by the primitive church as the means of preserving its purity, and of enforcing obedience to its laws, was afterwards used for the extensive promotion of ecclesiastical power, and was converted into a means of oppression in those countries which were most subject to ecclesiastical power. (Robertson's *History of Charles V.*, vol. ii. p. 109.)

In England excommunication became at an early period the means of punishment under the authority of the bishops, and others who had ecclesiastical jurisdiction. It was divided into the greater and the less excommunication. The latter only removed the person from a participation in the sacraments, and is what was most commonly meant by the term excommunication; the other was called anathema, and not only removed the party from the sacraments, but from the Church and all communication with the faithful, and even deprived him of Christian burial. Subjects were absolved from their allegiance to an excommunicated prince. Gregory V. was the first prelate who ventured to excommunicate a reigning prince in the case of Robert, King of France, in 998. John and Henry VIII. are well-known instances in English history.

The following offenders were punished with the greater excommunication: diviners, heretics, their receivers and comforters; simoniacs; violators and plunderers of churches; those who spoiled clerks going to Rome; the plunderers of the property of a bishop which ought to go to his successor; those who gave aid, favour, or counsel to excommunicated persons; those who laid violent hands on clerks or religious persons, or commanded others to do so.

Those punished with the less excommunication were persons committing any mortal sin, as sacrilegious persons; those who received a church from lay hands; notorious offenders; those who talked with, saluted, or sat at the same table with, or gave anything in charity to persons excommunicated by the greater excommunication, unless they were familiars or domestics.

Excommunication was also pronounced for other matters which belong to ecclesiastical jurisdiction, such as adultery and fornication, or for contempt of any ecclesiastical order or sentence. A sentence of excommunication was preceded by three monitions at due intervals, or one peremptory, containing the legal space of time, with a proper regard to the quality of the person and the nature of the offence. But, as Blackstone in his usual manner remarks, "heavy as the penalty of excommunication is, considered in a serious light, there are, notwithstanding, many obstinate or profligate men, who would despise the *brutum fulmen* of mere ecclesiastical censures, especially when pronounced by a petty surrogate in the country, for railing or contumelious words, for non-payment of fees or costs, or other trivial causes. The common law therefore compassionately steps in to the aid of the ecclesiastical jurisdiction, and kindly lends a supporting hand to an otherwise tottering authority." This was effected by the writ "de excommunicato capiendo," or for seizing the excommunicate. But before the writ for taking the excommunicated person could be granted, the contumacy and contempt of the party were to be certified by the bishop to the court of Chancery by letters under his seal; and by 5 Eliz. c. 23, the writ was made returnable into the King's Bench. By the statute just cited the cause of excommunication was to be stated in the writ, in order that the court might judge as to the justice of the case. The sentence of excommunication might be revoked by the judge who passed the sentence, or upon appeal the party might be absolved. Absolution generally belonged to the same person who passed the sentence, unless in some particular cases, which were referred to the pope or a bishop. (Reeves's *Hist. of English Law*; Sullivan's *Lectures*.)

By a sentence of excommunication, both greater and less, the excommunicated were excluded from the right of Christian burial, from bringing or maintaining actions, from becoming attorneys or jurymen, and were rendered incapable of becoming witnesses in any cause. But since the 53 Geo. III. c. 127 (54 Geo. III. c 68, for Ireland), excommunication cannot now be pronounced in England or Ireland, except in certain cases (as spiritual censures for offences of ecclesiastical cognizance); and by the 3rd section of that statute "no person who shall be pronounced or declared excommunicate (pursuant to the second clause of this statute) shall incur any civil penalty or incapacity, in consequence of such excommunication, save such imprisonment, not exceeding six months, as the court pronouncing or declaring such person excommunicate shall direct." The proceedings in those cases, in which excommunication may still be pronounced, are the same, as to the issuing and return of the writ, as they were before the act of 53 George III. By the same act (53 George III. c. 127), in all cases cognizable by the laws of England in ecclesiastical courts, when any person shall refuse to appear when cited by such court, or shall refuse to obey the lawful order or decree of such court, no sentence of excommunication, except in the cases above alluded to, shall be pronounced; but a writ "de contumace capiendo" shall issue, which in effect is the same as the old writ "de excommunicato capiendo" was.

EXECUTION is the effect given to the judgments and other proceedings analogous to judgments of courts of law in civil suits. This term denotes the process by which a party is put into the possession of that to which the judgment of a competent court declares him to be entitled.

As a judgment of a court of common law ascertains that the party is entitled to the possession of some object of a real or personal nature; or to recover damages in respect of property withheld or injuries done, so the execution founded upon such judgment will be framed with a view to putting the party in whose favour the judgment is given either in the possession of the thing in dispute, or to enable him to obtain pecuniary compensation.

For this purpose a written command issues in the name of the king or other lord of the court, to an officer of the court. When the judgment is in one of the king's superior courts at Westminster, the officer of the court for this purpose is the sheriff of the county in which the property is situated, or, in the case of pecuniary compensation, the sheriff of the county in which the party from whom such compensation is due is supposed to reside; which, until the contrary is shown, is taken to be the county in which the litigation was carried on.

When lands or other corporeal hereditaments are recovered, the process of execution varies according to the nature of the interest recovered. If a right to a freehold interest has been established, the writ commands the sheriff to give the recoverer seisin of the lands, &c., and is called Habere facias seisinam. If a chattel interest in land is recovered, the writ does not affect to authorize the sheriff to intermeddle with the freehold, and directs that officer merely to give possession of the land, &c. This is called Habere facias possessionem.

A judgment in the action of Detinue establishes the right of the recoverer to the possession of a specific personal chattel, and the writ of execution called a Distringas ad deliberandum issues, which requires the sheriff to coerce the defendant by his distringas (distress) to restore the specific chattel or its value.

A judgment for the defendant in Replevin establishes his right to the possession of the personal chattel which formed the subject of the litigation. In the ordinary case of an action of replevin after a distress, the right of the defendant in respect of the chattel distrained is merely to hold it as a security for the payment of the debt or duty, the payment or performance of which is sought to be enforced by the coercion of a distress. The writ of execution requires the sheriff to cause the chattel to be restored to the possession of the defendant. This is called a writ De retorno habendo, and in case the sheriff is unable to find the chattel, further process issues commanding him to take other chattels of the plaintiff as a substitute for that which is withheld, by a writ called a Capias in withernam.

The most ordinary cases of execution are those in which pecuniary compensation is to be obtained, but in these cases the sheriff is not authorized directly to take money from the party by whom it is to be paid. Formerly the only mode of obtaining this compensation was by process of distringas or distress. And this is still the case in inferior courts; but in the superior courts execution of judgments or other records which establish pecuniary claims, may be had by a writ of Fieri facias, which affects the personal property; by writ of Elegit, which affects both real and personal property; and by Capias ad satisfaciendum, by which compliance with the pecuniary demand is enforced by detention of the person of the defaulter in prison until the claim be satisfied, or the adverse party consents to his discharge.

A subject is not entitled to pursue all these remedies at once; but in the case of the crown, the right to obtain satisfaction from the goods, lands, and person of its debtor may be enforced simultaneously, by writ of Capias, and Extendi facias, or Extent.

Execution is also the term applied to denote the giving effect to the sentence of a court of criminal jurisdiction. In this sense it is most commonly used with reference to the execution of sentence of death. [SHERIFF.]

EXECUTOR. An executor is he to whom another man commits by will the execution of his last will and testament. The origin of executors seems to be traceable to a constitution of Manuel Comnenus (περὶ διοικητῶν τῶν διαθηκῶν). All persons who are capable of making a will, and some others besides, as married women and infants, are capable of being made executors; but infants are by statute rendered incapable of acting in the execution of the will until they attain the age of twenty-one.

An executor can derive his office from a testament alone, though it is not necessary that he should be appointed by any particular words. If no executor is appointed by the will, administration is granted by the ordinary, with the will annexed, in which case the administrator is bound to obey the directions of the will. An executor may decline to act; but having once acted, he cannot divest himself of the office or its liabilities; nor can an administrator who has accepted the office get rid of his responsibility.

The first business of an executor is to prove the will, as it is termed, which is done before the proper ecclesiastical court, which furnishes him with a Probate, or approved copy of the will, which is his authority for acting. The original will is deposited in the registry of the court. An executor may do many acts in execution of the will before probate, as paying and receiving debts, &c., but he cannot, before probate, sustain actions or suits. An administrator can do nothing till the letters of administration are issued; for he owes his appointment to the ordinary. If an executor die before probate, administration must be taken out to his testator, with the will annexed; but if an executor, having proved the will, die, his executor will be the executor and representative of the first testator, unless, before proving the will of the second testator, he expressly renounces the execution of the will of the first. If the executor dies intestate, his administrator is not the representative of the testator, but an administrator *de bonis non*, as it is termed, of the testator must be appointed by the ordinary. If there are several executors, the office survives, and is transmitted ultimately to the executor of the surviving executor, unless he dies intestate. Executors have a joint and entire interest in the effects of their testator; any one of them is capable of acting by himself; and the receipt of a debt, or the transfer of property by one, is as valid as if it had been done by all.

If a stranger takes upon himself to act as executor without any authority, he is called an executor *de son tort* (of his own wrong), and is liable to all the trouble of an executor without any of the advantages attached to the office. He is chargeable with the debts of the deceased, so far as assets come to his hands; and is liable not only to an action by the rightful executor or administrator, but also to be sued as executor of the deceased by the creditors and legatees. The only advantage which an executor derives from his office is the right to retain any debt due to him from the testator, as against creditors of equal degree, and this privilege is allowed him, because he cannot take any legal steps to recover payment.

The duties of executors and administrators are in general the same. Their duties are to bury the deceased, to prove his will (which of course only an executor has to do), to get in his goods and chattels, to pay his debts in the order appointed by law, and also his legacies, if he has bequeathed any, and to dispose of the residue of his goods and chattels in the manner by the will directed, or according to the statutes for the distribution of the effects of intestates, if there should be a total or partial intestacy. Executors and administrators are liable to an action at law, and also to a suit in equity, for the payment of the debts and liabilities of their testator or intestate; and to a suit in equity and the Ecclesiastical Court for the legacies bequeathed by him, and the due administration of his estate: but no action at law lies for a legacy, at least not until after the executor has assented to it, as it is called, that is, has acknowledged the sufficiency of the assets after providing for the payment of the debts.

The Ecclesiastical Courts are the only courts in which, except by special prescription, the validity of wills of personalty can be established or disputed. If all the goods of the deceased lie in the diocese or jurisdiction within which he died, the will is proved before the bishop or ordinary of that diocese or jurisdiction; but if he had *bona notabilia* (that is, goods and chattels to the amount of 5*l.*) within some other diocese or jurisdiction than that in which he died, then the will must be proved before the archbishop or metropolitan of the province by special prerogative; and if there be *bona notabilia* in different provinces, there must be two prerogative probates. A will should be proved within six months after the death of the testator, or within two months after the termination of any dispute respecting the probate. (55 Geo. III. c. 184, § 57.)

Executors and administrators are treated by the courts of equity as trustees for the creditors, legatees, and next of kin of their testators or intestates. They are bound to administer the assets according to their due order of priority, and to pay the debts of the deceased in like manner; and though the ecclesiastical courts will entertain suits for the payment of debts or legacies and the due administration of the assets, yet, where there is any trust to be executed, or any charge on the real estate to be established, a court of equity will interfere by injunction or prohibition; for the constitution of the ecclesiastical courts is not adapted to the administration of trusts, and over real estate they have no jurisdiction. The probate is exclusive evidence of a will of personalty; but courts of equity assume the jurisdiction of construing the will in order to enforce the performance of the trusts by the executor: hence they are sometimes styled courts of construction, in contradistinction to the ecclesiastical courts, which, although they also are courts of construction, are the only courts of probate. Formerly, the personal estates only of persons deceased were liable for the payment of their simple contract debts; but now, since the statute 3 & 4 Wm. IV. c. 104, real estates are liable for the payment of debts of that nature; and it may be broadly stated that all the real and personal estates of the deceased are assets for the payment of his debts. The personal estate is liable in the first instance, unless the testator direct otherwise. Estates descended are applied before estates devised; and in other respects the estates of the deceased are administered in the order laid down by the courts.

The debts are payable in a certain order, which is fixed by law, and the executor should observe it. If he finds any difficulty in this matter, he ought to take the best legal advice that he can get.

The next duty of an executor or administrator is to pay the legacies, and to distribute the personal estate of the deceased pursuant to his will; and if there is no will, to dispose of it pursuant to the Statute of Distributions. [ADMINISTRATION, p. 24.] In this part of his duty also, if he find difficulties, the safe and proper course is to take legal advice.

Full information upon these subjects will be found in the works of Williams and Toller 'On Executors,' and Went worth 'On Administrators.'

EXEMPLIFICATION. [EVIDENCE.]

EXETER, or EXON DOMESDAY, the

name given to a record preserved among the muniments and charters belonging to the dean and chapter of Exeter cathedral, which contains a description of the western parts of the kingdom, comprising the counties of Wilts, Dorset, Somerset, Devon, and Cornwall. It is supposed, as far as it extends, to contain an exact transcript of the original rolls or returns made by the Conqueror's commissioners at the time of forming the General Survey, from which the great Domesday itself was compiled. It is written on vellum in the form of a book of the small folio size, containing 532 double pages. The skins or sheets of vellum of which it is composed vary in the number of leaves which they comprise from one to twenty; the lands of each of the more considerable tenants begin a new sheet, and those of almost every tenant a new page. The lands in the counties of Devon, Somerset, and Cornwall belonging to one tenant, are classed together, and the counties follow each other, though not always in the same order; and, in like manner, the summaries of property in Wilts and Dorset are classed together.

Upon collating the returns of lands which form the great body of the Exeter Survey with the Exchequer Domesday, they have been found, with a few trifling variations, to coincide; one entry of property alone is discoverable in the Exeter which is omitted in the Exchequer Domesday, relating to Sotrebroc in Devonshire. The Exeter manuscript, however, is not complete in its contents. There are considerable omissions of lands in Wiltshire, Dorsetshire, and Devonshire; but these have evidently been cut out and lost. In Cornwall every manor mentioned in the Exchequer occurs in the Exeter Domesday. One leaf of this record was accidentally discovered in private possession within these few years, and has been restored to the manuscript. In the writing of the names of places and persons there is a remarkable difference between the two records.

The most striking feature of the Exeter Domesday, in which it uniformly supplies us with additional knowledge to that in the Exchequer Survey, is the enumeration of live stock upon every estate; there is an account of the number of oxen, sheep, goats, horses, and pigs, exactly in the same manner as it is given in the second volume of the Great Domesday. The reason for omitting this enumeration in the breviated entries of the first volume of the Great Survey is self-evident. The live stock was altering every day and year; the enumeration of it therefore could be of no further use than for the exact time when the survey was made. A comparison of this part of the Exeter with the second volume of the Great Survey tends greatly to corroborate the notion that the returns of the counties of Essex, Norfolk, and Suffolk were transcribed in full from the original rotuli, in the same manner as the Exeter Domesday. The difference between the two surveys as to expression, when they agree in sense, is likewise remarkable; as for instance,

Exchequer Domesday.	Exeter Domesday.
Acra . . .	Agra
ad arsuram .	ad combustionem
censores .	gablatores
clerici .	sacerdotes
geldabat .	reddidit Gildum
leuca . . .	leuga
manerium .	mansio
ad opus militum .	ad soldarios
molendinum .	molinus
nummi . .	denarii
in paragio . .	pariter
portarii .	portatores
pastura . .	pascura
poterat ire quo volebat (tom. i. fol. 97 b.) . .	poterat sibi eligere dominum secundum voluntatem suam cum terra sua (fol. 383).
quarentena .	quadragenaria
sylva . . .	nemusculum
T. R. E. (tempore regis Edwardi)	Die qua rex Edwardus fuit vivus et mortuus
tainus . .	tagnus
Terra est viii. car.	possunt arare viii. carr.
Terra Regis. .	Dominicatus Regis (and in one instance), dominicatus Regis ad regnum pertinens

Exchequer Domesday.	Exeter Domesday.
Totum valet xxi. lib.	Hæc mans. reddit ad opus abb. x. & viii. lib. et ad opus tagnorum iii. lib.

The utility of this record for the purpose of comparison with the Exchequer Domesday is obvious. The Exeter Domesday was published, with several other surveys nearly contemporary, by order of the Commissioners upon the Public Records, under the direction of Sir Henry Ellis, in a volume supplementary to the Great Domesday, folio, London, 1816. Our account of this record is chiefly derived from the Introduction to that volume.

EXHIBITION. [SCHOOL.]
EXILE. [BANISHMENT.] .
EXPORTS. [BALANCE OF TRADE.]
EXTRA-PAROCHIAL. [PARISH.]
EYRE. [COURTS, p. 711.]

www.ingramcontent.com/pod-product-compliance
Lightning Source LLC
Chambersburg PA
CBHW020739020526
44115CB00030B/630